ART IN THE MAKING

Underdrawings in Renaissance Paintings

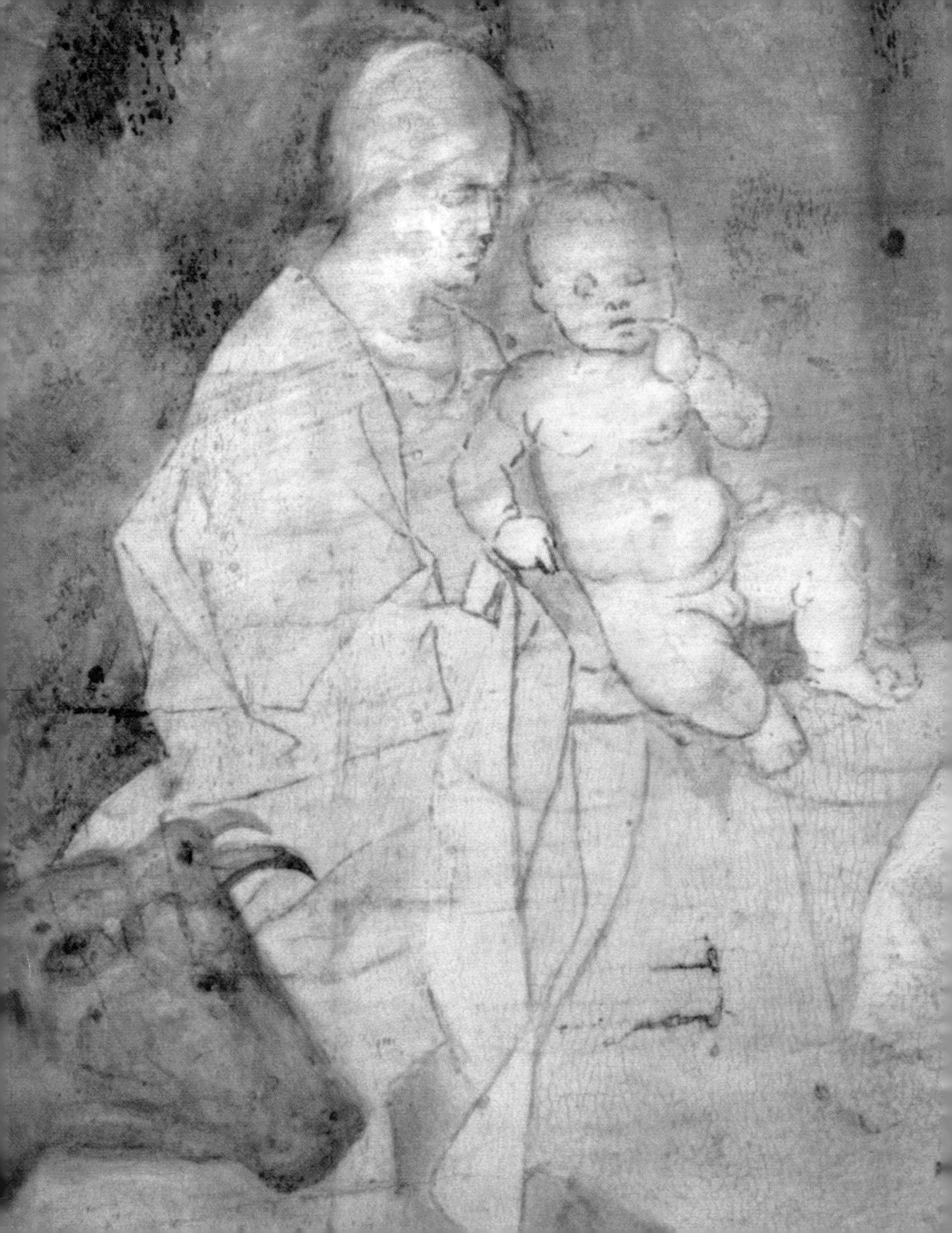

ART IN THE MAKING

Underdrawings in Renaissance Paintings

Edited by David Bomford

*With contributions from
Rachel Billinge, Lorne Campbell,
Jill Dunkerton, Susan Foister,
Jo Kirby, Carol Plazzotta,
Ashok Roy, Marika Spring*

NATIONAL GALLERY COMPANY, LONDON
Distributed by Yale University Press

Exhibition supported by

GlaxoSmithKline

First published in Great Britain in 2002 to accompany an exhibition at the National Gallery, London, 30 October 2002–16 February 2003

National Gallery Company Limited
St Vincent House, 30 Orange Street,
London WC2H 7HH
www.nationalgallery.co.uk

ISBN 1 85709 987 7
525106

British Library Cataloguing-in-Publication Data.
A catalogue record is available from the British Library.
Library of Congress Catalog Card Number: 2001095556

COMMISSIONING EDITOR David Bomford
EDITOR Diana Davies
DESIGNER Isambard Thomas
PROJECT MANAGER Jan Green
PICTURE RESEARCHERS Catharina Tesdorpf, Xenia Corcoran

Printed and bound in Great Britain by Butler and Tanner

COVER ILLUSTRATIONS
Carlo Crivelli, *The Dead Christ supported by Two Angels*
FRONT Detail from infrared reflectogram mosaic (Fig. 169)
BACK Detail of Fig. 168

Acknowledgements

The authors would like to thank the following for their help in the preparation of this catalogue: Maryan Ainsworth, J.R.J. van Asperen de Boer, Peter van den Brink, Bodo Brinkmann, David Alan Brown, Stephanie Buck, Edwin Buijsen, Richard Charlton-Jones, Peter Eikemeier, Molly Faries, Jacques Foucart, Rosamund Griffin, Daniel Hess, Fritz Koreny, Sally Korman, Patrick Le Chanu, Philippe Lorentz, Adri Mackor, Antonio Natali, Ute Neidhardt, Hans Nieuwdorp, Ulrike Nürnberger, Nicholas Penny, Allegra Pesenti, François Quiviger, Catherine Reynolds, Jochen Sander, Jennifer Saville, Cécile Scaillierez, Christoph Schölzel, Roger van Schoute, Sarah Staniforth, Hélène Verougstraete, Elizabeth Walmsley, Margreet Wolters – and all our colleagues at the National Gallery who have worked so hard on this catalogue and the exhibition it accompanies.

Essays

Catalogue

Sponsor's Foreword

GlaxoSmithKline is proud to be supporting *Art in the Making: Underdrawings in Renaissance Paintings*, a revelatory exhibition that manages to combine the scholarly with the accessible. Using infrared reflectography, the National Gallery has explored what lies beneath the surface of each painting, often with dramatic and unexpected results. As a company for whom science is fundamental, it is particularly appropriate that GSK should be identified with an exhibition that uses scientific techniques to help us understand and define the artistic practices of some of the Gallery's treasures.

Art in the Making: Underdrawings in Renaissance Paintings is the latest in a series of exhibitions that GSK has supported in recent years, which includes *American Sublime* and *William Blake* at Tate Britain, *Grinling Gibbons and the Art of Carving* at the V&A, and *Spanish Still Life* at the National Gallery. Our partnerships with Britain's galleries and museums are built on a shared commitment to excellence, innovation and access. GSK is also committed to supporting arts projects that involve the participation of young people from an early age. Through our support we hope to attract new audiences and encourage those already familiar with the arts to take a fresh look.

Themes of innovation and discovery are fundamental to a research-based company; we hope that both themes will also be evident in this exhibition. One of our objectives in supporting *Art in the Making: Underdrawings in Renaissance Paintings* is to help reveal to new audiences how closely art and science can be linked. We hope that visitors to the exhibition will be intrigued by the connection.

gsk GlaxoSmithKline

Director's Foreword

The three *Art in the Making* exhibitions between 1988 and 1991 were among the most popular small exhibitions in the history of the National Gallery. Devoted to Rembrandt, Italian painting before 1400 and Impressionism, they presented to the widest possible public the results of technical research by the Scientific, Conservation and Curatorial departments into key areas of the collection. The catalogues that accompanied them have been reprinted many times and are recognised as standard texts in the field.

We are delighted that the series is now being revived with *Art in the Making: Underdrawings in Renaissance Paintings*. The revelation of artists' preliminary drawings beneath the paint layers by infrared techniques is not a new discovery, but the National Gallery is one of the few museums in the world to have examined its collection in depth. Computer technology developed here at the Gallery as part of the VASARI and MARC programmes has helped produce images of underdrawings of startling clarity that are as remarkable visually as they are valuable for art-historical research.

The infrared reflectogram mosaics of underdrawings assembled in this catalogue are the work of Rachel Billinge, formerly Leverhulme Research Fellow and latterly Rausing Research Associate here at the National Gallery. The paintings shown and discussed in these pages represent only a small part of the systematic survey that Rachel has carried out over the last decade and we are very grateful for the dedication she has shown in producing this unique archive of images. It is no exaggeration to say that our view of these paintings has been illuminated and transformed by the results of her work.

Finally, we would like to acknowledge the help of our friends at GlaxoSmithKline for their continuing support for the National Gallery – and in particular for their enthusiastic sponsorship of this exhibition.

Charles Saumarez Smith, *Director*

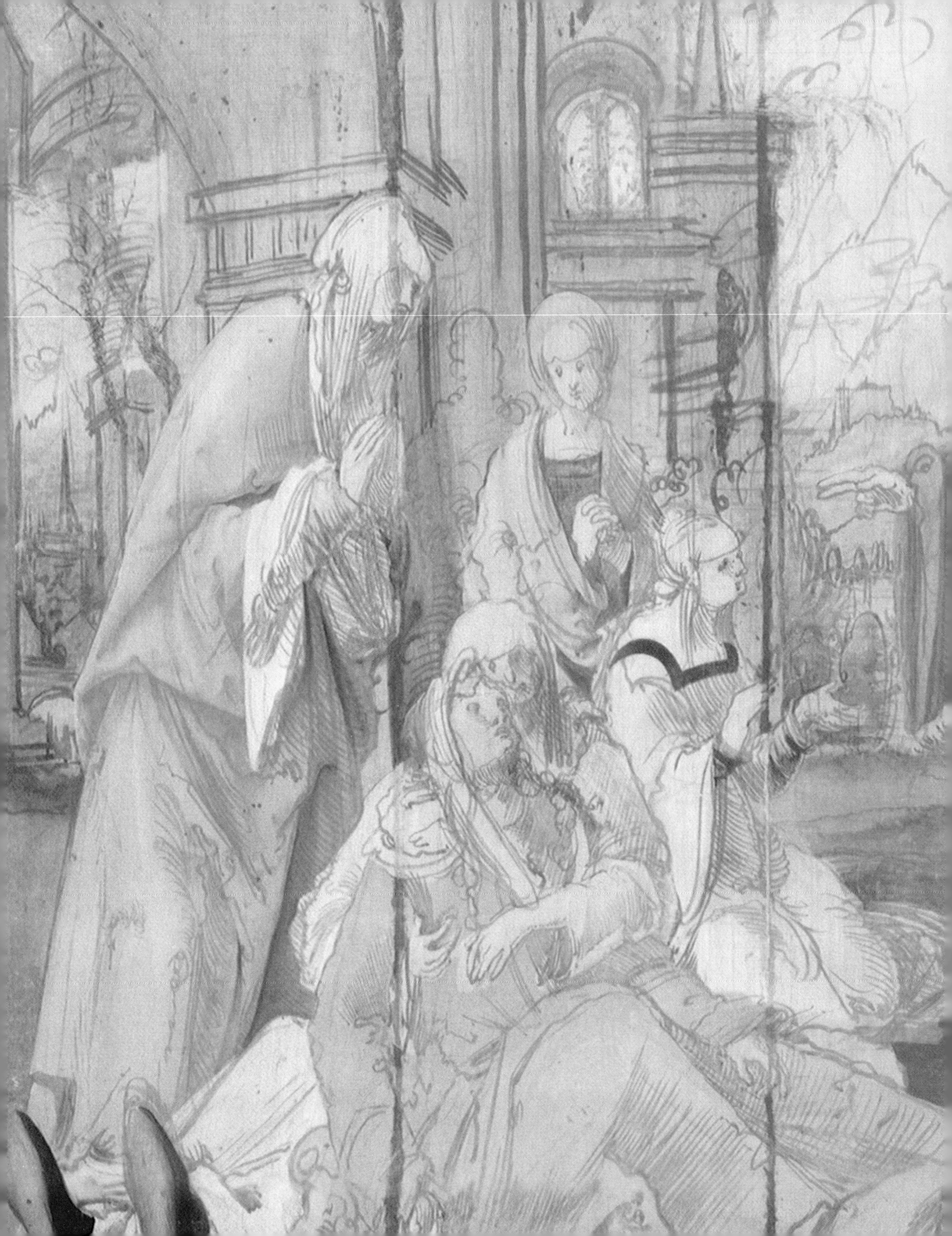

Essays

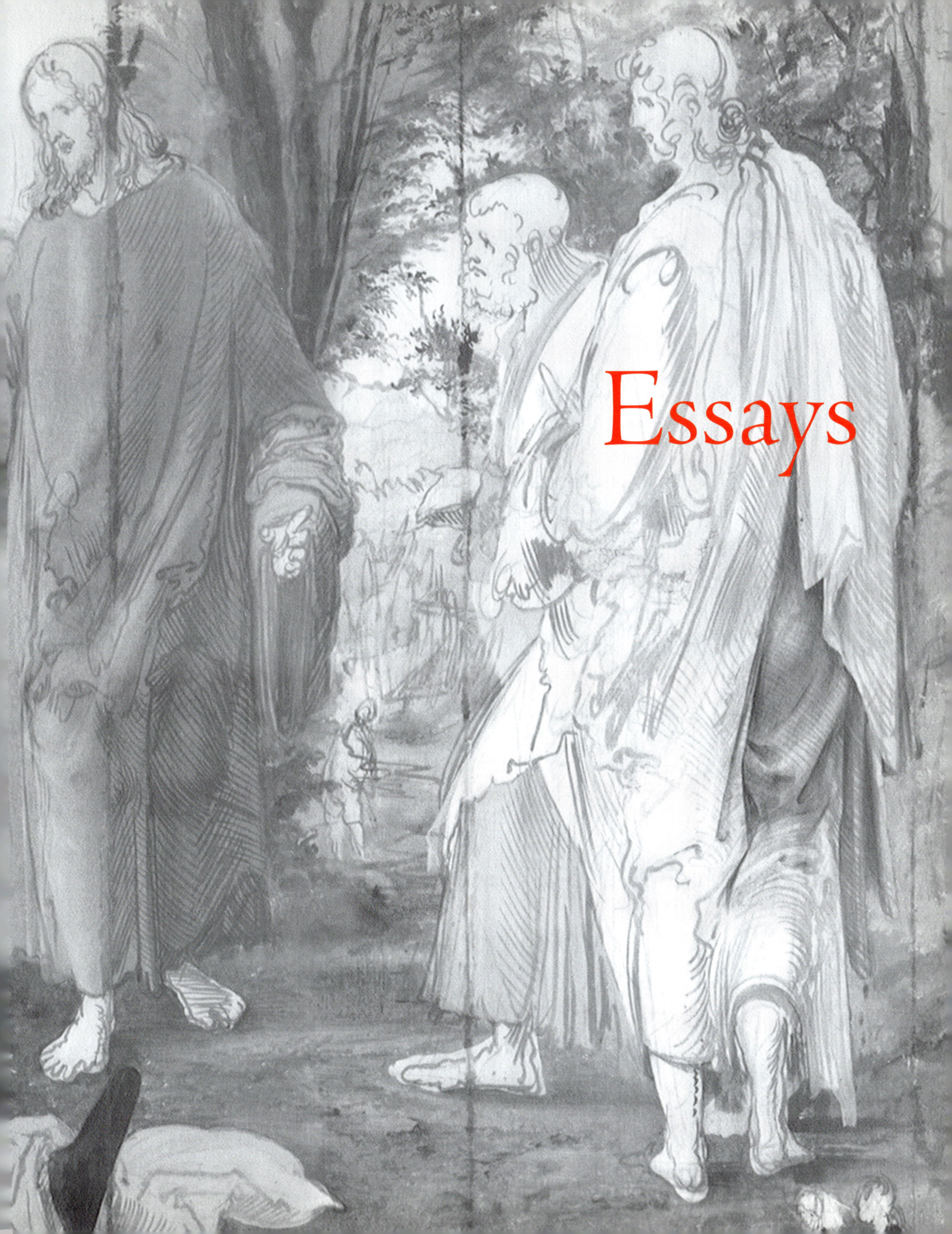

1 Introduction

Fig. 1
JAN VAN EYCK, *Portrait of Giovanni (?) Arnolfini and his Wife* [NG 186], 1434, detail

Fig. 2
Infrared photograph of Fig. 1

In 1940, the first Scientific Adviser of the National Gallery, Ian Rawlins, published a pioneering book of technical photographs entitled *From the National Gallery Laboratory*. It was a notable event in that it began the tradition of publishing the results of the technical examination of paintings in the Gallery that has continued ever since. The images in the book were mostly of X-radiographs, a technique that had been used for examining paintings almost since the discovery of X-rays in Germany in 1895. Two images were infrared photographs of the head and hand of one of the angels in Cosimo Tura's *Virgin and Child Enthroned*. Infrared photography had been developed as an examination tool in the 1930s, when it was observed that it was capable of revealing layers just below the visible surface of a painting. In his brief commentary on the photographs of Tura's paintings, Rawlins made this clear: 'These details ... bring out the capacity of the infrared to reveal sub-surface modelling in the form of shading scarcely visible in the picture itself, and little seen in ordinary photographs.' What Rawlins described as the 'modelling' and 'shading' below the surface of the Tura is the underdrawing that is the subject of this catalogue.

By 1950, infrared photography was beginning to be a routine examination method – especially for early Netherlandish paintings, which yielded significant results. In that year, an infrared photograph was taken of Giovanni Arnolfini's upraised hand in van Eyck's double portrait of Giovanni(?) Arnolfini and his wife (NG 186; Figs 1 and 2). It shows the hand in two positions and two stages of evolution. The position towards the right corresponds with the painted hand that we see in the finished picture – edge-on, the fingers behind each other and a ring on the forefinger. The other position, partly obscured by the painted hand, is quite different: it is angled more towards the viewer, is shown in outline only and has no ring.

What is revealed here is van Eyck's underdrawing, the first sketching-out of Arnolfini's hand. Underdrawings are the preliminary drawings on the panel (or canvas) that has been prepared for painting: subsequently they will be covered by the paint layers themselves. As will be seen in this catalogue, underdrawings vary enormously in extent, complexity, style and technique. Close examination of the underdrawn lines of Arnolfini's hand shows that they have a particular character – they are broad and have a continuity that suggests a fluid rather than a dry process. This distinction will be discussed in the sections that follow and it will be seen that underdrawings described in this catalogue are much more likely to be in a fluid medium than a dry one. Often, as Arnolfini's hand shows,

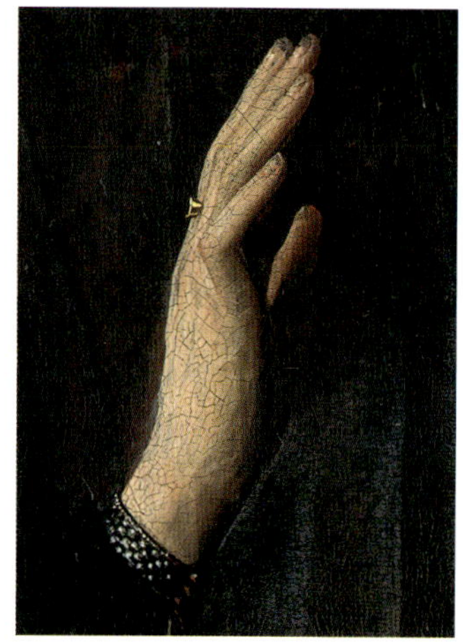

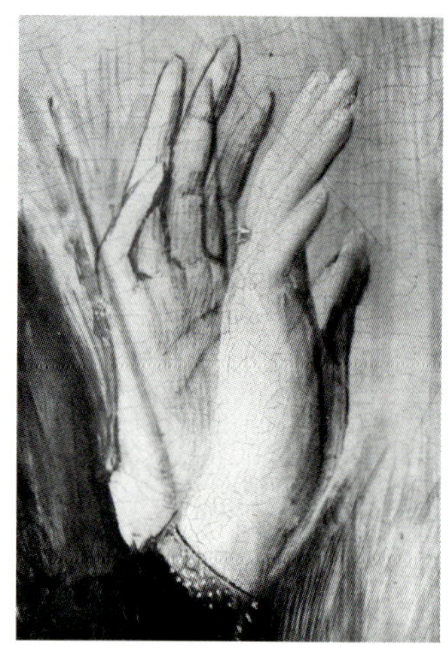

Fig. 3
HANS WERTINGER, *Summer* [NG 6568], *c.*1525. Oil on wood, 23.2 × 39.5 cm

Fig. 4
Detail of Fig. 3

underdrawings are not followed precisely at the painting stage: occasionally they differ dramatically from the finished composition. Much of the interest in studying underdrawings lies in what they reveal about the creative processes of the artist. Understanding the genesis of a painting may involve following the evolution of an artist's ideas from preliminary sketches and drawings on paper, through preparatory underdrawings and revised outlines to the complexity of the final painting. All of these stages represent a continuing development of the design process.

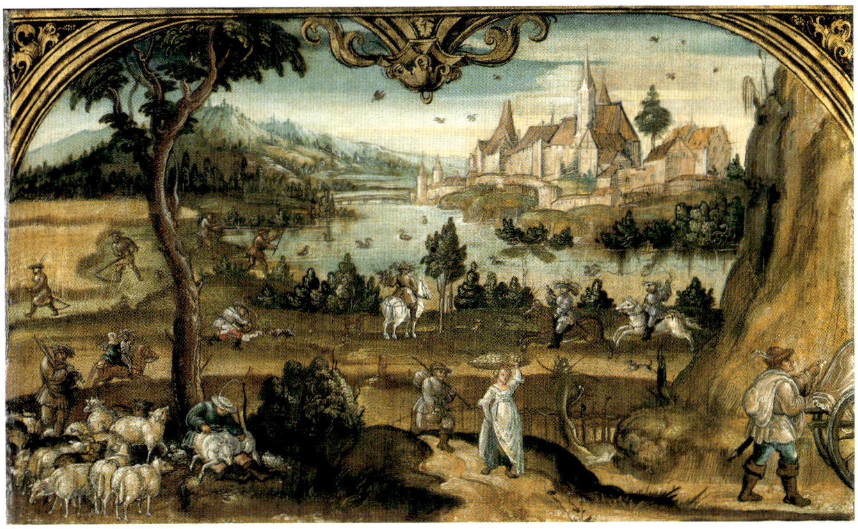

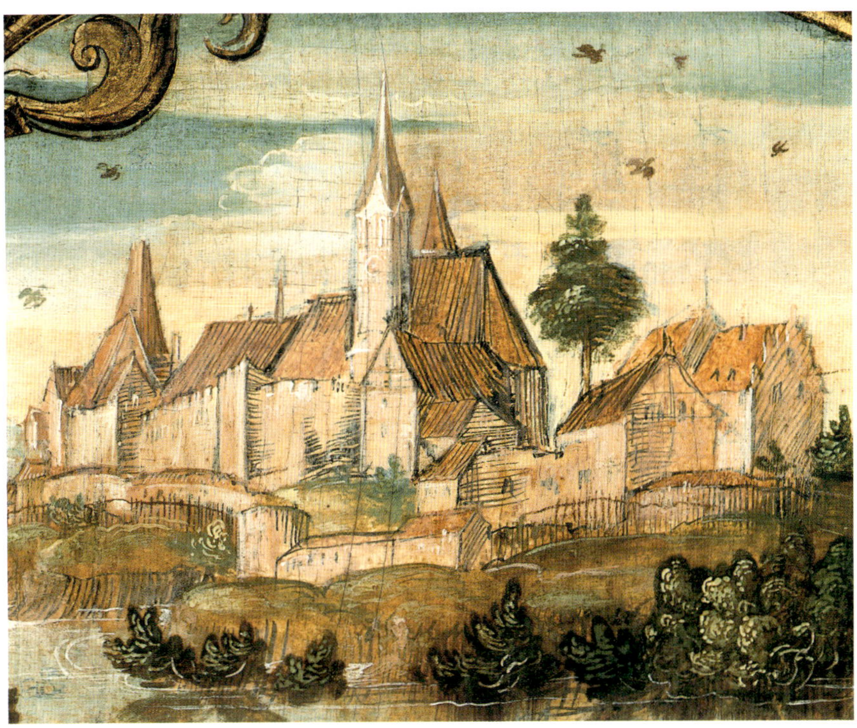

Visible Underdrawings

One problem with studying underdrawings is that they are usually concealed by the paint layers and must be revealed by technical photography. Sometimes, however, the paint may be thin enough for the drawn lines to show through directly. A clear example of this is Hans Wertinger's small panel, *Summer* (NG 6568; Figs 3 and 4), painted around 1525, in which a detailed drawing can be seen through the paint, especially in the distant buildings and bridge, and in the foreground at the right. In these areas, the painting now has the appearance of a delicate pen-and-ink drawing covered by thin washes of colour. In fact, the underdrawing was probably made using a very fine brush with black paint and is visible only because the overlying colour layers have become more transparent with time. Although the present appearance of the work is not exactly what Wertinger intended, it is a striking instance of an underdrawing that can be seen unaided.

Unfinished paintings also yield evidence about layers that would normally be covered. Albrecht Dürer's *Salvator Mundi* (New York, Metropolitan Museum, Fig. 5), recorded as incomplete in an inventory as early as 1573, has a startlingly visible underdrawing. Traditionally, it is said that Dürer left it unfinished when he went to Italy in 1505, but it now seems more likely that it was started in Italy and left uncompleted when he returned to Nuremberg: the fact that the panel seems to be of poplar suggests an Italian origin. The painting was apparently 'finished' by an unknown hand in the nineteenth century, but was freed from its repaint in the mid-twentieth. As can be seen from its present state, only the draperies were completed: the head and hands were left at an early stage in which Dürer has hardly begun to cover his preliminary drawing with paint. The drawing is highly detailed; features and modelling are delineated with successions of fine lines of black paint or ink.

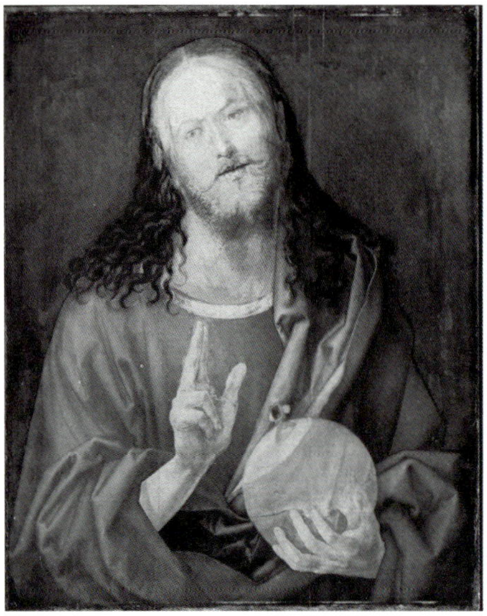

with many preliminary drawings on paper, since the underdrawing is direct and confident.

Underdrawings may also become visible through damage, whether accidental or deliberate. A regrettable but highly informative example is the *Virgin in Majesty with Four Saints* by a follower of Hugo van der Goes (Private Collection; Fig. 8) – once owned by Horace Walpole at Strawberry Hill and attributed at that time to Gossaert. More than thirty years before Walpole bought the painting, an unscrupulous dealer had apparently scraped away substantial areas of original paint in the centre and at the left – uncovering the entire underdrawing in these parts – and repainted it as a more saleable *Marriage of Henry VII and*

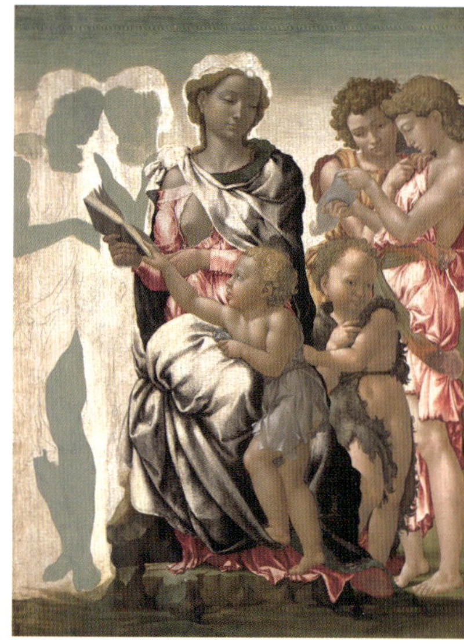

Shadows are indicated with hatching. Infrared techniques have revealed similar meticulous drawings beneath the surfaces of finished Dürer paintings.

Michelangelo's *Manchester Madonna* (NG 809; Fig. 6) in the National Gallery is another notable example of an unfinished picture. The seven figures in this panel painting are in various stages of completion: some parts are highly finished, especially towards the right, while others are hardly begun. The two angels at the left are present on the gesso ground only in outline and the preliminary green earth tone has been laid in for the flesh colours. A careful underdrawing, which presumably underlies the whole composition, is clearly visible in the unpainted draperies of these angels (Fig. 7). The drawing is entirely linear, the folds indicated with long, confident strokes made with a brush and thin black paint. There is no indication of form or shadow in the drawing, no hatching or shading. Detail and form were added at the painting stage: for example, the Virgin's robe is modelled in black paint and awaits its blue finishing layers. Michelangelo must have planned the composition of *The Manchester Madonna* carefully

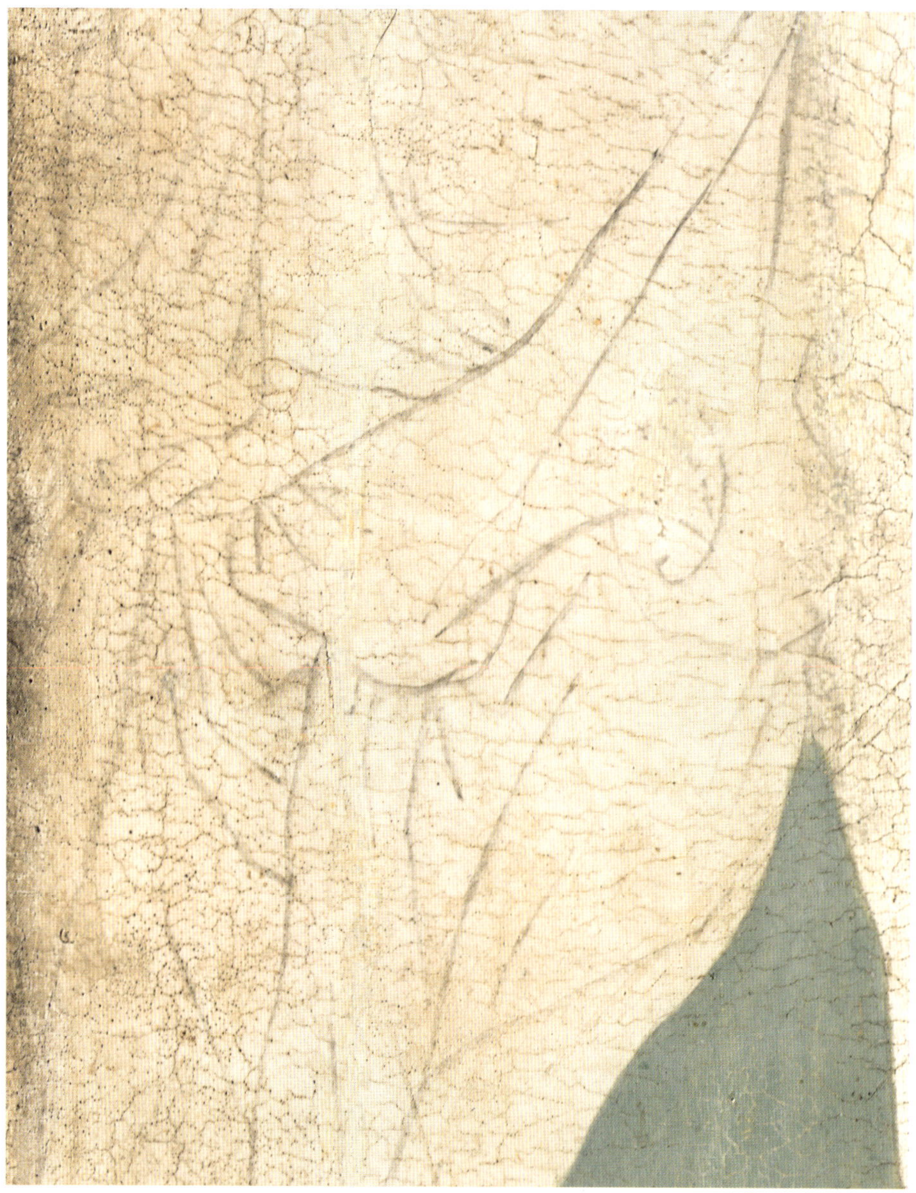

Fig. 5 (far left)
ALBRECHT DÜRER, *Salvator Mundi*
Oil on wood, 58.1 × 47 cm. New York, The Metropolitan Museum of Art
The Friedsam Collection, Bequest of Michael Friedsam, 1931, inv. 32.100.64

Fig. 6 (left)
MICHELANGELO, *The Virgin and Child with Saint John and Angels (The Manchester Madonna)* [NG 809], *c.*1497
Egg and oil on wood, 104.5 × 77 cm

Fig. 7
Detail of Fig. 6

Fig. 8 (right)
Attributed to HUGO VAN DER GOES, *The Virgin in Majesty with Four Saints*
Oil on wood. Private Collection

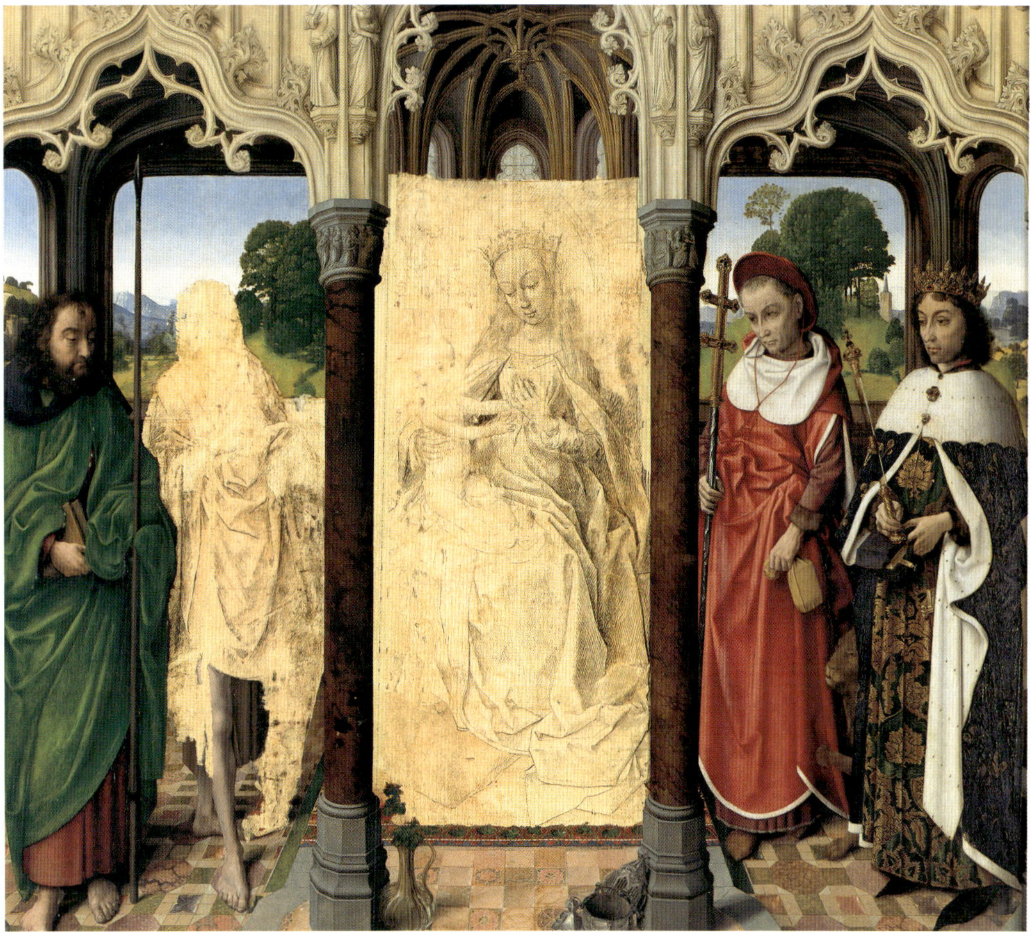

Elizabeth of York. The eighteenth-century repaint was removed in recent years and the underdrawing exposed again. Delicate outlines, with refined cross-hatching for the shadowed parts, define the figures and the cloth of honour behind the Virgin. It is an extraordinary sight: the meticulous drawing for the Virgin and Child and Saint John the Baptist is revealed exactly as the artist set it down on the chalk ground, ready for painting. The underdrawing for one saint, even though somewhat damaged by scraping, lies alongside the fully finished figure of another, under which must lie something very similar.

Infrared Photography

Underdrawings concealed beneath paint layers can be revealed by the use of infrared radiation, which is the portion of the electromagnetic spectrum just beyond visible light – commonly encountered as the radiant heat present in sunlight and tungsten light. Paint that is opaque in the visible part of the spectrum becomes increasingly transparent in the longer wavelengths of the infrared and, therefore, infrared light may be capable of penetrating below the visible surface of a painting to the level of the underdrawing. However, because infrared light cannot be seen by the human eye, some sort of imaging technique must be used to make it visible: the two methods generally used for this purpose are infrared photography and infrared reflectography.

For infrared photography, an infrared-sensitive film is used in a conventional camera and the image only becomes apparent once the film is developed. Certain conditions favour the successful detection of underdrawings by infrared photography. Ideally, the paint layers should be thin and relatively transparent to infrared radiation, which is then reflected back to the camera from a light-coloured ground beneath. Any underdrawing on the ground done in a material that absorbs infrared – especially one that contains carbon black in some form – will register as a dark line on the photographic image.

A small panel painting that exactly fulfils these requirements is *Christ appearing to the Virgin with the Redeemed of the Old Testament* by the Hispano-Flemish artist Juan de Flandes (NG 1280; Fig. 9). A beautifully clear infrared photograph (Fig. 10) shows a complete drawing below the paint in which every feature is outlined and every form fully modelled to indicate light and shade. The red bed hanging is particularly detailed where it is tucked and gathered at the right. The shadow of each fold here is so diligently hatched that the design has

Fig. 9
JUAN DE FLANDES, *Christ appearing to the Virgin with the Redeemed of the Old Testament* [NG 1280], before 1505
Oil on chestnut, 20.9 × 15.3 cm

Fig. 10
Infrared photograph of Fig. 9

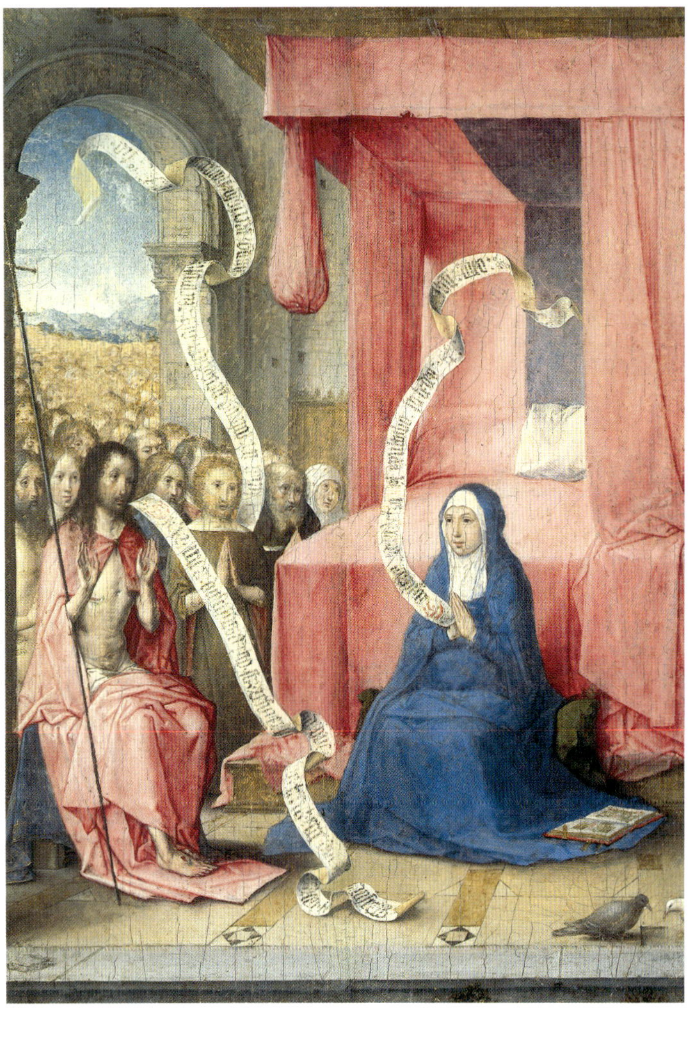

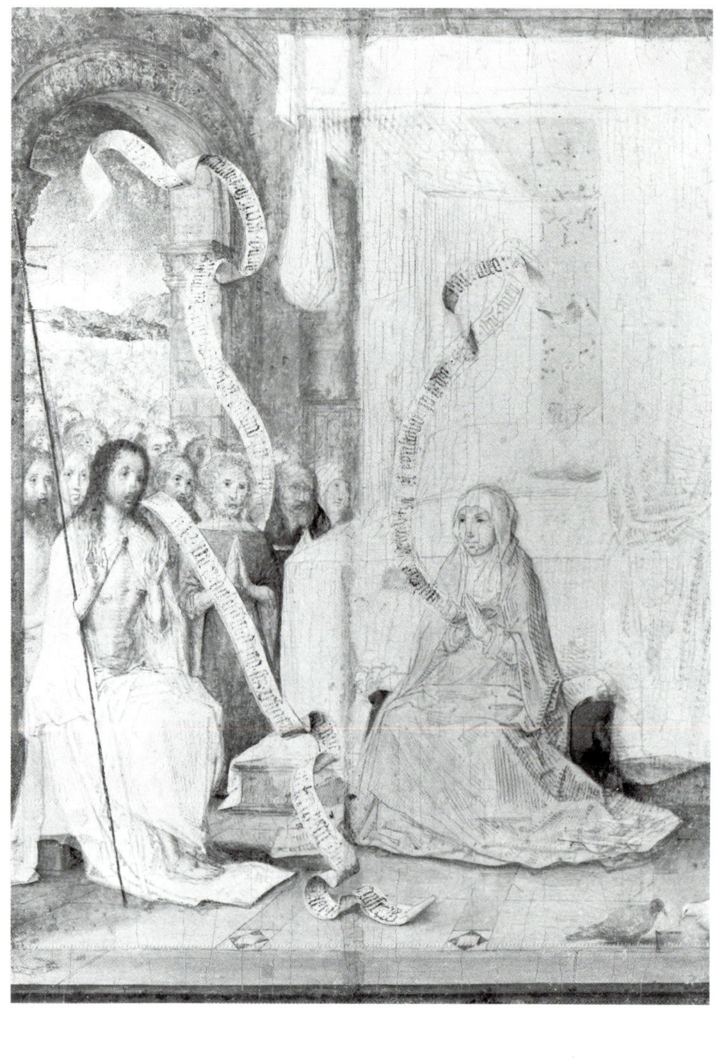

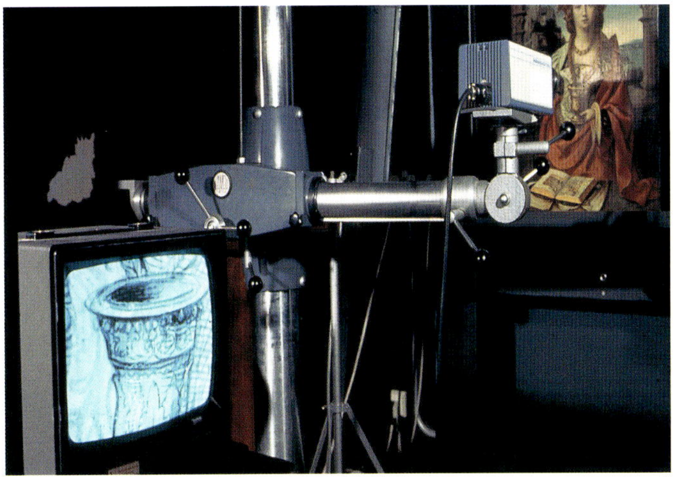

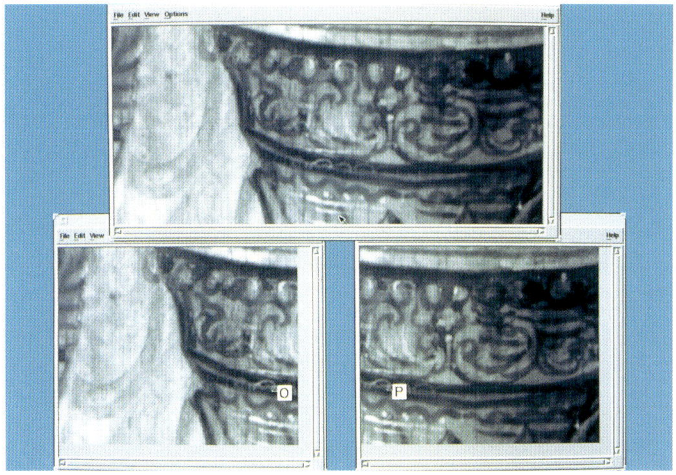

Fig. 11
Apparatus for infrared reflectography

Fig. 12
Joining of images on computer screen

become over-complex and has been sharpened and simplified at the painting stage. The Virgin's blue robe, too, is more detailed in the underdrawing than in the final painting – but the opposite is true of Christ's red robes, which became more intricate between drawing and painting.

The range of infrared radiation that can be recorded by infrared film is limited, and penetration of some pigments, especially the copper-containing blues and greens favoured by European artists in the fifteenth and sixteenth centuries, is poor. A major practical problem with infrared photography is that it has become difficult to obtain suitable infrared film.

Infrared Reflectography

Longer wavelengths in the infrared are capable of penetrating these colours and revealing what lies beneath. In the 1960s, J.R.J. van Asperen de Boer, a physicist working in the Netherlands, developed the use of an industrial infrared camera sensitive to the longer wavelengths of infrared, linked to a television monitor to produce instantaneous images – a technique he named *infrared reflectography*. The system uses a highly sensitive video tube (called a *vidicon*) housed in a television camera. The special coating on the tube converts the infrared radiation into electronic signals, which generate a black and white image on a monitor (Fig. 11). The vidicon is also sensitive to visible light but this is prevented from entering the camera by a filter – so that what is shown on the monitor results only from the infrared. Such a system remains the basis of most underdrawings research today, although the specialised cameras have developed significantly and computer-assisted recording of the images has transformed their clarity (see Appendix, p. 181).

Cameras used for infrared reflectography are rather low in resolution so that only small areas – just a few centimetres across – are studied at a time. These individual frames viewed on the monitor and recorded in some way are known as *reflectograms*. Dozens, or even hundreds, of reflectograms are systematically recorded to cover a whole painting.

In the earlier days of infrared reflectography, the reflectograms were photographed one by one directly from the television screen with black and white film, developed, carefully printed and then painstakingly assembled by hand into composite *mosaics*. This laborious process was not only very slow, but could produce uneven patchwork images that were difficult to interpret. More recently, the ability to digitise the individual reflectograms and use computer programs to join them together (Fig. 12) has made it easier and quicker to produce clear, uninterrupted composite images.

Reading Reflectograms

Infrared reflectography has become the primary tool for revealing underdrawings. The interpretation of reflectograms is the key to understanding their nature and significance and for evaluating the role of underdrawing in the creative process. Reading reflectograms seems straightforward but the image can be more complex than it first appears.

Infrared reflectograms can reveal more than infrared photographs because they result from a detector sensitive to a more penetrative range of radiation. This is immediately apparent if we look at a reflectogram of Giovanni(?) Arnolfini's hand. In the infrared photograph we saw in Fig. 2, part of the underdrawing was obscured by the opaque painted hand on top. In the reflectogram (Fig. 13), the painted hand is still apparent, but the drawn hand can be seen through it more fully. However, this increased visibility is achieved at a cost: it will be noticed that the reflectogram is less sharp, partly due to its origin as a television image. The greater sharpness of infrared photographs as compared with the greater penetration of reflectograms is one of the reasons why they are best considered as complementary rather than alternative techniques.

The ability of reflectograms to reveal underdrawings below areas of paint not penetrated in infrared photographs is demonstrated by looking at blue or blue-green draperies or green landscapes painted using copper-containing pigments. The Virgin's robe in *The Adoration of the Kings* by Gerard David (NG 1079), for example, appears dark and opaque in an infrared photograph, whereas a reflectogram reveals clear preliminary drawing (Figs 14–16).

The most important point to bear in mind when examining infrared images is that we are looking at and through superimposed layers – partially transparent paint over drawing. The infrared radiation is absorbed by the same materials wherever they appear in the layer structure and, once absorbed, cannot continue through to reveal anything about lower layers: a black line on the surface effectively hides all below it. It is sometimes difficult to distinguish which features belong to which layer. A line clearly visible in an infrared image may indeed belong to the underdrawing, or it may be a line in the surface paint – which may or may not be hiding underdrawing. If possible, infrared images should always be compared directly with the painting itself so that such ambiguities can be resolved. Studying reflectograms in isolation can lead to errors of interpretation.

It is also important to remember that the absence of visible underdrawing in an infrared image does not necessarily mean that no underdrawing is present. It may simply be concealed by opaque paint, or it may be that the underdrawing was executed in a material that is transparent to, and does not register in, infrared. This is clearly demonstrated in the small triptych, *The Virgin and Child with Saints* (NG 6497), from the workshop of the Master of the Saint Bartholomew Altarpiece, in which some of the underdrawing is clearly visible to the eye and yet does not show in infrared reflectography (Figs 17 and 18). The underdrawing here was done in iron-gall ink, which is transparent to infrared.

Infrared images not only give us information about what the artist painted but can also show some of the picture's subsequent history. Damages to paintings show clearly in infrared images. If paint and ground are both missing, then the underdrawing will also have been lost from that area and a line of underdrawing may be interrupted. Where a restorer has repainted the loss, even if the restoration matches perfectly on the surface, it is unlikely that materials with

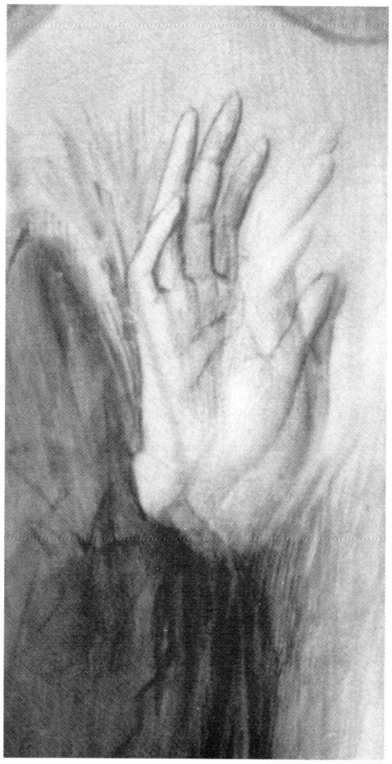

Fig. 13
JAN VAN EYCK, *Portrait of Giovanni(?) Arnolfini and his Wife* [NG 186], 1434
Detail from infrared reflectogram mosaic (Fig. 62)

Fig. 14 (right, top)
GERARD DAVID, *The Adoration of the Kings* [NG 1079], 1515–23, detail

Fig. 15
Infrared photograph of Fig. 14

Fig. 16
Infrared reflectogram mosaic of Fig. 14

Fig. 17 (right)
WORKSHOP OF THE MASTER OF THE SAINT BARTHOLOMEW ALTARPIECE, *The Virgin and Child in Glory with Saint James the Great and Saint Cecilia* [NG 6497], c.1480, detail

Fig. 18
Infrared reflectogram of Fig. 17

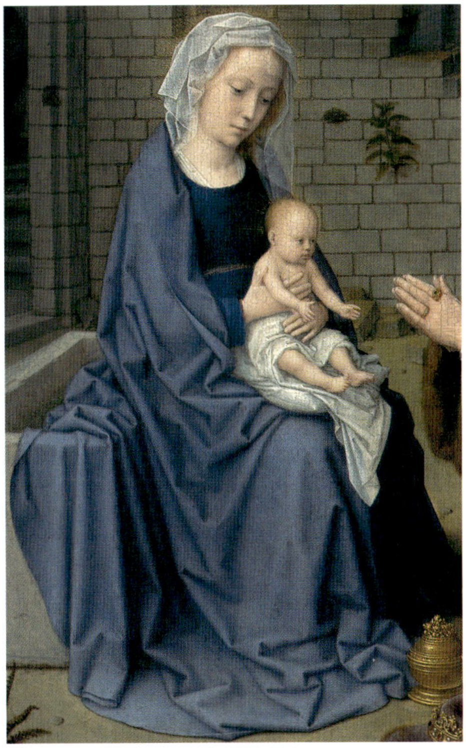

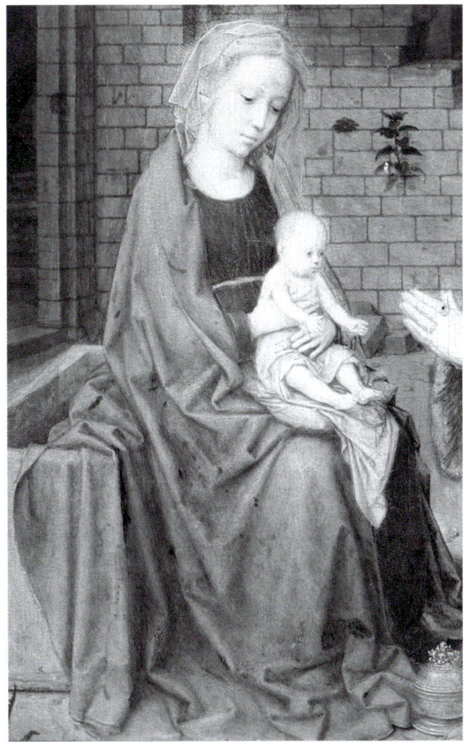

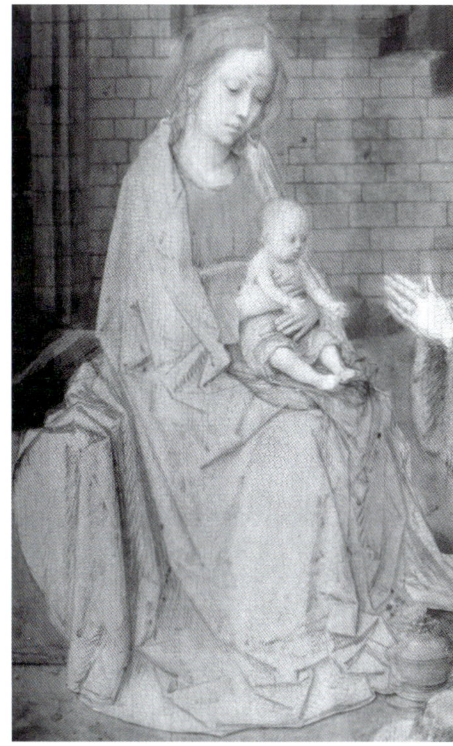

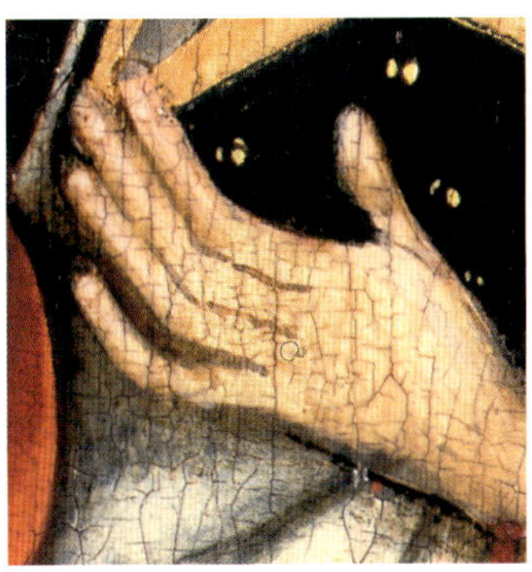

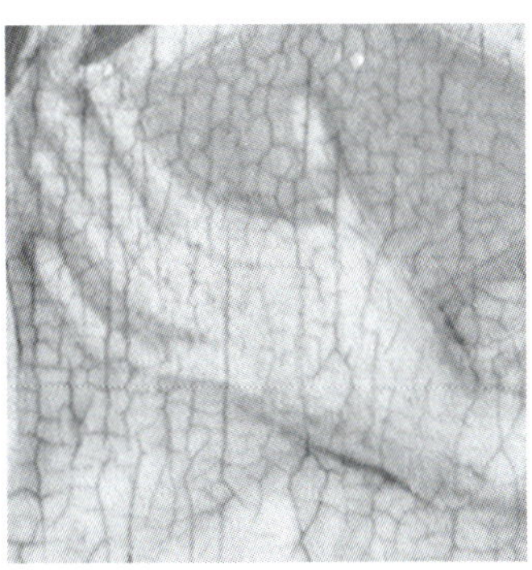

exactly the same infrared-absorbing properties will have been used, and so the restoration will show.

The Magdalen, by an unknown sixteenth-century Netherlandish painter (Fig. 19), is a good example of the different types of information obtainable from infrared photographs and reflectograms. Examined in normal light, a few lines of cross-hatching can be seen in the deeper shadows of the Magdalen's red cloak. The infrared photograph penetrates the cloak completely, showing extensive underdrawing following the form of the drapery, reinforcing the folds and boldly cross-hatched in the shadows (Fig. 20). It is a superb example of a confident, expert, functional underdrawing by an unknown artist. But elsewhere in the painting the infrared photograph shows little that is not visible to the naked eye. In the Magdalen's face and hands, her jar, the architectural surround and the landscape background all that is seen is the paint. To penetrate these areas, a reflectogram mosaic of the painting is necessary (Fig. 21). It reveals not only an extensive drawing beneath almost every part of the composition, but also significant changes.

The Magdalen's face is drawn in a schematic, idiosyncratic style using serpentine 'w'-shaped lines for the end of her nose, her lips and chin. The underdrawn features do not correspond exactly with the painted ones on top. Two positions are clearly visible for the figure's right eye – the underdrawn eye is lower, visible only in outline; when it came to painting the artist moved the eye up slightly, using black for the pupil and a dark blue (which also absorbs infrared) for the iris. Curving lines in the area of the figure's neck indicate alternative ideas for the necklace and décolletage that were not pursued. A more significant change has taken place in the Magdalen's jar. The infrared reflectogram mosaic clearly shows drawing for a jar decorated with a simple pattern of overlapping leaf shapes. The

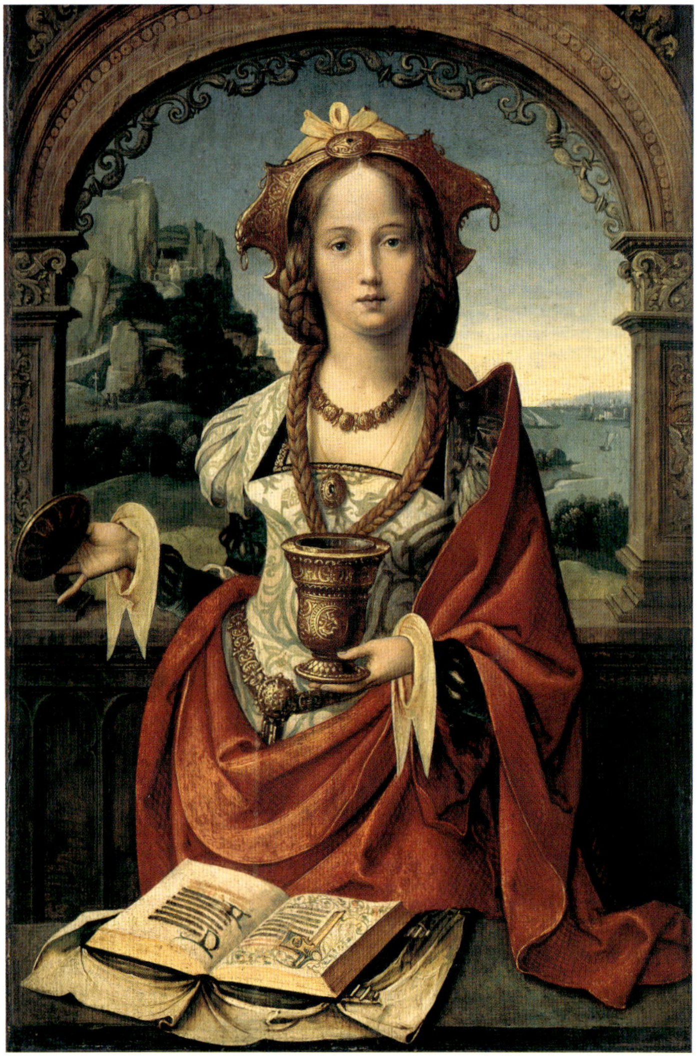

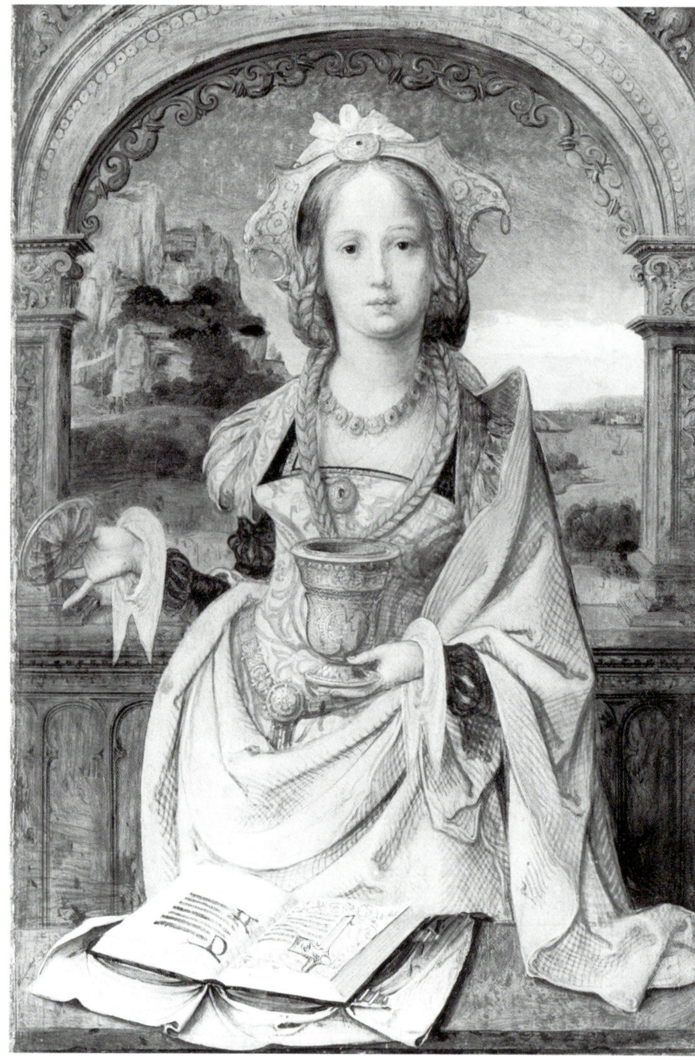

Fig. 19
NETHERLANDISH, *The Magdalen* [NG 719], *c.*1530. Oil on oak, 52.7 × 34.9 cm

Fig. 20
Infrared photograph of Fig. 19

Fig. 21
Infrared reflectogram mosaic of Fig. 19

circular design showing Cain slaying Abel which is visible in the finished picture was painted directly over the drawing of the leaves: its position can just be seen in the reflectogram because the thick yellow paint reflects infrared radiation and shows up as white.

Examples of surface paint appearing in the infrared reflectogram which could be mistaken for underdrawing include the circles decorating the arch near the top and the two small figures in the landscape at the left.

Comparison of the mountains painted to the left of the Magdalen's head with the underdrawing revealed in the reflectogram shows that the artist completely changed this area of the background landscape. The drawing shows a series of tall, pointed peaks, the highest reaching to the top of the Magdalen's head. The flatter, squarer mountains are a depiction of La Sainte-Baume in Provence where the Magdalen is said to have spent many years in penitence.

To the right of the Magdalen's head, level with her chin, is a disturbed area where a lighter patch cuts through some underdrawing. This is a damage – where the paint and ground have been lost – which was subsequently retouched by a restorer. The area now shows empty sky. An X-radiograph shows the damage clearly, but also

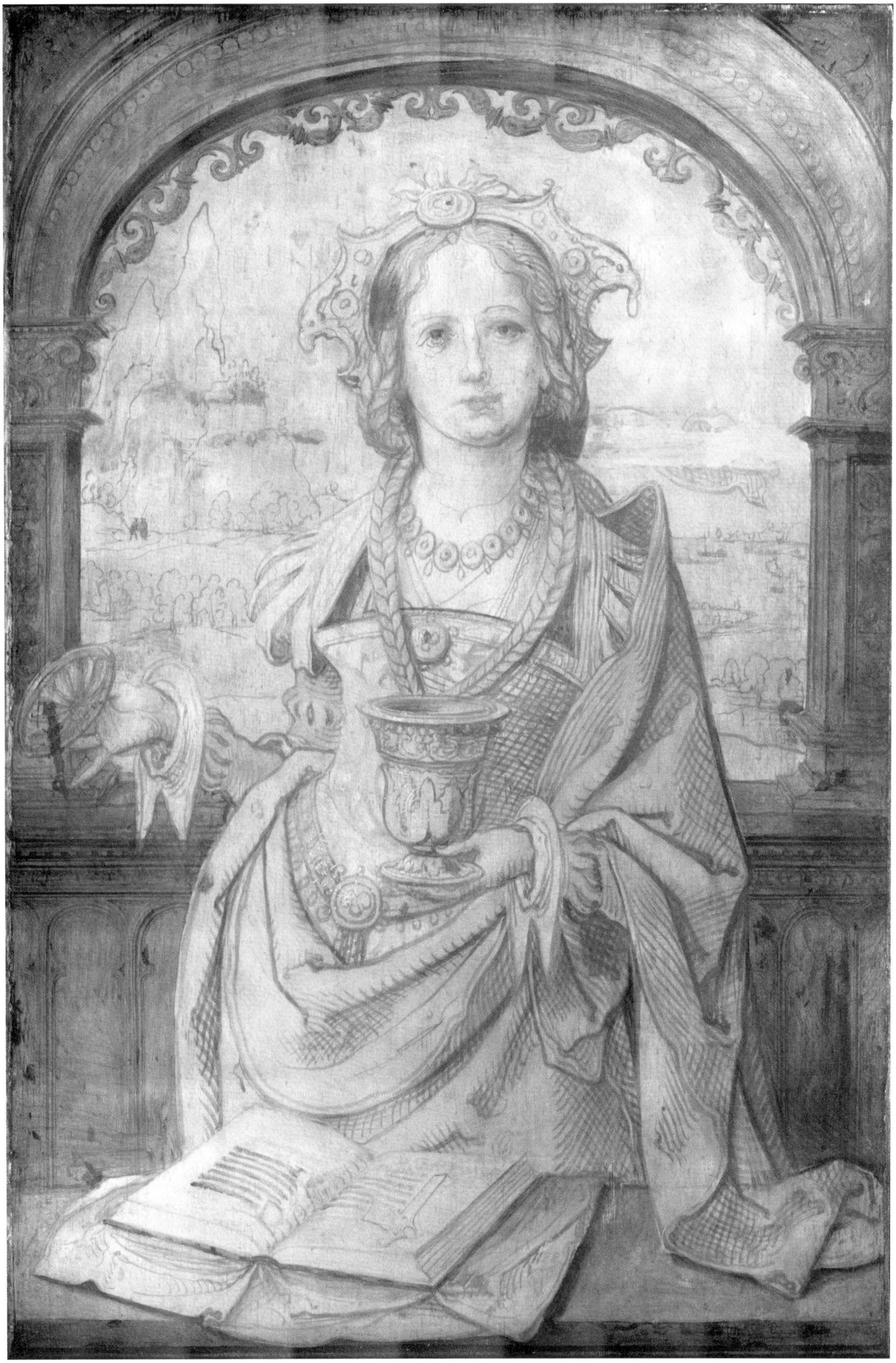

indicates that nothing else was ever painted here. It is difficult to make sense of the underdrawing because of the damage, but it seems to be for a billowing headscarf that was abandoned before painting was carried out.

Underdrawing: Style and Technique

In examining underdrawings, certain types of question are of particular interest and are addressed in the individual catalogue entries that follow. First, how is the underdrawing developed and how does it relate to other drawings that may exist for the composition? What changes are evident in the underdrawing itself and between the drawing and painting stages? And which parts of the painting are underdrawn and which are not?

Secondly, what is the style of the under drawing itself? Who is it by? Is it freehand and sketchy or methodical and orderly? Has the artist used a copying process such as *tracing*, *pouncing* or *squaring* to transfer a design from a drawing on paper or from another painting? How has the artist used line and hatching to suggest form?

Thirdly, what material or materials have been used to make the drawing? Is it dry or fluid – or, perhaps, a fluid reinforcement of a dry sketch? If fluid, was a brush or a pen used? The materials of underdrawing are discussed in detail below (p. 26) and it must always be remembered that underdrawings are rarely observed directly: an imaging process is relied on to make them visible. We must therefore be cautious about characterising drawing lines too precisely on the basis of a processed image: usually the nature of underdrawing materials is confirmed by microscopy or by micro-sampling and analysis. Where it is not possible to take a sample, identification must be based on an educated guess, comparing the appearance of the lines revealed with those in other underdrawings for which material has been identified, and with examples of the materials used on paper.

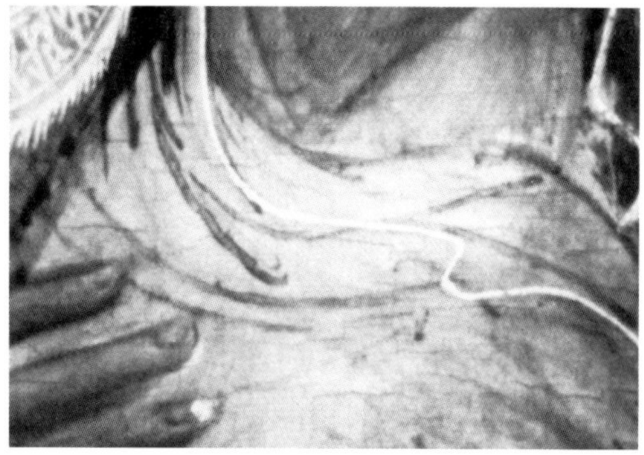

Fig. 22
DUCCIO, *The Virgin and Child with Saints Dominic and Aurea* [NG 566], *c.*1315, infrared reflectogram

Fig. 23
ROGIER VAN DER WEYDEN, *The Magdalen Reading* [NG 654], probably *c.*1435, detail

Fig. 24
Infrared reflectogram mosaic of Fig. 23

Sometimes a drawn line in a reflectogram has such an obvious character that the technique can be confidently described. Wet-brushed lines tend to be smooth and continuous and often appear to have puddled slightly at the point where the brush left the surface (see, for example, Figs 16 and 21). Pen drawing can show a line loaded towards the edges by the divided nib: a clear example of this is observed in Duccio's *Virgin and Child with Saints Dominic and Aurea* (NG 566), in which the split line made by the quill is readily apparent (Fig. 22).

It is worth emphasising that dry lines are rare in the pictures so far examined in the National Gallery. Sometimes, traces of a material similar in appearance to black chalk can be observed in passages of preliminary sketching, the design subsequently being developed more fully in a fluid material. But, often, what appears to be black chalk, with a somewhat granular appearance, turns out to be a 'dry brush' technique, using lean dark paint. A lightly charged brush passed over the ridged brushstrokes of the priming layers leaves a broken mark similar in appearance to black chalk or charcoal on paper. Charcoal was certainly used to make quick indications of a composition or for the transfer of designs (see below), but it would then deliberately be brushed away as the underdrawing developed, or became blurred or washed away in the painting process – so it is rarely found in any quantity.

The stylistic analysis of underdrawings, like all forms of connoisseurship, relies on the

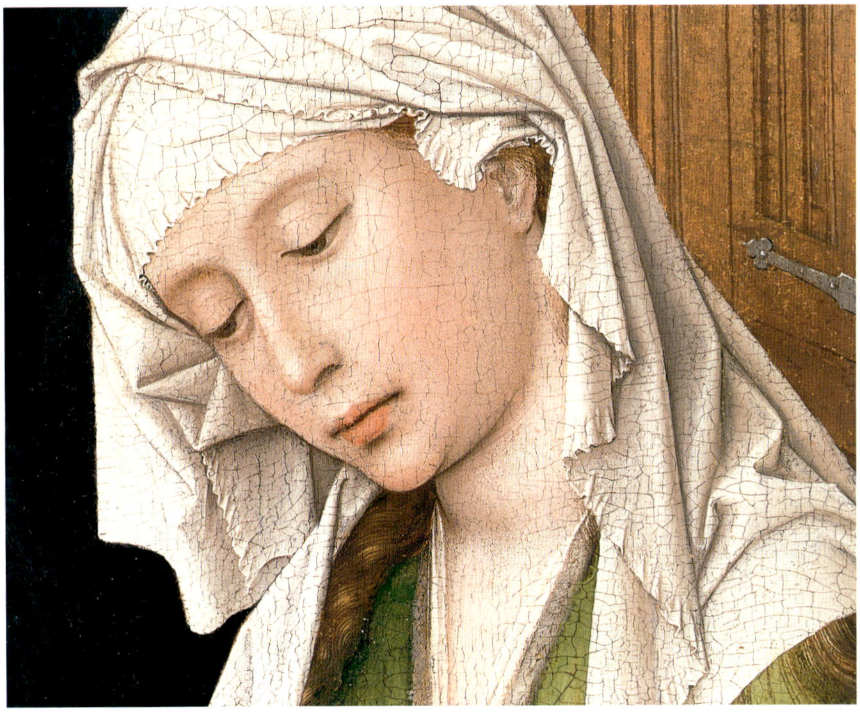

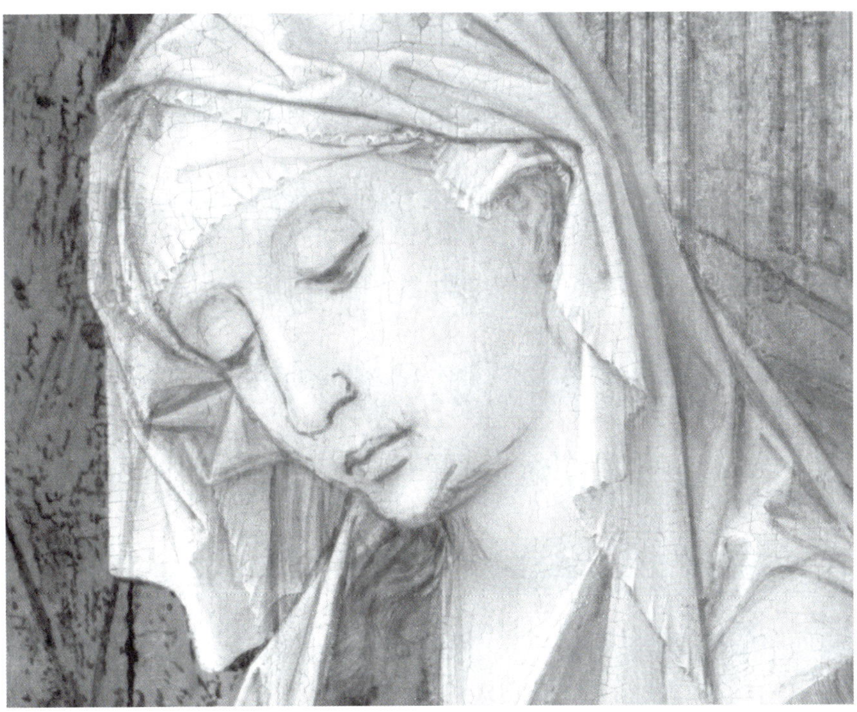

description and classification of visual effects. By interpreting the appearance of drawn lines in an infrared image, an attempt is made to clarify individual cases. Such visual analysis may also be used as a tool for attribution, although this can be fraught with difficulties in a workshop product where underdrawing and painting may be collaborative efforts.

One distinction that can usually be made is between a freehand underdrawing and a design that has been transferred to the panel from another drawing by some mechanical method. Freehand drawing can be characterised by an exuberant setting down of outline, as in Altdorfer's *Christ taking Leave of his Mother* (Cat. 13) or even a scribbled reworking such as that beneath Memling's *Young Man at Prayer* (Cat. 4). It can also be more controlled as when copying an existing compositional idea, such as in *The Virgin and Child with Musical Angels* by the Master of the Saint Bartholomew Altarpiece (Cat. 7).

Underdrawings followed similar conventions to drawings on paper: the contours of a form were outlined, half tones and light shadows were hatched, and deepest shadows were more closely hatched or sometimes cross-hatched for emphasis. In drawings, artists frequently used liquid wash or the stumping (rubbing) of chalk to create light, shade and form. Although such techniques were generally employed for the finishing stages of a drawing, they may also have played a role in underdrawing. However, infrared reflectography is best at detecting linear underdrawings and so the extent of such methods is unclear. Even within the broad conventions of underdrawing, very distinct styles can be distinguished between one artist and another and were reflected in the practice of a workshop. Outlining could be very complete, with every contour scrupulously drawn, as in Crivelli's *Dead Christ supported by Two Angels* (Cat. 3), highly stylised like that of Raphael's *Garvagh Madonna* (Cat. 9); or barely indicated, like the beautifully spare marking-out of the features in Rogier van der Weyden's *Magdalen Reading* (NG

654; Figs 23 and 24). Then again, the short, curved, comma-like hatching of the Master of the Saint Bartholomew Altarpiece (Cat. 7) is quite different to the geometric hatching of Stephan Lochner (Cat. 1), the expansive hatching of the Netherlandish School *Magdalen* (Fig. 21), or the bold, sculptural hatching of Cosimo Tura (Cat. 2).

Transfer Processes

Sometimes it is apparent from an infrared image that an underdrawing is the product of a mechanical transfer process. Two methods were commonly used for transferring full-scale drawings or cartoons from paper to the painting support. One was *tracing*, which involved blackening the back of a drawing with charcoal or black chalk, laying it down on the prepared panel and following the outlines with a stylus. Alternatively, an intermediate sheet of paper blackened on the underside could be placed between drawing and panel. The result was a schematic map of the design that could then be

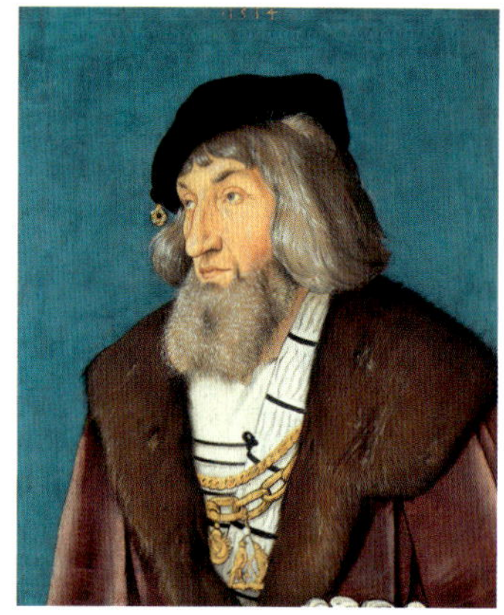

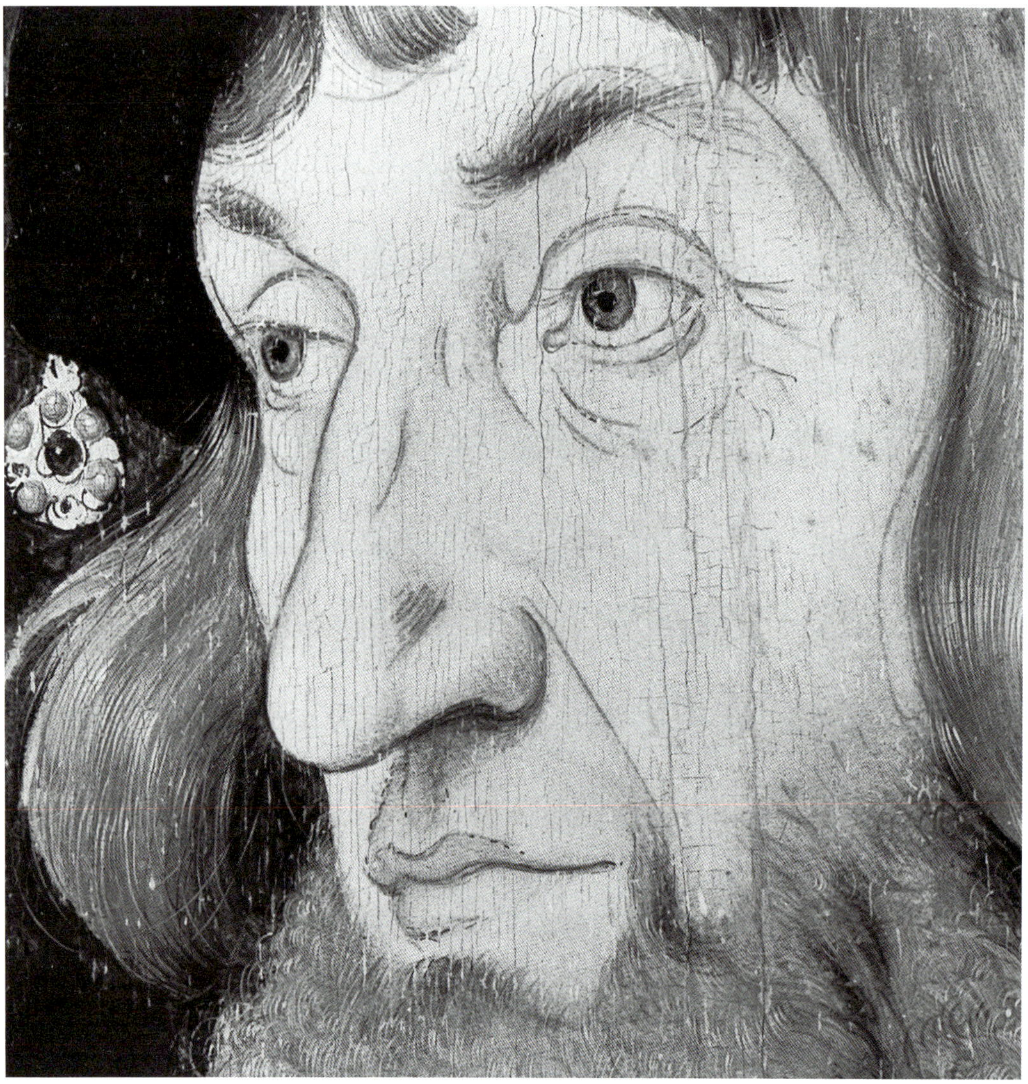

Fig. 25
HANS BALDUNG GRIEN, *Portrait of a Man* [NG 245], 1514. Oil on lime, 59.3 × 48.9 cm

Fig. 26
Infrared photograph detail of Fig. 25

reinforced with a drawing in a more fluid material. Exactly this method is evident in Hans Baldung Grien's *Portrait of a Man* (NG 245; Fig. 25). An infrared photograph of the face shows the carefully traced outlines of all the features, slightly smudged by subsequent painting, and darker, freehand reinforcing lines in a fluid material on top (Fig. 26). Marinus van Reymerswale's *Two Tax Gatherers* (Cat. 15) is a more complex example of a design traced from an almost identical version of the same composition.

A second method of transferring designs directly from paper to painting support was *pouncing*, a technique more commonly used in Italy because of its traditional role in the design of wall paintings. Pouncing involved pricking the outlines of a drawing on paper (the cartoon), laying the pricked drawing on the prepared panel and dusting charcoal or dark pigment through the holes by means of a pounce bag – a porous fabric bag full of the charcoal or dark pigment. The resulting dots on the panel (*spolveri* in Italian) would then be joined up to make the underdrawing. The dots would usually be brushed away as the artist worked, but sometimes their remains can be seen in infrared photographs or reflectograms. They are clearly visible in Raphael's *Procession to Calvary* (Cat. 8) and in his *Allegory (Vision of a Knight)*. Although the cartoon for the *Procession to Calvary* does not survive, that for the *Allegory* is in the British Museum (Figs 217 and 218, pp. 126–7).

Another method used to transfer drawings on to painting supports was *squaring*. It could be used where a change of scale was required, usually progressing from a smaller drawing to a larger painting. A grid was drawn across the drawing on paper and another of the same relative proportions was made on the prepared panel; the design was then copied freehand from one to the other in small, manageable sections, square by square. Infrared photographs of two wings from an altarpiece by Martin van Heemskerck (NG 6508) show a distinct grid pattern under the paint (Figs 27 and 28); the lines have the smudged appearance of charcoal, the presence of which has been confirmed by

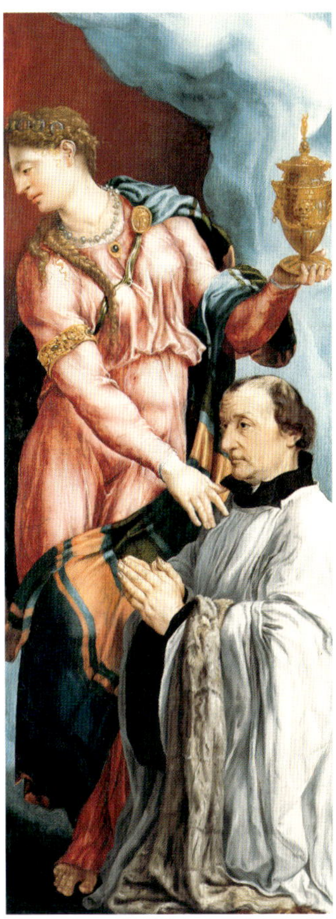

Fig. 27
MARTIN VAN HEEMSKERCK,
The Donor and Saint Mary Magdalene [NG 6508.2], *c.*1540. Oil on oak, painted surface 123 × 46 cm

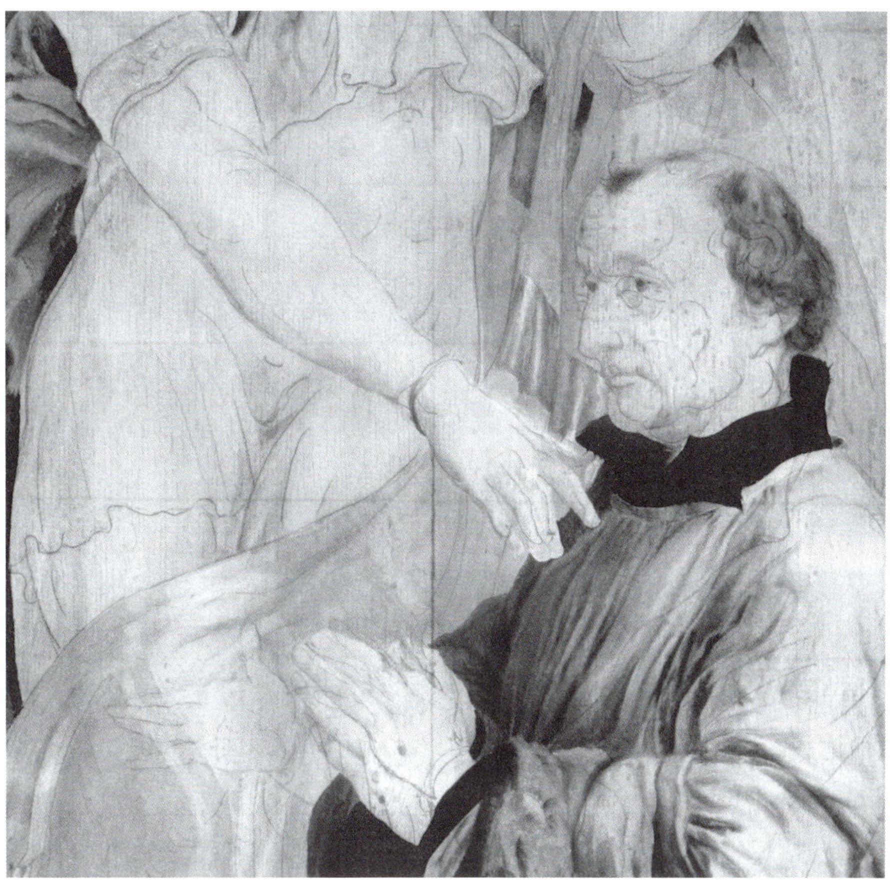

Fig. 28
Detail from infrared reflectogram mosaic of Fig. 27

sampling. Squared drawings by Heemskerck for other altarpieces are known, so his use of the technique here is not surprising.

Changes of Composition

An insight into the creative processes of artists is gained by mapping revisions or changes in a composition (*pentimenti* in Italian). These can occur during the underdrawing stage, between underdrawing and painting, and during painting. The majority of the paintings in this catalogue have changes at one or more of these stages, some quite minor, some extensive. In the Master of the View of St Gudula's *Portrait of a Young Man* (Cat. 5), for example, figures in the background were drawn but not subsequently painted. In Giorgione's *Adoration of the Kings* (Cat. 10), another drawing becomes apparent if the reflectogram is turned upside down. In the most complex example described in the following pages, the background of Pontormo's *Joseph with Jacob in Egypt* (Cat. 12) was completely reversed and redrawn so that key elements were switched from one side of the picture to the other.

Frequently, parts of a composition would be added at the painting stage, without being underdrawn first: this may suggest improvisation in some cases, but an underdrawing was often simply a guide that was intended to be developed and elaborated in the paint layers that followed. The identification of underdrawings as key intermediate stages – reflecting the preliminary ideas and drawings that preceded them and anticipating the paintings that cover them – gives profound insights into the methods and ambitions of the artists that made them.

The Catalogue

This catalogue examines in detail sixteen paintings of the fifteenth and sixteenth centuries, from the Netherlands, Germany and Italy, in more or less chronological order. .

The selection of works has been dependent to some extent on the systematic examination and cataloguing programme in progress at the National Gallery and reflects the different stages this has reached for different areas of the collection. It has been possible, for example, to choose works that illustrate aspects of Netherlandish and German workshop production, since cataloguing of these areas is advanced or completed. However, examination of corresponding Italian paintings is at an earlier stage and the well-known paintings included here, all of them clearly executed by the artist without signs of workshop assistance, have been chosen more for their fascinating and distinctive underdrawings than to explore workshop production in Italy. Moreover, outside the National Gallery the methodical study of underdrawings, and their implications for workshop practice, has also tended to be applied principally to paintings from the Netherlands and Germany. On the other hand, many more drawings on paper, of every type, ranging from first sketches to detailed studies and full-scale cartoons, survive from Italy than from Northern Europe. In particular, a tragically small number of fifteenth-century drawings survive from the Netherlands, and those that do tend to be highly finished and developed designs, revealing few traces of earlier stages in their creation. This disparity in the available evidence means that the two essays on drawing and underdrawing practice in Northern Europe and Italy are written from somewhat different standpoints. Nevertheless, as will become apparent, painters from both sides of the Alps shared in common many techniques such as methods for transfer of designs. They also used similar drawing materials, which are discussed in the following essay.

Other Underdrawings

The use of underdrawings is by no means confined to the period described in this

Fig. 29 (below)
UNKNOWN ENGLISH/FRENCH artist,
The Wilton Diptych [NG 4451], *c*.1395–9
Egg on oak, 53 × 37 cm
Right panel (diptych open)

Fig. 30
Infrared reflectogram, detail of
Fig. 29

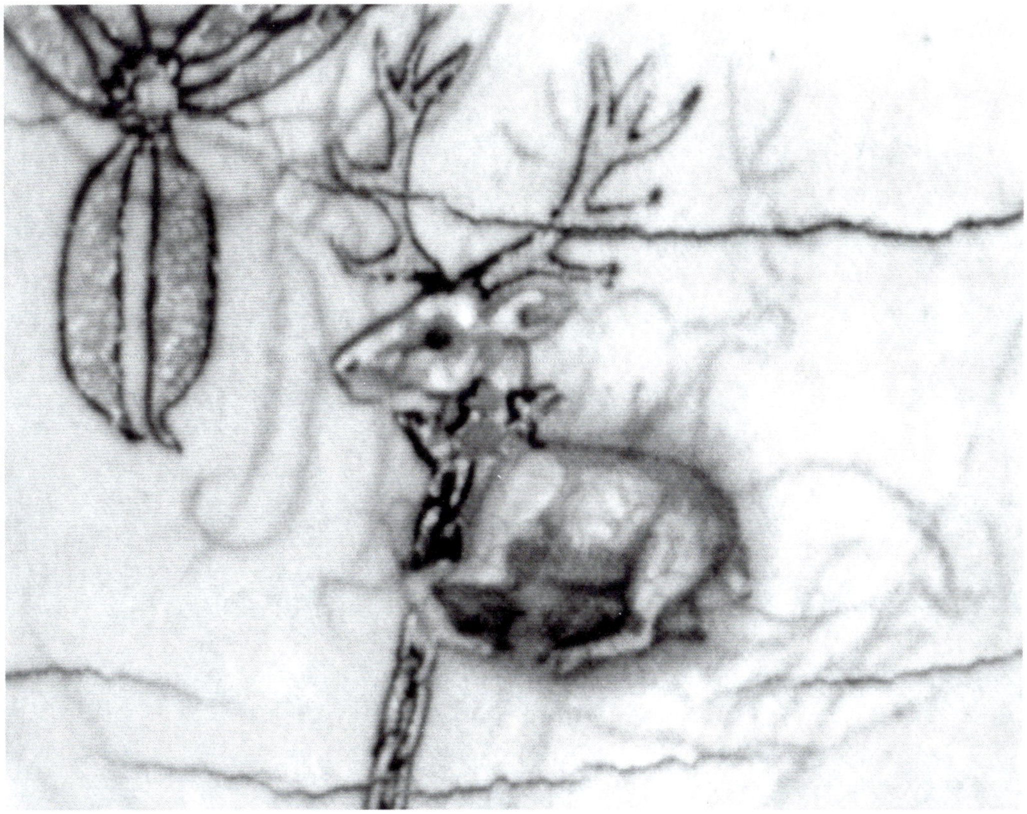

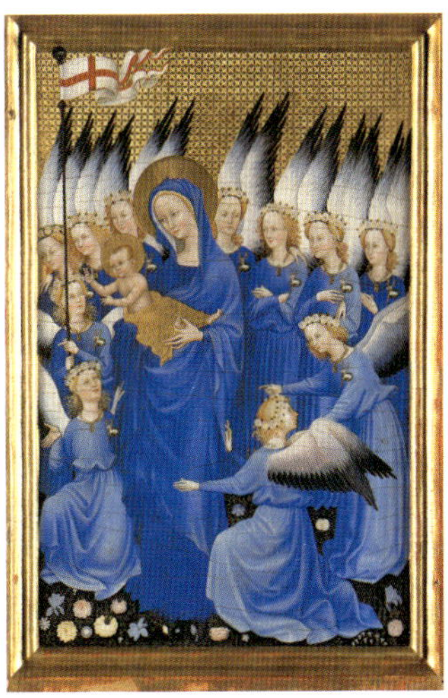

catalogue – although, by the nature of its painting techniques, this has traditionally been the most fruitful area for underdrawings research. Infrared reflectography is increasingly being applied to paintings outside the scope of this catalogue and significant results have been achieved for paintings earlier and later than those discussed here. At the National Gallery earlier examples include the Wilton Diptych, which has an extensive drawing beneath many of the principal features (Figs 29 and 30), and the paintings of Duccio (see Fig. 22). Later examples examined have included seventeenth-century Dutch and Flemish artists, especially architectural painters like Bartholomeus van Bassen and Pieter Saenredam. Infrared reflectography was also instrumental in distinguishing between two almost identical Rembrandt 'self portraits' in The Hague and in Nuremberg. What had been considered to be the prime version in The Hague was shown to have an underdrawing, quite uncharacteristic of Rembrandt, traced from the other version in Nuremberg – and, as a result of this observation, the status of the two paintings was dramatically reversed. Many underdrawings have also been identified beneath nineteenth- and twentieth-century paintings.

2 The Materials of Underdrawing

'Their workroom is quite full of pictures, painted and to be painted, and many fine tools. There are charcoals, pencils, pens, brushes ... pencils of silver which make many a fine line . . .'
Jean Lemaire de Belges, *La Couronne Margaritique*, 1504–5.[1]

Identification of Materials

The identification of the materials used for underdrawing presents a particular problem because the drawing is located beneath layers of paint and consequently it is difficult to gain direct access to it for the purpose of microscopical or analytical examination. Even with early drawings on paper and other flexible supports, which are often described as being executed with, for example, 'red chalk' or 'charcoal with white heightening' and so on (Figs 31 and 32), these materials are seldom identified by some positive means other than the general appearance of the lines or shading.[2]

Infrared images showing underdrawings are often used to draw inferences about the nature of the materials used, and on occasion the inability to see the underdrawing in the infrared image, when it is known to be present, can also be indicative of the material used. The character of the drawing seen by infrared radiation – whether the lines appear fluid and continuous, or broken and granular; the definition of the

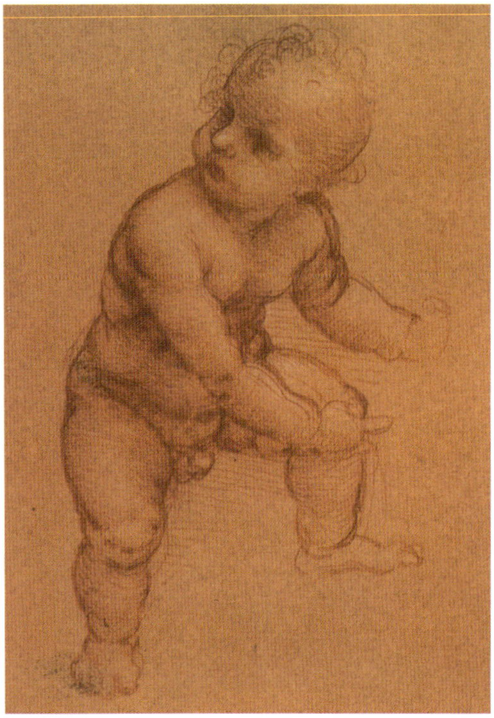

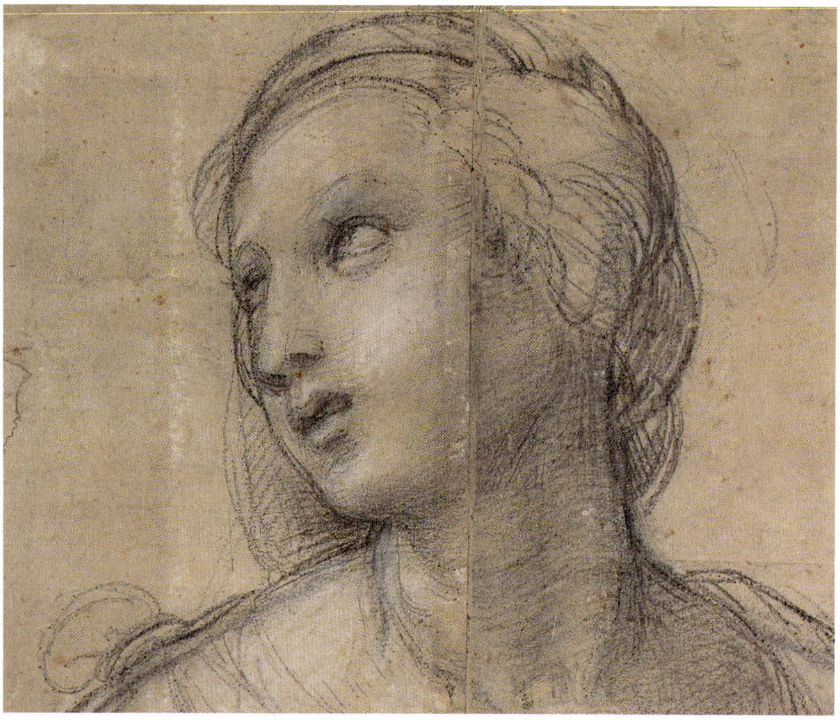

Fig. 31
LEONARDO DA VINCI, *Studies of a Child and Parts of a Child*, detail of Fig. 102

Fig. 32
RAPHAEL, *Saint Catherine*, detail of Fig. 105

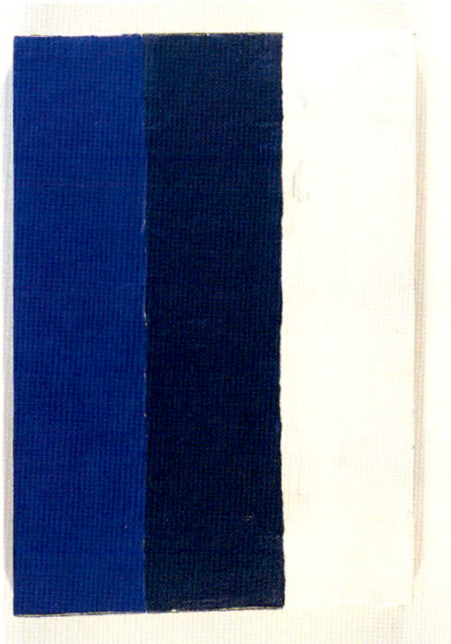

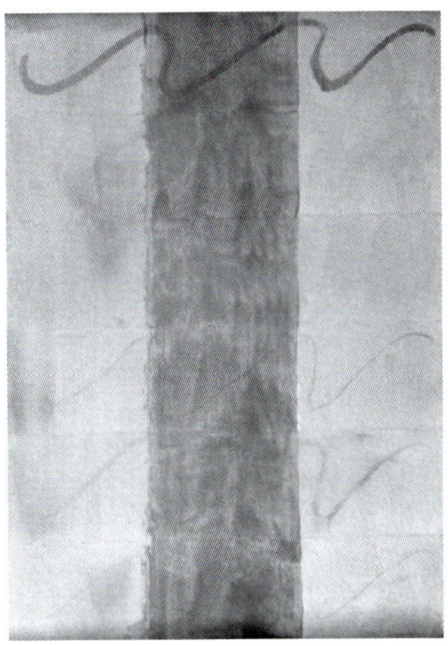

Fig. 33
Ultramarine (left) and azurite painted over six types of underdrawing

Fig. 34
Infrared reflectogram mosaic of Fig. 33

lines; and the degree of contrast compared to the ground layer, as well as other factors – can be interpreted in terms of the materials present in the drawing layer. This approach amounts to a form of connoisseurship of infrared images, and while reasonably reliable does not provide unambiguous identification of materials. More certain deductions can only be achieved by confirmatory microscopical and analytical study and even then the results may not be wholly conclusive.

Two further problems in firm identification present themselves. First, the quantity of drawing material that might be present within a microsample of paint taken from a picture is frequently exceedingly small, and second, because a number of materials used to create both drawings and underdrawn designs are based on some form of carbon, analytical identification of the material on its own does not provide sufficient information to pin down the origin or source of the carbon used. In these cases, careful microscopical examination of the particle form of the carbon can reveal its origin, but this method does not always provide certain results. It is, however, very helpful to examine samples of underdrawing and to relate either firm or more qualified identifications of the materials used to the appearance of the underdrawings as they are recorded in infrared images. When a body of information is acquired in this way, the results should make deductions based on the images alone more certain in future and it is one of the purposes of this catalogue to record studies of this kind.

It is also helpful to examine the appearance in infrared light of different types of drawing materials beneath layers of paint on test panels as an aid to interpreting the materials used for underdrawings in fifteenth- and sixteenth-century paintings. The materials are most conveniently divided between those that are fluid in nature, in which some kind of colouring matter is suspended in a liquid medium, and a second group consisting of a dry drawing material. The first category includes thin or dilute paint and a variety of inks, while the second group comprises materials such as charcoal, various kinds of chalks, graphite and metal-point.

Fig. 33 illustrates a panel on which lines have been drawn with six different types of material. A priming was applied over the lines, and sections of them were then covered with two types of blue paint, one containing ultramarine and the other containing azurite. These pigments, which occur frequently in fifteenth- and sixteenth-century paintings, have different infrared-absorbing properties. In the infrared reflectogram mosaic of the same panel, shown in Fig. 34, a line lying beneath the ultramarine-containing paint is more clearly seen than the line beneath the azurite-containing paint, because the azurite absorbs some of the infrared light, while the ultramarine allows most to be transmitted. The first line, at the top of the panel, is a fluid black paint (carbon black in watercolour). The second line is also fluid, but painted with iron-gall ink; this can barely be seen in the infrared image. Dry materials have been used for the other lines: red and black chalks, charcoal and, lastly, silver-point, the line at the bottom of the panel. The red chalk line disappears in the infrared image unlike the black chalk line because it is based on iron oxide rather than carbon black. The fluid lines are characteristically continuous and vary in width. There is some pooling of the paint at the edges of the lines, and sometimes also where the line turns a corner or the brush is lifted off. The softer dry materials also show some variation in width, but the line made with the harder metal-point is fine and very even. The charcoal line has been picked up by the paint above, smudging it.

The great majority of fifteenth- and sixteenth-century European paintings on which underdrawings have been detected have white grounds. In most Italian examples, the ground is gesso (mineral calcium sulphate) bound with animal-skin glue, while paintings produced in

Northern Europe usually have white grounds consisting of natural chalk or calcium carbonate, also bound in glue. Oil paintings frequently had a further thin, priming layer, usually in oil, to reduce the absorbency of the principal ground layer. Although coloured grounds came into use during the sixteenth century, in the majority of paintings from this period the priming layer was light in colour.[3] In canvas paintings where the binding medium of the paint was an aqueous material like glue or egg tempera, the canvas was often simply sized before any underdrawing was executed.[4] As the painter was working on a white or light-coloured ground, a drawing material that would show clearly on this surface was required. Although this ruled out the use of white 'chalks' made from a number of possible mineral whites, or sticks of compressed white pigment (discussed below), there remained a wide range of possible choices.

It was common practice to execute the drawing stage over the first layer of ground, before any priming or 'sealing' layer (*imprimitura* in Italian, *primuersel* in Dutch) was applied. The priming layer was generally applied as a thin veil of paint over the drawing layer, through which the drawn design could still be seen (Figs 35 and 36). Sometimes, however, particularly in the sixteenth century, the underdrawing was executed on top of the priming.[5] Examples include Jan Gossaert's *Adoration of the Kings* (NG 2790) and Raphael's *Procession to Calvary* (Cat. 8). The lines often appear broken in the infrared

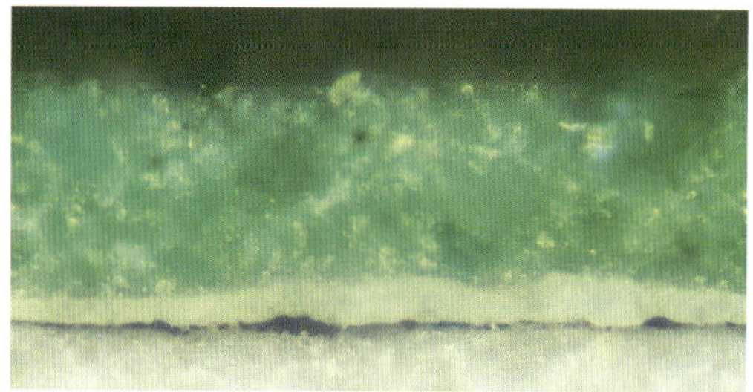

Fig. 35
Cross-section from Fig. 36 showing underdrawing below priming layer

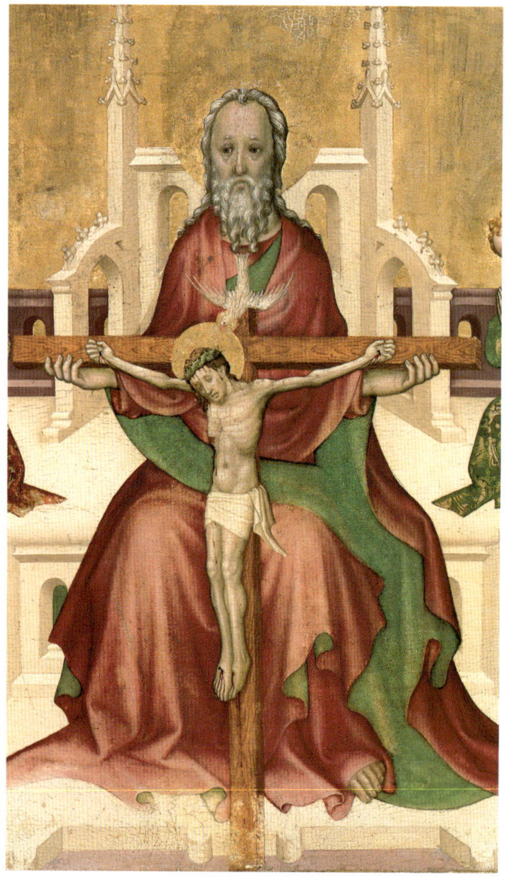

Fig. 36
AUSTRIAN SCHOOL, *Trinity with Christ Crucified* [NG 3662], *c.*1410, detail

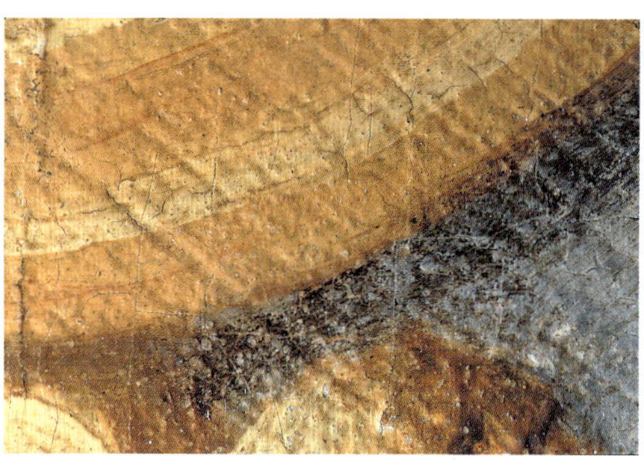

Fig. 37 (bottom left)
Detail of Fig. 42

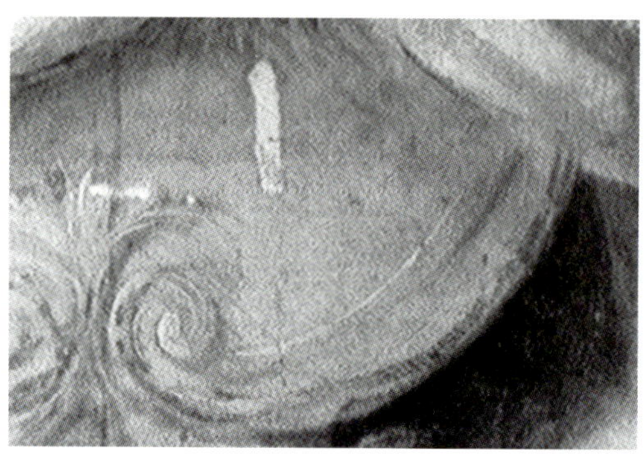

Fig. 38 (bottom right)
Infrared reflectogram, detail of Fig. 42

Fig. 39 (right)
NETHERLANDISH, *The Magdalen* [NG 719], *c.*1530, detail of Fig. 19

Fig. 40 (far right)
Infrared reflectogram mosaic, detail of Fig. 21

Fig. 41
WORKSHOP OF THE MASTER OF THE SAINT BARTHOLOMEW ALTARPIECE, *The Virgin and Child in Glory with Saint James the Great and Saint Cecilia* [NG 6497], detail

Fig. 42
GAROFALO, *The Holy Family with Saints John the Baptist, Elizabeth, Zacharias and (?) Francis* [NG 170], *c.*1520. Oil on canvas, 60.5 × 47.2 cm

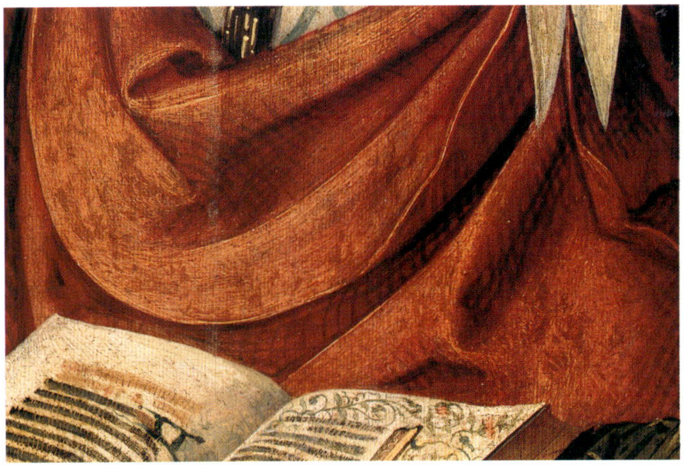

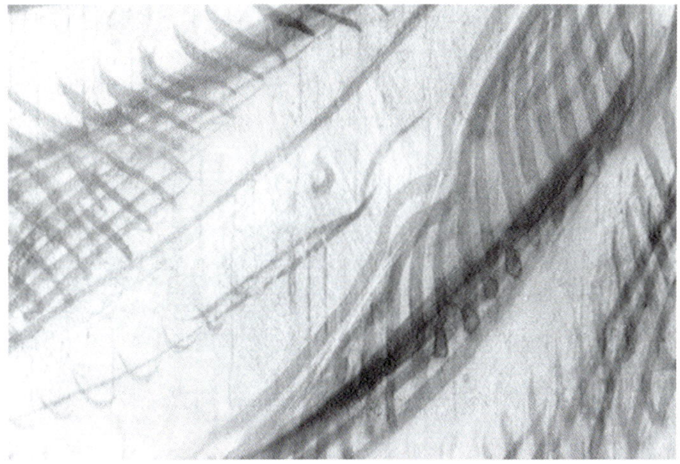

image because they are interrupted by the brushstrokes of the uneven priming layer, as illustrated by a detail of the paint at the foot of the cradle in Garofalo's *Holy Family* (NG 170; Figs 37, 38 and 42). Sometimes more than one drawing material was used, and in some cases different drawing media were deployed for different parts of a composition, for example draperies, architecture and landscape, the figures and so on.

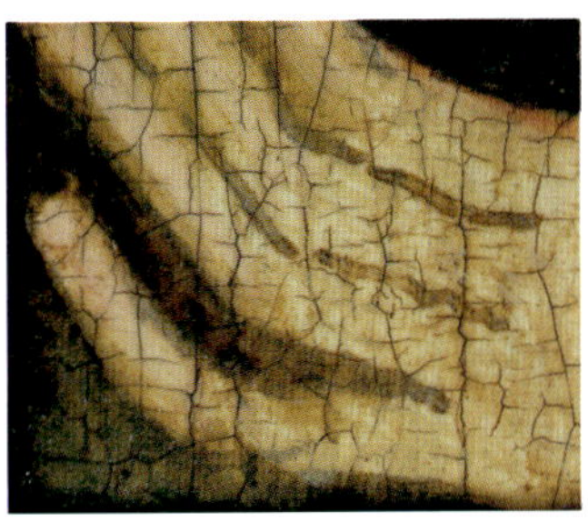

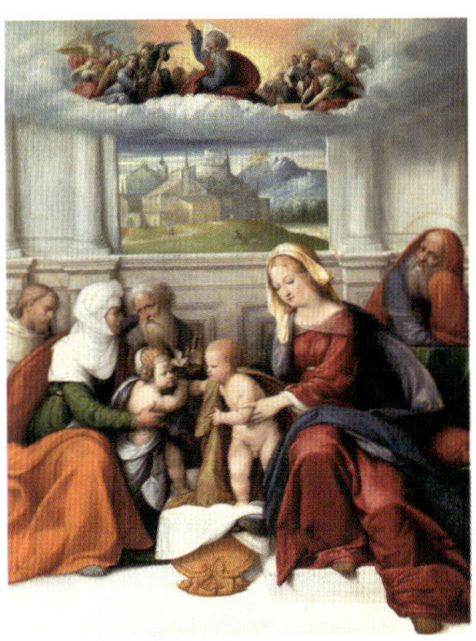

Fluid Drawing Media

Underdrawings for paintings in the fifteenth and sixteenth centuries were most frequently executed in fluid drawing media. These are distinguished from dry types of drawing material by the presence of some kind of binding medium for a colouring matter in the form of pigment. One of the main advantages of inks and fluid paints in the preparation of an underdrawing on panel is that they are very easy to use, both for linear design and for rapid, free shading. When the paint or ink is very fluid the lines are characteristically continuous in nature, vary in width and density, and form a droplet at the end of a brush- or pen-stroke (Figs 39 and 40). It is not always easy to distinguish between drawn lines produced by a pen or brush; however, in the underdrawing for *The Virgin and Child in Glory with Saint James the Great and Saint Cecilia* (NG 6497) from the workshop of the Master of the Saint Bartholomew Altarpiece (Fig. 41), the fact that the drawn lines appear denser at the edges and have markedly square ends suggests that a pen was used.[6]

The dividing line between an ink and a paint of fluid consistency is not a sharp one and it is often not possible to distinguish the precise form of fluid material from the infrared image, or in samples of paint. Indeed, it is sometimes difficult to see any evidence of the presence of binding medium in the thin layer of underdrawing visible in a paint cross-section, even though it appears clear from the infrared image that a fluid drawing material was used. It seems likely that the inks used for underdrawings are mostly aqueous, like those used for drawings on paper. Oil-based 'inks' – in this context essentially a very liquid oil paint – would have been perfectly possible, however, and may have been quite commonly used for underdrawings in the later fifteenth and sixteenth centuries. Most inks are theoretically distinguishable from paints either by the very fine particle size of the pigment content, or by the complete dispersion or dissolution of colouring matter in the medium. A paint, used as such rather than as an ink, is likely to have rather larger pigment particle sizes; if the material is to be used as an ink, the pigment needs to be quite finely ground so that the paint can flow freely from the brush or quill.

Carbon-based inks

Inks were often based on carbon as the colouring matter. The most common form of carbon was some variety of lampblack – essentially soot collected on a cool surface by condensing a smoky flame from burning oil, resin, wax or some other similar material such as pitch.[7] The carbon particles collected in this way are exceedingly fine and relatively even in size, leading to good dispersion in the medium and an ink that flows easily. Examination of cross-sections of samples taken from fifteenth- or sixteenth-century paintings has so far suggested that, in spite of its ideal properties, lampblack was used rather less frequently than another source of black pigment: burnt plant matter. Peach stones, almond shells or, indeed, vine or other forms of charcoal, finely ground, were all suitable and suggested for use. The resulting colouring matter was not greasy – therefore easily miscible with water – and was a bluish black. Karel van Mander, writing at the beginning of the seventeenth century but discussing the practice of earlier painters of the North and South Netherlands, describes the 'most skilled' practice of those who drew their design all at once with charcoal ground in water, before applying the first thin layer of oil paint (the priming or *primuersel*) (Fig. 44).[8] Charred paper, ground finely, is also mentioned as a source of carbon to prepare water-based inks.[9]

An ink containing carbon seems to be the type recommended by Cennino Cennini as the drawing medium to be used to fix and reinforce an initial underdrawn design, first worked up in charcoal, on a panel (see pp. 73–4).

Iron-gall inks

Iron-gall inks, the colours of which are produced by the formation of complex salts of iron, have been in use from about the third century BC.[11] In essence, the ink is made by extracting compounds called tannins from insect galls. Galls are roughly spherical excrescences produced by certain plants and trees in response to the irritant action of various parasitic insects laying their eggs in some part of the tree, frequently the leaves or leaf stems; oak galls caused by the female gall wasp are probably the most familiar in Europe, although many other types exist (Fig. 43). As well as their use in the production of ink, galls (and other sources of tannin) were used in dyeing in the fifteenth and sixteenth centuries and beyond. Aleppo galls, from the so-called gall oak (*Quercus infectoria* Oliv.), have a notably high tannin content (50–70%) and were imported into Europe from the Eastern Mediterranean regions on a large scale.[12] The gall contains soluble gallotannins which, when reacted with iron sulphate in solution, often in the presence of acidity (wine or vinegar), form dark-coloured compounds (ferric 'tannates'), although they do not develop their fullest depth of colour immediately. These dark brown and blackish materials, stabilised as fine suspensions in aqueous solution by the addition of gum arabic (gum from species of *Acacia*), constitute the iron-gall ink.[13]

By medieval times numerous fairly standard recipes for iron-gall ink are recorded in treatises from all over Europe. Examples include the collection made by the Paris lawyer Jehan Le Begue in 1431; the tract on the preparation of inks and colours included in the various editions of the homely collections of useful recipes and instructions – *Kunstbüchlein* – which had an enormous circulation in Germany and the Low Countries; compilations made by scribes, often in monastery scriptoria; and more elegant manuals on calligraphy.[14] Minor variations in the procedure involved, for example, heating the solutions with wine, the addition of other sources of tannins, such as chestnut or oak bark, sumach leaves or pomegranate peel, filtration and so on. Although iron sulphate – sal martis,

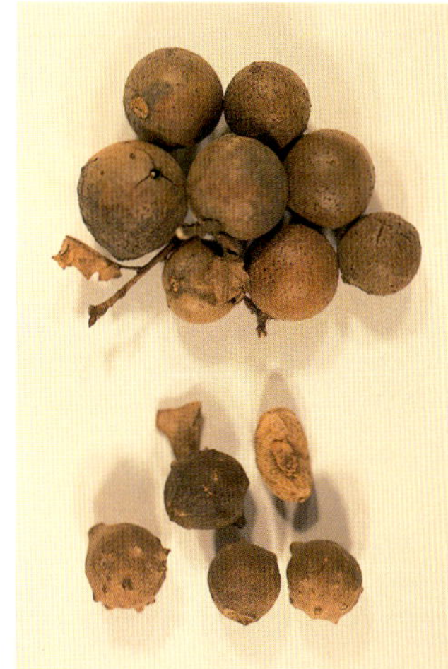

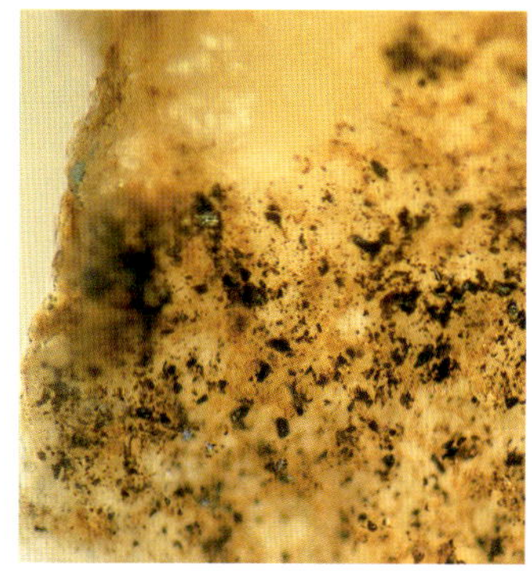

Fig. 43
Oak galls from English oak (top), Aleppo galls (below)

Fig. 44
Charcoal in a liquid medium, paint sample, from *The Coronation of the Virgin* [NG 2154], by the Master of Cappenburg

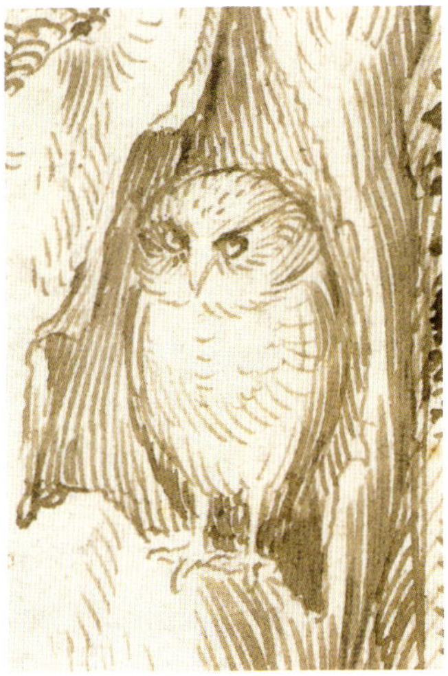

Fig. 45
HIERONYMUS BOSCH, *The Wood has Ears, the Field has Eyes*, detail of Fig. 92

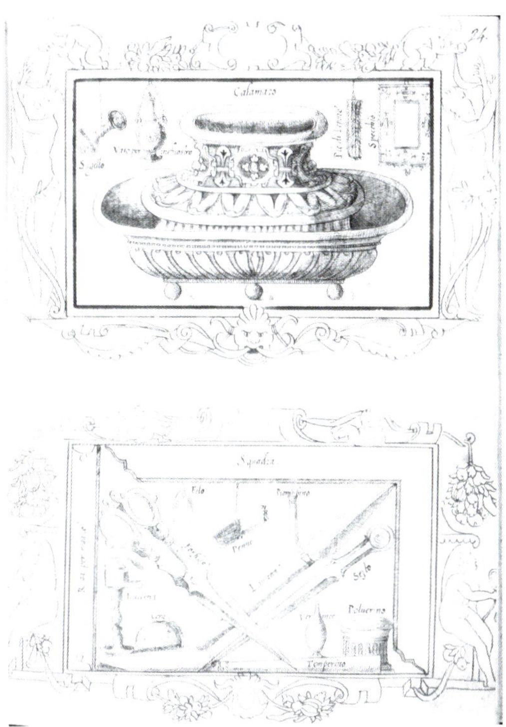

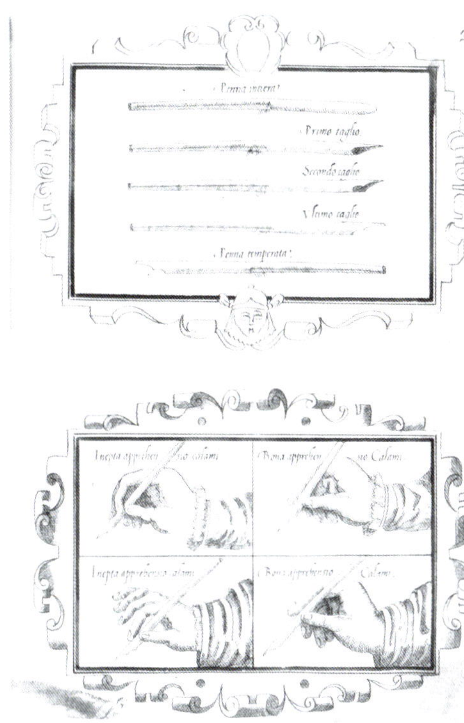

Figs 46 and 47
Illustrations of pens and pen-cutting from *Modi di perfettamente scrivere del R.P. Maestro Fra Cherubino Ghirardacci Bolognese Eremitani*
Siena, Biblioteca Comunale degli Intronati
inv. MS H.VII 39, folios 24 and 25

copperas, *vitriolium cyprinum*, Roman vitriol, English vitriol: the salt is given various names in early recipes – was usually used, the copper salt, which forms similar compounds, was occasionally used instead. Some Northern European recipes include an ingredient known as *substancie*, which consisted, for these water-based inks, of an aqueous extract of some source of tannin such as the bark of trees or walnut shells, boiled down to give a dark, tarry material, which could be added as desired to alter the colour or consistency of the ink.[15] Although the chemistry involved is complex, the basic reactions are common to all the variants in preparation; however, the stability of the ink, particularly in response to fading, was variable according to the method used for its making.

Iron-gall inks are exceptionally important in the history of written documents: the colour of the ink is deep and intense, and when correctly prepared, very stable to light. Furthermore, iron-gall inks are indelible since they enter the fibres of paper and parchment, in contrast to carbon-based aqueous inks which lie on the surface and smudge when moistened or if subjected to high humidity. A serious drawback of their use, however, is that the iron compounds can induce complex oxidative reactions which corrode paper and parchment, in severe cases eating through the support entirely. All types of inks can be applied with pens or brushes, and Renaissance drawings executed in pen and iron-gall ink are well known (Figs 45, 46 and 47). In the same way, iron-gall inks were used in underdrawings, but they are often not recorded or recognised as they register very poorly in infrared images of paintings.

Iron-gall inks are also difficult to identify analytically in underdrawings, generally because only small quantities of the drawing material are present in samples. The iron content, and an absence of carbon, are characteristic, and can be demonstrated by analysis in favourable cases. Iron-gall ink underdrawing has been confirmed, by this means, in the predella panels of the high altarpiece painted, probably in the mid-1420s, for the church of San Domenico, Fiesole, by Fra Angelico (NG 663.1–5; Figs 48 and 49), and also in Giovanni Battista Cima's large altarpiece, *The Incredulity of Saint Thomas* (NG 816; *c.*1502–4), originally in the church of San Francesco in Portogruaro. In both cases, the underdrawing in ink lies directly on a gesso ground. It is rarely possble to detect any compounds related to the tannin component of the ink; however, in Piero di Cosimo's *A Satyr mourning over a Nymph* (NG 698), painted in about 1495, the ink drawing was present in a sufficiently substantial layer in some areas to cause disruption and cracking of the paint above (Fig. 50). In this case it was possible to separate, examine and identify some of the tannin-related constituents.[16] Iron-gall ink has also been found as an underdrawing material on a painting in the style of the Antwerp painter Joachim Patinir, *The Virgin and Child with a Cistercian Nun* (NG 945), and here too it has caused cracking of the paint layers above.

Dry Drawing Media

Charcoal

The second broad category of drawing materials consists of those that are dry in nature. One of the most familar and, perhaps, earliest in use in this group is wood charcoal. Charcoal had many industrial uses, such as smelting metals, and was made on a large scale. The choice of wood was important: charcoal made from soft or young woods was not suitable for processes that required prolonged heating at a high temperature, and oak or beech, or the wood of other large trees, was used.[17] For artists' charcoal, however, softer woods like willow, or even vine twigs, were suitable and the charcoal could be made on a smaller scale. Its use for drawing, as well as in pulverised form as a black pigment for painting, is mentioned by Cennino Cennini who describes its preparation from small bundles of strips of willow, tied with wire, and heated in the baker's oven overnight in a closed earthenware 'casserole' sealed with clay.[18] Whatever kind of wood was used, it is a usual feature of the preparation of charcoal that air should be excluded, otherwise only grey ashes are produced. The length of heating time is also important: it must be long enough to allow complete carbonisation of the wood, but not so long as to reduce the sticks to powder. Raffaello Borghini, writing in 1584, describes the use of a small iron box, with a closely fitting lid, which could be heated in a furnace or fire. He favoured the use of lime wood for this purpose, cut into pieces roughly the size of a finger.[19]

The dry impermanent nature of a line drawn in charcoal was often seen as an advantage since, unless fixed in some way, it could be corrected by dusting away with a feather. Cennino Cennini recommends an initial sketch on paper or on panel in charcoal, worked over until the drawing has been perfected. The lines were then gone over with silver-point, in the case of paper, or with dilute ink, for a panel, and the charcoal drawing brushed away.[20] For sketching on panels he suggests that the sticks of charcoal, sharpened to a point, should be fixed to a wooden holder to allow the painter to work some distance from the composition. This would have the added advantage that the painter would keep his hands clean; the charcoal could also be put in a goose-quill holder.[21]

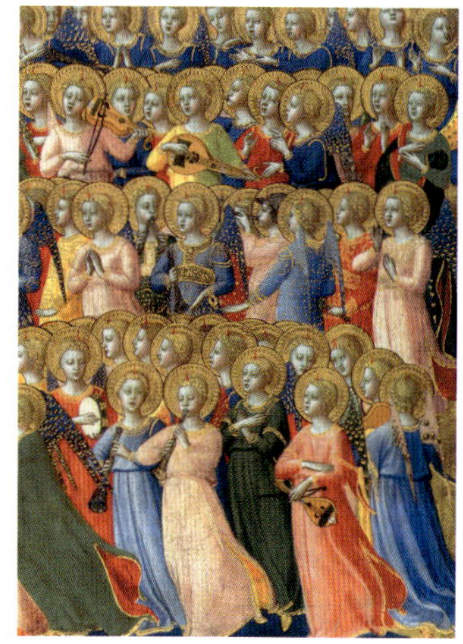

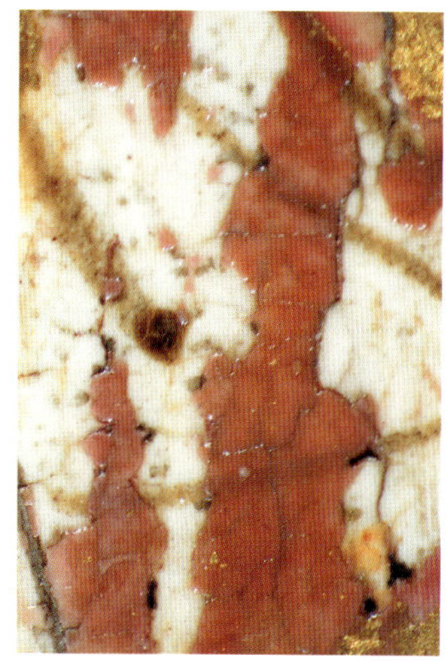

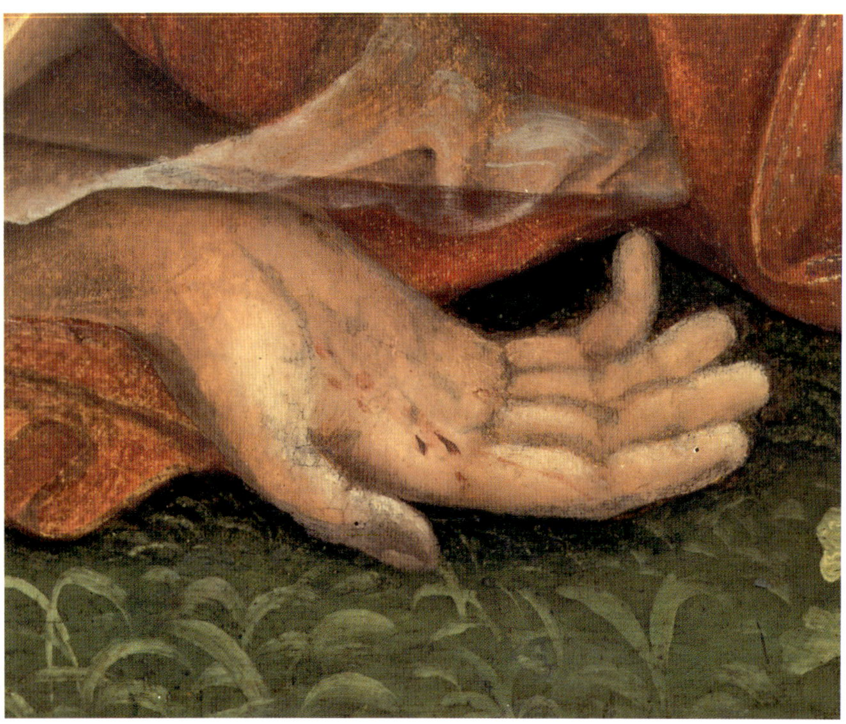

Fig. 48 (top)
FRA ANGELICO, *Christ Glorified in the Court of Heaven* [NG 663], early 1420s, detail

Fig. 49
Macro detail of Fig. 48

Fig. 50 (left)
PIERO DI COSIMO, *A Satyr mourning over a Nymph* [NG 698], *c.*1495, detail

Fig. 51 (top right)
Paint sample from *The Family of Darius*, Fig. 52, showing charcoal

Fig. 52
VERONESE, *The Family of Darius before Alexander* [NG 294], 1565–70, detail

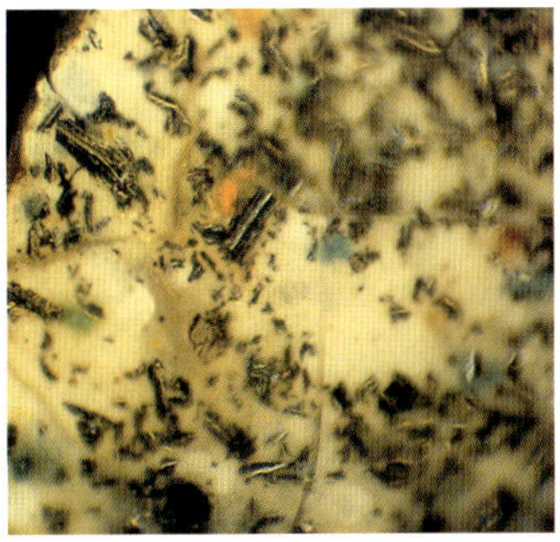

Charcoal encourages very free styles of drawing and allows heavy shading, rapidly produced, of the type often seen in sixteenth-century drawings on paper. Its use for underdrawing in paintings was probably most common in larger-scale works, including works on canvas. Veronese's very large work on canvas, *The Family of Darius before Alexander* (NG 294), painted probably in the late 1560s, for example, has extensive underdrawing in wood charcoal for the architectural background (Fig. 52).[22] There are several ways in which charcoal might be used in the design preparation of paintings: directly as a drawing material on the grounded support; by transfer from a design on paper which has been blackened on its reverse with charcoal as described, for example, by Vasari;[23] and as a result of the use of powdered charcoal to 'pounce' a pricked cartoon (see p. 23). The first two cases cannot be distinguished by the examination of paint samples, whereas pouncing generally leaves evidence of the transfer procedure.

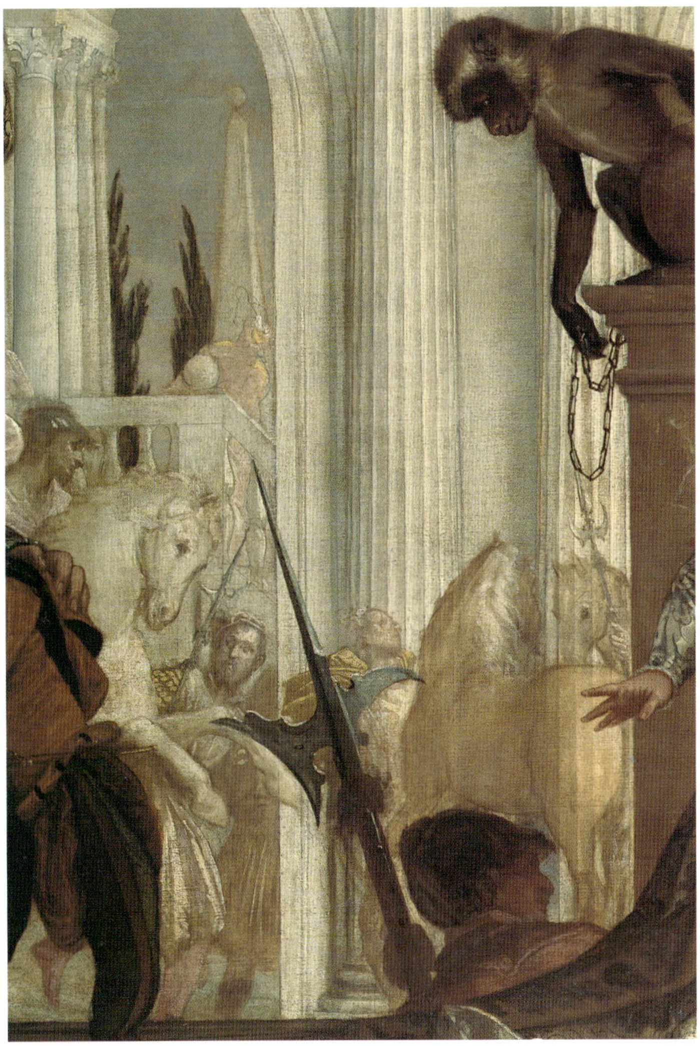

Wood charcoal has a characteristic appearance under the microscope. The intense black particles are usually sharp, splintery fragments, with a considerable range of particle sizes. In large particles the residual wood cell structure can be made out under the microscope. A paint sample from Veronese's *Family of Darius before Alexander* (Fig. 51) shows the use of charcoal black. Underdrawing in charcoal can produce a comparatively substantial layer in paint cross-sections, and may absorb oil medium from the paint layers above. It is possible also, of course, for charcoal to be used as a pigment bound with a fluid medium and employed as a paint for underdrawing a design, as discussed above.

Black chalk

The second dry drawing material of importance is also a carbon-containing substance, although naturally occurring rather than artificially prepared. Black chalk is described briefly in Cennino Cennini's treatise. Writing at the very end of the fourteenth century, he implies it is at that time a novel material: 'I have come across a certain black stone, . . .and it can be sharpened with a penknife, for it is soft. It is very black. And you can bring it to the same perfection as charcoal. And draw as you want to.'[24] The source is recorded by Cennini as Piedmont, but later treatises mention other locations, such as *terra nera di Roma* and *terra nera di Venezia* – this last was said to have come from Verona rather than Venice. Vasari recommends black and red natural chalks for drawing, stating that the black variety came from 'the hills of France'.[25] Germany (Thüringen) and Spain (Andalucia) were other early sources of supply.[26]

Black chalk is clay-like shale or schist deposit containing carbon, partly in the form of graphite, as the black colouring material. The composition is variable, and the suitability of the material for drawing relies on a balance between sufficient hardness and cohesivity for the material to be cut into sticks and sharpened for drawing, and sufficient carbon, which makes the chalk friable. Black chalk of the right character can produce thin clear dark lines on paper or gesso- and chalk-grounded panels and, while also able to produce thick lines, can be used with greater refinement than wood charcoal. By the fifteenth and sixteenth centuries it appears to have become a standard material in both Northern and Southern Europe for the execution of independent drawings on paper. However, its identification is difficult and recognition of black chalk based on the appearance of infrared images tends to rely on the elimination of other forms, particularly the characteristic look of fluid types of underdrawings and the very fine appearance of metal-point. Those underdrawings which do not show any of these characteristics, and are evidently in a dry material, are assumed to have been produced with black chalk. Occasionally, in samples there will be black particles in the underdrawing layer with the slightly metallic sheen of graphite, and a fine, flake-like character which suggests the use of black chalk. Several samples from Joachim Beuckelaer's four large paintings of *The Four Elements* (NG 6585–8), dating from 1569–70, contain just such a material used for drawing (Figs 53 and 54). Sometimes a few obviously mineral particles may be present, including fine iron-oxide particles, but the analytical detection of these associated materials in very thin underdrawing layers is challenging.

Although purer forms of graphite – a crystalline mineral form of carbon with a characteristic flake-like structure – were known in Germany as early as the thirteenth century, graphite did not become widespread as a drawing medium until well after the discovery and exploitation of well-known deposits at Borrowdale (Cumbria, England) in the 1580s and was not common until the later seventeenth century. Drawings and underdrawings in true graphite pencil form detectable infrared images; however, their occurrence is outside the scope of this catalogue.

Coloured chalks

Chalks of colours other than black, particularly red and white, have been used as drawing media, but are particularly difficult to detect as underdrawings, since they often do not register in infrared images.[27] The chances of recognising chalk underdrawings in paint cross-sections are also limited. Red chalk has a similar mineral character to the black form, with crystalline red iron oxide (haematite) replacing carbon as the colouring matter. In the same way, the pigment is contained within a clay-like matrix, and the chalk can be cut into sticks for drawing; the Italian word *matita* (pencil), which Borghini uses in the sense of a drawing material, red or black, is derived from the word for haematite.[28] The texture of the chalk – black or red – was important as, if too spongy or friable, it tended to break into thin pieces or flakes. It was suggested that rough or hard outer matter should be trimmed away, making it easier to cut to shape and to sharpen. The pieces could be used in a brass holder.[29] The colours vary from pinkish and fiery orange-reds to deep maroon and brownish-red tones depending partly on the proportion of haematite present.

Deposits of red earths are extremely widespread, notable sources being Provence in Southern France, Siena in Italy and the west of England.[30] According to Vasari, and also the seventeenth-century writer Filippo Baldinucci, the best *matita rossa* came from Germany.[31]

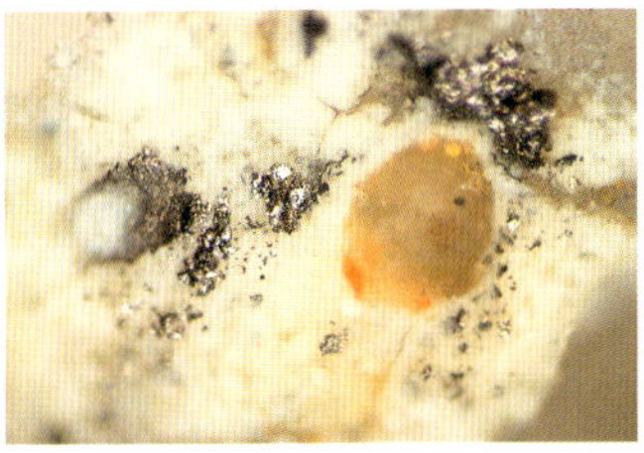

Fig. 53
Paint sample from *The Four Elements: Water*, Fig. 54, showing graphite particles contained in black chalk

Fig. 54
JOACHIM BEUCKELAER, *The Four Elements: Water* [NG 6586], 1570, detail

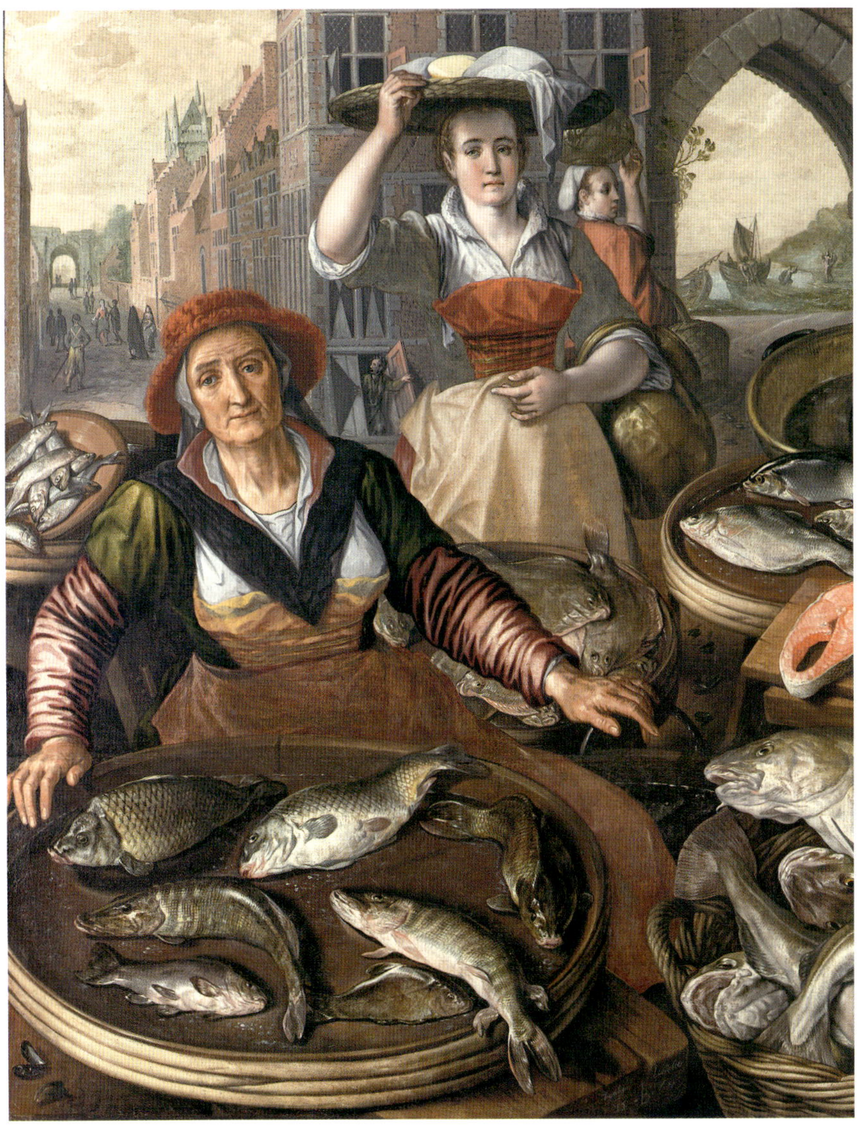

Giovanni Paolo Lomazzo mentions a red stone 'much used by Leonardo da Vinci', mysteriously called *apisso*, perhaps a local Milanese name for the material.[32] A few cases are known where red chalk underdrawing can be glimpsed through overlying thin, relatively transparent layers of paint; Lucas Cranach the Elder is one painter who is known to have used red chalk in this way in some of his later paintings, including *The Close of the Silver Age* (?) (NG 3922, *c.*1527–35), *Cupid complaining to Venus* (NG 6344, probably early 1530s; Figs 55 and 56) and *Charity* (NG 2925, 1537–50),[33] and it is safe to assume that the technique must be more common in sixteenth-century paintings than has been established firmly. There was, after all, a long tradition of use of the red earth known as *sinopia* in Italian fresco painting for laying in the main elements of the composition on the wall.[34] The great many surviving drawings on paper in red chalk – among the best known of which are those by Leonardo (see, for example, Fig. 31) – implies wider general use of the material.

White chalk

White chalk based on natural calcium carbonate (limestone and chalk), calcium sulphate (gypsum) or a white alumino-silicate mineral, steatite (soapstone; tailor's chalk) may also have been used to make underdrawings for paintings, but its application would be limited of necessity to coloured grounds.[35]

One kind of white chalk, which could be used for making corrections to manuscripts, was made from powdered chalk lightly bound with, for example, egg white or milk; this could have been used in place of natural chalk.[36] The same method may have been applied to making red or black chalks; or indeed chalks or pastels of any colour.

Pastels

Italian references to *pastelli* appear during the second half of the sixteenth century. According to Lomazzo, pointed pastels composed of powdered pigments were particularly effective on paper, although the work was easily damaged. They were much used by Leonardo da Vinci and Lomazzo cites drawings of the heads of Christ and the Apostles by Leonardo as examples.[37] Benvenuto Cellini and Giovanni Battista Armenini both refer to the use of *pastelli* made of lead white bound with a little gum arabic (in the first case) and fine gypsum and lead white (in the second) for applying highlights to drawings. Pastels were also useful for trying out colours a painter proposed to use in a fresco, or for making sketches of paintings seen.[38] Leonardo himself gives a recipe for a wax-based 'point for colouring' of ground pigment mixed with a little wax in hot water; the water was then distilled off as steam. With this ever-inventive artist, it is impossible to be sure how far this was unique to him, and how extensive the use of such 'crayons' may have been.[39]

Metal-point

The third important group of dry media used for drawings and underdrawings relies on sharpened metal styli. Metal-point drawn lines can be produced by a variety of soft malleable metals and alloys, the most important of which are silver, lead, tin, copper and lead-tin alloys.[40] Gold can also be used, but this seems to have been quite rare. The metal stylus must be sufficiently soft to allow the slightly abrasive 'tooth' of the drawing surface to rub off particles of metal and so create a fine greyish-silver line as the stylus is drawn over the support. Paper and parchment need to be prepared with some kind of thin ground to take metal-point, except for the softest metal-point materials such as lead, but gesso and chalk grounds, even when smoothed, have the right hardness and abrasive quality to be suitable without further preparation.[41]

Metal-point executed with silver-coloured metals and alloys characteristically produces a greyish, fine unbroken line, the width of which depends slightly on the degree of pressure applied and also on the softness of the metal (Fig. 57). Lead styli blunt quickly and need to be re-sharpened, and the drawn line can be expected to be broader as the tip of the stylus becomes more rounded in use. However, it was usual to prepare lead-point styli as double-ended with a sharp tip and a more rounded end for the executions of lines of differing widths. Cennini states that the stylus should be drawn so lightly over the panel that the line is hardly visible, repeating the strokes to strengthen the line.[42] In practice, during the preparation of the experimental panels at the Gallery (see Fig. 33), it was indeed found that, using silver for example, the lighter the pressure exerted, the easier it is to draw the line; increasing the pressure does not give a markedly darker line and can score the ground on the panel.

Oxidation of the deposited metals also affects the appearance of the drawn lines in metal-point, particularly those in silver-point, which darken with time as a result of the formation of brown silver sulphide; the final product of oxidation can be virtually black. Tin and lead, and their alloys, also react with the atmosphere to produce darker lines over time, and this phenomenon even appears to take place in silver and tin metal-point underdrawings in paintings, in spite of their protection beneath layers of paint. Copper-point lines on paper

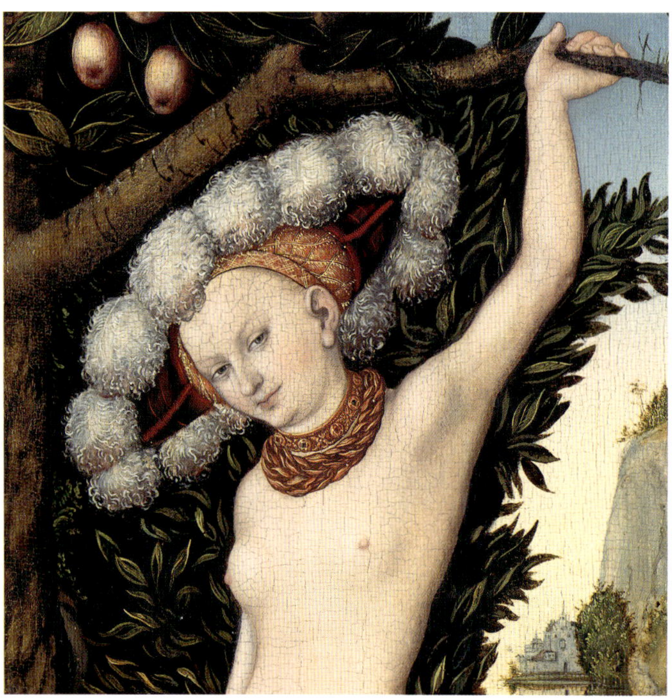

Fig. 55
LUCAS CRANACH, *Cupid complaining to Venus* [NG 6344], probably early 1530s, detail

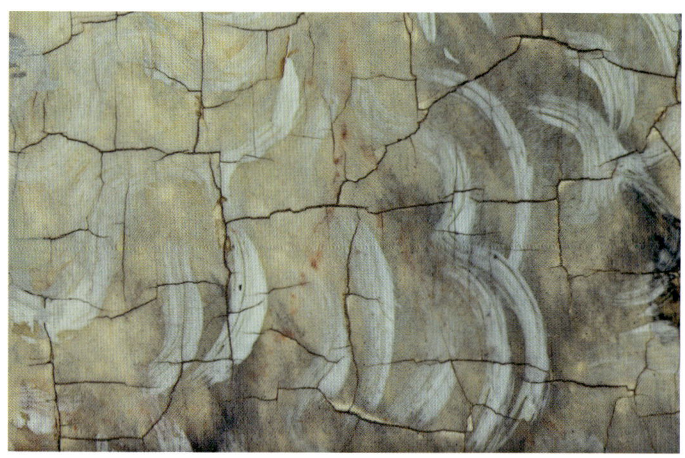

Fig 56
Macro detail of Fig. 55 showing red chalk

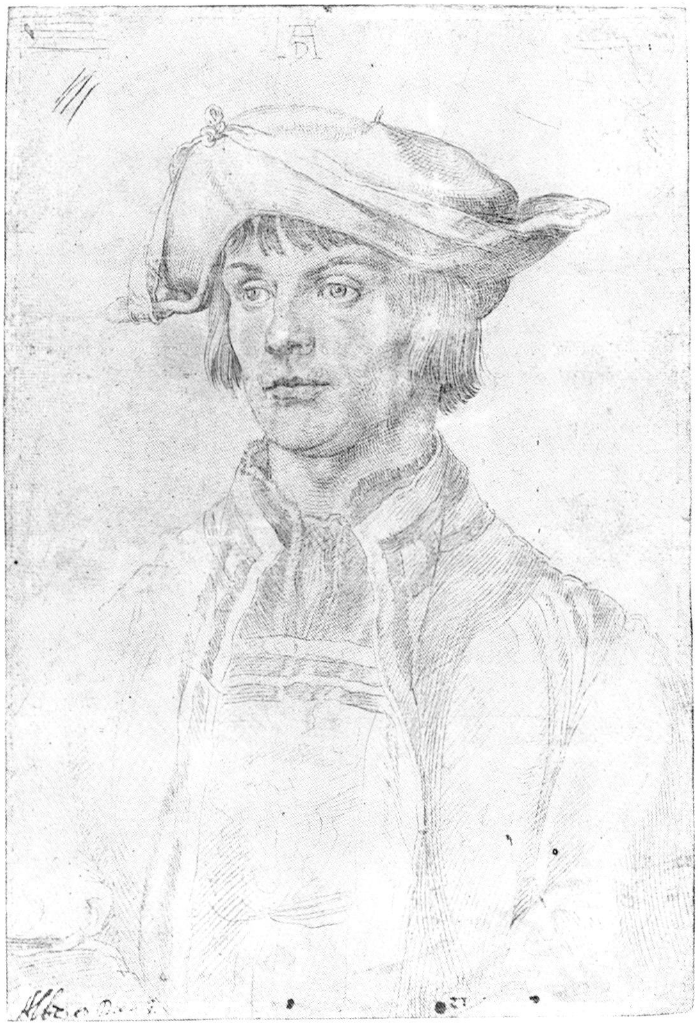

Fig. 57
ALBRECHT DÜRER, *Lucas van Leyden*.
Metal-point, described as silver-point, 24.4 × 17.1 cm
Lille, Musée des Beaux-Arts
inv. Pl. 918

evolve a faint greenish tinge over a period of time, while gold remains immutably grey.

Infrared images of metal-point underdrawings are usually not very strong and clear, partly because of the fineness of the lines. The oxidised products, particularly silver sulphide, absorb infrared radiation more strongly, and will therefore produce clearer images. The difficulty of identifying them resides in the minuscule amounts of material that may be present in paint samples, but there is greater chance of identifying metal-point in underdrawings by analysis than some of the other underdrawing materials, since the metal content can be detected by instrumental methods of microanalysis. Metal-point underdrawing using a lead-tin alloy has been confirmed in Raphael's *Garvagh Madonna* (Cat. 9).

Conclusion

Individual painters no doubt followed their own preferences in their choice of drawing materials for use on a prepared panel or canvas, which might differ from what they chose to use on paper. Albrecht Dürer is a particularly interesting example. In his journal of his trip to the Low Countries in 1520–1, he noted down the materials he had used to draw some of the people he met and various other subjects; some of these drawings, including those in his sketchbook, still exist. In September 1520, for example, he made a drawing of the artist Jan Provost '*mit dem kohln*' (charcoal, probably), the material he used most frequently.[44] He also used black chalk, *schwarczen kraiden* (various spellings) and metal-point, *stefft*; the latter was used for a drawing of the artist Lucas van Leyden in 1521 (see Fig. 57).[45] In September 1520, while in Antwerp, he bought *stain kohln und schwarcze kreuden* (charcoal and black chalk).[46] Once only he referred to a drawing made on a large sheet of paper in a liquid drawing material with the brush: '*auf ein gross papier mit dem pensel schwarcz und weiss*'.[47] The scale on which he was working may have been a significant factor in his choice of drawing material. Examination of his paintings in the Alte Pinakothek, Munich, has shown that dry materials were rarely used for the underdrawing: usually it was executed using a liquid paint or ink and a pen or brush, with great fluency and confidence.[48] In the hands of such a supreme draughtsman any material could be used with ease and its own intrinsic properties manipulated at will.

JK, AR, MS

3 The Artists of 'the North', their Drawings and Underdrawings

The drawings revealed under the painted surfaces of pictures often show many changes and sometimes appear very rough and sketch-like. This may seem to indicate that the prepared panel or canvas was used like an artist's sketching pad on which first ideas for a composition were made. However, this is to misunderstand the way in which paintings were created in artists' workshops in both Northern and Southern Europe in the fifteenth and sixteenth centuries. Far from signalling the physical manifestation of the artist's first ideas, the underdrawings show the final adjustments in a series of preparatory stages before paint was first applied to the panel or canvas. These preparations made use of an abundance of reference material available in the workshop to the artist and his assistants, and such material could be used both in the creation of the underdrawing and as a supplement to the underdrawing after painting had begun. Underdrawings were not invariably made by the principal artist who headed the workshop but were sometimes delegated to assistants. Few people would have seen the underdrawings: the master; his assistants; clients visiting the workshop. Concealed for centuries beneath paint, they can now be revealed in infrared photographs and reflectograms.

Although the artists of Northern Europe undoubtedly produced vast numbers of paintings and drawings during the fifteenth

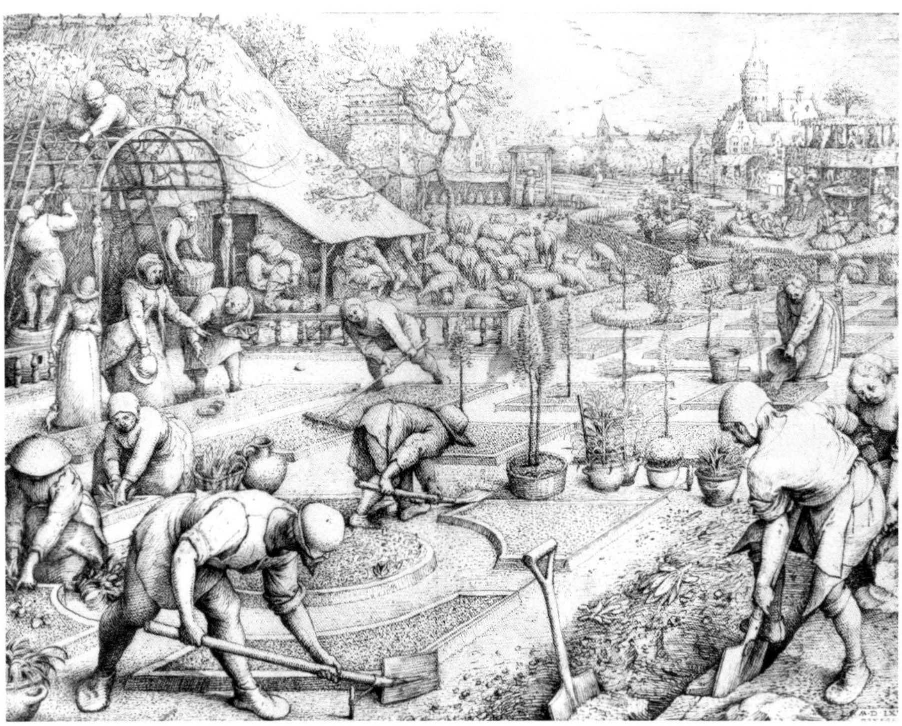

Fig. 58
PIETER BRUEGEL, *Spring*, 1565
Pen and ink on paper, 22 × 29 cm
Vienna, Albertina, inv. 23.750

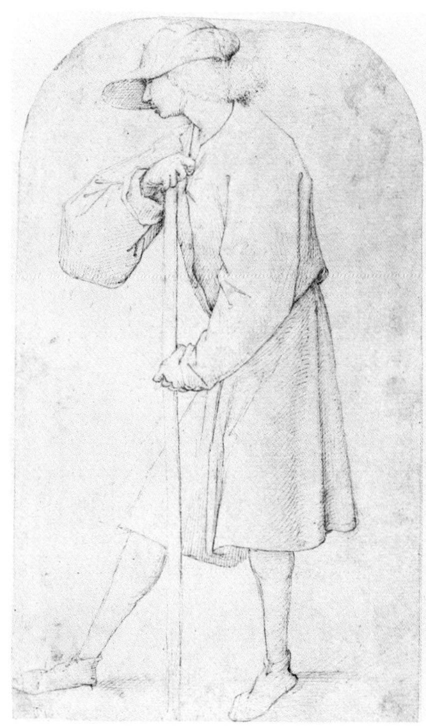

Fig. 59
PIETER BRUEGEL, *Gooseherd*, *c.*1565
Pen and ink over traces of black chalk on paper, 24.6 × 14.8 cm Dresden, Staatliche Kunstsammlungen, Kupferstichkabinett, inv. C2128

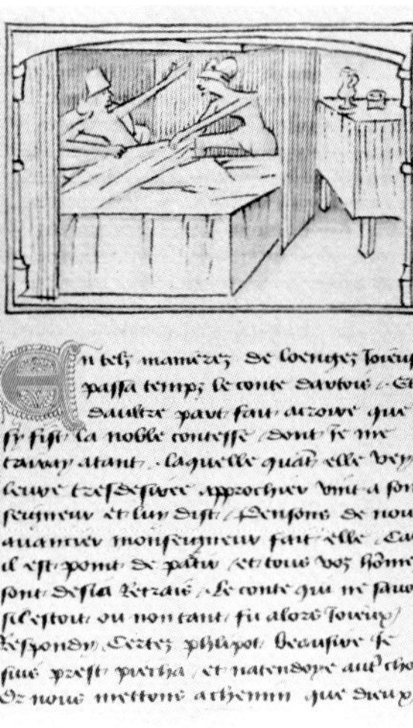

Fig. 60
MASTER OF WAVRIN, *The Countess of Artois, disguised, gets into Bed with the Count*, from the *Livre du très chevalereux comte d'Artois et de sa femme, fille du comte de Boulogne*, Lille, *c.*1455
Pen and ink with watercolour washes on paper, 29.5 × 20.5 cm
Paris, Bibliothèque Nationale de France
MS fr 11610, fol. 97 verso

Fig. 61
ALBRECHT DÜRER, *Death Riding*, 1505
Charcoal on paper, 21.1 × 26.5 cm
London, The British Museum, inv. P&D 1895-9-15-971

and sixteenth centuries, relatively little of their work has survived. Countless pictures have been destroyed: during the iconoclast outbreaks of the Reformation and subsequent periods; and during wars and revolutions. Paintings exported from the Low Countries to Italy and Spain before the iconoclasm of 1566 had better chances of survival than those that remained in the North. When fashion favoured classicising and Italianate styles, Northern pictures were everywhere in danger. Treated with contemptuous neglect, they must have been thrown away in their thousands. Those paintings that still exist do not constitute an adequate or representative sample of what was produced. Their underdrawings have not been exhaustively investigated, though the works of some artists, for example Rogier van der Weyden, Nuno Gonçalves and Gerard David, and paintings in certain collections, have been studied systematically and with exemplary care.[1]

The extant drawings likewise do not constitute a representative selection: survival rates are better for certain types of drawing, certain periods, certain areas and certain artists. Dürer, who realised that later generations would take great interest in his work, preserved and annotated his drawings with unusual care, and subsequent owners valued and looked after them. Other artists were less careful and less fortunate. Considerable numbers of drawings by Bruegel, for example, still exist, but they are not representative samples of his output. Most of them are designs for engravings (Fig. 58); we have only one or two drawings done from life or based on sketches of posed models (Fig. 59).

Lost to us are almost all the drawings that could have been classified as sketches: the initial jottings of first ideas or inspirations. We can form some notion of their appearance from the rapid pen drawings in the manuscripts of the Master of Wavrin, active in Lille in the 1450s. They are sketches in pen and ink with watercolour washes. He was a draughtsman of genius, who, working with singular economy and at enormous speed, could catch in the minimum of lines the telling essentials of an expression, a gesture or a movement. On folio 97v of his *Livre du comte d'Artois*, the Countess of Artois, pretending to be the King of Castile's daughter, climbs with gleeful energy into the bed of her estranged and surprised husband, whom she is about to seduce (Fig. 60).[2]

Dürer did not routinely keep his first sketches, though some of his letters include interesting doodles.[3] Very occasionally, he must have recognised in a rapid sketch something worth keeping. The early pen drawing of his wife, inscribed 'my Agnes', must have been the work of a few minutes.[4] The charcoal drawing of *Death Riding*, dated 1505, must again have been the work of a few inspired moments, but despite the apparent spontaneity, the drawing has its own more tentative 'underdrawing', where Dürer has lightly explored a few alternative contours before fixing his vision in bold and broad lines (Fig. 61).[5]

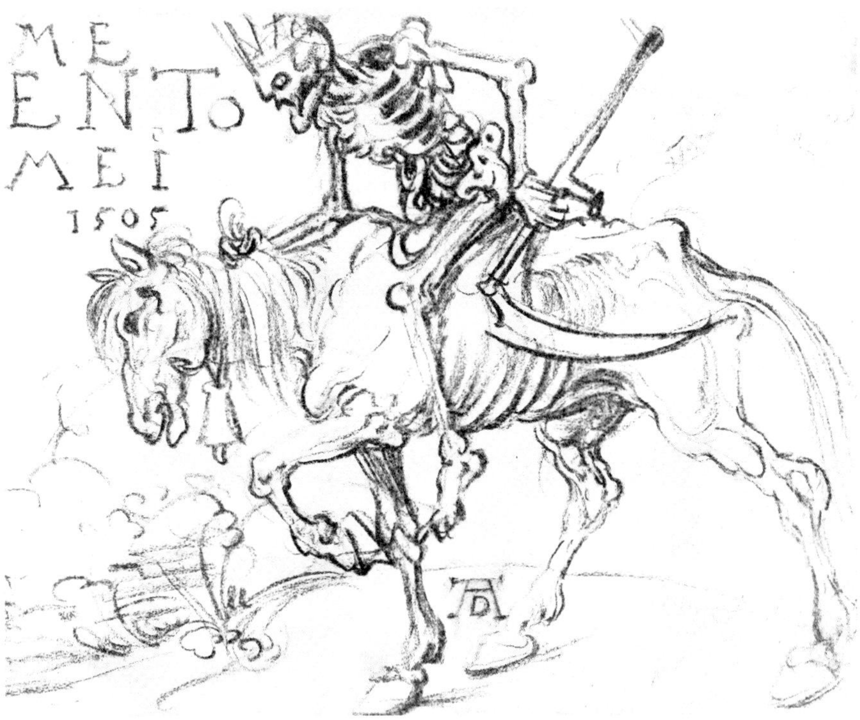

Design Procedure

Generally, painters would have made small-scale designs of their major works; some, though by no means all, made full-size cartoons.[6] They seem to have followed practices similar to those used by manufacturers of tapestries. When

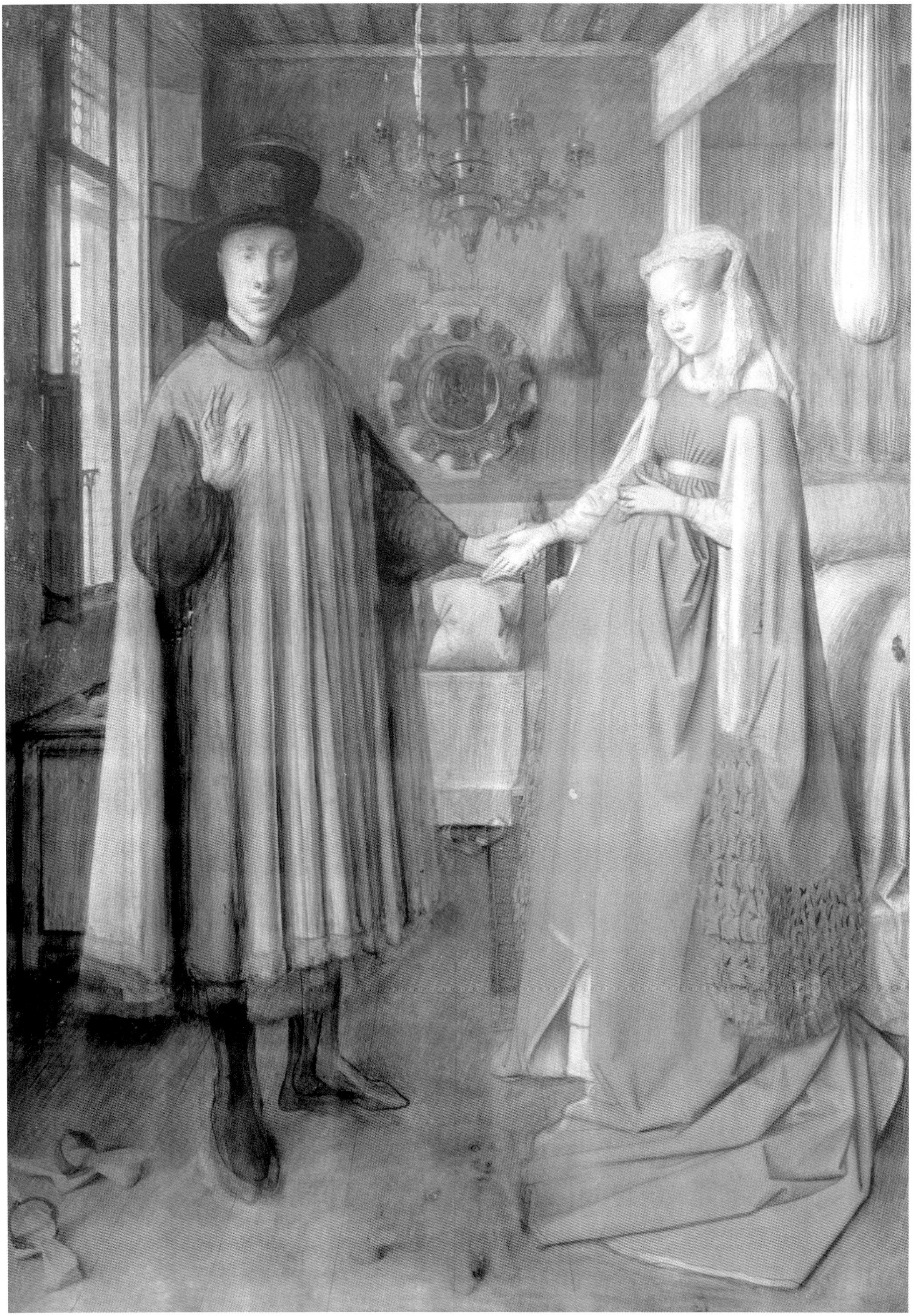

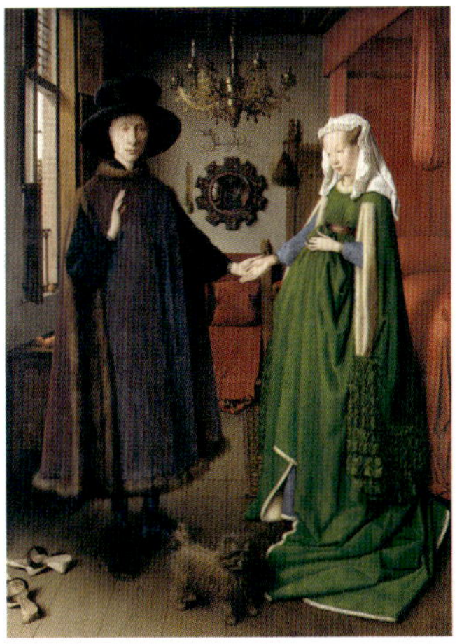

Fig. 63
JAN VAN EYCK, *Portrait of Giovanni(?) Arnolfini and his Wife* [NG 186], 1434
Oil on oak, 84.5 × 62.5 cm

Fig. 62 (left)
Infrared reflectogram mosaic of Fig. 63

tapestries were commissioned, the merchants showed to their clients small-scale designs on parchment or paper, called in French *petits patrons*.[7] Once they had been approved, the full-size cartoons or *grands patrons* were painted on cloth or on paper.[8]

When Jan van Eyck decided to paint Giovanni(?) Arnolfini and his wife, he and the couple must have agreed that he would show them in full length, standing in a reception room. He would have made sketches in which he resolved his first ideas for the portrait and a drawing to show them what they might expect in the finished picture. Before beginning work on the panel, he would probably have made drawings of their faces, figures and clothes. When he started his underdrawing, he could have referred to all those preliminary drawings.

We can chart with some degree of confidence the stages by which the composition evolved. The first underdrawing showed the couple, the window, the chest, the bench and the bed. The mirror was larger and eight-sided; the brush was much bigger and hung from the wall; the carpet was smaller. There may have been a slight indication of a smaller chandelier in a higher position. All these objects, except the bed, were to be radically altered; the painted chandelier, the beads, the high-backed chair between the bench and the bed, the oranges, both pairs of discarded pattens and the dog were not underdrawn and were included as afterthoughts (Figs 62 and 63). Some of the most dramatic changes occurred in the two heads and in the man's body. At first, Arnolfini had an even bigger head, a taller hat and even narrower shoulders; the hem of his tabard was higher and he stood with his legs and feet much further apart. He turned his right palm outwards and grasped his wife's hand more firmly with his left hand. Van Eyck altered his underdrawing before and after he began to paint; he then made more changes as he painted, without amending his underdrawing. The final version of Arnolfini's face, for example, was underdrawn but the completed right hand was not. The woman's head, more intricately underdrawn, was altered during painting: the finished head, with the features placed higher and at slightly differing angles, was not underdrawn. Van Eyck's reasons for making all these changes were doubtless many and various. He evidently wanted to make Arnolfini look less ungainly and to diminish the distortions which, in the underdrawn heads, were perhaps too obtrusive and would have impaired the impression of complete credibility which, while manipulating reality for aesthetic purposes, he was anxious to evoke.[9]

The Painter's Workshop

Jan van Eyck's double portrait of the Arnolfini, Altdorfer's *Christ taking Leave of his Mother* (Cat. 13) and Bruegel's *Adoration of the Kings* (Cat. 16) seem to have been drawn and painted without any help from collaborators. These artists, painting with immense skill and at great speed, were exceptional. Most of their contemporaries – some of them no less skilled – relied a good deal on their assistants, who worked under their supervision on drawings, underdrawings and paintings. Indeed very few successful painters can have worked without assistants. The two principal classes of assistant were the apprentices, who were mostly very young and who were undergoing training, and the journeymen, who were fully trained but who had not the means, or perhaps even the desire, to set up their own businesses. They therefore took employment with the master painters, who alone had the right to market pictures.[10]

The painter's establishment consisted of a dwelling where he and his assistants lodged, a studio and a shop – or at least a shop window, for the privilege of exhibiting pictures for sale was an important and jealously guarded one.[11] It is very difficult to establish how many assistants worked in any one workshop. According to the regulations prevailing in Cologne in the early fifteenth century, painters could have only one apprentice at a time, and elsewhere in Germany a maximum of two was commonly set.[12] No limits were set for the numbers of journeymen, however, and their presence must have enabled some workshops to produce large quantities of pictures, and to take on the production of complex altarpieces. Journeymen were often involved in the carved work of altarpieces, as well as in the production of stained glass and manuscript illumination, despite the fact that they were expensive to hire and could not be laid-off at short notice if work became scarce.[13]

Some German painters evidently ran workshops with a well-organised production line. Lucas Cranach the Elder, for example, whose two sons worked with him, must have required further assistants in order to execute bulk orders such as the sixty pairs of portraits of the Electors of Saxony produced in 1533.[14] Dürer worked with at least four assistants in the early years of the sixteenth century: as well as his brother Hans whom he trained, he had help from painters who were already capable of independent work, Hans Baldung Grien, Hans von Kulmbach and Hans Schäufelein.[15] Frans Floris, the most successful Antwerp painter of the mid-sixteenth century, was said to have trained over 120 pupils during a career of about twenty-five years.[16] Floris's 'pupils' were not apprentices; as far as the Antwerp Guild was concerned, they must have had the status of journeyman.

In the Low Countries pictures of standard subjects were produced, sometimes mass-produced, for sale from painters' workshops, or at the great annual fairs held at Antwerp and elsewhere in the fifteenth and sixteenth centuries, or through dealers.[17] However, the production of copies was not invariably to be associated with the lower end of the market. Fine copies of works by much-prized artists might also be in demand. Gossaert's small *Virgin and Child*, itself a collector's piece, was frequently copied by later artists and it is interesting to

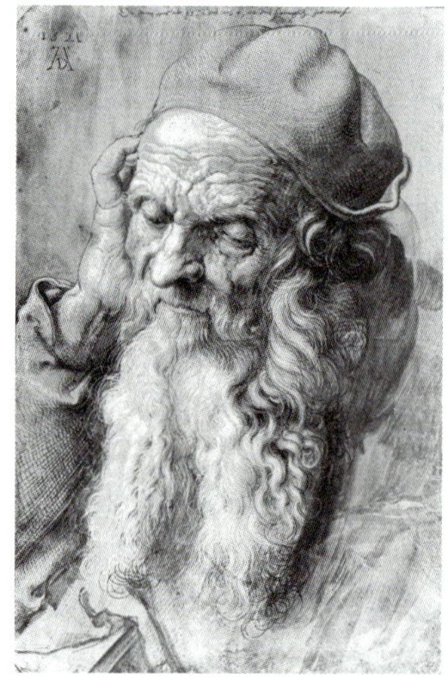

Fig. 67
ALBRECHT DÜRER, *Man aged Ninety-Three*, 1521. Brush and ink, heightened with white, on dark purple prepared paper, 42 × 28.2 cm
Vienna, Albertina, inv. 3167

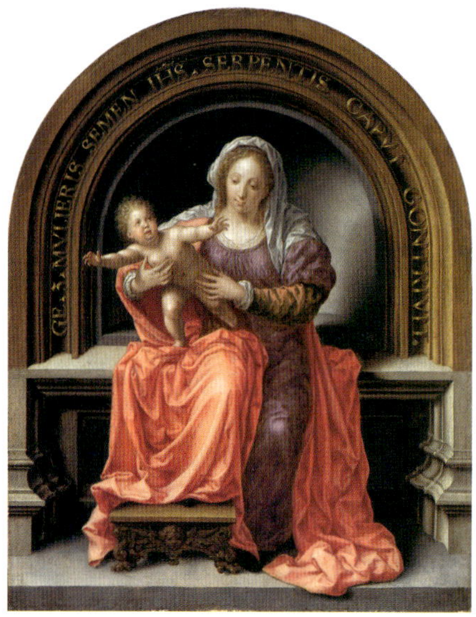

Fig. 64
JAN GOSSAERT, *The Virgin and Child* [NG 1888], 1527. Oil on oak, 30.7 × 24.3 cm

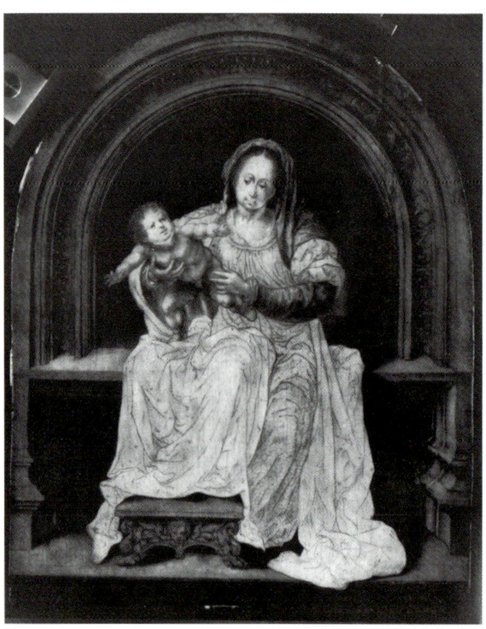

Fig. 65 (bottom left)
AFTER JAN GOSSAERT
The Virgin and Child, digital infrared photograph. Oil on oak, 30.6 × 24.6 cm
Sold London, Sotheby's, 15 April 1999, Lot 36

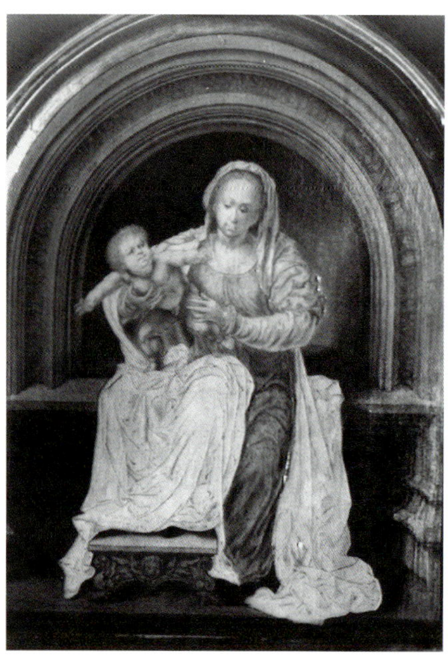

Fig. 66 (bottom right)
AFTER JAN GOSSAERT, *The Virgin and Child*, infrared reflectogram.
Oil on oak, 30 × 24 cm
Munich, Alte Pinakothek, Bayerische Staatsgemäldesammlungen, inv. WAF 306

Fig. 68 (below)
WORKSHOP OF DÜRER(?),
The Virgin and Child (The Madonna with the Iris) [NG 5592],
early 16th century. Oil on lime,
149.2 × 117.2 cm

Fig. 69 (bottom)
ALBRECHT DÜRER, *Irises*
Watercolour, 77.5 × 31.3 cm
Bremen, Kunsthalle, inv. 35

Fig. 70
Detail from infrared reflectogram mosaic of Fig. 68

Fig. 71
Detail of Fig. 68

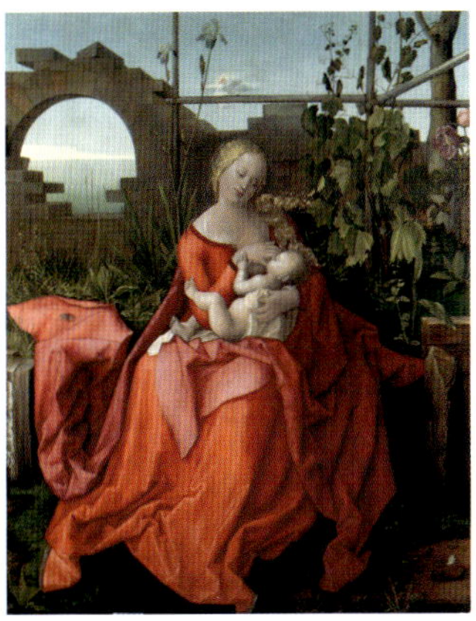

observe that two of the copies have exceedingly similar underdrawings.[18] One is at Munich;[19] the other was sold at Sotheby's in London on 15 April 1999 (lot 36).[20] These two copies may have been produced at the same time, from the same tracing and in the same workshop (Figs 64–66).

'Pattern' Drawings

A vital part of the equipment of any studio was the collection of reference material – probably mainly in the form of drawings but perhaps including paintings and coloured drawings – which would have been constantly consulted by the master and his assistants.[21] The writer and painter Karel Van Mander describes in his *Schilderboeck* (1604) how Frans Floris used his patterns and delegated work to his assistants. 'Frans set his journeymen to do the dead-colouring after he had indicated to them his intention somewhat with chalk, letting them get on with it, after having said: Put in these or those heads; for he always had a good few of those to hand on panels. In this way they gained courage and experience so that they saw no problem in setting up canvases and designing something themselves and painting from their imagination.'[22]

Some drawings were executed for specific purposes. At Antwerp in 1521, Dürer met a man aged ninety-three, 'still healthy and active'. Apparently paying him to sit, Dürer made at least three brush drawings on purple prepared paper of his head, arms and hands (Fig. 67). He used these drawings for a painting of *Saint Jerome*, which (in March 1521) he gave to a Portuguese friend and which is now in the Lisbon museum. Dürer may have been planning his picture when he met the ninety-three-year-old or, just possibly, the old man may have inspired him to conceive the painting.[23]

In the *Madonna with the Iris*, apparently produced in Dürer's workshop (Figs 68 and 71), there are four different types of flowers and foliage, each with their origins in a separate drawing by Dürer or associable with him. For example, the famous watercolour study known as the 'Great Piece of Turf' provides the model for the foliage to the left of the Virgin. The irises in the background are based on Dürer's watercolour study of *Irises* in Bremen (Fig. 69), but are not copied exactly; the underdrawing shows a different version of the flower again (Fig 70). The bugle on the right with a lily of the valley leaf was taken from a drawing of a bugle and lily of the valley now in the British Museum: although no underdrawing for these plants is visible, a tracing of the motif in the painting corresponds to the drawing, the lower part needing to be turned slightly to produce an exact fit, the kind of manipulation that would often have occurred when patterns were traced. The white bells of the lily of the valley in the watercolour study, however, were never painted

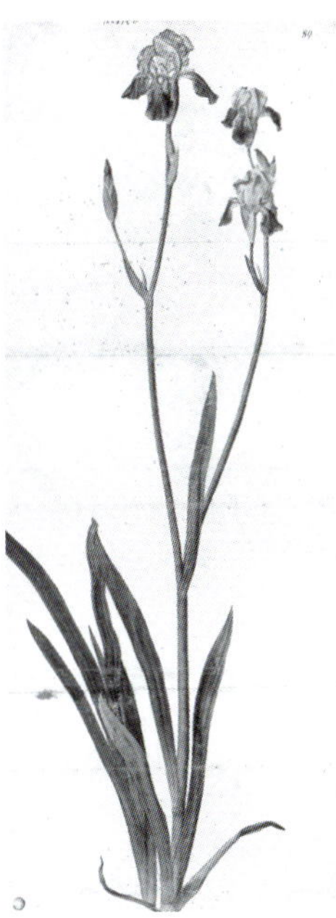

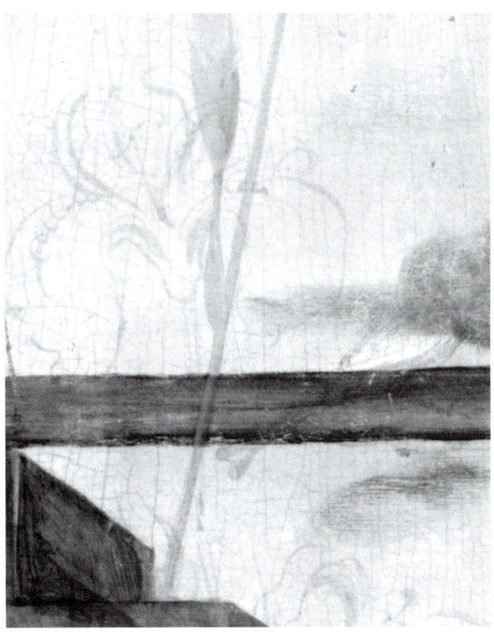

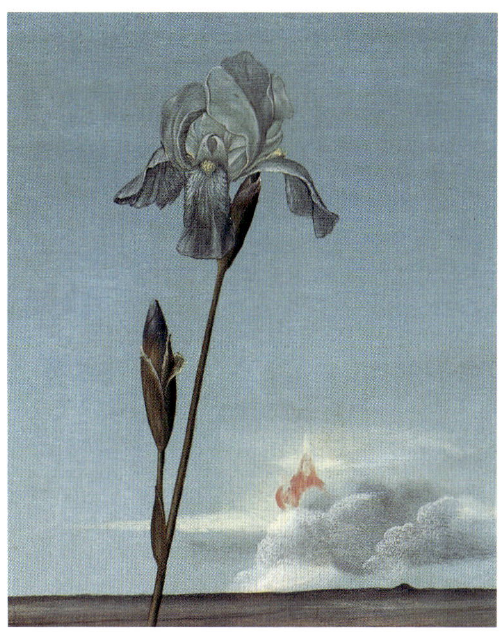

over the leaves in the painting.[24] Conversely, the peonies on the right were painted but not underdrawn; however, they are similar to a number of studies of this flower which appear to have been copied after a lost drawing by Dürer. This must have been itself modelled on, or extremely similar to, the watercolour by Schongauer which Dürer appears to have owned, and which Schongauer had used in the creation of his altarpiece of the *Virgin in the Rosebower* in Colmar .[25] Dürer himself clearly made many such coloured studies including the landscape with the *Weierhaus* now in the British Museum which was used in the creation of the background of the engraving of the *Virgin with the Monkey*.

In the National Gallery painting of *Saints Peter and Dorothy* by the Master of the Saint Bartholomew Altarpiece, Dorothy carries a basket of flowers which has no handle (Fig. 74). In another painting by the artist, the *Baptism of Christ* in Washington, a very similar basket is shown, but this time with a handle (Fig. 73). The underdrawing for the basket in the National Gallery picture also shows it with the handle, which was never painted (Fig. 72). Presumably a workshop pattern existed for a basket with a handle, which the underdrawing followed, and the decision was then taken to remove it to improve the composition.[26]

A contemporary of the Master of the Saint Bartholomew Altarpiece in Cologne, the Master of the Holy Kindred, appears to have had access to the Saint Bartholomew Master's patterns, and the two painters perhaps worked closely together. The illuminated book held by a female saint in the Master of the Holy Kindred's *Circumcision* altarpiece (now in Munich) is taken from the one held by Saint Columba in the painting now at Mainz which forms a pair with the National Gallery's *Saints Peter and Dorothy*.[27] The figure of Saint John on the back of the National Gallery panel, which appears to have been produced by a member of the workshop of the Master of the Holy Kindred, is based on the Saint John in the Saint Bartholomew altarpiece now in Munich.[28]

Dürer shared his workshop drawings with his assistants. In some instances it is known that the assistants undertook to paint altarpieces based on drawings provided by their master, for example the Saint Sebald altarpiece in Nuremberg for Sebald Schreyer. In the case of the Ober-Sankt-Veit altarpiece, now in Vienna, commissioned by the Elector Frederick the Wise, Dürer prepared the drawings and Hans Schäufelein executed the painting. Similarly for the epitaph for Lorenz Tucher in St Sebald in Nuremberg, Dürer created the design but Hans von Kulmbach carried out the painting.[29] In

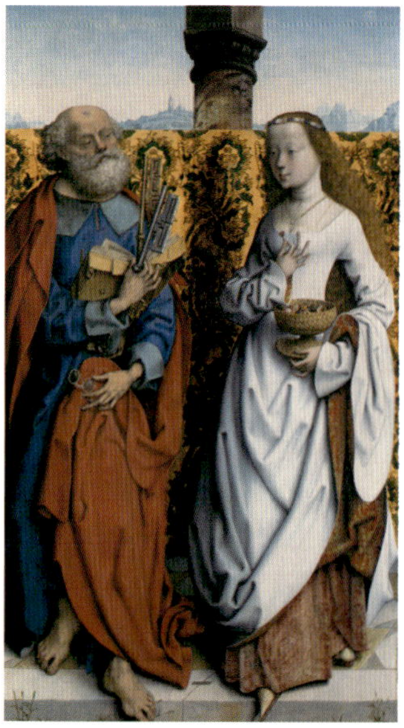

Fig. 74
MASTER OF THE SAINT BARTHOLOMEW ALTARPIECE, *Saints Peter and Dorothy* [NG 707], probably 1505–10
Oil on oak, 125.7 × 71.1 cm

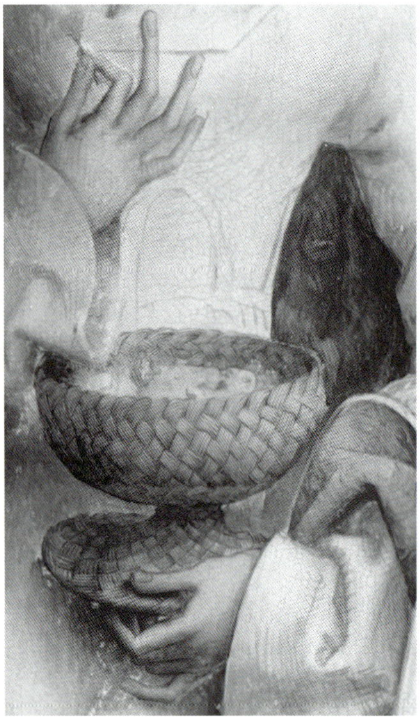

Fig. 72
Infrared reflectogram mosaic detail of Fig. 74

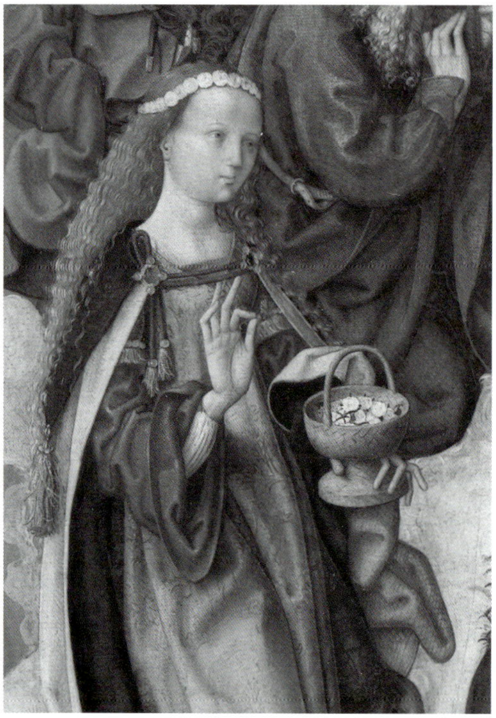

Fig. 73
MASTER OF THE SAINT BARTHOLOMEW ALTARPIECE, *The Baptism of Christ*, *c.*1485/1500
Oil on wood, detail
Washington, National Gallery of Art
Samuel H. Kress Collection 1961
inv. 1961.9.78 1630

other paintings it is clear that they owed inspiration to a model provided by him: the *Lamentation* by Baldung in New York, for example, is based on Dürer's *Lamentation* in Munich, which in turn provided a model for the painter who produced the Düreresque *Lamentation* now in Edinburgh.[30] The production of portrait images which would have been in frequent demand, such as that of the Emperor Maximilian, one of Dürer's patrons, was certainly facilitated by the use of workshop patterns, as investigation has shown.[31]

Cranach's workshop too must have included many patterns available for reference, although it is a distinctive feature of his production that there is rarely any exact repetition, even among subjects such as Venus and Cupid, of which many versions survive, including one in the National Gallery. Cranach must have employed patterns in the production of such versions, but he seems to have encouraged small variations each time a version was repeated. The small painting of three female heads on paper today in Truro must have functioned as such a workshop pattern (Fig. 75): it can be shown to have a precise relationship to the heads in at least one painting by Cranach of the Three Graces, which were based on them and subsequently elaborated and varied. It is possible that different combinations of patterns for heads, bodies and other details were used in the Cranach workshop.[32]

As Cranach was also a court painter who, as mentioned above, was sometimes called upon to produce multiple images of his patrons, he would have needed to retain workshop patterns for the production of such portraits. The portrait of Elector Johann the Steadfast which forms the left-hand panel of the portrait diptych of the elector and his young son painted by Cranach in 1509 is based on such a pattern: the same pattern was used in Cranach's depiction of the *Holy Kinship* in Frankfurt.[33]

The elevated wooden bridge to the tower in Altdorfer's landscape in the National Gallery is very similar to the small wooden bridge to a gatehouse in the background of Wolf Huber's *Christ taking Leave of his Mother*, also in the National Gallery. The bridge and tower reappear in drawings by Altdorfer, Huber and others, suggesting that such topographical motifs were recycled and copied among groups of artists, probably by means of drawings which circulated among them.[34]

Prints could very usefully augment a stock of patterns and broaden its range and must have been avidly collected. The Louvain painter Gord van den Dale, who died in about 1469, owed a large sum of money for 'prints and images' bought from a dealer, who in 1472 brought an action to recover the debt.[35] Prints by Schongauer were used by German artists in their work. The dog in *Christ before Pilate* by the Master of Cappenberg in the National Gallery is based on the engraving by Schongauer of the same subject.[36] Similarly, the small painting of the *Virgin and Child in a Garden* (NG 723) probably by a workshop assistant of Schongauer is close to an engraving by Schongauer, though it does not follow it exactly. The central panel of the small triptych in the National Gallery attributed to the Master of the Saint Bartholomew Altarpiece

Fig. 75
CRANACH, *Three Heads of Women*
Oil on paper mounted on oak panel, 12.5 × 26.9 cm
Truro, Royal Institute of Art, 1824.4

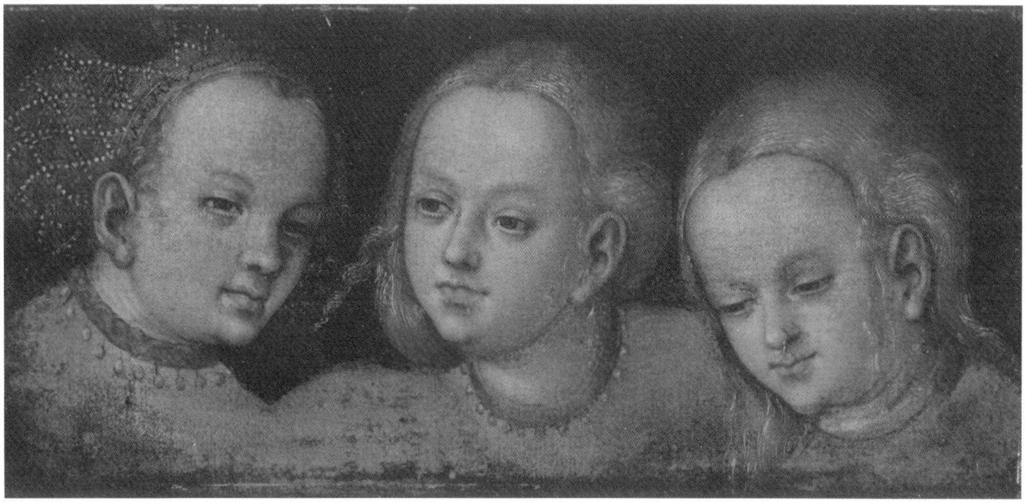

(NG 6497) derives from two separate engravings by Schongauer of the Virgin and Child. One of these provided the basis of the composition of the Virgin holding the Christ Child, where the apple held by the Child in the engraving has been transformed into an orb in the painting. The other provided the motif of the angels crowning the Virgin (Fig. 76). These are shown in the painting without the trailing sashes which Schongauer has given them, but close examination reveals their presence at the underdrawing stage; they were probably suppressed at the painting stage because they obscured the clarity of the painted composition (Fig. 77).[37]

Contracts and Contract Designs

In 1460 the Valencian painter Jaume Baço Jacomart contracted to make a retable for the church of Catí, north of Valencia, and promised to draw (*deboxare*) the desired compositions, which he was then to gild and paint. This retable survives in the parish church at Catí. It is not clear why so much stress was laid on the drawing but it is possible that from the start Jacomart and his client realised that most of the painting might be delegated to assistants.[38] In Germany in the early sixteenth century some contracts indicate that clients sometimes thought it essential to bind the master to produce the work in question himself, rather than passing it to others to execute, perhaps on the basis of a drawing, as Dürer did on a number of occasions; when accepting a commission for an altarpiece for Jakob Heller in 1508 he had to agree he would paint it himself. Similarly, the contract with Wolf Huber for the Saint Anne altarpiece in Feldkirch in 1515 stipulated that Huber must himself do the work.[39] Such agreements were designed to prevent sub-contracting with other workshops as well as ensuring work of quality by the master himself.

At Bruges in 1517 Aelbrecht Cornelis contracted to execute an altarpiece of the *Nine Choirs of Angels* for the church of St James and to 'execute well and with artistry all the principal and naked parts' of the picture. During lawsuits in 1519, it emerged that he had subcontracted the work to another painter but he claimed in his defence that he had indeed executed the principal and naked parts, which he defined as the faces.[40] At Brussels in June 1546, Jan Vermeyen promised to execute the cartoons or

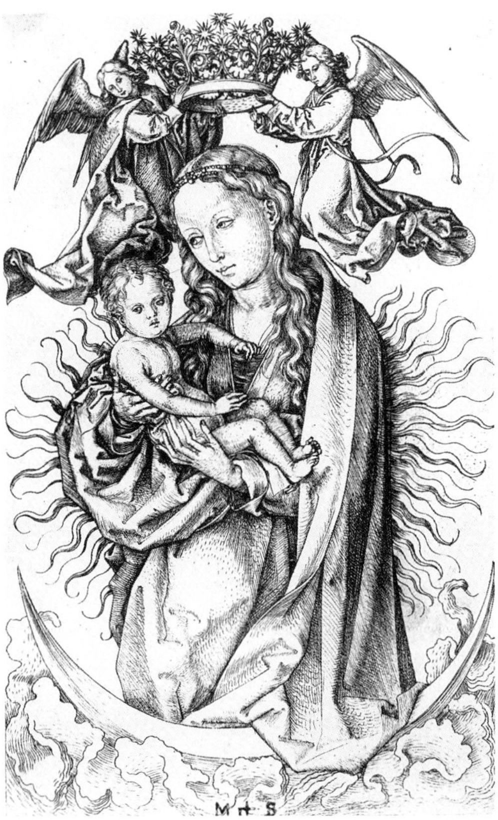

Fig. 76
MARTIN SCHONGAUER,
The Virgin and Child with Angels
Engraving
London, The British Museum, inv. P&D B. 31

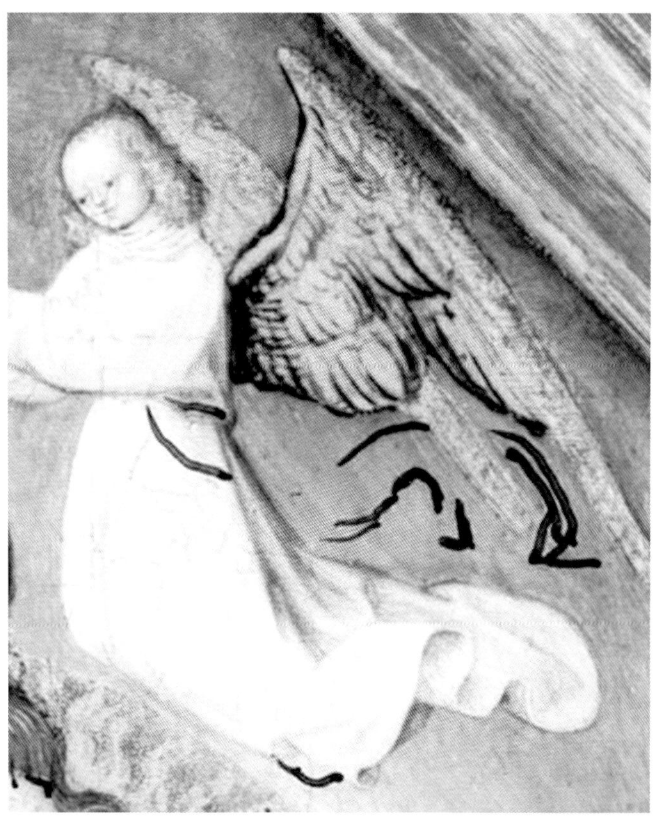

Fig. 77
WORKSHOP OF THE MASTER OF THE SAINT BARTHOLOMEW ALTARPIECE,
The Virgin and Child in Glory with Saint James the Great and Saint Cecilia
[NG 6497], *c.*1510–15, detail of centre panel, with overlay showing underdrawn but unpainted sashes

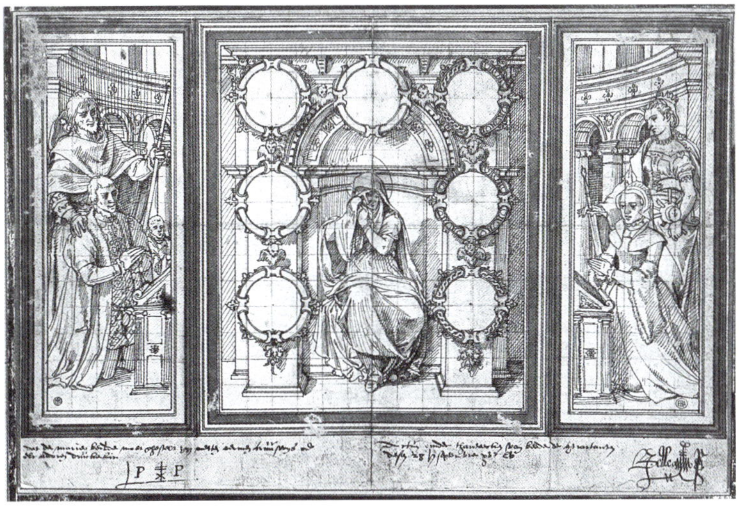

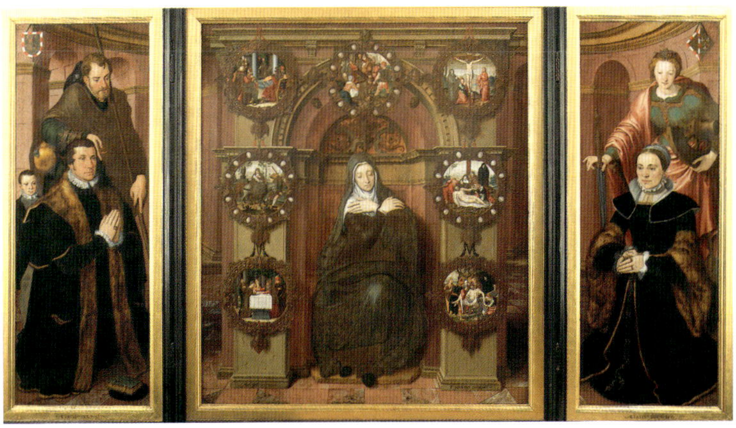

Fig. 78
PIETER POURBUS, *Drawing for the van Belle triptych*, 1555. Pen and ink and wash on paper, 20.3 × 35.5 cm
Paris, École Nationale Supérieure des Beaux-Arts, inv. M. 552

Fig. 79
PIETER POURBUS, *Triptych of Joos van Belle*, 1556. Oil on oak, centre panel 140.5 × 124 cm, wings 141.5 × 52.5 cm
Bruges, Sint Jakobskerk

grands patrons for a series of twelve tapestries of the *Conquest of Tunis* (ten of the cartoons survive in the Vienna Museum; ten of the tapestries belong to the Patrimonio Nacional in Madrid). The cartoons were to follow the *petits patrons* already approved. Confusingly, though Vermeyen was to execute the *grands patrons* with his own hand, he was to be assisted by 'knowledgeable and competent assistant painters, whatever the cost, so that the said cartoons may be made in the best possible way'.[41]

When a large painting was commissioned, it seems to have been normal practice to draw up a contract and to prepare a contract design, called in French a *patron*, in Dutch a *patroen*, in German a *Visierung* and in Spanish a *mostra*. The term *vidimus* was also used, epecially for designs for stained and painted glass.[42] At Barcelona in 1443, Lluís Dalmau contracted to execute the *Virgin of the Councillors* according to a *mostra*. The painting, the contract and the *mostra* have all survived (Barcelona, Museum of Catalan Art and Municipal Archive), though the *mostra* is merely a diagram.[43] Normally the design was a drawing: the client could then see exactly what he would be getting. The design itself remained the property of the artist, but on at least one occasion the painter was paid to copy his design for the client, who could then keep checks on the progress of his commission.[44] Changes could of course be introduced, with the agreement of all parties.

Usually the design was prepared before the contract was signed and was the work of the artist who was to execute the commission. In Paris in 1507, the painter and carver Jean Hamelet signed a contract for a double-winged altarpiece of the life of Saint Vincent which was to include fourteen or fifteen scenes from the saint's life. Hamelet was to make for his clients' approval a sketch on paper, which was to be coloured in wash.[45] In Paris in 1518 the painter Hans Secundefer agreed to paint a panel of the *Crucifixion* for Antoine de La Roche, Lieutenant of the Bastille, who handed over the *patron* which Secundefer was to follow and which he was to give back when he delivered his painting.[46] This *patron* seems not to have been by Secundefer.

In 1555 Pieter Pourbus and his client Joos van Belle signed the contract drawing (Paris, Ecole Nationale Supérieure des Beaux-Arts; Fig. 78) for a triptych of the *Virgin of the Seven Sorrows* (Bruges, Sint Jakobskerk; Fig. 79), completed in 1556. On the drawing is the note that the Virgin, here wiping the tears from her eyes, is to be shown with crossed hands, as indeed she appears in the finished triptych.[47]

During his first visit to England in 1526–8, Holbein was commissioned to paint a group portrait of Sir Thomas More and his family, now lost. As well as separate studies of the individual heads, taken from the life, as was Holbein's usual practice, a drawing survives (Basel, Kupferstichkabinett, Öffentliche Kunstsammlungen) which shows the entire composition (Fig. 80). Divergences from the reality shown in the individual sketches, such as the chair on which Anne Cresacre (More's daughter-in-law) sits in the sketch, but which is removed in the drawing of the group, where she is shown standing, make it clear that this drawing has an entirely artificial composition. This was apparently shown to Holbein's client for his approval. On the drawing are notes in Holbein's own hand, indicating the changes to be made: Lady More is to sit rather than kneel, while the viol seen hanging up in the background was to lie on the sideboard with other instruments. The notes seem to have been made at the same time as very hasty sketches which amended the original drawing: adding a monkey to Lady More's side, showing the hanging viol, and striking through the candle in the window. Holbein must have discussed the form of the amendments with the Mores and made sketches on his design at the same time, in their presence. A copy of the painting made around 1590 by Rowland Lockey shows precisely these amendments, although other divergences from the drawing may be later interpolations.[48]

In 1404 Pere Nicolau, a painter of Valencia, agreed to paint for Gil Sanxes, a draper of Teruel, a retable for the high altar of the church of St John the Baptist at Teruel. Sanxes seems to have been an unusually demanding client. His altarpiece was to be more beautiful and more refined in its carpentry than any retable in Valencia and was to follow exactly the approved design. Sanxes was to examine and approve the carpentry before the grounds were applied, the grounds before Nicolau began to draw, and the drawings before he began to paint.[49] Such repeated inspections may have been common; there is, however, no indication that underdrawings were examined and approved in the same way as contract designs or that underdrawings ever took the place of contract designs.

From Drawing to Underdrawing

As we have seen, some artists would on occasion paint from full-size cartoons but others worked freehand from preliminary drawings, contract designs or pattern drawings. Transferring the design to the support was in fact a routine task, which may often have been entrusted to well-trained assistants. Though Rogier van der Weyden must himself have executed the very beautiful, very bold underdrawing of his *Descent from the Cross*, now in the Prado, he must have asked his assistants to take charge of the underdrawing of his Columba Triptych, now in Munich. Clearly, the compositions of the triptych were created by Rogier, but, equally clearly, the underdrawings are in a style totally unlike his, typified by that of the Prado *Descent*.[50] Joachim Beuckelaer, in his paintings of the *Four Elements* (NG 6585–8), avoided the time-consuming processes of tracing, squaring or pouncing, for he was quite capable of enlarging, diminishing or reversing as he copied his pattern drawings of vegetables, birds and the like. He made radical changes to the composition of *Earth*. The two heroines, who now face each other, originally looked in opposite directions, towards the vegetables and the fruit in the lower corners of the painting. Though the

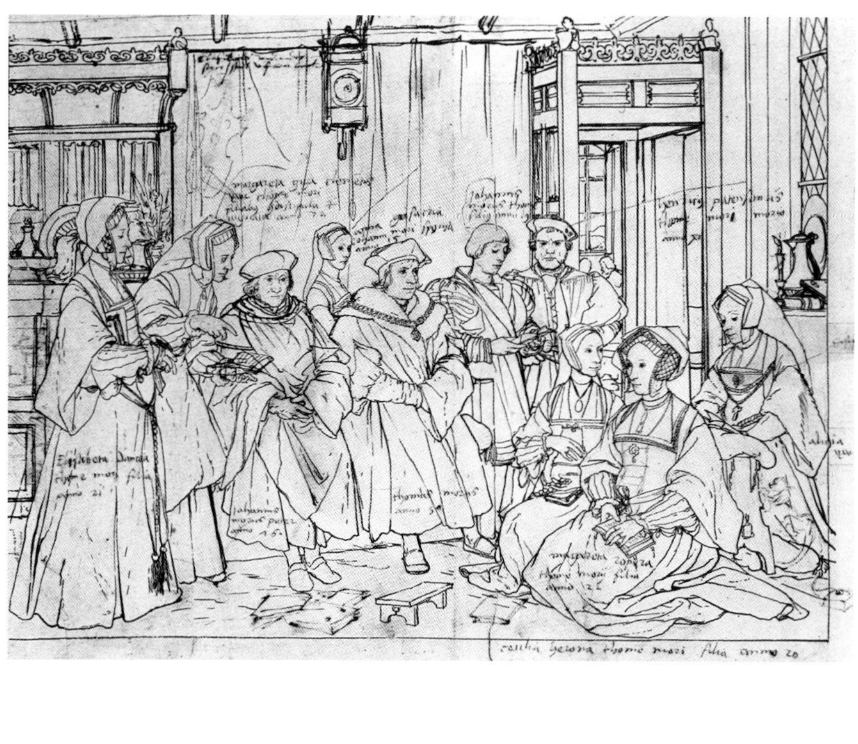

Fig. 80
HANS HOLBEIN *Sir Thomas More and his Family*, 1527. Pen, brush, brown and black inks and black chalk on paper, 38.9 × 52.4 cm Basel, Oeffentliche Kunstsammlung inv. 1662.31

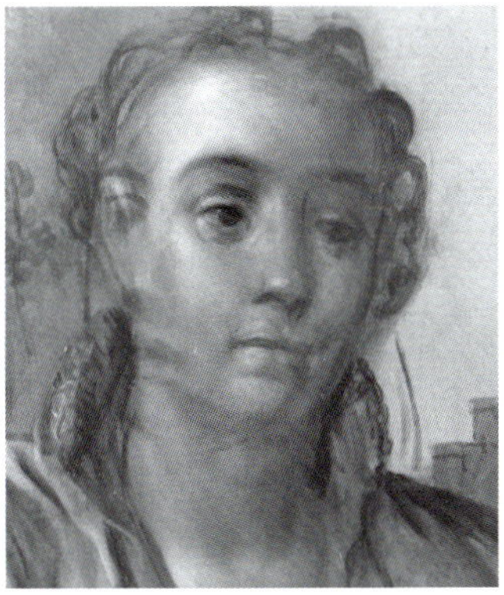

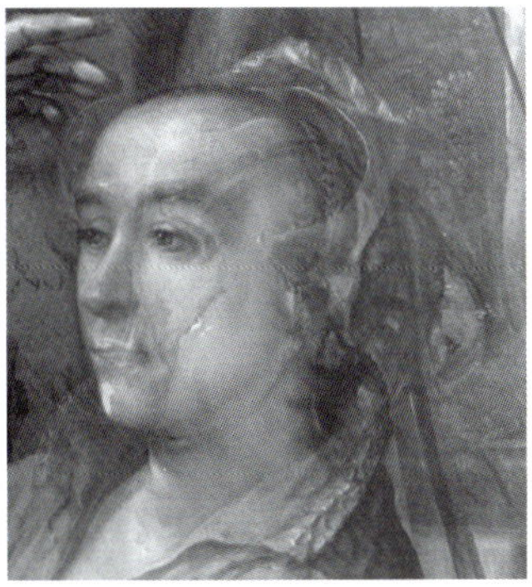

Figs 81 and 82
Infrared reflectogram mosaic details of Fig. 83

Fig. 83
JOACHIM BEUCKELAER
The Four Elements: Earth [NG 6585], 1569
Oil on canvas, 158 × 215.4 cm

underdrawn heads are not distinguishable in the reflectograms, they were almost certainly in the same positions as the underpainted heads which, boldly indicated with broad blackish and whitish brushstrokes, are easily detected (Figs 81–83).[51]

Squaring provides the simplest means of altering the scale of a design. Pieter Pourbus's contract drawing of 1555 for the *Virgin of the Seven Sorrows* is squared for transfer (Fig. 78). The underdrawings of Heemskerck's wing panels, *The Virgin and Saint John the Evangelist* and *The Donor and Saint Mary Magdalene* (NG 6508.1 and 2), are squared and have been enlarged from smaller drawings (Figs 27 and 28). The drawings, now lost, had doubtless been approved by the client – an unidentified canon. Important changes, however, were made after the underdrawings had been completed. In the underdrawing, the donor's hands had been raised in a gesture of pious awe; in the painting, they are folded in prayer. His face was drawn below and slightly to the left of the painted face and his head was inclined downwards, whereas the painted head is on a vertical axis. Heemskerck's grid is drawn in charcoal;[52] Aertsen, who also squared some of his compositions, used both black and red grids.[53] Altdorfer also used this method, as can be seen in the underdrawing revealed in his painting *Susanna Bathing* in Munich, which has a design transferred from a drawing which survives.[54]

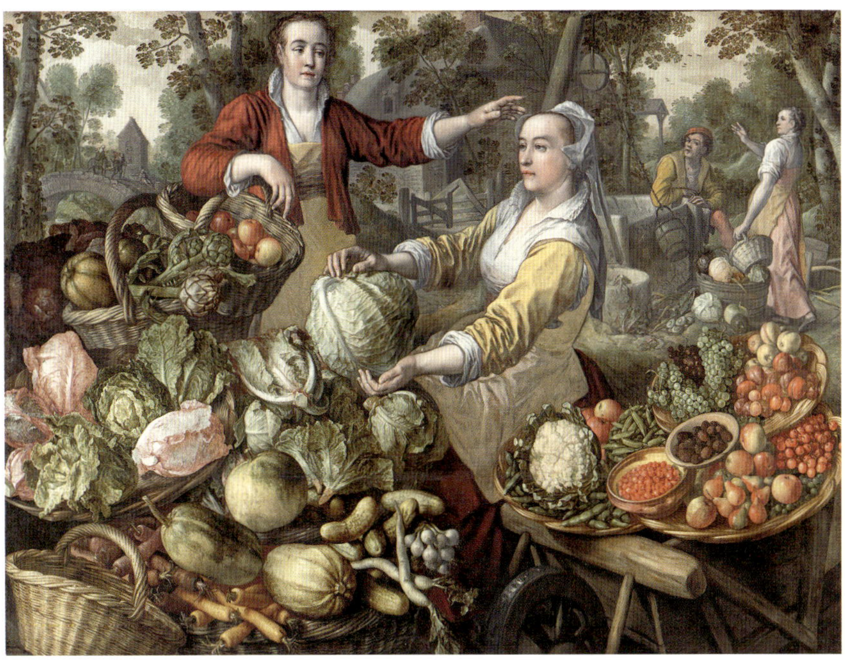

Some artists, including Aertsen, made and preserved full-size cartoons. Aertsen's altarpiece of the *Nativity*, painted for the Nieuwe Kerk in Amsterdam, was destroyed by iconoclasts. Van Mander recorded: 'The cartoon of this painting is still preserved in Amsterdam, as large as the original work; it was a particularly grand work, masterful and manfully conceived, in which the nude parts and other elements were often completed, straight onto the drawing, at one go, and so precisely that from a distance (as indeed it must be viewed) it looks outstanding.[55]

Hans Holbein the Younger made a full-size cartoon for the dynastic wall-painting he carried out for King Henry VIII at Whitehall Palace (destroyed in 1698), of which the left-hand portion survives today in the National Portrait Gallery. The representation of the king's head in the cartoon is an enlarged and exaggerated version of the three-quarter-face image seen in a smaller individual portrait of the king (Madrid, Thyssen Museum). However, copies of the finished painting show a completely frontal view of the king. Evidently this view was substituted for the initial one after the cartoon had been used for transfer, presumably with royal approval. Copies of the image which prevailed must subsequently have been made available, as several frontal images of the king appear to have relied on it.[56] Holbein's cartoon was transferred by pouncing, a method fairly commonly used by Northern European artists in the fifteenth and sixteenth centuries (see p. 23).[57]

However, Holbein seems normally to have employed tracing as his preferred method of transferring his individual portrait drawings taken from life to his panels for painting. Comparisons between surviving examples of corresponding drawings and paintings show clearly that the painted outlines must depend upon the drawings: not only do they match precisely in size, but examination of the underdrawings of the painted portraits strongly suggests the presence of traced lines.[58] Baldung too used this method of transfer: the underdrawing of his portrait of an unknown man in the National Gallery shows the presence of traced lines (see p. 22).[59]

Pieter Bruegel the Elder must have made full-size cartoons for his larger and more complex compositions. Otherwise it seems impossible to explain how his two sons, Pieter and Jan, who were small children when their father died, were able to make accurate and full-size copies of his compositions long after the originals had left the workshop and, in some cases, after they had left the Low Countries. Bruegel's *Proverbs* of 1559 (Berlin) must have been painted from a cartoon which was coloured or carried colour notes and which would have been inherited by his son Pieter the Younger, who used it to manufacture his own full-size versions of his father's composition. All this has been established by comparing Pieter the Younger's copies with his father's underdrawing as well as with his finished picture. The copies correspond to the underdrawing and not to the painted surface. Figures and objects which Pieter the Elder altered or suppressed when he was painting reappear in the copies just as they had been underdrawn; while details which Pieter the Elder added to his painting after completing his underdrawing are not included in the copies.[60]

Although Pieter the Elder seems to have kept images of most or all of the pictures that he created, he is unlikely always to have made and kept full-size cartoons. For his less complicated compositions, such as the *Adoration of the Kings* (Cat. 16), he would have made sketches on a smaller scale. He would have worked up from a sketch the very free and creative underdrawing of the *Adoration*, which is much less precise than the underdrawing of the *Proverbs*. It seems plausible to suggest that, in cases where he had not made a full-size cartoon, he would have made a 'record copy' of the finished painting. Pieter the Younger's copy of the *Adoration* corresponds more closely with his father's finished picture than with its underdrawing; it must therefore have been taken from such a 'record copy'.

Jan Brueghel also used several figures from his father's composition, which he would have known from the same 'record copy', in various similar *Adorations*, including one dated 1598 in the National Gallery (see Fig. 305, p. 180). There the figures of the halberdier, Joseph, the man whispering to him and the black king come from his father's picture; the foreground figure on the extreme right is taken from his father's drawing now in Dresden and usually known as *The Gooseherd* (Fig. 59: it was also copied by Jan's brother Pieter the Younger).[61] Jan took the general idea for the crowded groupings and several of his figures, including the Virgin and Child, the two older kings and several of their attendants, from a much-repeated composition attributed to Pieter the Elder: the best version is probably the damaged *Adoration* in watercolour on linen in the Brussels museum.[62] Jan's stable, however, comes from the centre panel of the triptych of the *Adoration of the Kings* by Hieronymus Bosch, now in the Prado. Its early history is obscure, but as Philip II of Spain gave it to the Escorial in 1574,[63] it was not directly available to Jan Brueghel.

It seems reasonable to suppose that Pieter Bruegel the Elder owned and bequeathed to his sons, besides cartoons for many of his paintings,

Fig. 84 (below, left)
FOLLOWER OF HUGO VAN DER GOES
Virgin and Child, *c*.1490
Brush and ink over black chalk(?) on paper, 51.2 × 20.1 cm
Dresden, Staatliche Kunstsammlungen, Kupferstichkabinett, inv. C 811

Fig. 85 (below)
Detail of Fig. 8

Fig. 86 (right, top)
JAN VAN EYCK, *Cardinal Albergati*, *c*.1435
Silverpoint on prepared paper, 21.4 × 18.1 cm
Dresden, Staatliche Kunstsammlungen, Kupferstichkabinett, inv. C 775

Fig. 87 (right, centre)
HANS HOLBEIN *Lady with a Squirrel and a Starling* [NG 6540], detail from infrared reflectogram mosaic

Fig. 88
MASTER OF THE MORNAUER PORTRAIT, *Portrait of Alexander Mornauer* [NG 6532], infrared reflectogram mosaic, detail

Fig. 89
AUSTRIAN SCHOOL, *Trinity with Christ Crucified* [NG 3662], *c*.1410, detail from infrared reflectogram mosaic

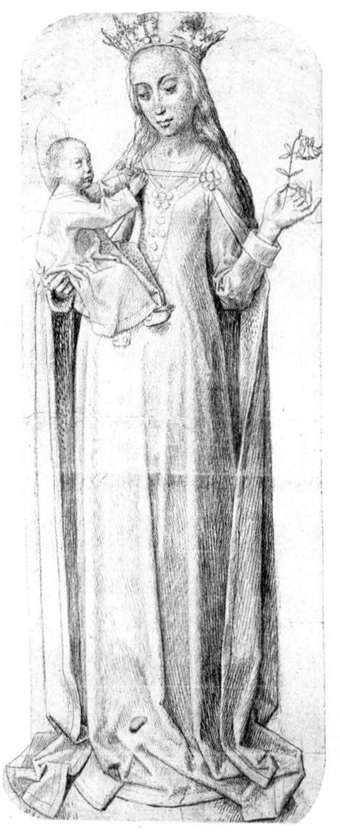

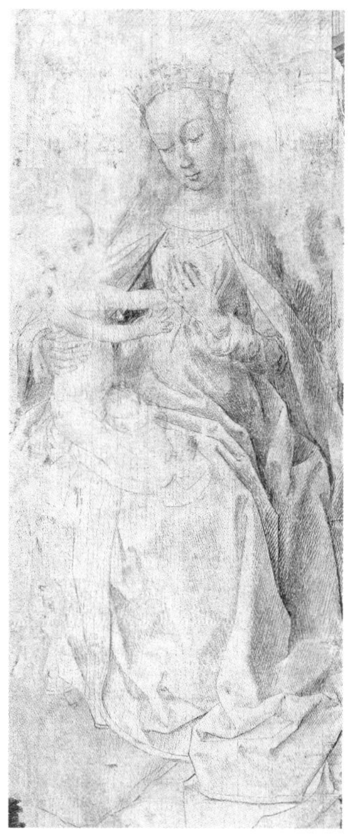

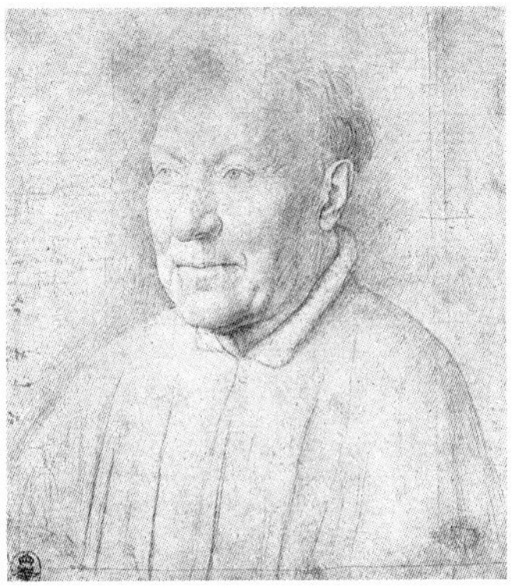

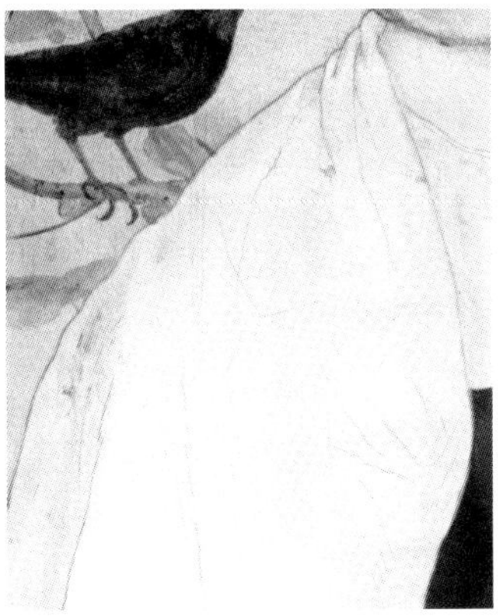

a copy of Bosch's *Adoration*, his own drawing of the *Gooseherd*, a version of the Brussels *Adoration* and a full-size record copy of his London *Adoration*.

Underdrawing and Drawing Styles

Some similarities between drawing styles on paper and underdrawings at different periods can be observed: for instance the underdrawing of the Austrian *Trinity* (NG 3662; Fig. 89) from the early 1400s shows a linearity that can be matched in drawings on paper of the same period. The extremely detailed hatching to indicate light and shade which can be observed in the underdrawing of the *Portrait of Alexander Mornauer* by the Master of the Mornauer Portrait (NG 6532) working in Austria much later in the fifteenth century shows a style of drawing similar to that which can be seen in many surviving drawings by German and Austrian artists from the same period (Fig. 88). The underdrawing of drapery seen in the *Madonna with the Iris* (NG 5592) can for example be matched by drawings on paper by Dürer himself, as well as those of his assistants. The brush underdrawing of the *Virgin and Child with Four Saints* by a follower of Hugo van der Goes, painted in about 1480 (see p. 13, Fig. 8; Fig. 85),[64] is very similar indeed to a brush drawing on paper of the *Virgin and Child* (Fig. 84).[65] As this is a very large drawing, the techniques are comparable even if the drawn Virgin is on a slightly smaller scale than her underdrawn counterpart.

But it can be misleading to draw conclusions about authorship from comparisons of drawings on paper and underdrawings: the relationship between initial drawings on paper, workshop patterns and underdrawing need not have been consistent in a single workshop. The same artist might well use differing procedures on different occasions.

A silver-point drawing by Jan van Eyck exists which is a preliminary study, complete with colour notes, for his painted portrait of Cardinal Albergati (Fig. 86). The drawing was evidently done from life, but it corresponds only in a very general way to the painting, which presents a carefully reconsidered likeness. The changes seem to have been made before van Eyck began the underdrawing for the painting.[66] Van Eyck's *Saint Barbara*, dated 1437, is a brush drawing on a prepared panel. Though it may have started out as an underdrawing, van Eyck is most unlikely to have completed such an

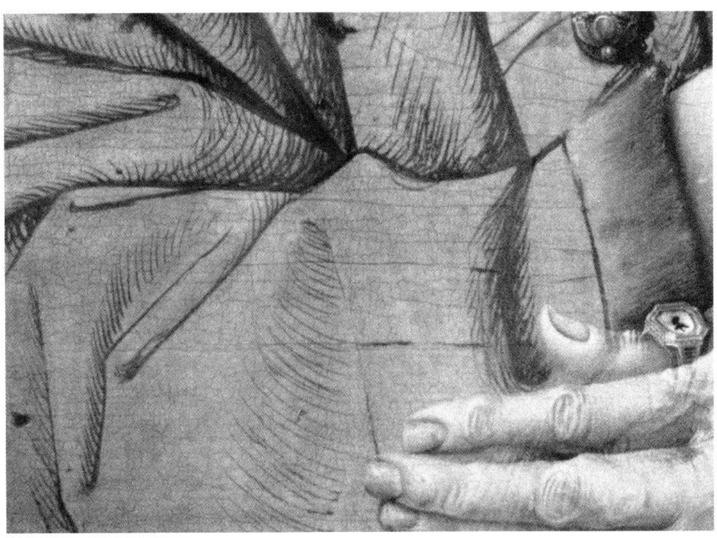

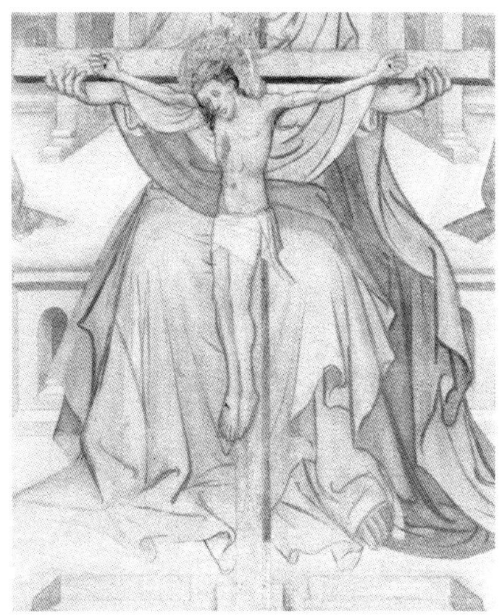

exquisitely finished underdrawing with the intention of concealing it beneath layers of paint.[67] The Albergati drawing and the *Saint Barbara* differ from the underdrawing of *Giovanni(?) Arnolfini and his Wife* (Fig. 62), though there can be no doubt that all three drawings were executed by the same artist.

Pieter Bruegel, too, drew in various different ways. His pen drawing of a *Gooseherd* (Fig. 59), evidently based on sketches of a posed model, is very different from his *Spring*, a highly finished pen drawing made to be engraved (Fig. 58). Neither bears much resemblance to the rapidly and boldly executed brush underdrawing of his *Adoration of the Kings* (Cat. 16). All three drawings are undoubtedly by Bruegel, one of the most versatile of draughtsmen.

The portrait drawings Hans Holbein made in England are executed with varying mixtures of coloured chalks, ink and metal-point outlines and the occasional use of washes. The underdrawings of his painted portraits appear very different, and reflect the fact that he would trace the outlines of his drawings from life onto his prepared panel in order to convey the features of his sitters with accuracy. For example, in the case of the *Lady with a Squirrel and a Starling* (NG 6540) the outlines of the head appear to have been fixed by tracing, but the folds of the sitter's shawl are outlined with the brush in a manner reminiscent of many of the drawings on paper (Fig. 87). These folds are not followed slavishly in the painting, and there were a number of adjustments to the sitter's arm during painting, apparently to accommodate the last-minute addition of the squirrel to the design.[68]

Similarly Bosch could use different graphic techniques and styles, even on the same panel. His painting of *Christ Mocked* (NG 4744; Fig. 91) lies over an underdrawing executed mainly with broad brushes and showing Christ's tormentors behaving even more cruelly and violently. Beneath that underdrawing lies a second, earlier underdrawing, executed mainly with a finely pointed brush and showing Saint Christopher carrying the Christ Child (Fig. 90).[69] The brush drawing of the naked Child has a number of points in common with a pen drawing on paper which is also attributed to Bosch and which illustrates a proverb: *The Wood has Ears, The Field has Eyes* (Berlin, Kupferstichkabinett; Fig. 92).[70] The assurance with which the contours are drawn in broken arcs – the arms of the Child, the branches of the hollow tree – may be compared, as well as the rapid but disciplined hatching of the drawing and the second underdrawing.

The Berlin drawing bears a Latin inscription written at a very early date, conceivably by Bosch himself: 'It is indeed a mark of a most wretched spirit always to use the discoveries of others and never to think of anything new.'[71] This observation, taken from a thirteenth-century text, was paraphrased by Dürer in the dedication of his *Four Books on Human Proportions* (1528).[72] While Italian painters became increasingly imitative of antique precedent and increasingly aware of Pliny's injunctions to copy nature faithfully, Northern European artists such as Jan van Eyck, Dürer, Holbein, Bruegel and their colleagues held inventiveness and originality in great respect[73] and made some of the most beautiful drawings and underdrawings ever created.

LC, SF

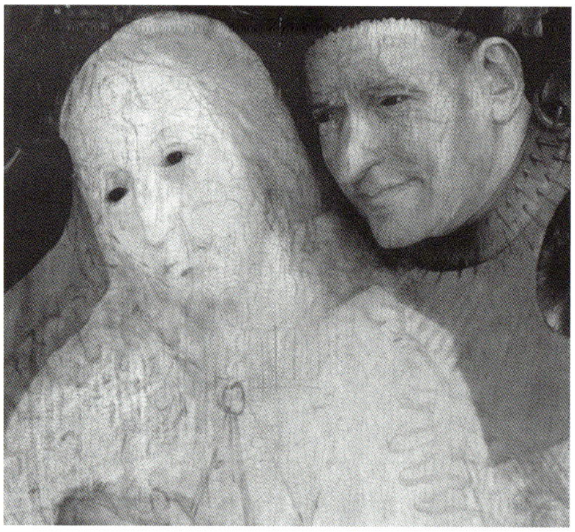

Fig. 90
Detail from infrared reflectogram mosaic of Fig. 91

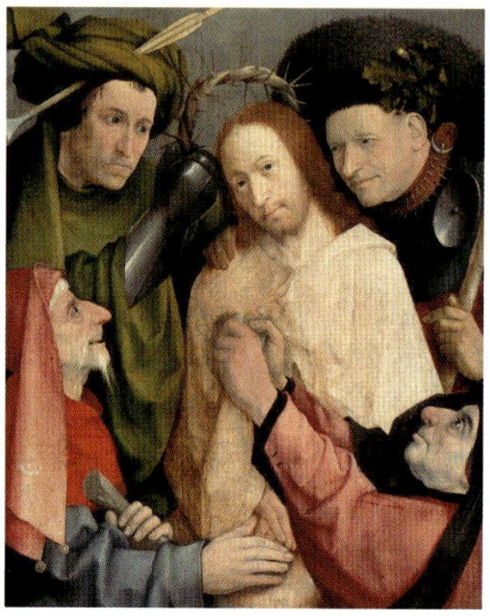

Fig. 91
HIERONYMUS BOSCH, *Christ Mocked (The Crowning with Thorns)* [NG 4744], *c*.1500. Oil on oak, 73.8 × 59 cm

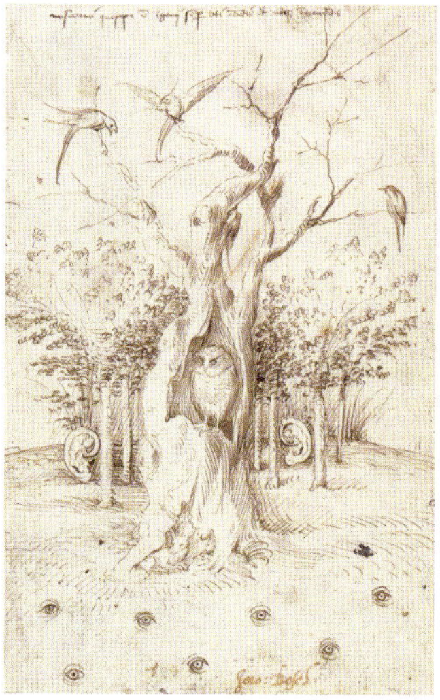

Fig. 92
HIERONYMUS BOSCH, *The Wood has Ears, the Field has Eyes*, *c*.1500
Pen and ink on paper, 20.4 × 12.9 cm
Berlin, Staatliche Museen, Kupferstichkabinett, inv. KdZ 549 recto

4 Drawing and Design in Italian Renaissance Painting

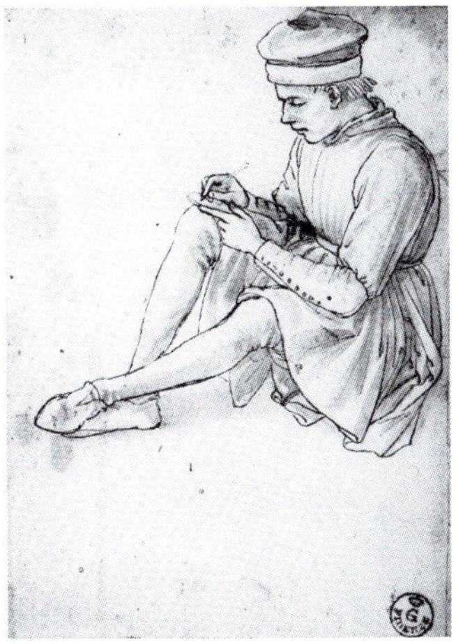

Fig. 93
MASO FINIGUERRA,
Young Man seated on the Ground, 1450s
Pen and brown ink, brown wash, over traces of black chalk on white paper, 18 × 13.6 cm
Florence, Galleria degli Uffizi
Gabinetto dei Disegni e delle Stampe
inv. 68 F

Disegno: Drawing and Design

In English, *drawing* is the execution by the hand of a *design* conceived in the mind. This distinction between conception and execution is blurred in Italian, which expresses both drawing and design by a single term: *disegno*.[1] By calling the visual arts 'arts of *disegno*', the sixteenth-century artist and writer Giorgio Vasari underlined the fact that Italian Renaissance artefacts were the result of a continuous creative and technical process, rooted in a tradition of drawing.[2] Paintings were not spontaneous creations, but were carefully prepared in advance, in sketches and studies, and even sculptural models. Underdrawings are one of the stages in this design process, and for this reason cannot be discussed in isolation from other kinds of drawings made by artists.

In the late fifteenth century, and through much of the sixteenth, writings on art were aimed not at artists but at an educated public of patrons, collectors and connoisseurs. Written descriptions of works of art therefore focused on subject, truth to nature, style and quality, but rarely considered materials and techniques. Practical aspects of artistic production, on the other hand, were passed on from master to pupil in the workshop, making the publication of formal technical manuals redundant. Thus Cennino Cennini's fourteenth-century *Libro dell'Arte*, our most valuable surviving source on early painting practice, was not published until 1821, although it must have circulated among his contemporaries in manuscript copies.[3] The first comprehensive account of painting technique to appear in print was part of the introduction to Vasari's *Lives of the Artists* (first published in 1550, and expanded in the second edition of 1568).[4] Even here, however, technique constitutes a small proportion of the whole book, which is mainly biographical and art historical in focus. Giovanni Battista Armenini's *De veri precetti dell'arte della pittura* (*On the True Precepts of the Art of Painting*), of 1586, much influenced by Vasari, was the first entirely practical work on painting to be published in Italy.[5] Although never intended to replace practical instruction in the workshop, these texts, in conjunction with analyses of surviving drawings and underdrawings, shed much light on how Italian Renaissance painters prepared and developed their compositions.

The Practice of Drawing

For Cennino, drawing was fundamental to the painter's practice. In his view, ability in drawing was innate (the product of what he termed 'natural enthusiasm'), but required practice and training to achieve perfection.[6] The exercise of this natural aptitude for drawing, which Cennino equated with 'nobility of spirit', was itself capable of delighting the intellect of the practitioner; and it was this delight and enthusiasm, rather than a wish to profit by his trade, which would lead him to find an appropriate master and succeed in the field.[7] Cennino recommended that before embarking on a full term of training in a master's workshop, the fledgling apprentice should spend a full year as a shopboy, devoting himself exclusively to the exercise of drawing on small boxwood panels (Fig. 93).[8] Only then could he proceed to the lengthy training required to become a painter.[9] Throughout this long apprenticeship, Cennino prescribed the continual practice of drawing alongside workshop tasks, 'never leaving off, either on holidays or on workdays', although he sensibly advised moderation in the daily practice, 'so as not to lose taste for it or get tired of it'.[10] Having mastered metal-point, students could graduate to drawing with a quill pen, which would make them, 'expert, skilful, and capable of much drawing out of your own head'.[11]

Despite Cennino's emphasis on the importance of drawing practice, very few fourteenth-century drawings survive, and none that can certainly be linked with any known panel. Many are lost because they were made as exercises, on reusable surfaces, such as wooden panels, prepared with a thin coating of ground bone, or on erasable parchment tablets, prepared with gesso and lead white in oil.[12] Drawings on such supports were made in metal-point, usually of silver, which deposited a thin coating of metal that rapidly tarnished, producing a hard grey line not unlike that of graphite pencil.[13] The practice of drawing in metal-point on a prepared ground prevailed even after paper became more widely available. Not only did the ground help preserve the paper by reinforcing and stiffening it, but it could also be coloured with a wide range of pigments to produce a mid-tone between the shaded lines and highlights, thereby enhancing the illusion of relief.[14]

Before the mid-fifteenth century, paper was too scarce and expensive a commodity to be used by artists in any quantity.[15] Only occasionally might it be selected as a support for a composition at an advanced stage of development. Taddeo Gaddi's highly finished drawing (Fig. 94) relating to his fresco of *The Presentation of the Virgin* in the Baroncelli Chapel in Santa Croce, Florence, may have been made as a demonstration for the patron's approval, or simply as a record of a complex and valuable architectural design.[16] Paper had been imported

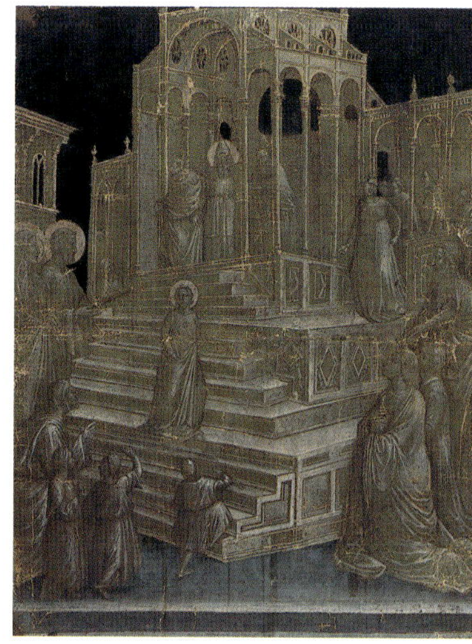

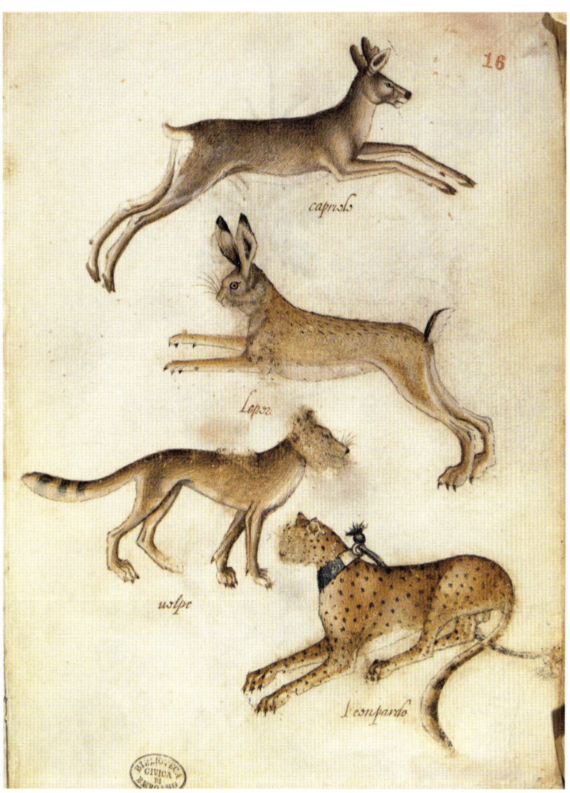

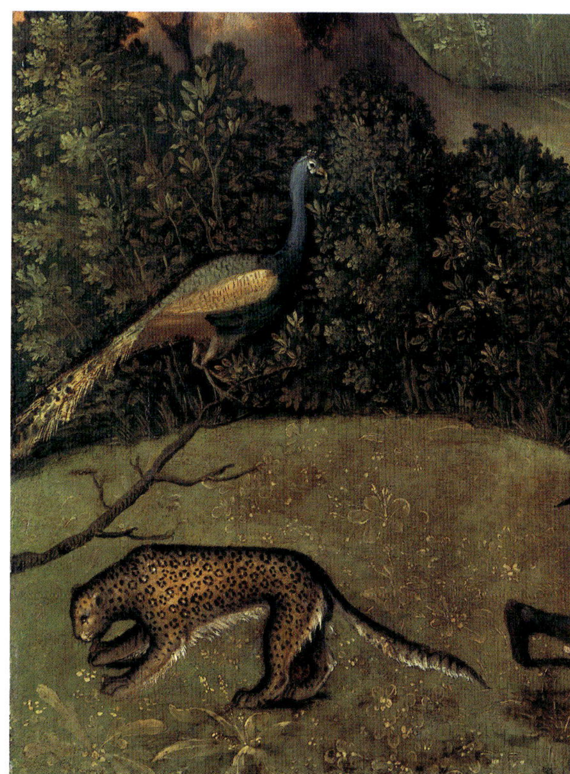

Fig. 94 (left)
TADDEO GADDI, *Presentation of the Virgin*, *c.*1328. Silver-point, with white heightening, dark green and blue pigments, on green prepared paper, 36.4 × 28.3 cm
Paris, Musée du Louvre inv. 1222

Fig. 95 (bottom, far left)
WORKSHOP OF GIOVANNINO DE' GRASSI, *Roebuck, hare, wolf, leopard*, *c.*1389–98. Pen and washes, silver-point with white heightening on parchment, 26 × 17.5 cm. Bergamo, Civica Biblioteca Angelo Mai, inv.MS. D.VII.14 (formerly Cassafa. 1.21), folio 16

Fig. 96 (bottom, left)
FOLLOWER OF GIORGIONE, *Homage to a Poet* [NG 1173], early 16th century, detail

Fig. 97 (below)
PISANELLO, *Head of a Horse*, *c.*1434–42
Pen and ink over black chalk, 26.6 × 17.1 cm. Paris, Musée du Louvre, inv. 2359

Fig. 98 (below, right)
PISANELLO, *The Vision of Saint Eustace* [NG 1436], mid-15th century
Tempera on wood, 54.5 × 65.5 cm

into Europe for several centuries, but its manufacture is not recorded in Italy until the late thirteenth century, when paper mills were first established at Fabriano.[17] Production became widespread only after the first printing presses were set up in Rome and elsewhere on the peninsula in the early 1470s, in response to the invention of printing by movable type. The new availability of paper coincided with the emergence of a more experimental approach to design by artists. In his treatise on painting, *De Pictura*, of 1435, Leon Battista Alberti encouraged painters to produce clear, well-composed narratives, in perspectivally convincing spaces, populated by figures in a variety of lifelike poses, with animated expressions.[18] In the pursuit of these new aims, drawing became ever more essential for artists, not just for recording, but also for exploring, analysing and – ultimately – for inventing figures and compositions, as well as for mastering perspective and the illusion of relief. Alberti perceived how restrictive it was to draw on small tablets, where mistakes could be concealed. He saw the value in 'drawing things large', so that errors could be exposed and corrected, before they found their way into finished paintings.[19] Although paper was produced in sheets of a predetermined size, these could be cut or pasted together to suit the purpose of the project in hand. By the end of the fifteenth century, paper was still relatively expensive, but it was still considerably cheaper than parchment[20] and (except in the case of metal-point drawing) required no preparation.

Copying from Models and Drawing from Life

The relatively few fourteenth- and early fifteenth-century Italian drawings in existence today survive because they were made with preservation in mind, on durable surfaces such as prepared or papered panels or parchment. Drawings on parchment are usually in pen and ink, and are detailed and highly finished, often with watercolour washes. Although some have come down to us as single sheets, originally they would have been bound into pattern or model books.[21] These contained collections of designs, motifs and individual figures, which could easily and rapidly be incorporated into paintings without recourse to the original models. The battered condition of most surviving pattern books indicates that they were in constant use and an essential part of workshop equipment. In Northern Italy, and especially Lombardy,

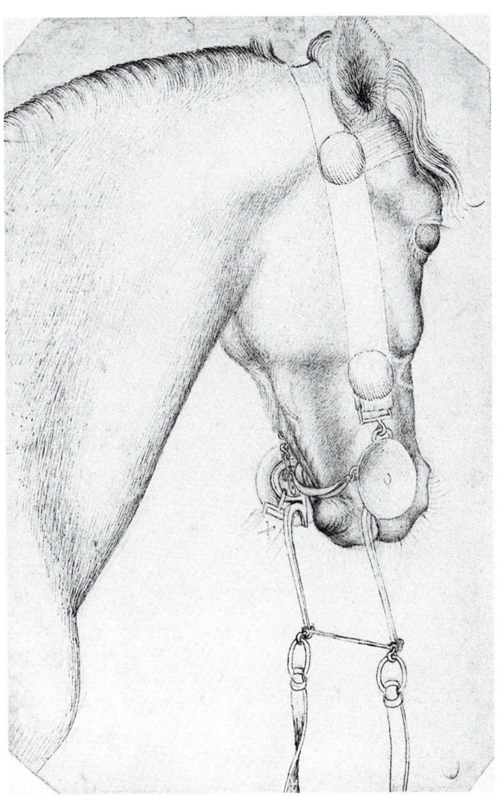

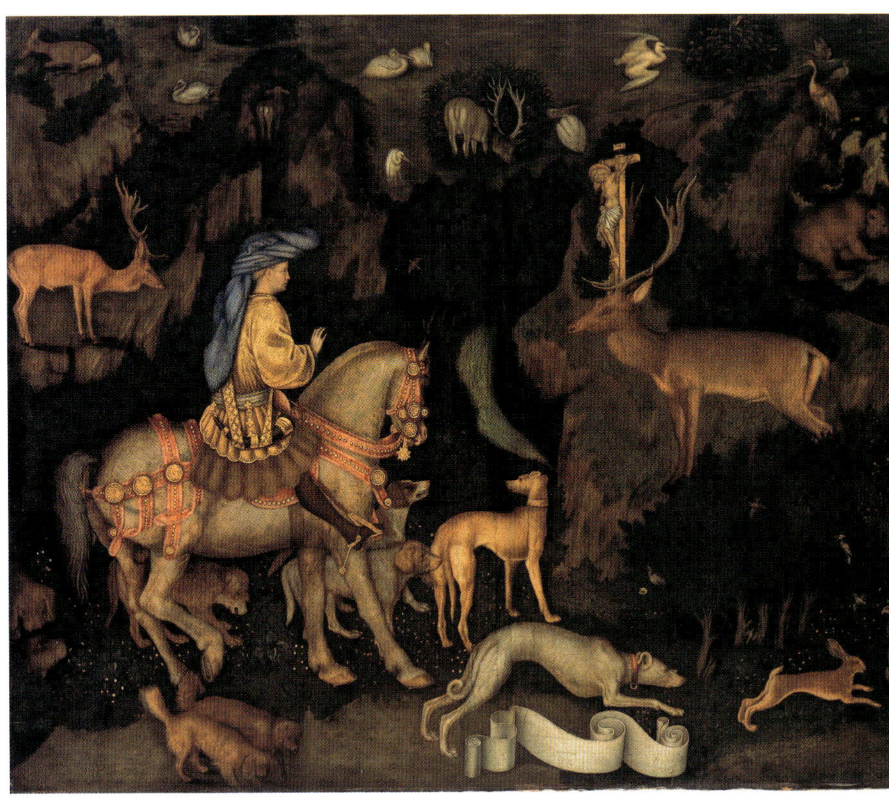

early model books consisted principally of studies of birds and animals. Exotic animals such as leopards and cheetahs, for example, would only have been known from model book prototypes in circulation (Fig. 95). Breathtakingly fresh studies of horses, hounds, birds and other animals by Pisanello demonstrate his outstanding visual acuity and sensitivity to nature, for which he was fêted by the intellectuals of his day. He is the first Italian artist whose drawings survive in large numbers.[22] Numerous more imitative drawings in a variety of distinct hands attest the existence of several assistants and pupils in Pisanello's workshop.[23] Even though relatively small in scale, the animals that inhabit the landscape in his *Vision of Saint Eustace* (NG 1436) all depend upon drawings made directly from nature, several of which survive (Figs 97 and 98). Only a few of them would have been made specifically for such a work, and these in turn would have been kept as reference for future works.[24] The integration of all these separately studied motifs into a single composition (now only a fragment of the original, more panoramic, scene) gives the painting its rich, tapestry-like effect. The far more formulaic animals in the National Gallery's Giorgionesque *Homage to a Poet* illustrate how the model-book tradition survived well into the sixteenth century (Fig. 96).[25]

Drawing in this early period enabled artists to record the work of their predecessors and contemporaries, which they often had to travel to see. Until the introduction of printmaking in the later fifteenth century, there was no other way of transmitting visual ideas and information. Cennino recommended copying the best works by great masters, though in his view the development of a personal style depended on restricting oneself to a few, and ideally only to a single great master.[26] This tradition was still current at the end of the fifteenth century. Michelangelo's early drawings show him building up form by means of a dense network of hatching and cross-hatching very similar in technique to the drawings of his master, Domenico Ghirlandaio.[27]

It was only in the later fifteenth century that new demands for perspective and verisimilitude in painting led to the increase in drawing from sculptural models and from the life. The rediscovery of classical texts and sculpture provided new source material and inspired artists to imitate the natural world more closely.[28] Alberti, writing only thirty years after Cennino, censured the slavish practice of copying the works of other painters, recommending sculpture or ideally nature as a model instead.[29] For Vasari, the practice of drawing from good painted and sculptural models and from the life gave rise to dexterity, which in turn enabled the artist to express his invention freely, harmoniously, and with lightness of touch.[30] Subjects for study included 'figures in relief either in marble or stone, or else plaster casts taken from the life, or from some beautiful antique statue, or even from models in relief of clay, which may either be nude or clad in rags covered with clay to serve for clothing and drapery'.[31] Leonardo and Fra Bartolommeo made exquisite drapery studies in gouache on fine linen by this method (Fig. 99).[32] The study of drapery was particularly important for endowing figures with convincing monumentality. The practice of copying from sculpted models became widespread in the sixteenth century and ultimately became one of the most important components, with life drawing, of academic study.

Although, with a few notable exceptions, Italian painters rarely practised engraving or etching themselves (at least until the later sixteenth century), prints were nevertheless an important stock item in the workshop, providing access at little cost to a broad range of subjects and compositional solutions, both from within and outside Italy.[33] Armenini recommended that novice draughtsmen should practice making copies of prints in pen and ink at an early stage in their training. Antonio

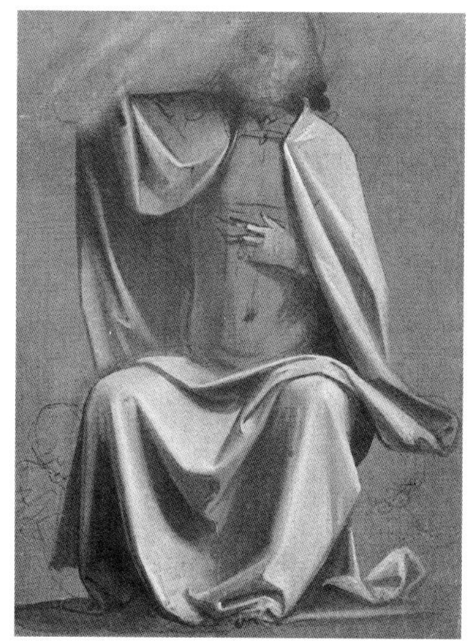

Fig. 99
FRA BARTOLOMMEO, *Drapery Study for a Figure of Christ in the Last Judgement*, 1499
Brush drawing in grey-brown and white distemper on dark-grey tinted linen, 30.7 × 21.3 cm
London, The British Museum, inv. P&D 1895-9-15-487

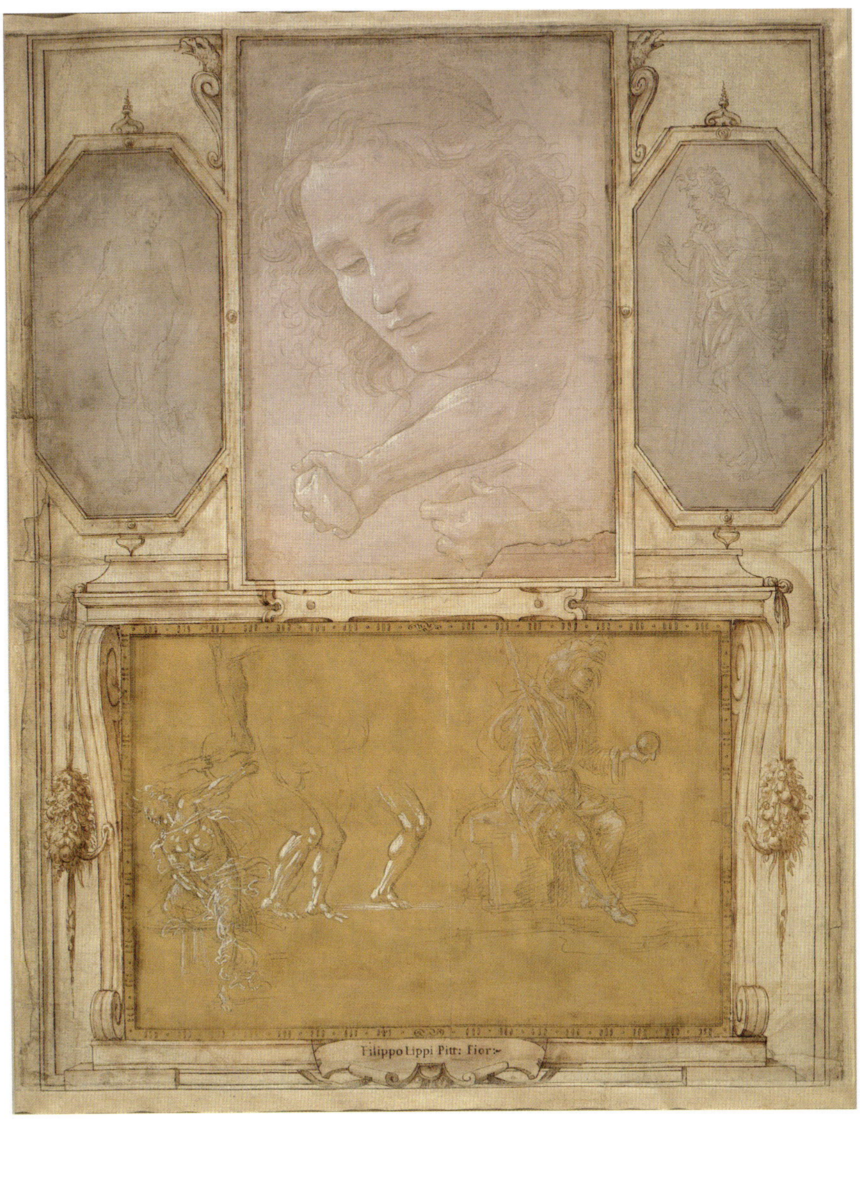

Fig. 100
GIORGIO VASARI and FILIPPINO LIPPI,
Page from *Libro de' Disegni* (recto), sheets by Lippi: probably 1480–1500; the decorative framework added by Vasari after 1524
Pen and brown ink, brown and grey wash, on light buff paper,
56.7 × 45.7 cm
Washington, National Gallery of Art, Woodner Family Collection, Patrons Permanent Fund, 1991
inv. 1991.190.1.a-d

Pollaiuolo's *Battle of Nude Men*, of about 1470, circulated among artists in Italy as a vivid demonstration of his skills as a draughtsman of the male nude in movement, and was plundered for motifs.[34] Mantegna's *Battle of the Sea Gods*, which may have circulated only in a few rare impressions, was copied by many artists, including Dürer.[35] Raphael was the first artist to use the print medium systematically and on a grand scale to broadcast his skills as a draughtsman and designer.[36] Botticelli and Pontormo were among many Italian artists who sought inspiration in Northern prints.[37]

When describing the vital role of 'drawings and models' in the creative process, Alberti used the analogy of notes and quotations jotted down by writers in their private notebooks.[38] Leonardo, too, recommended painters always to carry a small book for sketching.[39] By recording 'the circumstances and behaviour of men' in everyday situations, the artist would learn how to compose narrative painting.[40] Such books, filled with rapid sketches, were to be carefully preserved for later use.[41] The degree to which Leonardo practised what he preached is borne out by the vast numbers of informal drawings and jottings from life that survive from his hand. Vasari also extolled the benefits of studying from the life, once the student had developed a facility for fluent drawing: 'for the things studied from nature are really those which do honour to him who strives to master them, since they have in themselves, besides a certain grace and liveliness, that simple and easy sweetness which is nature's own, and which can only be learned perfectly from her, and never to a sufficient degree from other things of art.'[42] This recalls Alberti's striking observation that a well-known face drawn from nature attracts the eye above 'other [invented] figures of a much more perfect art, and more pleasing than this one'.[43]

Collecting Drawings

Before 1500, drawings were preserved in workshops, where they were used for copying and perpetuating designs. They were inherited with other workshop equipment by an artist's family or pupils after a master's death.[44] Because of their negligible material value and purely practical function, drawings of this period were of little interest to contemporary patrons and connoisseurs.[45] However, with the wider availability of paper, artists began to draw not only to develop specific compositions, but frequently studied the natural world, either for practice, for future reference, out of opportunism or for sheer pleasure; and as 'invention' – fuelled by classical and literary models – gradually replaced the imitation of stock motifs, drawings became more attractive to collectors. It was in Northern Italy that the collecting of drawings first became common, perhaps because there they were more frequently worked up to a high degree of finish to make them attractive. Mantegna made highly finished drawings comparable in appearance to his own monochrome paintings, and self-consciously signed one of them (the vast majority of fifteenth- and sixteenth-century drawings are unsigned).[46] Gabriele Vendramin was the first patrician connoisseur known to have collected drawings and prints (he owned the drawing book by Jacopo Bellini now in the British Museum, London).[47]

Artists themselves were among the first to become aware of what a drawing could convey to an educated friend, connoisseur or fellow professional. Vasari tells us of a drawing of Neptune (now lost) made as a present by Leonardo for Antonio Segni as early as *c.*1501.[48] Raphael exchanged drawings with the painters Francesco Francia and Dürer, and offered them as gifts to important patrons.[49] For special friends, such as the young Tommaso Cavalieri and Vittoria Colonna, Michelangelo also made highly worked drawings as gifts.[50] His designs, even when translated by others, had enormous cachet. Sebastiano del Piombo was selected by Cardinal Giulio de' Medici to paint an altarpiece in competition with Raphael for the Cathedral of Narbonne largely on the strength of his association with Michelangelo, who had provided him with his designs in the past and did so again in this instance.[51] Pontormo and Marcello Venusti also benefited from designs provided by Michelangelo.[52]

The first truly great collection of drawings was that assembled by Vasari, as a visual counterpart to his biographies of artists.[53] The value he placed on drawings is reflected in the care with which he mounted them in his *Libro*, with woodcut portraits from the *Vite* and fanciful drawn borders (Fig. 100). Since *disegno* represented for Vasari the true intellectual achievement of the artist, first formed in the mind and then transferred onto paper, it was only natural for him to acquire examples of this direct expression of artistic achievement. His pioneering collection, like the *Lives* themselves, was heavily biased in favour of Central Italian, and especially Tuscan, drawings (the lack of North Italian and Northern European drawings has to some extent affected the overview of the subject we have today). He seems to have preferred quite careful, finished drawings, to rapid sketches. Of these, the vast majority are of figures and architecture, reflecting his own artistic pursuits as history painter and architect at the Medici court.

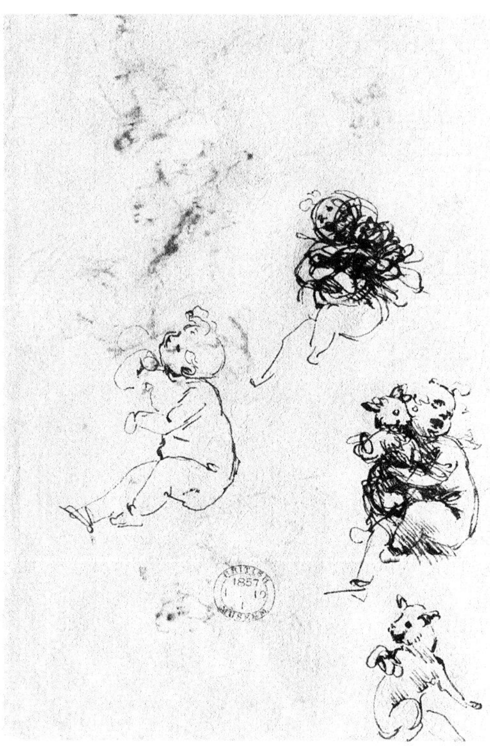

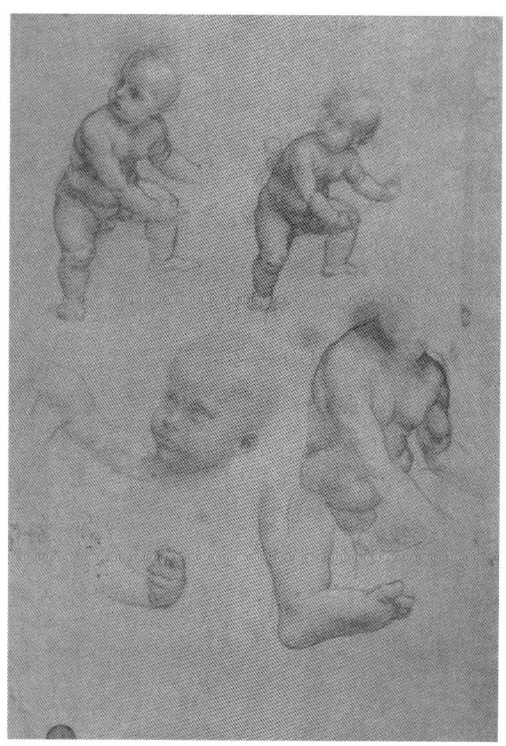

Fig. 101
LEONARDO DA VINCI, *Studies of the Child, the Virgin and Child with a Cat, the Child with a Cat, and a Cat*, *c.*1478–81,
Pen and ink over stylus sketches, 20.8 × 14.3 cm
London, The British Museum
inv. P&D 1857-1-10-1 (verso)

Fig. 102
LEONARDO DA VINCI, *Studies of a Child and Parts of a Child*, *c.*1508–10
Red chalk, 28 × 22 cm
Venice, Galleria dell'Accademia
inv. B.B.1109A

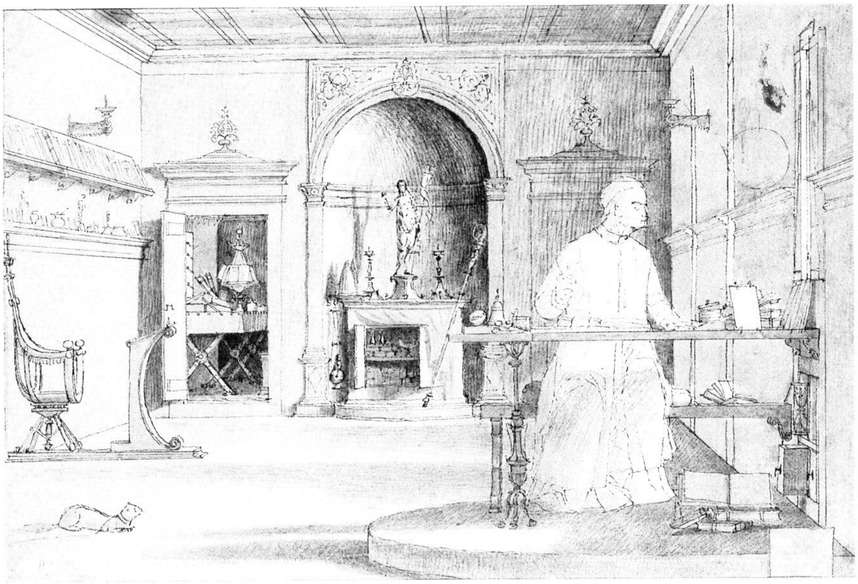

Fig. 103
VITTORE CARPACCIO, *The Vision of Saint Augustine*, design for Carpaccio's mural in San Giorgio degli Schiavoni, 1502
Pen and grey wash, 27.7 × 42.7 cm
London, The British Museum
inv. P&D 1924-12-8-1

Vasari on Preparatory Drawings

Vasari's introduction to the two editions of his *Lives* contains the first complete summary of the design process of paintings in the artistic literature of the Renaissance. The progression he describes from rapid sketches to highly finished scale drawings (cartoons) reflects Central Italian practice, which was predominantly linear and compositional in approach. The different types of drawings he collected aptly illustrate the preliminary design stages he describes (though not all artists, even those close to Vasari, necessarily adopted his method). Northern Italian painters may not have been so systematic in the preparation of their painted works, and certainly far fewer North Italian drawings survive (not much more than a couple of dozen by Titian, for example).[54]

For Vasari, the very first step in the process of designing a painting was the sketch: 'Sketches [*schizzi*] ... are in artists' language a sort of first drawing, made to find out the manner of the pose, and the first composition of the work. They are made in the form of a blotch, and are put down by us only as a rough draft of the whole. Out of the artist's impetuous mood they are hastily thrown off, with the pen or other drawing instrument or with charcoal, only to test the spirit of that which occurs to him...' (Fig. 101).[55] At this initial stage, the artist had to work fast and approximately in order to capture the essence of his idea. The term '*primo pensiero*' or 'first thought', coined in the seventeenth century, aptly sums up the predominantly conceptual nature of this stage. It is interesting to note that Vasari and other early collectors owned few such *schizzi*, probably because they lacked the degree of finish associated with collectable artefacts. This may also have been the category of drawing most frequently destroyed by artists themselves.[56]

The next stage in the design process was the production of more finished studies, in which the initial idea was fleshed out and developed in more detail ('drawings in well formed relief, in the doing of which the artist tries with all possible diligence to copy from the life, if he does not feel himself strong enough to be able to produce them from his own knowledge'[57]). Since, in these studies, the modelling of light and shade played a key role, Vasari recommended the use red chalk, black chalk, pen and ink, or pen and ink with wash on tinted paper, highlighted with white, all of which could achieve a tonal or what Vasari calls pictorial ('*alla pittoresca*') effect.[58] The vast majority of fifteenth- and sixteenth-century drawings that have survived are preparatory studies in this category. These would include figure studies (Fig. 102), either made from life, or less frequently the imagination. The figures might be nude, clothed or draped, and, especially in the fifteenth century, were often based on workshop assistants ('*garzoni*' in Italian) (see Fig. 93). The study of figures would extend to more detailed studies of heads and facial features, hands and limbs, and to the structure beneath the skin, in the form of anatomical studies and *écorchés*. Separate studies of drapery were, as we have seen, also made, though often artists would only 'dress' their figures in the last stages of composition (or even occasionally during painting).[59] The settings of paintings were anticipated at this stage by architectural and landscape studies. Vasari owned many examples of all these different types of preparatory drawing.

From Drawing to Underdrawing: the Cartoon

Before proceeding to draw the design on the prepared painting support, whether a wall or a panel or canvas, painters often distilled their sketches, studies, stock drawings and elements drawn from the imagination into some form of small compositional drawing on paper. This category of drawing (which later became known as the *modello*) was distinct from the initial compositional sketch in being much more worked up, with the overall design fully resolved and the poses of the figures established. In the late fifteenth century, finished composition drawings were produced particularly when an artist was working on important large-scale commissions that required careful planning (Fig. 103). As well as assisting in the process of scaling up the overall design for painting, compositional drawings could be shown to patrons as demonstrations of projected works, for approval or amendment. Sometimes such drawings would form part of a legal contract, as a more precise visual record of a verbal agreement. A finished drawing by Francesco Salviati for his *Incredulity of Saint Thomas* in the Louvre (Fig. 104) is stated in an inscription by the artist to be the design (*disegno*) for an altarpiece that he was bound by contract to make for Albizzo del Bene, a Florentine merchant banker living in Lyon.[60] The contract also survives, cross-referring to the inscribed drawing as the model (*modulo*) for the commission.[61] Prior to the cartoon phase, Vasari also recommends making three-dimensional models (*modelli*) in clay, particularly for establishing the balance of light and shade across the whole composition.[62]

From the later fifteenth century onwards, and particularly in Central Italian painting, the preparatory process was sometimes extended to include drawings on the same scale as the

Fig. 104
FRANCESCO SALVIATI,
The Incredulity of Saint Thomas, *c.*1544–5
Pen, brown ink, brown wash, with white heightening, over black chalk
Paris, Musée du Louvre
inv. RF 31139

Fig. 105
RAPHAEL, *Saint Catherine*, *c.*1507–8
Black and white chalk, pricked for transfer, 58.7 × 43.6 cm
Paris, Musée du Louvre
inv. 3871

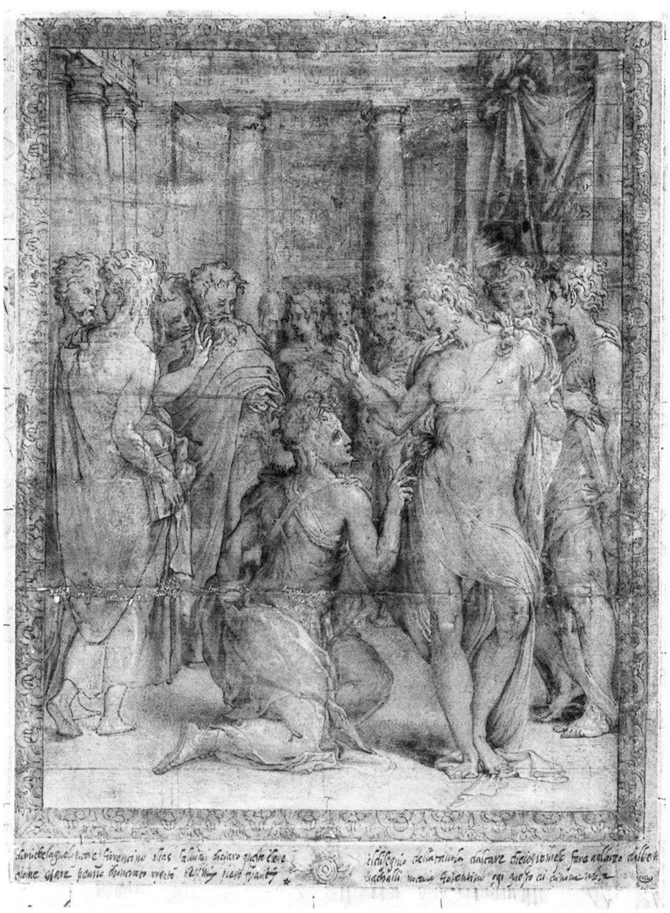

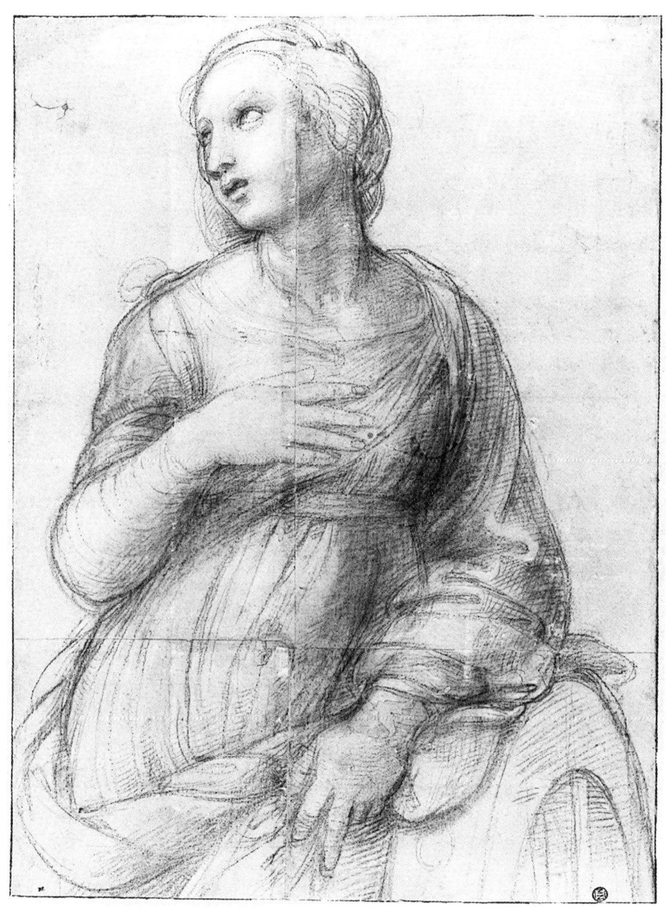

painting. These drawings, known as cartoons ('*cartone*' in Italian meaning literally 'big paper'), were initially invented as practical devices for the efficient transfer of parts of the design (see below), but by the early sixteenth century they had developed into highly worked drawings, which were much admired and collected (Fig. 105).[63] Vasari describes the cartoon as the point where 'painters go through all the processes of their art';[64] while for Armenini, it was the most authentic, highly distilled expression of the artist's idea.[65] For him, the cartoon was 'the last and most perfect manifestation of everything which the art of design can express',[66] and he goes so far as to say, 'but for the colours the cartoon is the work itself.'[67] Three highly influential cartoons exhibited in Florence at the beginning of the sixteenth century demonstrate how cartoons were sometimes treated with the awe and enthusiasm usually reserved for finished works of art. Shortly after his return to Florence in 1500 or 1501, Leonardo gained instant fame by displaying in his private rooms a cartoon of the Virgin and Child with Saint Anne and the Infant Baptist with a Lamb. According to Vasari, 'not only were artists astonished...but for two days the chamber where it stood was crowded with men and women, young and old, as they might do in going to solemn festivals, all hastening to behold the marvels of Leonardo.' Leonardo's *Battle of Anghiari* and Michelangelo's *Battle of Cascina* for the Sala del Gran Consiglio of 1503–4 were even more celebrated. In one account of the Cascina cartoon's fate, Vasari suggests it was torn to pieces by copyists, a casualty of its own astounding originality.[68] However, such cartoons were probably exceptional, and the inflation of their value by subsequent writers on art should not lead to the assumption that they were common in the process of picture making. A cartoon as elaborate and exquisite as Leonardo's *Virgin and Child with Saint Anne and Saint John the Baptist* in the National Gallery (Fig. 106) may not even have been made with a finished work in mind (it shows no signs of the transfer process), and is itself not entirely finished.

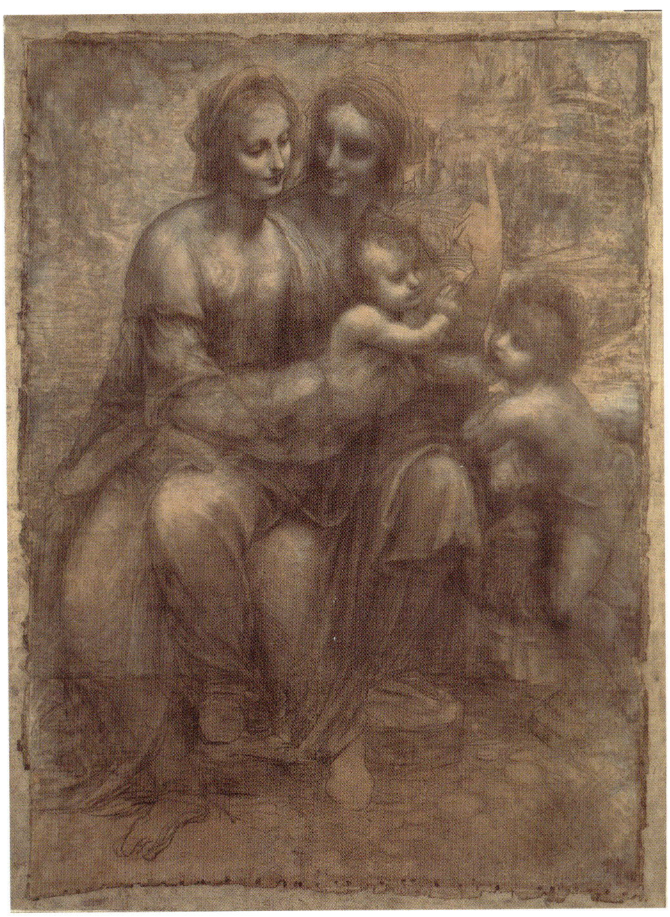

Fig. 106
LEONARDO DA VINCI, *The Virgin and Child with Saint Anne and Saint John the Baptist* [NG 6337], perhaps *c.*1499–1500
Charcoal, black and white chalk on tinted paper, 141.5 × 104.6 cm

Transfer of Drawings: the Development of the Cartoon

Since parchment and paper were so expensive in the fourteenth century, drawings made on the same scale as the eventual painting for transfer were small and used for repetition of motifs. Cennino is the first western source to describe the technique of pouncing (which seems to have been introduced to the west from China, probably in connection with woven silk textiles),[69] and in using the diminutive form *spolverezzi* (little pouncing patterns) to describe these drawings, he implies their small dimensions. To make the repeats for a cloth of gold to be executed using the technique of *sgraffito* as described by Cennino,[70] a *spolverezzo* representing only one quarter of the textile motif needed to be pricked and pounced, the full pattern being achieved by reversing it and pouncing through both sides – the *spolverezzo*

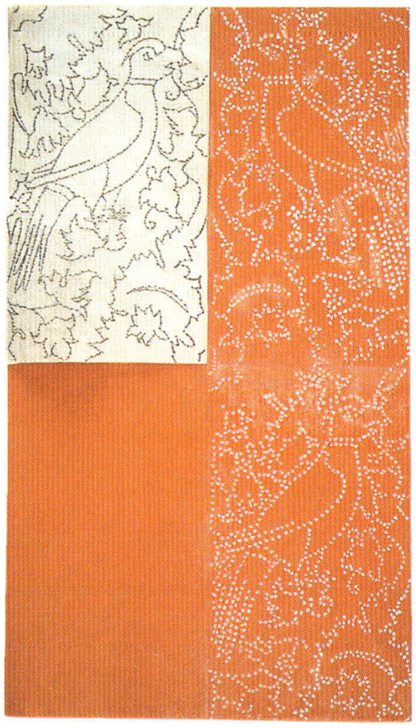

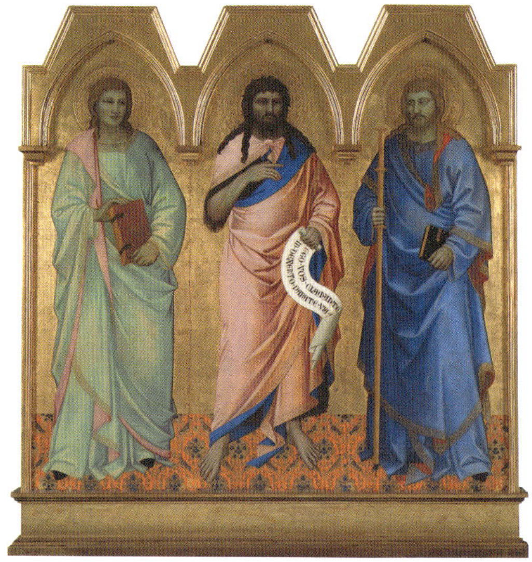

Fig. 107 (far left)
Pouncing textile repeats, using the method described by Cennino

Fig. 108
NARDO DI CIONE, *Saint John the Baptist with Saint John the Evangelist(?) and Saint James* [NG 581], *c.*1365
Egg on poplar, 159.5 × 147.5 cm

Fig. 109 (below)
Detail of Fig. 108

Fig. 110 (right)
PIERO DELLA FRANCESCA, *Saint Michael* [NG 769], completed 1469
Oil on poplar, 133 × 59.7 cm

Fig. 111
Infrared reflectogram mosaic, detail of Fig. 110

used for the floor covering in Nardo di Cione's *Saint John the Baptist with Saint John the Evangelist(?) and Saint James* (Figs 108 and 109), for example, was probably no larger than 11.5 x 6.5 cm (Fig. 107).[71] The design was almost certainly transferred by pouncing but the inevitable loss of the dots of pounced powder in the process of scraping away the paint and of tooling the exposed gold means that no evidence for this remains. Furthermore, no small pouncing patterns survive, even though parchment instead of paper (as mentioned by Cennino) was probably often used since it was stronger and less likely to tear, especially along the perforations. The fact that a textile pattern with the same paired parakeets was used in paintings by the brothers Andrea, Nardo and Jacopo di Cione[72] indicates that *spolverezzi* could be reasonably robust, and were likely to have been passed on and inherited from workshop to workshop. Certainly this particular pattern continued to be used in Florentine workshops right through into the early years of the fifteenth century, but in some of its later appearances details of the design tend to disappear or become distorted – although its dimensions do not change – which suggests that the original *spolverezzo* was much copied and recopied.

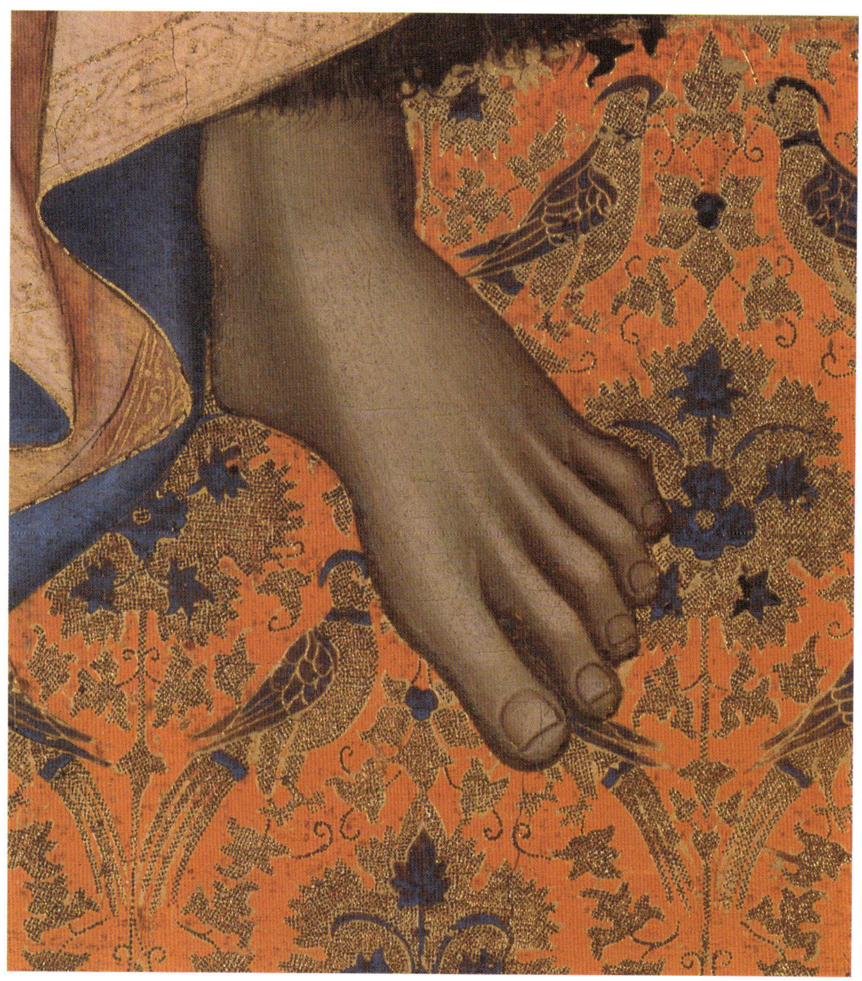

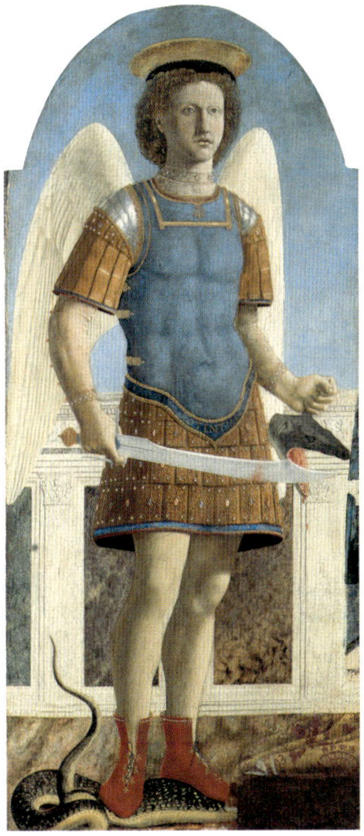

Spolverezzi also had obvious practical advantages for details of buildings, such as capitals, which might be repeated across a composition, and especially for the decorative semi-architectural borders which frame and separate the scenes of fresco cycles. Here pounced dots – easily detected because the black pouncing powder is absorbed by the damp plaster – have been observed on fourteenth-century wall paintings,[73] and pounced patterns continued to be used for repetition of architectural motifs in subsequent centuries. They were equally valuable for the duplication of *imprese* and coats of arms, and were used by Pisanello for the repeated pattern of the emblematic frieze which runs across the top of his murals in the Palazzo Ducale, Mantua.[74]

Piero della Francesca began his career with a painter who included among his many activities the painting of coats of arms, and it has been suggested that this, together with the extreme care with which he seems to have planned his pictures, may have predisposed him towards the extensive use of pounced drawings.[75] In the panel of Saint Michael (Fig. 110) from his polyptych for the church of Sant'Agostino in Borgo San Sepolcro, now in the National Gallery, he employed them for repeated elements such as the mouldings and architectural detail of the balustrade which runs behind the figure – traces of pouncing have been detected on all the surviving panels[76]– as well as for the red velvet pattern of the textile which appears in the lower right corner (probably the trailing end of the draperies worn by the Virgin in the lost centre panel) (Fig. 111). This very traditional application of pounced transfer for textile repeats continued into the next century, a notable example appearing in the cloth of honour behind the Virgin in an altarpiece painted in Cremona in 1507 by Marco Marziale (Figs 112 and 113).

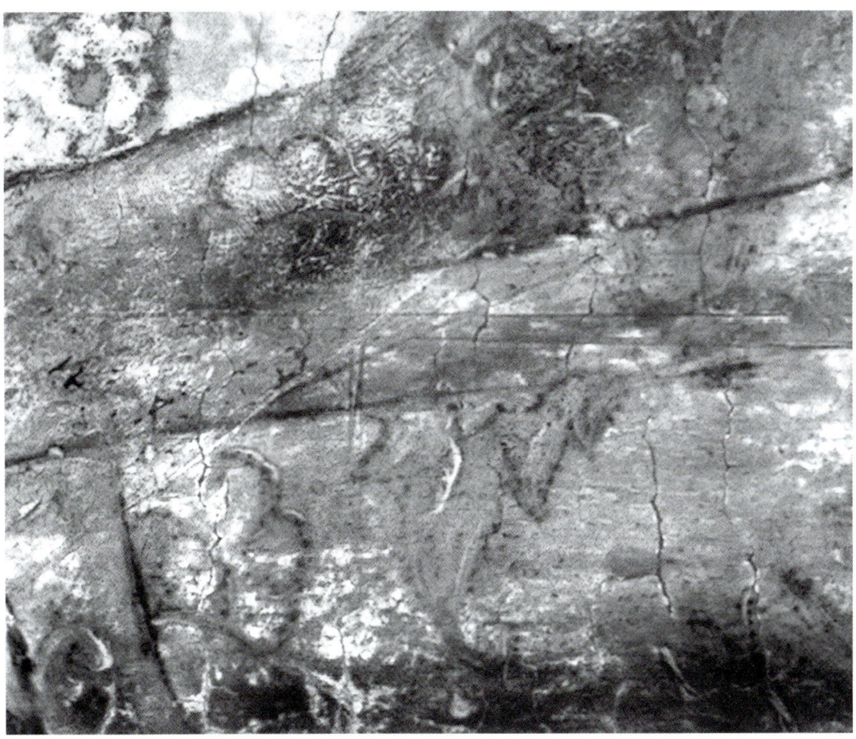

Evidence of pouncing on Piero's panel paintings, however, confirms that he also made specific drawings on the same scale as the painting for particular heads or complex areas of drapery. A pricked drawing was used for the head of Saint Michael, although the rest of the figure seems to have been drawn freehand, while in the *Baptism of Christ* (NG 665) the pounced dots made in the transfer of a study of the bunched folds of the tunic of the angel on the left are visible even to the naked eye. For his murals Piero made sophisticated use of pounced drawings of various sizes, ranging from *spolverezzi* for textiles and repeated architectural detail to cartoons for heads, and also for larger areas, which must have involved the pasting together of several sheets of paper.[77] It appears that larger pounced cartoons were first used for wall paintings by artists of the generation of Paolo Uccello and Domenico Veneziano,[78] with whom Piero had worked in 1439 on the decoration of the choir of Sant'Egidio, Florence. Subsequently it often seems to have been painters with considerable experience of working on walls who exploited pounced drawings in their panel paintings as well. Luca Signorelli, for example, used a pricked cartoon for the bowl and book in the foreground of his *Circumcision* (NG 1128), in this case added over the completed painting of the floor so that the pouncing dots are clearly visible where the black powder has stuck to the slightly soft paint beneath. Vincenzo Foppa pounced some of the heads in the *Adoration of the Kings* (Figs 114 and 115)[79] (otherwise underdrawn with fluid freehand lines, often not followed in the painting) in a way that is exactly analogous to his use of pounced drawings in his wall paintings in the Portinari Chapel in the Church of Sant'Eustorgio, Milan.[80] The sharp definition of the pounce marks on the *Adoration of the Kings* suggests either that they were made with a liquid medium, perhaps dotted through the holes of the cartoon with a brush, or that the heads were pounced not onto the gesso but onto the *imprimitura* before it had completely dried.

Until the sixteenth century the cost of paper appears to have restricted the use of cartoons incorporating entire compositions for paintings, unless they were relatively small.[81] Raphael, in the early part of his career, generally pounced comprehensive cartoons for small pictures of the Virgin or predella scenes (see Cat. 8), but made freehand underdrawings on the main panels of his altarpieces, often using squaring (see page 23) as an aid in the enlargement of his compositional drawings on paper. Large cartoons that covered the complete composition were probably first made by painters supplying designs to be executed in other media, for example stained glass and marquetry[82] and, above all, embroidery and tapestry. Here the enormous cost of the final product (far greater than that of murals and panel paintings) would have justified the expense of making full-scale paper cartoons. Between November 1457 and December 1458 the Este accounts show that Gregorio de Gasparino, *cartolaro* (paper merchant) of Ferrara, supplied to Cosimo Tura several dozen sheets of '*carta reale*' (large sheets,

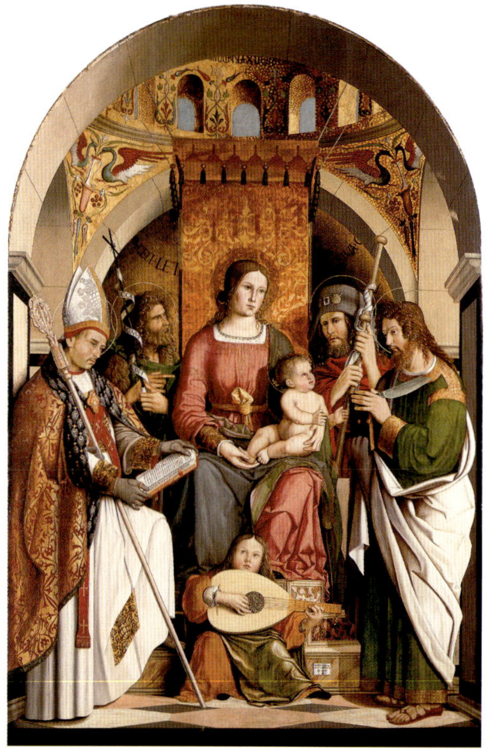

Fig. 112
MARCO MARZIALE,
The Virgin and Child with Saints [NG 804], 1507. Oil on wood, 221 × 142.2 cm

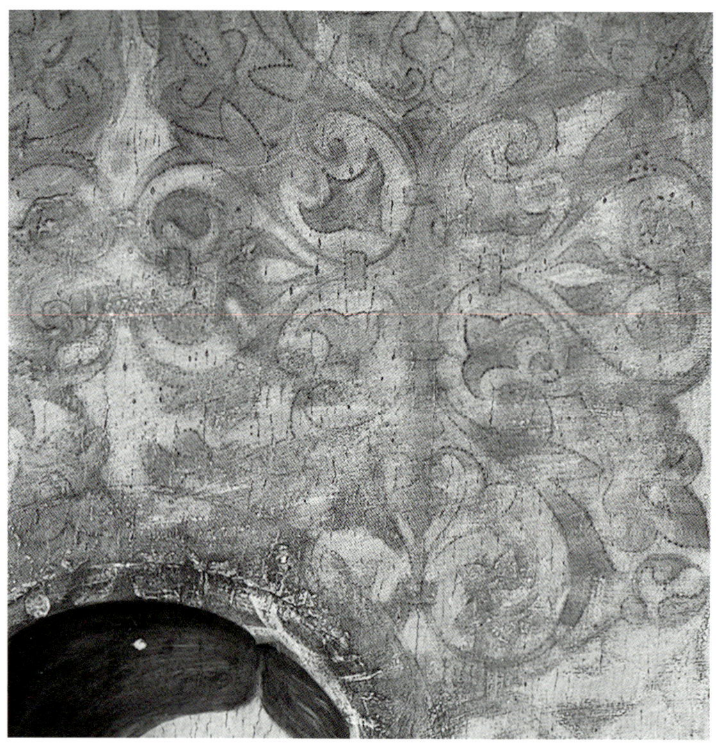

Fig. 113
Infrared photograph detail of Fig 112

Fig. 114
VINCENZO FOPPA,
The Adoration of the Kings [NG 729],
1480s or 1490s. Oil on poplar,
241 × 212.8 cm

Fig. 115
Infrared photograph detail of Fig. 114

possibly measuring as much as 50 by 63 cm) for him 'to make designs' for tapestries to be woven by the Northern European weavers working for the court in Ferrara. Tura also produced full-scale *patroni* (patterns) for tapestries (the equivalent of the *grand patron* in the Netherlands) which were painted in colour on linen canvas, the pigments bound in a glue-size medium.[83] It is possible that the painting of tapestry cartoons on canvas represents an earlier practice which was gradually displaced as paper became cheaper and more available, so that by the time Raphael came to make his celebrated cartoons, now in the Victoria and Albert Museum, for the tapestries to be hung in the Sistine Chapel, it had become normal procedure to paste together sheets of paper in very large quantities.[84]

For his prestigious Roman commissions Raphael was able to use compositional cartoons for large-scale paintings as well. The surviving portion of the cartoon in the Pinacoteca Ambrosiana, Milan, for the fresco of the *School of Athens* in the Vatican Stanze, consists of nearly 200 sheets of paper, and the architectural setting of the upper part of the fresco may originally also have been included.[85] There was no question of taking this enormous and magnificently worked drawing and transferring it direct to each day's worth of damp plaster (the *giornate*). Instead, a series of substitute cartoons must have been made, probably by the simple process of laying blank sheets of paper behind the full cartoon and then pricking along the outlines of the design, perforating both layers of paper.[86] It did not matter if these secondary cartoons were soiled by pouncing powder or torn in the process of indenting the lines with a stylus into the damp plaster. The surface of the fresco reveals that both these transfer techniques were used for the *School of Athens*, together with direct freehand incision in certain areas.[87]

Secondary cartoons would also have been used to transfer designs to panels, especially

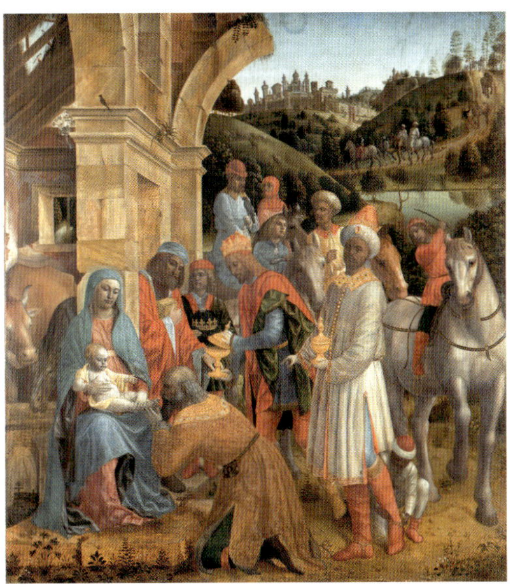

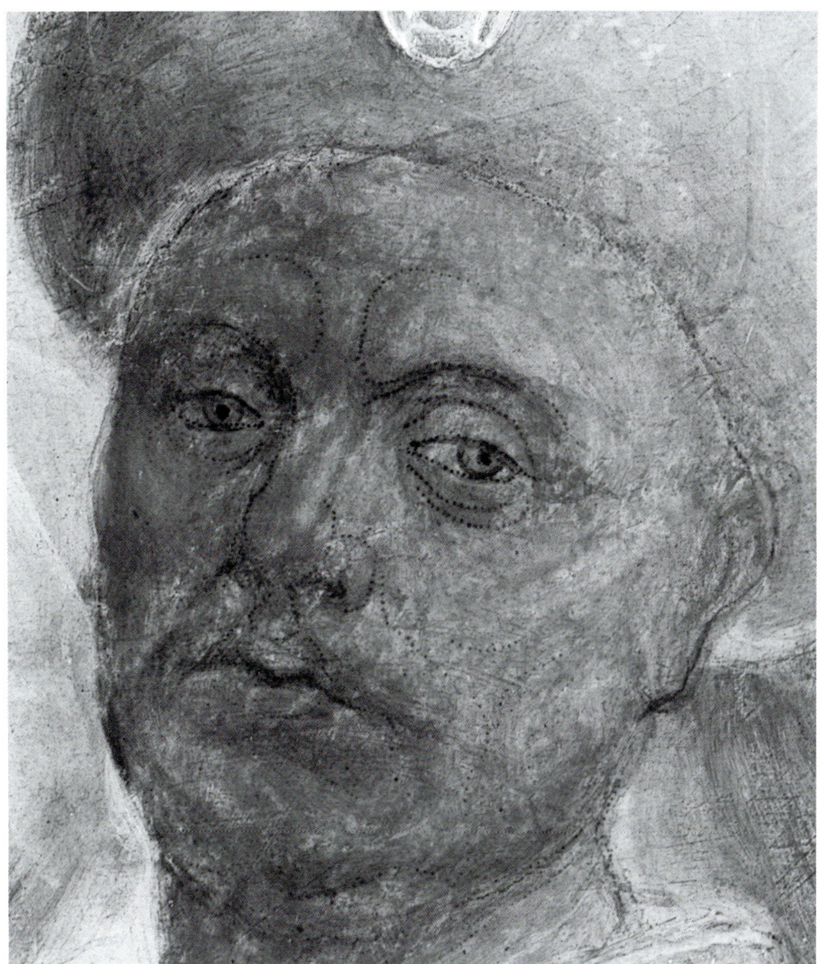

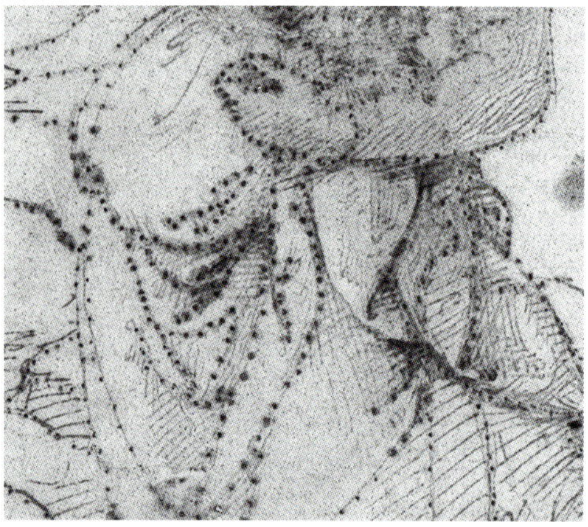

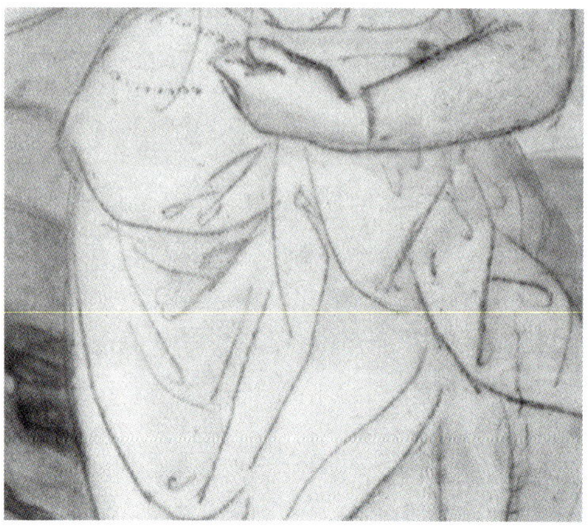

when the cartoon was drawn in a medium vulnerable to abrasion such as charcoal or black chalk. However, traces of black powder in the perforations in Raphael's little pen-and-ink cartoon for *An Allegory ('Vision of a Knight')* (Figs 116 and 117) show that it was pounced directly,[88] as in this instance the pouncing dust could be brushed away from the drawing's surface without causing damage. The cartoon, with its shading to model forms and establish the lighting, was still needed for reference during execution of the painting, since the information transferred to the wall or panel could only be linear.

Making Replicas

In the later part of his career Raphael ran a large and productive workshop, his role becoming increasingly restricted to the design process rather than to the actual production of paintings. Cartoons would have been an efficient aid in the deployment of assistants, especially for the execution of murals, but his earlier experience in their use when in the workshop of Pietro Perugino had a rather different emphasis. Greatly in demand, and running workshops in both Florence and Perugia in the 1490s, Perugino often worked for relatively conservative patrons who were likely to ask for a painting similar, if not virtually identical, to one of his extant works. As well as creating near replicas both of large altarpieces and smaller devotional panels, he frequently took figures and reorganised them into different compositions (for which he was later censured by Vasari). Since it has been shown that many of these repetitions are on the same scale,[89] it is clear that he made extensive use of cartoons, with pouncing most probably the usual method of transfer.[90]

The three panels in the National Gallery from the polyptych commissioned from Perugino for the Certosa di Pavia in 1496 (Fig.

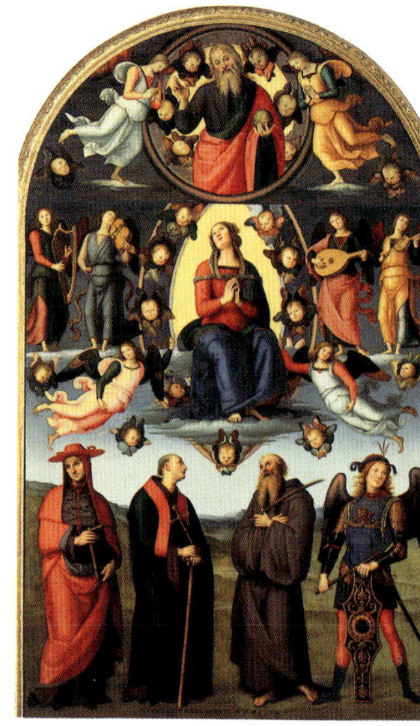

Fig. 116 (top left)
RAPHAEL, Cartoon for *An Allegory ('Vision of a Knight')*, detail of Fig. 218

Fig. 117 (left)
RAPHAEL, *An Allegory ('Vision of a Knight')*, detail from infrared reflectogram mosaic (see Fig. 217)

Fig. 118 (below)
PERUGINO, centre panel of Fig. 122, infrared reflectogram, detail

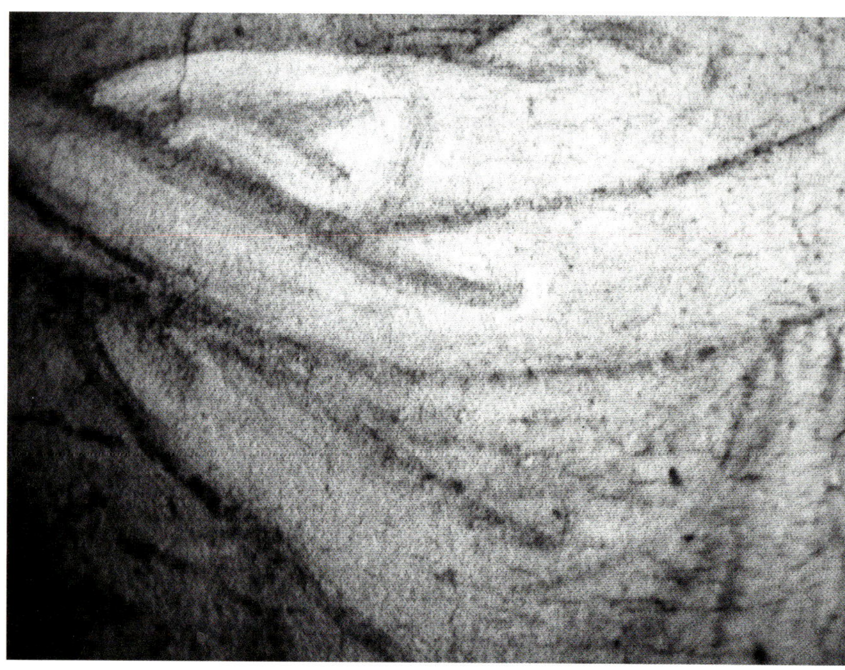

Fig. 119 (left)
PERUGINO, Vallombrosa Altarpiece, 1500
Oil on wood, 415 × 246 cm
Florence, Palazzo Pitti, Galleria Palatina

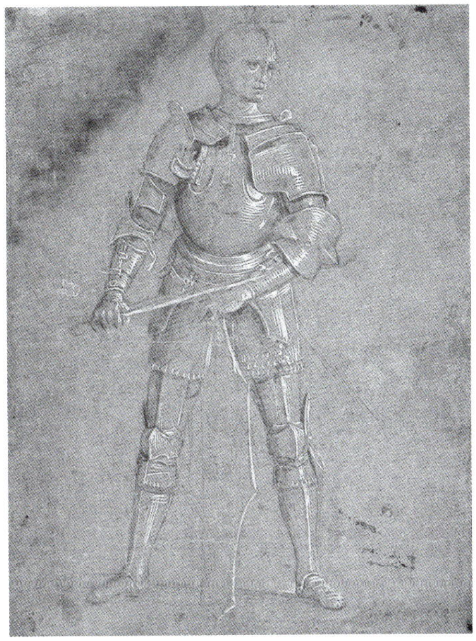

Fig. 120 (right)
PERUGINO, *A study of a man in armour (Saint Michael)*
Metal-point with white heightening on blue prepared paper, 24.9 × 18.5 cm
Windsor, The Royal Collection RL 12801 P&W 21

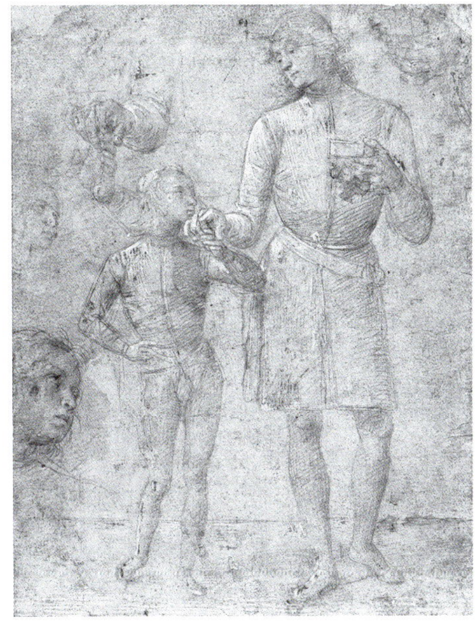

Fig. 121 (far right)
PERUGINO, Studies for *Raphael and Tobias*
Metal-point with white heightening on cream prepared paper, 23.8 × 18.3 cm
Oxford, Ashmolean Museum inv. Parker 27

Fig. 122 (below)
PERUGINO, Fragments from the Certosa di Pavia Altarpiece [NG 288.1–3], *c.*1496–1500. Oil on poplar, 114 × 56 cm, 113 × 64cm, 113 × 56 cm

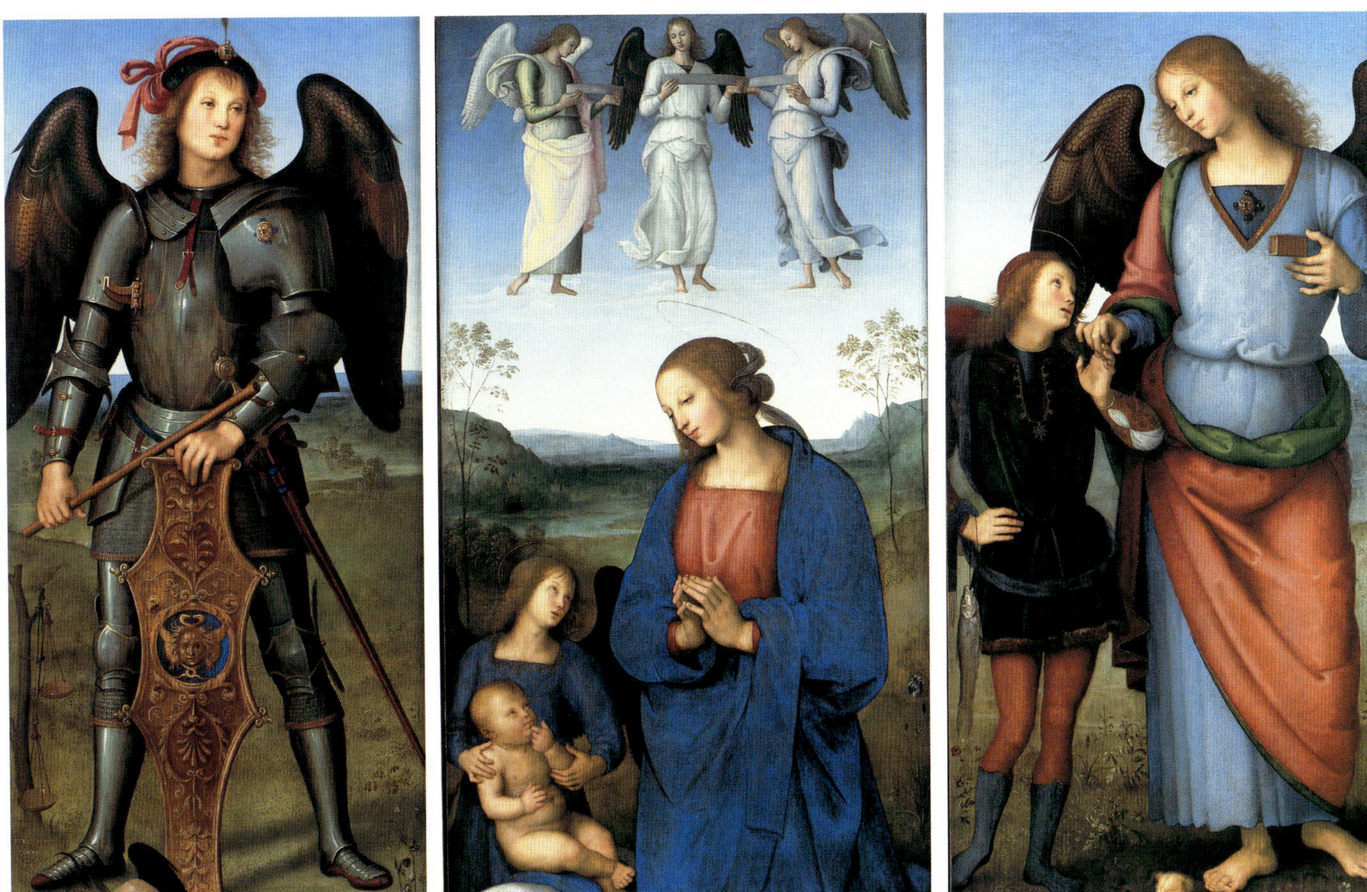

122), but generally thought to have been painted a few years later, illustrate how the artist both created new models and recycled extant designs. The figures of the Archangel Raphael and Tobias appear to be unique in his output, and so special preliminary studies had to be made; a metal-point drawing shows two workshop assistants in contemporary dress adopting the poses selected for the painting (Fig. 121). A study of a man in armour holding a shield (Fig. 120) is clearly connected with the panel of the Archangel Michael, but it is less certain that it was made specifically for the Certosa di Pavia polyptych, since a closely similar Saint Michael, but on a larger scale, appears in the line-up of saints in the Vallombrosa altarpiece which is dated 1500 (Fig. 119).[91] The armoured figure then makes a third appearance, on the same scale as in the Vallombrosa altarpiece, but with modifications to convert him into the Roman Lucius Sicinus in the frescoes of the Collegio del Cambio, Perugia, on which Perugino worked from about 1496 to 1500.[92] However, an argument in favour of the study initially having been made for the Certosa project (and therefore for dating the National Gallery panel to before 1500) is that the saint's armour in the painting, although fanciful, is still close to the presumably real armour worn in the drawing, whereas in the larger scale versions much of the armour has been shed. The cartoons were almost certainly enlarged or reduced (depending on the precedence of the versions) by freehand copying, probably with the aid of squaring.

The principal figures in the central panel of the Certosa di Pavia polyptych appear on the same scale, but slightly further apart and with the addition of an infant Baptist, in a painting known as the *Madonna del Sacco* (Florence, Galleria Palatina), usually dated to between 1495 and 1500.[93] Whichever version was painted first, it is clear that cartoons were made with the intention of repeating the design, for pounced dots have been found in the head and drapery of the angel in the London panel.[94] Pouncing has also been detected in the trio of singing angels (Fig. 118) above the main group, and they in turn feature – with some variations – in the *Adoration of the Shepherds* in the Collegio del Cambio. Furthermore, this fresco also includes a Virgin that is very close to those in the panel paintings. Edited versions of the *Adoration* composition recur in later frescoes for Umbrian churches, and so Perugino's designs continued to be recycled and repeated.

The rival Florentine workshop headed by Domenico Ghirlandaio appears to have been more inventive, at least when Domenico himself was involved. Cartoons clearly played an important role in the execution of frescoes, but principally as a practical aid for the rapid transfer of designs on to the freshly laid plaster, thus maximising the amount of time for applying the colours. Repetition of Domenico's designs seems mainly to occur in paintings executed by the workshop; for example the Child in his National Gallery *Virgin and Child* (NG 3937), a panel with a confident freehand underdrawing, perhaps enlarged from a study by eye, recurs, slightly altered and balanced somewhat precariously on the Virgin's knee, in an altarpiece apparently painted entirely by the workshop for the church of San Girolamo dei Gesuati, Pisa (now in the Museo Nazionale di San Matteo).[95]

The situation in Giovanni Bellini's Venetian workshop seems to have been broadly similar. Infrared examination has shown that pictures painted largely by Giovanni himself tend to have elaborate and carefully shaded underdrawings (discussed more fully below), at least until around 1500 when he simplified his underdrawing style.[96] He made occasional use of pounced drawings for repetition of architectural detail and sometimes for hands (with which he always had some difficulty), but when pounced (and sometimes possibly traced) underdrawings have been found on pictures associated with his circle – often derived from known or presumed lost works by him – the painting is not usually

Fig. 123
ANDREA DEL SARTO, *The Virgin and Child with Saint Elizabeth and Saint John the Baptist* [NG 17], *c.*1513
Oil on wood, 106 × 81.3 cm

Fig. 124
ANDREA DEL SARTO, *The Virgin and Child with Saints Catherine, Elizabeth and John the Baptist (The Tallard Madonna)*, *c.*1511–18
Oil on canvas (transferred from panel), 102 × 80 cm
St Petersburg, The State Hermitage Museum, inv. 62

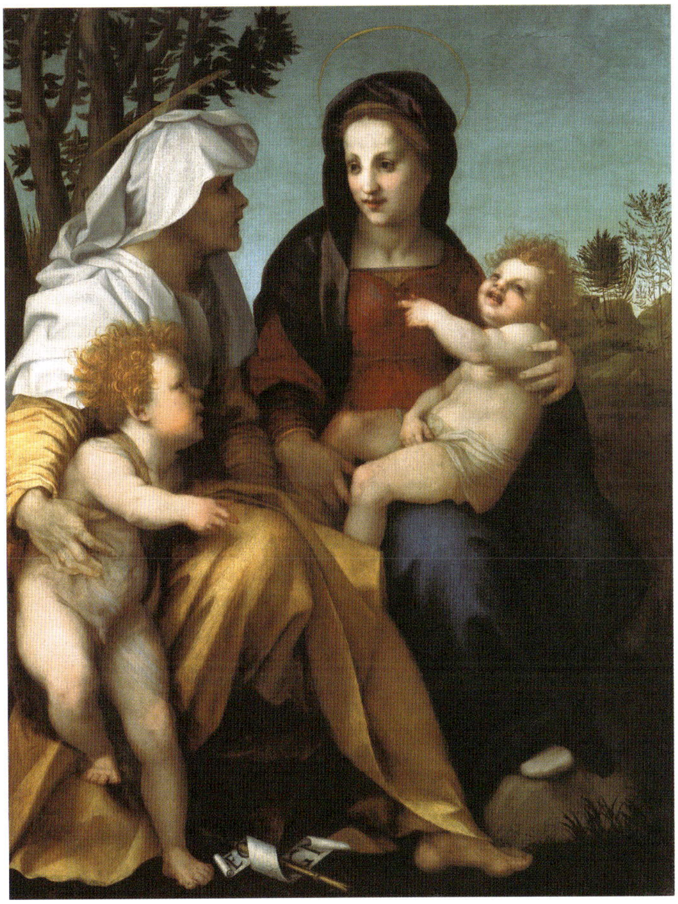

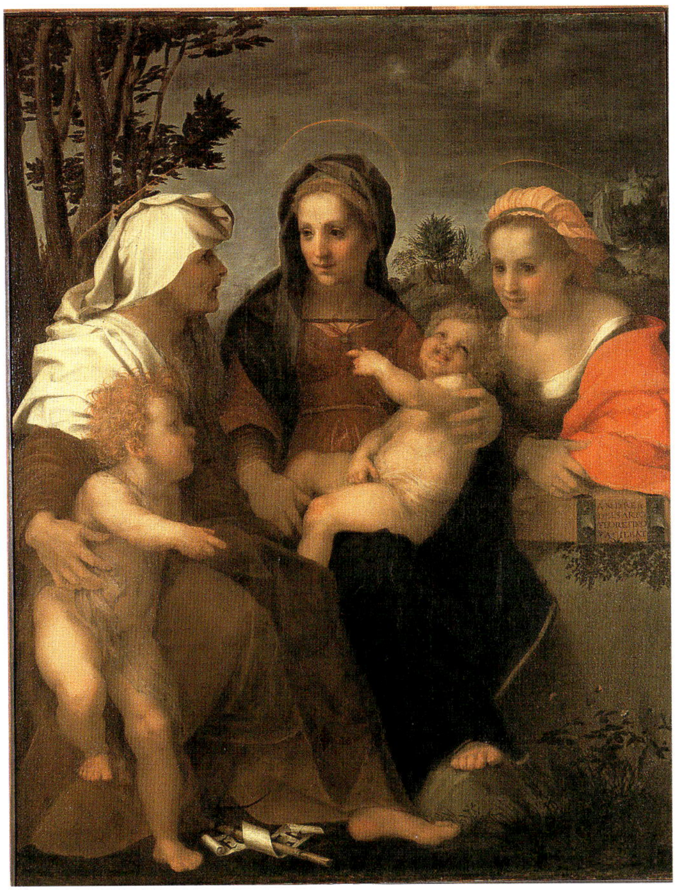

of sufficient quality to suggest that he played much part in their execution. More often, however, the drawings and cartoons that were used to repeat Bellini's inventions are likely to have been made by copying and tracing his finished paintings or sometimes perhaps even his underdrawings. Certainly they became increasingly debased and incoherent as they were recopied and transmitted from workshop to workshop, not only in Venice itself, but also on the Venetian mainland.[97]

The sixteenth century is often thought of as a period when 'invention' was more highly valued than previously, but many artists, among them Andrea del Sarto, remained as efficient and ingenious in their use of cartoons for the replication and adaption of designs as Perugino had been. Like Perugino, del Sarto repeated his compositions – usually with some variations – both for altarpieces and smaller devotional pictures. *The Virgin and Child with Saint Elizabeth and Saint John the Baptist* in the National Gallery is based on the same cartoon as a similar painting in St Petersburg, which includes the additional figure of Saint Catherine (Figs 123–126).[98] The design seems to have been transferred by the so-called *calco* method as described by Vasari, in which either the reverse of the cartoon, or more probably a second sheet of paper, was blackened with powdered charcoal, and laid (blackened face down) over the gessoed and primed panel – Vasari mentions that the *imprimitura* was applied first, and this does indeed usually seem to be the case with sixteenth-century paintings. The most important outlines of the cartoon could then be transferred to the panel surface by tracing over them with a stylus. As Vasari pointed out, 'the cartoon is not spoiled, and all the figures and other details on the cartoon come out very well outlined on the panel.'[99] The charcoal marks could then be fixed by going over them with a brush and black ink. Confirmation that this method was used in del Sarto's London and St Petersburg paintings is supplied by the slight variations between the underdrawn lines: since the stylus does not mark the cartoon, other than by a slight indentation, the painter or workshop member responsible for transferring the design is unlikely to choose to go over exactly the same lines each time that the transfer is repeated. Furthermore, in an elaborately shaded cartoon such as was probably behind this composition, del Sarto's soft *sfumato* contours would not have been specific.

In North Italian workshops stock designs were similarly repeated and modified, presumably with the aid of cartoons, although more of these survive in Florence. Leonardo seems to have directly supervised, and perhaps participated in, the production in his Milanese workshop of at least two versions of the much-repeated composition known as the *'Madonna of the Yarnwinder'*, both of which exhibit differences between the underdrawing and the painting,[100] and multiple versions exist of paintings by his followers, such as Luini, Cesare da Sesto and Giampietrino.[101]

In a different category are replicas made during or after the completion of the prime version of a composition, a case in point being the two versions of Lorenzo Lotto's *Virgin and Child with Saints Jerome and Nicholas of Tolentino* (Fig. 127).[102] Lotto seems to have started work on the canvas which is now in the Museum of Fine Arts, Boston, making a freely improvised underdrawing, with several fairly radical revisions. At this stage, or possibly shortly after he began painting, a replica was ordered, and so he prepared a second canvas, the National Gallery one, and copied onto it a simplified version of the underdrawing of the Boston picture. He may have done this by eye, since the principal elements of the design are not always in exactly the same position (Fig. 128). Lotto then seems to have painted both versions concurrently, for the same pentimenti made in the course of painting occur on both, and paint cross-sections reveal the same paint layer structures.

Such a procedure would not have been

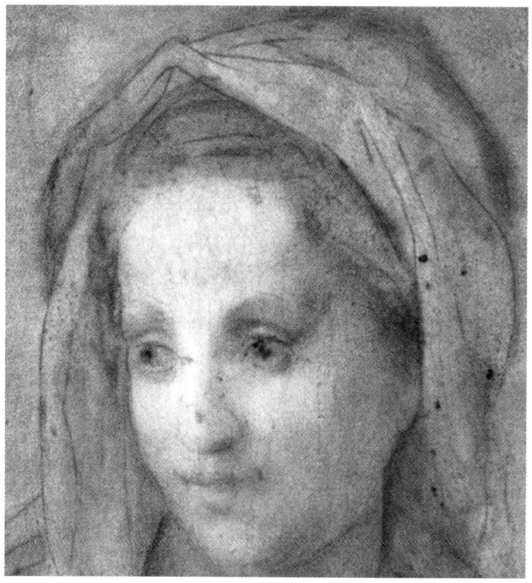

Fig. 125
Infrared reflectogram mosaic, detail of Fig. 123

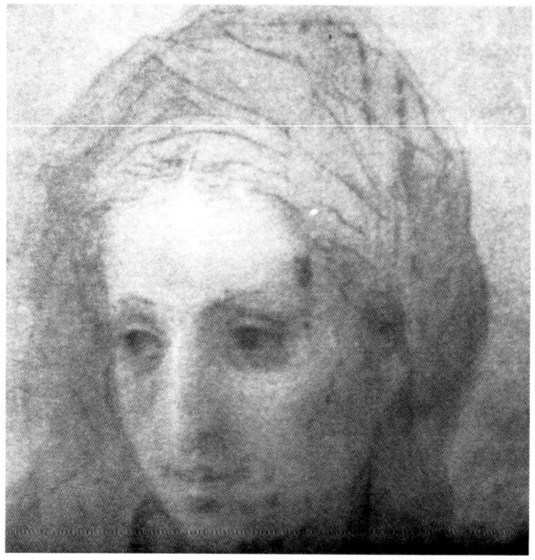

Fig. 126
Infrared reflectogram mosaic, detail of Fig. 124

Fig. 127 (right)
LORENZO LOTTO, *The Virgin and Child with Saint Jerome and Saint Nicholas of Tolentino* [NG 2281], probably 1522
Oil on canvas, 89.5 × 74.3 cm

Fig. 128
Infrared reflectogram mosaic, detail of Fig. 127

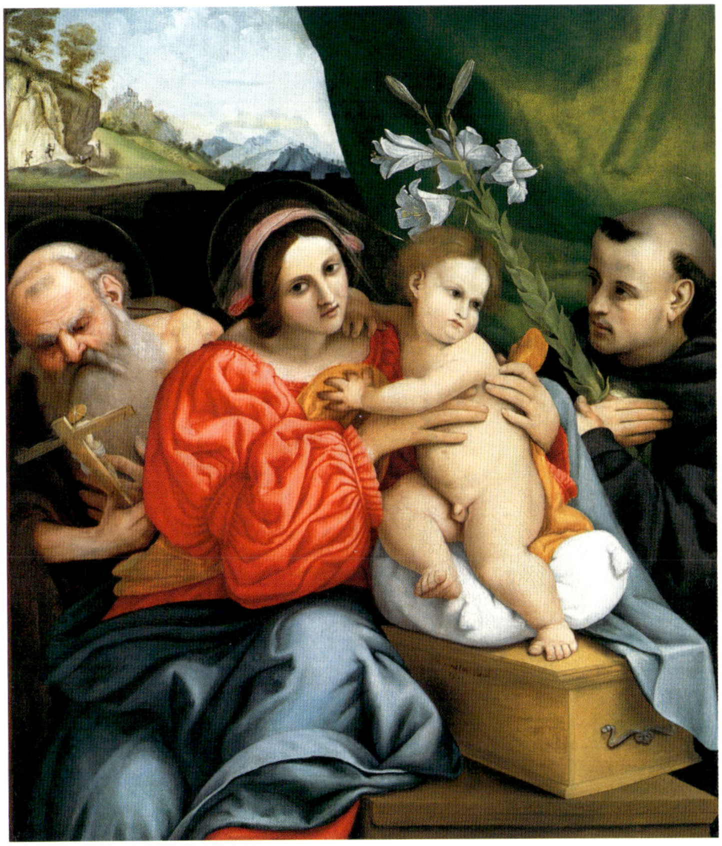

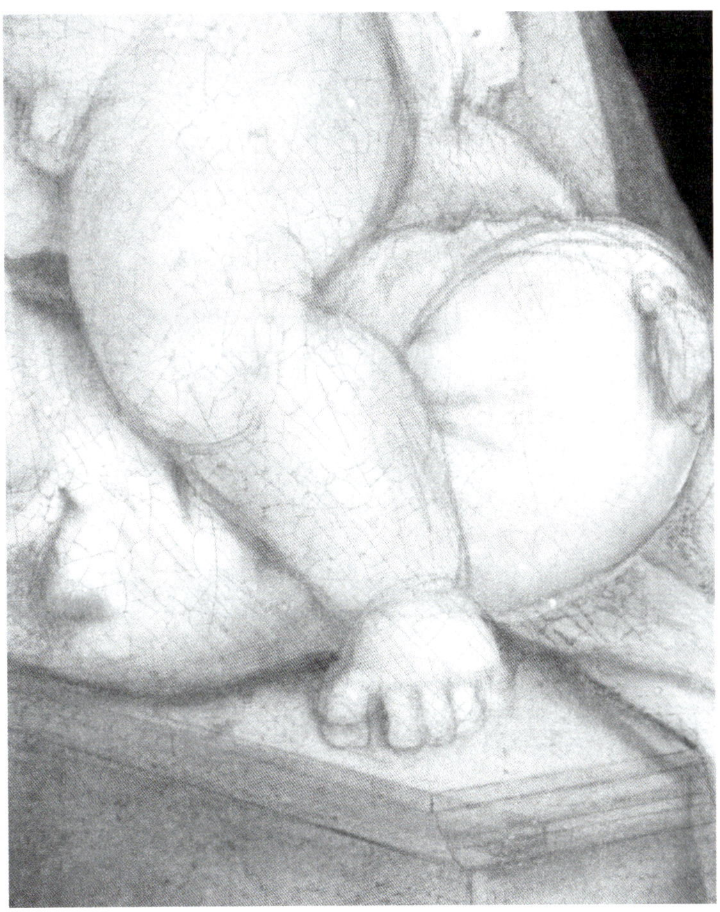

possible in Titian's workshop. Although he began his paintings with an underdrawing, this was usually sketchy and approximate, and was seldom followed closely in the course of painting. Invariably he continued to make extensive alterations as he painted. Therefore replicas must have been made only when the original painting was more or less complete. Sometimes tracings taken from the finished painting may have been used; the figure of the female saint in *The Virgin and Child with the Infant Saint John and a Female Saint or Donor* (NG 635) reappears on the same scale in variations on this composition – apparently painted by the workshop, but possibly with some intervention by Titian himself – in the Galleria Palatina, Florence, and the Kimbell Art Museum, Fort Worth.[103] These seem to be among the first products of a practice that became increasingly common in Titian's workshop, with replicas and variations made both on similar and quite different scales.[104] There is little evidence to indicate how his original paintings were recorded (especially when they had left Venice), and the relationship between versions, including variations in scale, has yet to be fully investigated by technical means such as infrared reflectography.

In common with most Renaissance portraitists Titian was sometimes called upon to make replicas of portraits, and many of these exist, some clearly executed by the workshop. When Cardinal Granvelle, writing to Titian in 1549 in the hope of obtaining a copy of the portrait of Philip II of Spain that he had painted in Milan, asked 'if you have retained a drawing of it, let me have a version',[105] it is not clear whether he knew Titian to have made and kept portrait drawings, or whether he assumed that he did on the basis of the practice of other painters. These drawings could, of course, have been made either before painting or during a sitting with the subject or they could be *ricordi* drawn after the painting, and made precisely so that replicas could be supplied if requested. The

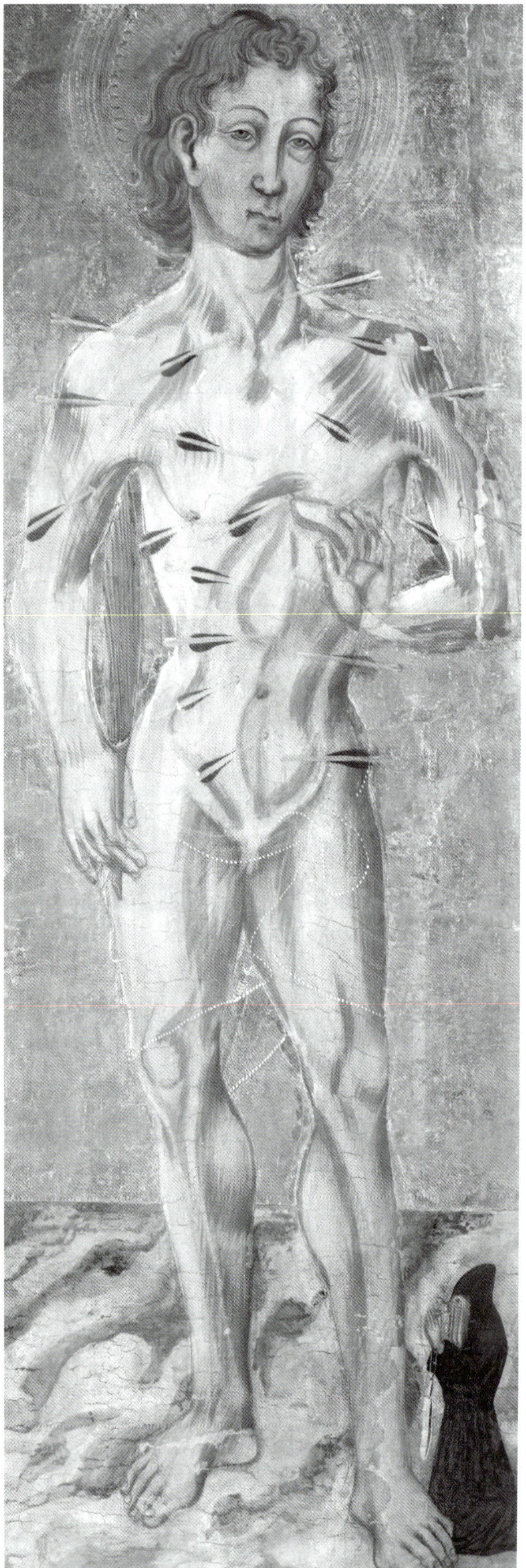

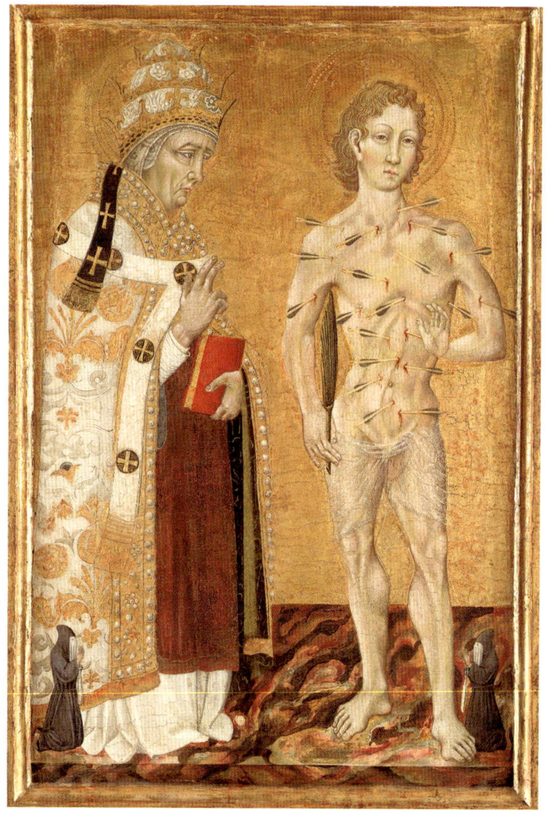

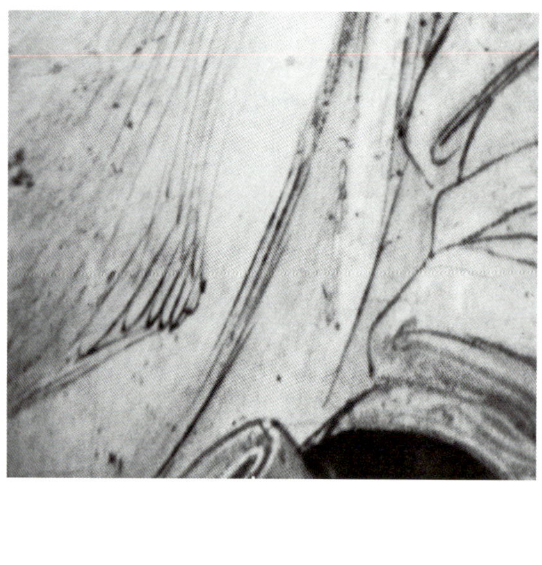

Fig. 129 (far left)
Infrared reflectogram mosaic, detail of Fig. 130

Fig. 130 (left)
GIOVANNI DI PAOLO,
Saints Fabian and Sebastian [NG 3402], *c.*1475–82. Egg on wood, 84.5 × 54.5 cm.

Fig. 131
Infrared reflectogram, detail of Fig. 108

Fig. 132 (below)
MICHELANGELO, *The Virgin and Child with Saint John and Angels (The Manchester Madonna)*, detail. Raking-light photograph of Fig. 6 showing incised lines

Fig. 133
VINCENZO FOPPA,
The Adoration of the Kings, detail
Raking-light photograph of Fig. 114 showing incised lines of architecture

highly detailed drawing in black chalk, heightened with white, by Francesco Bonsignori that matches closely his painted *Portrait of an Elderly Man* of 1487 in the National Gallery, repeats so exactly the lighting of the painting that it may well be such a record.[106] The other way of making repetitions was to work from a cartoon; the discovery of *spolveri* on several fifteenth-century portraits, including Leonardo's portraits of *Ginevra de' Benci* and *Cecilia Gallerani*,[107] and the survival of a number of portrait drawings pricked for transfer[108] confirm that this was common practice.

The Freehand Underdrawing

Although cartoons of every type played an important role in the production of paintings in some Italian workshops, infrared examination has shown that, when dealing with original productions by competent painters who intended to undertake much, if not all, of the execution of the paintings themselves, the design frequently appears to have been drawn directly onto the painting surface. Any material used for drawing on paper might also be used for underdrawings, as well as every graphic technique, ranging from simple outlining to elaborate shading with hatched strokes, or, less commonly, with dilute washes of ink. Enlargement from studies on paper was by eye, aided, if necessary, by measuring with dividers or calipers[109] and by drawing horizontal and vertical plumblines (especially important for large wall paintings) and squaring grids. Since these were usually ruled in a dry drawing material, the lines seldom survive on panels or canvases, and their use often has to be deduced from drawings on paper marked up with such grids.

Before cheaper paper made the large cartoon a possibility, freehand underdrawing was the only option. Cennino's instructions for making underdrawings for frescoes and panels are essentially the same.[110] For a fresco the complete composition was drawn on the *arriccio* (the first rougher layer of plaster, which was applied to the whole wall and allowed to dry). The drawing was made initially in charcoal, and then fixed by going over it with a brush and a liquid medium, often using a natural red iron oxide, called *sinopia*, hence the use of this term for these underdrawings. The *intonaco*, the second layer of plaster which carried the colours, was applied in patches (known as *giornate*, enough for a day's worth of painting), over the *arriccio*, thereby gradually obscuring the *sinopia*. Many of these *sinopie* have subsequently been revealed by the removal of the upper fresco layers and their transfer to new supports, and they now represent the best evidence for how painters

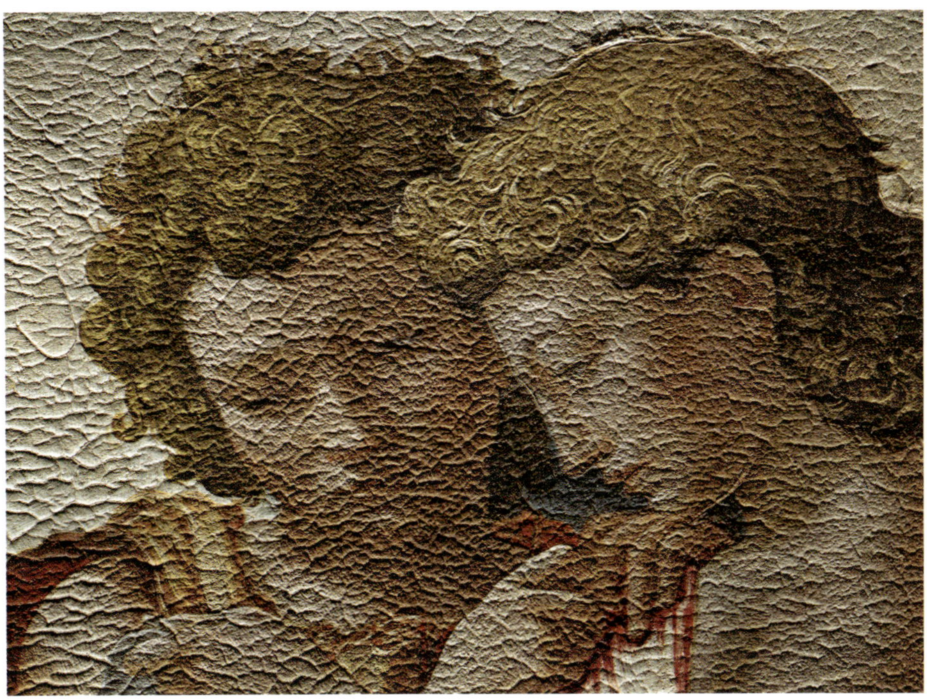

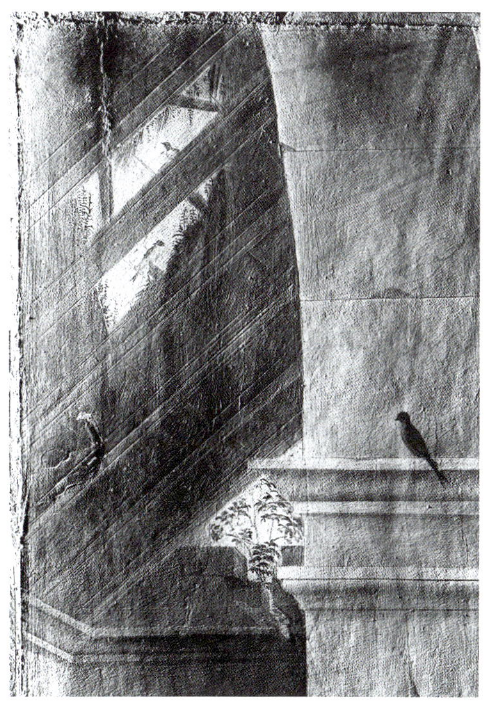

drew in the fourteenth century. Underdrawings on panels were also to be sketched first in charcoal, generally willow charcoal, the stick tied to a cane to encourage the artist to stand back a little, 'for it is a great help to you in composing'. Any erasures could be made with the feathered end of a quill. Cennino recommended putting the underdrawing aside for a few days, and once it had been considered afresh, and amended if necessary, most of the charcoal was to be dusted off, leaving a faint trace of the drawing. This could then be reinforced by going over it with a dilute ink applied with a fine-pointed brush, and any remaining charcoal swept away. Finally the drapery folds and the faces were to be shaded with washes of ink applied with a blunt soft brush, resulting in 'such a handsome drawing ...that you will make everyone fall in love with your productions'.

In fact, underdrawings shaded with washes do not appear to be all that common in the fourteenth century[111] and among paintings at the National Gallery, the drawing which perhaps conforms best to Cennino's account is a fifteenth-century one, that found on the votive panel of *Saints Fabian and Sebastian*, a late work by the technically conservative Sienese painter, Giovanni di Paolo (Figs 129 and 130).[112] Underdrawings on fourteenth-century panels in the collection generally consist of simple outlining of contours and drapery folds, drawn either with a quill or a brush, or, as seems to be the case with panels by Duccio, both used interchangeably.[113] The only shaded drawing of note is that by Nardo di Cione for his *Saint John the Baptist with Saint John the Evangelist(?) and Saint James* (NG 581), where the drapery folds are hatched with a quill pen, the lines sometimes drawn without lifting the nib so that they appear as a series of calligraphic U-shaped loops (Fig. 131).

As part of the underdrawing process, Nardo

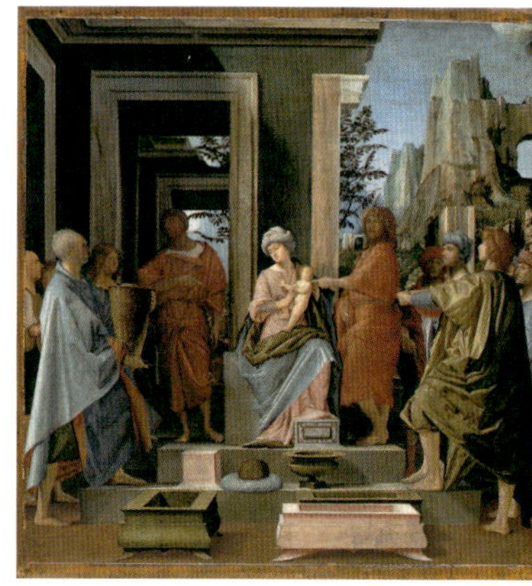

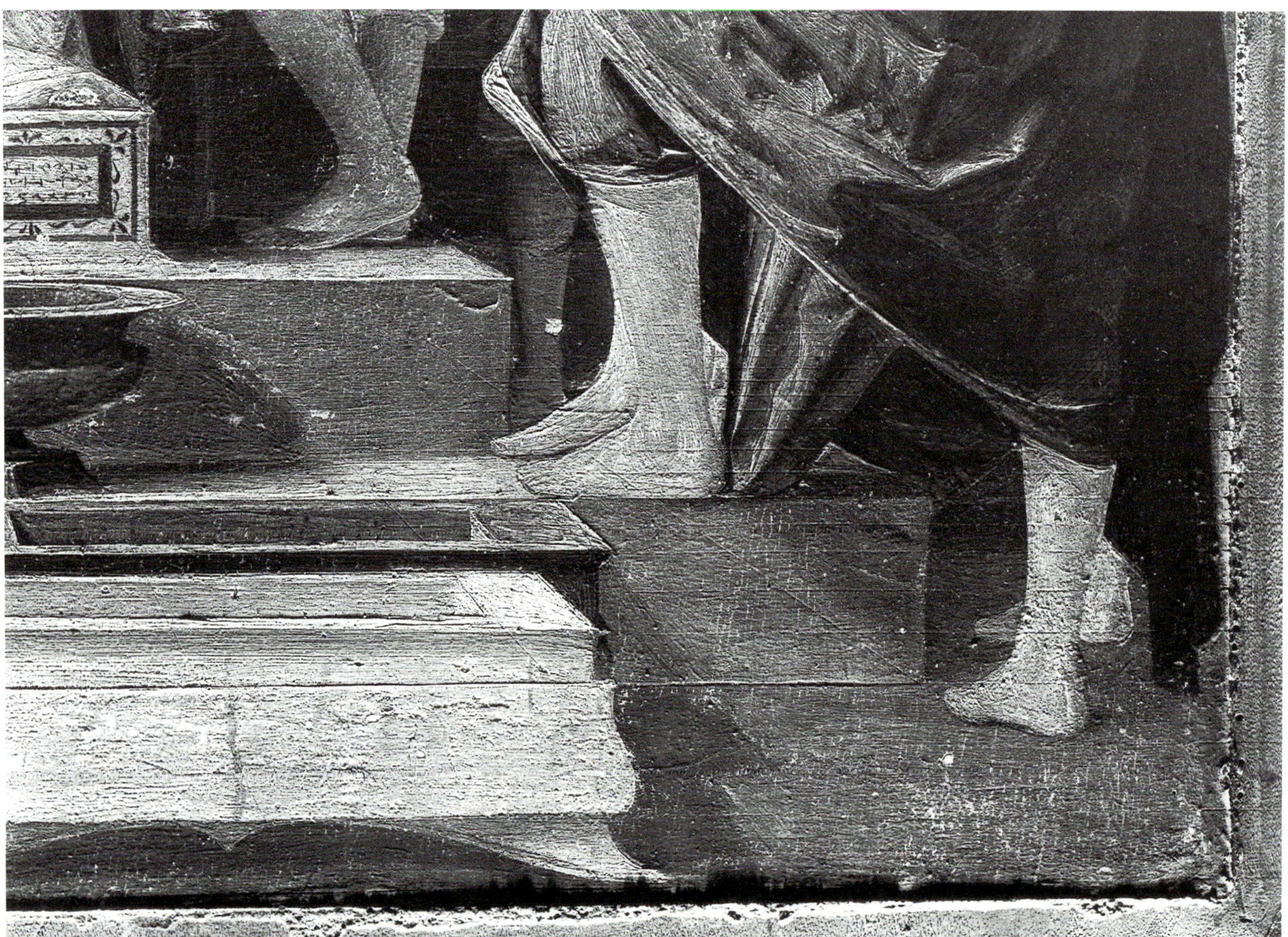

Fig. 134 (bottom left)
Raking light photograph of Fig. 135 showing incised lines

Fig. 135 (left)
BRAMANTINO, *The Adoration of the Kings* [NG 3073], *c.*1500. Oil on poplar, 56.8 × 55 cm

Fig. 136 (below)
Infrared reflectogram mosaic, detail of Fig. 137

Fig. 137
FILIPPINO LIPPI and SANDRO BOTTICELLI, *The Adoration of the Kings* [NG 592], *c.*1470. Tempera on wood, 50.2 × 135.9 cm

also scratched the contours of his figures into the gesso, distinguishing between areas to be painted and those that were to be gilded, and this practice, prescribed by Cennino, continued to be usual. The folds of any drapery that was to be executed by *sgraffito* and therefore covered with gold leaf, and also areas of blue and green that might be underpainted with black, were also usually incised, and incisions of this type were still being made in the late fifteenth century, for example on the altarpiece by Foppa (see Fig. 114).[114] Probably for similar reasons Michelangelo lightly incised the profile and features of the angel on the right in the *Manchester Madonna* (Fig. 132), thereby reinforcing his underdrawing before it was submerged under the green earth underpaint for the flesh.[115] The incision is most unlikely to be associated with stylus transfer of a cartoon, since it is difficult to mark the hard surface of scraped and polished gesso even through relatively thin paper.[116]

As it is much easier to score a line along a straight edge than to rule it with a quill and ink, architectural settings were commonly incised (Fig. 133), but when harder black drawing stones or 'chalks' became more available, they were increasingly used for this purpose. In the background of Veronese's *The Family of Darius before Alexander* the ruled lines of the columns may have been made with a hard drawing 'chalk' rather than charcoal which was used for the outlines of the horses and figures in front of them (Fig. 52).[117] It is generally assumed that complex perspective settings were worked out first on paper, as in Leonardo's celebrated drawings for his *Adoration of the Kings*, but in the National Gallery's small panel of the same subject by Bramantino (NG 3073), author of a lost treatise on perspective, the entire perspective construction was set out (or perhaps repeated) on the surface of the panel (Figs 134 and 135).[118] The regular division of the base line with vertical strokes of ink along the unpainted lower edge of the panel, and the incised orthogonals and progressively receding horizontals confirm this as a model application of Albertian single-point perspective. The buildings and figures could then be placed in the setting, the latter drawn in a summary manner with short broken strokes and zigzags, the abrupt changes between thick and thin lines suggesting the possible use of a quill rather than a brush.

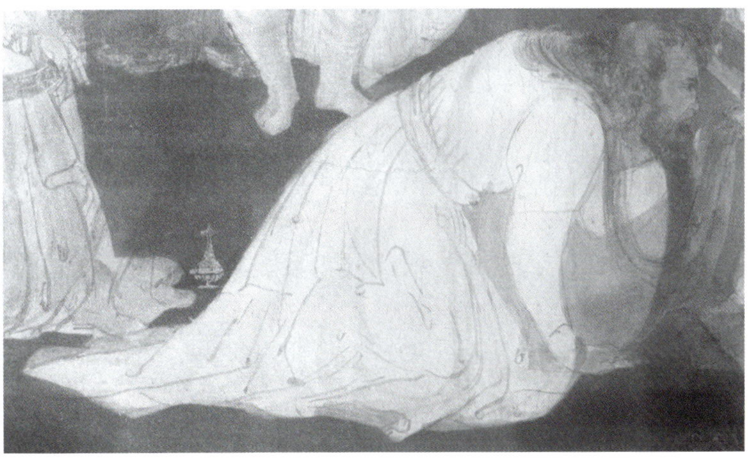

Even when made freehand, the underdrawing on Italian paintings tends to be relatively simple, often consisting of little more than basic contours and a few of the more important drapery folds (one reason, perhaps, why they

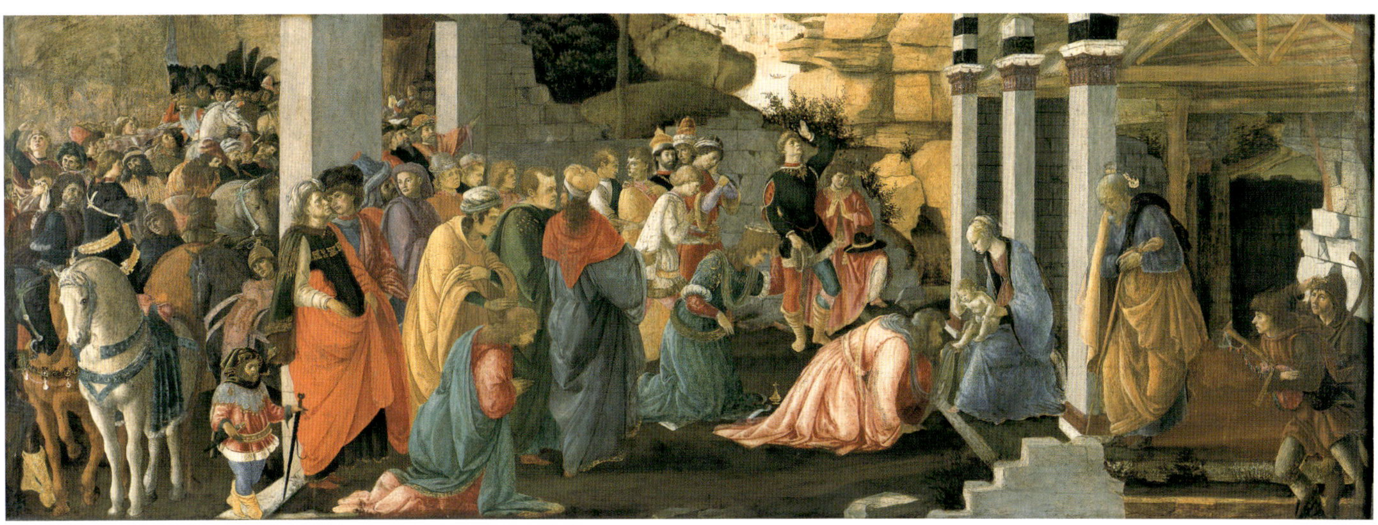

have been less intensively studied by infrared methods than the more rewarding Netherlandish and German underdrawings). The outlines may be fluent, but careful, as in Michelangelo's underdrawing for the *Manchester Madonna* (see Fig. 7, p. 12), or spontaneous and approximate, as in the figures drawn by the young Filippino Lippi for the *Adoration of the Kings* which he painted in collaboration with Sandro Botticelli (Figs 136 and 137).[119] Presumably this more schematic approach can be explained by the existence of extensive preliminary drawings which had already been made, although not necessarily worked up to full-scale cartoons, but it may also be associated with the widespread use of a tempera-based technique during the fourteenth and fifteenth centuries. The practice of building up the

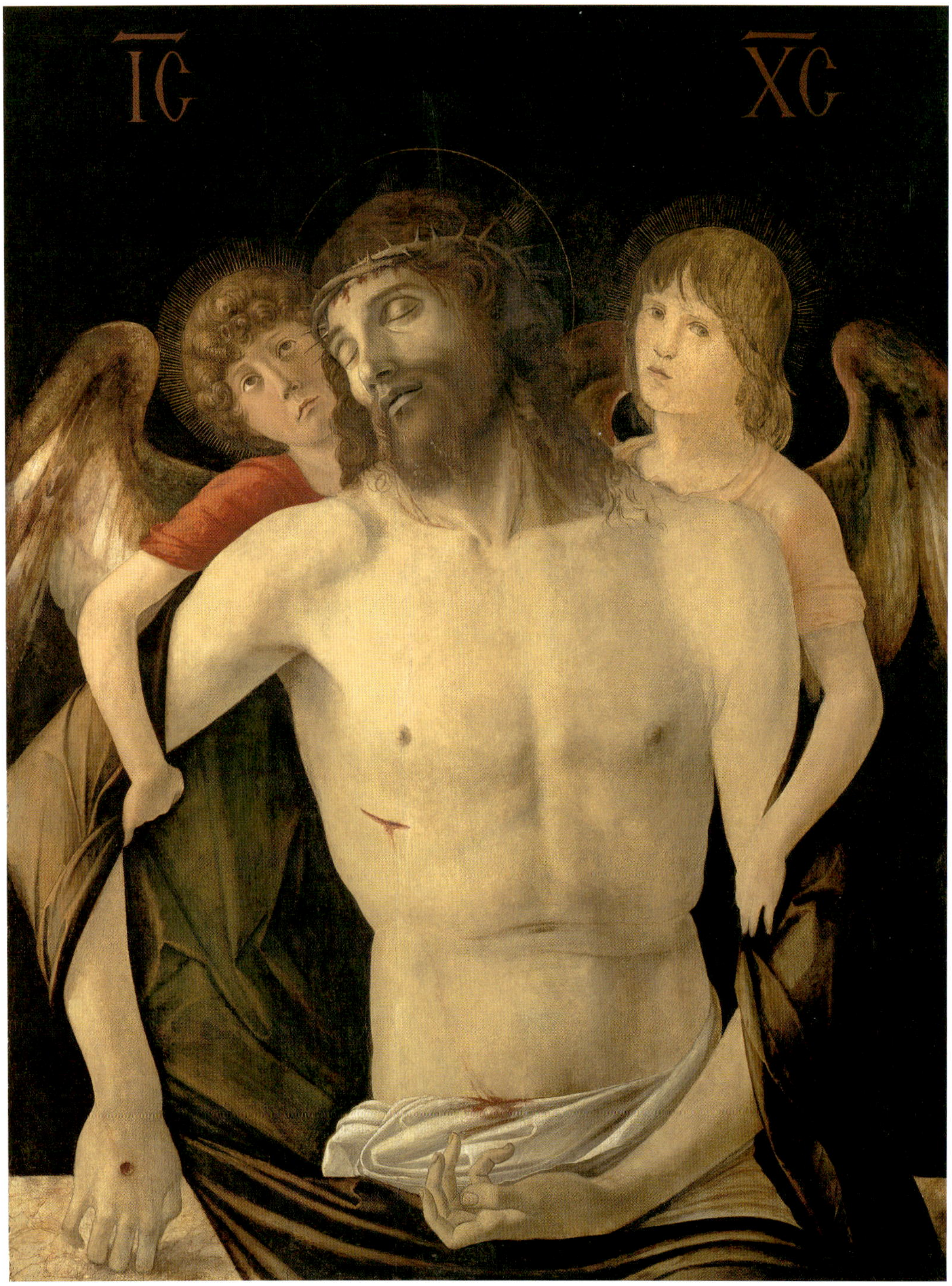

Fig. 138
GIOVANNI BELLINI,
The Dead Christ supported by Angels
[NG 3912], perhaps 1465–70. Oil on wood, 94.6 × 71.8 cm

modelling of a drapery by shading with hatched brushstrokes, gradually blending a sequence of pre-mixed shades of colour, starting with the shadows and working through the mid-tones to the highlights, is very close to the process of shading a drawing, especially one heightened with white and on a tinted drawing surface to supply the mid-tone (as described by Cennino). If this exercise had already been carried out on paper, then there would have been little need to repeat it in an underdrawing.

The exception to this general rule are the underdrawings made by certain North Italian painters, most notably Giovanni Bellini, Cosimo Tura (Cat. 2) and Carlo Crivelli (Cat. 3), although the last named has not yet been as thoroughly investigated. Their intricate underdrawings, with extensive use of hatched shading, often seem closer in approach to those of Netherlandish and German painters; it may not be a coincidence that all three are likely to have spent time in Padua where artists from north of the Alps are known to have been active.[120] For Giovanni Bellini the underdrawing was an opportunity to elaborate on the effects of light that so interested him. His short diagonal strokes of shading (Figs 138 and 139) establish the illumination of figures and draperies as much as their forms, and this was therefore an important stage in the evolution of his paintings.[121]

An explanation for the elaborate, but more volumetric, character of Tura's underdrawings (see Cat. 2) is that this approach to drawing had simply become habitual for a painter who spent much of his time supplying drawings and cartoons for works to be made by other craftsmen and in both two and three dimensions. His facility and inventiveness as a draughtsman meant that his underdrawings are unlikely to have taken long to execute and they never appear laborious. In their completeness the underdrawings of Tura and Bellini correspond with the worked-up cartoons on paper that were being developed by their Tuscan contemporaries. In both cases, the execution of the painting seldom departed to any great extent from the design as fixed in the drawing.

From the early years of the sixteenth century, however, some painters began to draw on their panels without yet having committed themselves to a final solution to the design. As well as making considerable alterations to the underdrawing, they often continued to make changes while painting. According to Vasari, Pontormo would not allow anyone to see his works 'unless completely finished', presumably because of his tendency to rework his ideas at a very late stage (well illustrated by Cat. 12).[122] Despite giving the appearance of having been carefully planned down to the last detail, the immaculate surfaces of the works of Pontormo's pupil Bronzino conceal many daring revisions, improvisations and refinements made during painting. Most of the iconographic attributes of the figures in Bronzino's *Allegory with Venus and Cupid* (NG 651) and *The Madonna and Child with Saint John the Baptist and a Female Saint* (NG 5280) were added when painting was well advanced, and in the case of the former work, Bronzino even increased the size of his panel.[123] When in 1545, Duke Cosimo de' Medici asked

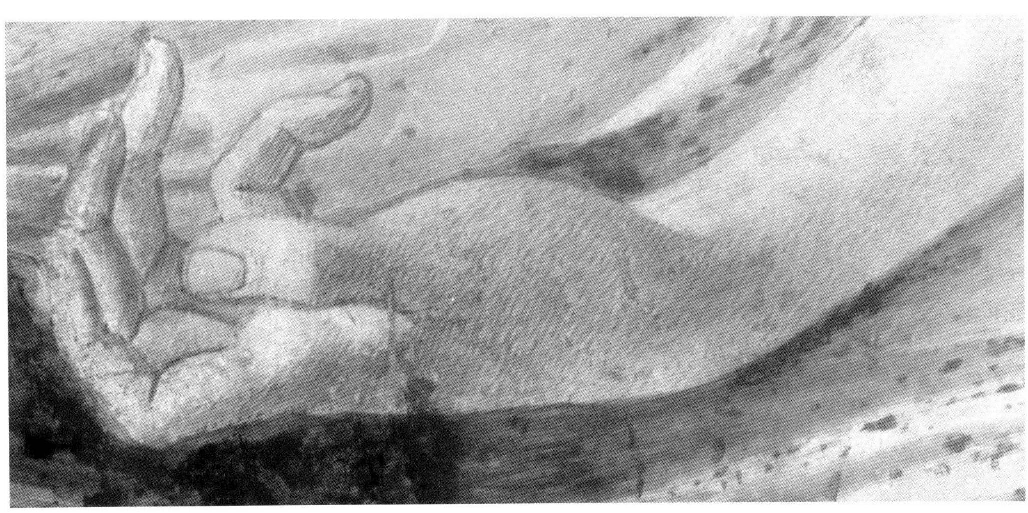

Fig. 139
Infrared reflectogram mosaic, detail of Fig. 138

the artist to make a copy of the *Lamentation* altarpiece he had painted for the chapel of Eleonora di Toledo, he explicitly forbade him to add any new invention because the original was to his liking.[124] This may well have been in response to Bronzino's habit of inserting new inventions and refinements to his works beyond the design stage.

The few drawings by Titian that exist confirm that he made sketches and studies for his pictures in much the same way as other painters. Several of these have squared grids for enlargement, and although no evidence for such grids has been found on his paintings, works that have been examined by infrared methods nearly always reveal some underdrawing, however rudimentary. Titian seems always to have begun his paintings by positioning his principal figures with rapid sweeping strokes in a black ink or paint, leaving undeveloped any details such as hands and feet (Figs 140 and 141). The many changes that he made when painting mean that the underdrawing often no longer coincides with the painted forms. When working on the alterations he sometimes brushed in lines of black over completed paint layers, and also lines of white paint, which, since they contain lead white, can be detected in X-radiographs.

As painters in the sixteenth century increasingly began to work on coloured preparations[125] they were less likely to make their underdrawings in black since they would not show particularly well, and, even if they did, they are not usually visible by infrared methods since there is insufficient contrast between the drawing and its background. They could, however, sketch in their designs with lines of lead white paint; X-radiographs have revealed such underdrawings, and also revisons made when painting, in canvases by Dosso Dossi and Tintoretto.[126] Underdrawings on coloured surfaces in white chalk[127] or other coloured chalks and drawing materials are impossible to detect, unless by chance an area of drawing is exposed by damage or a gap in the paint film.

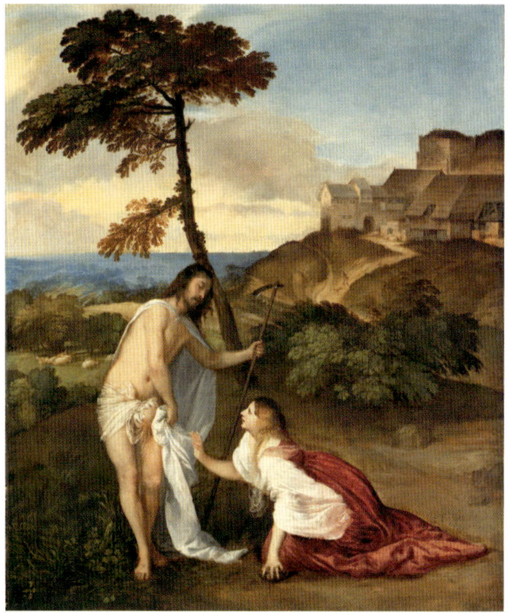

Fig. 140
TITIAN, *Noli me Tangere* [NG 270], probably 1510–15. Oil on canvas, 108.6 × 90.8 cm

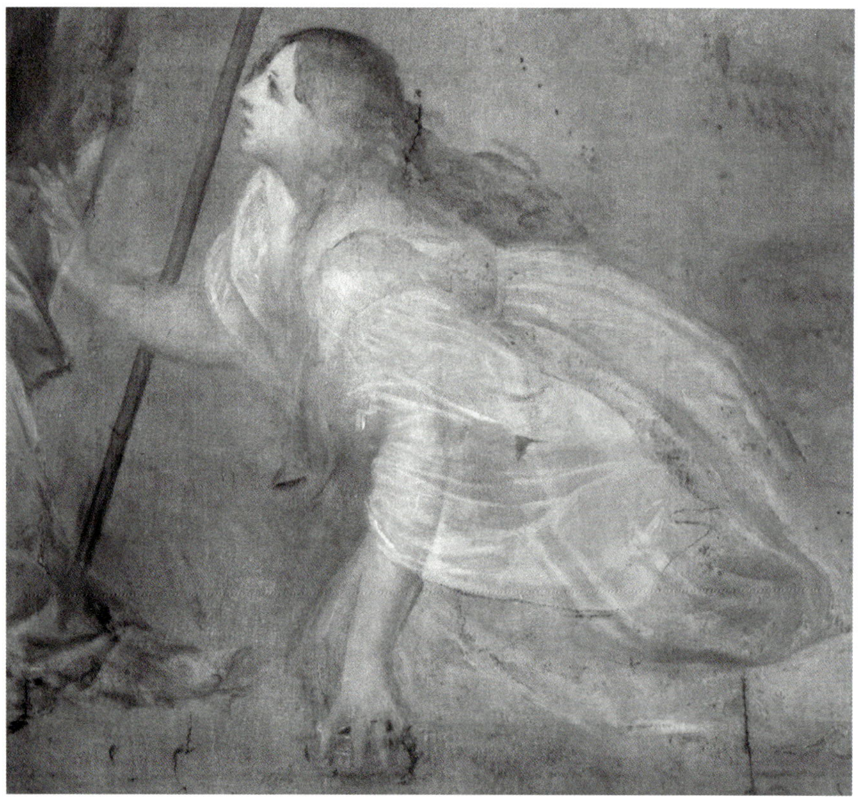

Fig. 141
Infrared reflectogram mosaic, detail of Fig. 140

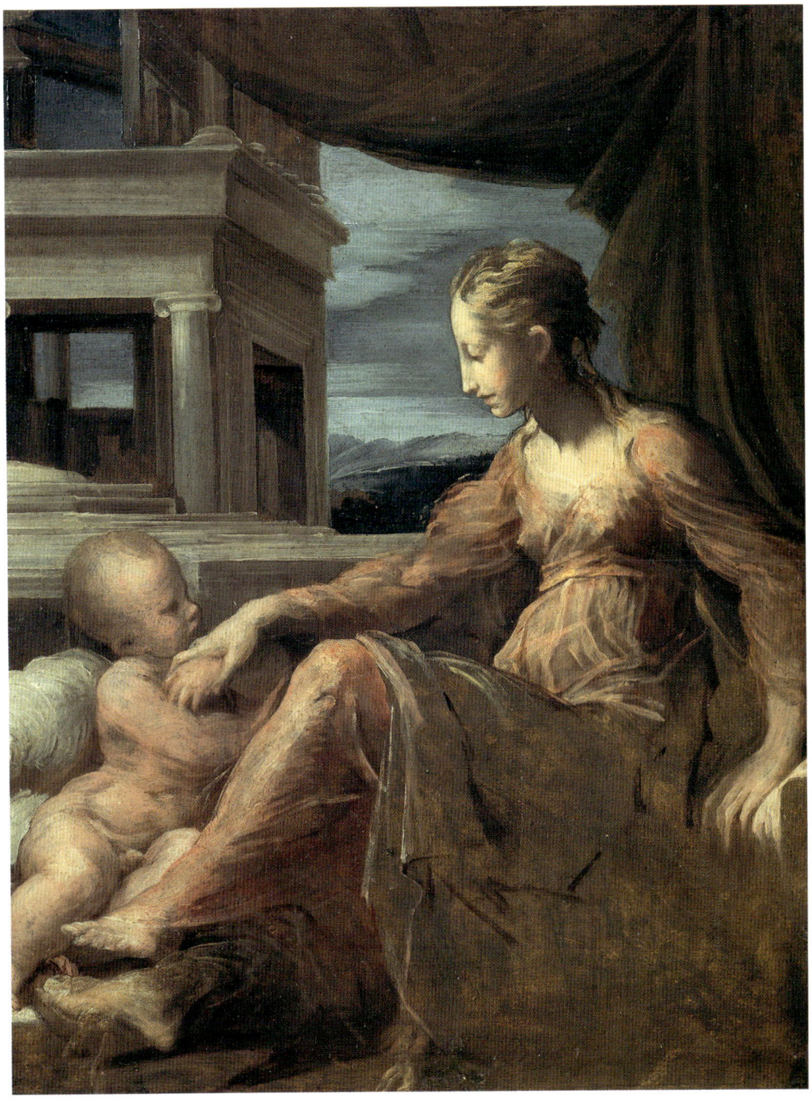

On Parmigianino's unfinished *Virgin and Child* (London, Courtauld Institute, Fig. 142) a few blackish lines dashed in over the streaky brown priming are all the underdrawing to be seen, yet the colours are applied with absolute confidence and control. A great many drawings on paper by Parmigianino survive, – among the most beautiful ever made.[128] Although his, as also Correggio's, drawing procedure did not necessarily follow the sequence from *schizzo* to cartoon prescribed by Vasari, without constant exploration through drawing Parmigianino could not have attained this fluency and facility in paint. For, as Leonardo pointed out, 'when you have schooled your hand and judgement by such diligence [in drawing], you will acquire rapidity before you are aware of it.'[129]

Michelangelo made the same discovery when, in painting the lunettes of the Sistine Chapel, he abandoned the laborious process of working from cartoons with which he had begun the project. Freed too from the discomfort of working with his head tilted back, he was able in a single day to paint areas as large as those that had previously taken a week or more.[130] Yet sketches and studies were as important as ever (Fig. 143);[131] *disegno* in all its meanings remained fundamental to his art.

JD, CP

Fig. 142
PARMIGIANINO, *The Virgin and Child, c.*1525–7
Oil on wood, 63.5 × 50.7 cm
London, Courtauld Institute Gallery
inv. 336

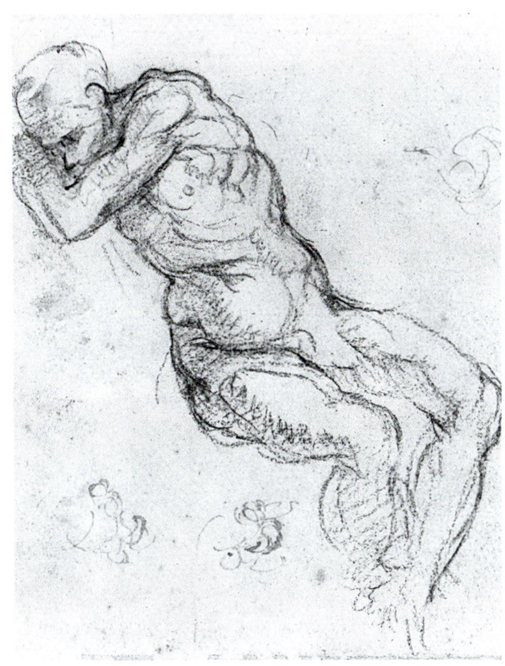

Fig. 143
MICHELANGELO, *Study for a Figure in the destroyed lunette of Esrom and Aram on the altar wall of the Sistine Chapel*
Charcoal or black chalk on paper, 14 × 14.5 cm
Oxford, Ashmolean Museum
inv. Parker 305 (recto)

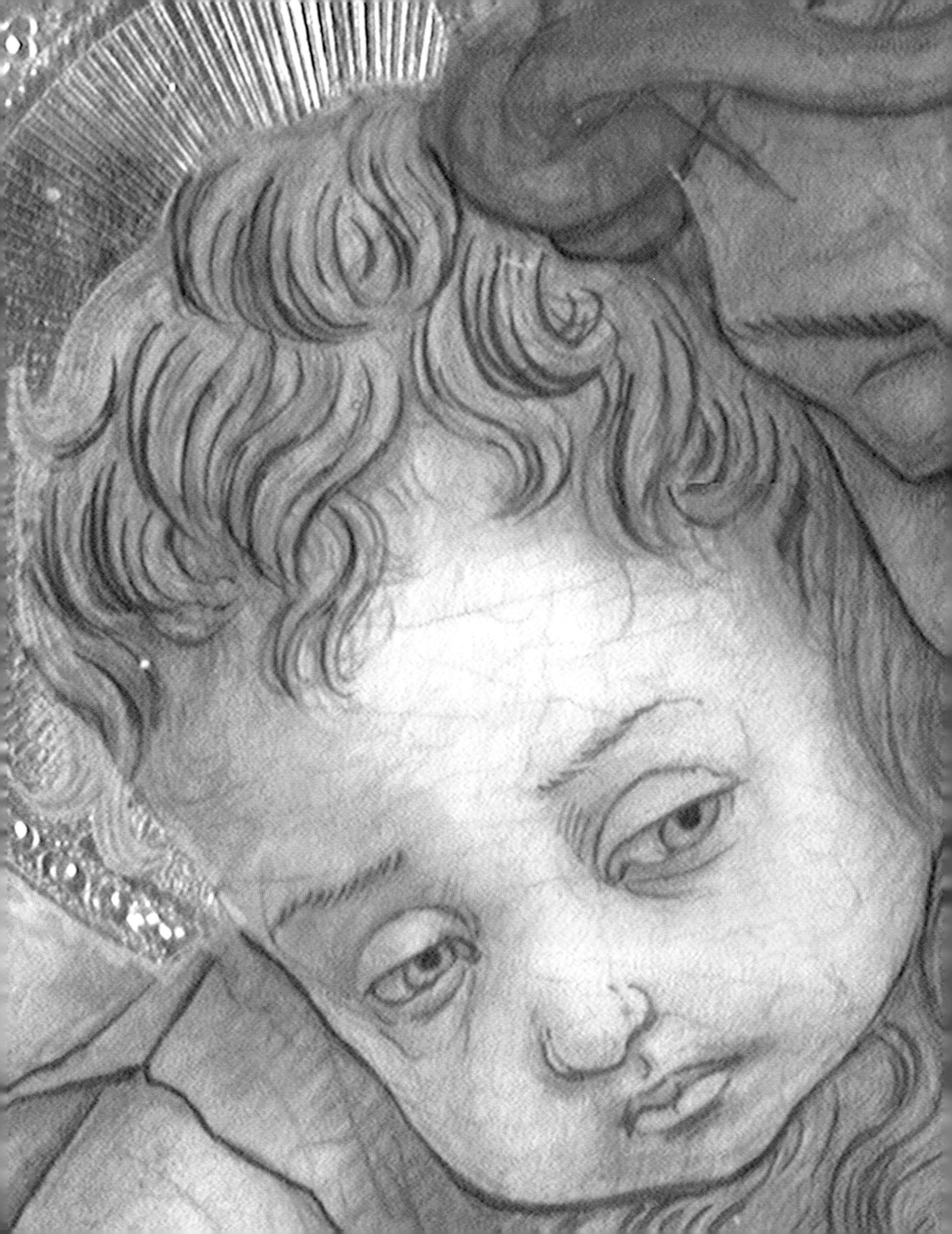

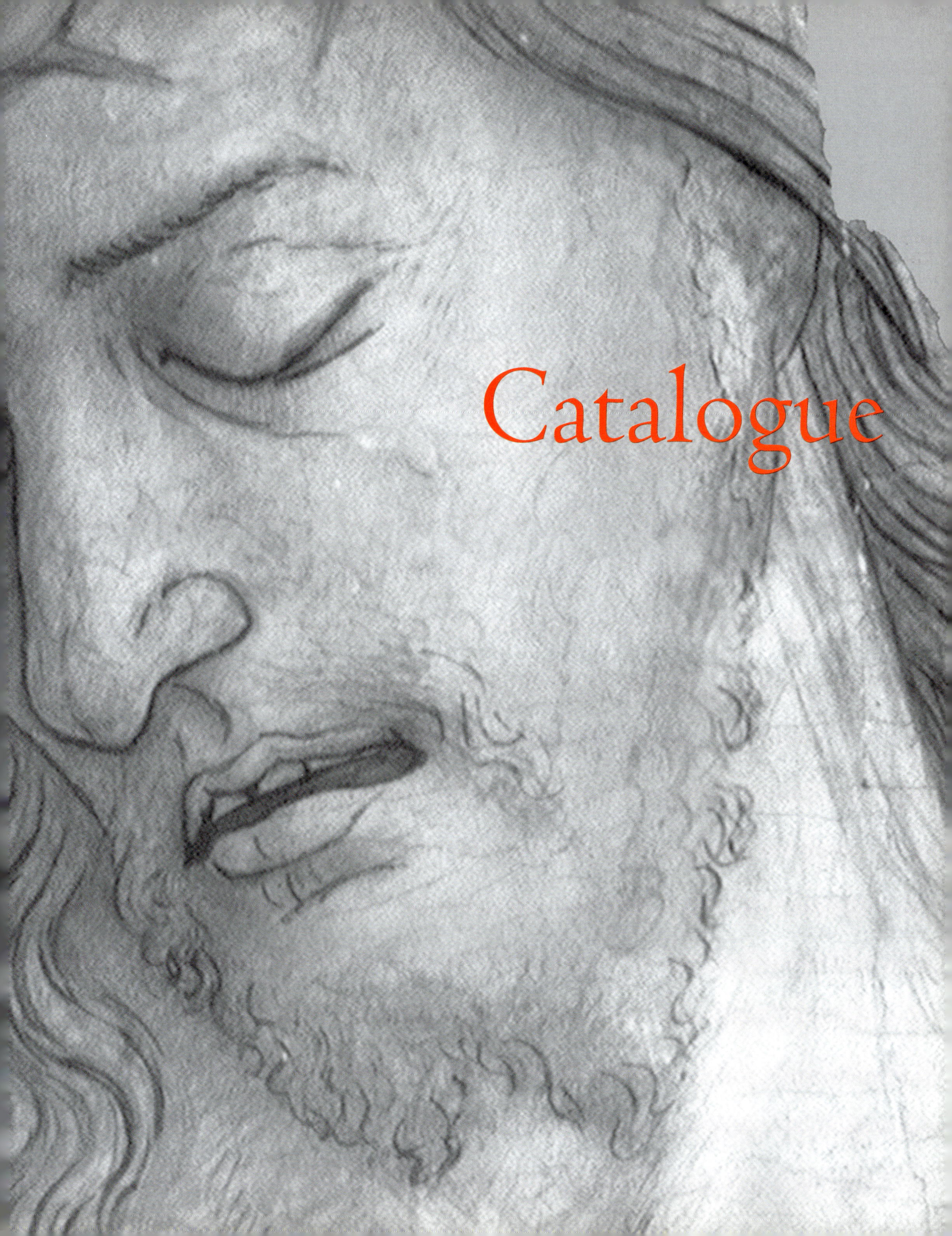

Catalogue

1 Stephan Lochner

active 1442; died 1451

Saints Matthew, Catherine of Alexandria and John the Evangelist (on the reverse, Saints Gregory, Cordula? and Jerome), *c.*1450

Oil on oak, *c.* 68.6 × 58.5 cm
NG 705

STEPHAN LOCHNER was the most important painter working in Cologne in the middle of the fifteenth century. The paintings attributed to him include the great altarpiece of the *Adoration of the Magi*, painted for Cologne Town Hall, and now in Cologne Cathedral. A document mentioning Lochner's parents at Meersburg in the region around Lake Constance has led to the presumption that he was not a native of Cologne. However, it is not entirely certain that the historical figure Stephan Lochner should be associated with the paintings grouped around the *Adoration of the Magi;* the argument for this rests solely on an assumption that a record made by Dürer of a painting he saw at the Town Hall by 'Maister Steffan' was the *Adoration of the Magi.* The paintings associated with Lochner include a number of altarpieces made for Cologne churches, and the artist must have had a large workshop.

The three saints, Matthew, Catherine of Alexandria and John the Evangelist, are depicted against an elaborate gilded background. They are shown with their attributes – the angel who inspired his gospel for Matthew, the wheel on which she was tortured (here lying broken at her feet) for Catherine, and the eagle for John the Evangelist, who also holds a chalice with a serpent, referring to his feat of drinking poison without harm.

This panel and another in the Wallraf-Richartz Museum in Cologne (Fig. 144) are the shutters of a small altarpiece. The Cologne shutter still has carved and gilded Gothic tracery in its uppermost part; the top of the National Gallery panel is cut, but presumably once had similar tracery. Both panels are painted on both sides (Figs 146 and 147). The reverse of the National Gallery panel is in a very damaged condition. The central panel of the altarpiece is lost and might have consisted of a sculpted rather than a painted scene. When opened the altarpiece would have shown the four Evangelists, Matthew, Mark, Luke and John, and two female saints, Catherine and Barbara. When closed it would have shown six saints with two male donor figures kneeling in prayer. The donors, who were members of the Zeuwelgyn family of Cologne, are wearing the robes of the Order of the Knights of Saint John. It is not known for certain for which church the altarpiece was commissioned, but it is usually assumed that it was the church of Saints John

Fig. 144 (below)
STEPHAN LOCHNER,
Saints Mark, Barbara and Luke
Oak, 100.5 × 58 cm
Cologne, Wallraf-Richartz-Museum
inv. WRM 68

Fig. 145 (opposite)
STEPHAN LOCHNER, *Saints Matthew, Catherine of Alexandria and John the Evangelist* [NG 705], *c.*1450

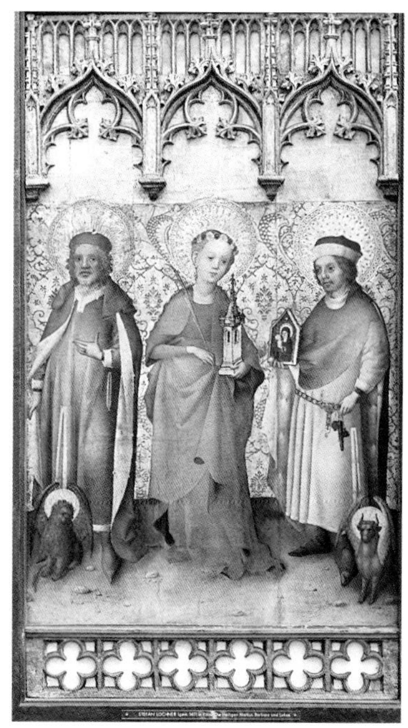

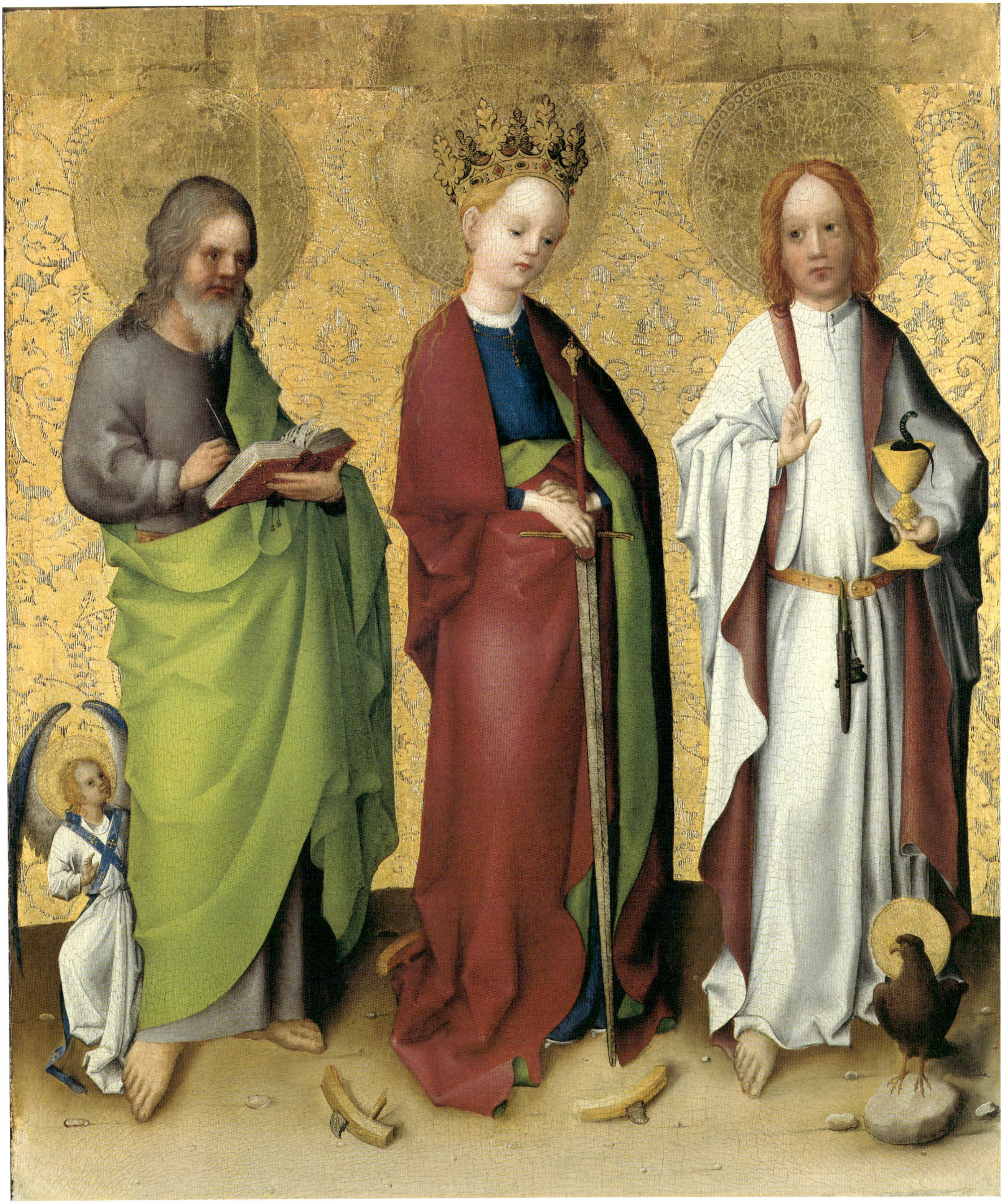

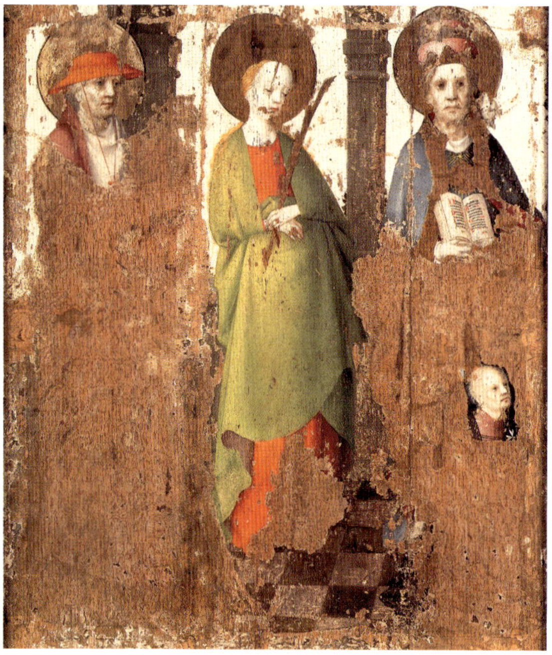

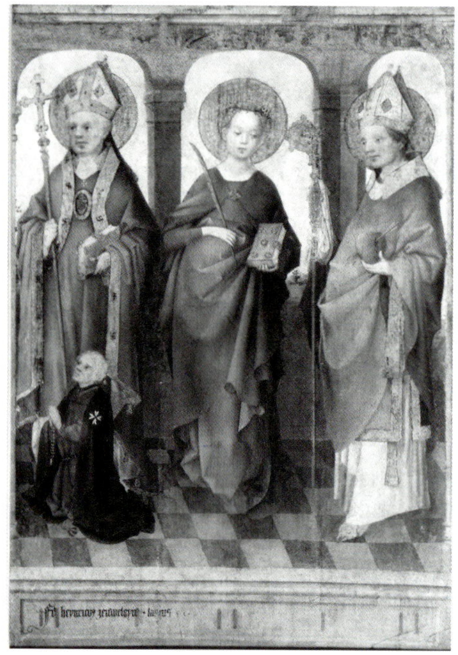

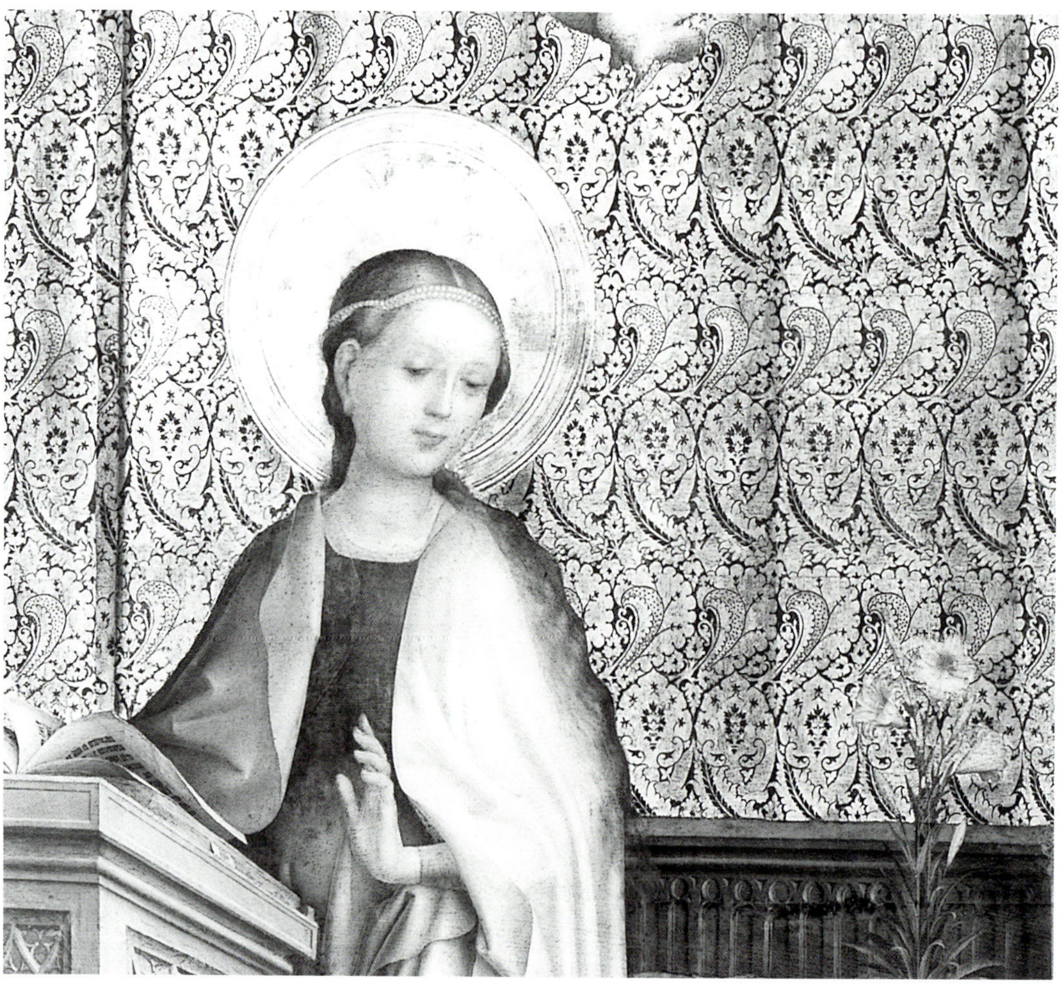

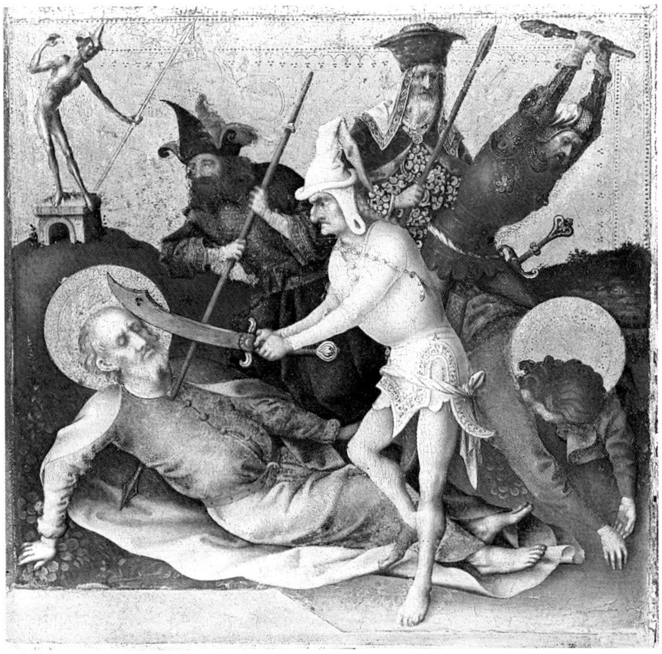

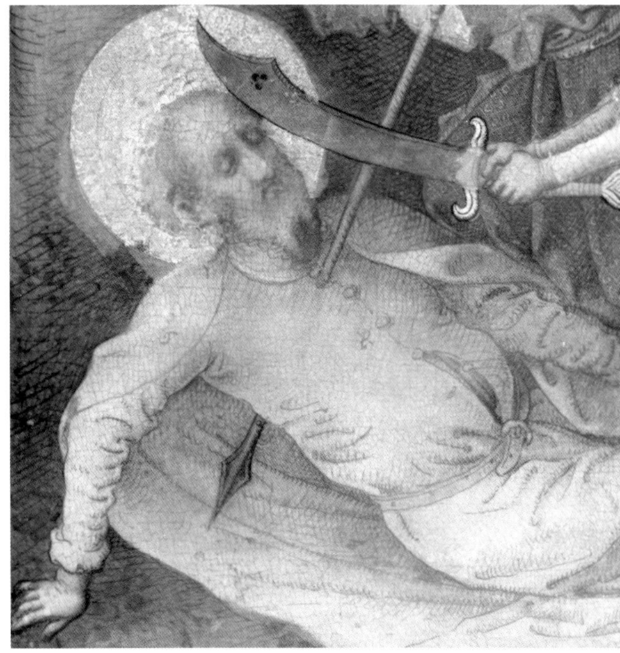

Fig. 146 (top, far left)
STEPHAN LOCHNER, *Saints Gregory, Cordula? and Jerome*, *c.*1450. Reverse of Fig. 145

Fig. 147 (top, left)
STEPHAN LOCHNER *Saints Ambrosius, Cecilia(?) and Augustine and a donor*.
Reverse of Fig. 144
Oak, 86 × 57.5 cm
Cologne, Wallraf-Richartz-Museum inv. WRM 69

Fig. 148
STEPHAN LOCHNER, *Annunciation*
Detail of reverse of the left-hand shutter of the *Adoration of the Kings*, *c.*1440–5. Oak, 261 × 142 cm
Cologne Cathedral

Fig. 149 (above)
STEPHAN LOCHNER, *Martyrdoms of the Apostles*
Detail of the *Martyrdoms of Saints Simon and Judas*
Walnut, 120 × 80 cm
Frankfurt am Main, Städelsches Kunstinstitut
Inv. 490905

Fig. 150 (above, right)
Detail from infrared reflectogram mosaic of Fig. 149
Courtesy of Städelsches Kunstinstitut, Frankfurt am Main

and Cordula of the Order of Saint John in Cologne, given the order worn by the donors.

The production of pictures in which gilding played a prominent role in the finished effect necessitated considerable planning. The elaborate, decorative gilded background of the National Gallery picture is extensive and occupies a substantial area of the panel. In one section of the background, coinciding with a border line in the design, where the gold has been worn away, charcoal particles, elsewhere sparsely scattered on the ground, form a black dot clearly visible under a microscope; this suggests that pouncing was used to transfer the design (see p. 23). Underdrawing here has two distinct functions, to mark out the pattern of the gilded background, and to create the figures to be painted. The boundaries between the areas to be painted and those to be gilded were marked by incisions into the chalk ground, as also seen in Lochner's *Martyrdoms of the Apostles* in Frankfurt (Fig. 149). The preparation of the gilded areas could then be embarked on.

The main part of the gold background has a brocade-like design created by carving into the chalk preparation on the panel. The design alternates flat areas and deep vertical grooves, mimicking gold thread, and is based on one which appears in other Cologne paintings, including the backs of the shutters of the great altarpiece of the *Adoration of the Kings* today in Cologne Cathedral (see Fig. 148). The design for the National Gallery painting must have been created from a pattern kept in the workshop. The pattern, or perhaps a reproduction of it made for this specific picture, was pricked along its outlines with small holes, carefully applied to the areas of the panel in which it was needed, and charcoal dust sprinkled over it. When removed, very small dots of charcoal marked the edges of the pattern, which was then incised freehand, followed by the carving of the grooves. Gold leaf was then applied over the carved pattern. A very fine round punch was used to create beautiful and intricate patterns for the haloes, which themselves must have been recorded in workshop pattern books: the patterns are all variations of motifs using stars, except for that of Saint Catherine's halo, which has a more complex outer border of flowers and clouds. The compass point marking the centre of each halo is visible in the X-radiograph.

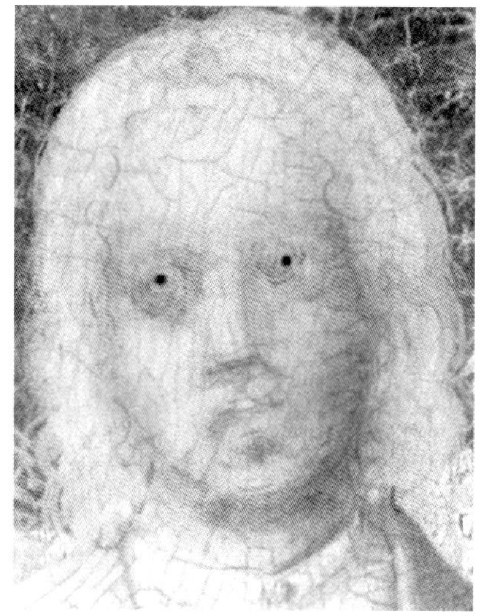

The design for the painted part of the picture was also laid out on the white chalk ground and executed in a fluid medium with a brush. The composition with three standing figures on each side of each shutter was a straightforward one. It is probable that the underdrawings for both sides of the panel followed workshop models: similar standing saints occur in a number of other works associated with Lochner. For example the Magdalene in Rotterdam is shown in drapery closely resembling that of Matthew, while her face is similar to that of Saint Catherine.

Although the figure pattern is straightforward, the underdrawing for each figure is worked up in some detail, with hatching and cross-hatching indicating the extent of shadow in the drapery for each figure, as well as for the small angel (Fig. 152). Noses and mouths are indicated by dashes and eyes are drawn merely as circles (Fig. 151), though in other Lochner works eyes are drawn in more detail. Hands are indicated using short strokes rather than a continuous outline (Fig. 153). The shadows on Saint Catherine's wheel are also indicated with hatching (Fig. 154). There is no detectable underdrawing for the rocky ground. The static nature of the composition would have allowed little scope for changes in pose, and with such a simple figure arrangement there was little need for adjustment once the outlines and areas of light and shade had been underdrawn. There are, however, small adjustments, for example in the position of Saint Matthew's head on the front of the panel and Saint Gregory's head on the reverse. Saint Matthew's pen has also been shortened (see Fig. 153). In some of Lochner's more complex narrative compositions, however, such as the *Martyrdoms of the Apostles* in Frankfurt (Fig. 149) or the *Last Judgement* in Cologne, there are numerous changes of details at the underdrawing stage, and in the *Presentation in the Temple* (Darmstadt) a child seen in the underdrawing was eliminated in painting.

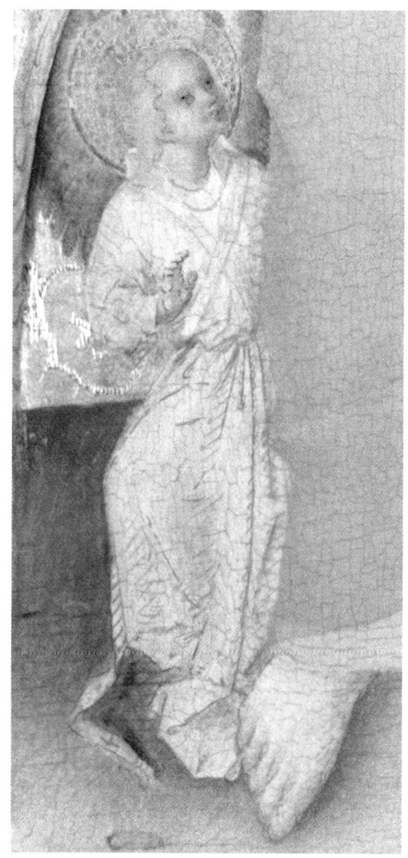

The use of a sophisticated system of hatching and crosshatching is a distinctive feature of paintings by Lochner and his workshop (Fig. 155). Although such a method for representing shadow is visible in gilding in earlier painting, as well as on metalwork, it does not appear to be a common feature of German underdrawings until later in the fifteenth century, and it does not appear widely in drawings and engravings until the mid-fifteenth century. In the earlier period, both drawings on paper and underdrawings tend to be correspondingly linear (for example, the Austrian School *Trinity* in the National Gallery, Fig. 89, p. 51), though drawings on paper show shadows represented through the use of washes.

Lochner's paintings are distinguished by an exceptional range of colour, balanced and contrasted with great skill, and ranging into variations of blues, violets and greens rarely seen in works by other artists. In the *Martyrdoms of the Apostles* the underdrawing (Fig. 150) includes a large number of notes about the colour to be

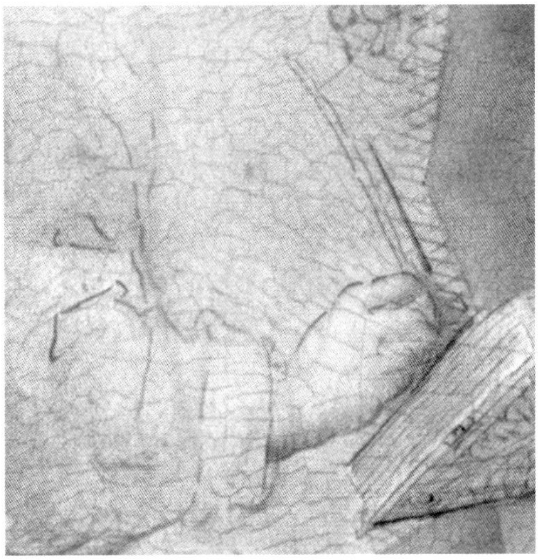

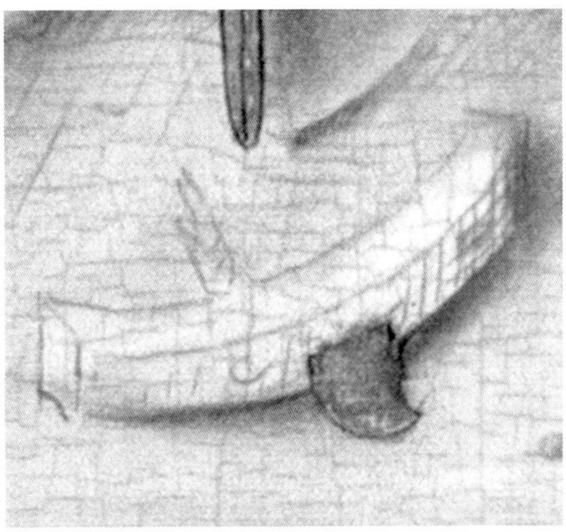

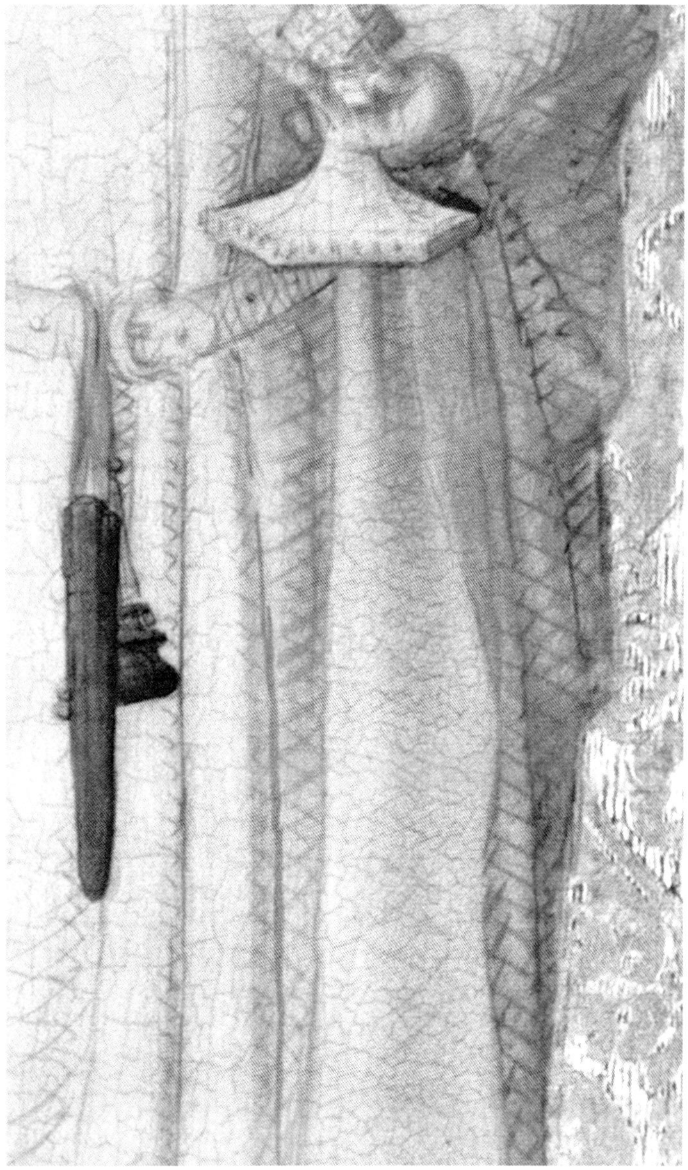

Figs 151 and 152 (left)
Details from infrared reflectogram mosaic of Fig. 145

Figs 153, 154 and 155 (above)
Details from infrared reflectogram mosaic of Fig. 145

used for the painting, but no such notes are visible in the London saints. The colour notes in the *Martyrdoms* were not always followed in the finished composition, suggesting that, as with alterations to the underdrawn compositions, the workshop master kept the work constantly under review, but may not always have been responsible for drawing every figure or scene. The degree of damage to the reverse of the London panel makes its quality difficult to assess but, in the case of the saints on the front, the high quality of the painted surface and its detail suggests Lochner's personal involvement, although the underdrawing might well have been carried out by assistants.

SF

2 Cosimo Tura

before 1431–1495

Saint Jerome, *c.*1470

Oil and egg tempera on poplar,
101.2 × 57.4 cm
NG 773

Fig. 156
COSIMO TURA, *Saint Jerome* [NG 773], *c.*1470

COSIMO TURA was the first, and greatest, painter of the Ferrarese School. In his own lifetime he was a celebrated artist, accumulating considerable personal wealth. He worked for Borso and then Ercole d'Este, dukes of Ferrara, and also for important functionaries of both court and Church. Nothing is known about his early training, but it probably took place in Ferrara. As a young painter he may have worked in Padua and possibly Venice. He was much influenced by the works by Rogier van der Weyden known to have been in Ferrara, and he was among the first Italian painters to adopt the new ways of using the oil medium as developed by Netherlandish artists. Documents show that he was extremely prolific and was able to work in many media and on every scale, ranging from tiny panels – some believe that he also made manuscript illuminations – to large altarpieces, canvases and wall paintings. Much of his work for the court involved making designs to be executed by other craftsmen. These included designs for three-dimensional objects such as a lavish silver-gilt table service, as well as many cartoons for tapestries and embroideries, and he clearly spent a great deal of his time exercising his skills as a draughtsman.

The National Gallery has four panels by Tura, the largest and arguably the most important group of his works to have survived. Among them is this panel representing a kneeling Saint Jerome, who holds a stone in his raised hand, poised to strike at his chest as part of his penance. He is shown in a rocky landscape, representing the desert to which he withdrew, accompanied by the lion, from whose paw, according to legend, he withdrew a thorn. On the ground beside him are his cardinal's hat and a book, presumably the Bible, which he translated into Latin from the original Hebrew and Greek. Perched in the hollow dead tree behind him are a wall creeper – a bird that inhabits barren and rocky places – and a barn owl, clutching in its talons a dark green frog. Behind the tree, to the right, a kneeling figure, dressed in pink and scarlet, presumably the donor, is accompanied by a friar in a grey-brown habit, his arms outstretched in a gesture which appears to echo that of Saint Francis during his stigmatisation. Originally they looked up at a figure of

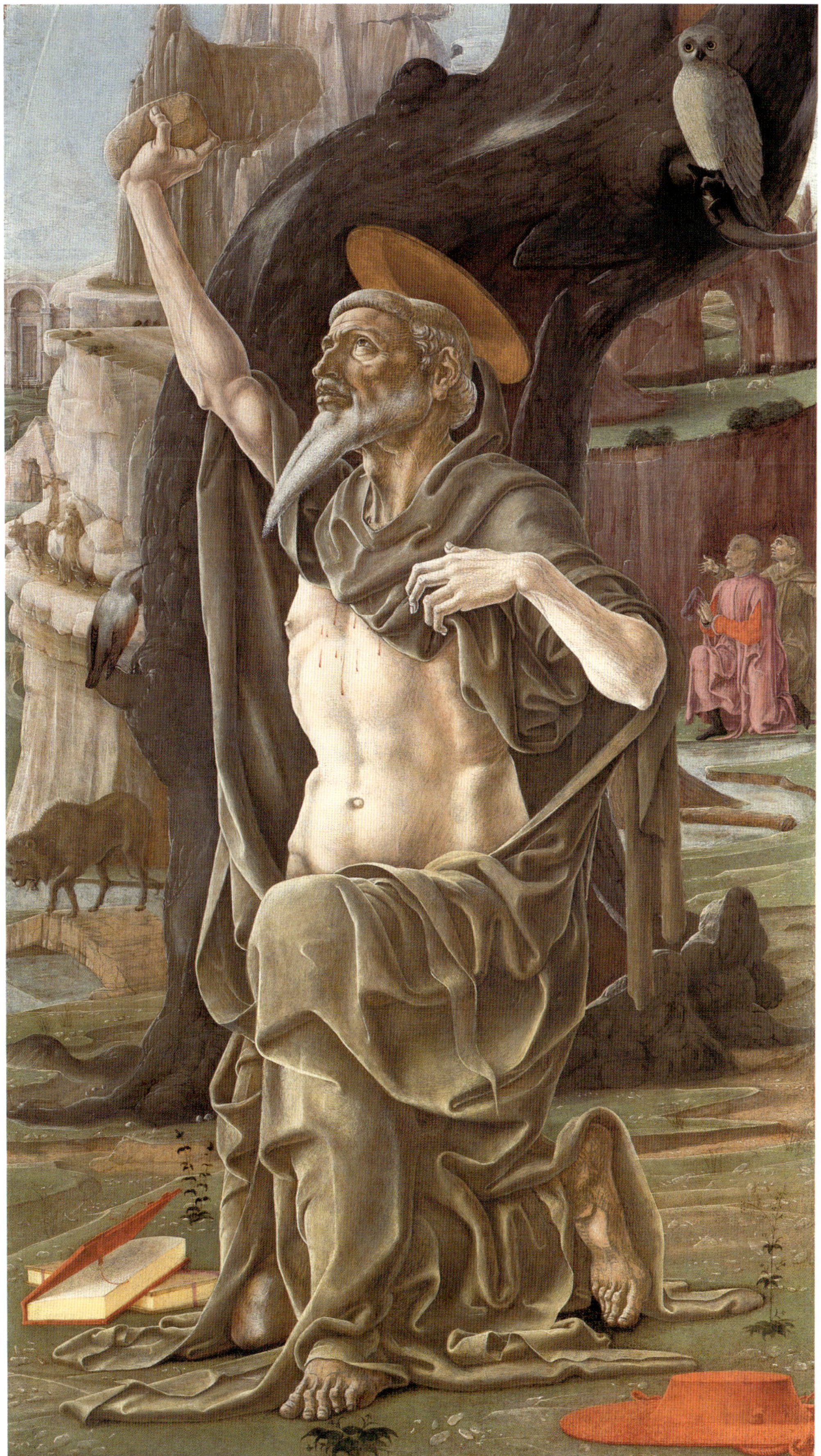

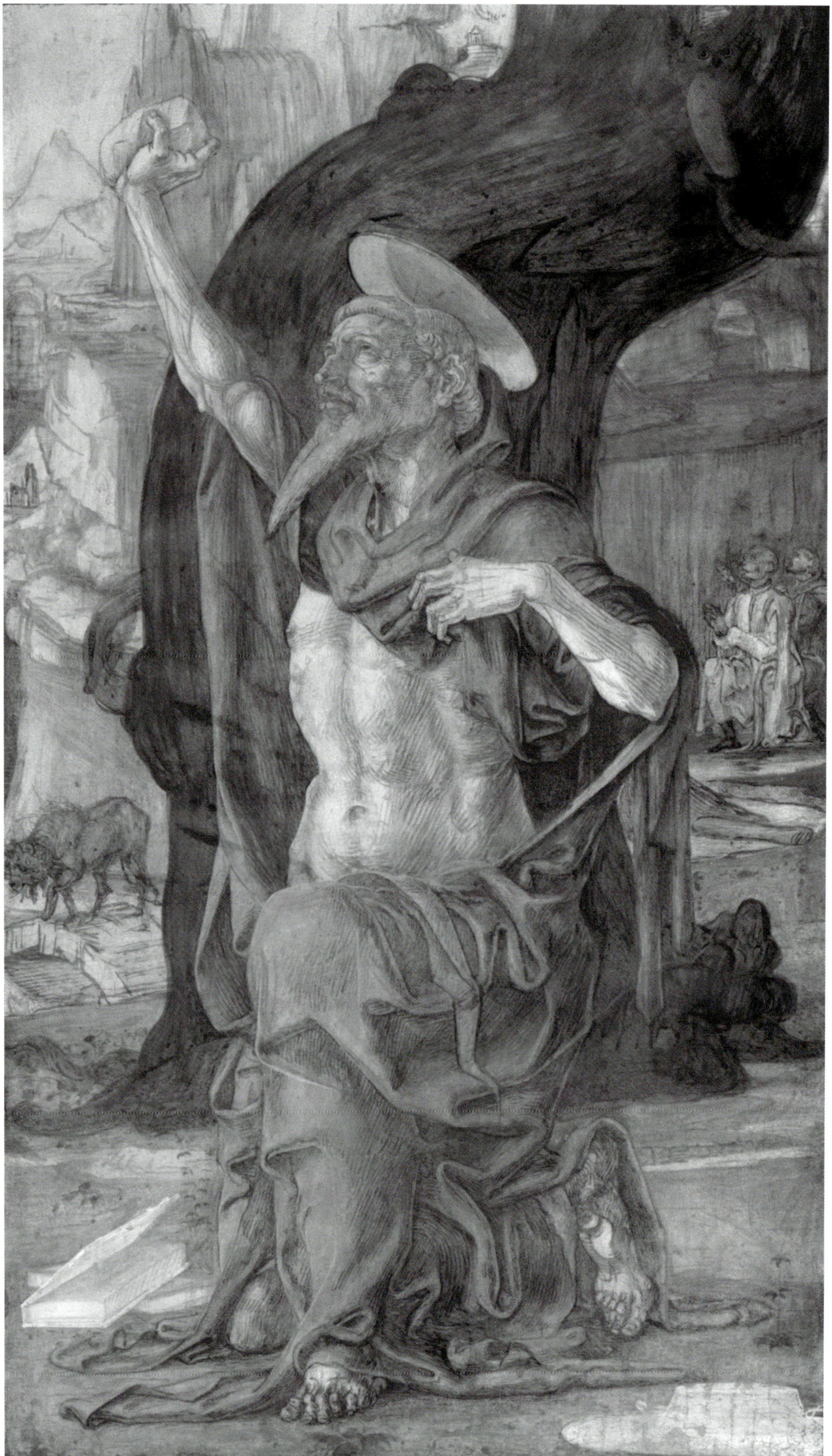

Fig. 157
Infrared reflectogram mosaic of
Fig. 156

Fig. 158
Photomontage of *Saint Jerome* with the
fragment *Christ Crucified*
Poplar, 21.5 × 17 cm
Milan, Pinacoteca di Brera
inv. 6044

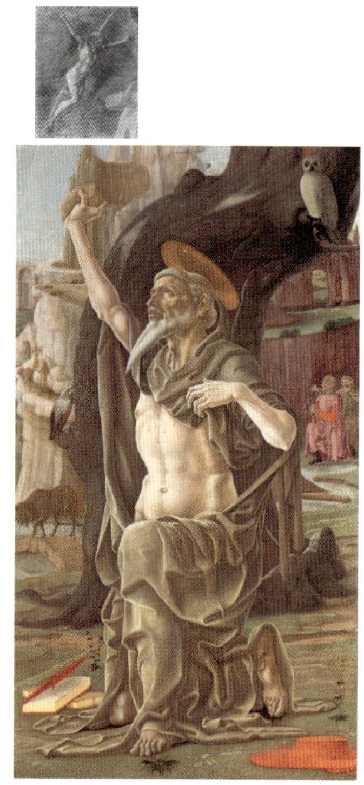

Fig. 159
Detail of Fig. 157

Fig. 160
Detail of Fig. 157

Fig. 161
Detail of Fig. 157

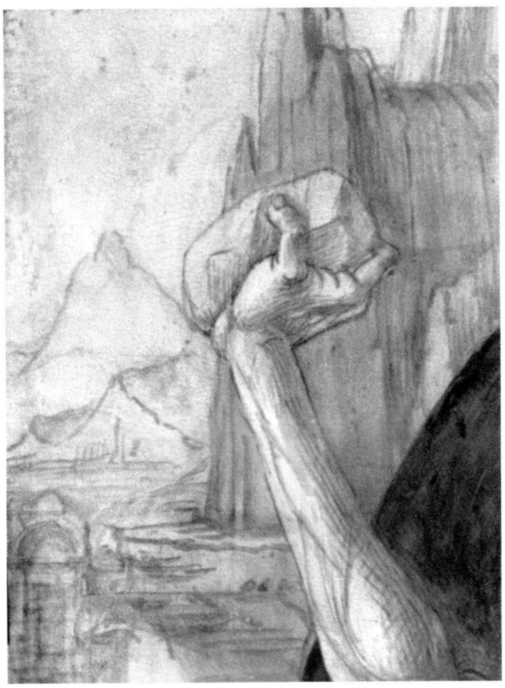

the Crucified Christ suspended on an arc of light across the sky, but this section has been cut from the main panel and is now in the Brera, Milan (Fig. 158). The end of the arc can be seen in the upper left corner of the *Saint Jerome*, while a branch of the tree and a corner of the distant mountain appear in the Milan fragment. The missing section was probably filled by the curving tree trunk, which was perhaps inhabited by more birds and animals. The National Gallery panel is definitely not cut at the sides, or at the lower edge, although here it is much damaged.

The tall narrow panel might have been part of a polyptych, but more probably it was an independent devotional piece, and not necessarily for an altar. A clue as to its possible original location is provided by the habits worn by the friar in the background and, most unusually, by Saint Jerome, who more commonly wears a simple cloak or hair shirt. These habits are often taken to be Franciscan, but in their structure, with a front panel hanging from the cowl (Jerome's is flung back over his left arm), they are more like those worn by members of Hieronymite congregations (some of which evolved from Franciscan orders). More of these friars appear in the background on the left, carrying building materials up the mountain path, apparently heading for the impressive Albertian church in the distance. The identity of the presumed donor in red and pink is not known, but he may be a member of Borso d'Este's court – certainly he is not Borso himself as was traditionally claimed. There is little agreement about the dating of the panel, but it has several features in common with Tura's great organ shutters painted on canvas in 1469 for the Duomo of Ferrara. A date of around 1470 therefore seems possible.

The panel consists of a single wide plank of poplar, prepared for painting in the usual way with layers of gesso. Before painting began, almost every aspect of the composition was established in the underdrawing (Fig. 157) – the only details added during the painting stage, and so not underdrawn, are the branch with the wall creeper and the friars climbing the path on the left. Tura was a supremely confident draughtsman, and there is no evidence in his underdrawings of the use of any aids for the reproduction of cartoons or the enlargement of studies on paper. Instead, he seems to have drawn directly on the gesso, making his first marks with a brush and very dilute ink or paint, perhaps guided by a smaller scale sketch on paper. In infrared reflectograms it can be difficult to distentangle these faint marks from the welter of lines made as the underdrawing was elaborated, but in the *Saint Jerome* a zigzag line in the sky, linking the peak of the most distant mountain with the rocky

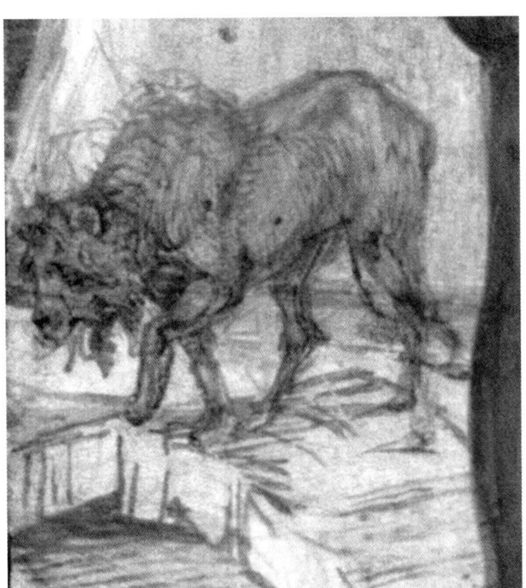

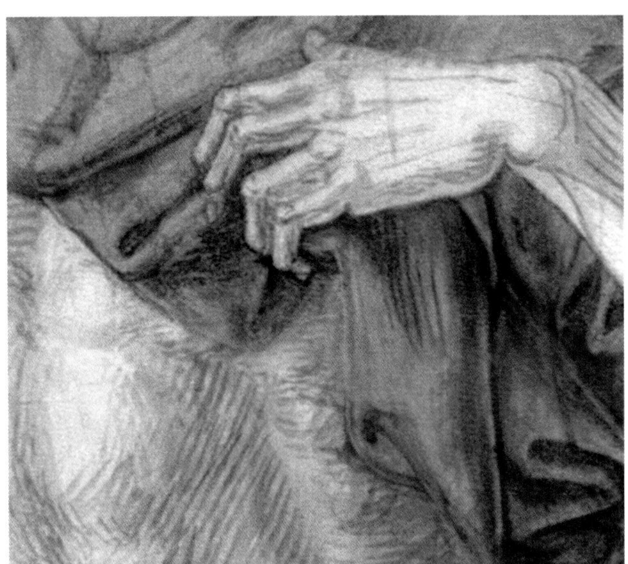

pinnacle above the saint's raised hand, seems to be a first rough indication of the outline of the mountains (Fig. 159). The lion too seems to have been sketched with this more dilute material; initially his legs were longer and his head and shaggy mane were drawn in a higher position (Fig. 160).

Once the placement of the main features was settled, Tura then developed the underdrawing using a darker, more pigmented liquid drawing material, still applied with a brush. Contours were defined with broad, fluent lines and the modelling of forms indicated with bold strokes of parallel hatching. Sometimes, as on the shadowed side of the saint's torso, the hatching appears as diagonal strokes, which serve to establish the fall of light on the figure (Fig. 161). Often, however, the parallel lines curve around the forms, defining the musculature of the figure and scooping out the drapery folds as if they were being excavated with a chisel. Areas of cross-hatching occur where the different planes of the forms intersect.

This sculptural approach to drawing reminds us that Tura supplied designs for goldsmiths and perhaps also for sculptors, but the origins of this boldly hatched underdrawing style may in fact lie in wall-painting techniques in use in Northern Italy. Tura's documented murals are all lost but we know that at least one decorative scheme by him was painted not in fresco, but in oil, probably on a dry *intonaco*, that is the second smoother layer of plaster which in true fresco technique is painted while it is still damp. North Italian painters generally preferred to paint only a few areas in fresco, executing the rest, which might include elaborate decoration with metal foils, on dry plaster (*a secco*). Pisanello, when painting his huge murals of Tournament Battles in the Palazzo Ducale, Mantua (*c.*1439–42), worked in this way, often making elaborately shaded underdrawings on the *intonaco*, especially for the suits of armour which were to be finished in tin or silver leaf (Fig. 162). He also made detailed drawings on the rougher *arriccio*, the layer of plaster subsequently covered by the *intonaco*. Tura's distinctive underdrawing style has more in common with these murals than with underdrawings that have been revealed on panel paintings, even those by the Netherlandish artists who so inspired him. He may have known of Pisanello's wall painting methods through contact with Bono da Ferrara, who had been Pisanello's pupil and assistant, both in Ferrara and in Mantua.

Even with all the hatched shading, the underdrawing of the *Saint Jerome* was still not complete. Over the drawn lines Tura then applied a monochrome yellow-brown undermodelling, consisting of washes of dilute paint, probably in an egg medium, and pigmented with carbon black, yellow ochre and possibly a translucent yellow lake (Fig. 163). The carbon black in the mixture means that these washes can be seen in infrared reflectograms, particularly as they contrast with areas in full light where the white gesso was left exposed. One such area is the triangular shape on the arch of the saint's right foot, while on the back of his left hand a dribble of the liquid wash has evidently run down the picture surface.

As the final stage in making the underdrawing, Tura picked out the highlights with fine lines of lead-white paint. These run mainly along the lit edges of forms, but there are also areas of hatching to indicate relief on the draperies. This highlighting cannot be detected in infrared, but during restoration of the painting it was exposed in places where the upper paint layers had flaked away, for example

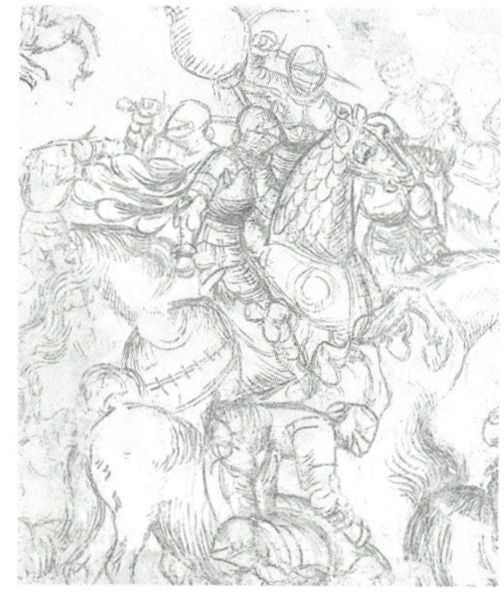

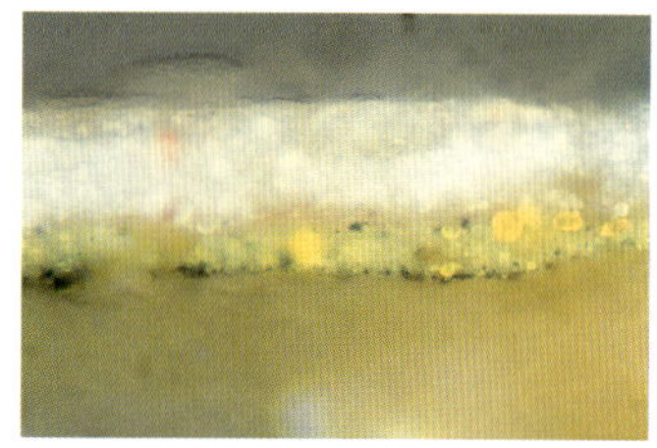

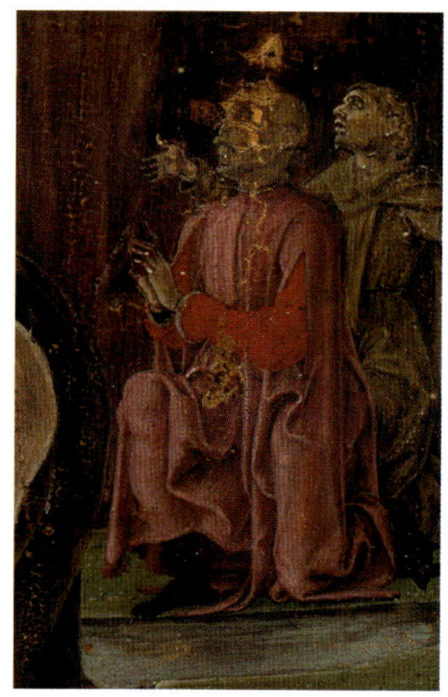

Fig. 162 (top)
PISANELLO AND WORKSHOP, detail of underdrawing on *intonaco*, from the Sala del Pisanello, Mantua, Palazzo Ducale.

Fig. 163
Cross-section from Saint Jerome's right knee showing a line of underdrawing on the gesso, followed by the yellow-brown undermodelling

Fig. 164
Detail of Fig. 156 after cleaning, before restoration

Fig. 165
X-ray detail of *pentimento*

Fig. 166
COSIMO TURA, *Hercules and the Nemean Lion, c.*1470
Black chalk, pen and ink, with washes and white highlights on ochre prepared paper, 21.2 × 15 cm
Rotterdam, Museum Boijmans Van Beuningen, inv. I-180

Fig. 167
Detail of Fig. 156

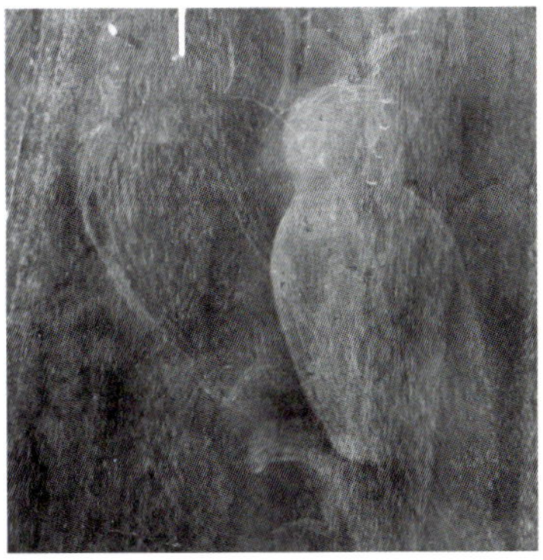

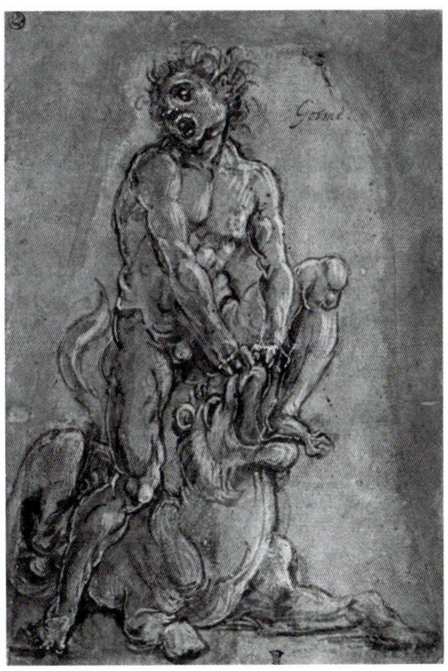

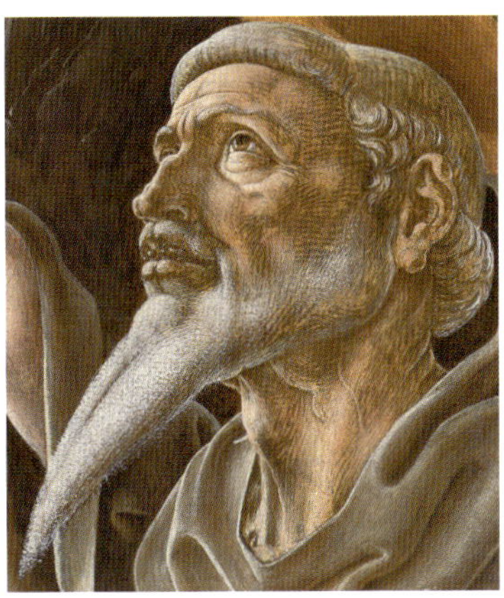

the figure of the donor (Fig. 164). Since the lines contain lead white, they register in X-rays, and are most easily seen in an alteration to the barn owl (Fig. 165). Originally it was drawn to the left of its present position: the black lines of the underdrawing can be made out with difficulty in the infrared reflectogram (because of the large amount of black pigment in the paint of the tree painted over it), but the white highlights show clearly in the X-radiograph. Following completion of the underdrawing, the appearance of the *Saint Jerome* must have resembled Tura's study of *Hercules and the Nemean Lion*, one of only three drawings on paper that are widely accepted as by him (Fig. 166). The heavy black outlines, modelled with parallel curved hatching and ink washes, and finished with thread-like white highlights, are strikingly similar.

Apart from moving the owl and adding the wall creeper and the friars (who were perhaps too small to be worth drawing), Tura generally followed his underdrawing closely when applying the paint layers. These are mainly in walnut oil, but with some egg tempera for the lighter colours and in the lower layers. In some areas, notably the shadowed side of the saint's head, the hatched shading of the underdrawing can be seen through the translucent paint film (Fig. 167). The underdrawing is often visible on other paintings by Tura and this has led to the suggestion that it was intended to be seen, with the black lines of hatching contributing their vibrancy to the final optical effect. Against this, however, is the fact that on a few very well-preserved panels by him the drawing barely shows. Furthermore, if it was supposed to be a visible part of the structure of the painting, then it should be evident under all colours, whereas it tends to show only beneath certain pigments, notably red lakes and the translucent brown mixtures that Tura used for shading areas of flesh. These are the colours that are most likely to have become more transparent with time as a result of changes in the paint medium and pigments. An indication of the increase in transparency of some of the paint in the *Saint Jerome* is supplied by a small *pentimento* in the brown-pink arched rock in the landscape on the right. Here Tura extended the rocks down slightly over the layer of malachite green laid in for the grassy meadow. The extension now appears as a dark band, with the underlying green showing through and contrasting with the area above where the luminosity of the gesso has become more apparent because of the loss of covering power of the pink paint.

If Tura did not intend his underdrawings to be visible, then why are they so fully elaborated? There is no indication on the *Saint Jerome*, and other paintings securely attributed to him, that these detailed drawings were made so that the paint layers could be applied by his workshop – the painting is always of exceptional and unmistakable quality. However, he was continually making designs for other craftsmen, who needed all that information and detail, and so he may simply have become accustomed to drawing in this way. Moreover, the underdrawing is never laborious, but is carried out with an invention and facility that suggests that he took pleasure in its execution. Since so few of his drawings on paper survive, it is only through infrared examination that we have come to know these extraordinary drawings, products of one of the greatest draughtsmen of the fifteenth century.

JD

3 Carlo Crivelli

*c.*1430/5–*c.*1494

The Dead Christ supported by Two Angels, *c.*1470–5

Egg tempera on poplar, 75 × 59.5 cm, painted and gilded area 73 × 55 cm
NG 602

Fig. 168
CARLO CRIVELLI, *The Dead Christ supported by Two Angels* [NG 602], *c.*1470–5

Carlo Crivelli was born in Venice. He may have trained with his father, also a painter, as was his brother Vittore. In addition, he seems at some point to have had contact with artists who studied in the Padua workshop of Squarcione. In 1457 he was fined and imprisoned for cohabiting with the wife of a Venetian sailor. Soon after he appears to have left Venice, working first in Zara in Dalmatia, before moving to the Marches. He was established there by 1468, the date on a polyptych painted for Massa Fermana, near Ascoli Piceno. He remained at Ascoli, and died there probably in 1494 (in September 1495 his brother, Vittore, made a claim to be his legitimate heir). Crivelli's career was distinguished and in 1490 he was knighted by Prince Ferdinando di Capua, the future King Ferdinand II of Naples. His production was limited to altarpieces and small devotional panels. He seems never to have painted secular subjects, and no canvas or wall paintings exist. His altarpieces usually consisted of complex polyptychs with ornate frames and gilding often richly decorated with tooling, *pastiglia* and applied carved ornament.

The Dead Christ supported by Two Angels was originally the centre panel of the upper tier of a polyptych painted probably in the early to mid-1470s for the church of San Francesco at Montefiore dell'Aso, not far from Fermo. In the first half of the nineteenth century the altarpiece was partially dismembered. Six panels, together with sections of the frame, remain at Montefiore, transferred to the church of Santa Lucia. The others were placed on sale by the Roman dealer Cavaliere P. Vallati, from whom the National Gallery acquired the *Dead Christ* in 1859, choosing it over two panels from the main tier, the central *Virgin and Child* and the *Saint Francis* (both now Brussels, Musées Royaux d'Art et d'Histoire), and a predella of Christ with seven apostles, then apparently still a single plank, but soon after cut up and dispersed as individual panels (see Figs 175, 176 and 181). Most unusually, the *Dead Christ supported by Two Angels* carries the inscription CAROLUS. CRIVELLUS. VENETUS. PINSIT on the parapet on the left, although the same form of words also appears on the central *Virgin and Child*, where it would normally be expected.

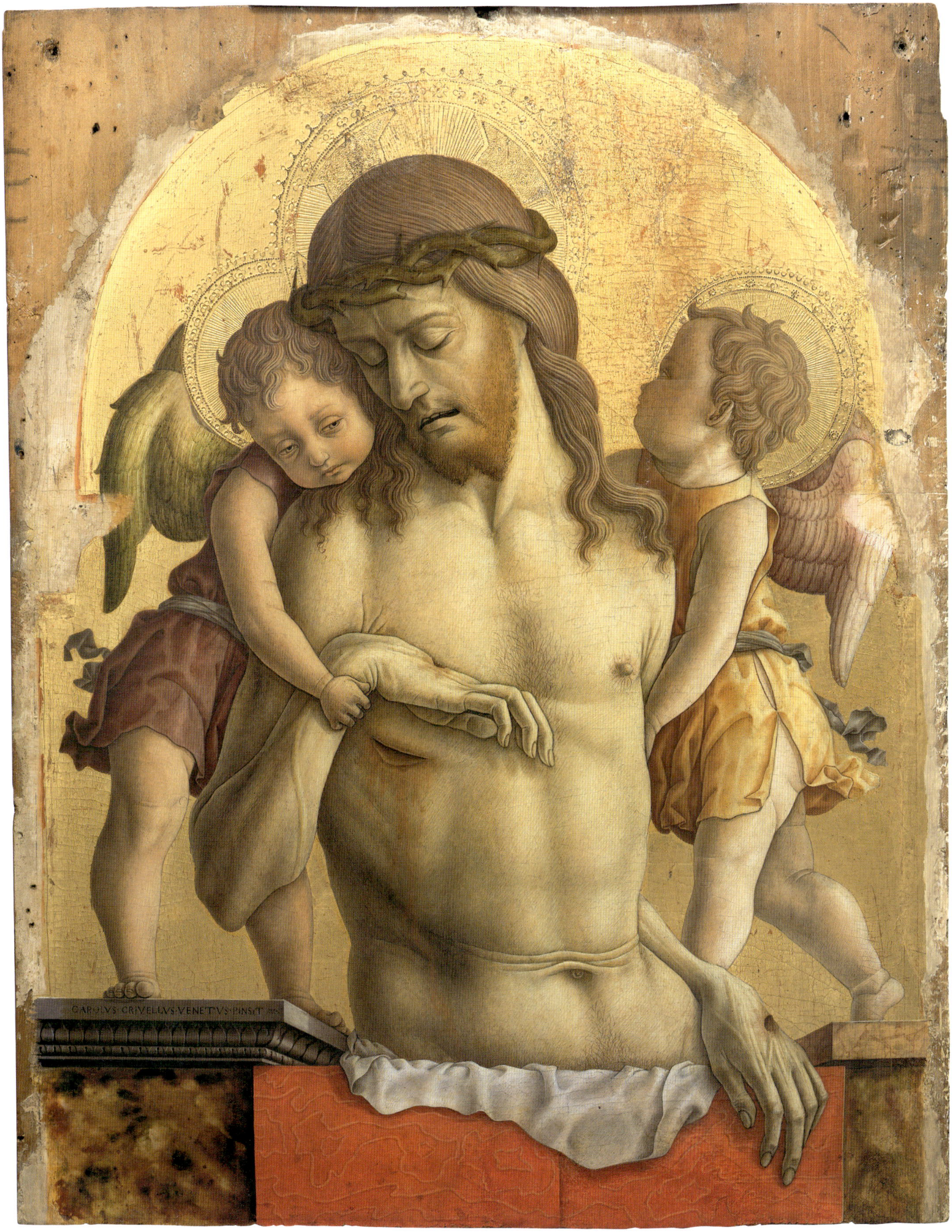
CAROLVS·CRIVELLVS·VENETVS·PINSIT

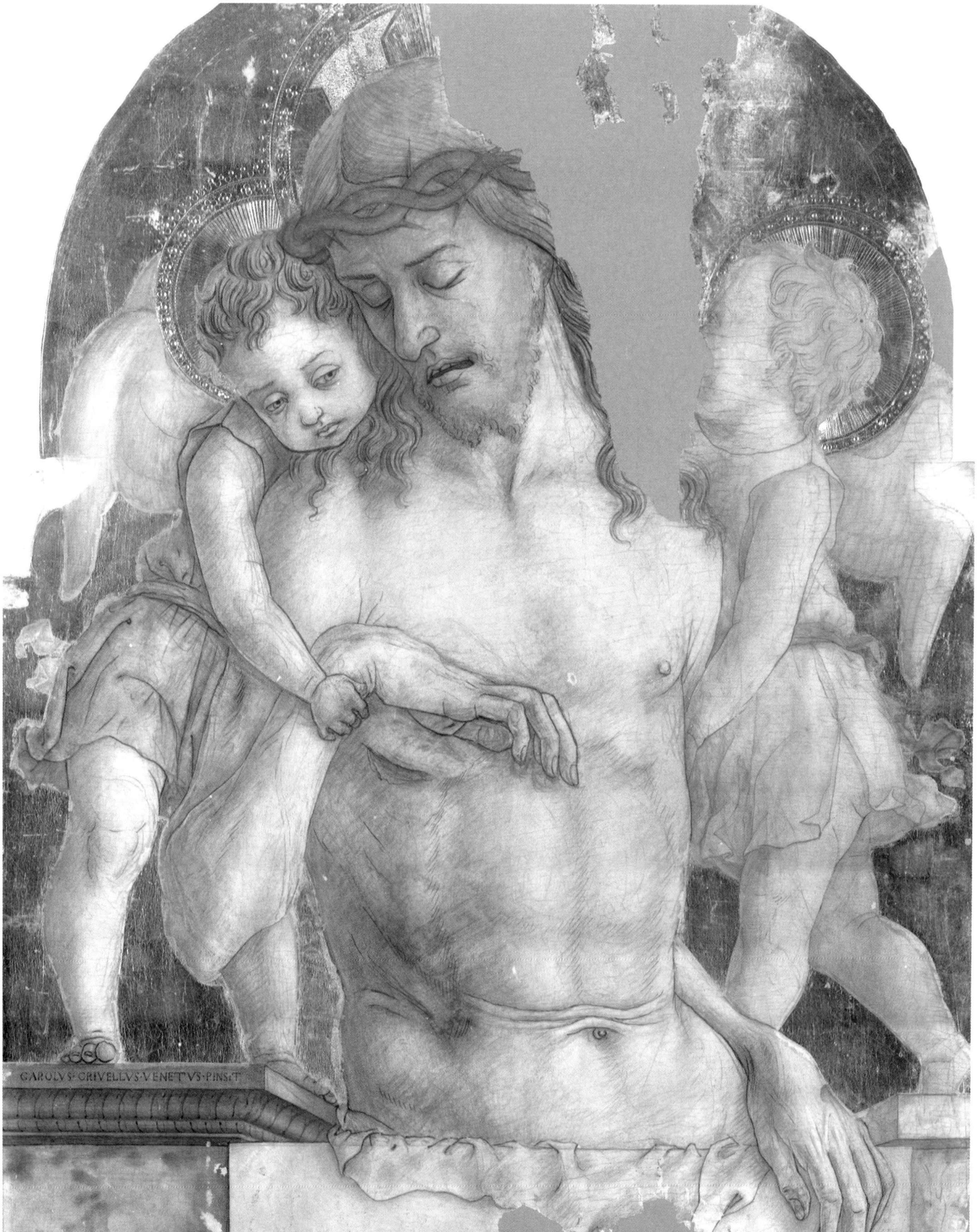
CAROLVS·CRIVELLVS·VENETVS·PINSIT

Fig. 169 (left)
Infrared reflectogram mosaic

Fig. 170
Detail of Fig. 169

Fig. 171
Detail of Fig. 169

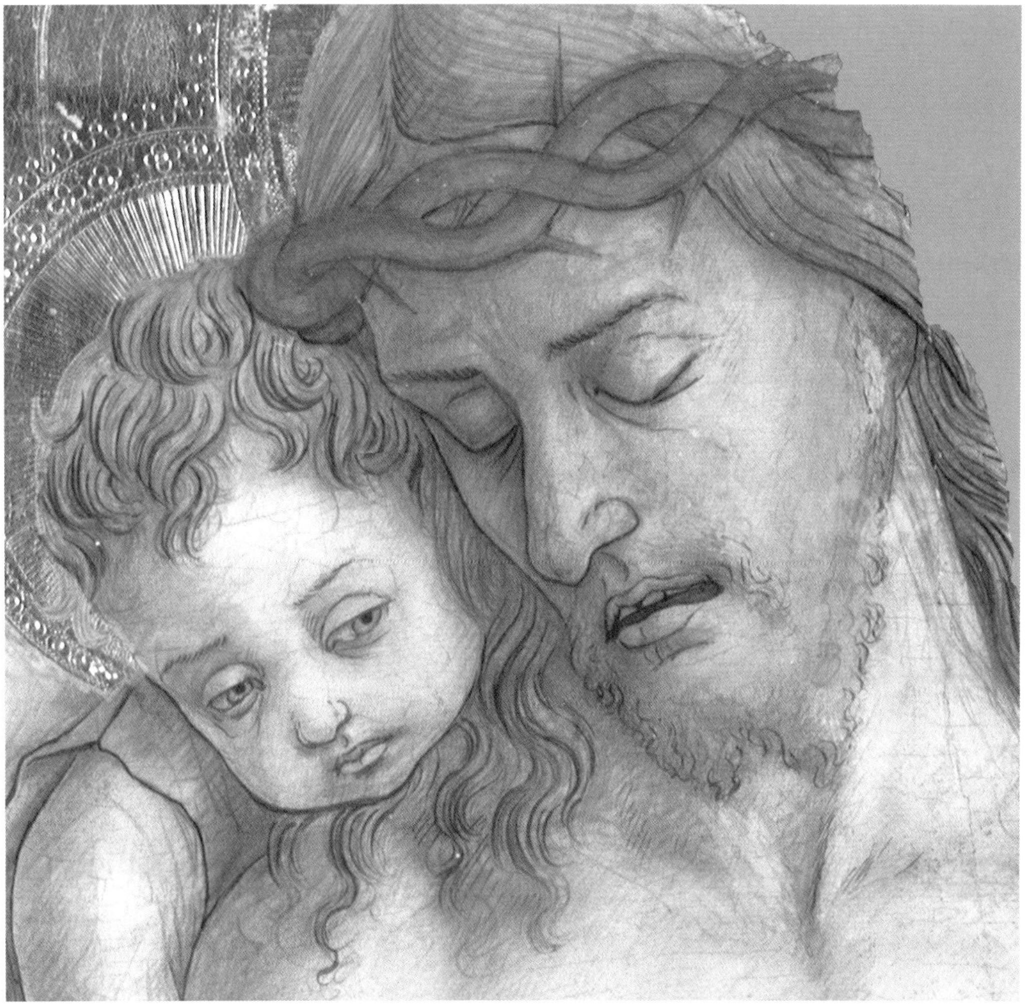

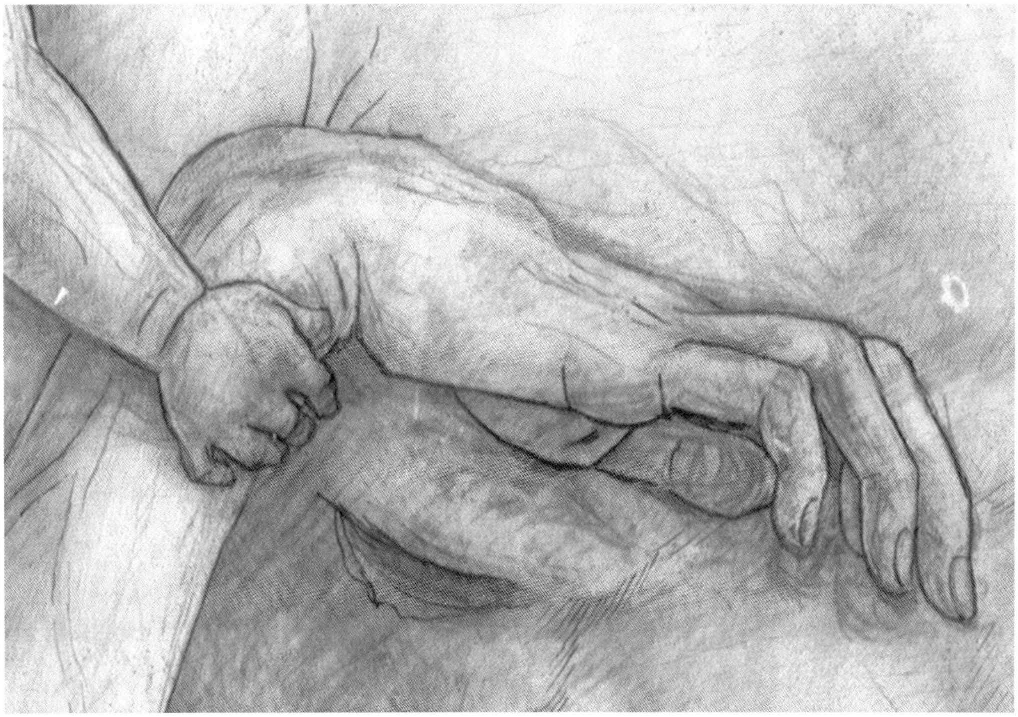

Formerly, the signature on the *Dead Christ* was suspected to be a later addition, but recent removal of the nineteenth-century varnish and restoration has established that not only is the paint original but that it lies under a very old varnish, composed of materials used for varnish-making in the fifteenth century. The exceptional survival of this varnish layer – barely discoloured despite its age – means that much of the paint film is in immaculate condition, having escaped the damage often caused in the past by attempts to remove these old and now insoluble varnishes. Unfortunately, however, there are two very large losses where the paint and ground have flaked away from the wood: the first, and most evident, is roughly triangular in shape and includes the top and right side of Christ's head, the right shoulder of the angel on the right together with part of the angel's profile, and all the gilding in-between. The second loss is along the lower edge and comprises parts of Christ's loincloth and the red watered-silk fabric draped over the tomb. These missing areas are now reconstructed, but in the infrared reflectogram (Fig. 169) they have been filled in with a flat grey tone.

By restricting his output mainly to altarpieces, Crivelli inevitably found himself repeating certain subjects: for example, the figure of the Dead Christ in his tomb, either alone, or supported by angels, or by the Virgin and other mourners, appears as the lunette or the centre of the upper tier of eleven surviving (although often dismembered) altarpieces, as well as a small devotional panel now in the Louvre, Paris. He painted many versions of the Virgin and Child, and the same saints frequently reappear in different altarpieces. Therefore he might be expected to have made use of cartoons, and perhaps even of templates, in the production of his paintings. Analysis of his designs, however, shows that, although at first sight they often appear closely related, he seems never to have duplicated exactly his own inventions.

The impression that each design was largely recreated afresh is confirmed by the underdrawing revealed by infrared examination of *The Dead Christ supported by Two Angels*. Like his Ferrarese contemporary Cosimo Tura (see Cat. 2), Crivelli seems to have begun his underdrawing with little to guide him other than perhaps a small preliminary study on paper. He also started with a dilute ink applied with a brush, but was clearly not such a decisive draughtsman as Tura. As he sought to place his figures, their contours were repeatedly redrawn with rapid light strokes, the multiple lines most evident down the side of Christ's neck, in the arm of the angel to his right, and above all in the search for the correct angle for the expressively drooping hand, arguably the focal point of the picture in the way that it frames the wound in his side (Figs 170 and 171). Faint, almost scribbled, lines can also be seen on Christ's torso, the legs of both angels and down the arm of the angel on the right, initially marked out with a series of short curved strokes.

As Crivelli moved towards a resolution of the design, he began to work out the fall of light on the figures, shading with diagonal lines of parallel hatching, still with a dilute ink or paint. Occasionally, as on the forearm of the angel on the left, the lines are fine and closely spaced, but generally the hatching is loose and open. Eventually he committed himself to a final version by taking up a fine-pointed brush and a much blacker, more concentrated ink to fix the principal contours,

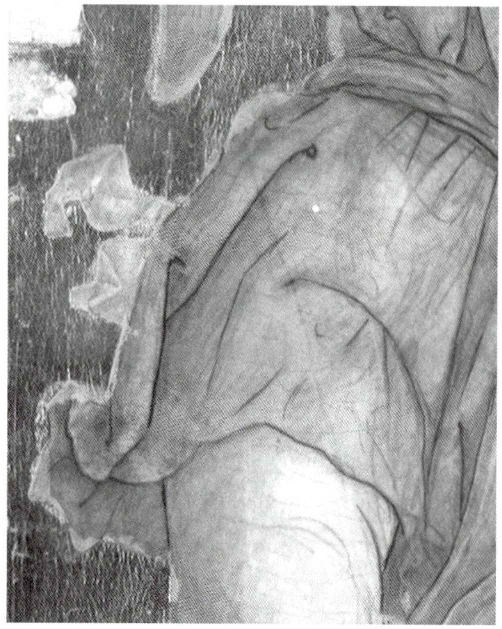

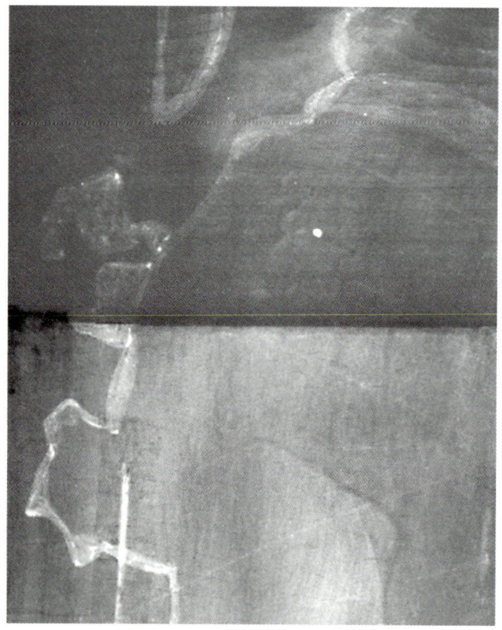

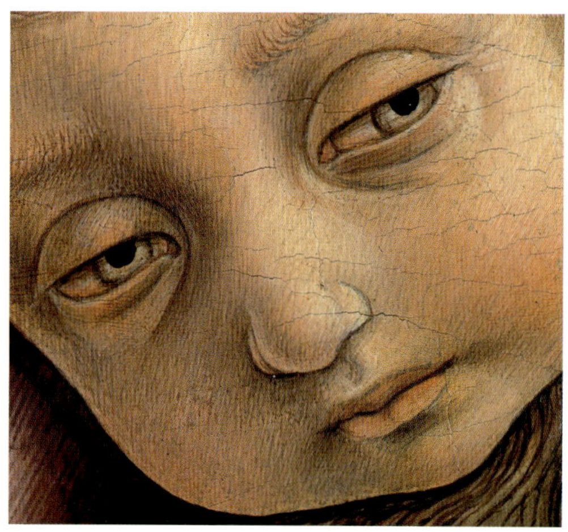

Fig. 172 (left)
Detail of Fig. 169

Fig. 173
X-ray detail of area shown in Fig. 172

Fig. 174
Detail of Fig. 168

Figs. 175 and 176 (below)
CARLO CRIVELLI, *Apostles*, *c.*1470–5
Egg tempera on poplar, 31.5 × 23.8 cm
Upton House, The Bearstead Collection, The National Trust

features and details and to add a few small areas of shading. In contrast to the improvisatory earlier stages of underdrawing, these lines are schematic – indeed, in places, especially on the loincloth, they have the character of lines usually interpreted as having been transferred from a cartoon by tracing, although here this cannot be the case.

In this most sculptural of Crivelli's paintings – probably influenced by the reliefs by Donatello that he is likely to have seen in Padua – the outlines, especially where the figures meet the gold background, are important for the illusion of volume (although in fact the composition is spatially impossible). Therefore, it was essential that they were firmly established with these darker reinforcing lines, even though they were not incised, as had been the normal practice with paintings with gold backgrounds. Inevitably the pieces of gold leaf encroach over the outlines, which remain visible in infrared in only a few places, for example along the skirt of the angel on the left, just above the fluttering ribbons of his sash (Fig. 172). Gold is highly reflective in infrared and so the edges and corners of the leaf can be seen where it overlaps the figures. To reclaim their contours (and to ensure that the subsequent paint layers did not flake from the gold) Crivelli painted over the overlaps with a pale grey paint containing mostly lead white (which seems to ensure better adhesion to metal leaf). This shows clearly in the X-radiograph (Fig. 173).

The dark reinforcing lines also played a role in the painting process. Generally the painted contours follow the drawn ones with absolute precision, and in many places the underdrawn lines are allowed to show through the paint to contribute to the final effect: for example, the creases of Christ's armpit or the lines around the nostrils and under the eyes of the angel on the left (Fig. 174). Sometimes they are then strengthened with a fine stroke of brown-black paint, but confirmation that it is the underdrawn lines that register in the infrared reflectogram is supplied by a small difference between the underdrawing and painting along the edge of Christ's loincloth at the top of his right thigh; originally drawn as a simple curve, the fabric was painted as though twisted to form small folds. Similarly, it is the underdrawn version of Christ's eyebrows, indicated with short almost vertical strokes, that

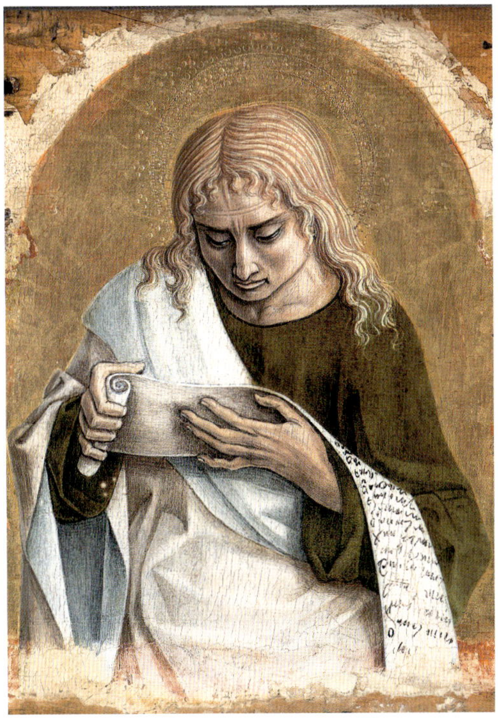

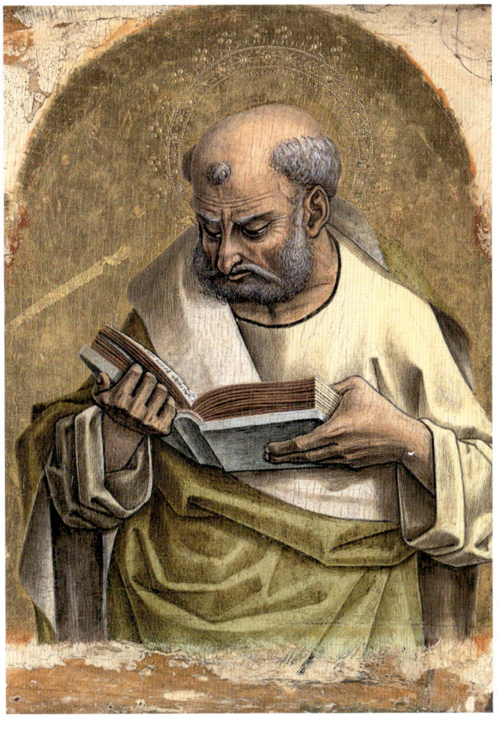

shows in infrared and not the painted one, where the minute hairs are depicted growing along the brow as they should. The darker areas of hatched shading were almost certainly not intended to be visible. They remain well covered where the paint includes sufficient lead white, for example the shading of the eye socket of the angel on the left, but in some of the shadowed parts of the flesh painting on Christ, which have almost certainly become slightly more translucent, the lines can now be seen with the naked eye. They are too dark and heavy ever to have blended with the delicate hatched strokes of the tempera paint and they must therefore once have been obscured.

The Dead Christ supported by Two Angels stands out among Crivelli's paintings for its refinement and attention to detail in both planning and execution (he may have recognised this in adding the superfluous signature) and the underdrawing may not be entirely typical. On some panels by him areas of parallel hatched underdrawing can be discerned with the naked eye, but they disappear in infrared, an indication that the underdrawing was made in an iron-gall ink. However, the National Gallery has been able to examine two fragments showing apostles from the predella of the Montefiore polyptych, now in the care of the National Trust at Upton House, Banbury (Figs 175 and 176). Although they are less refined in execution, both in the painting and the underdrawing, Crivelli seems to have taken much the same approach to establishing their design as he did for the upper tier panel. In both, the underdrawing was worked up from freehand try-outs made on the gesso and using a dilute ink or paint (Figs 177 and 178). On the younger apostle the folds of the sleeve were sketched in several positions, possibly with a different, higher opening, resulting in a flurry of haphazard lines, which are most visible in the area of the scroll. His right hand was modified, and may even have been tried with the fingers extended, while similar approximate placement lines can also be seen in the

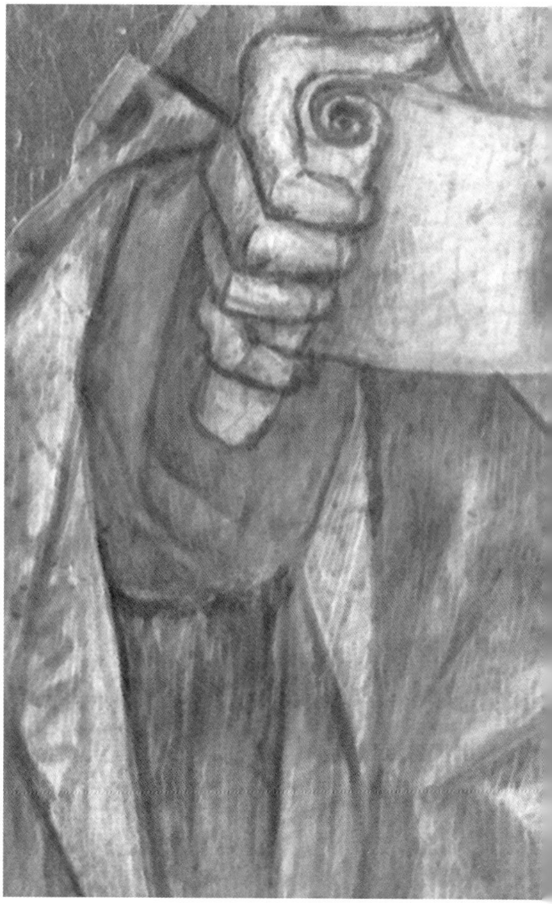

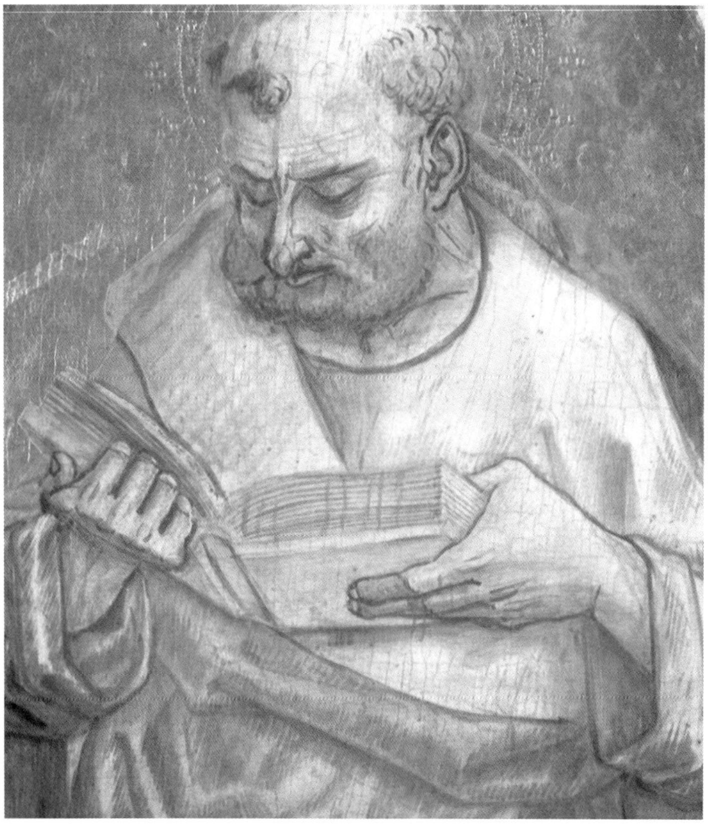

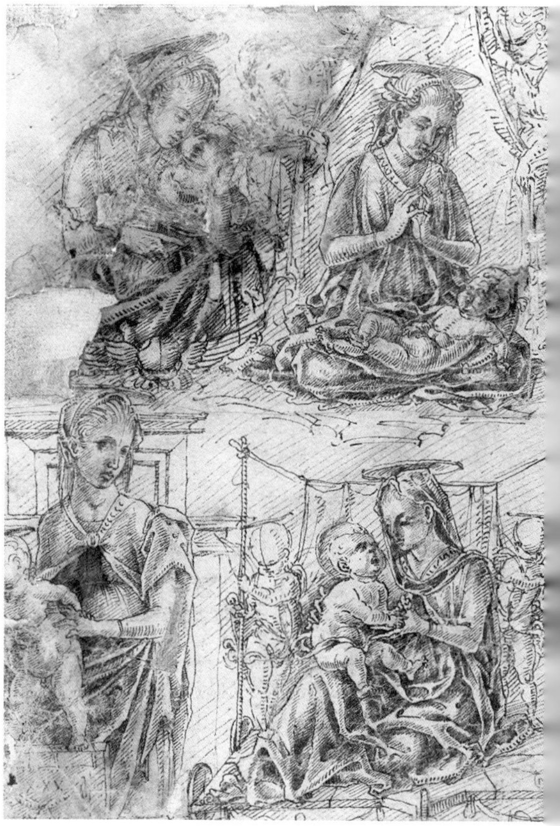

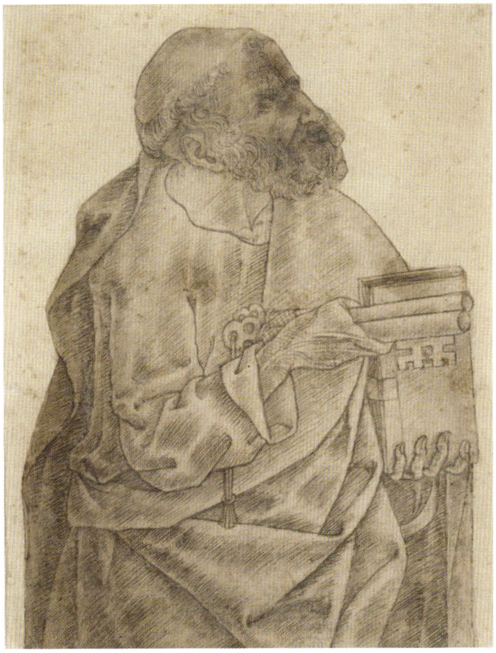

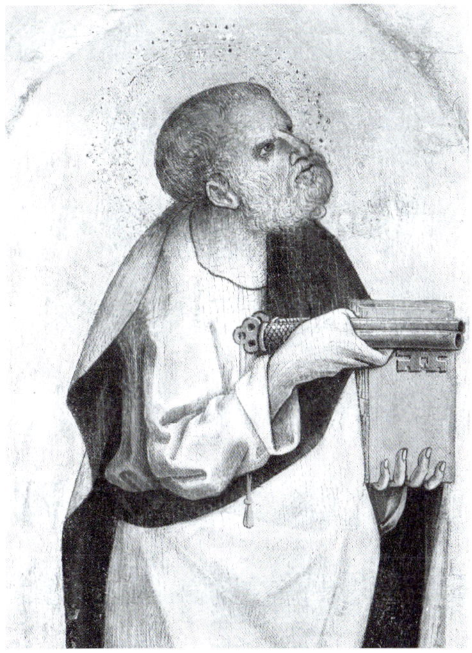

Fig. 177 (bottom, far left)
Detail from infrared reflectogram mosaic of Fig. 176

Fig. 178 (left)
Detail from infrared reflectogram mosaic of Fig. 175

Fig. 179 (bottom, left)
MARCO ZOPPO,
Studies of the Virgin and Child
Pen and ink with wash on pink prepared paper, 28.8 × 19.6 cm
London, The British Museum
inv. P&D 1904-12-1-1 recto

Fig. 180 (above)
After CRIVELLI, *Saint Peter*
Brown ink, brown wash and white gouache on cream paper,
20.5 × 14.5 cm
Cambridge, Massachusetts, Harvard University Art Museums, Courtesy of the Fogg Art Museum
Bequest of Charles A. Loeser, 1932
inv. 1932.280 recto

Fig. 181
CARLO CRIVELLI, *Saint Peter*, *c.*1470–5
Wood, 31.8 × 23.2 cm
Detroit, The Detroit Institute of Arts, Gift of E.M. Sperling 1928
inv. 28.8

reflectogram of the older apostle with a book. Crivelli may have been creating these figures, and the other apostles on the predella, directly on the gessoed panel; alternatively, he may have worked from a series of small studies, probably not unlike the sheets showing variations on the theme of the Virgin and Child by Marco Zoppo (Fig. 179), who may have been a contact of Crivelli's in Padua and subsequently in the Marches.

The underdrawings of the apostles were then gone over with a darker ink, generally with a heavier, coarser line than that seen on the *Dead Christ*, but applied with considerable panache and a notable command of the structure of the heads. The draperies were more extensively shaded than the upper tier panel, using a loaded brush, which left blobs of surplus ink at the beginning or end of strokes. Although clearly drawing at greater speed – towards the left edge of the younger apostle a fold of drapery is shaded with a hasty zigzag flourish – the artist was still in complete control of his design and materials.

The discovery of such extemporised underdrawing on the predella as well as on the upper tier means that the only drawing on paper or parchment to have been attributed to Crivelli, a version in pen and ink of the figure of Saint Peter from the Montefiore predella (Figs 180 and 181), cannot be by him. As has been demonstrated, no such careful study lies behind the National Gallery and Upton House panels. The scratchy, rather uncontrolled hatching, always at the same angle, and including the head – when shading in Crivelli's underdrawings is limited mainly to the draperies – suggests that the drawing is a copy, made after the painted predella.

JD

4 Hans Memling

active 1465; died 1494

A Young Man at Prayer, *c.*1475

Oil on oak, 39.0 × 25.4 cm
NG 2594

Fig. 182
HANS MEMLING, *A Young Man at Prayer* [NG 2594], *c.*1475

MEMLING was from Seligenstadt near Frankfurt. He became a burgess of Bruges in 1465 and pursued a prosperous career there until his death in 1494. The altarpiece of the Two Saints John and the Floreins Triptych (both now in the Memlingmuseum in Bruges) are both inscribed with Memling's name and the date 1479. The Donne Triptych in the National Gallery probably dates from around the same time. Memling's patrons included local dignitaries, lay and ecclesiastical; persons associated with the Burgundian court; and members of the foreign communities of Bruges. His paintings were in demand all over Europe, particularly in Italy. A highly successful painter, he clearly ran a large and well-organised workshop. Very little is known about his collaborators.

This portrait was apparently the left wing of a diptych or triptych, where the donor worshipped a religious image, probably of the Virgin and Child, which would have been shown in the adjoining panel.

There are no indications of the young man's identity, though he was clearly very wealthy. He wears a red velvet doublet and over it a black robe. On his right, the robe is turned back into a sort of lapel; his right sleeve is folded over above his wrist to reveal a dark grey lining with a damask-like pattern. His shirt appears through openings in the armhole seams of doublet and robe. From the gold chain around his neck, worn under the robe, hangs a cross set with sapphires and surrounded by pearls. In his book, only a blue initial D is legible; the other inscriptions, in red and in black, were never intended to be read. The two coloured marble columns have golden capitals and bases; they are not convincingly related, in terms of structure or perspective, to the figure or the surface on which his book rests, but they suggest a luxurious setting.

Examination with infrared reflectography reveals a great deal of free, scribbled underdrawing, probably in a dry material such as black chalk. However, as sometimes happens when underdrawing is discovered in a painting, it cannot be fully understood. Such is the case with the *Young Man at Prayer*. The drawing is clearly visible in the face and hair (Fig. 183) and in the hands and book (Fig. 184), but the

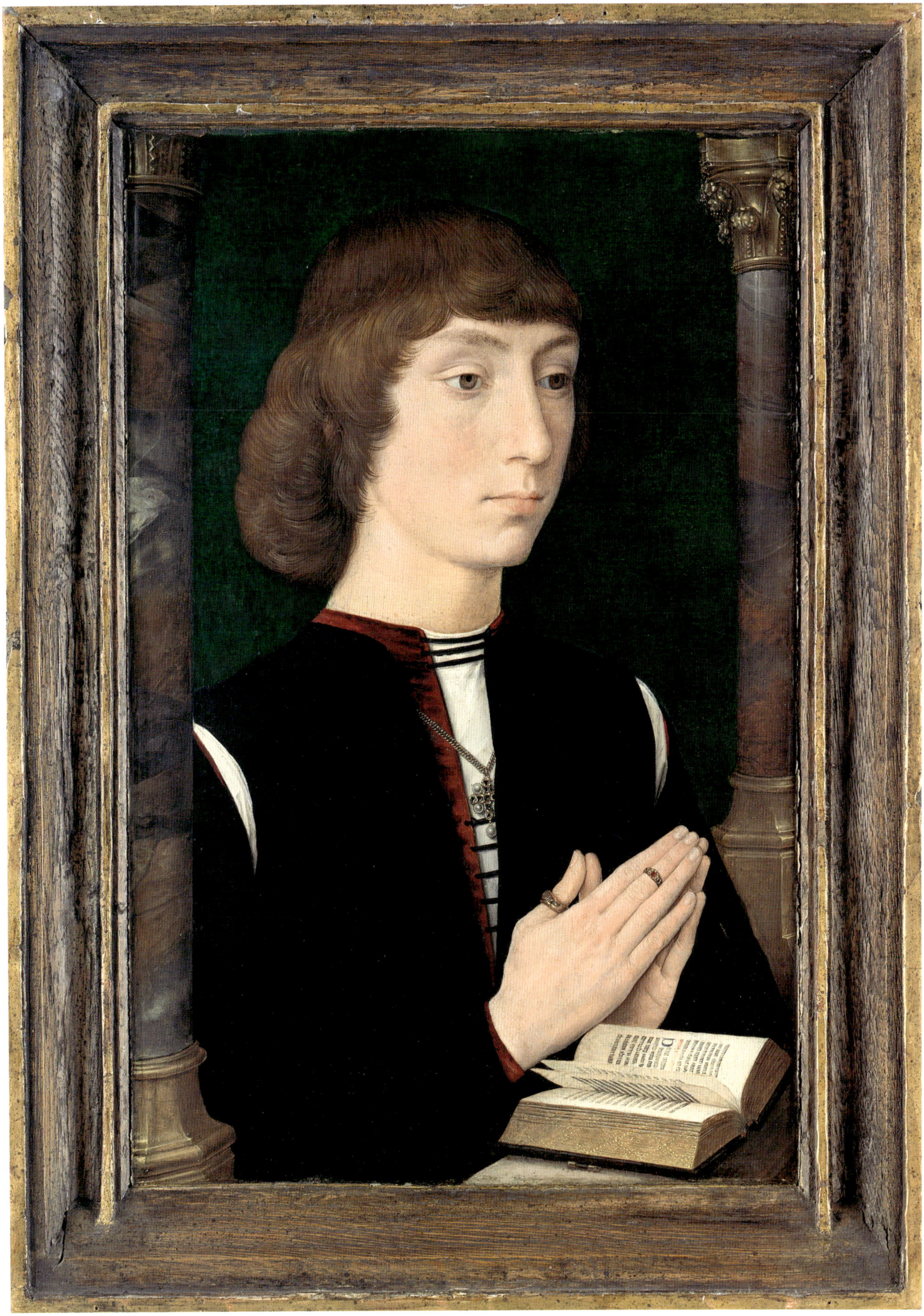

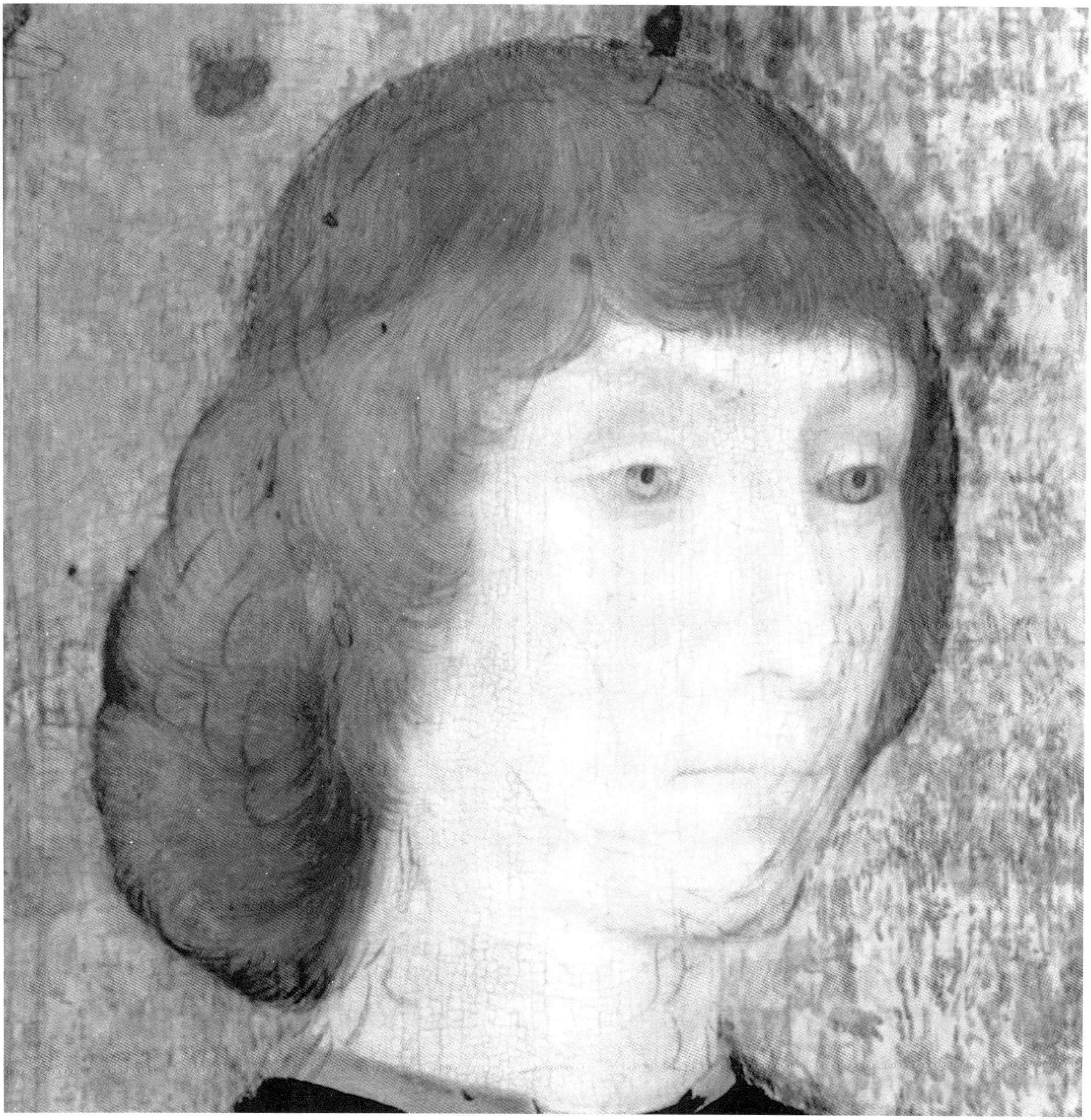

Fig. 183
Infrared reflectogram mosaic, detail

Fig. 184
Infrared reflectogram mosaic, detail

black paint of the young man's clothing conceals any underdrawing in that area. The whole composition, however, is underdrawn. In the drawing, the column on our left is wider and the base of its capital is a little lower; drawing for the base of the column on our right is also visible. In the head and neck, the underdrawing consists of short, slightly curving lines that indicate roughly where the head is to go. Memling has made numerous attempts to establish the positions of the young man's chin, cheek, left eye and temple. The lines in the hands and book are very much more confusing but probably record various ideas for the placing of the hands, the surface on which the book rests, and the book itself.

Some of Memling's portraits have comparable underdrawings, for example his portrait of Maarten van Nieuwenhove of 1487 (Bruges, Memlingmuseum), with multiple lines for the contours of the figures. If we could see the underdrawing beneath the black paint in the London portrait, we could doubtless make greater sense of Memling's scribbled lines. He may have been trying out on the panel his first ideas for the pose; it is probable that he also made fairly detailed drawings of the sitter. When he was painting the portrait, he would have used them to elaborate details of texture and shadow omitted from the underdrawing. Few changes were made at the painting stage, although there are adjustments in some of the contours, for example those of the hair and the garments.

LC

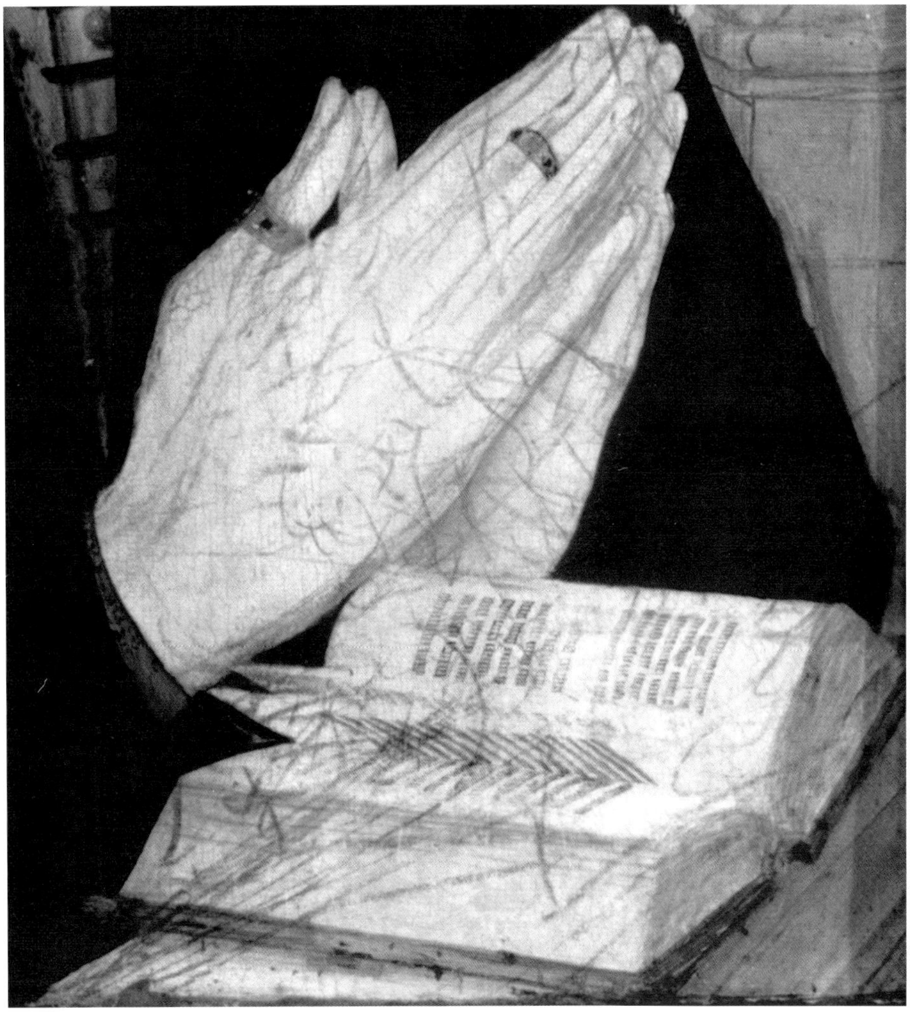

5 Master of the View of St Gudula

active 1470s–1480s

Portrait of a Young Man, *c.*1480–5

Oil on oak, 22.8 × 14.0 cm
NG 2612

This unknown Master is named after a picture in the Louvre of a saint preaching, in the background of which is a view of Brussels, dominated by the west front of the Collegiate Church of St Gudula (now the Cathedral of Saints Michael and Gudula). The Master seems to have specialised to some extent in relatively accurate views of Brussels and to have worked there in the 1470s and 1480s.

The young man is seen through the arched window of a brick-built house; a pen-case and ink-well lie on the stone sill. Though the writing in his book is fictive, this book, and the book in a similar portrait in the Metropolitan Museum in New York (Fig. 185), also attributed to the Master of the View of St Gudula, resemble an Amiens Book of Hours of about 1500 (Paris, Bibliothèque Nationale de France, MS lat. 10536), which similarly opens into the shape of a heart and has some decorated initials, alternately red and blue (Fig. 189). In the book in the London picture, the numerous initials and divisions in the text suggest a devotional rather than a secular manuscript, and the young man may be at his devotions. The portrait is probably the right wing of a small diptych and the sitter's gaze may then be directed towards the image in the missing left wing. In this and in the similar portrait in New York, however, the sitters wear hats. It would be unusual, but by no means exceptional, for a praying donor to wear a hat.

The church in the background is Our Lady of the Zavel (Notre-Dame du Sablon) in Brussels; it is seen from the south. The painter's viewpoint is apparently the present rue des Sablons. The church is in an unfinished state: the aisles were not constructed until after 1494 and the south portal was not completed until the nineteenth century (Fig. 187). The open space is the cemetery of the Zavel. Beyond the cemetery a line of houses descends towards a crossroads where a rectangular stone cistern has been erected. It is apparently one of the *poelen* – or pools – dug for the town authorities of Brussels. The water from the *poelen* was not for human consumption but was evidently used for fire-fighting and for watering animals. The structure depicted here is probably the *poel* situated outside the Inner Coudenberg Gate. The landscape behind would be the open space between the inner and outer walls of the town and on the horizon is a section of the outer wall. The winding

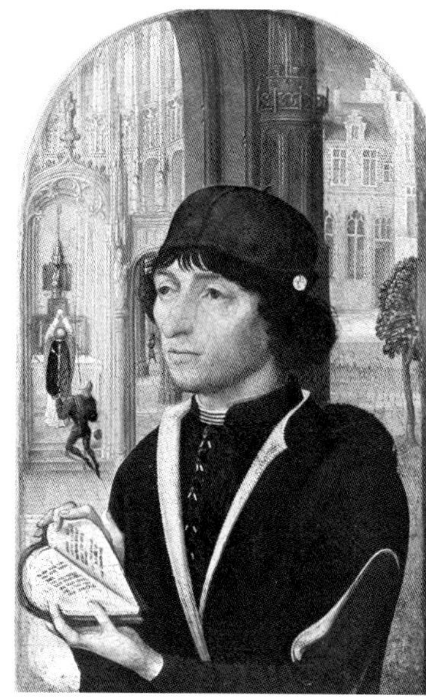

Fig. 185
MASTER OF THE VIEW OF ST GUDULA, *Portrait of a Young Man holding a Prayer Book*, *c.*1480.
Oil on panel, 21 × 13 cm. New York, The Metropolitan Museum of Art Bequest of Mary Stillman Harkness, 1950. 1950.145.27

Fig. 186 (opposite)
MASTER OF THE VIEW OF ST GUDULA, *Portrait of a Young Man* [NG 2612] *c.*1480–5

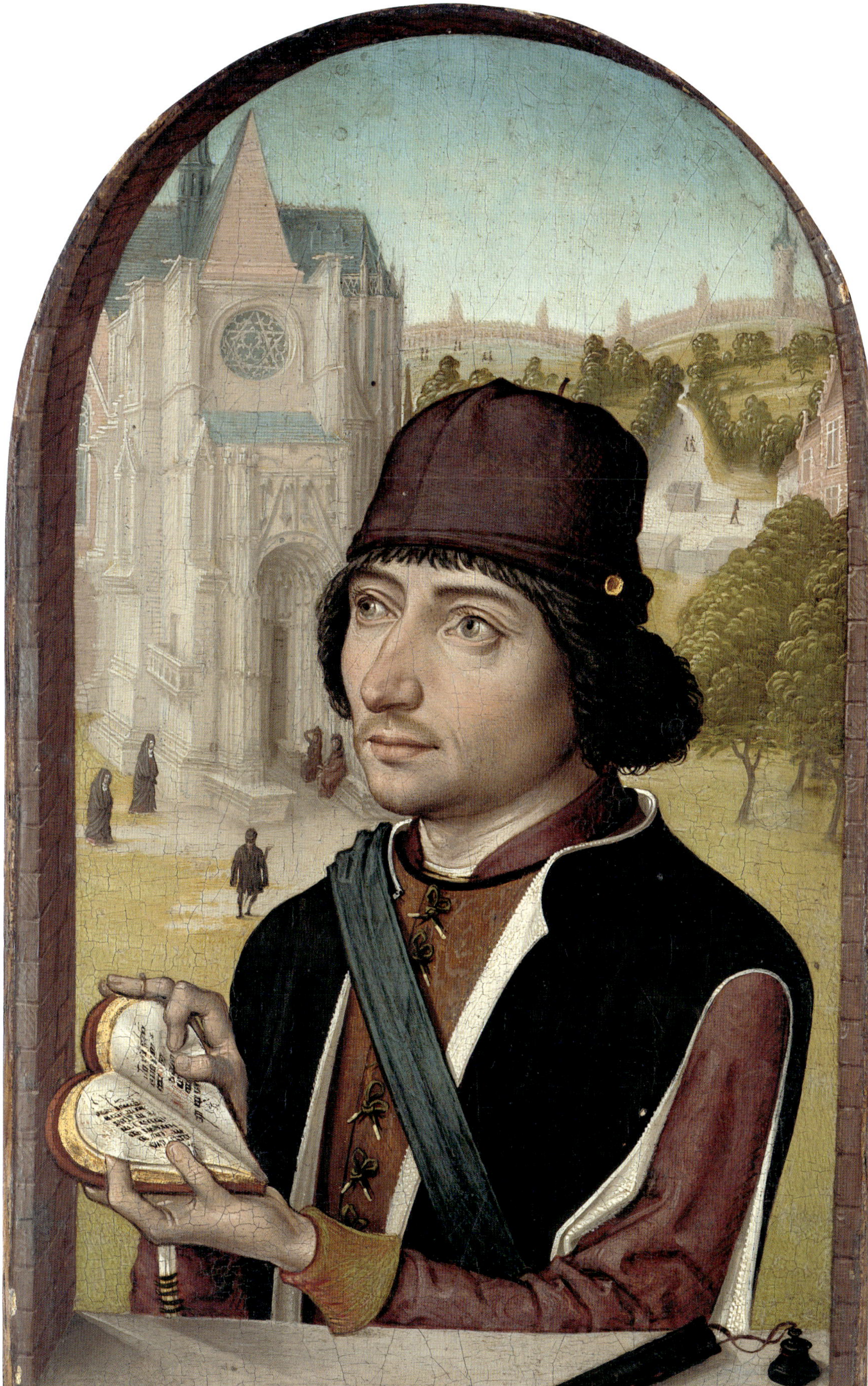

road seems to be the 'little street' which did not continue to the outer walls but led into the park of the ducal palace. Similar backgrounds recur in two paintings of the *Marriage of the Virgin* which are likewise attributed to the Master of the View of St Gudula (Utrecht, Catharijneconvent, and Brussels, Musées des Beaux-Arts; Fig. 188).

The young man may be Philippe Cottereau, who became in 1484 Keeper of the Charters of Brabant and whose family probably owned the houses on the right. The landscape must have been of particular importance to the sitter and it is certainly of the greatest interest now as one of the earliest known views of Brussels.

The painting is on a single piece of oak, prepared with a chalk ground onto which the composition was drawn. Because the paint has become more transparent as it has aged, some of the underdrawing is now visible to the naked eye in lighter areas: for example, along the side of the young man's nose and in the church. The infrared reflectogram mosaic gives a more complete image of the underdrawing, which is extensive and detailed, executed with bold, rapid strokes in a liquid medium (Fig. 190). Blobs where liquid has collected as the brush was lifted can be seen at the ends of many of the brushstrokes: for example, in the horizontal hatching on the buttress on our left (Fig. 191). In important areas such as the face and the church, the drawing is particularly detailed with extensive use of short parallel hatching to indicate shadow. Elsewhere the drawing is more stylised: the hatching for shadows sometimes becomes continuous zigzags, and squiggles or loops indicate trees and bushes.

There are many differences between the underdrawing and the painting. The underdrawn lines in the sky above the sitter's head have been interpreted as feathers in his hat but they do not touch his cap. They seem rather to denote tall trees, similar to the two painted trees which cross the horizon in the background of the Brussels *Marriage of the Virgin* and which appear out of scale with the rest of the landscape (Fig. 188). Though the main elements of the landscape have not been radically altered, the positions of several have been shifted and some small buildings have been suppressed. Also, the large trees at the right, indicated only schematically in the drawing, conceal a long wall that disappears out of the right edge of the composition. The painter has slightly extended the church at the right and elaborated certain architectural details: the steeple is drawn as a narrow tower with parallel sides; the tracery of the rose window is simpler in design in the underdrawing than in the painting. The little figures in front of the church have all

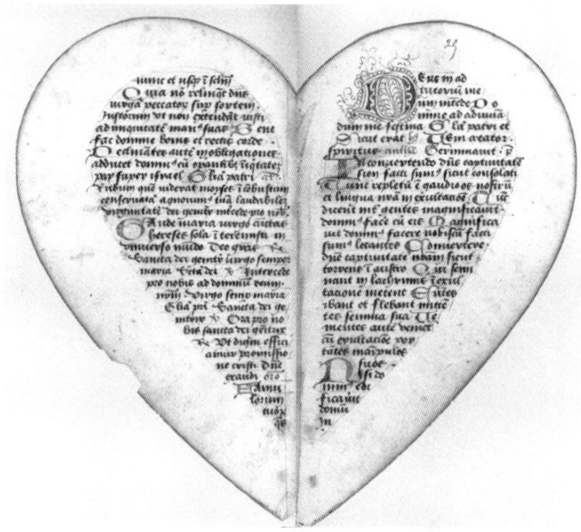

Fig. 189
Heart-shaped Book of Hours, Amiens, late 15th century, paper folios each 16.5 × 9 cm
Paris, Bibliothèque Nationale de France
MS lat. 10536. fols 24v–25

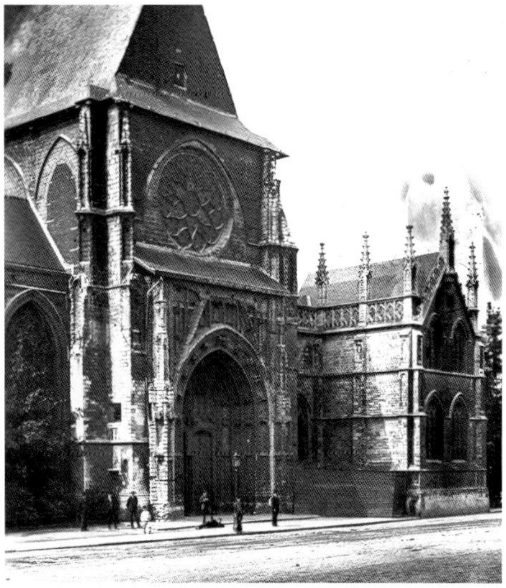

Fig. 187 (bottom left)
South portal, Our Lady of the Zavel, Brussels, state in *c.*1850

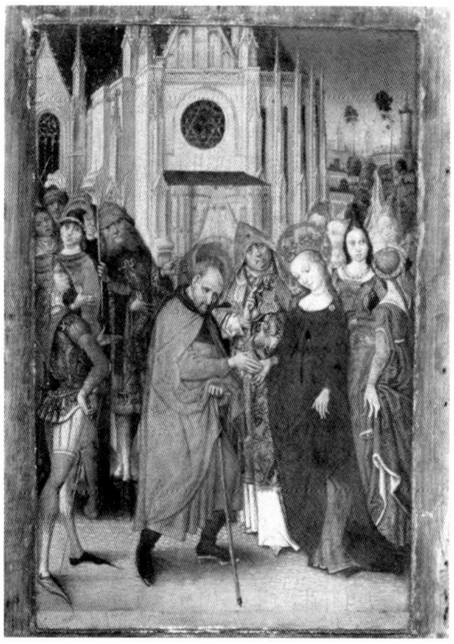

Fig. 188 (bottom right)
MASTER OF THE VIEW OF ST GUDULA, *Marriage of the Virgin*, *c.*1485
Oil on panel, 47.2 × 83 cm
Brussels, Musées des Beaux-Arts, inv. 7559

Fig. 190 (opposite)
Infrared reflectogram mosaic of Fig. 186

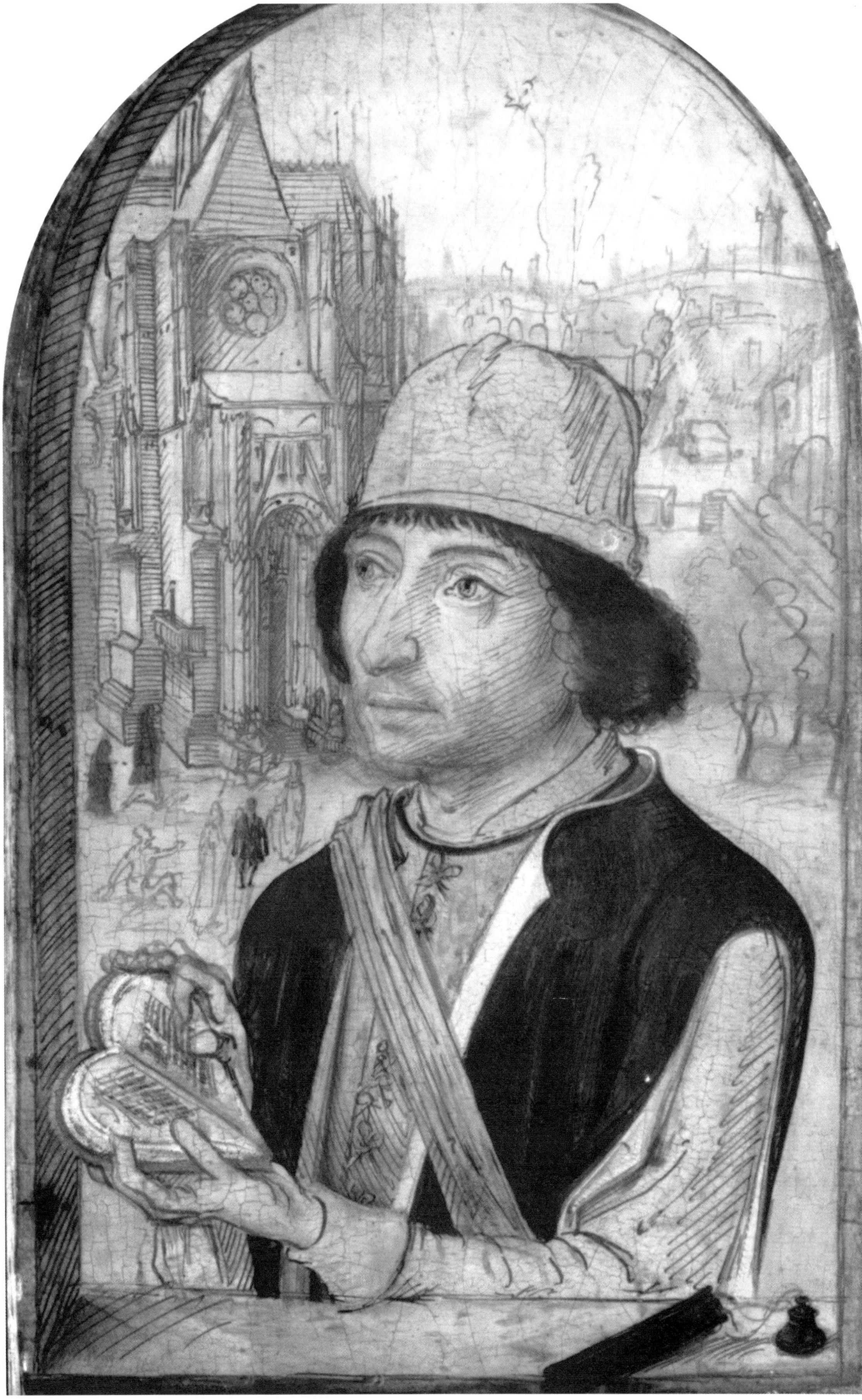

been changed; none of the small painted figures is underdrawn (Fig. 191). The underdrawn figures, larger in scale than those painted, include a seated beggar, extending his right hand towards two standing women seen from the back. Between them and the church is another standing woman, again in back view, who may be leading a child by her left hand. Behind the beggar is a fourth woman: the lower parts of her skirts are clearly seen, though the upper part of her figure is concealed beneath the second of the two painted women. The bench on which the two figures in the portal are seated was fully drawn before they were included. Lines at the opposite side of the portal are difficult to interpret but may be indications for other figures which were never painted.

There are fewer changes to the young man himself. Though his eyes have not been altered, his nose and chin are drawn within their painted contours and what seems to be hair, drawn in a curiously stylised way, intrudes further across the near

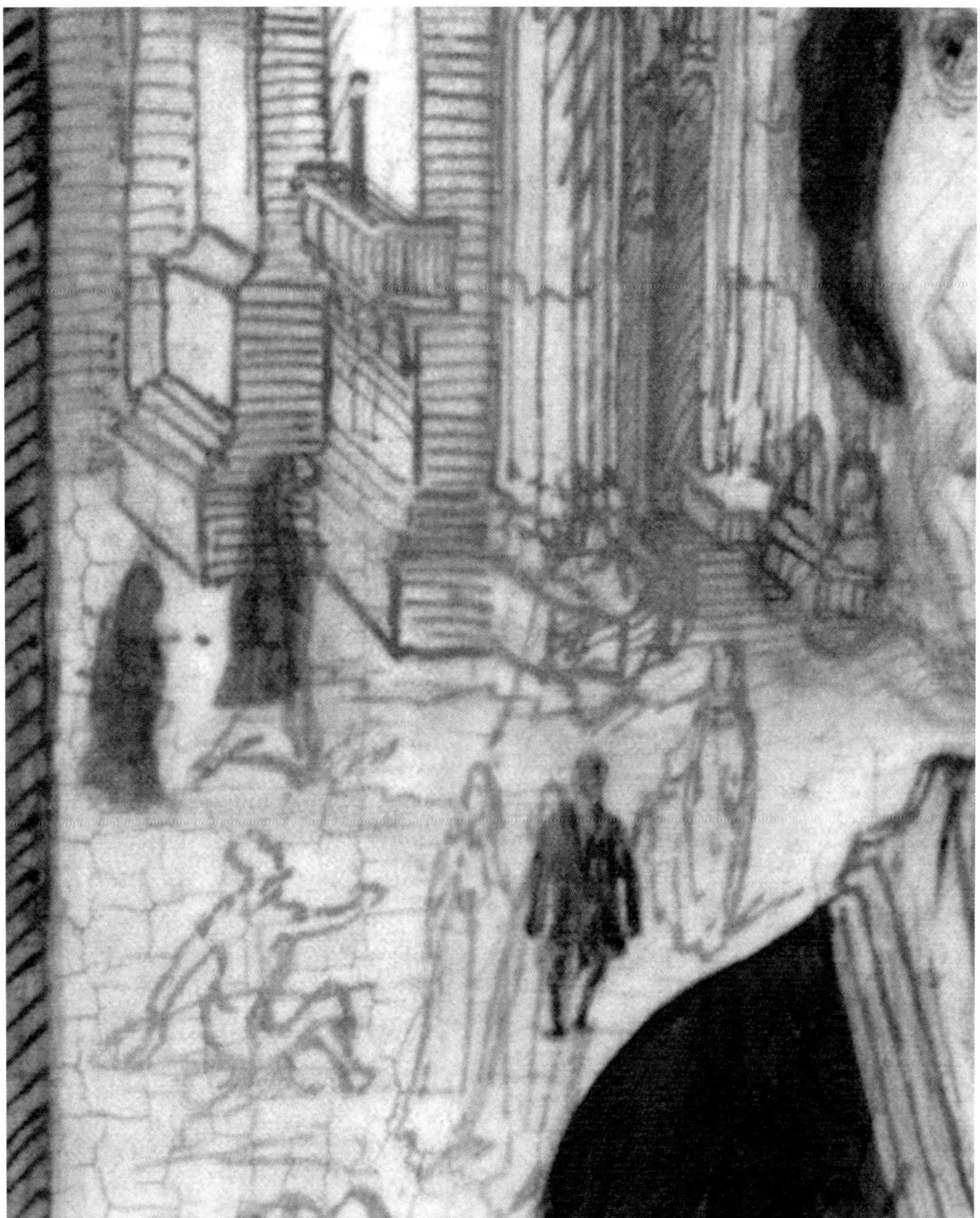

Fig. 191
Detail of Fig. 190

Fig. 192
X-radiograph of Fig. 186

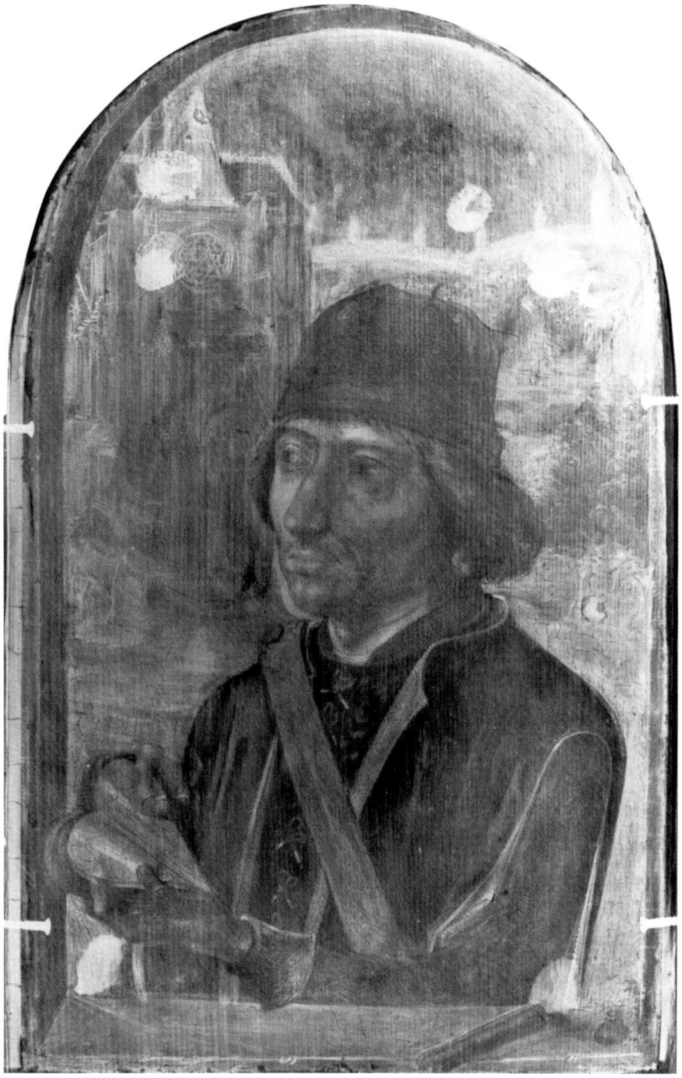

side of his face. In the underdrawing his chin is rather smaller than the painted one, but the artist seems at one stage to have experimented with an even larger chin: in the X-radiograph the lighter area of an earlier painted chin can be seen on the left of his completed mouth and chin (Fig. 192). The fingers of both his hands have been rearranged.

Such alterations may have been made in order to improve the likeness and to tighten up the composition. Though the figure of the young man would always have dominated by virtue of its scale, its strong colours and its deep tone, there had been a danger that the background might have become overcrowded with distracting incident.

LC

6 Master of the Life of the Virgin

active second half of the 15th century

The Conversion of Saint Hubert, *c.*1480

Oil on oak, 123.9 × 83 cm
NG 252

The Master of the Life of the Virgin is named after a series of panels depicting the Life of the Virgin, seven of which are in the Alte Pinakothek Munich, and one (*The Presentation in the Temple*) is in the National Gallery, London; these are datable to the mid-1470s. A great many paintings in similar styles appear to have been produced in the workshop of this painter using a number of assistants and a repertoire of common patterns. The workshop, one of the largest and most important in Cologne in the last three decades of the fifteenth century, adopted many figure and compositional patterns from near-contemporary Netherlandish painters such as Rogier van der Weyden and Dieric Bouts.

The painting is one of two panels from an otherwise lost altarpiece made for the important abbey church of Werden in the Rhineland. These have since been split into four. Two of the panels show scenes from the Life of Saint Hubert – *The Mass of Saint Hubert* and the *Conversion* and two, which must have formed the reverses, show saints; all are in the National Gallery (NG 250–3; Figs 193–195). The story of the Conversion relates how the nobleman Hubert (d.727) turned to the monastic life. Rather than praying or fasting during Holy Week, he had gone out hunting in the Forest of the Ardennes where he saw a

Fig. 193 (bottom left)
WORKSHOP OF THE MASTER OF THE LIFE OF THE VIRGIN, *The Mass of Saint Hubert* [NG 253], *c.*1480. Oil on oak, 123.9 × 83 cm

Fig. 194
WORKSHOP OF THE MASTER OF THE LIFE OF THE VIRGIN, *Saints Jerome, Bernard(?), Giles and Benedict* [NG 250], probably 1485–90. Oil on canvas, transferred from wood, 123.8 × 82.5 cm

Fig. 195
WORKSHOP OF THE MASTER OF THE LIFE OF THE VIRGIN, *Saints Augustine, Ludger(?), Hubert and Gereon(?)* [NG 251], probably 1485–90. Oil on oak, 123.8 × 82.2 cm

Fig. 196 (opposite)
MASTER OF THE LIFE OF THE VIRGIN, *The Conversion of Saint Hubert* [NG 252], *c.*1480

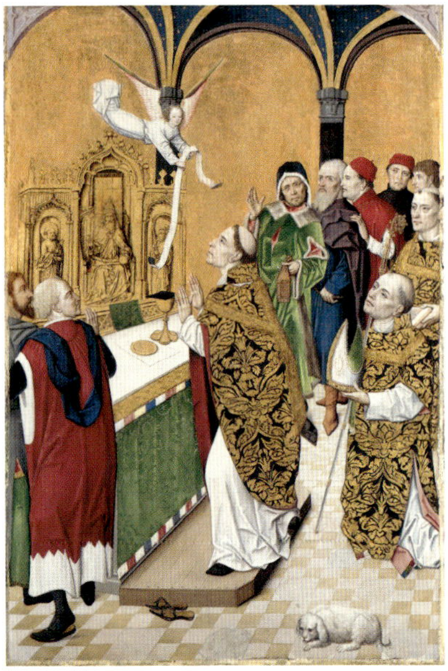

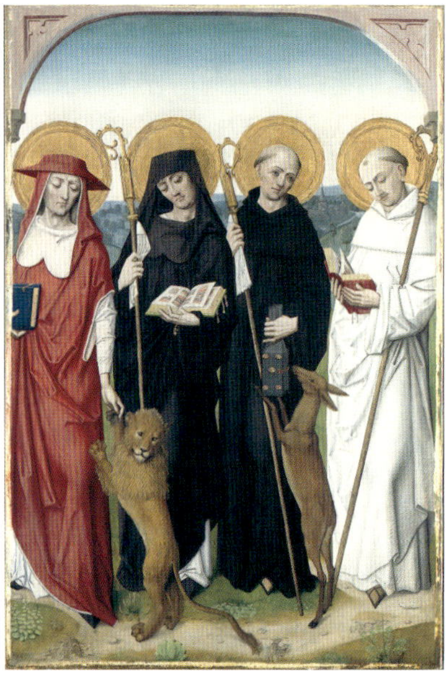

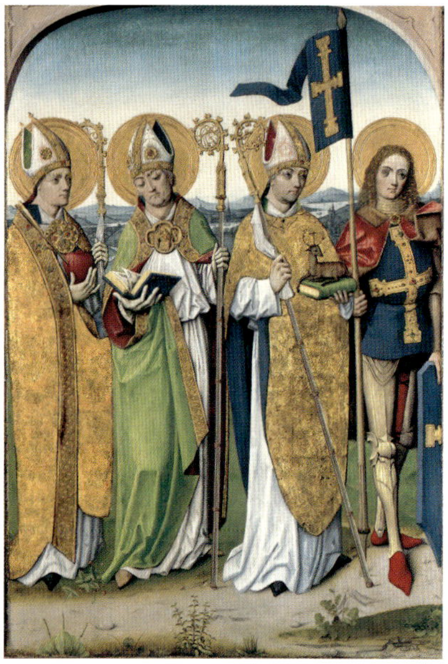

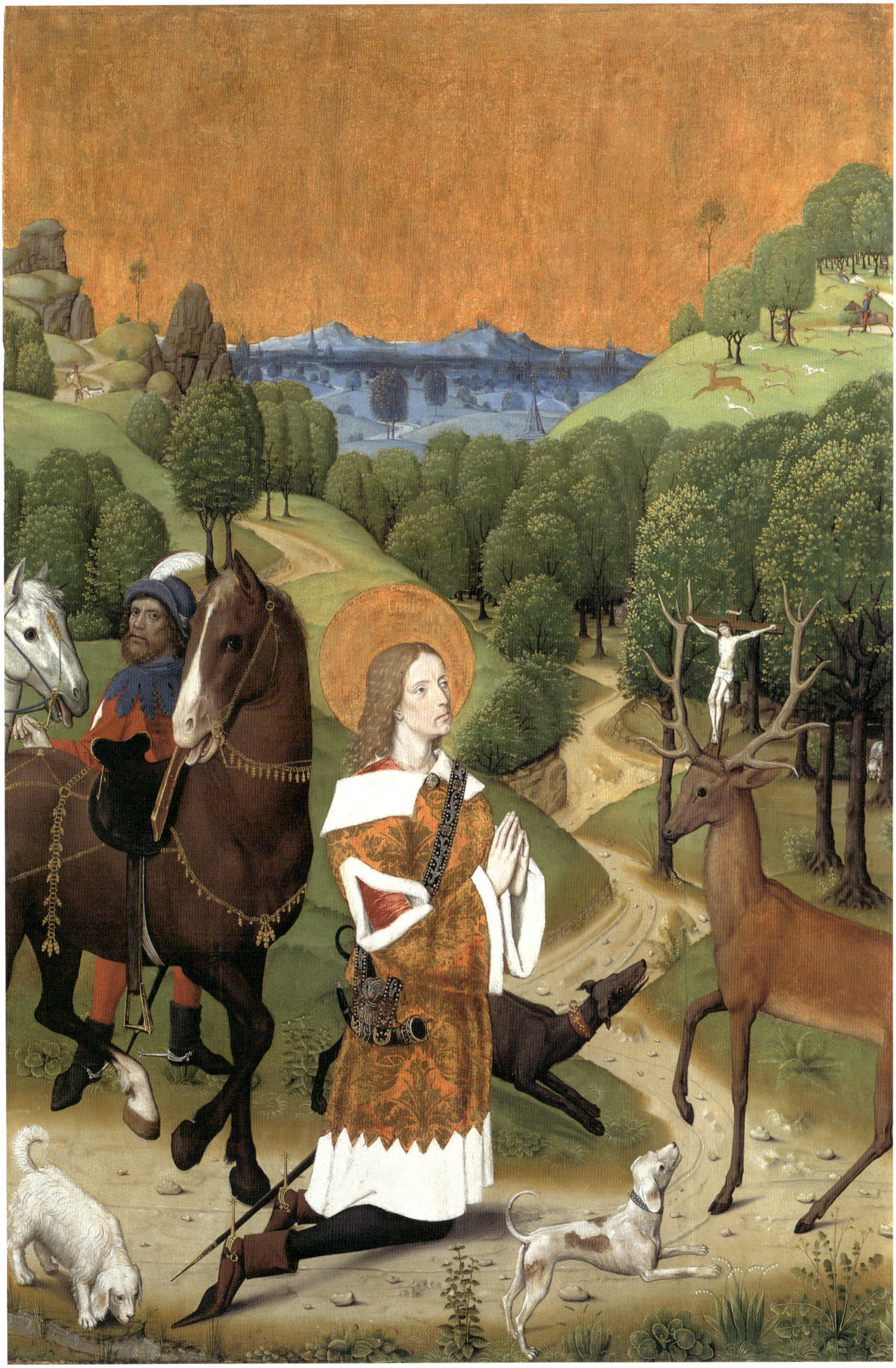

7 Workshop of the Master of the Saint Bartholomew Altarpiece

active *c.*1470 to *c.*1510

The Virgin and Child with Musical Angels, *c.*1500

Oil on oak, 53.6 × 37.4 cm
NG 6499

THE MASTER OF THE SAINT BARTHOLOMEW ALTARPIECE was the most important painter working in Cologne at the end of the fifteenth century. He is named after an altarpiece now in the Alte Pinakothek, Munich. He carried out two altarpiece commissions for the Carthusian Church in Cologne and his patronage appears to have extended beyond Cologne to the Northern Netherlands, so he must have had a large workshop. The range of work produced included manuscript illumination as well as panel painting.

Fig. 203
WORKSHOP OF THE MASTER OF THE SAINT BARTHOLOMEW ALTARPIECE, *The Virgin and Child with Musical Angels* [NG 6499], *c.*1500

This small devotional painting depicts the Virgin as Queen of Heaven. The Latin inscription on the scroll held by the singing angels at the top of the picture reads: *regia.celi.letare* (The Queen of Heaven rejoice). Other angels play musical instruments in accompaniment, while one on the left scatters flower petals.

The painting is particularly rich in the number and combination of allusions it evokes: the columbine shown growing in the foreground was a symbol of the Virgin, and in the glass vase on the right are blue cornflowers, also associated with the Virgin, and deep pink carnations, a flower sometimes known as the 'nailflower', which symbolised Christ's sacrifice on the cross. The Virgin appears to look down towards this vase, as though meditating on the future sacrifice of her son. The sharpened shapes in the gilded tracery border at the top of the picture may be intended as simplified thorns. The mingled themes of joy for the mother of Christ and sorrow at the thought of their future suffering are characteristic of devotional literature in the fifteenth century. The morse or brooch which fastens the cope of the central singing angel for example includes a tiny image of God the Father, who in other compositions of this type looks down on the scene of rejoicing.
The owner of the painting would have used it to assist in prayer and meditation on these themes.

There is an extremely detailed underdrawing in a liquid medium, applied with a brush and apparently freehand (Fig. 204). The forms are outlined, and hatching and cross-hatching used to indicate shadows. Much of the hatching consists of short comma-like strokes Fig. 207). The edges of the folds of drapery are created

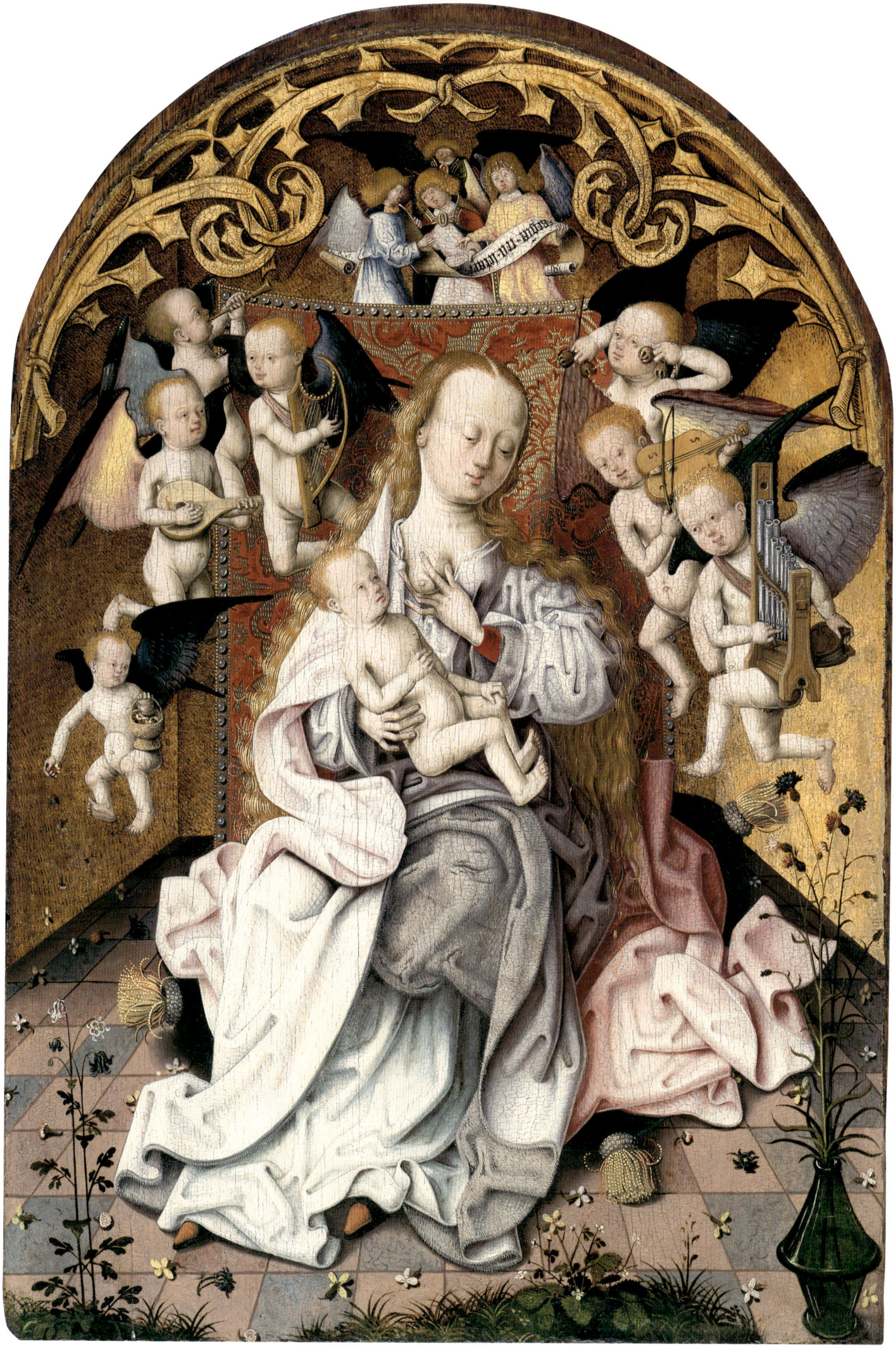

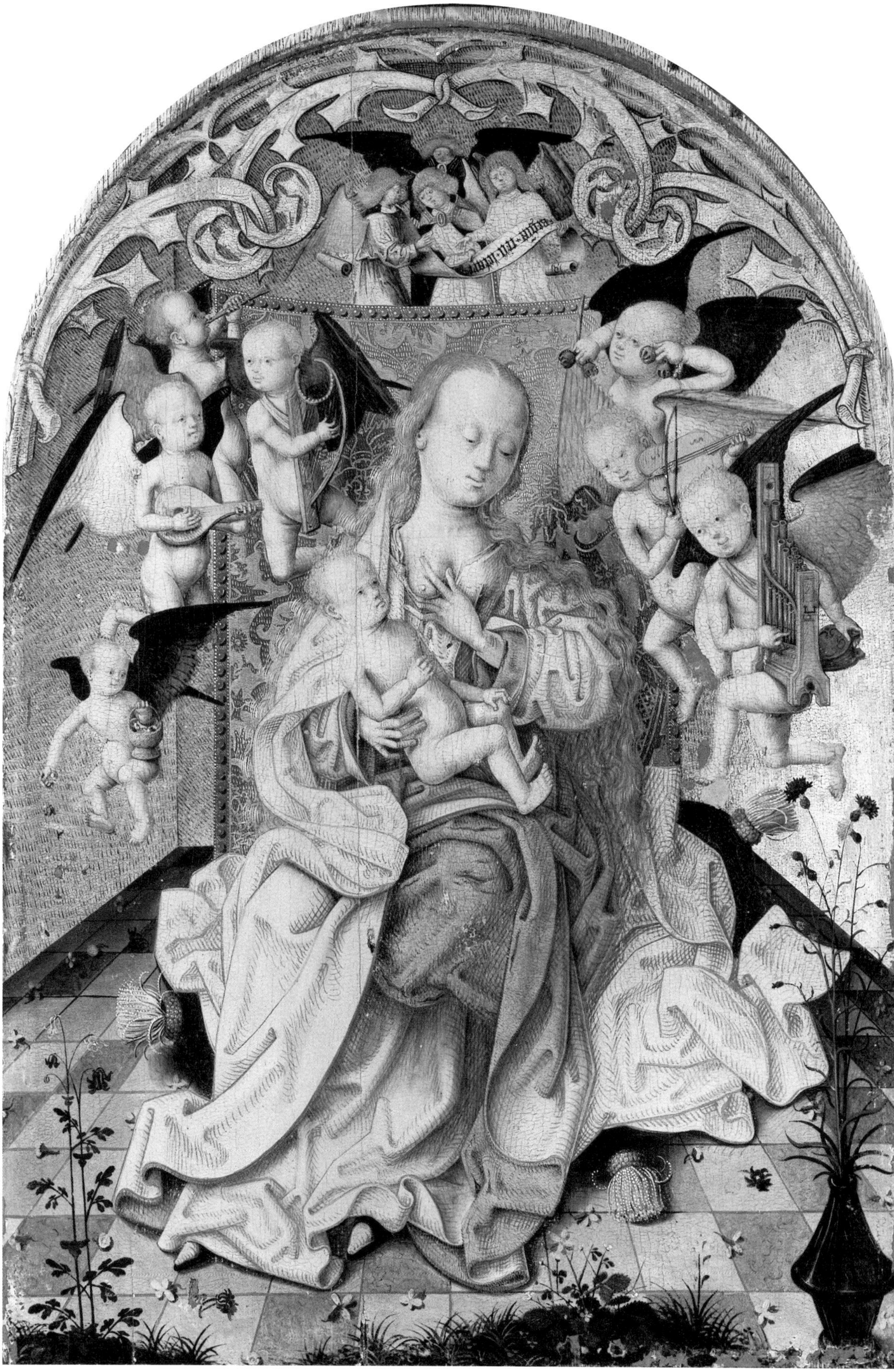

Fig. 204 (left)
Infrared photograph of Fig. 203

Fig. 205 (below)
THE MASTER OF THE SAINT BARTHOLOMEW ALTARPIECE,
The Virgin and Child with Saint Agnes, *c*.1495
Oak, 41.2 × 33 cm
Nüremberg, Germanisches Nationalmuseum
inv. Gm 1634

Fig. 206 (below right)
WORKSHOP OF THE MASTER OF THE SAINT BARTHOLOMEW ALTARPIECE,
The Madonna and Child with Saint Anne, and Saints Augustine and Jerome
Wood, 33.6 × 25.4 cm
Waddesdon, The National Trust, The Rothschild Collection

with continuous lines ending in hooks, along which, set at right angles, are neat sequences of short, curved parallel hatching. Variations in the spacing and thickness of the hatching indicate variations in the depth of shadow, with cross-hatching used for deeper shadow. Areas of cast shadow on the floor are hatched. The green vase is drawn, but not the plants or the scattered flowers.

Paintings associated with the Master of the Saint Bartholomew Altarpiece are characterised by the presence of extremely detailed underdrawings, making extensive use of hatching and cross-hatching. The underdrawing of the *Virgin and Child with Musical Angels* is particularly notable for the degree of precision used: there are no alterations visible, either to the drawing or at the painting stage, and it is clear that the composition was established from the start, and must have followed workshop models.

There is no single exactly similar composition to the *Virgin and Child with Musical Angels* elsewhere in the group of paintings associated with the Master of the Saint Bartholomew Altarpiece. Nor has an engraving been discovered which corresponds with the composition here. However, there is an obvious relationship with parts of other pictures by the Master or the workshop which implies that patterns were used to create this composition and to vary it from others. For example the Virgin's head is similar to that of Saint Agnes in a painting now in Nuremberg (Fig. 205) – though Saint Agnes is in reverse – as well as to the Virgins in paintings of the Virgin and Child in Darmstadt, Cologne (the Saint Thomas altarpiece), Frankfurt and Waddesdon. The position of the child is similar to the child in the picture at Waddesdon (Fig. 206), in reverse, and its head is similar to the child in the Saint Agnes picture. Similar deductions can be made in relation to the angels and the musical instruments.

As the precision of the underdrawing indicates, patterns incorporating these various motifs had already been prepared before the underdrawing stage, and might well have been those used to make other versions of the painting. Such compositional patterns would have been transferred to the prepared panel by

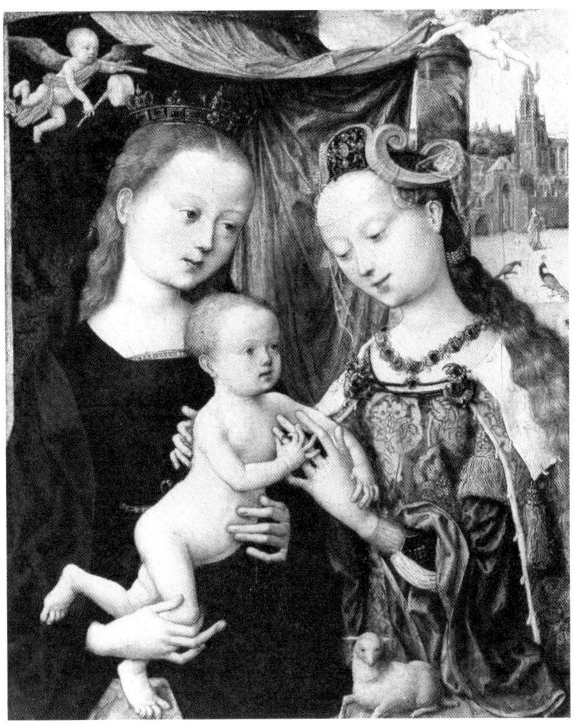

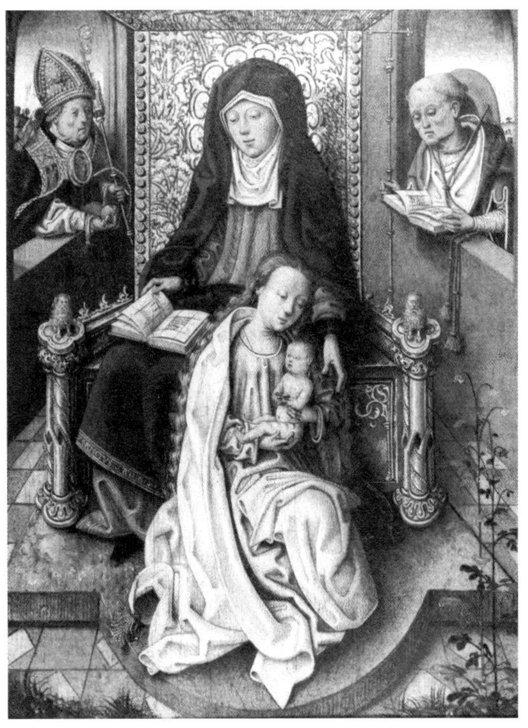

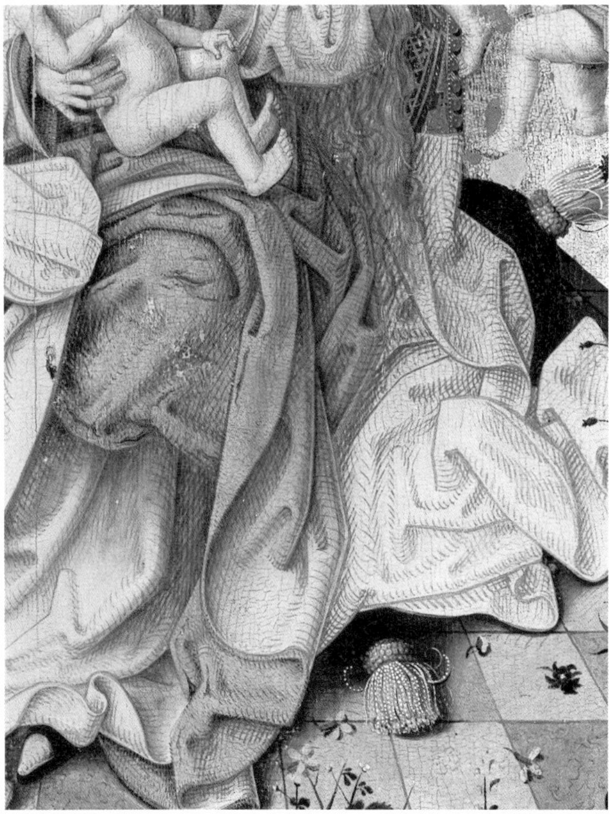

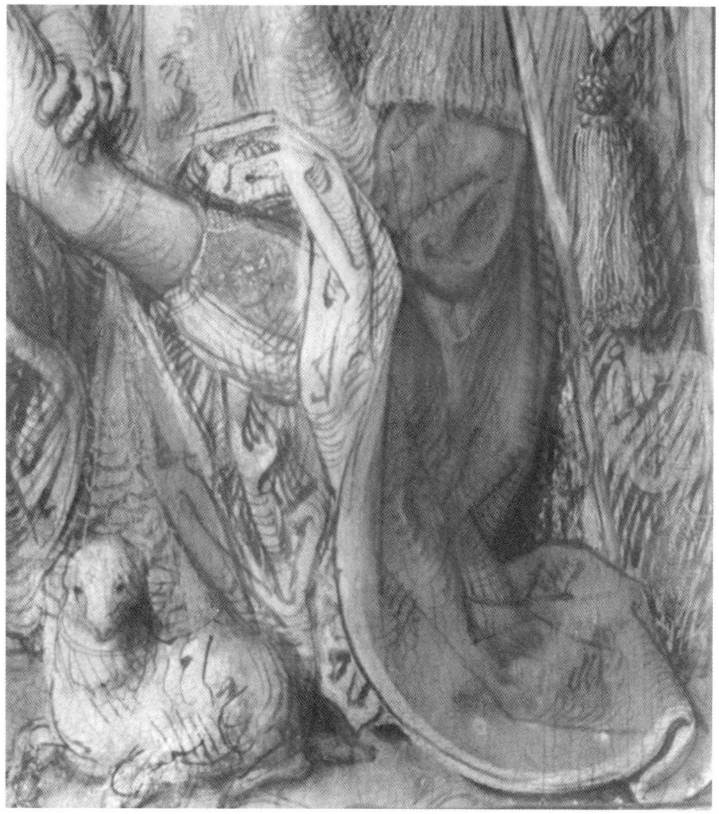

Fig. 207 (left)
Detail of Fig. 204

Fig. 208
Infrared reflectogram mosaic, detail of Fig. 205.
IRR © Prof. Dr Molly Faries/Stichting RKD; assembled by Rachel Billinge. Courtesy Germanisches Nationalmuseum, Nuremberg

tracing or some other mechanical means. In the small painting of the *Virgin and Child with a Nut* in Cologne (Fig. 209) there appears to have been a first outline underdrawing of the composition with chalk beneath the detailed brush drawing, which itself shows a number of alterations and adjustments. In the National Gallery painting the only indication of preparation for the composition is found in the fact that the tiles on the floor are ruled with lightly incised lines; in other compositions from the Master of the Saint Bartholomew Altarpiece group, including the *Virgin with a Nut*, a number of positional incision lines have been observed.

When the underdrawing of the *Virgin and Child with Musical Angels* is compared to other works associated with the Master of the Saint Bartholomew Altarpiece, in particular the large altarpieces, the greater freedom in the style of underdrawing in these other works is clear. The *Saints Peter and Dorothy* in the National Gallery, for example, which is the shutter from a large altarpiece, has a similar system of hatching and cross-hatching with parallel lines, but the underdrawing is far more complex, and a great deal less neat: hatching lines frequently cross the boundaries of contour and fold lines, while still making a controlled contribution to the depiction of shadow (Fig. 210). A similar freedom and assurance in underdrawing and in the making of changes are also seen in some small devotional paintings, such as the *Virgin and Child with a Nut* and the *Virgin and Child with Saint Agnes* (Fig. 208),

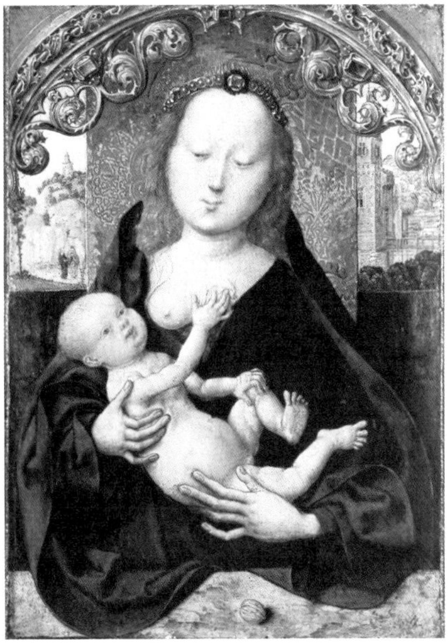

both of which are exceptionally refined in their painted surface. A system of underdrawing which has much in common with that in the National Gallery picture with its carefully arranged parallel hatching at right angles to outlines of folds and forms can be seen in some other small pictures associated with the Master of the Saint Bartholomew Altarpiece, but these are usually attributed to the workshop on the grounds of their inferior quality.

It seems unlikely that the underdrawing of the National Gallery picture was the work of the Saint Bartholomew Master himself, given its schematic nature and the clear differences from those with a more complex and ambitious underdrawing. However, if the *Virgin and Child with Musical Angels* was not executed by the Master, who was certainly responsible for the *Virgin and Child with a Nut* and the *Virgin with Saint Agnes*, it is by an extremely talented member of his workshop.

SF

Fig. 209 (above)
THE MASTER OF THE SAINT BARTHOLOMEW ALTARPIECE,
The Virgin and Child with a Nut, c.1485
Oak, 31.2 × 21.7 cm
Cologne, Wallraf-Richartz-Museum, 200258

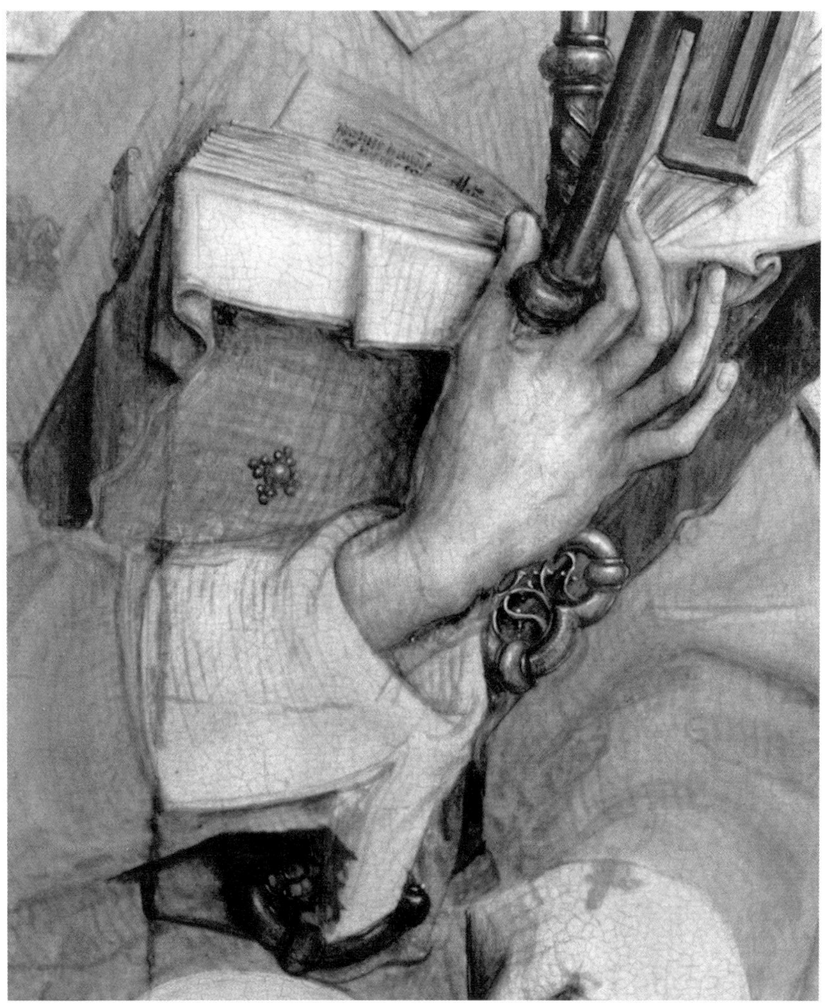

Fig. 210
THE MASTER OF THE SAINT BARTHOLOMEW ALTARPIECE,
Saints Peter and Dorothy [NG 707],
infrared reflectogram mosaic, detail

8 Raphael (Raffaello Santi)

1483–1520

The Procession to Calvary, *c.*1504

Egg tempera and walnut oil on wood
24.4 × 85.5 cm
NG 2919

RAPHAEL was born in Urbino, where his father, Giovanni Santi, was court painter. As a youth, Raphael probably spent a period in the workshop of Perugino. He went on to paint altarpieces for churches in Umbria and Tuscany, as well as exquisite small-scale works for courtly patrons. His style was transformed by his study of works by Leonardo and Michelangelo in Florence. He was summoned to Rome in 1508 to work for Pope Julius II, whose library and private apartments (the Stanze) he decorated with monumental frescoes in a grand classical style. His friends were intellectuals, poets and members of the papal court, who shared his interest in antiquity. He ran a large workshop, which increasingly carried out the commissions he received according to his designs. After Julius's death he was retained at the court of Pope Leo X and also worked for important private patrons, painting frescoes, portraits, altarpieces, and designing tapestries and buildings. His amorous exploits were said to have been the cause of his premature death, at the age of thirty-seven.

Fig. 211
RAPHAEL, *The Procession to Calvary* [NG 2919], *c.*1504

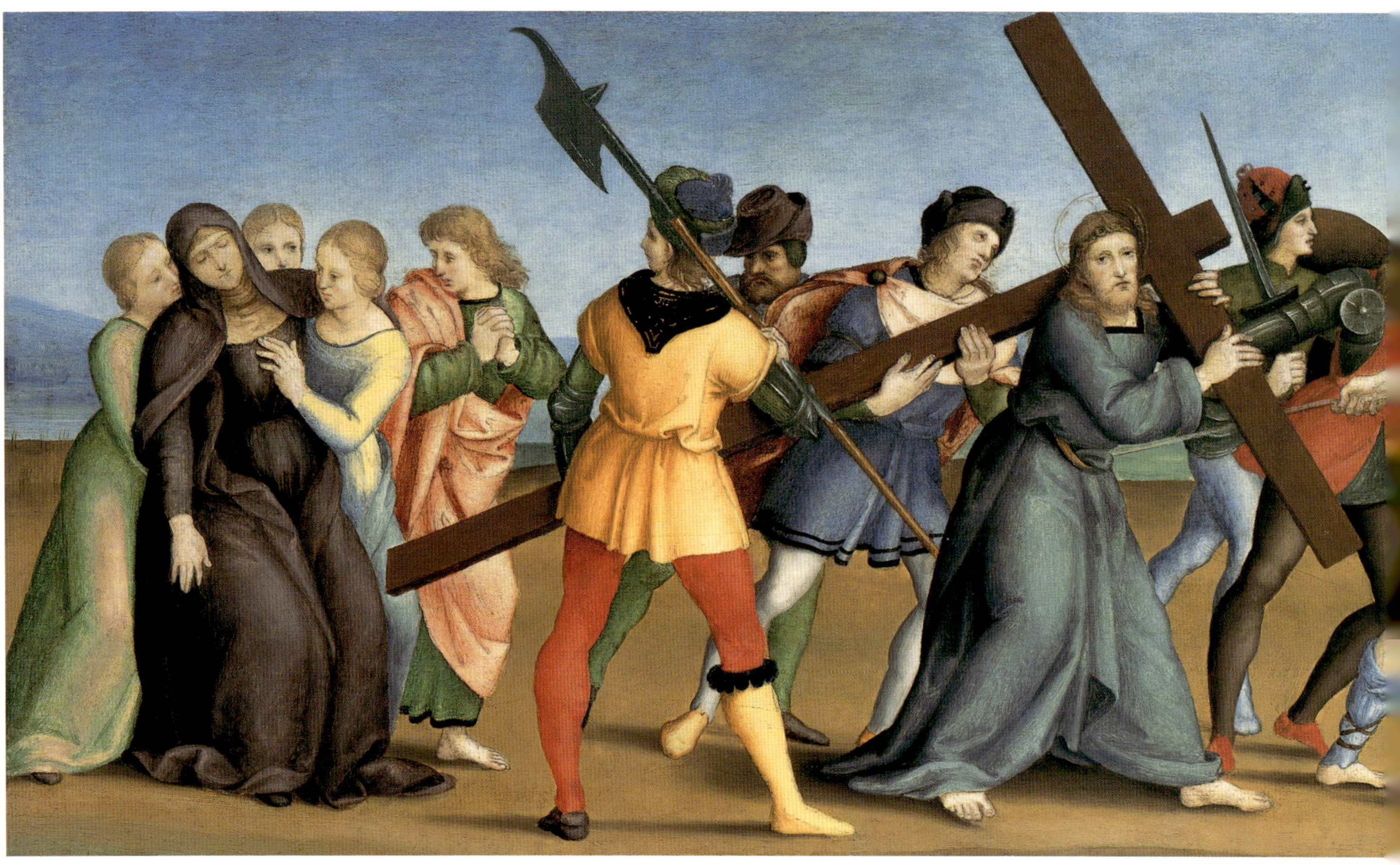

The *Procession to Calvary* shows the scene mentioned briefly in all four Gospels in which Christ, having been interrogated by Pilate and condemned to death by the crowd, is led away to Golgotha to be crucified. Christ, carrying the cross, is accompanied by five foot-soldiers, one of whom drags him along by a rope. Behind him, Simon of Cyrene helps bear the weight of the cross. The procession is led by two horsemen, the foremost of whom is turbaned and carries a standard. On the left, the Virgin Mary, fainting at the spectacle, is supported by the other three Maries. Saint John the Evangelist, beside her, wrings his hands in distress.

The *Procession to Calvary* was the centrepiece of the predella of an altarpiece painted by Raphael for the Franciscan church of Sant' Antonio, Perugia. The main panel, showing the *Madonna and Child enthroned with Saints* (Fig. 213), along with a lunette depicting *God the Father blessing with Two Angels*, are in the Metropolitan Museum of Art, New York. Five elements of the predella survive. The *Procession to Calvary* was originally flanked on the left by the *Agony in the Garden* (also in the Metropolitan Museum; Fig. 214) and on the right by the *Pietà* (Boston, Isabella Stewart Gardner Museum). Two smaller panels depicting the Franciscan saints Francis and Anthony of Padua are in the Dulwich Picture Gallery. There are no documents for the commission, but the altarpiece was most likely carried out by Raphael between 1503 and 1505. It remained intact *in situ* until 1663 when the nuns of Sant' Antonio sold the predella to an agent of Queen Christina of Sweden. A few years later (1677–8), they also sold the main panel and lunette to Antonio Bigazzini of Perugia, who in turn sold them to the Colonna family in Rome (the altarpiece subsequently became known as the 'Pala Colonna').

The panel with the *Procession to Calvary* consists of a single plank of wood, probably poplar, horizontal in grain, with a slight convex warp. The gesso ground is covered by a creamy-white priming, composed of lead white mixed with a small amount of lead-tin yellow. This priming mixture, apparently favoured by Raphael,

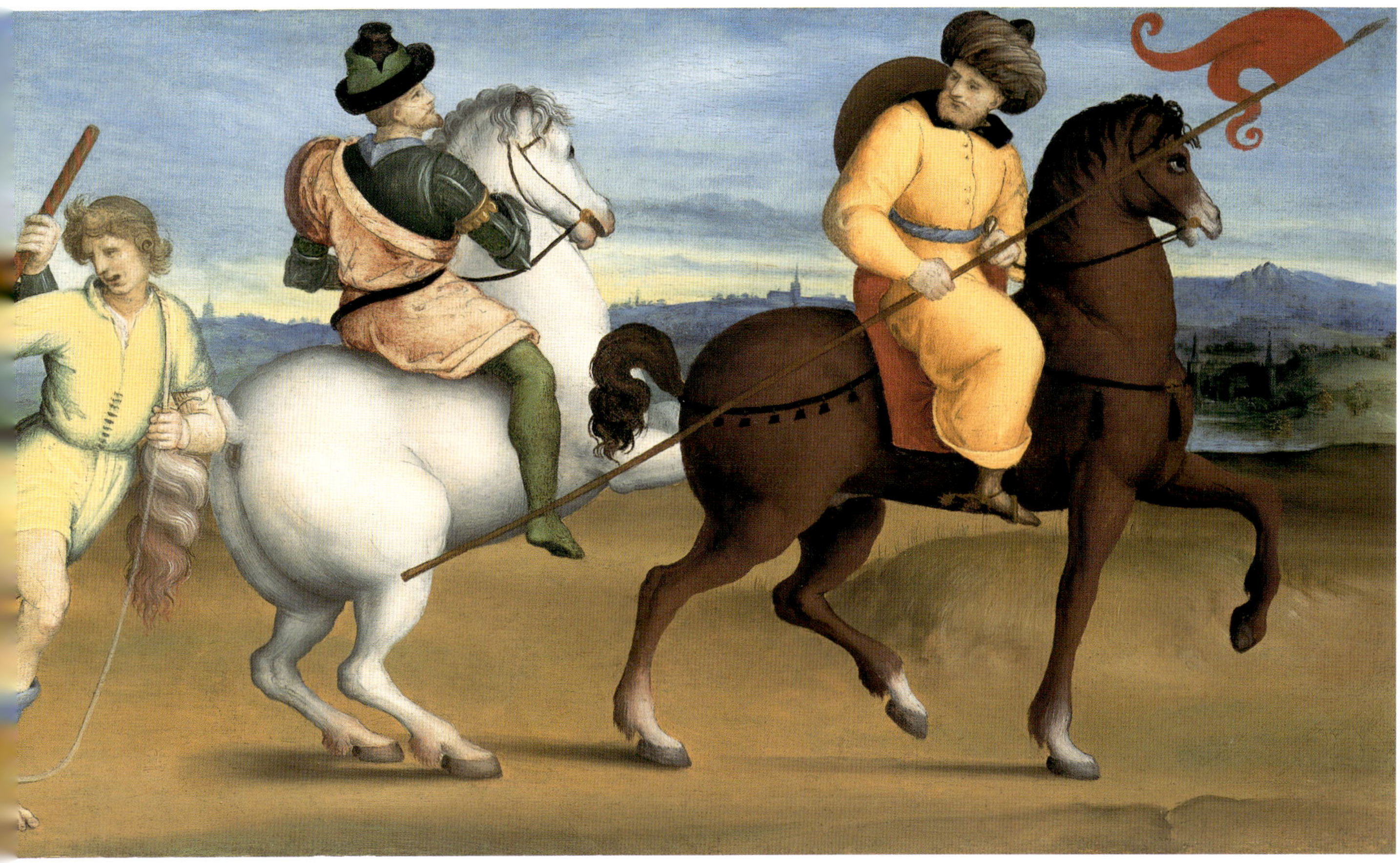

has been observed on three other paintings by him in the National Gallery: the *Garvagh Madonna* (Cat. 9), the *Mond Crucifixion* (NG 3943) and the predella of the *Ansidei Madonna* depicting *Saint John the Baptist Preaching* (NG 6480). It was, however, also used by other artists, not just in Italy.

The infrared reflectogram mosaic (Fig. 212) reveals that the composition was bisected horizontally and vertically with ruled lines in what appears to be a dry black material. These lines may have helped with the alignment of the cartoon that was used to transfer the design to the panel, though such marks are present in many other drawings and underdrawings by Raphael (see Cat. 9), regardless of whether the design was to be transferred or not. Raphael seems frequently to have marked out his compositional fields in this way before embarking on a work, to assist him in laying out the design (here for example the horizontal establishes the waist level for all the figures on foot). The reflectogram confirms that a pricked cartoon was used, since traces of pouncing are clearly evident beneath the underdrawn outlines of the figures (see for example Fig. 219). Although the cartoon for the *Procession to Calvary* does not survive, a pricked cartoon for the flanking predella scene of the *Agony in the Garden*, in the Pierpont Morgan Library, New York (Fig. 215), offers further evidence that this was indeed the method of transfer used for these small narrative paintings.

The reflectogram of the *Procession to Calvary* reveals that the lost cartoon must have been very extensively pricked, with large numbers of closely spaced holes along every outline. Such painstaking pricking is evident in many surviving cartoons for Raphael's small-scale paintings of this period. Two outstanding examples are the cartoon for the National Gallery's '*Vision of a Knight*' of 1504–5 (Figs 217 and 218), and that in the Uffizi for the *Saint George* in the National Gallery of Art, Washington, of 1505–6. The delicacy and sensitivity of the pricking in these and

Fig. 212 (below)
Infrared reflectogram mosaic of Fig. 211

Fig. 213 (right)
RAPHAEL, *Colonna Altarpiece*
Madonna and Child Enthroned, with Saints
Tempera, oil, gold on wood, 172.4 × 172.4 cm
New York, The Metropolitan Museum of Art
Gift of J. Pierpont Morgan, 1916
inv. 16.30a

Fig. 214
RAPHAEL, *Colonna Altarpiece*
Predella panel: *The Agony in the Garden*
Tempera and oil on wood, 24.1 × 28.9 cm
New York, The Metropolitan Museum of Art
Funds from various donors, 1932
inv. 32.130.1

Fig. 215
RAPHAEL, Cartoon for *The Agony in the Garden*
Pen and wash, pricked for transfer, 22.6 × 26.5 cm
New York, The Pierpont Morgan Library, inv. I,15

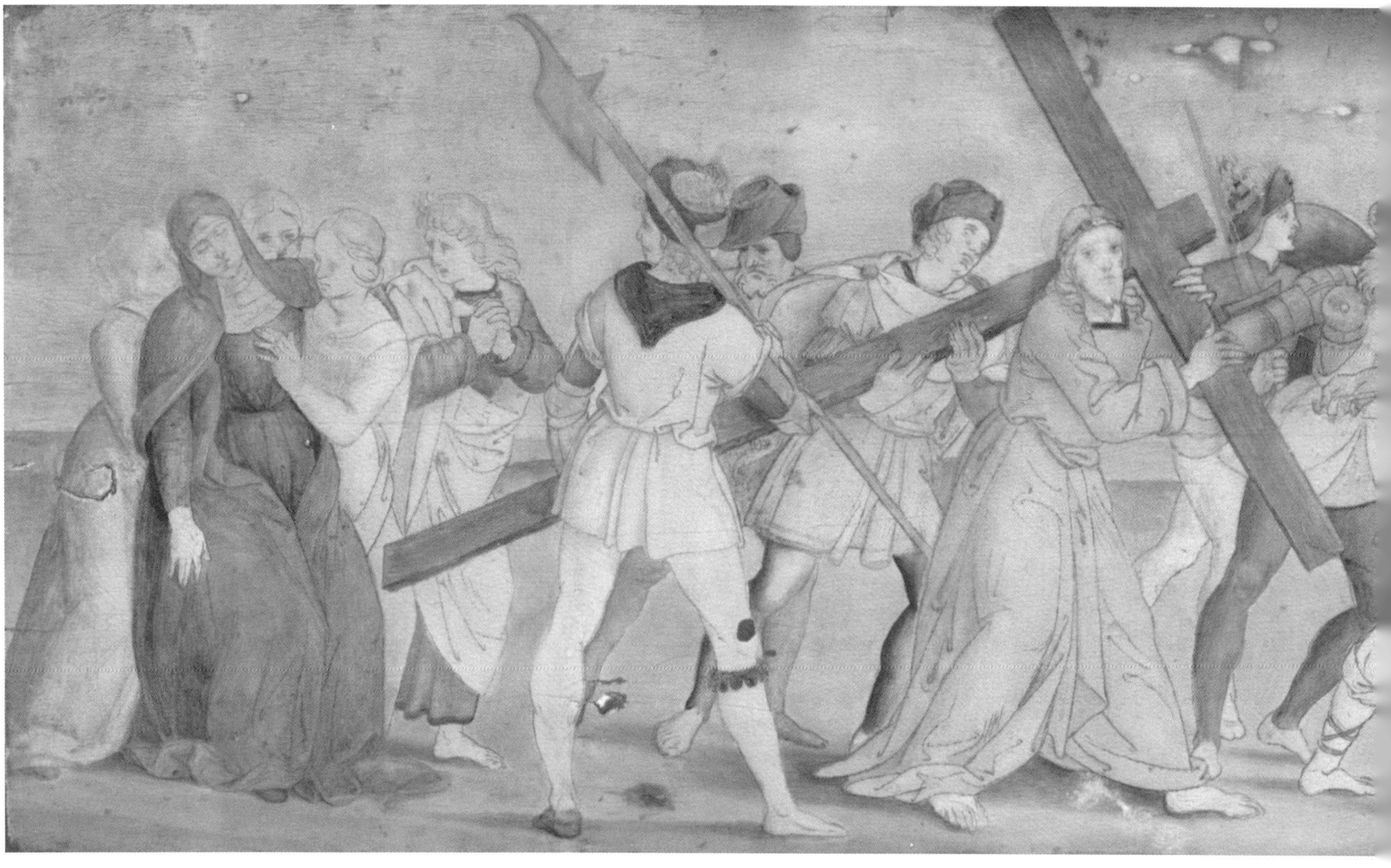

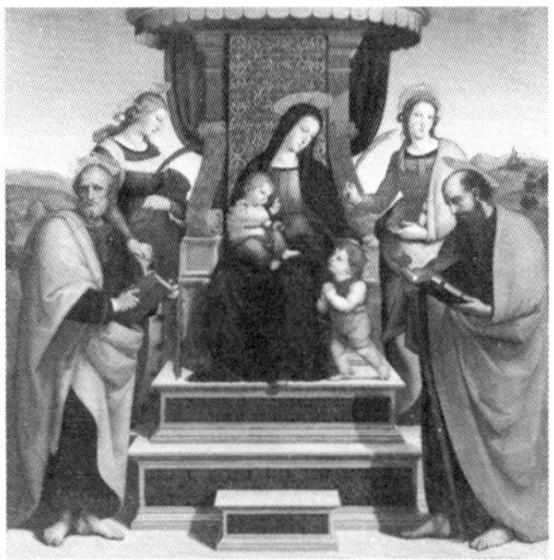

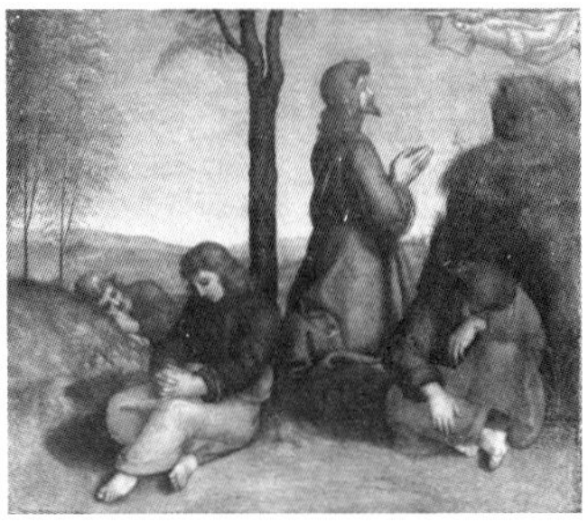

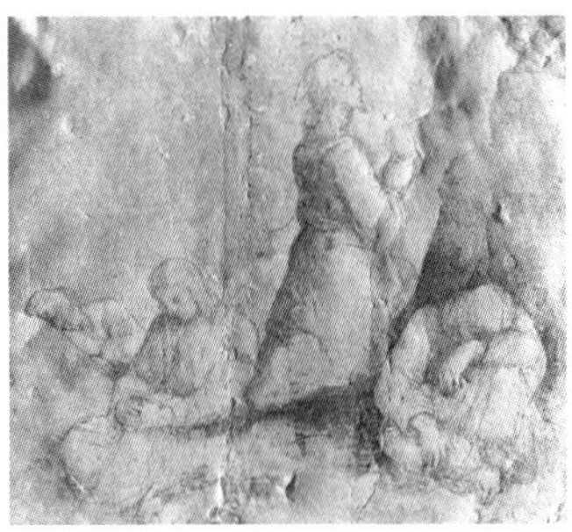

other examples suggest that Raphael consistently carried out the transfer of the designs himself (the quality of his cartoons is such that Raphael might reasonably have been reluctant to delegate this invasive and potentially hazardous procedure to an assistant). In the case of the *Procession to Calvary*, it is remarkable just how many outlines Raphael actually pricked. Every drapery fold (right down to the Peruginesque pot-hook flourishes at their ends), and each curl of hair, was anticipated with a dense sequence of underlying pounced dots. The way in which they were subsequently joined with a fine line in a liquid medium is characteristic of Raphael's own drawing style. Raphael's cartoons always include indications of light and shade, conveyed either by hatching and cross-hatching when using pen, or a mixture of hatching and stumping (smudging) when using chalk. However, since only the linear elements of a composition could be reproduced by pouncing, Raphael frequently added freehand hatchings to his transferred designs, to provide additional modelling. These touches are well illustrated in the underdrawing of the *Procession to Calvary*, in the soldier dragging Christ (Fig. 219), whose figure is enlivened by passages of rapid parallel hatching in the folds down the right side of his torso, and in the flesh above and below his left knee, as well as by cross-hatching in the folds of his tunic where it billows out from his hips.

Features in the *Procession to Calvary* that required geometrical instruments such as a ruler and compass were omitted from the cartoon stage (that is, they were not pounced) and were incised into the gesso with a fine needle-like point after the design had been transferred. The haloes of Christ, the Virgin and the Holy Woman behind her left shoulder were incised with the aid of a compass (the two other Holy Women and Saint John do not have incised haloes).

In addition to these minor interventions, Raphael introduced certain more fundamental modifications to the composition thus far delineated. It appears, for instance, that in the cartoon, the Virgin was supported by only one of the Holy

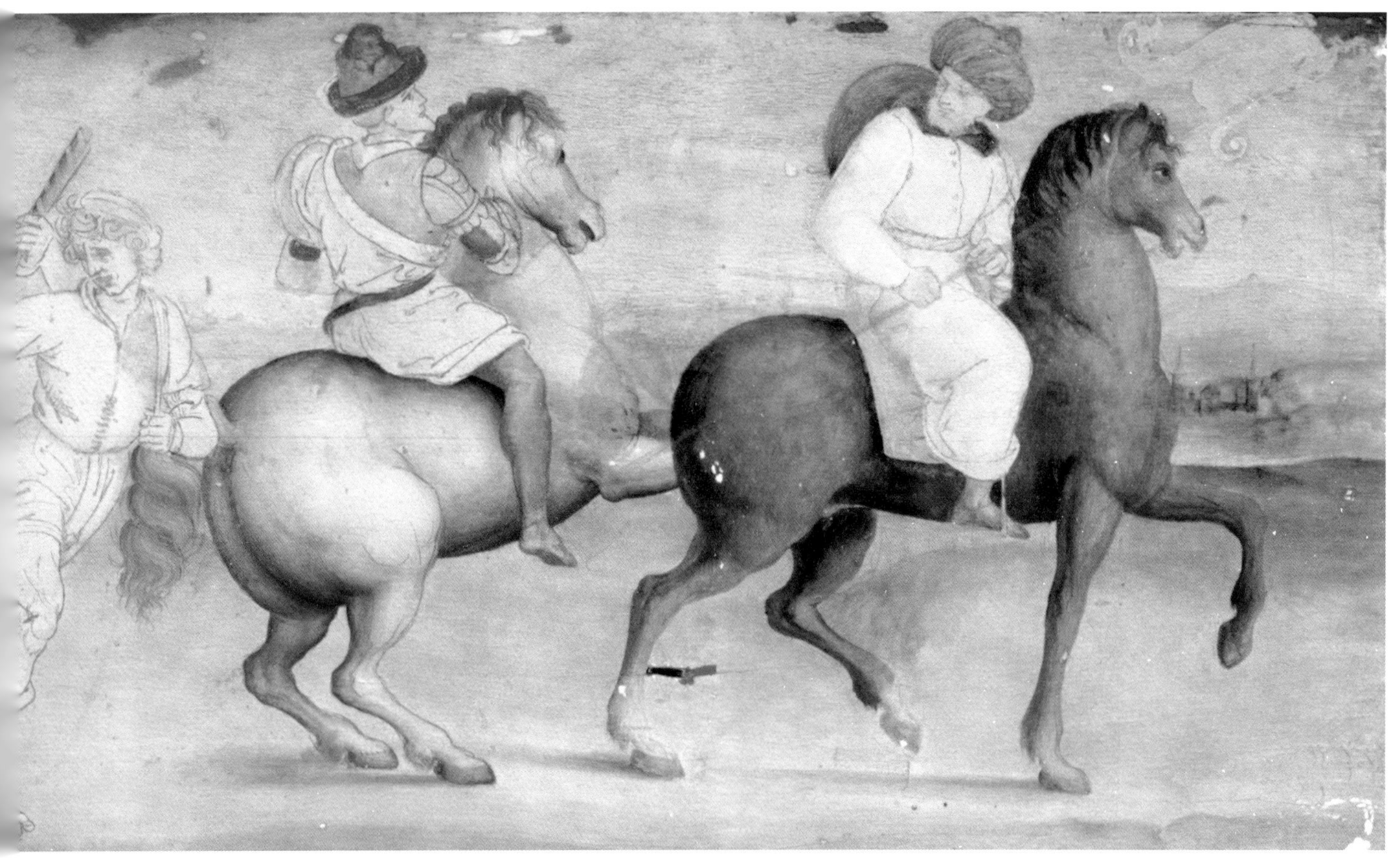

Women (the one who bears the Virgin's arm on her shoulder), with Saint John the Evangelist looking on. This can be deduced from the fact that there is no trace of pouncing beneath the female figures whose heads flank that of the Virgin (Fig. 216). Raphael drew these two figures directly onto the panel around his transferred design, before he began painting. He subsequently left the figures in reserve, painting the sky and ground around their drawn contours. The underdrawing for both these figures is more fluent in appearance than the lines joining up the pounced dots, and there is a *pentimento* for the leg of the woman on the left, offering further evidence that she was a late addition to the transferred design. The fact that the incised profile of the Virgin's halo passes through her head confirms this.

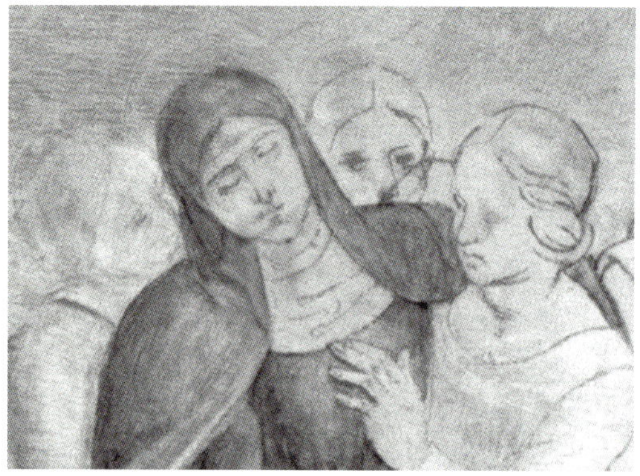

Although pounced dots are clearly evident beneath the contours of the two horsemen, their mounts do not appear to have been transferred using a cartoon. In fact, there are faint indications of changes to the positions of the horses' legs, implying a more freehand type of drawing. It is odd that the riders should have been transferred to the panel independently of their mounts, and the reason for this remains a mystery.

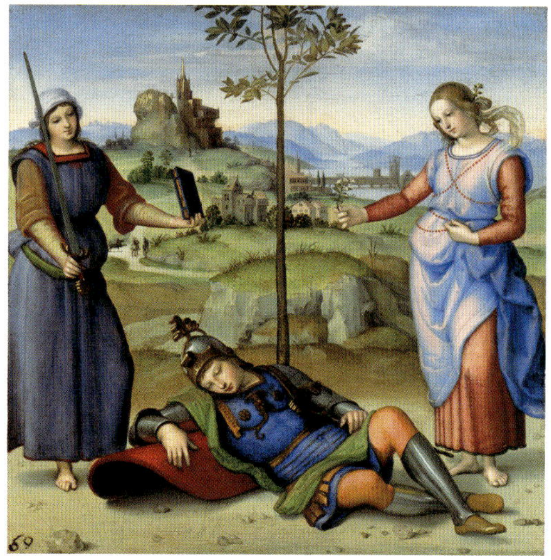

In addition to the pouncing, incisions and freehand additions, certain elements were painted directly onto the panel without any prior preparation. The most significant of these is the background landscape, which was neither transferred by pouncing nor subsequently drawn in. This implies that prior to the cartoon stage, Raphael conceived the composition purely in terms of the figures. When re-examined, these can be seen to divide into three distinct groups: the two horsemen at the front of the procession; Christ, Simon of Cyrene and the five soldiers; and the Virgin, the Holy Women and Saint John. It is therefore possible that the composition was composed using more than one cartoon. Smaller square cartoons would have been easier to store and could have been reused in a variety of permutations or combined with other cartoons for different projects. There is no underdrawing or incising beneath the brown horse's tail, and the similarly calligraphic tips of the pennant fluttering in the breeze; these were dynamic elements that Raphael knew he was going to include, but did not bother to draw in advance, presumably preferring to improvise these passages in order to convey an impression of fluidity and spontaneity. The leaves of the tree and the flower held by the voluptuous woman on the right in the *Vision of a Knight* were similarly omitted from the cartoon (Fig. 218).

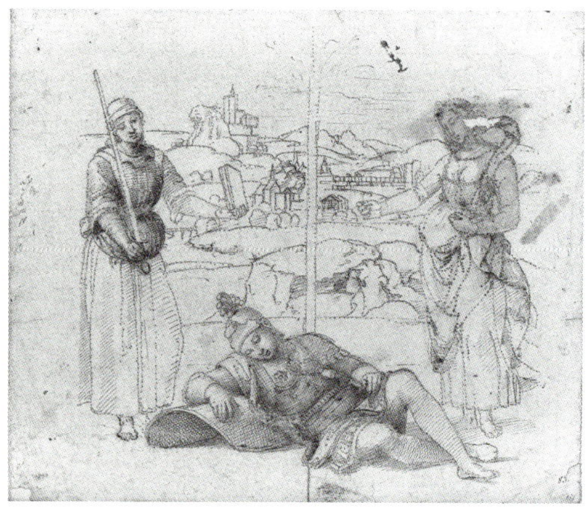

Of Raphael's numerous surviving drawings, as many as one sixth are either pricked for transfer or drawn over pounce marks, while further evidence of his systematic use of pricked cartoons is emerging as more paintings are examined with infrared reflectography. Raphael's practice of reproducing his designs by means of pouncing, as well as his use of plumblines and horizon lines for design construction, have their roots in his early association with Perugino's workshop. The tradition of design replication in Umbria and the Marches was strong and reflected the conservatism of patronage in these regions. Two features of Raphael's method are exceptional, and represent a departure from such derivative and repetitive practices. The first is the degree of personal control he exercised – at least in this early period – throughout the design and transfer process. Not only are his

Fig. 216 (left)
Detail of Fig. 212

Fig. 217
RAPHAEL, *An Allegory* (*'Vision of a Knight'*) [NG 213], *c.*1504
Tempera on poplar, 17.1 × 17.1 cm

Fig. 218
RAPHAEL, Cartoon for *An Allegory* (*'Vision of a Knight'*)
Pen over silver-point, pricked for transfer, 18.2 × 21.4 cm
London, The British Museum

Fig. 219 (below)
Detail of Fig. 212

surviving cartoons exquisite, but so also is the meticulous pricking of the outlines, which frequently affords evidence of intelligent choice in the selection of the lines to be pricked or left unpricked. The second remarkable feature of Raphael's practice is that, unlike Perugino, whom Vasari criticised for the repetitive nature of his designs, his methods of design replication were not ends in themselves, but part of an ongoing creative process. In addition to making very detailed cartoons, and faithfully transferring them to his chosen support, Raphael continued subtly to enliven, alter and improve his designs, both at the underdrawing stage, and during the course of painting, as the infrared reflectogram of the *Procession to Calvary* vividly demonstrates. It was precisely the dynamic design of this composition which caught Vasari's eye, when, in his description of the altarpiece, he singled out 'the very beautiful movements of the soldiers' in this predella panel for particular praise.

CP

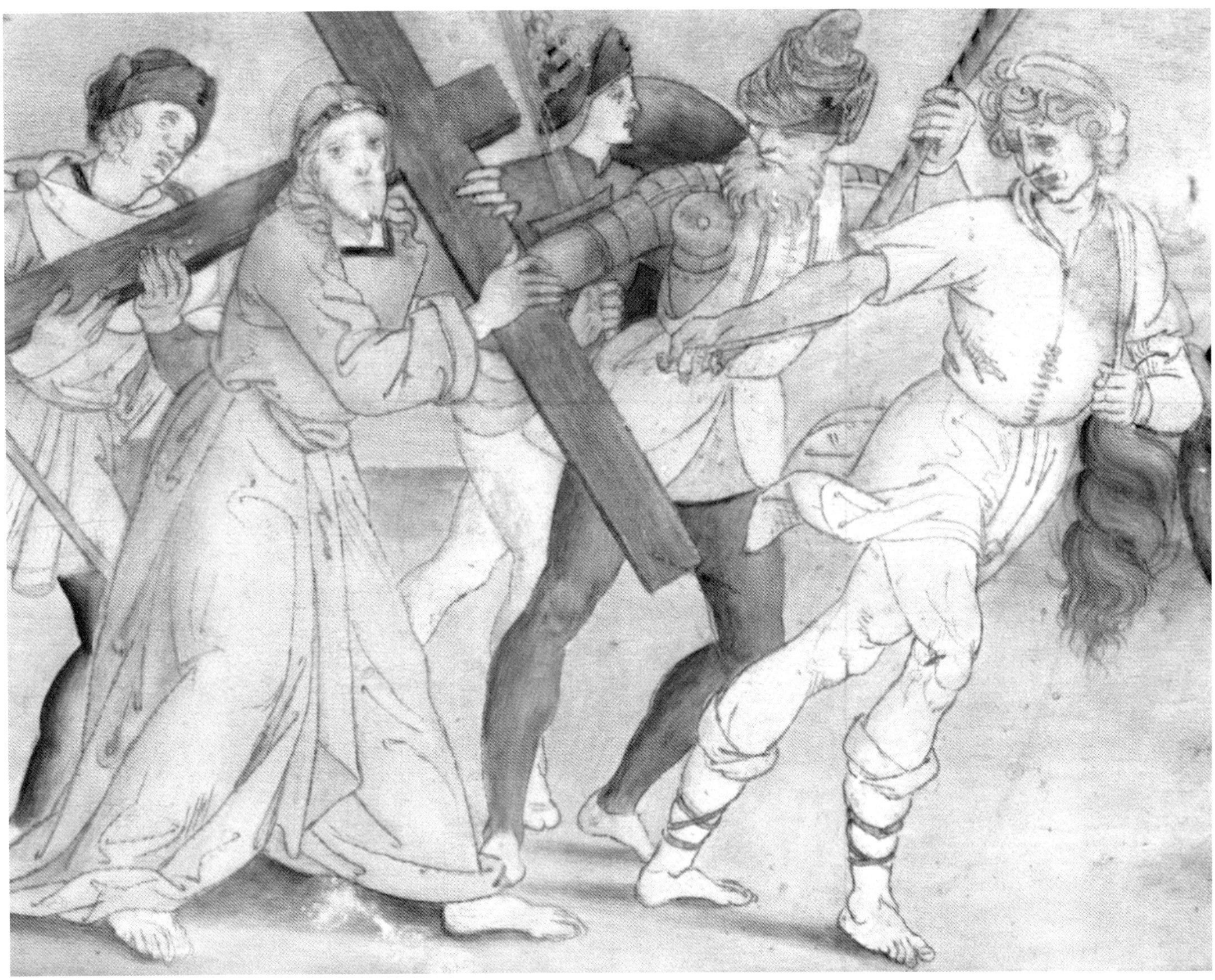

9 Raphael (Raffaello Santi)

The Madonna and Child with the Infant Baptist
(The Garvagh Madonna), *c.*1509–10

Oil on wood, 38.9 × 32.9 cm
NG 744

The Virgin is seated on a simple bench or plinth with her left leg tucked beneath her body. She wears a full-sleeved blue undershirt beneath a red dress, the neck and sleeve of which are trimmed with a simple gold border. She is wrapped about in a darker blue drapery, the colour of which contrasts pleasingly with that of her undershirt. Her light brown hair is parted and gathered in braids at the nape of her neck. She wears a blue and green striped headscarf decorated with gold. With her right hand she gathers a bunch of drapery and draws it around the bare back of her son, the infant Christ, who is seated naked on her lap. Both mother and son gaze down at Christ's cousin, the infant John the Baptist, who proffers the Christ Child a red carnation, a symbol of his future Passion. Saint John is also nude but for a camel skin pelt wrapped loosely about his torso. The Virgin holds it in place, her left hand plunged into its furry texture. In his right hand, Saint John holds a green reed cross bound with twine, another allusion to Christ's future sacrifice. Christ's halo is decorated with a cross, for the same symbolic purpose.

Behind the figures, to left and right, two arched openings give onto a distant landscape. Visible through the left arch is a church with a bell tower and a hemispherical apse, and a misty landscape and mountains beyond. Visible through the right arch is a larger building, perhaps also a church, buttressed and ringed by perimeter walls. Beyond what appears to be a stretch of water, more of the city can be seen, including a fortified keep.

The *Madonna and Child with the Infant Baptist* is first recorded in 1787 in the apartments of Prince Aldobrandini in the Palazzo Borghese in Rome. Sometimes referred to as the 'Aldobrandini Madonna', it is also known as the 'Garvagh Madonna' from the English family who subsequently owned it in the nineteenth century. The original circumstances of its commission are not known, but its small scale and exquisite finish imply a discriminating patron and a private context. Although it is not signed, it has always been accepted as by Raphael on grounds of style and quality. The underdrawing (Fig. 223) provides further proof of Raphael's authorship (as well as revealing much about the genesis of the composition).

The painting is generally acknowledged to date from the early years of Raphael's stay in Rome. It is very similar in style to a tondo of the same subject, but with the

Fig. 220
RAPHAEL, *The Madonna and Child with the Infant Baptist (The Garvagh Madonna)* [NG 744], *c.*1509–10

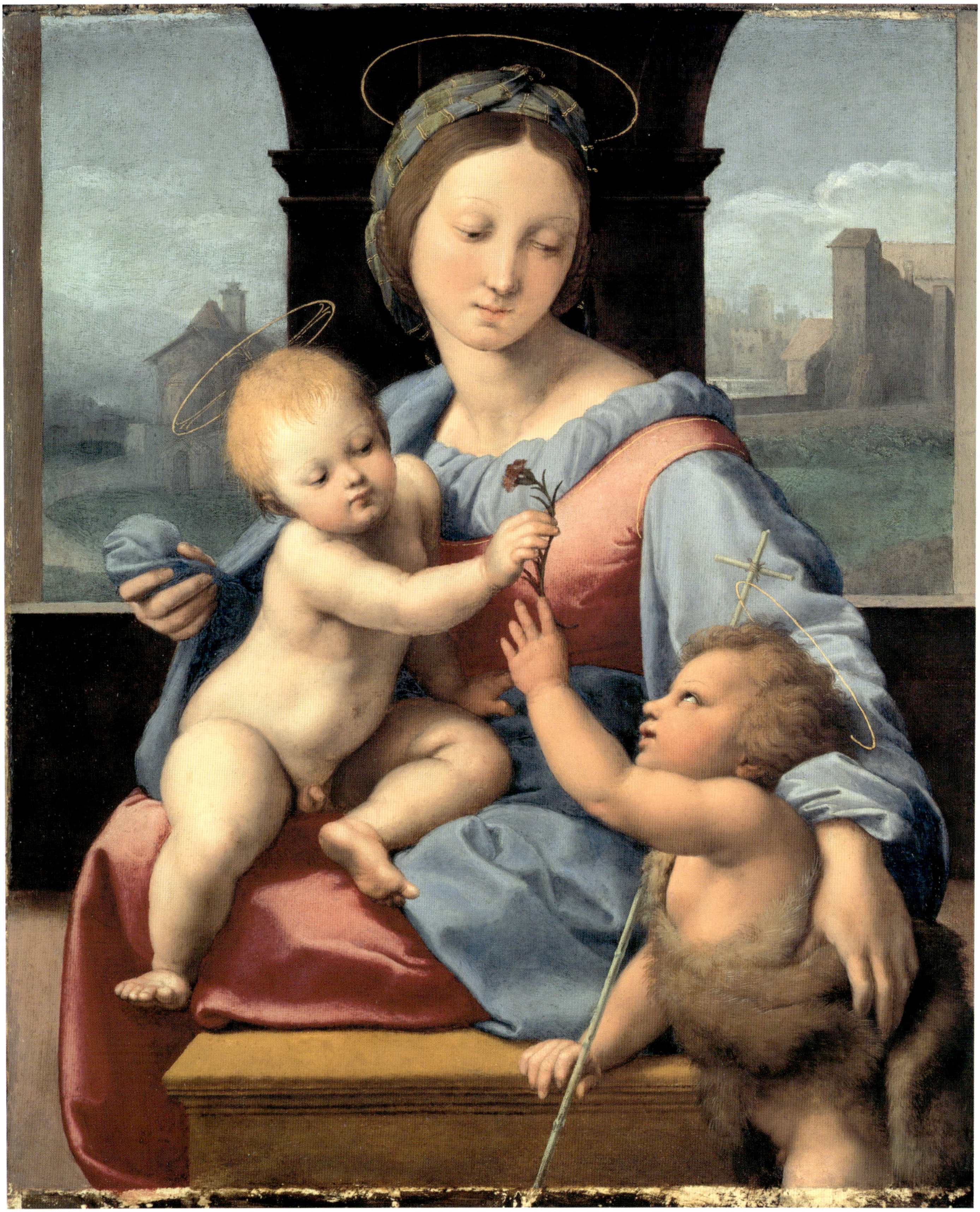

Virgin seated on the ground and in an open landscape, known as the *Alba Madonna*, in the National Gallery of Art in Washington (Fig. 221). The paintings have many points in common, such as the pose of the Christ Child, the treatment of the Baptist's pelt and the misty landscape, as well as the cool colouring and geometric harmony. The *Garvagh Madonna* and the *Alba Madonna* are usually compared to the frescoes in the Stanza della Segnatura, the first room in the Vatican that Raphael was given to decorate by Pope Julius II (1508–11).

The panel is a single plank of wood, probably poplar, and was prepared for painting with layers of gesso and a creamy-coloured priming extending to all four edges. Before embarking on the underdrawing, Raphael ruled a border inside all four edges (with a slightly wider margin along the bottom) to delineate the confines of the picture field.

The extensive underdrawing for the composition, executed in a dry material, is visible in places to the naked eye, where the paint has become more transparent over time, but the infrared reflectogram mosaic allows us to appreciate its full beauty (Fig. 223). Since the first comprehensive discussion of the underdrawing, samples have been taken from the bottom edge where underdrawn lines for Saint John extend outside the painted area. Contrary to expectations, the underdrawing was not executed in silver-point or black chalk, but in an alloy composed of tin and lead. This was one of several different varieties of metal-point available in Raphael's lifetime that were used for drawing by inserting a short piece of wire into a holder. Both lead and tin make a soft, slightly smudgy line, but in this combination produce the soft, fluent quality of line seen here.

Much of the harmonious effect of Raphael's paintings derives from his habit of careful geometric preparation. The infrared reflectogram mosaic reveals that he divided the picture field vertically and horizontally into four quadrants by means of ruled lines (as in *The Procession to Calvary*, Cat. 8). This may have been done to aid the positioning of his figure group as he copied the design onto the panel (a simplified form of squaring – another technique Raphael often used for scaling up larger works such as the *Ansidei Madonna* in the National Gallery and the Baglioni *Entombment* in the Galleria Borghese). However, the ruled registration lines so frequently employed by Raphael both in his drawings and in the underdrawings of his paintings were more than just an aid to copying. He seems to have found them useful as a means of structuring and anchoring his designs. In the *Garvagh Madonna*, the figure group forms a tall pyramid about the central axis, a formula established by Raphael in the Madonnas of his earlier Florentine period (1504–8). The ruled vertical bisecting the picture field acts as a plumbline around which the twisting pose of the Virgin coils. A similar vertical line provides the foundation for the serpentine pose of Raphael's *Saint Catherine*, also in the National Gallery (interestingly this features in the underdrawing of the painting (Fig. 222), but not in the scale cartoon for the work in the Louvre). The ruled horizontal in the underdrawing of the *Garvagh Madonna* coincides with the top of the parapets of the two window embrasures in the background. The geometrical centre of the composition, established by the intersection of the ruled lines, is located in the gap between the hands of the two infants, giving an extra charge to the symbolic impact

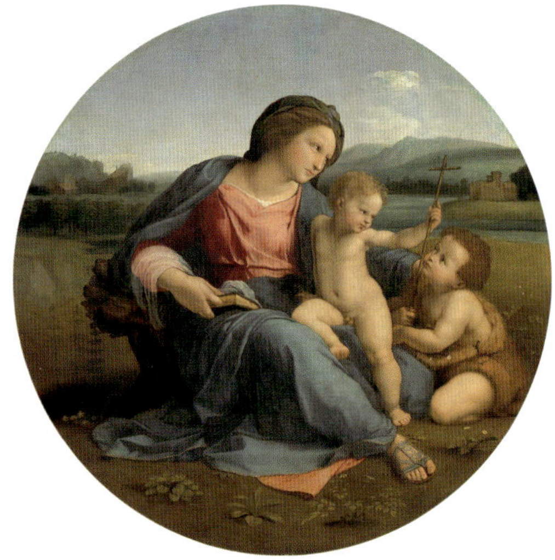

Fig. 221
RAPHAEL, *The Alba Madonna*, *c.*1510
Oil on panel transferred to canvas, diameter 94.5 cm
Washington, National Gallery of Art
Andrew W. Mellon Collection, 1937
1937.1.24

Fig. 222 (below)
RAPHAEL, *Saint Catherine* [NG 168], *c.*1507–8
Infrared reflectogram mosaic, detail

Fig. 223 (opposite)
Infrared reflectogram mosaic of Fig. 220

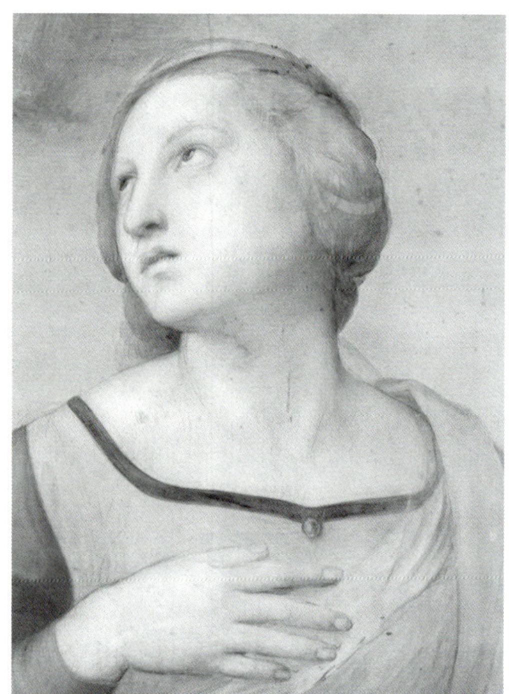

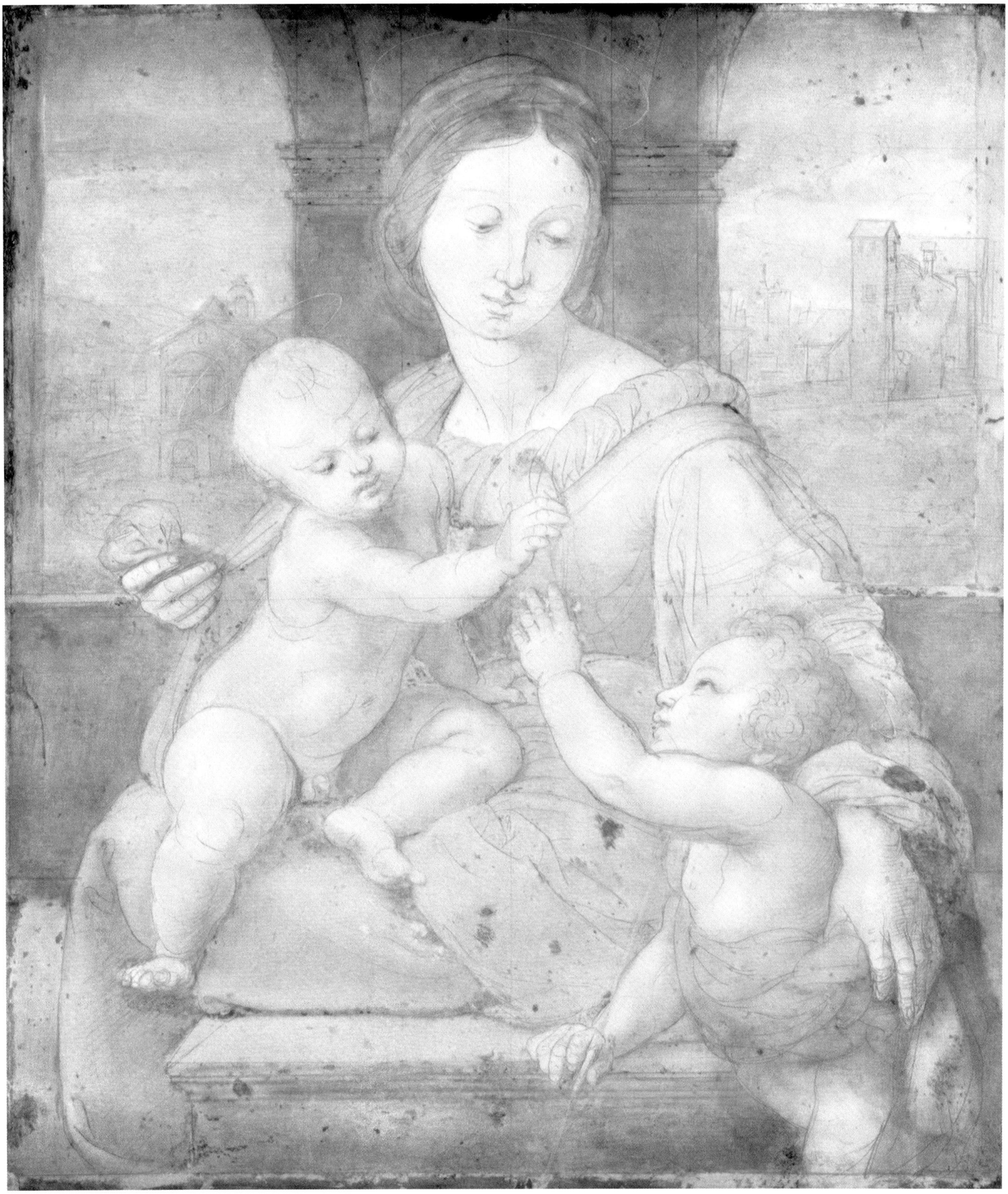

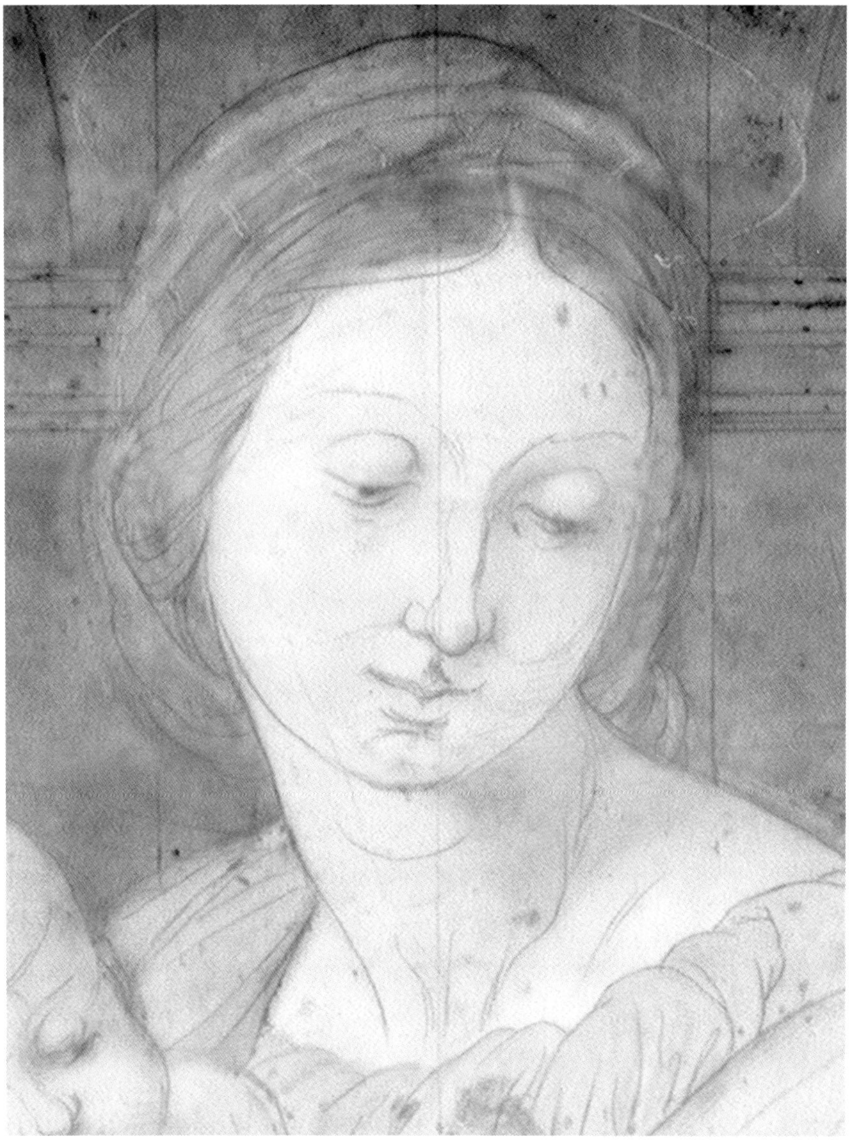

Fig. 224
Detail of Fig. 223

Fig. 225
Detail of Fig. 223

of the Baptist's gift. Raphael adapted the perspective of the plinth on which the Virgin is seated to conform to this vanishing point, as can be seen from the *pentimento* in the underdrawing at its corner. The Baptist is neatly confined to the bottom right quadrant, the diagonals of which determine his pose.

Raphael drew out the whole design on the panel in some detail, not omitting to indicate drapery folds and landscape details in the background. The drawing is confident, with relatively few revisions. There is no indication of pouncing and the design does not give the impression of having been traced using a cartoon. On the contrary, it seems likely that the composition was drawn freehand, probably with reference to a pre-existing compositional study. This freedom is particularly evident in the plump forms of the children, some of whose outlines he drew several times,

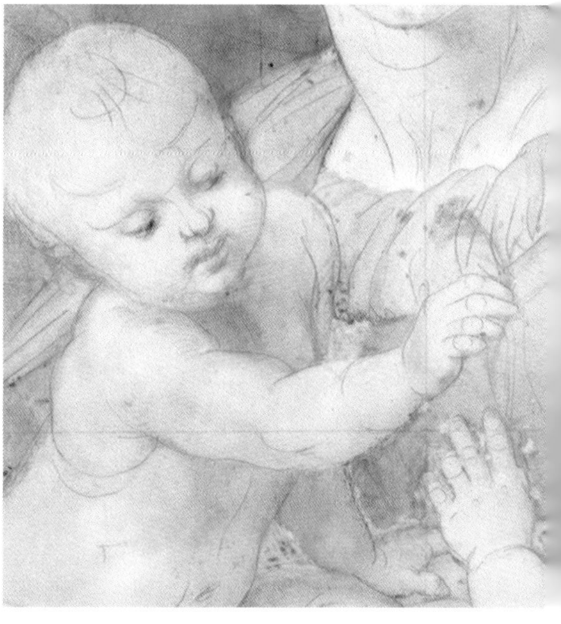

searching for the optimum contour (see for example the curve of Christ's right hip, or the upper contour of the Baptist's raised left arm). As well as defining the outlines of his composition in the underdrawing in some detail, Raphael also used parallel hatching to indicate the internal modelling of the figures, which he planned to be strongly lit from the left.

The underdrawing, while full, is at the same time relatively schematic, particularly in the features of the figures. These are broken down into loose circles and arcs, as in the drawing of the Virgin's cheeks and eyelids (Fig. 224), the forehead and crown of Christ's head (Fig. 225), the muscles of his right arm, and the knuckles of all the figures' hands. The slightly stilted appearance of some of the lines, for example in the Virgin's drapery, may be explained by the act of copying.

Raphael made a few alterations to the composition as he drew on the panel. At an early stage, he adjusted the positions of the figures themselves. All three were originally drawn slightly further to the right. This is most easily seen in the first outline of the long side of the Virgin's neck, and more faintly her chin and jaw (Fig. 224). The hatching visible in the region of her right temple is a remnant of her hair in this first configuration. The position of the Baptist's head was also altered, his features just discernible tilted into more of a three-quarters view slightly further to the right. The contour of the Christ Child's right side (running from his shoulder through his thigh) is also visible to the right of its present position. It is noteworthy that these preliminary outlines are very difficult to see, perhaps because Raphael tried to erase them. Another more minor adjustment, which Raphael did not erase, is visible in the Christ Child's right foot, which was originally lower.

One of the most significant changes Raphael made was in the landscape background which in the underdrawing can be seen extending uninterrupted across the entire width of the upper half (Fig. 226). He subsequently introduced the central pier, presumably in order better to offset the Virgin's head. The dark brown

Fig. 226
Detail of Fig. 223

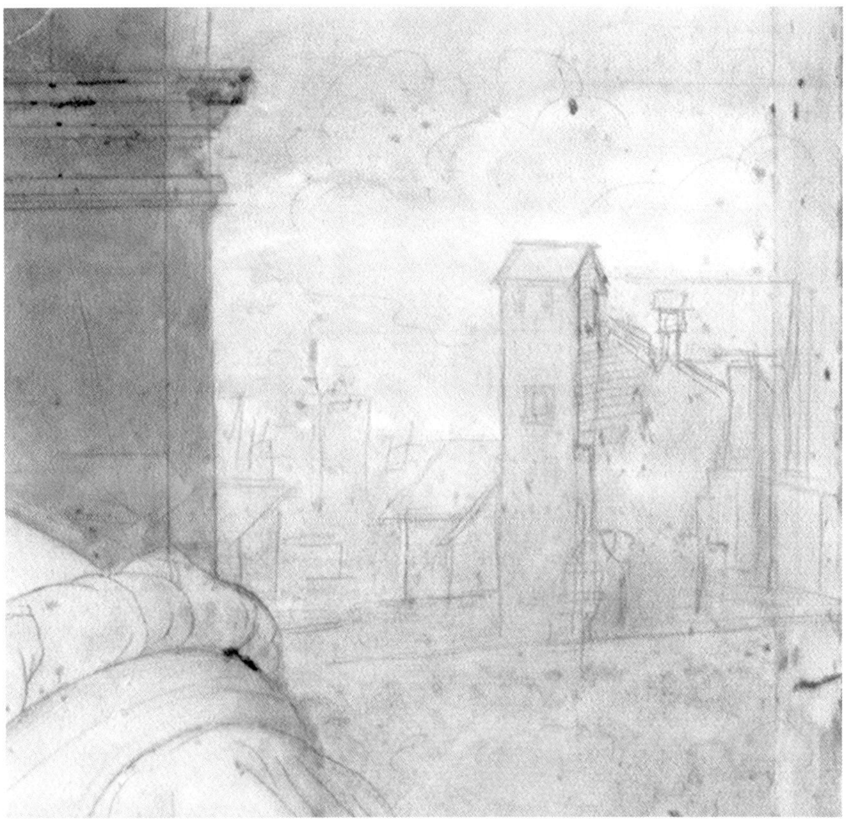

of the pier in the painting acts as a foil to her face, which would otherwise have lost definition against the pallor of the sky and the distracting shapes of the distant townscape. The underdrawing reveals how the perfect oval of the Virgin's head is 'held' in place between two ruled verticals of the background architecture. The vertical architectural members to the left and right of the window embrasures are on top of the painted landscape and thus must have been an even later afterthought introduced at the painting stage. They are presumably intended to be read as projecting elements of the building, but Raphael's principal motive in adding them was probably to contain and push back the landscape views.

The only elements of the painting which were not underdrawn are the two symbolic attributes of the Baptist. The graceful S-shaped carnation is simply painted with a swift calligraphic touch where Christ's fingers had been drawn to receive it. The Baptist's reed cross is drawn only in the section that passed beween his finger and thumb. The rest of the shaft was not drawn but incised subsequently (using an extraordinarily fine point and a ruler) into the paint. As in the case of the standard in the *Procession to Calvary*, Raphael knew he could easily improvise the positioning of the slender cross and the sinuous flower, once the arrangement of the figures had been settled.

The sure touch of the underdrawing in the *Garvagh Madonna* implies that the composition had already been rather fully worked out elsewhere, but no studies exactly anticipating the finalised design – whether composition studies or figure studies drawn from life – survive. During his early Roman period, Raphael made many drawings on the theme of the Madonna and Child in which he experimented with ideas for a range of different compositions. Some hints as to the genesis of the *Garvagh Madonna* can be gleaned from a group of drawings now in Lille which may once have formed part of a drawing book, known as the 'Pink Sketchbook' (from the pink ground with which the paper is prepared). Among these are studies showing the Virgin seated with one leg folded under her (Figs 227–230), which may contain the seeds of ideas for the *Garvagh Madonna*, though they also have points in

Fig. 227 (below left)
RAPHAEL, *Study for a Virgin and Child* (detail)
Brush and brown ink over stylus indentations and leadpoint, 12 × 16.2 cm
Lille, Musée des Beaux-Arts
inv. Pl. 455 (verso of Fig. 229)

Fig. 228
RAPHAEL, *Study for the Virgin and Child*
Metal-point on pink prepared paper, 16.2 × 11.2 cm
Lille, Musée des Beaux-Arts
inv. Pl. 436

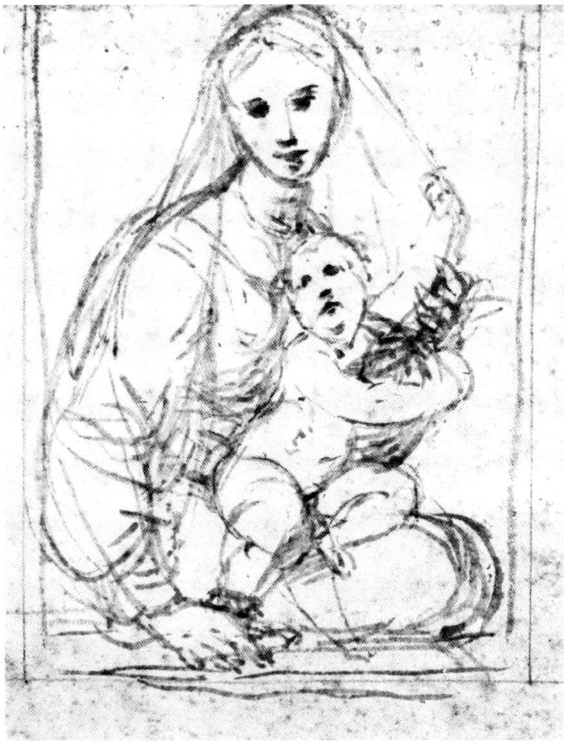

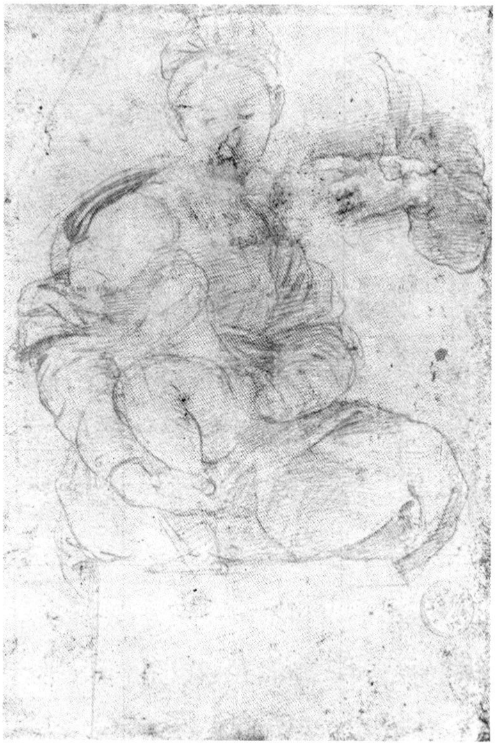

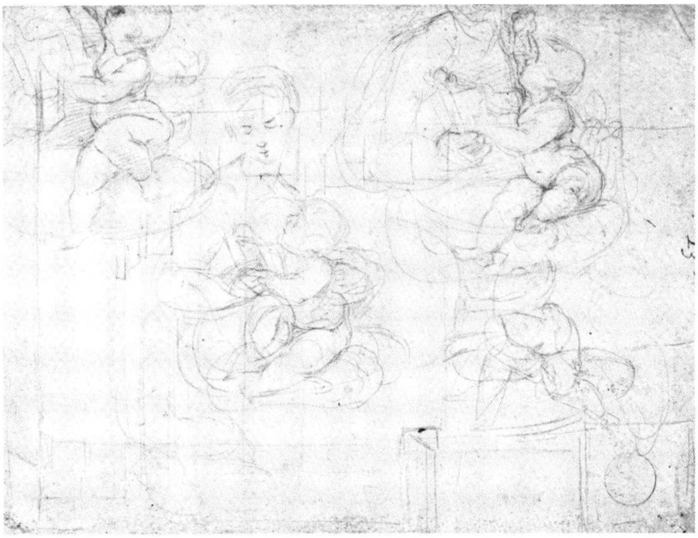

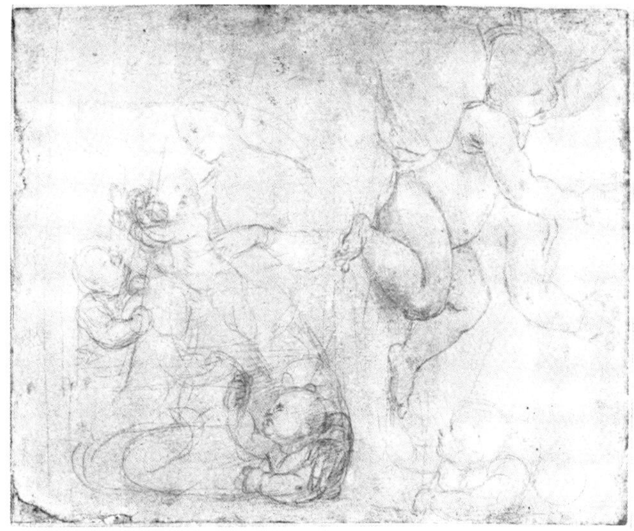

Fig. 229 (above)
RAPHAEL, *Studies for the Virgin and Child*
Metal-point on pink prepared paper,
12 × 16.2 cm
Lille, Musée des Beaux-Arts
inv. Pl. 454 (recto of Fig. 227)

Fig. 230 (above right)
RAPHAEL, *Studies for the Virgin and Child and the Infant Saint John the Baptist.*
Metal-point on pink prepared paper,
11.1 × 14.3 cm
Lille, Musée des Beaux-Arts,
inv. Pl. 437

common with the *Alba Madonna* and other Madonnas. One sheet containing several rapidly executed studies of the Virgin and Child (Fig. 229) shows Raphael exploring a similar arrangement in reverse, with the Virgin's knees to the right. The Baptist is not present and the Virgin is holding a book. Although more freely drawn, there are notable similarities between the studies on this sheet and the underdrawing of the *Garvagh Madonna*. The schematic facial features (particularly of the Virgin), the tendency to reduce the forms to simple arcs and circles, the quest for outline, especially in the contours of the baby, and the controlled cross-hatching in areas of shadow, all find parallels in the underdrawing. These studies are also comparable to the underdrawing in technique: although they were executed in metal-point (usually hard and scratchy), the line is nevertheless similarly soft and fluent.

Raphael was one of the greatest draughtsmen of the Italian Renaissance and his innate feeling for design underpins his entire oeuvre. His method of working out compositions with a series of drawn preparatory studies, usually culminating in a scale cartoon, derives from Central Italian working procedures, which he absorbed from Perugino's workshop and during his Florentine sojourn. Few painters were as particular as he in planning his compositions and adhering closely to his prepared designs. Although he favoured the use of cartoons, even for small-scale works (and this was the secret of his success in Rome where he increasingly delegated the execution of his designs in different media to his huge workshop), the *Garvagh Madonna* offers a fascinating example of Raphael bypassing the cartoon process. The underdrawing was almost certainly copied from a well-worked up compositional draft, no longer extant, but Raphael continued to elaborate and modify his design on the panel. The assured yet delicate touch of the underdrawing is reflected in the fresh, dynamic quality of the painting, and is a measure of Raphael's growing confidence, during his early years in Rome, in his unique talent for graceful and harmonious design.

CP

10 Giorgione
probably 1478–1510

The Adoration of the Kings, *c.*1505

Oil on wood, 32 x 84.3 cm
NG 1160

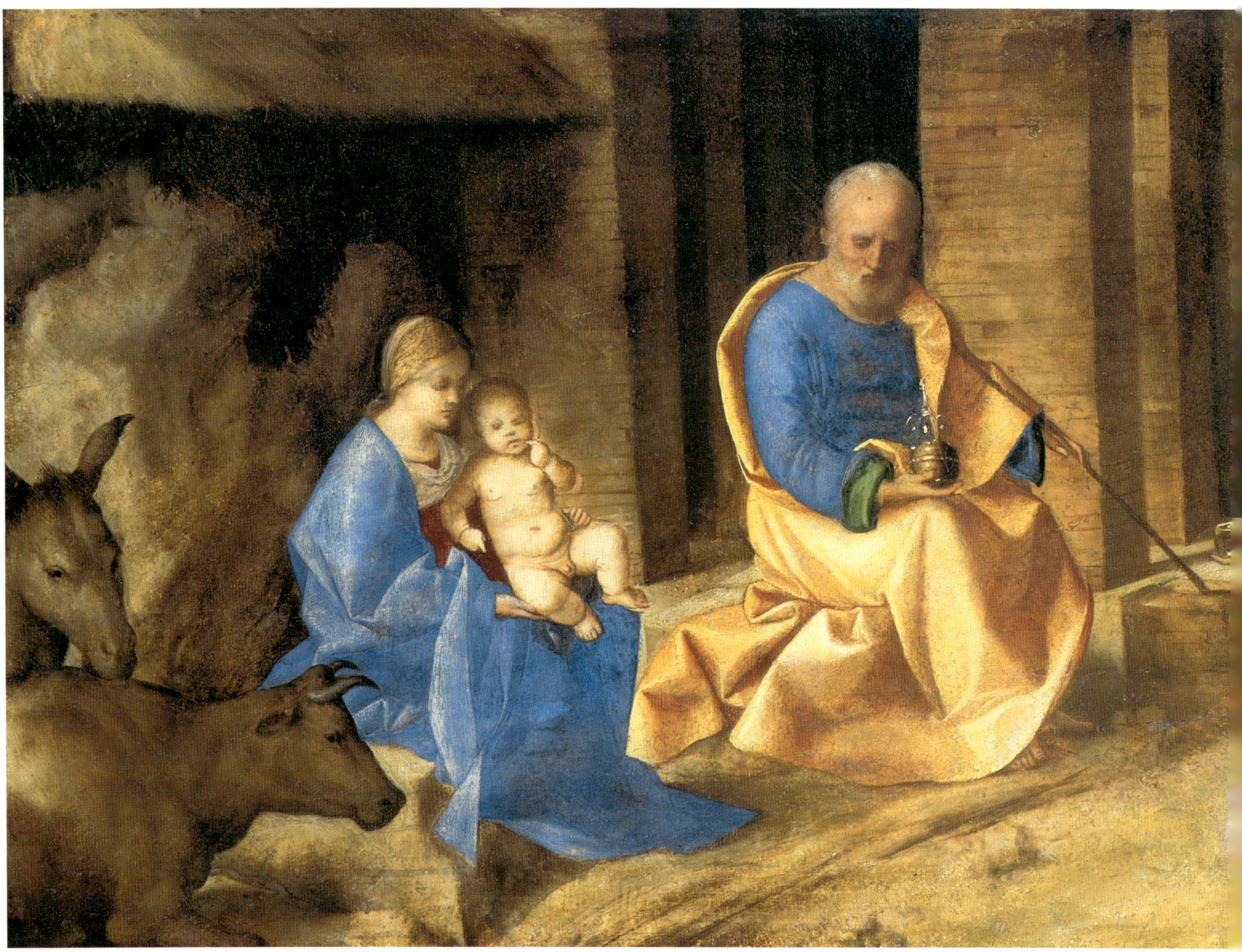

Fig. 231
GIORGIONE, *The Adoration of the Kings* [NG 1160], *c.*1505

In his own lifetime Giorgione was known simply as Giorgio (in Venetian dialect, Zorzi or Zorzo) from Castelfranco, where he was born, possibly in 1478, the corrected date given by Vasari in the second 1568 edition of his *Lives*. Vasari also stated that he was brought up in Venice and studied with Giovanni Bellini. By Vasari's time, however, Giorgione's biography was already confused and was certainly coloured by the myths that had grown up around his abbreviated career. He is not mentioned in a document until a commission of 1507 for a canvas for the Palazzo Ducale, Venice, and in 1508 he was engaged to paint the main façade of the Fondaco dei Tedeschi, of which only a few fragments survive. By October 1510 he was dead. One painting, the *Laura*, in the Kunsthistorisches Museum, Vienna, is dated 1506, according to an inscription on the back of the panel on which Giorgione's canvas is mounted. No other painting is securely dated, and attributions, even of the core group of paintings accepted by all scholars, have mostly been made by associating surviving works with descriptions and inventories of Venetian collections compiled several years after the painter's death. Giorgione seems to have been prized among collectors for his inventive approach both to traditional themes, including religious paintings and portraits, and to novel subjects – the meaning of some paintings attributed to him remains elusive to this day.

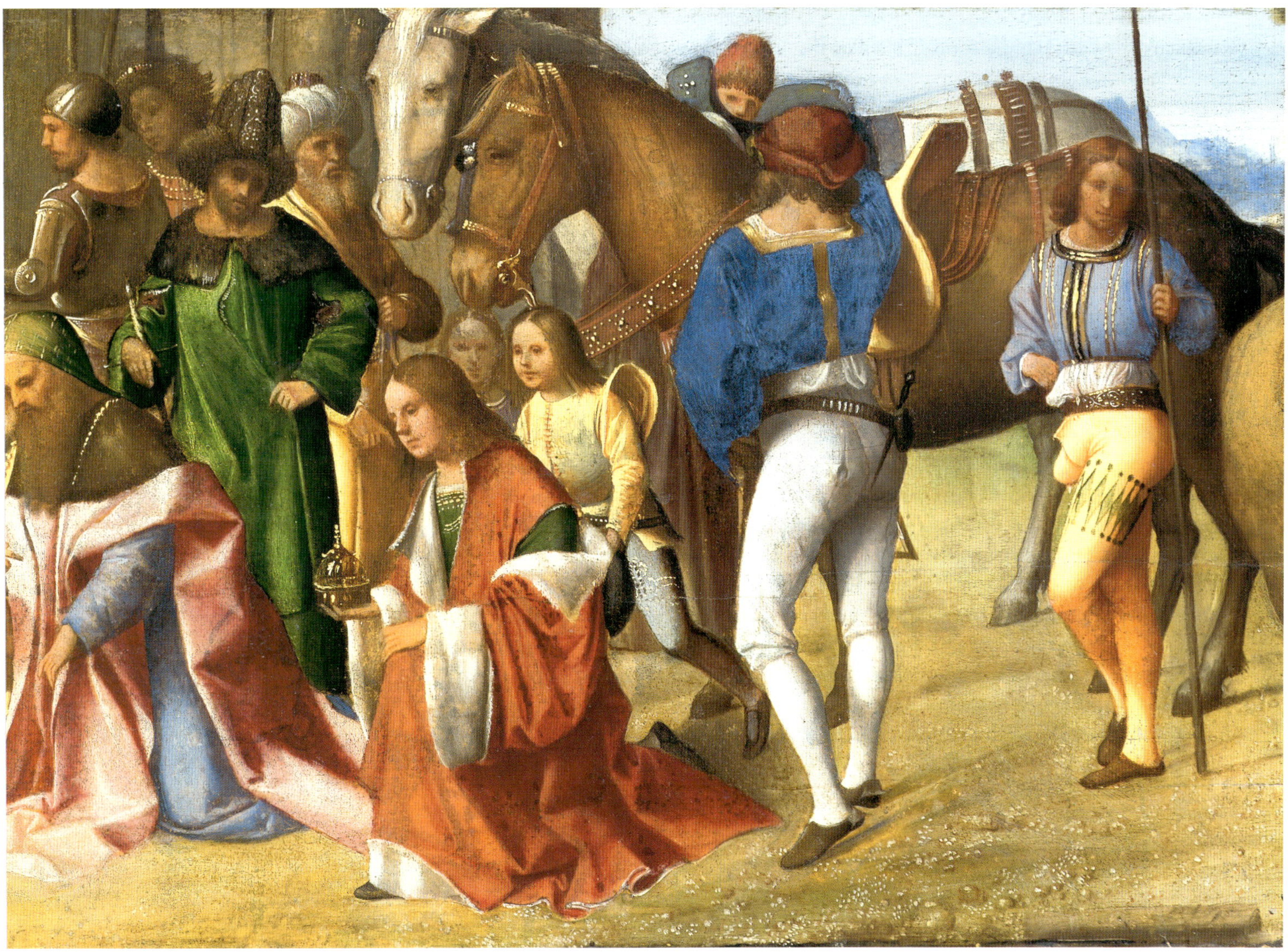

painted hand – itself poorly drawn and impossibly undersized, a common feature of hands in small-scale paintings attributed to Giorgione.

The underdrawn lines of the inverted image that appear to be related to drapery folds spread over too extensive an area to belong only to Joseph and it is likely that a kneeling king was drawn in front of him; there is a hint of a bearded head in profile. Further to the right, and much more visible, is a standing figure, which appears to have been drawn as a nude, but the arrangement of his arms suggests that he may be holding a gift. To his right another head can be distinguished, with one or two lines that probably represent drapery, and this may be the third king. Over the other shoulder of the nude figure, the faint outline of the head of a bystander appears, and then the boldly drawn horse, his casually posed attendant, arm slung over the saddle, a relation of the youths in the final painting. The head of this figure seems originally to have been sketched further to the right, but after that the underdrawing peters out, with only a few faint marks, such as the curves in the area of the Virgin's lap which might be rough indications of the rumps of more horses. Above the heads of the figures in the main group on the left are a few vertical lines, presumably to indicate the structure of the stable. Other marks, such

Fig. 236 (below)
Infrared reflectogram mosaic of Fig. 231

Fig. 237 (right)
GIORGIONE, *'The Three Philosophers'*, detail from infrared reflectogram mosaic

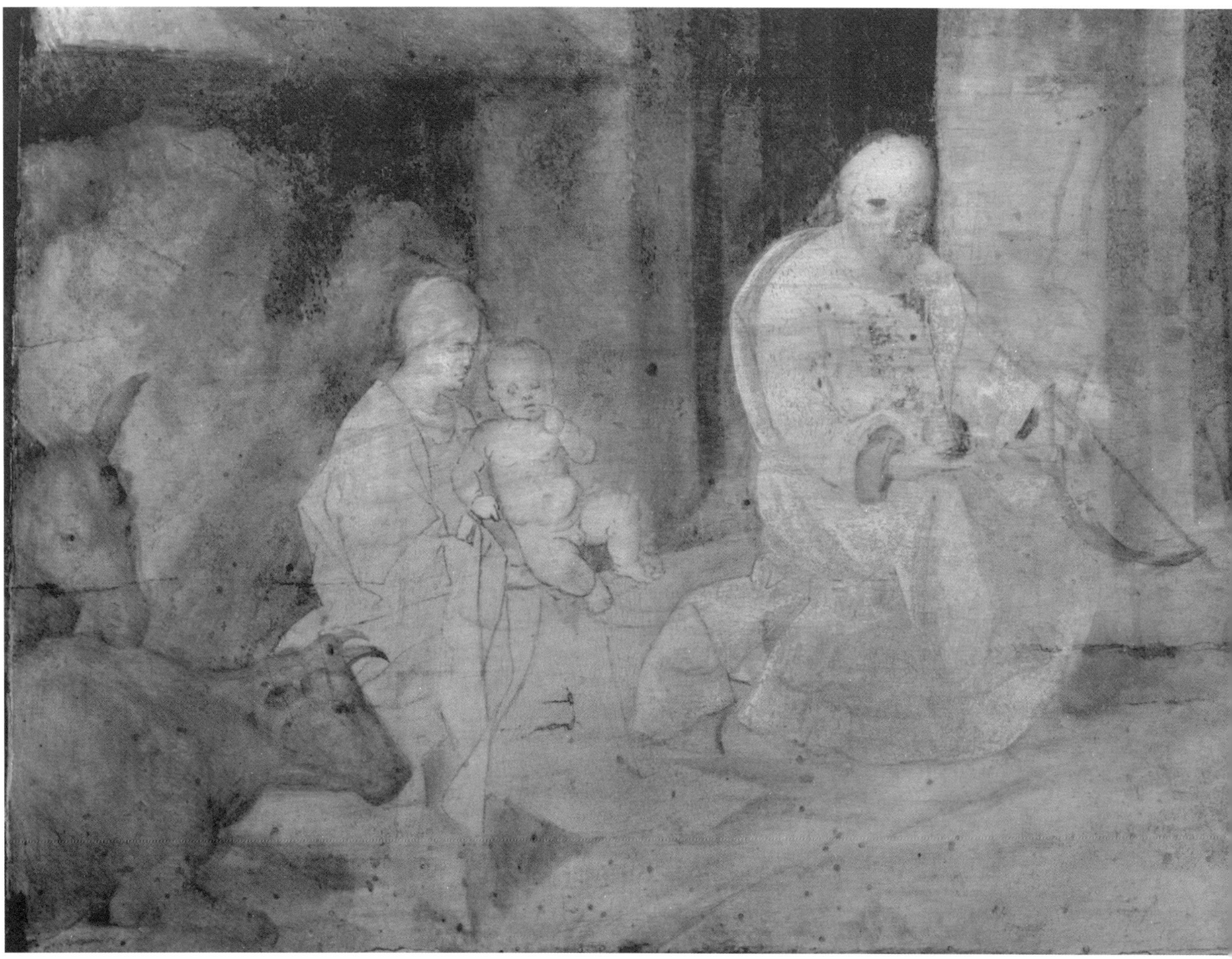

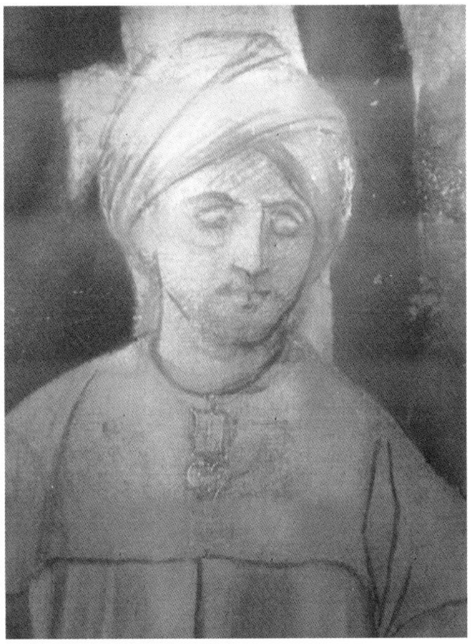

as those to the left of the Virgin, are too summary to be interpreted.

There is no reason why this drawing should not be by the same artist who executed the eventual painting, but it is questionable whether it can be considered as a first, rejected underdrawing. Instead it seems more likely to be a free improvisation on the theme of the Adoration of the Kings, and indeed it cannot be excluded that it was drawn after, rather than before, the careful underdrawing made for the painting. It would have been difficult to superimpose such delicate, fine drawing over the heavy dark lines of the inverted image, even if Giorgione were working from studies on paper. Several features make it probable that the artist was simply using the prepared panel as a surface on which to explore the subject: unless the panel has been cut, the placing of the Virgin so close to the edge would be unusual, while an Adoration of the Kings in which the Virgin and Child remain absorbed with one another, ignoring both the kings and the viewer of the picture, would be a remarkable invention, even for Giorgione. Furthermore, the obvious speed of execution, with many forms barely indicated or left incomplete, indicates that this was a rapid sketch, created from the artist's mind. The horse, for example, is a fantastic imagined beast, whereas those in the painting seem to be based on

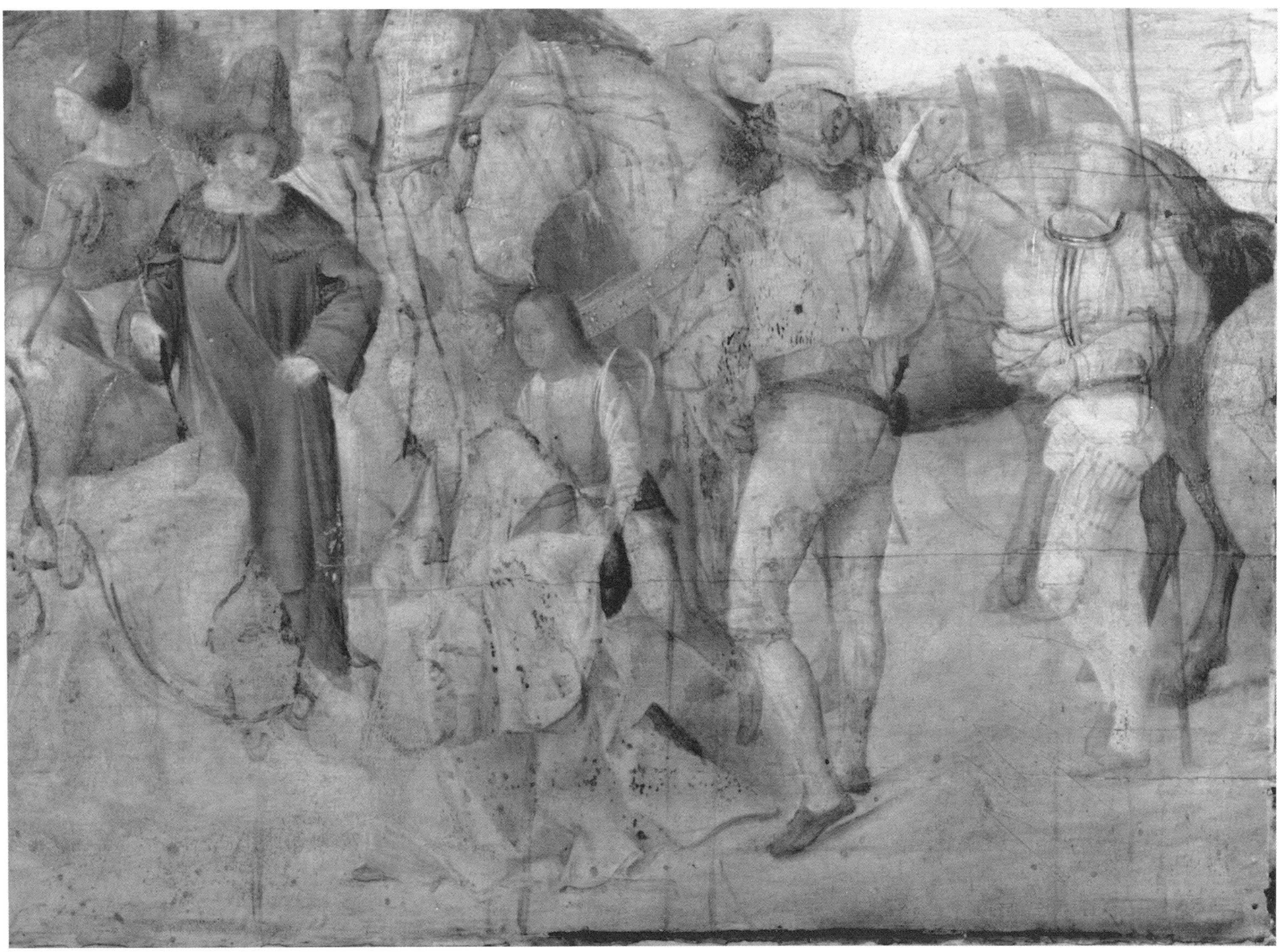

11 Lucas Cranach the Elder

*c.*1472–1553

Saints Christina and Ottilia, 1506

Oil on lime, 121.3 x 63.8 cm
NG 6511.2

CRANACH was born at Kronach in Upper Franconia. Around 1500 he appears to have travelled through Bavaria to Vienna, where he painted portraits of subjects associated with the university. On 14 April 1505 he was taken into the service of the Elector Frederick of Saxony at Wittenberg. In 1509 he travelled to the Netherlands for a short stay. On his return he continued to work in Wittenberg for successive electors of Saxony: Johann the Steadfast, who ruled jointly with his brother Frederick the Wise, and Johann's son, Johann Friedrich the Magnanimous, who became elector in 1532. Cranach ran a large workshop in which his sons Hans (d.1537) and Lucas the Younger (1515–1586) played a part. His work ranged from altarpieces, portraits and mythological subjects to wall-paintings for the electors' castles. In 1552 Cranach retired to Weimar, where he died on 16 October 1553.

Saint Christina of Bolsena (fourth century) stands on the millstone to which she was tied when thrown into the Lake of Bolsena; she miraculously floated. Her hair is brown and she wears a dress of patterned gold. Saint Ottilia (died *c.*720) holds a book on which are a pair of eyeballs, a reference to her blindness, miraculously cured on baptism; she wears the black habit of a Benedictine abbess: she was the abbess of the convent of Hohenburg and patron saint of Alsace.

This is one of two panels which once formed the outside of the wings of Cranach's Saint Catherine altarpiece, signed and dated 1506. The other panel, also in the National Gallery, shows Saints Genevieve and Apollonia (Fig. 244). The central panel, showing the martyrdom of Saint Catherine, and the inner faces of the two wing panels (of which the National Gallery panels formed the reverse sides before they were sawn apart), each showing three female saints, are in the Gemäldegalerie,

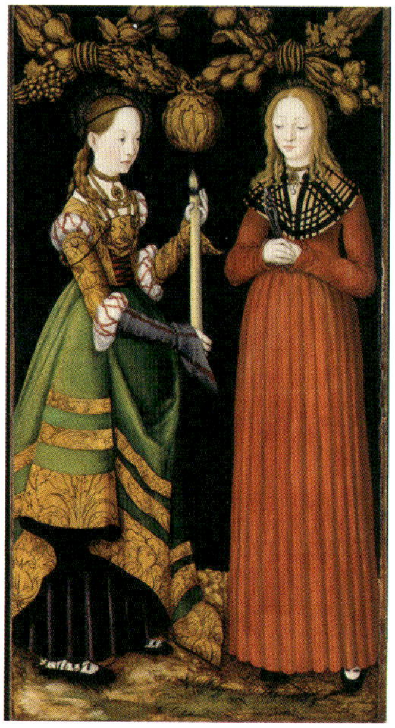

Fig. 244
LUCAS CRANACH,
Saints Genevieve and Apollonia [NG 6511.1], 1505–8. Oil on lime, 120.5 × 63 cm

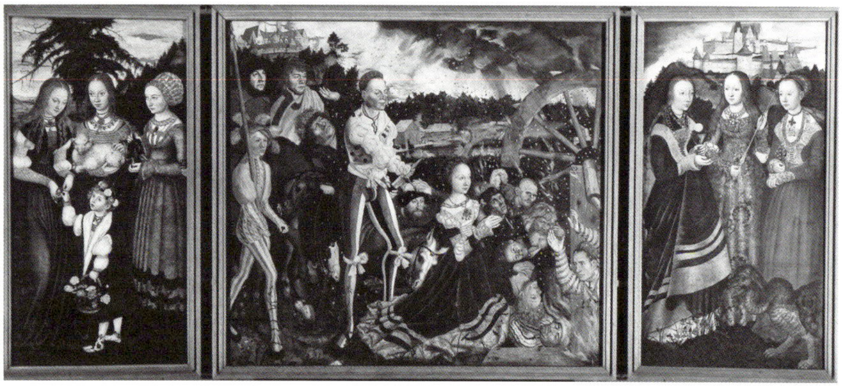

Fig. 243 (left)
LUCAS CRANACH,
Saint Catherine Altarpiece,
Centre panel: 126 × 139 cm; shutters: 124 × 66.5 cm each
Dresden, Staatliche Kunstsammlungen, Gemäldegalerie Alte Meister

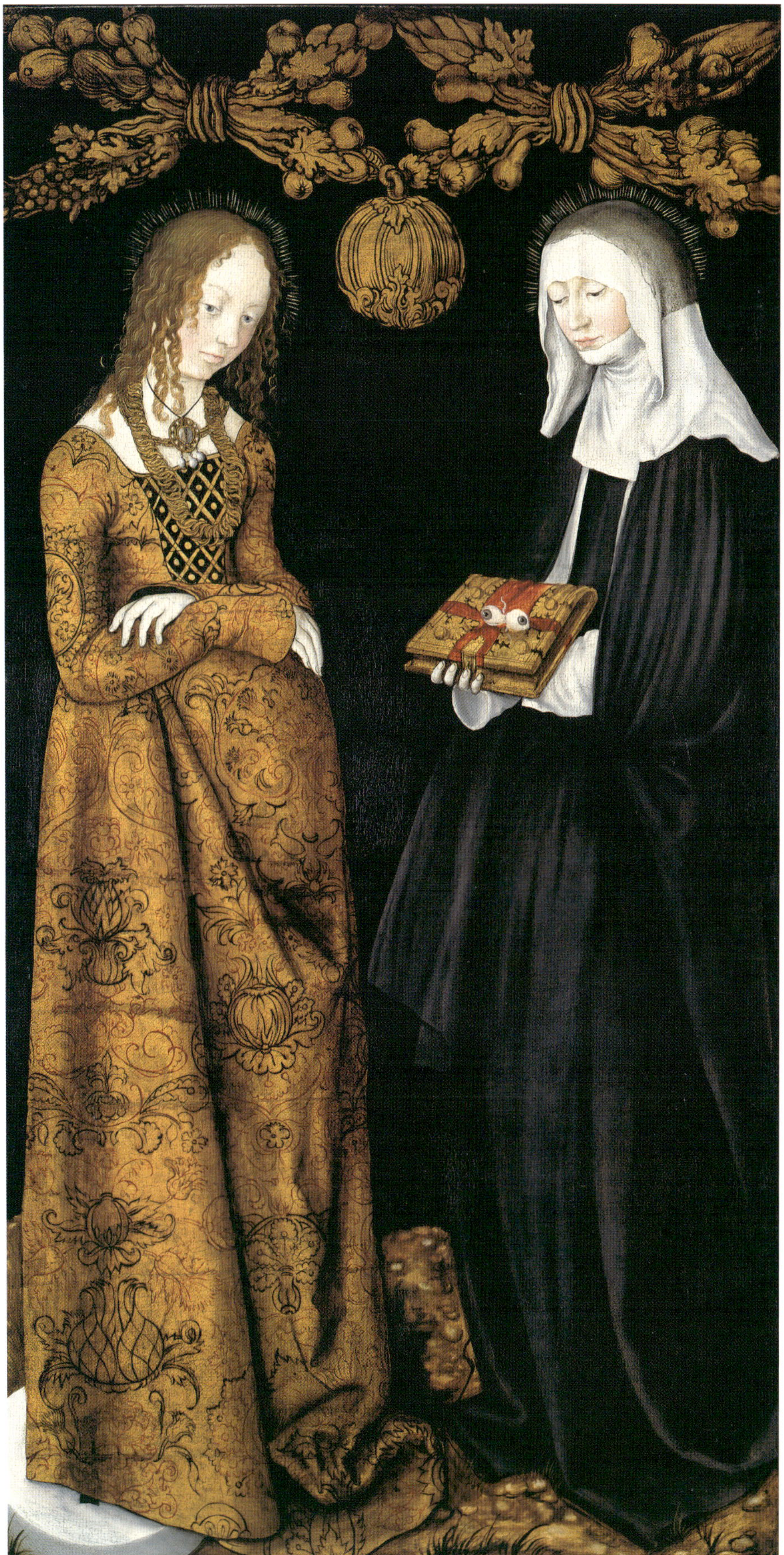

Fig. 245
LUCAS CRANACH,
Saints Christina and Ottilia
[NG 6511.2], 1506

Dresden (Fig. 243). The Saint Catherine altarpiece was one of Cranach's first and most important commissions after becoming court painter in 1505 to the electors of Saxony. It shows the highly dramatic martyrdom of Saint Catherine of Alexandria, who was condemned to be killed by being bound to a spiked wheel. However, by divine intervention the wheel broke apart, its splinters killing some of the spectators. Catherine herself was then beheaded.

The central panel of the altarpiece includes portraits of the Elector Frederick the Wise; the boy represented on the inner wing with Saint Dorothy appears to be a portrait of the young future elector, Johann Friedrich. In the background are two of the electors' castles or hunting lodges. The original location of the altarpiece is uncertain, but it is likely that it was intended for the chapel at Wittenberg castle. The female saints in the altarpiece are those whose relics the electors owned. While in the service of the electors Cranach made an illustrated catalogue of their enormous collection of saints' relics in their ornate reliquaries.

The Saint Catherine altarpiece was dismembered before 1786, and the fronts and backs of the shutters were sawn apart. The present arrangement of the shutters, with Saints Dorothy, Agnes and Cunigunde on the left and Saints Barbara, Ursula and Margaret on the right is conjectural but is presumed to be Cranach's original intention, as it appears to be the more visually harmonious solution. However, there is no doubt concerning the relationship of the now separated fronts and backs of the shutters, since the joins of the National Gallery panels and those of the Dresden panels can also be shown to match exactly. The National Gallery panel with Saints Genevieve and Apollonia matches the Dresden panel with Saints Dorothy, Agnes and Cunigunde, and this panel, with Saints Christina and Ottilia, matches the Dresden panel with Saints Barbara, Ursula and Margaret.

There is a rather free, linear underdrawing visible in both National Gallery panels, done in a liquid medium using a brush (Fig. 247). Saint Christina's eyes were originally shown looking to the right, not directly at the viewer as painted. The drawing of the eyes includes details of the circle of the iris as well as eyelashes. The position of the saint's left eye was drawn higher, and the contour of her left cheek narrower, than subsequently painted. There may also have been some adjustment to the shape or position of the lips. There is a large ear drawn under the hair, some of the curls of which are indicated with drawing, but the ear was not represented at the painting stage. The underdrawing of the features of Saint Ottilia are followed more closely in paint than those of Saint Christina, although there are adjustments to the drawing in the position of the eyelids (Fig. 246). The outlines of the saint's veil are drawn and this guide was followed in painting. The folds of the headdress are sketched with considerable freedom, and this was not always followed at the painting stage. The position of the saint's knuckles relative to the book she holds were adjusted at the underdrawing stage.

Similar linear brush drawings are characteristically found under the paint surface of Cranach's earlier works, often in a very detailed and precise form, although the underdrawing of the saints here is less detailed and rather more free. The undertaking of a large work like the Saint Catherine altarpiece clearly needed detailed preparation. No preparatory drawings for it by Cranach survive, but the

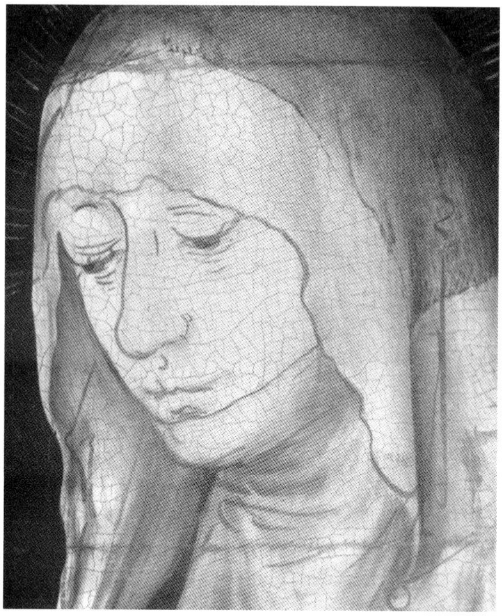

Fig. 246
Infrared reflectogram mosaic, detail of Fig. 245

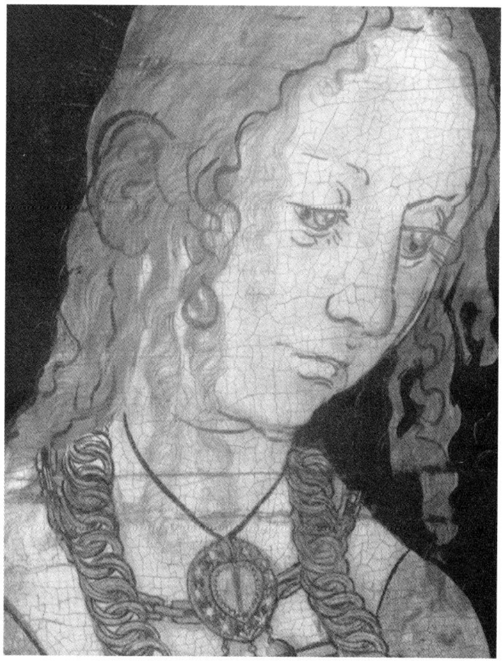

Fig. 247
Infrared reflectogram mosaic, detail of Fig. 245

Fig. 248
ALBRECHT DÜRER, *Saint Catherine*, *c.*1497–8
Woodcut, 39 × 28.8 cm
Dresden, Staatliche Kunstsammlungen, Kupferstichkabinett
A 1951-51 B. 120, M. 236

Fig. 249
Infrared reflectogram mosaic, detail of Saint Ursula's head from the right-hand shutter of the Saint Catherine Altarpiece (Fig. 243)
©SWE GmbH, Fulda
Courtesy Gemäldegalerie, Dresden

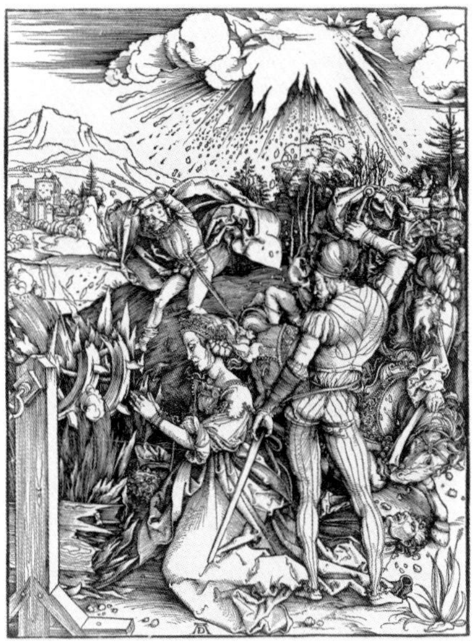

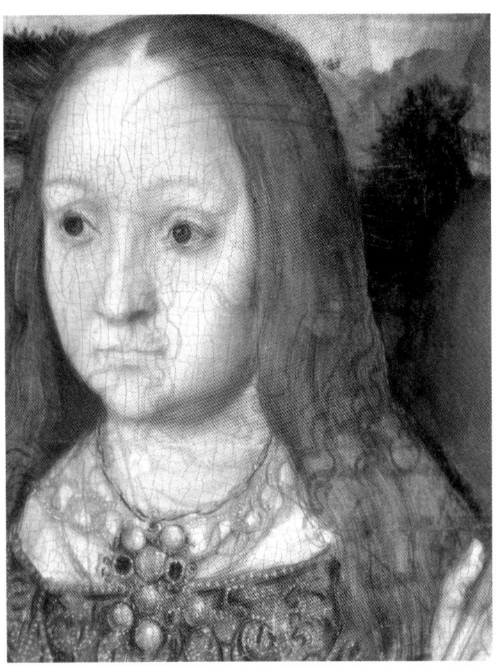

composition of the martyrdom scene in the central panel relies heavily on the woodcut of the same subject by Dürer, of about 1498 (Fig. 248). For the portraits which were included in the central scene, and presumably also for the portrait of the child Johann Friedrich on the left-hand shutter, Cranach must have relied on separate drawings or portrait patterns based on drawings from the life.

The underdrawing of the central panel and the fronts of the shutters show a number of radical changes to the positioning of individual figures, notably to the orientation of the heads in the central panel. In the left-hand panel, the figure of Johann Friedrich was drawn as a much smaller child: his head can be seen drawn at the height of the painted figure's shoulders. The head of this first child is shown in near-profile. As he was so much smaller, the hands of Saint Dorothy were originally drawn reaching much further down to take his hand. Conceivably this first sketch was made at a stage when it had not been decided that the child should be a portrait of Johann Friedrich.

The heads of all the female saints in the altarpiece were based on patterns or drawings which were transferred or copied to the panel, where slight adjustments were made at the underdrawing stage. The heads of the saints on the National Gallery panels, the reverses of the shutters, were based on patterns which correspond to the heads of the saints on the fronts of the shutters, and were therefore either taken from them, or derived from drawings used to create all the female saints. In the right-hand shutter the head of Saint Ursula was underdrawn turned to the right, her head inclined and eyelids lowered (Fig. 249). The underdrawing of the head of Saint Ursula is extremely similar to the finished head of Saint Christina, also bent to the right with downcast eyes (Fig. 247); the contour of Christina's left-hand cheek as originally drawn is narrower, like that of the underdrawing of Saint Ursula, but has been adjusted at the underdrawing stage to become slightly wider. Similarly, the head of Saint Ursula as painted is extremely like that of Saint Apollonia and the face pattern of Saint Barbara has been used for Saint Genevieve.

The difference between the styles of underdrawing in the fronts and backs of the shutters – that of the fronts more precise and detailed than that of the reverses – may reflect a difference in the use of patterns and the method of production. It may also reflect a greater use of assistants in creating the reverses, although presumably under the direction of Cranach himself. On the inner faces of the shutters the models for the saints' heads were followed precisely in detailed drawings which were then painted. On the National Gallery panels – the outer faces – models were used but the main features were indicated only roughly in the underdrawing and then adjusted in a similarly free manner at the painting stage.

SF

12 Jacopo Carucci, called Pontormo

1494–1557

Joseph with Jacob in Egypt,
probably 1518

Oil (identified) on wood, 96.5 x 109.5 cm
NG 1131

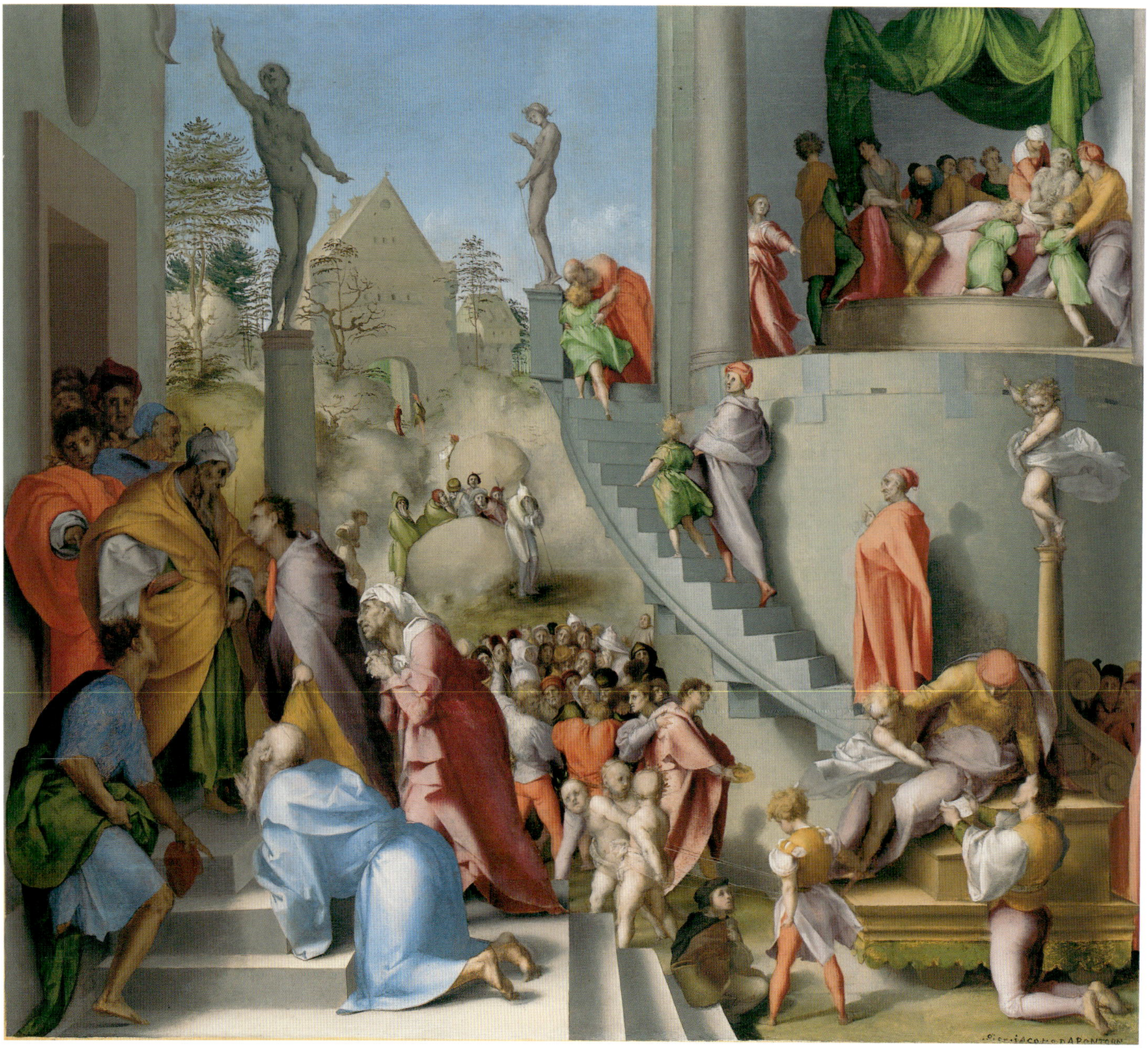

Fig. 250
PONTORMO, *Joseph with Jacob in Egypt* [NG 1131], probably 1518

Fig. 251
Infrared reflectogram mosaic of Fig. 250

Jacopo Carucci was called Pontormo after the Tuscan village of that name where he was born in 1494. He arrived in Florence in about 1507, and was based there for the rest of his life. The son of a painter, his early training was (according to Vasari) with Leonardo da Vinci. He subsequently studied with Piero di Cosimo, and by 1510 with Mariotto Albertinelli. His style was influenced by a longer period of apprenticeship, from around 1512, with Andrea del Sarto. Pontormo was already working as an independent artist by 1515, when he was engaged on the decorations celebrating the entry of the Medici Pope Leo X into Florence. Other Medici commissions followed, including fresco decorations at the Medici villas at Poggio a Caiano, Careggi and Castello. At the end of his life, Pontormo was commissioned by Duke Cosimo I to decorate the choir of San Lorenzo (1546–56). He never held an official position at the Medici court although he nevertheless gained a reputation as the leading painter in mid-sixteenth-century Florence, and was

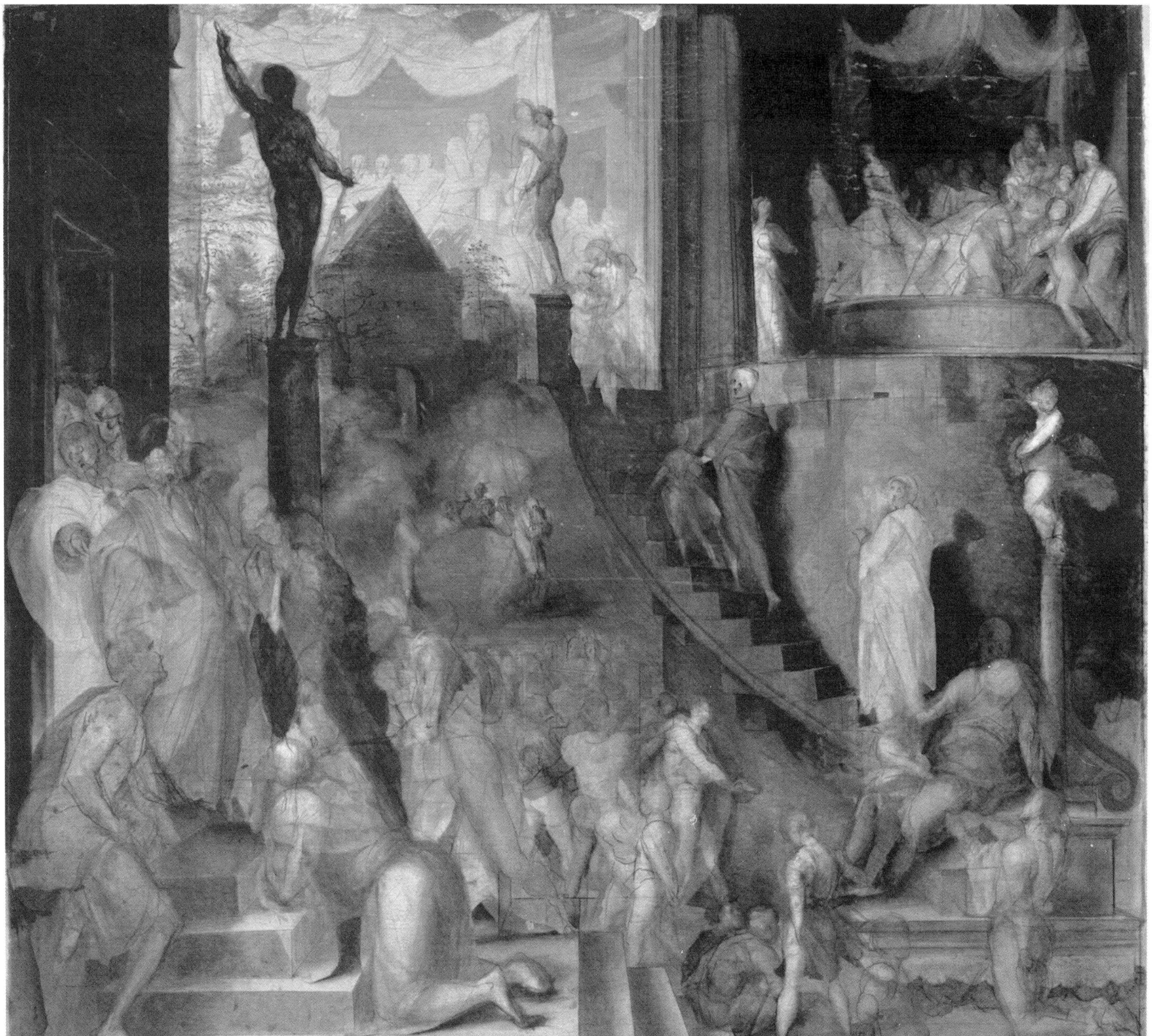

undoubtedly one of the most original and extraordinary artists of the period. He painted mainly religious works, including several prestigious altarpieces. His many surviving drawings, typically figure studies in red and black chalk, are a testament to his consummate draughtsmanship. His highly personal style was much influenced by Michelangelo, although he was also inspired by Northern art, especially the prints of Dürer and Lucas van Leyden.

Joseph with Jacob in Egypt is one of a series of paintings depicting the Old Testament story of Joseph made to decorate a bedroom in the Florentine townhouse of the wealthy banker Pierfrancesco Borgherini (1480–1558). Collaborating with Pontormo on the painted narratives were three other successful young artists of the day, Andrea del Sarto, Bacchiacca and Francesco Granacci. Baccio d'Agnolo, the architect of the house, was responsible for the intricately carved walnut furnishings of the bedroom, into which the paintings were set. These included panelling, seats, *spalliere* (backboards), *cassoni* (chests) decorated with carved putti, and a bed. The decorative ensemble was said by Vasari to have been the gift of Pierfrancesco's father Salvi made in honour of his son's marriage to the noblewoman Margarita Acciaiuoli in 1515. It remained intact until 1584 when four of the larger painted panels passed into the Medici collection. The dispersal of the other paintings followed. Although nothing now remains of the carved woodwork, fourteen paintings from the Joseph cycle survive, two by del Sarto (in the Palazzo Pitti, Florence), four by Pontormo (in the National Gallery), six by Bacchiacca (two also in the National Gallery, and four in the Galleria Borghese, Rome) and two by Granacci (in the Uffizi, Florence). The paintings are usually dated between 1515 and 1519. Pontormo's *Joseph with Jacob in Egypt*, probably the last of the works to be completed, was installed to the left of the entrance to the bed chamber.

Joseph with Jacob in Egypt depicts four scenes from the concluding chapters of the story of Joseph, when Joseph is joined in Egypt by his father and brethren (Genesis 47–49). Joseph, consistently clad in a red hat, an ochre tunic and a mauve mantle, appears in all four scenes. In the first, bottom left, he presents his father Jacob to Pharaoh who stands majestically at the top of the steps, swathed in ample ochre drapery and wearing a turban. Joseph approaches him, cap in hand, pointing to his father, the bald old man dressed in blue, kneeling on the steps at his feet. The identity of the female figure in a pinkish red dress and white headdress following Joseph up the steps is uncertain. The barefoot figure in the bottom left corner, who doffs his red hat to Pharaoh and also points to Jacob, may be one of Joseph's brothers. The second scene takes place in the bottom right corner. Joseph, with a child between his knees, is seated on a chariot drawn by three putti. Beyond them, soldiers restrain a crowd from surging towards the chariot. These are Egyptians, afflicted by the great seven-year famine predicted by Joseph, clamouring for bread (Genesis 47:15; 19). A representative, holding out his hat imploringly towards Joseph, is allowed forward. In the bottom right corner, a kneeling messenger holds out a letter to Joseph, presumably bearing news of his father's illness (Genesis 48:1). The putto atop the column of the chariot points to the continuation of the narrative in the third scene. Here Joseph accompanies one of his sons up the stairs,

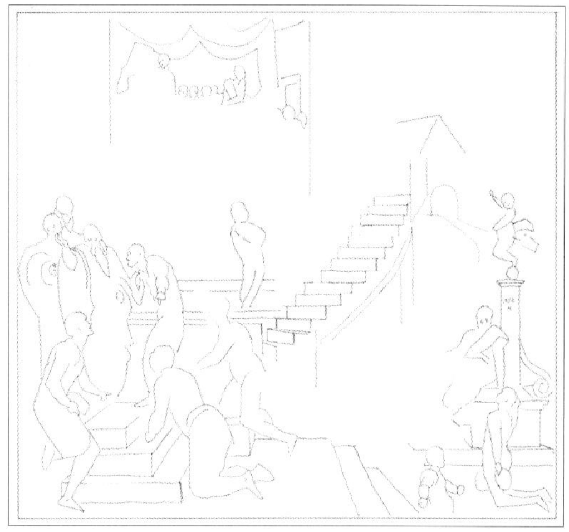

Fig. 252 (above)
Diagram of underdrawing

Fig. 253 (below)
Detail of Fig. 251

Fig. 254 (right)
Detail of Fig. 251

Fig. 255
Detail of Fig. 251

Fig. 256
Detail of Fig. 251

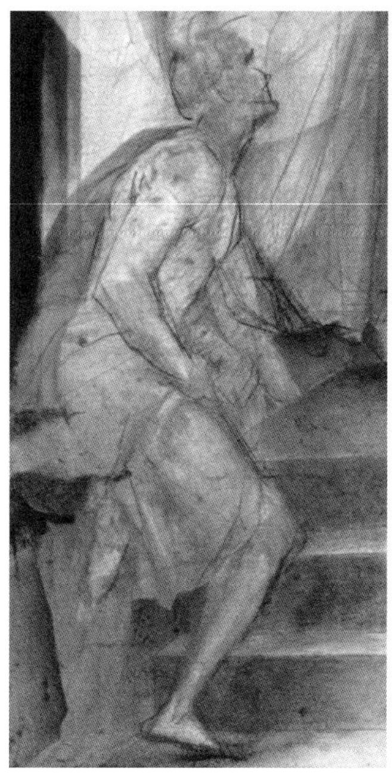

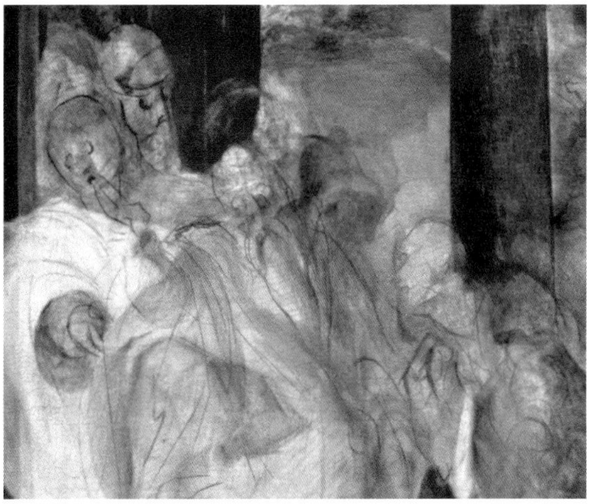

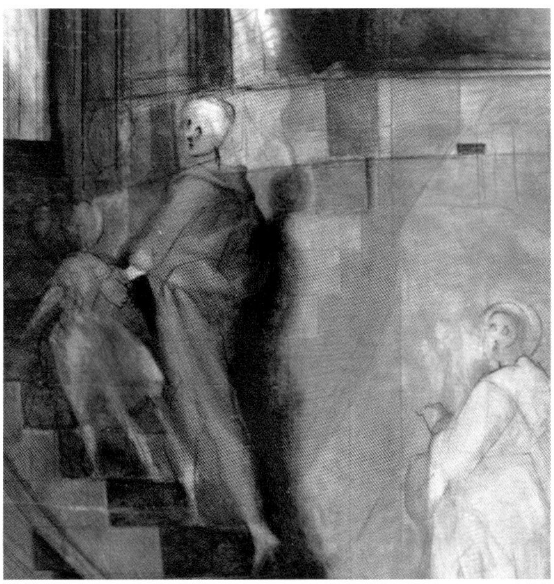

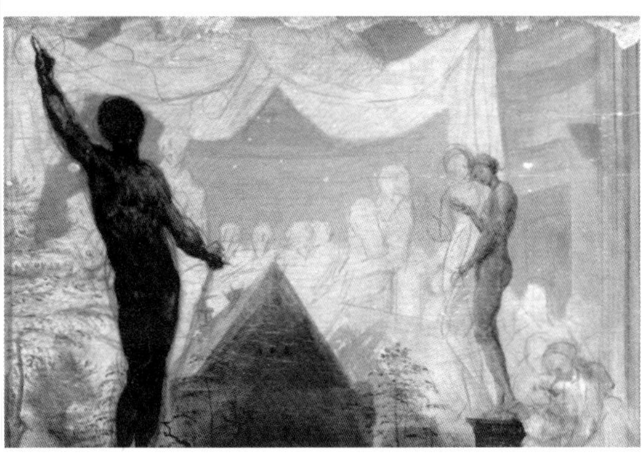

while the other is greeted at the top by their mother Asenath. The identity of the old man in red following them up is unknown. In the final scene (top right), Jacob is on his deathbed surrounded by his family. He blesses Joseph's sons (both dressed in green tunics as in the previous scene), but instead of blessing the eldest, Manasseh, with his right hand, he blesses the younger son Ephraim.

Joseph with Jacob in Egypt is painted on a wood panel formed from three planks, horizontally arranged. The panel was prepared for painting with a gesso ground. No paint samples have been taken for analysis so it has not been possible to establish whether there is a priming over the ground, nor, if such exists, whether the first underdrawing is below or above it in the layer structure. The three other panels by Pontormo in this series are, however, primed, making it likely that a priming exists in this case.

The infrared reflectogram mosaic (Fig. 251) provides an extraordinary insight into the genesis of the composition, suggesting that it was developed in an intense campaign of invention carried out not on paper in advance, but in an energetic welter of drawing on the prepared panel itself. At various stages of the underdrawing, Pontormo not only introduced, eliminated, or altered many of the figures – several of them undergoing at least two or three changes in position – but also radically rethought the entire design.

As the reflectogram mosaic reveals, the composition was initially organised very differently, with the background arranged in reverse (see also diagram, Fig. 252). In this first underdrawing, the deathbed scene was originally drawn on the left of the picture, in the larger area that is now sky (Fig. 256); the curved staircase swung up to the right (Fig. 255); and the gatehouse with the pitched roof occupied the space now filled by the deathbed scene. The foreground seems to have been planned broadly as it is now, with a group of large figures to the left and Joseph on his chariot to the right. It is more difficult to interpret the reflectogram mosaic in the middle ground. A series of ruled parallel lines behind the foreground figures may have been intended as some sort of balustrade closing off the steps. Behind the balustrade, in the area now occupied by the boulder with its group of onlookers, were at least one – or possibly two – standing figures similar in scale to the figures ascending the staircase in the finished painting (these are hard to see in the reflectogram). It is unclear whether these figures participated in the narrative or were perhaps statues.

Pontormo sketched in his figures rapidly in a characteristic shorthand, first drawing them nude, and afterwards adding the drapery (Fig. 253). He indicated their facial features with abbreviated marks (curves or circles for eyes, and short dashes for the tips of noses and mouths; Fig. 254). Hands were frequently left with no clearly defined fingers, and feet were denoted by rough triangles, with sharp 'v's for the ankle bones. Once the figure groups had been established, Pontormo indicated areas of shadow with parallel hatching, as can be seen in the canopy above the deathbed (see Fig. 256), and in the vertical edges of the curved staircase. Those parts of the architecture that required straight lines were ruled with a sharp point leaving incisions in the ground layer.

Apparently satisfied with this design, Pontormo then started to paint. In the

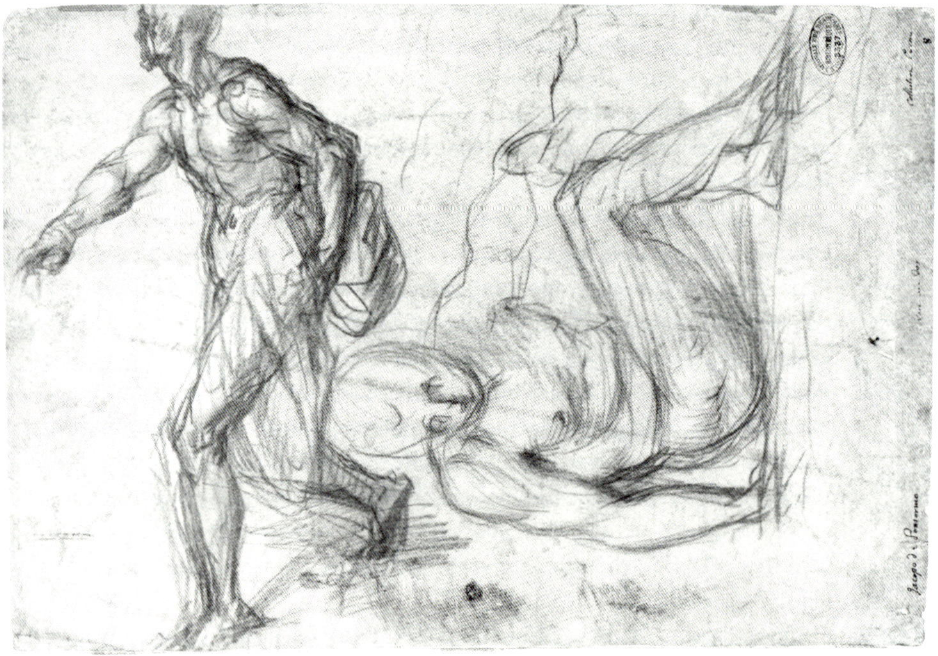

Fig. 263
PONTORMO, *Study for Joseph sold to Potiphar and for a seated figure*, *c*.1516
Red chalk, 26.5 × 39.5 cm
Paris, École Nationale Supérieure des Beaux-Arts
Inv. EBA 293

Fig. 264
PONTORMO, *Joseph sold to Potiphar* [NG 6451], probably 1515
Oil on wood, 61 × 51.6 cm

Fig. 265
PONTORMO, *Pharaoh with his Butler and Baker* [NG 6452], probably 1515
Oil on wood, 61 × 51.7 cm

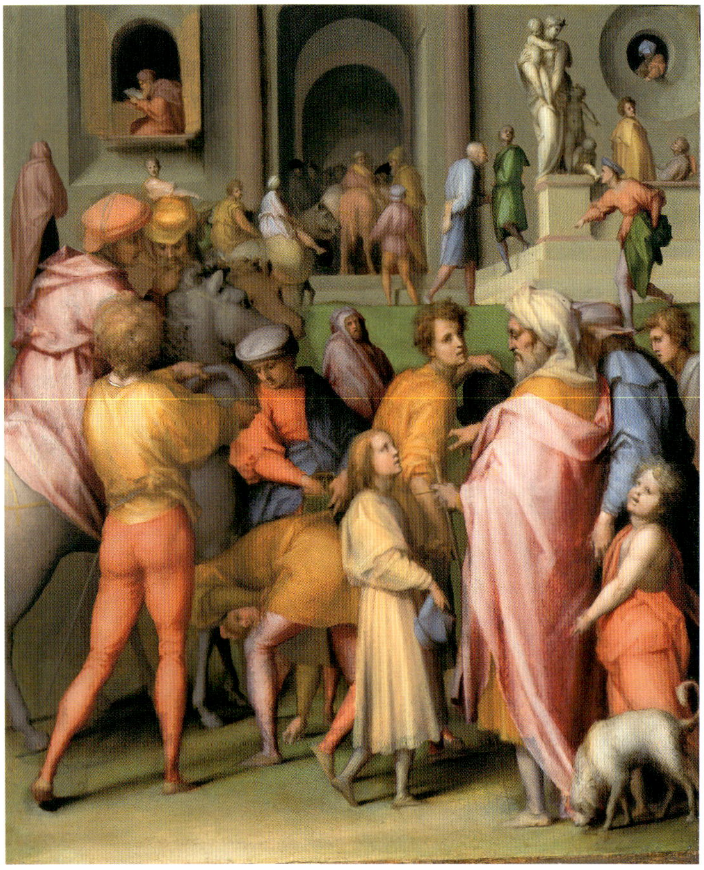

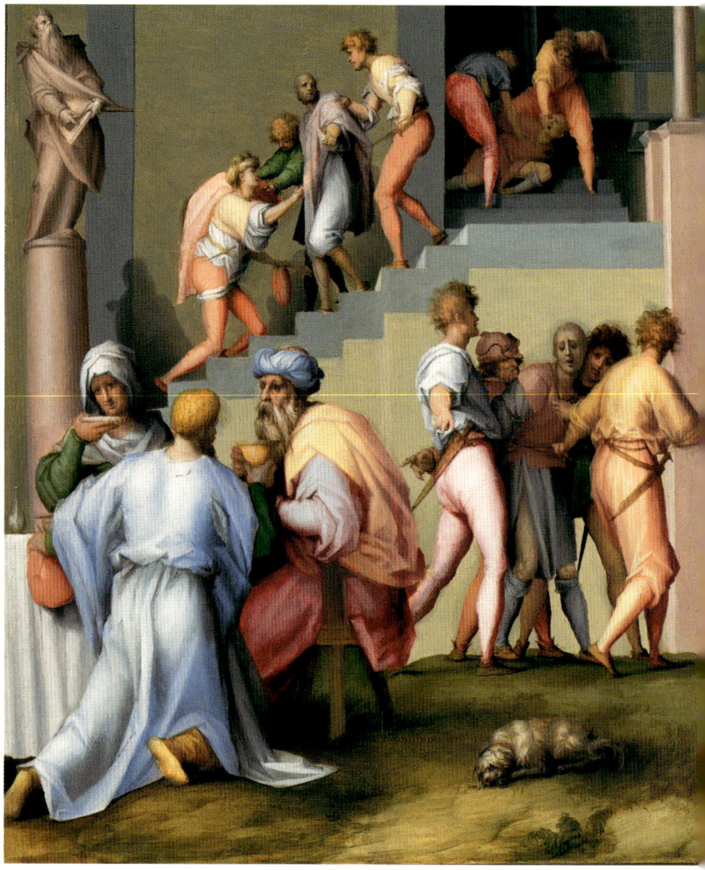

characteristically schematic underdrawing and some, far less dramatic, changes (though there is hardly any underdrawing on the first panel to have been executed, *Joseph's Brothers beg for Help*). All the preparatory drawings on paper that have been connected with Pontormo's four Joseph panels are individual figure studies, made in black or red chalk. In style, they compare extremely well with the underdrawings revealed in infrared reflectography, being rapidly executed, with strong outlines, rectilinear draperies, angular limbs, and some parallel hatching in the shadows (Figs 260, 261 and 263). Very few securely related studies for *Joseph with Jacob in Egypt* exist, and given the extent of improvised preparatory work revealed on the panel itself, this may be no coincidence.

Of all the paintings for the Borgherini bedroom, Vasari singled out *Joseph with Jacob in Egypt* for special praise, judging it the finest work Pontormo ever painted. He applauded the painter for his ingenuity and skill as demonstrated in the vivacity of the heads, the distribution of the figures, the variety of the poses, and the beauty of the invention. The underdrawing revealed by infrared reflectography provides startling evidence of how these qualities were achieved. Liberated by the absence of a cartoon, Pontormo worked with considerable freedom on the prepared panel, revising and improvising not just the poses of individual figures but the entire design of the composition as well. The underdrawing reveals an artistic personality by turns dashingly experimental and resolutely perfectionist. Such spontaneity, a kind of unremitting creativity reminiscent of Pontormo's first mentor Leonardo da Vinci, ran contrary to the Florentine tradition of preparing compositions by means of carefully worked-out designs. This approach is well exemplified by Bacchiacca's much more cautious technique in his panels for the series (Fig. 266). We know from existing cartoons (Fig. 267) that he worked everything out carefully in advance and transferred his designs mechanically to the panel by means of pouncing. Bacchiacca also colour-coordinated not just the main protagonist, Joseph, but all eleven brothers. Such rigorous discipline, both in terms of technique and design, is predictably betrayed in the somewhat laboured appearance of his contributions. Pontormo's courageous departure from this approach, on the other hand, and his increasing faith in his own flexible imagination, led to the creation of one of the most extraordinary and original compositions of its time.

CP

Fig. 266
BACCHIACCA, *Joseph pardons his Brothers* [NG 1219], probably 1515, detail

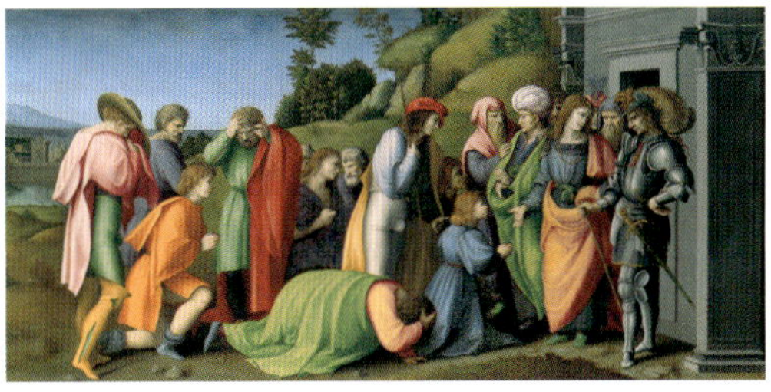

Fig. 267
BACCHIACCA, cartoon for *Joseph pardons his Brothers*, probably 1515
Black chalk heightened with white, on paper pricked for pouncing, 33 × 69 cm
Paris, Musée du Louvre
inv. 1967

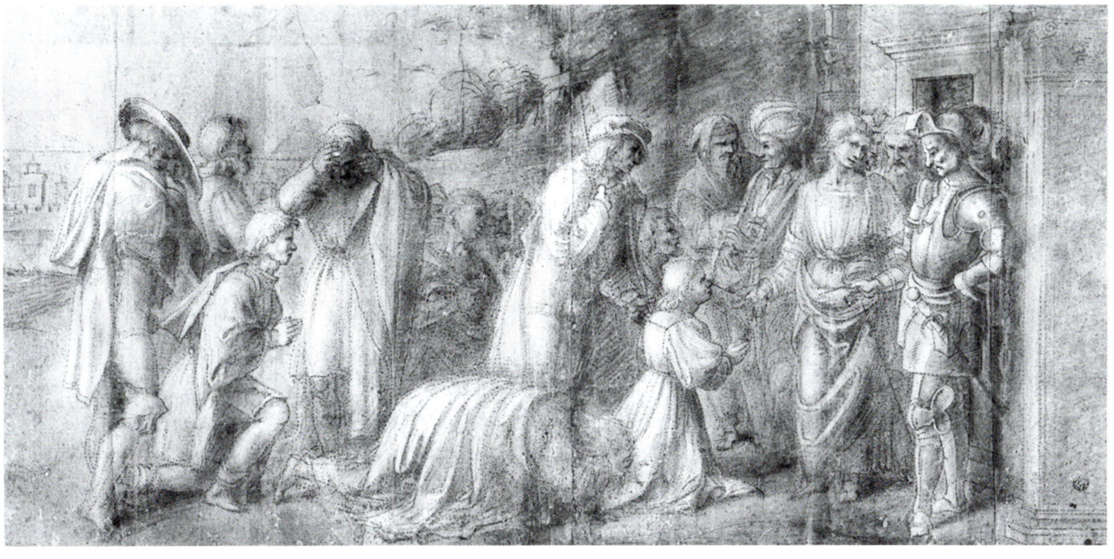

13 Albrecht Altdorfer

*c.*1482/5–1538

Christ taking Leave of his Mother, *c.*1515–20

Oil on limewood, 137 x 106.8 cm
NG 6463

Fig. 268
ALBRECHT ALTDORFER, *Christ taking Leave of his Mother* [NG 6463], *c.*1515–20

ALTDORFER is documented as a citizen of Regensburg in Southern Germany in 1505, and spent most of his life in the city, becoming a member of the city council in 1517. His father was probably the Regensburg miniature painter Ulrich Altdorfer. Altdorfer's work ranged from painted altarpieces to innovative prints and landscape drawings, apparently made for collectors, as well as architecture; he was employed as the city architect in Regensburg. From 1509 to 1516 Altdorfer was employed on a large altarpiece commission for the Augustine monastery of Saint Florian, near Linz in Austria, showing scenes from the Passion of Christ and the Life of Saint Sebastian, of which sixteen panels survive. With his workshop Altdorfer also undertook commissions for the Emperor Maximilian, contributing drawings for the margins of Maximilian's Prayer Book of 1515 and miniatures and designs for woodcuts to the Triumphal Arch of 1516–18. In addition he worked for Duke Wilhelm IV of Bavaria, contributing the *Battle of Alexander* of 1529 (Munich, Alte Pinakothek) to a series of battle paintings. His will refers to his collection of Italian engravings.

Christ, in a plum-coloured robe, stands in the centre of the composition, giving his blessing before departing for Jerusalem, while his mother, the Virgin Mary, in the knowledge that this will lead to his death, lies collapsed in grief, supported by one of the three Maries. On the right stand Saint John the Evangelist in a red robe, and the bearded Saint Peter. Mary Magdalene, in pale blue, kneels before Christ, as she pleads with him not to leave. The scene initiates the sequence of events which will lead to Christ's Passion. The left-hand side of the picture is dominated by a building with a Gothic arch and, to the right of it, a column which shows, at the top, a sculpted relief of the Flagellation of Christ, an intimation of the ordeal to come. Through the arch can be seen a landscape with a bridge over water and distant trees and mountains, as well as a few other buildings. The sky seen through the arch is red, and a halo of light on the extreme left probably indicates the position of the setting sun. At the bottom of the picture on the right are a kneeling donor family – husband, wife, four sons and a daughter, the children all dressed in green, the parents in black.

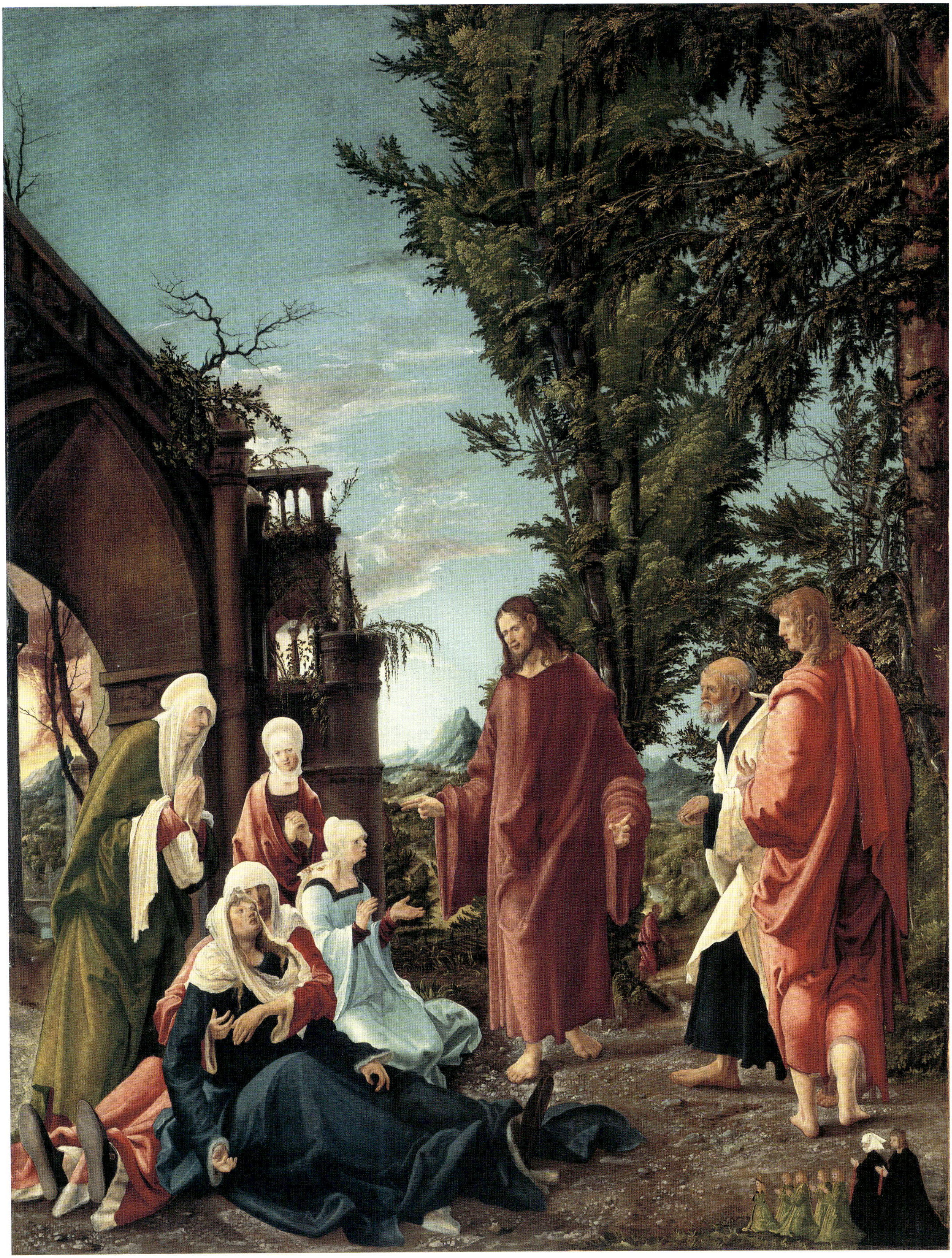

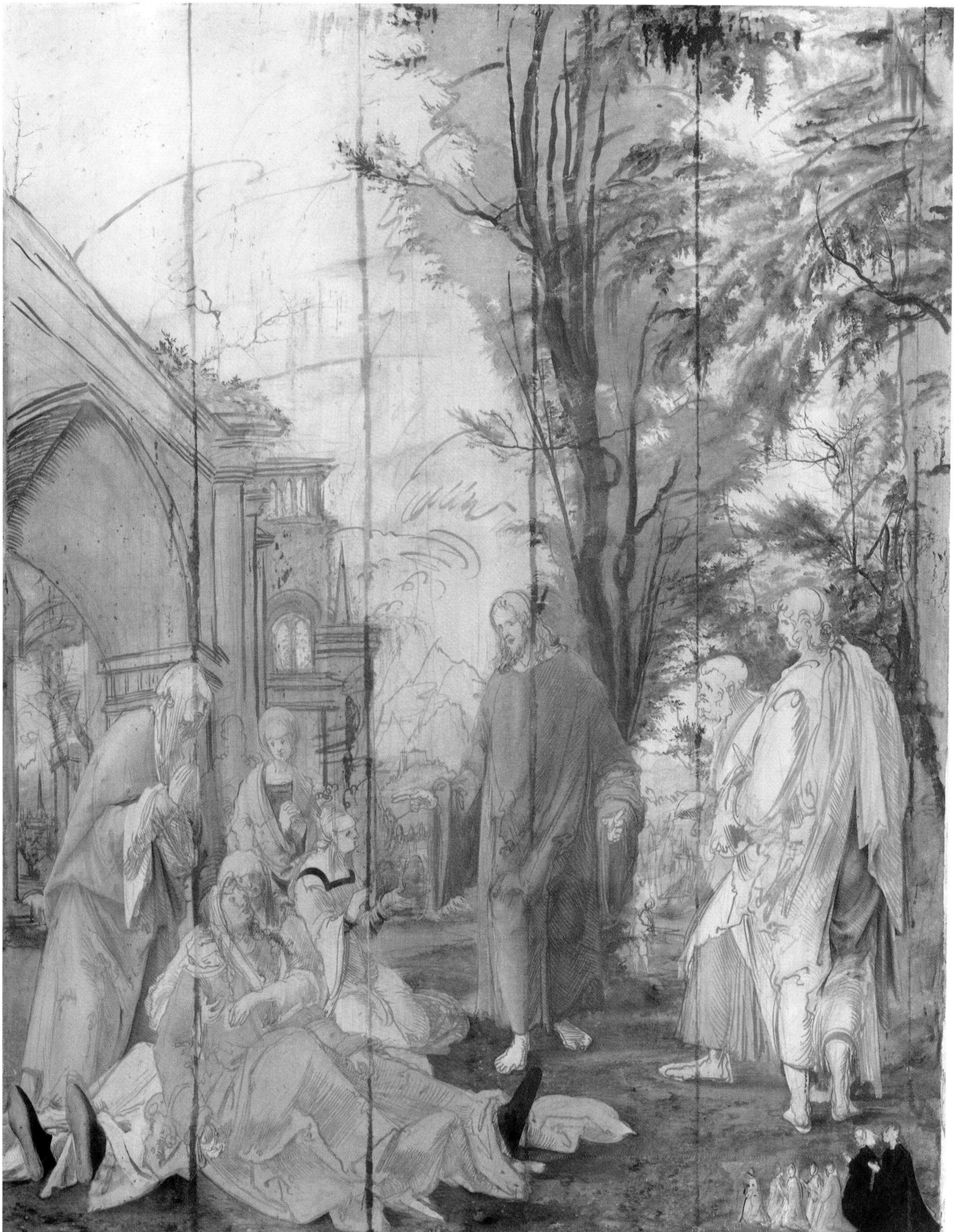

Fig. 269
Infrared reflectogram mosaic of Fig. 268

Fig. 270
Detail of Fig. 269

The subject of the picture is not of biblical origin, but is taken from devotional texts such as the Pseudo-Bonaventura *Meditations on the Life of Christ*. It was not an uncommon one in German art of the early sixteenth century and occurs for example in epitaphs made for Regensburg churches. Although the original location for which the picture was painted is not known, its history from the early nineteenth century connects it with the church of St Emmeram in Regensburg. It was presumably painted for the unidentified donor family, who must have been Regensburg citizens.

The painting was described in 1809 as bearing the date 1522 at the left edge, one foot up from the bottom, but no trace of this has been found in technical examinations. It has been suggested that the column in the background on which the Flagellation of Christ is depicted includes above it the numbers 520, standing for the date 1520. However, this date is not easily read, and close examination suggests that Altdorfer may not have intended to depict any numerals here. The painting shows a number of similarities with paintings forming part of the Saint Sebastian altarpiece for the Abbey of St Florian, commissioned in about 1509 and, in particular, with the *Resurrection* (Vienna, Kunsthistorisches Museum) from the predella, dated 1518. Elements in the composition of *Christ taking Leave of his Mother* can be closely related to drawings of around 1515–18 and the picture probably dates from around this time.

Extensive free underdrawing with the brush and a fluid medium is visible with infrared reflectography (Fig. 269). In some areas much fainter lines are just visible, which seem to be the outlines of a preliminary drawing possibly in a dry material such as chalk, although as has been observed (pp. 33–5), such identifications are difficult to confirm. These lines can be seen extensively in the architecture, in the sky just above it (Fig. 270), and in the cloak of Saint John.

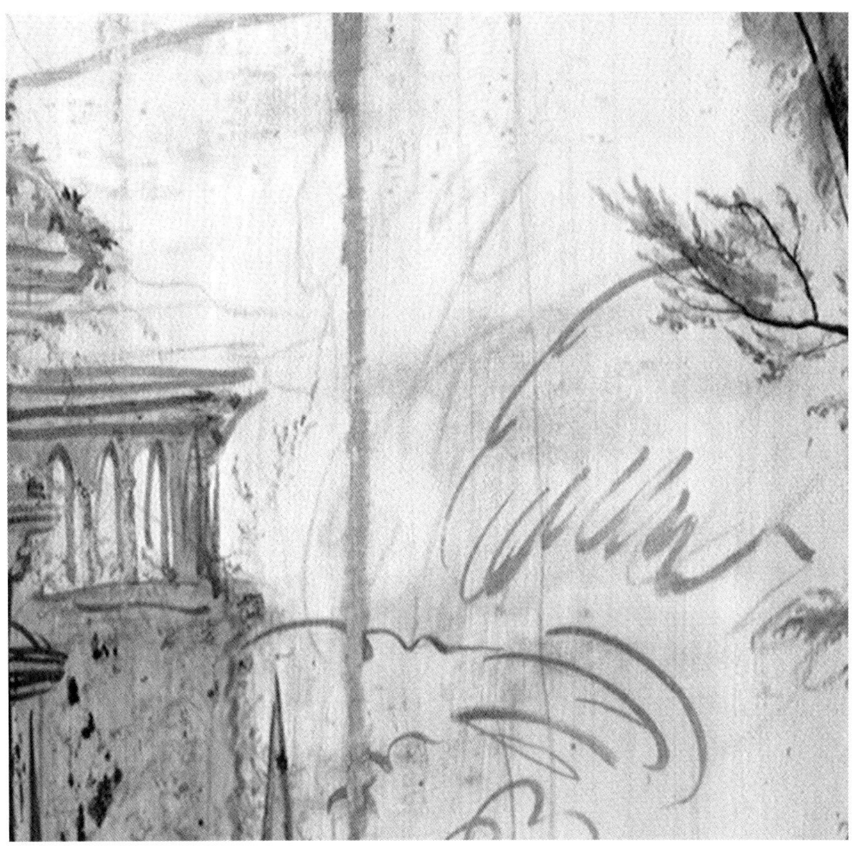

The brush underdrawing that underlies all the figures is highly distinctive: the draperies are drawn with the main folds outlined and extensive parallel hatching to indicate shadows, varied in direction to follow the folds in the cloth. There are a number of revisions in the drawing: for example, a late alteration to Saint John's cloak resulted in new fold lines crossing hatching for an older fold . The main architectural features are all underdrawn, but details such as the capitals were altered and elaborated during painting: the decoration of the capital supporting the arch was originally drawn with a simple vertical moulding (Fig. 271), and that at the top of the round pillar was drawn smaller with a series of concentric rings. Through the arch can be seen a small town with a church which has a tall spire (Fig. 271). In the middle of the painting a landscape scene is drawn with a number of buildings placed on a hillside and the peaks of distant mountains, reaching to a point beside Christ's head. The rest of the landscape background is indicated with great freedom: approximate positions for a branch of the tree and other foliage are sketched in with broad, rapid brushstrokes with loops and swirls. The style of the underdrawing is closely related to that of sketches on paper by Altdorfer, and it is certainly in his own hand. Small details such as the undulating profile of the distant mountains, even the unparticularised looping flourishes for the background elements, as well as larger elements such as the hatched figures, can all be paralleled in drawings by Altdorfer himself.

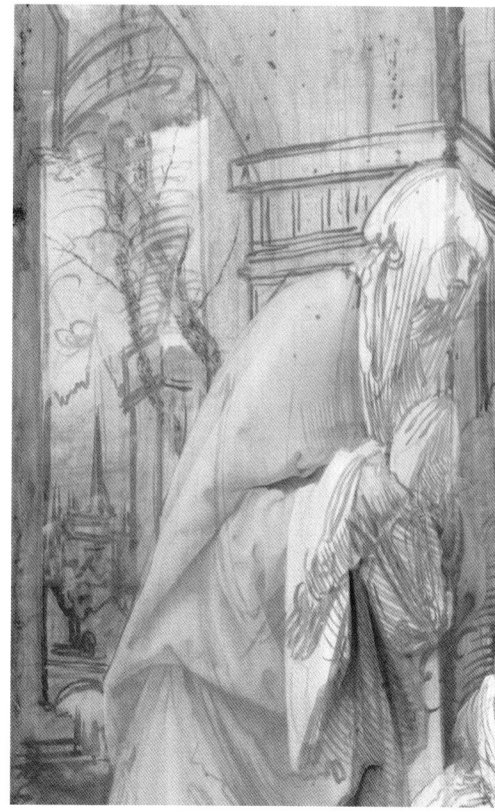

At the painting stage, the whole background landscape was radically altered so that it appeared emptier and more distant. The most striking change was the reduction in size of the mountains next to Christ, now well below the level of his shoulder. The underdrawing shows a long branch extending over Christ's head from the central tree and further branches from the bushes on the building at the left, but these were not painted. The building drawn in the landscape in the centre of the composition, above Christ's hand, is much smaller in the finished painting, and the church with the spire seen through the arch does not appear at all. There are also slight changes in every figure between the drawing and the final painted image: for example, many of the folds in the draperies were altered, and the size of the left foot of the figure supporting the Virgin was reduced. The outline for Christ's feet, drawn in the artist's distinctive looped manner, was enlarged at the painting stage, so that in the drawing the feet appear smaller. The rough indications of trees and bushes in the underdrawing were not followed precisely in the painting stage, and were largely composed afresh. The fence shown between Christ and Mary Magdalene was not drawn but introduced at the painting stage.

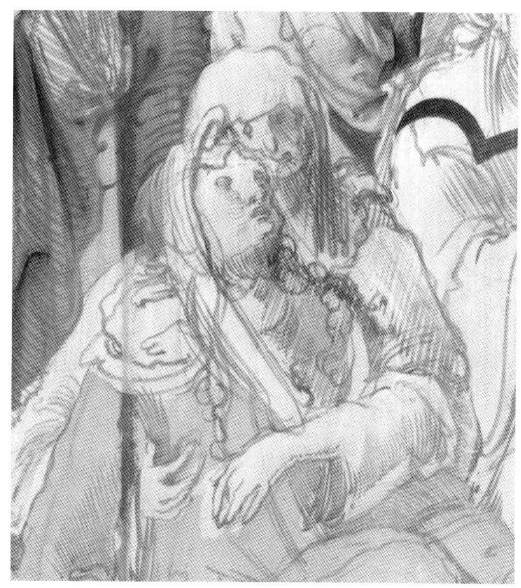

Despite the appearance of creative freedom in the brush underdrawing of *Christ taking Leave of his Mother,* Altdorfer appears to have been working with a detailed compositional plan, laid out in an initial rough sketch. From this it can be deduced that the overall composition had already been established before work on the panel began. This is consistent with the practice that has been observed in the *Susanna* in the Alte Pinakothek, Munich, where a detailed drawing on paper also survives, and the underdrawing shows squaring, of which there is no evidence here.

As we have seen, once the layout had been established, the brush underdrawing was begun, and the composition completed with details of architecture, landscape

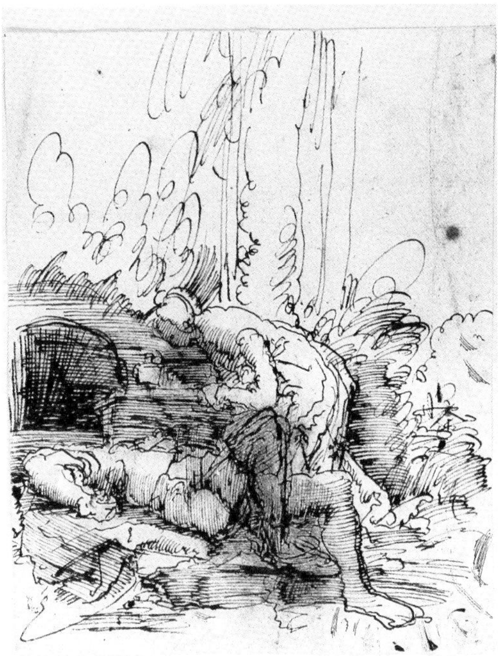

and figures. This detailed drawing was then amended at the painting stage, reducing the proportions of landscape to figures, ensuring that the background details did not conflict with the foreground narrative. The reasons for this may have had as much to do with drama as with clarity: departing from the convention of showing a detailed view of Jerusalem allowed Altdorfer to concentrate his effects on the rendering of the distance into which Christ was about to depart as a largely empty, unpopulated country lit by the red light of the setting sun. Rather than simply informing us that Christ is to travel to Jerusalem, Altdorfer encourages meditation on the journey towards his fate which is, as he conveys, a journey to a distant unknown destination, with a tragic and bloody end.

The pose Altdorfer uses for the Virgin, clearly established in the underdrawing, is also innovatory (Fig. 272). His Virgin is unusual in the extent of her distress, lying collapsed in the pose often adopted for the Virgin at the Crucifixion. The Magdalen in blue behind her occupies the kneeling pleading position more normally reserved for the Virgin in representations of this subject. The pose Altdorfer chose for the Virgin is one which seems to have preoccupied him in the second decade of the sixteenth century. Similar figures, lying with bent knees, occur in other works by Altdorfer, notably in drawings of Pyramus and Thisbe (Fig. 273), the *Lamentation* and Saint Florian rescued. The group of figures around the Virgin, and the Saint John, appear to derive from Mantegna's engravings, especially the *Deposition* (Fig. 274) and the *Entombment with Three Birds*. We know from his will that Altdorfer owned a collection of Italian engravings, and presumably he used these prints as inspiration for his drawings. A number of other compositional elements which occur in *Christ taking Leave of his Mother* were used elsewhere by Altdorfer, for example, the ruined arch occurs in the woodcut of the *Beheading of Saint John the Baptist*, dated 1512; these too imply reference to drawings which Altdorfer kept in his workshop.

SF

Fig. 271 (left)
Detail of Fig. 269

Fig. 272
Details of Fig. 269

Fig. 273 (above)
ALBRECHT ALTDORFER, *Pyramus and Thisbe*, *c.*1518
Pen and ink with wash on paper, 13.4 × 10.6 cm
Erlangen, Graphische Sammlung der Universität

Fig. 274 (right)
ANDREA MANTEGNA, *Deposition*, *c.*1465
Engraving
London, The British Museum
inv. P&D 1845-8-25-599

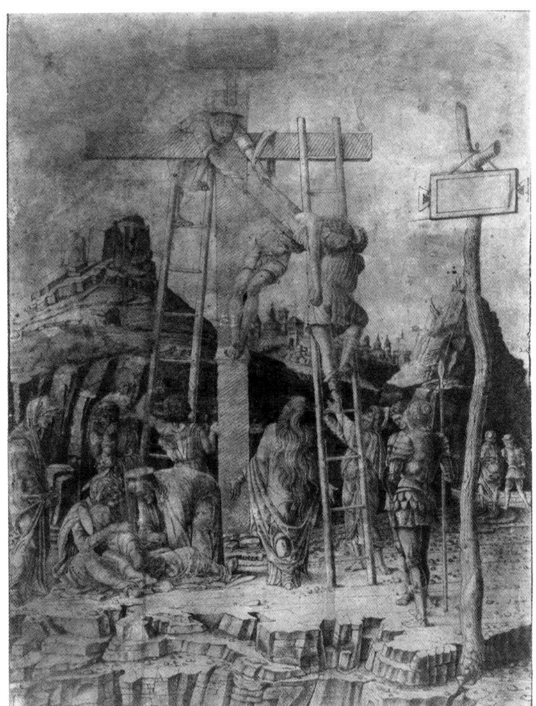

14 Workshop of the Master of 1518

active early 16th century

The Flight into Egypt, *c.*1525

Oil on oak, 80.2 x 69.7 cm
NG 1084

This unknown painter was named by Max Friedländer after the double set of painted wing panels of a large altarpiece in the Marienkirche in Lübeck, the carved central section of which bears the date 1518. These panels, one of which also shows the Flight into Egypt, include many borrowings from woodcuts by Dürer. They are in a style related to the fashionable trend misleadingly termed 'Antwerp Mannerism', although they are less extravagantly agitated and theatrical than typical 'Antwerp Mannerist' pictures. According to Friedländer, followed by many other art historians, the Master of 1518 also painted the triptych of the *Life of the Magdalen* (Brussels, Musées Royaux des Beaux-Arts), which came from the Abbey of Dielegem at Jette, now part of the western suburbs of Brussels. However, given the considerable stylistic differences between the triptych and the wing panels, it is likely that they are the products of two separate workshops, which can be tentatively assigned to a Master of 1518, probably active in Antwerp, and to a Master of Dielegem, possibly working in Antwerp but conceivably active in Brussels.

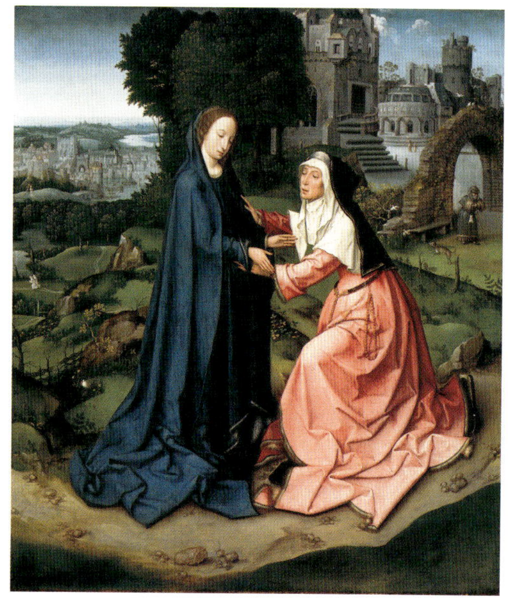

Fig. 275
WORKSHOP OF THE MASTER OF 1518,
The Visitation of the Virgin to Saint Elizabeth [NG 1082], *c.*1525
Oil on oak, 81.3 × 71 cm

The subject is from Saint Matthew's Gospel (2: 13–14) and various apocryphal texts. Saint Joseph advances down a rocky path and leads the donkey on which the Virgin is seated, nursing the Child. They have just passed a bronze statue of a nude pagan god, which has broken into several pieces and is falling from its pillar. According to legend, many idols were believed to have been broken as the Holy Family passed by on their way to Egypt. The dying tree on the right may refer to Ezekiel's prophecy (17: 24): '... I the Lord ... have made the dry tree to flourish', interpreted as a prediction of the Virgin birth. The spring and the stream over which the ass is about to step may refer to the Miracle of the Palm: a beautiful fountain sprang from the root of the palm tree which, at Christ's command, had lowered its branches so that the Virgin could pick its dates.

The town in the background is presumably Jerusalem; the village where soldiers are massacring the Innocents must be Bethlehem. In the valley below is taking place the Miracle of the Corn: legend tells us that when the Holy Family were on their

Fig. 276 (opposite)
WORKSHOP OF THE MASTER OF 1518,
The Flight into Egypt [NG 1084], *c.*1525

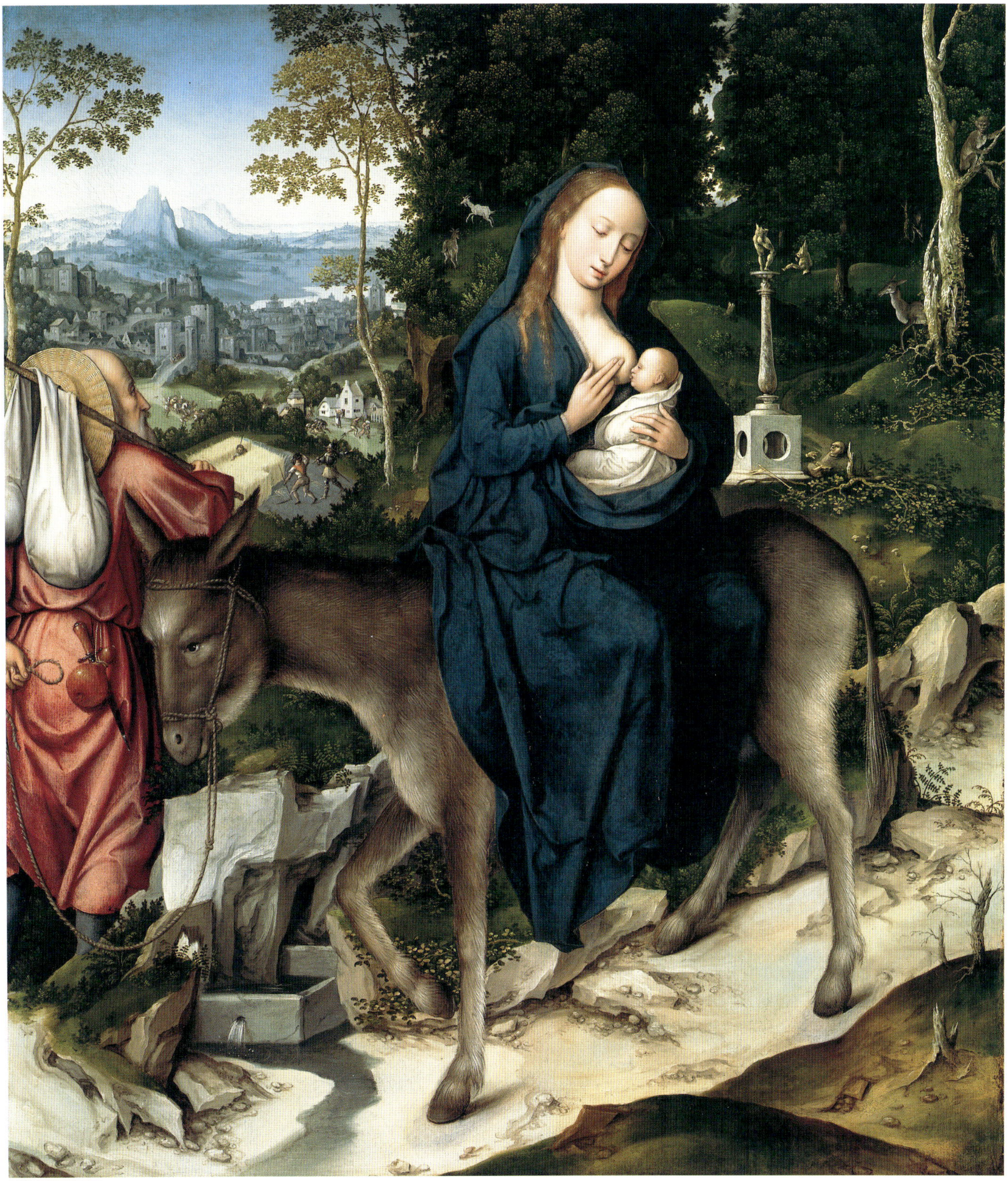

way to Egypt, they came upon a peasant sowing wheat. The Christ Child threw a fistful of the seed onto the road and immediately the wheat sprang up 'as tall and as ripe as if it had been growing for a year'. When Herod's soldiers, who were pursuing the Child in order to kill him, came upon the peasant, they asked him whether he had seen a woman pass that way who was carrying a child. 'Yes', he said, 'when I was sowing this wheat.' Since it appeared that the wheat had been sown over a year earlier, the soldiers returned to Jerusalem and the Holy Family escaped to Egypt.

The Flight into Egypt is painted on an oak panel made up of three vertical planks. Three other panels of the same dimensions and painted in similar styles have been identified as parts of the same series: the *Visitation* (NG 1082; Fig 275), the *Adoration of the Kings* (Honolulu; Fig. 277) and a *Christ and the Doctors* (Antwerp, Museum Mayer van den Bergh; Fig. 279). If they were from a cycle of scenes of the Infancy of Christ, the missing panels might have included an Annunciation, a Nativity and a Presentation in the Temple. As the reverses of the four panels seem never to have been painted, they cannot be from the shutters of a folding altarpiece. They may be from the central section of an altarpiece of the Infancy of Christ. In style, the National Gallery *Flight* resembles only distantly the *Flight into Egypt* of the 1518 altarpiece in Lübeck, which is itself closely based on the famous woodcut by Dürer. It also relates to the style of the Dielegem triptych, but again rather distantly. These are the grounds on which the London *Flight* and the paintings from the same series are associated with the workshop of the Master of 1518.

The underdrawing of the *Flight* (Fig. 280), executed in a liquid medium, is in two distinct styles and seems to be the work of two artists: one of them being responsible for the landscape; the other for the Holy Family and the donkey (Fig. 278). All the underdrawings appear to be freehand, although the artists would almost certainly have been working from preliminary drawings, especially for the figures. The underdrawings are essentially linear in style: forms are outlined, without much suggestion of volume. The artist who drew the landscape background has neatly outlined houses, trees and the distant horizon (Fig. 281); while in the denser trees behind the Virgin he has made the areas of deep shadow darker in the underdrawing by shading them with horizontal lines (Fig. 283). To indicate foliage on trees and bushes he has made great use of characteristically neat short curved strokes. In contrast, the foreground figures and the donkey are very

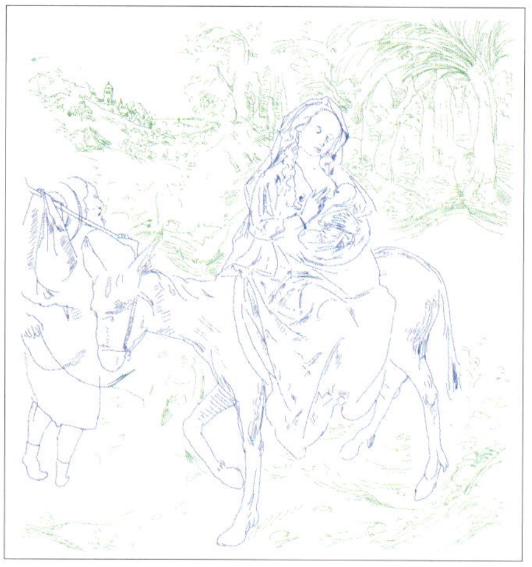

Fig. 278
Diagram of underdrawing

Fig. 277 (below left)
WORKSHOP OF THE MASTER OF 1518, *Adoration of the King*, *c.*1525
Oil on wood, 81.5 × 70.2 cm
Honolulu (Hawaii), Honolulu Academy of Arts Gallery Purchase, Acquisition Fund, funds given in memory of Mrs Richard A. Cooke, Alyce Hoogs, Wilhelmina Tenney, and Douglas Damon, the bequest of Alyce Hoogs, and contributions by the Charles and Anna C. Cooke Trust, Mrs Robert P. Griffing, Jr., cont: Robert Allerton and John Gregg Allerton, 1963 (3103.1)
inv. 1963.3103.1

Fig. 279 (below right)
WORKSHOP OF THE MASTER OF 1518, *Christ and the Doctors*, *c.*1525
Oil on oak, 81.7 × 70.5 cm
Antwerp, Museum Mayer van den Bergh
inv. 357

Fig. 280 (opposite)
Infrared reflectogram mosaic of Fig. 276

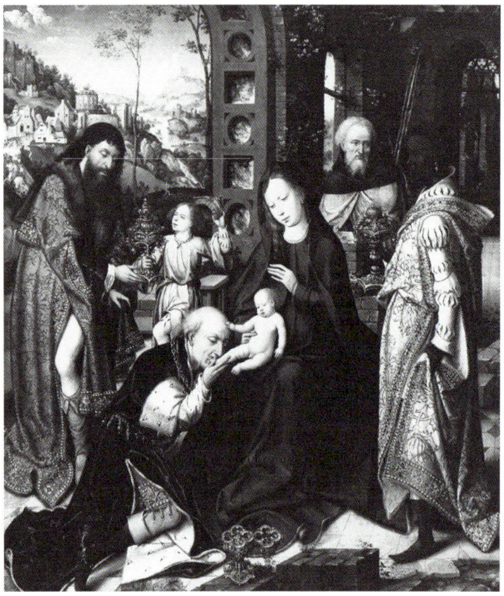

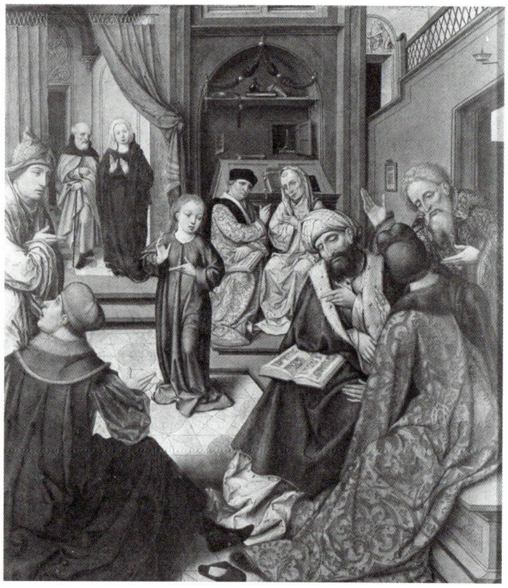

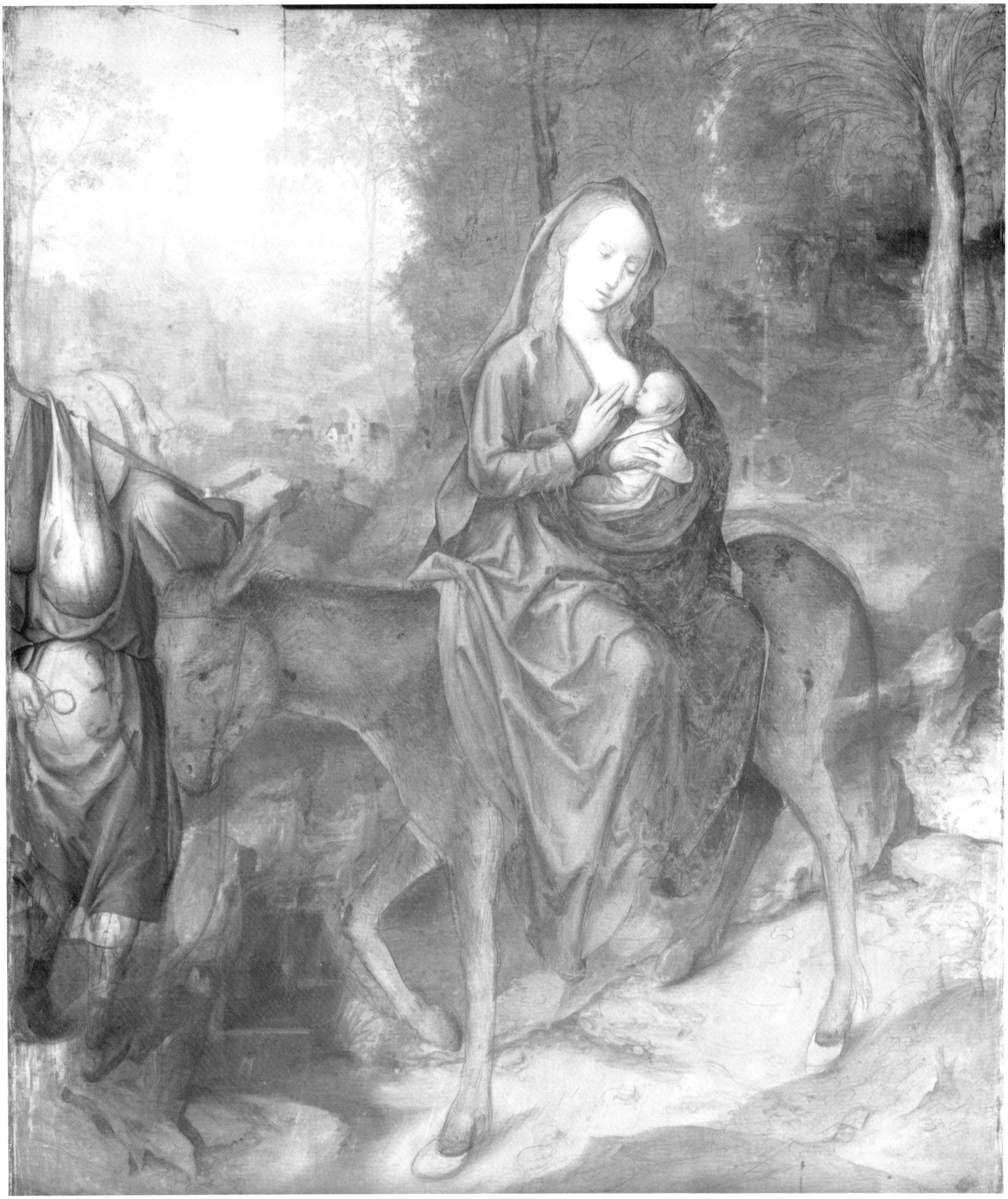

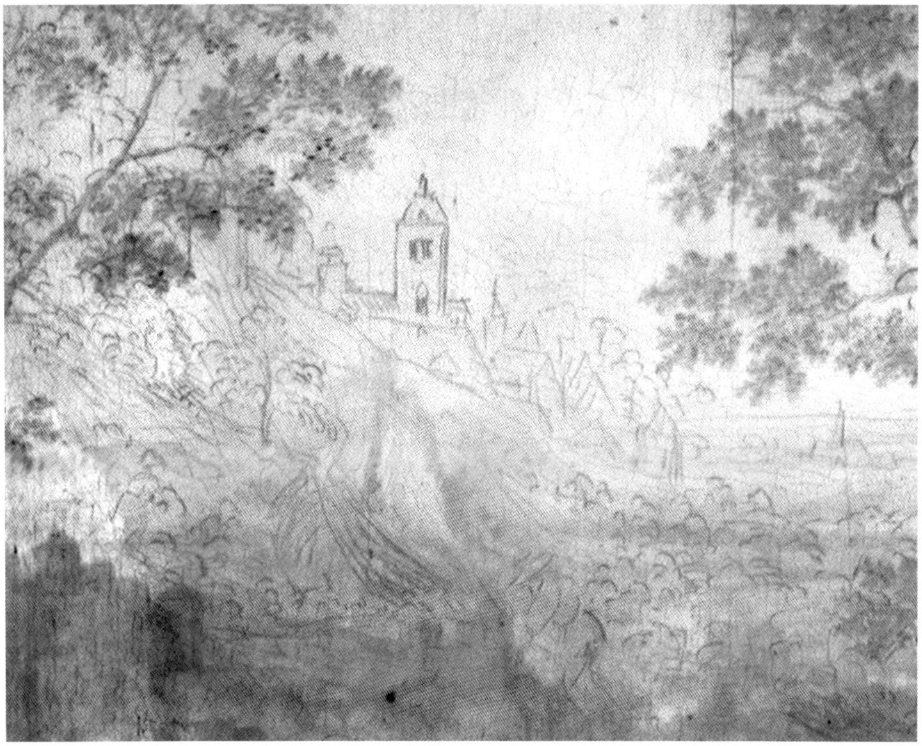

Fig. 281 (left)
Detail of Fig. 280

Fig. 282
Detail of Fig. 280

Fig. 283
Detail of Fig. 280

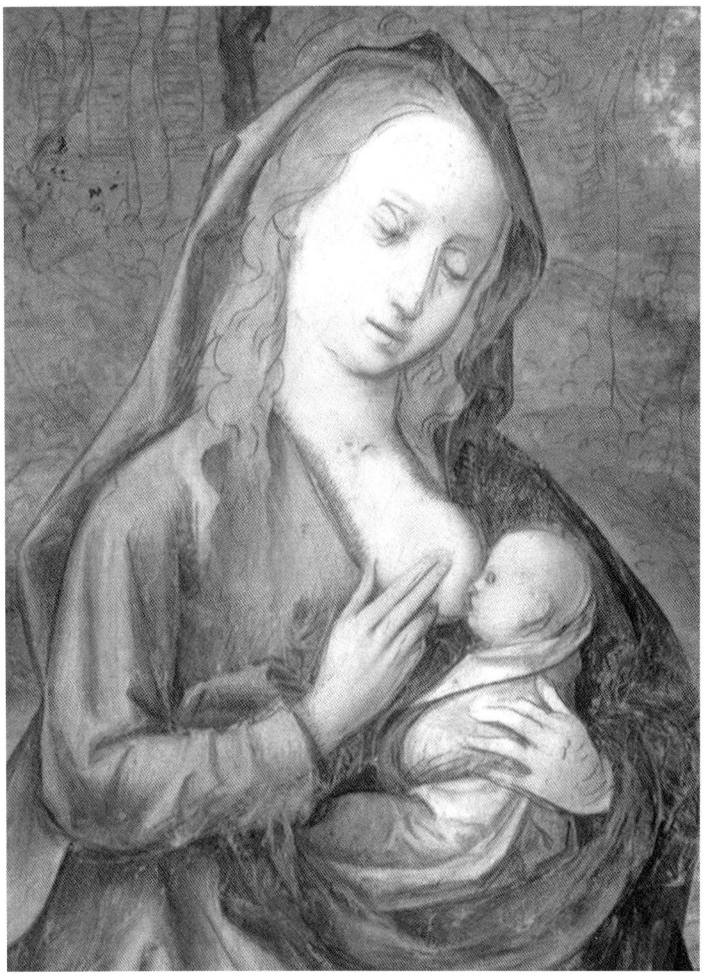

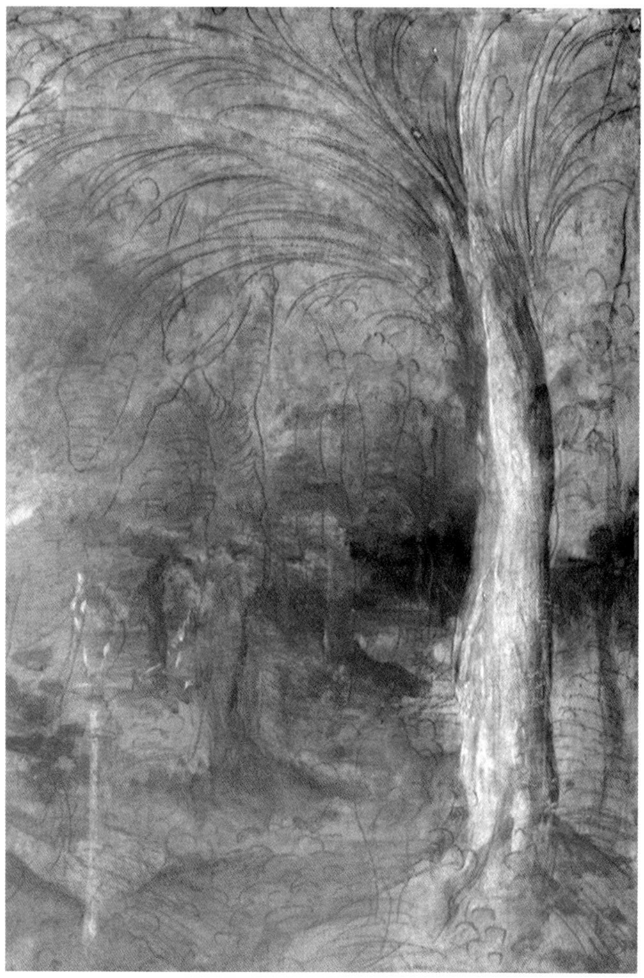

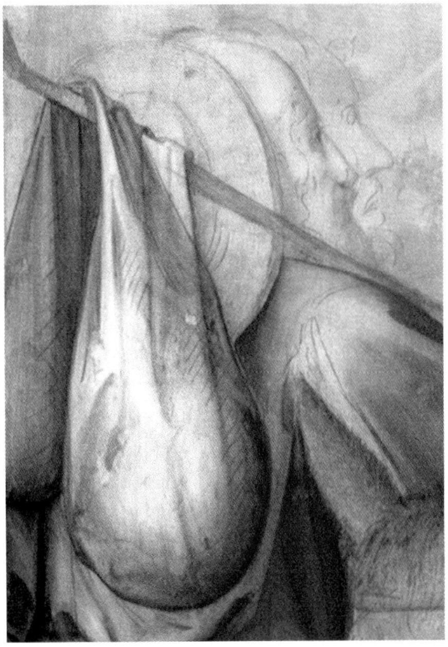

much more hesitantly and less neatly drawn. The facial features and the Virgin's hair are indicated very schematically (Fig. 282), while the folds in the draperies, for example the Virgin's mantle, are simply suggested by means of short lines and hatching following more or less the directions of the folds (Fig. 285).

The artist or artists who painted the *Flight* made various changes to the foreground figures. Joseph's profile has been moved to the left; his saddle-bags have been extended on the right (Fig. 284); his waist has been raised; his robe has been lengthened; and his feet, which have been begun in paint, were later concealed behind rocks. Neither his dagger nor his water-bottle has been underdrawn or reserved; the rope with which he leads the donkey has been repositioned. The donkey's ears are longer in the underdrawing, where it has a mane rather like a horse's mane (Fig. 286). Its rump has been lowered; both its near legs have been considerably shortened.

Alhough retaining the idea of combining a dark, wooded area behind the Virgin with a view across a distant landscape, the painter chose to ignore the underdrawing and to replace it with another landscape, not underdrawn, in a different style. On the left, he inserted a different vista with a lower horizon. Distant mountains appear to be much further from the spectator than the hilltop town in the underdrawing. The screen of trees behind the Virgin is very differently arranged in the underdrawing, which shows a dense wood of rather sculptural, often forked, trees in an undulating terrain with thick bushy undergrowth. An underdrawn palm tree (see Fig. 283), perhaps referring to the Miracle of the Palm (see p. 162), takes

Fig. 284 (above)
Detail of Fig. 280

Fig. 285 (right)
Detail of Fig. 280

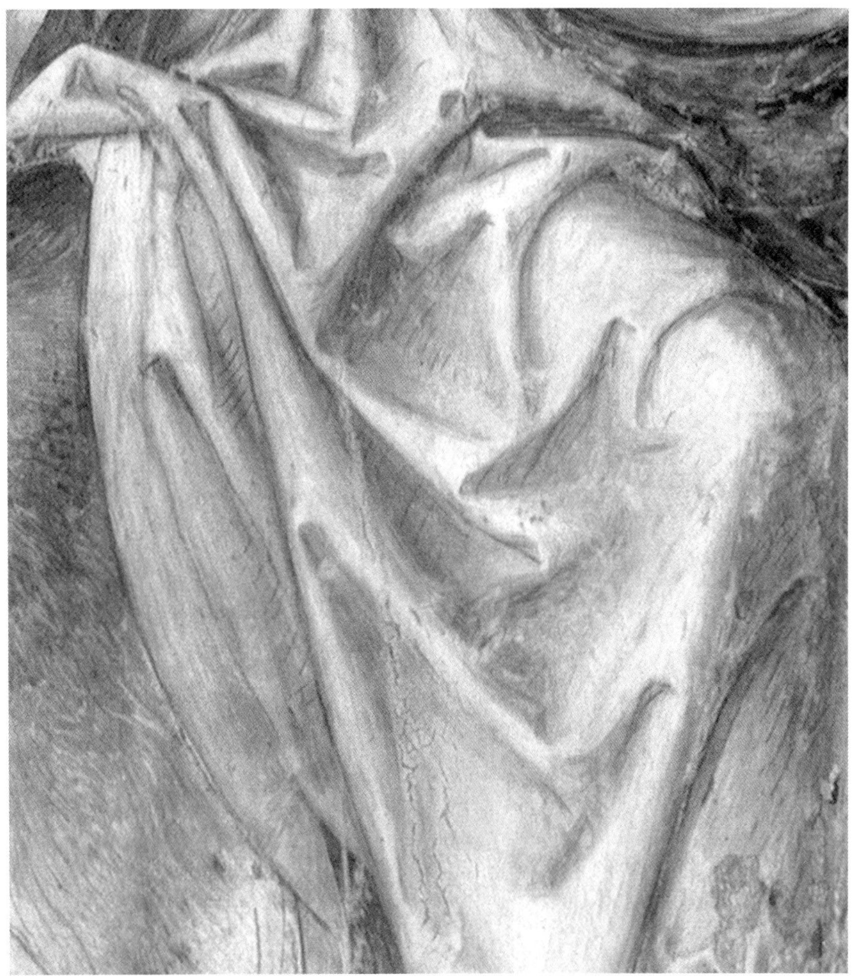

up much of the upper right corner but, in the painting, its trunk has been replaced by the half-dead tree. X-radiographs show that, during the first stages of painting, there were larger areas of sky above and to the right of the Virgin's head (Fig. 287). These areas of sky did not relate to the underdrawing and were probably the painter's first idea for the changed design.

The painted landscape was laid in around the underdrawn contours of the figures. When the figures were subsequently altered, adjustments had to be made to background areas then left exposed. The decision to lengthen Joseph's robe, and probably also to conceal his feet, was taken at a late stage, after the underdrawn robe had been underpainted in mixtures of vermilion, white and black. The underlayer in the addition contains less black; the addition therefore shows in the reflectogram as a much lighter band.

Some details were added at very late stages and are not underdrawn or reserved. They include the scenes of the Massacre of the Innocents and the Miracle of the Corn, the column and the falling idol – all passages which add to the narrative content. Other late additions which have no real narrative significance are the

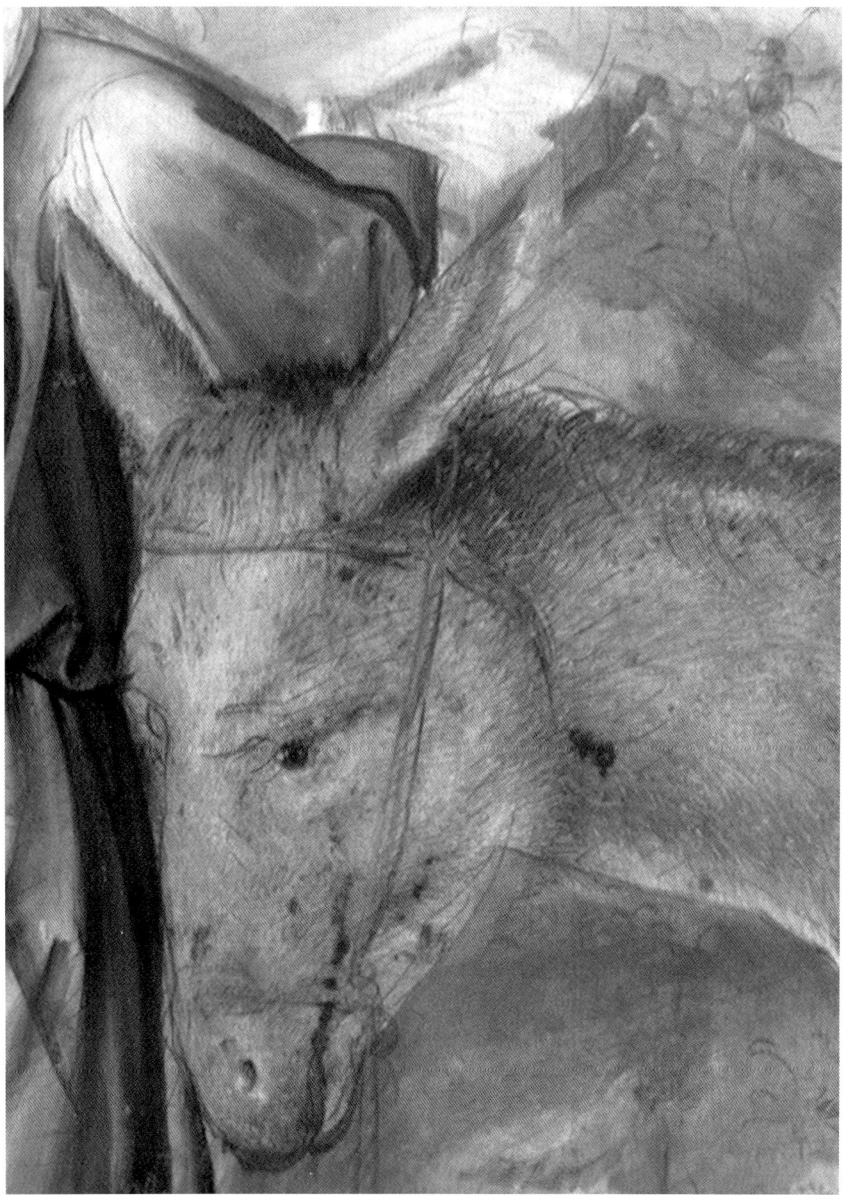

Fig. 286
Detail of Fig. 280

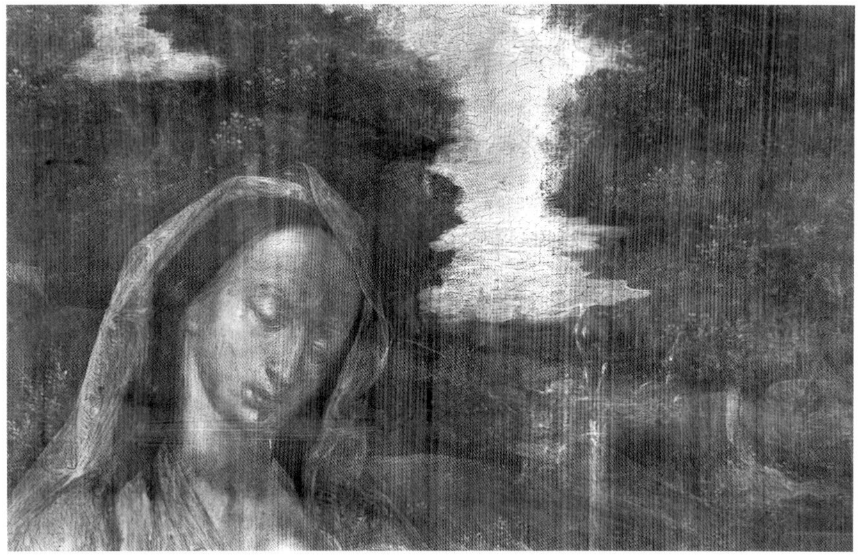

Fig. 287
X-ray detail of Fig. 276

animals, Saint Joseph's dagger and his water-bottle. In the lower right corner, the triangle of grassy verge is painted over an underdrawing of a wider roadway.

The *Visitation* is underdrawn and painted in similar ways and is probably the work of the same team of artists. The underdrawn landscape, perhaps less precisely rendered than that of the *Flight*, corresponds hardly at all with what has been painted. No infrared photographs are available of the *Adoration*. The published reflectogram of a section of *Christ and the Doctors* shows several of the foreground figures, where the untidy underdrawing bears some resemblance to that of the figures in the *Flight* and the *Visitation*. In the figure on the extreme right, however, are passages of fairly disciplined cross-hatching which do not resemble anything found in the *Flight* and the *Visitation*.

Friedländer and other art historians have considered that the *Flight* and the three related panels have much in common with the 1518 altarpiece and the Dielegem triptych. Indeed the resemblances are sometimes claimed to extend to the underdrawings. The published reflectogram and infrared photograph of parts of the 1518 altarpiece show very clear and disciplined underdrawings which are rather like prints in the ways in which shadowed areas are hatched and cross-hatched. The compositions of several of the panels are based on woodcuts by Dürer. The published reflectograms of the Dielegem triptych show a more tentative underdrawing which is perhaps a little closer in style to the underdrawing of the figures in the *Flight*.

As noted above, the underdrawing of the *Flight* is by at least two artists; the painting may have involved several more. They may have specialised to some degree. If so, there were at least two landscape specialists within this same workshop: the artist who made the underdrawing for the landscape and the collaborator who, ignoring the underdrawing, painted the visible landscape. The two employed very different formulae. Examination of the *Flight* serves to show how complicated the relationships could be among artists collaborating within one workshop.

LC

15 Marinus van Reymerswale

active 1535 to 1545

Two Tax Gatherers, *c.*1540

Oil on oak, 92.0 x 74.6 cm
NG 944

Signed works by this Netherlandish artist date from 1535 to 1545. Usually he signed simply 'Marinus' but occasionally he added the word 'Reymerswale'. He signed several almost identical paintings of *Saint Jerome in his Study*, several nearly identical pictures of *The Banker and his Wife* and two very similar paintings of *The Lawyer's Office*. He seems to have specialised in a rather narrow range of subjects and to have produced exact or nearly exact replicas of his few favoured subjects. In both respects he was unusual or unique among his contemporaries. Many of these paintings include representations of manuscripts and deeds. The writing is frequently, perhaps always, legible and in the texts many references have been found to the town and inhabitants of Reymerswale (Reimerswaal), which was once reckoned to be the third most important town in Zeeland but which was abandoned in 1631 and afterwards disappeared beneath the waters of the Ooster Schelde. Marinus probably lived in Reymerswale and must certainly have maintained contacts with the town. No certain reference to Marinus in contemporary sources has been found and nothing is known about his assistants. His work has many affinities with that of Quinten Massys and his son Jan Massys.

Fig. 288
MARINUS VAN REYMERSWALE, *Two Tax Gatherers* [NG 944], *c.*1540

Behind the two men is a wooden cupboard on top of which documents are piled. The folded document above the head of the man on the right is a deed issued, according to the inscription, in 1515 by two aldermen of Reymerswale. The name of the first is concealed by the folding of the document; the second, Cornelis Danielsz., was indeed an alderman in 1514–15 and died in 1530. The man on the left is writing in his ledger an account of the income of a town over a period of seven months from the excise duties on wine and beer, the 'fish-bridge', the weigh-house, the 'hall', the ferries, fees for deeds, charges raised for specific expenses, loans and the civic mills. It is clear that the town was Reymerswale, where there were a 'fish-bridge' – a fish-market on a bridge – a cloth-hall and a butchers' hall and from where ferries ran to Venusdam on the island of Tholen and to the mainland at Bergen-op-Zoom and Antwerp. The mills were water- and wind-mills. The man writing wears an elaborate heart-shaped hat of a kind worn by fashionably dressed

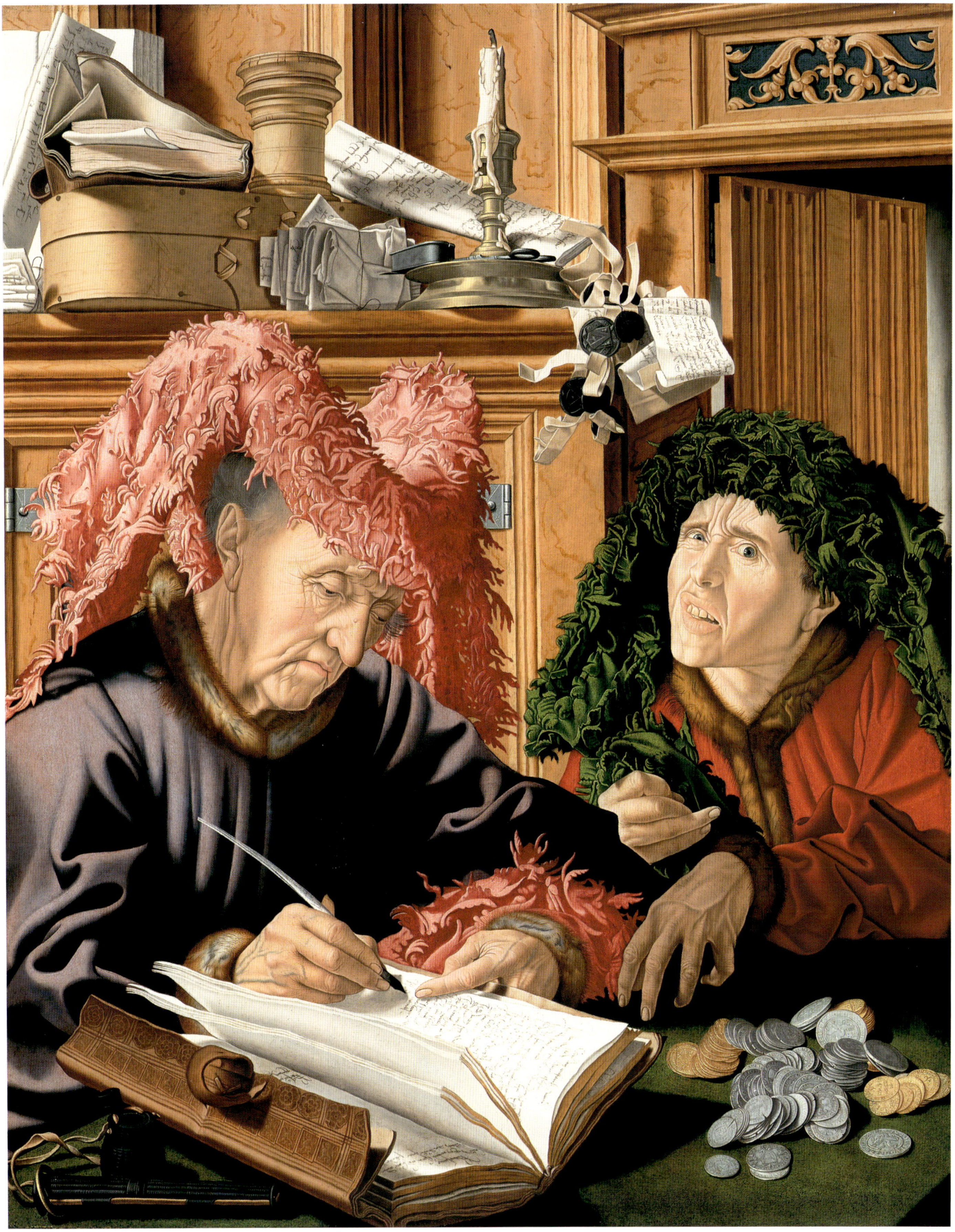

women in the mid-fifteenth century. The man on the right wears a hat of a shape fashionable for men during the first half of the fifteenth century. His sneering grimace and the grasping fingers of his left hand must indicate the extent of his avarice.

The man on the left is a municipal official who is writing an account of the revenues from various imposts put out to farm. He may be the Treasurer or Tax-Collector of Reymerswale and his companion may be one of the other collectors or tax-farmers. Alternatively the writing man may be the 'Counter-Book-Keeper', employed to keep a check on the activities of the Treasurer. Their extraordinary clothes remove them from contemporary reality, though the legible documents assert a connection with everyday life in Reymerswale.

A nearly identical picture, apparently also by Marinus, is in the Louvre (Fig. 289). The painted surface measures 91.5 x 75 cm, the panel 94 x 77 cm: this was probably the original size of the London picture, which has been slightly trimmed below and on both sides. Both the Paris and the London pictures are on panels of three oak planks. The two versions correspond closely in colour and in detail. The underdrawings, however, are very different.

It is not easy to date the London and Paris pictures but they are connected with and probably later than Marinus's paintings of *The Banker and his Wife*, the signed versions of which are dated 1538, 1539, 1540 and 1541 (Fig. 292). Exaggerated facial expressions, such as that of the man on the right, are not found in Marinus's pictures of the 1530s but become more apparent in the two signed examples of *The Lawyer's Office* dated 1542 (Munich) and 1546 (New Orleans). Perhaps during the 1540s Marinus was becoming more inclined to depict the grotesque extremes of facial expression. For such reasons, it seems plausible to suggest that the London and Paris pictures were painted in the 1540s.

Fig. 289 (bottom left)
MARINUS VAN REYMERSWALE,
Two Tax Gatherers, c.1540
Oil on oak, 94 × 77 cm
Paris, Musée du Louvre
RF 1989-6

Fig. 290
Infrared photograph of Fig. 289

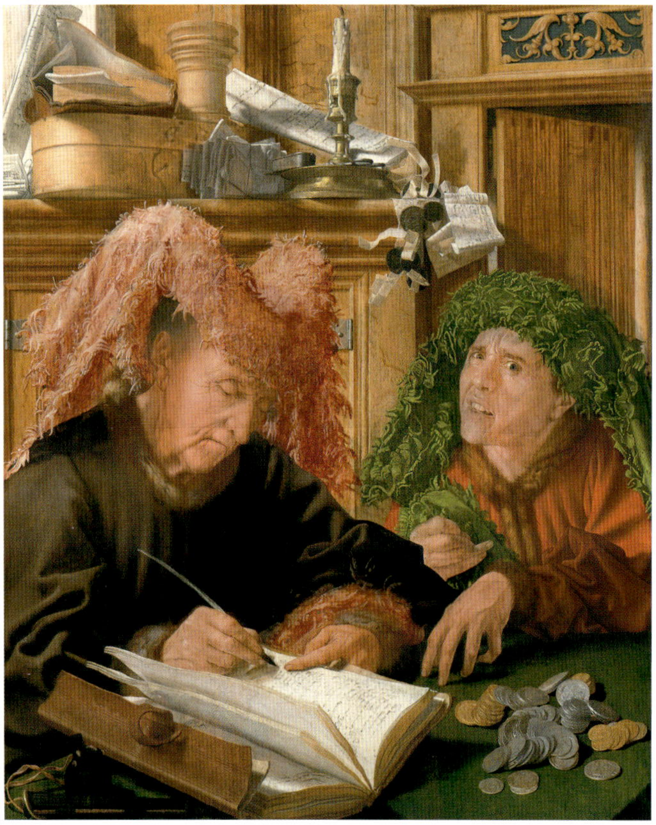

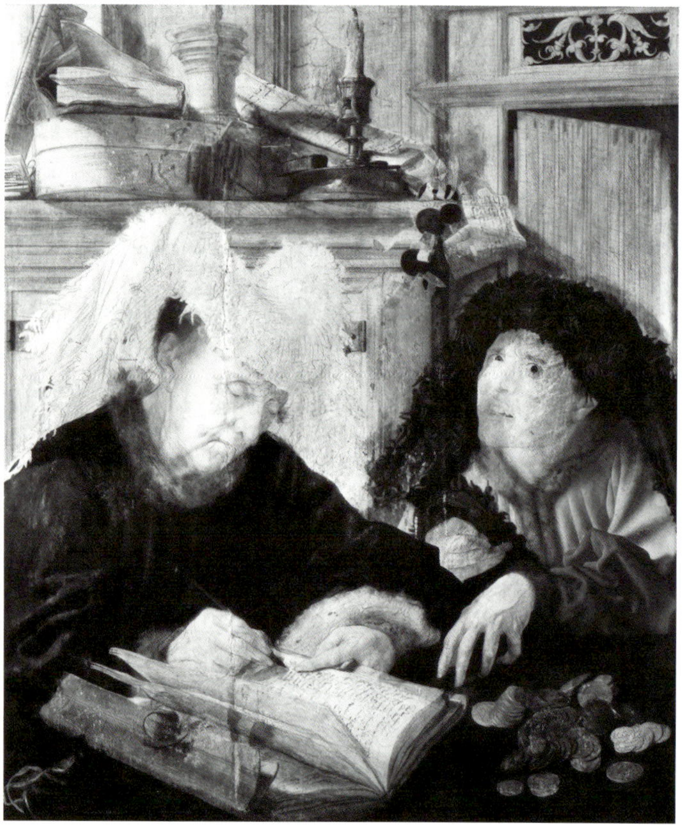

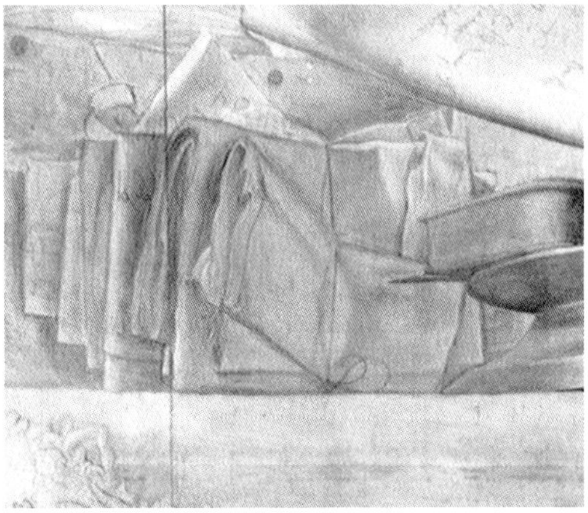

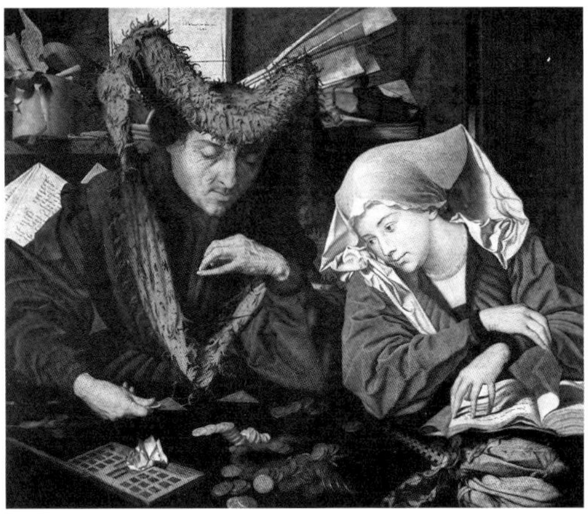

Fig. 291 (top)
Detail from infrared reflectogram mosaic of Fig. 288

Fig. 292
MARINUS VAN REYMERSWALE,
The Banker and his Wife
Oil on oak, 93.5 × 111 cm.
Dresden, Staatliche Kunstsammlungen, Gemäldegalerie Alte Meister
inv. 812

The popularity enjoyed by such pictures is difficult to explain but simplified versions of Marinus's composition went on being created by followers and imitators over a very long period. They must have served as warnings against avarice. Many people must have admired such paintings without fully understanding the references in the painted deeds to local affairs in Reymerswale or the puzzling fancy dress worn by the protagonists.

Infrared reflectography reveals a careful and detailed underdrawing (Figs 293 and 293): all the wrinkles and all the frills of cut fabric in the hats are meticulously outlined. Examined closely, the lines, drawn with brushes, look discontinuous and occasionally it is possible to see faint traces of other lines defining the same contours. These are signs that the underdrawing has been reproduced from a tracing. The artist has then 'fixed' the traced lines by going over them in a liquid medium. The underdrawing is faithfully followed in the painting. There are a few, very minor changes in the shapes of the cut decorations on the hat worn by the writing man and, in the bundle of papers above his head, the drawing for the loop formed by the string is smaller than, and to the left of, the painted loop (Fig. 291).

In contrast, infrared photographs of the Paris painting reveal a sketchy and nervous underdrawing (Figs 290 and 295). Though the artist probably made preliminary compositional drawings, the underdrawing was an important stage in the creative process. Working freely on the panel, he has tried out different positions for details, for example in the hands of the writing man and in his book (Fig. 296). During painting, he has continued to modify the design: he has, for instance, significantly enlarged the ear of the man on the left.

Marinus and his assistants were used to making exact copies of his pictures; Marinus was almost certainly responsible for both the London and the Paris paintings and clearly wrote both sets of inscriptions, where the handwriting is exceedingly similar. Interestingly enough, the inscriptions in the two ledgers are not precisely the same. In the Paris picture, the fifth item in the account is the *byerberye* – the barrow from which beer was sold: this entry does not occur in the London account. In the London ledger but not in the Paris ledger, *die fijne* – another tax – is entered as the ninth item, between the *omeslach* – a tax levied to meet specific municipal expenses – and the *molerije* or multures, charges for milling grain. Otherwise there is an almost exact correspondence between the inscriptions on the Paris and London paintings. The London picture is therefore a replica by Marinus and his assistants of his Paris composition; the London underdrawing appears to have been reproduced from a tracing of the Paris painting.

LC

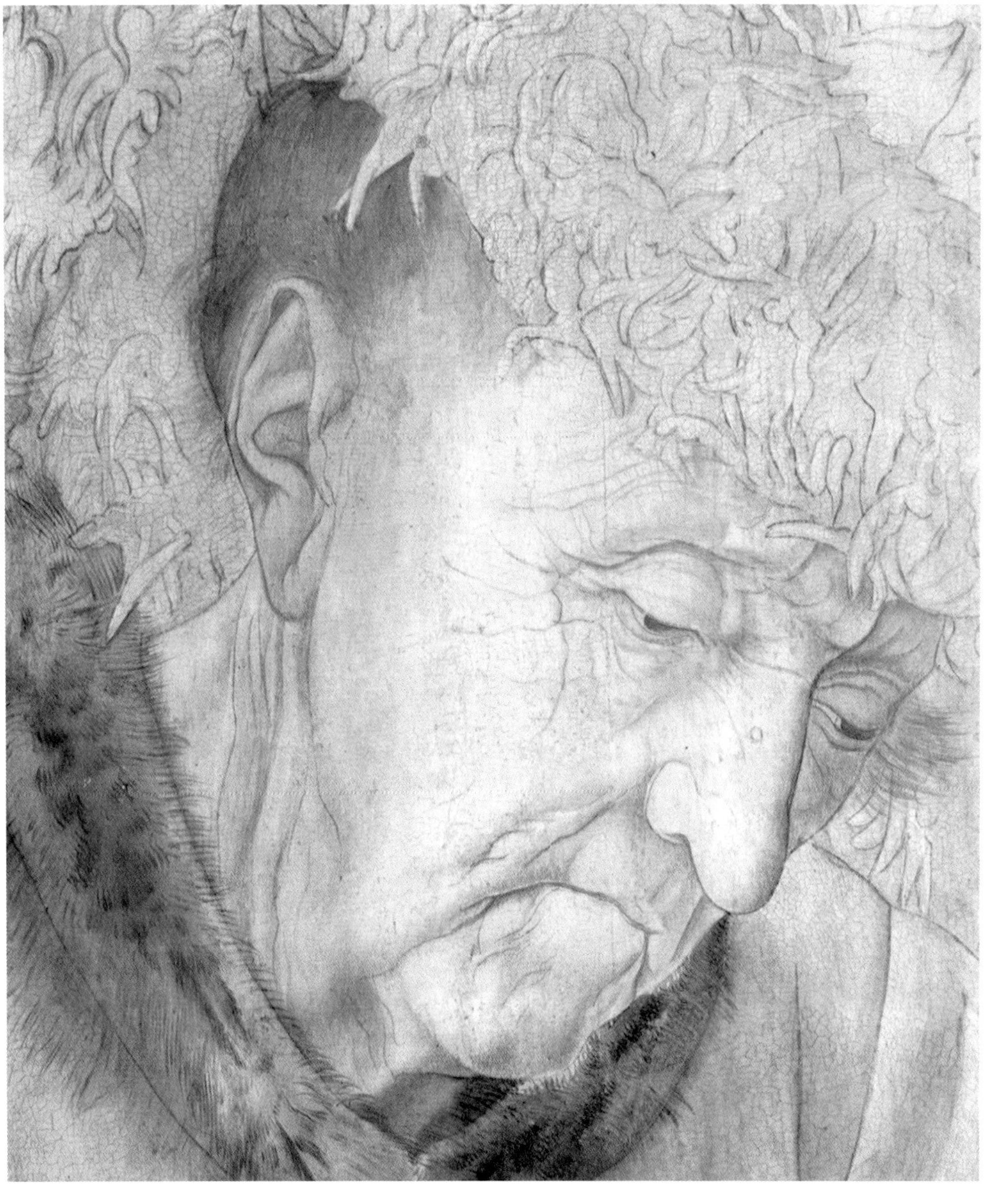

Fig. 293
Infrared reflectogram mosaic, detail of Fig. 288

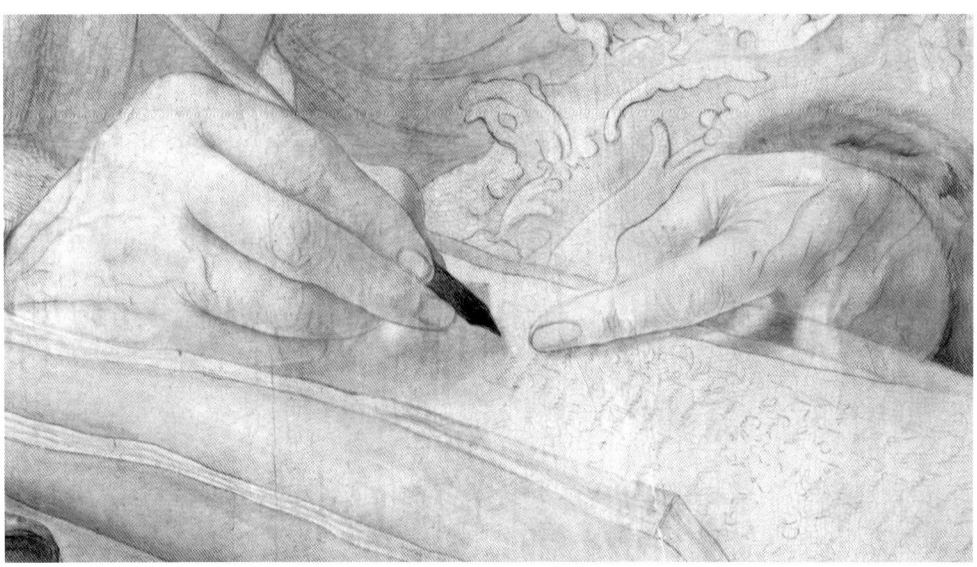

Fig. 294
Infrared reflectogram mosaic, detail of Fig. 288

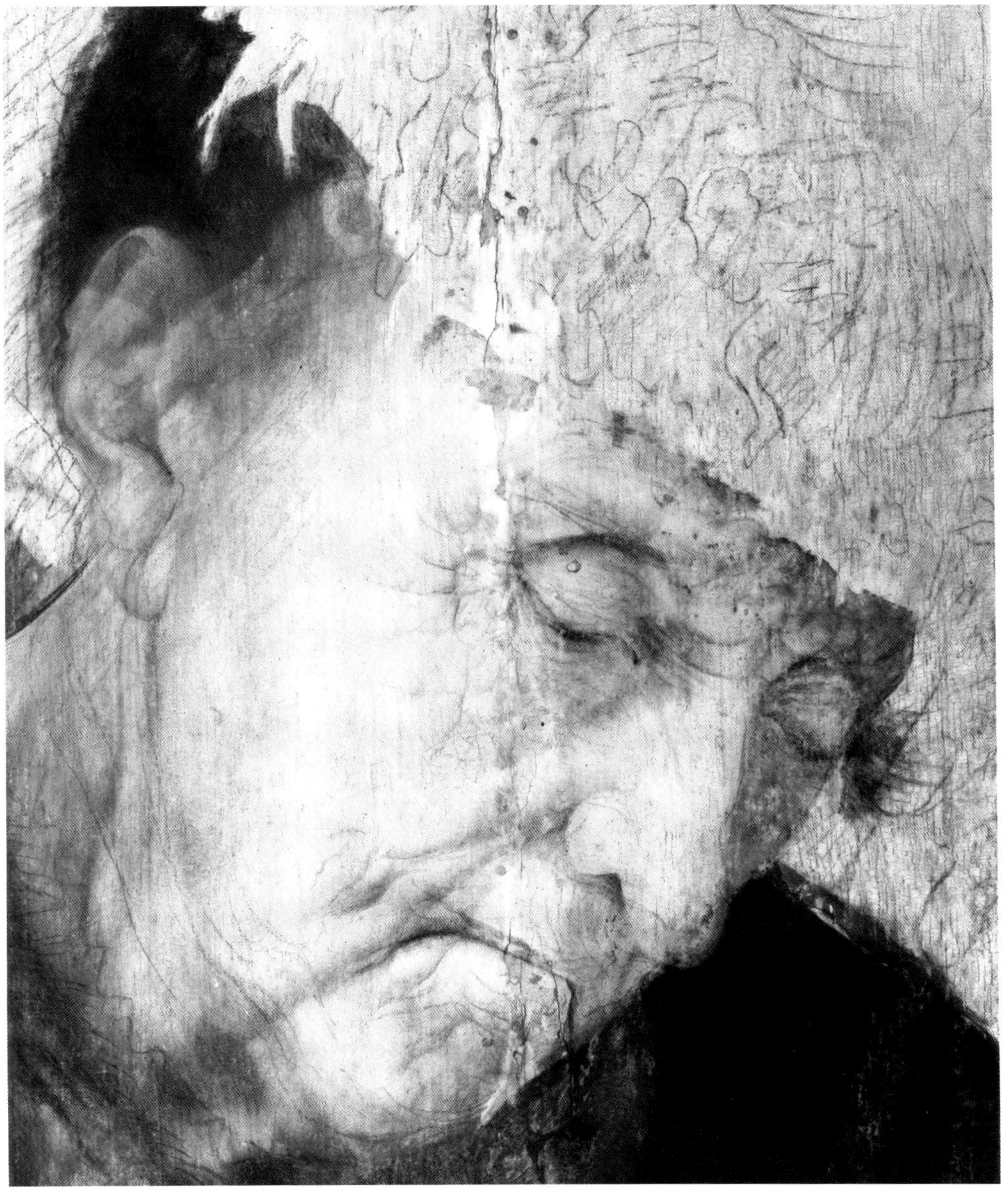

Fig. 295
Infrared photograph, detail of Fig. 289

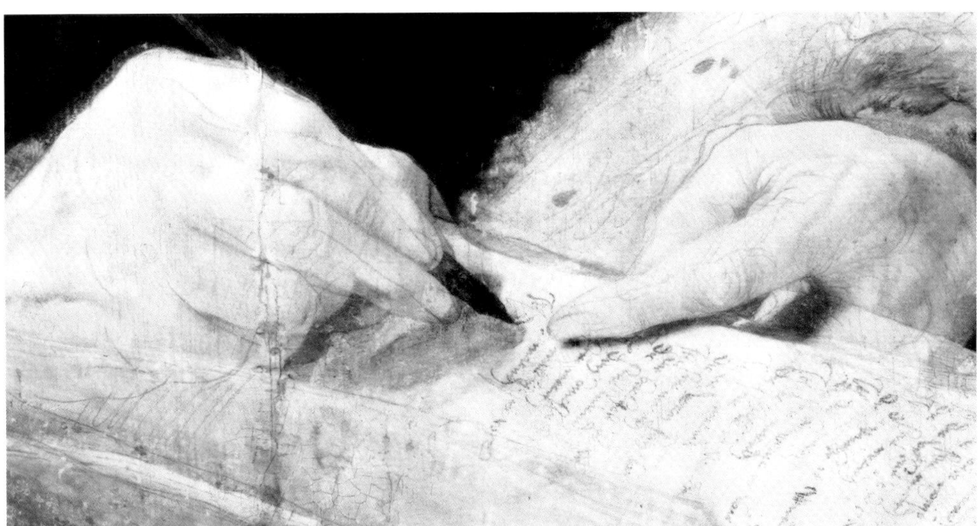

Fig. 296
Infrared photograph, detail of Fig. 289

16 Pieter Bruegel the Elder

*c.*1525?–1569

The Adoration of the Kings, 1564

Oil on oak, 112.1 x 83.9 cm
Signed and dated BRVEGEL MDLXIIII
NG 3556

The place and date of Bruegel's birth are unknown. In 1550–1, he was working with Pieter Baltens on an altarpiece for the church of St Rombout at Mechlin and in 1551 he became a master of the Antwerp Guild of St Luke. In 1552 and 1553, he was travelling in France, the Alps and Italy. On his return to Antwerp, he seems at first to have worked mainly as a designer of prints. His great paintings all date from the decade 1559–68. Having moved in about 1563 from Antwerp to Brussels, he died there in 1569. Although there are many signed paintings and drawings and many prints purporting to be after his designs, some of the 'signatures' are false and several attributions, especially of landscape drawings, are still being debated. Most of the surviving drawings are designs for prints; large numbers of drawings must have been lost, including life studies, preliminary studies for his pictures and full-size 'cartoon' or 'record' versions of his paintings.

Fig. 297
PIETER BRUEGEL THE ELDER,
The Adoration of the Kings [NG 3556], 1564

The Virgin is seated outside a dilapidated thatched stable, built of wood, wattle and daub and inhabited by an ass. Behind the Virgin stands Saint Joseph, elderly and fat. He holds a wide-brimmed hat and listens to the whispers of an unidentified man who, wearing old-fashioned headgear, echoes the shape made by the donkey behind him. On the right are a man in a turban and another man wearing spectacles – the lenses are painted with astonishing skill and economy – which may indicate his spiritual myopia. The oldest king, Caspar, wears a tunic trimmed with ermine, one of the tails of which has caught in the golden chain around his shoulders. The golden border of the tunic is decorated with strange figures of nudes in classicising styles. Caspar has removed his hat, laid down his sceptre and uncovered his gift, a golden vessel full of what is probably myrrh. Behind him, Melchior has not yet taken the lid off his gift. On the right stands the black king, Balthasar, wearing an improvised crown and a leather robe, its edges cut into fringes. His gift is in the form of a ship constructed around a green shell which contains a monkey and is surmounted by an armillary sphere. On the left the crowd of soldiers are probably part of the kings' retinue. One of them is an archer, wearing an arrow stuck into his hat, holding a crossbow and carrying its windlass at

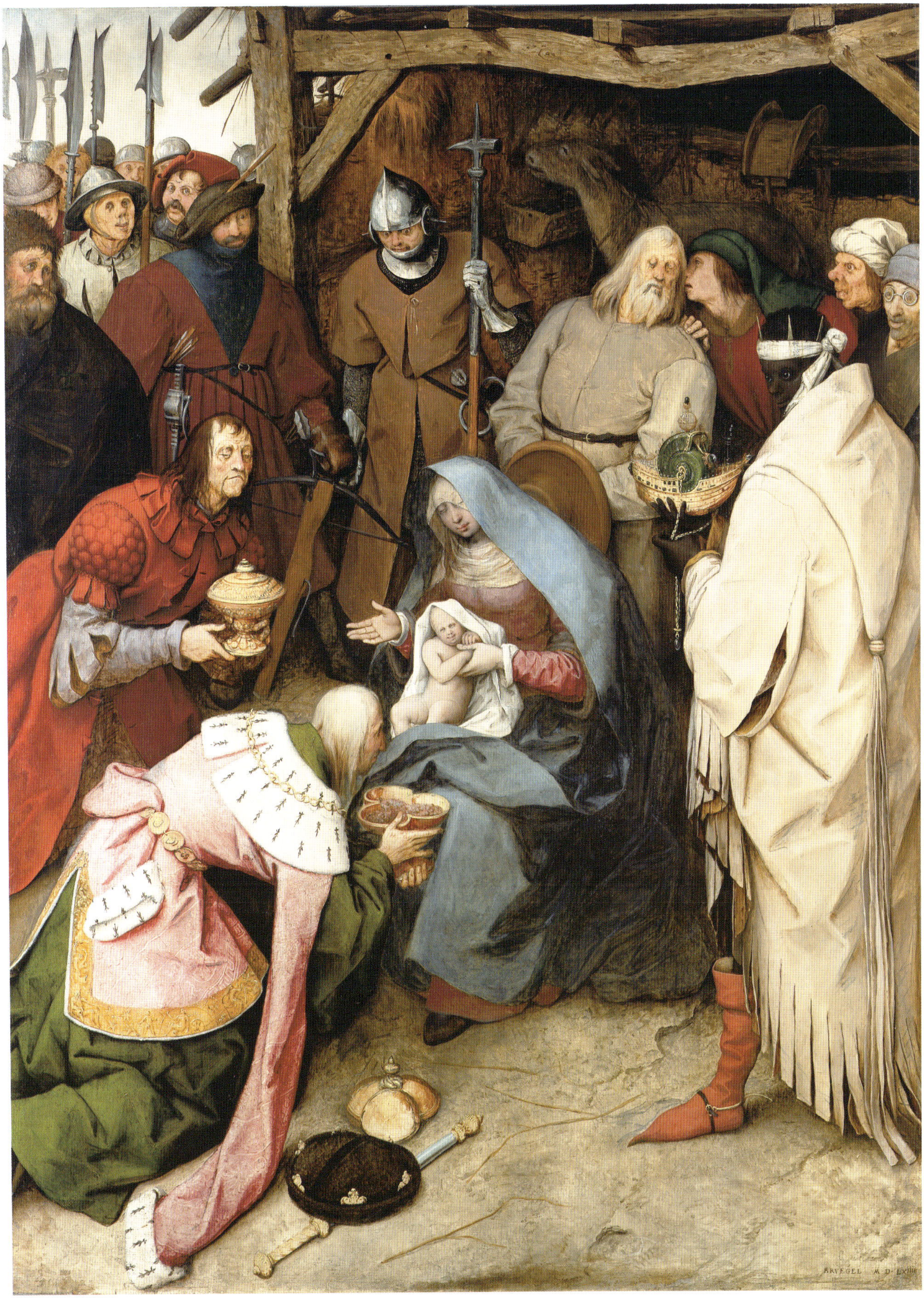

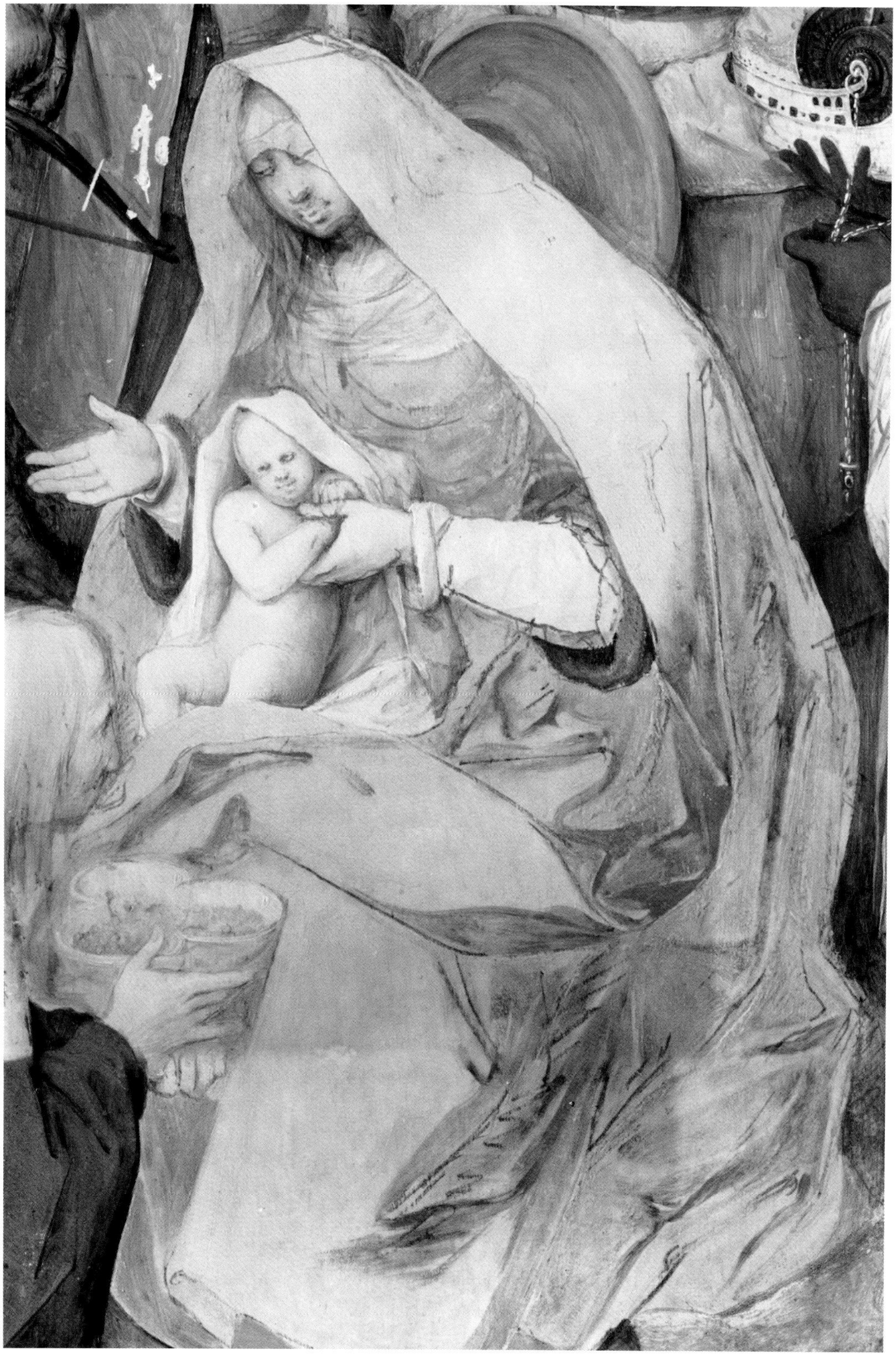

Fig. 298 (left)
Infrared photograph, detail of Fig. 297

Fig. 299 (right)
Infrared reflectogram mosaic, detail of Fig. 297

Fig. 300
Infrared photograph, detail of Fig. 297

Fig. 301
Infrared reflectogram mosaic, detail of Fig. 297

Fig. 302
Infrared photograph, detail of Fig. 297

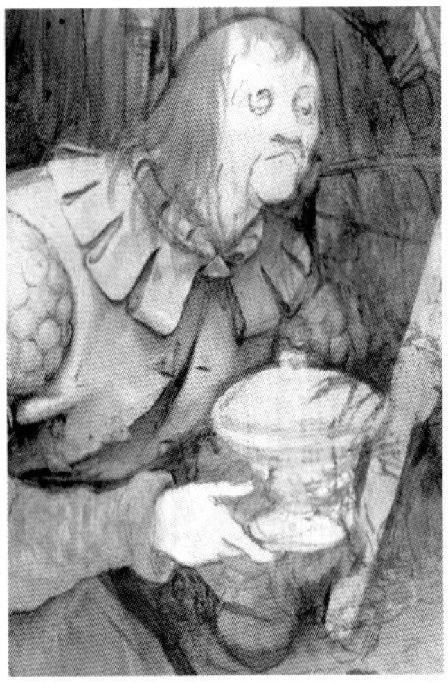

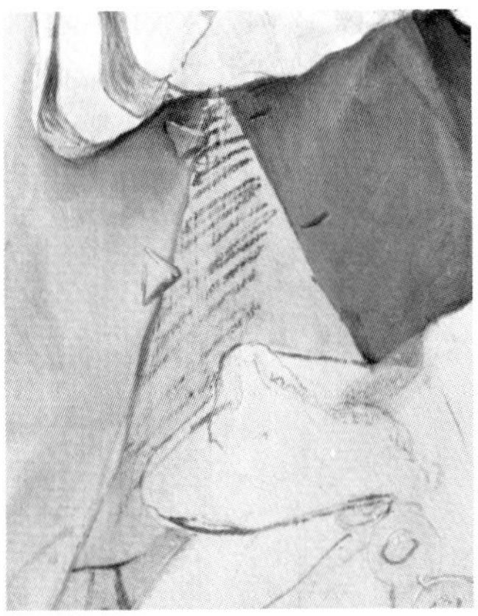

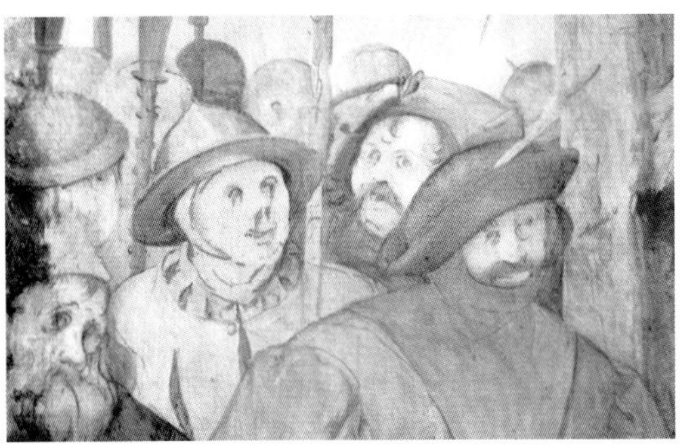

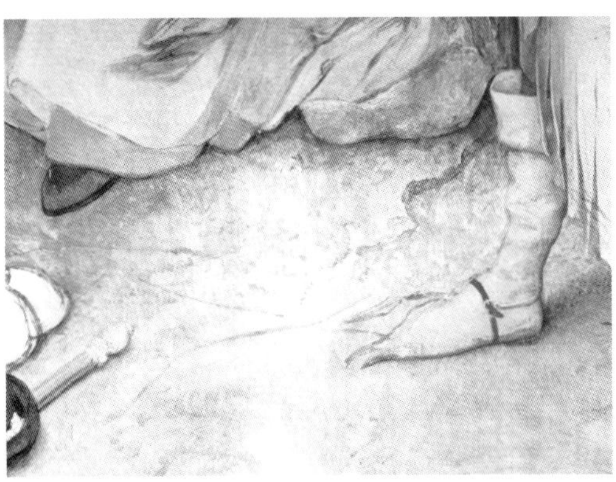

his belt. Next to him, another soldier, holding a halberd, gapes in astonishment at the Christ Child.

The *Adoration* is unusual among Bruegel's paintings because its format is upright and because its colour is relatively sumptuous. The format may indicate that it was designed as an altarpiece, while the splendour of the colour may have been considered appropriate for the subject. Because nothing is known about Bruegel's own beliefs and because the first owner of the *Adoration* has not been identified, it is impossible to explain the apparent tawdriness of the kings' magnificence, the strangely elongated proportions of the Virgin and Child, and the threatening crowding of the band of soldiers. It is, however, possible to analyse the complexities of the pattern-making and the superb skill with which Bruegel uses echoing and contrasting colours to punctuate and stress the forms of his patterns.

The underdrawing is boldly done with brushes in black paint on top of a thin whitish priming layer (Fig. 298). The brushmarks of this quickly applied priming often break the underdrawn lines and make them look as if they were executed in a dry material (Fig. 300). Everything is fully drawn, including the background figures (Fig. 301), the stable and the ass. Bruegel has used broad, rapid brushstrokes to outline figures and position folds; small areas of parallel hatching to indicate the deepest shadows; and circles and short lines for eyes, noses and mouths (Fig. 299).

Because there are few major alterations, it seems that the composition must have been worked out in advance on paper and that the underdrawing, done very quickly by Bruegel himself, must follow what had been established there. What differences there are between the underdrawing and the painting tend to be small refinements which often improve the pattern-making. Balthasar's left foot, for example, is drawn on a horizontal axis and has then been adjusted to point downwards, the curve of the toe of his boot echoing the contour of the Virgin's foot and skirt (Fig. 302). The whispering man was first underdrawn with the scarf of his hat dropping almost vertically to his shoulder, which was lower – closer to Balthasar. Bruegel's changes create a cruel parallel between the shapes of this head and the head and neck of the ass (Fig. 303). The most important changes are possibly those in the Virgin's head, which was drawn on an even smaller scale; the Child's head is also smaller in the underdrawing. His left hand, now resting on the Virgin's thumb, is drawn on a slightly smaller scale as a simple mitten shape, which grasps the Virgin's thumb. His right leg is painted in a different position. It may at first look as if Caspar's profile is underdrawn on the right of his painted profile (see Fig. 298). This is not the case, however, for the area between is hatched and appears to have formed part of the underdrawn draperies.

Bruegel's sons Pieter Brueghel the Younger (1564/5–1638) and Jan Brueghel (1568–1625), both of whom were small children when their father died, knew and copied from many of his compositions, including the *Adoration*, even though they are unlikely ever to have seen the original painting. Jan took from it only the figures of the central halberdier, Joseph, the man whispering to him and Balthasar; one of his copies is in the National Gallery (NG 3547, signed and dated 1598: Fig. 305). The younger Pieter's copy, signed P. BREVGHEL and thought to have been painted in or after 1616, was sold at Sotheby's on 19 April 1989 (lot 24: Fig. 304). It is very nearly the same size (108 x 86.5 cm) as his father's original (about 115 x 91 cm, before it was cut down to its present dimensions). Because Pieter has almost everywhere reproduced his father's colours with a fair degree of accuracy, it would appear that he had access to a replica of his father's picture and that it was coloured or had notes about the colours to be used in painting.

Pieter the Elder must have made full-size 'cartoons' for his larger and more complex compositions, for example his *Proverbs* of 1559 (Berlin). Such cartoons would have been inherited by his son Pieter the Younger, who used them to manufacture his own full-size versions of his father's compositions. All this has been established by comparing Pieter the Younger's copies with his father's underdrawing as well as with his finished picture. The copies correspond to the underdrawing and not to the painted surface. Figures and objects which Pieter the Elder altered or suppressed when he was painting reappear in the copies just as they had been underdrawn; while details which Pieter the Elder added to his painting after completing his underdrawing are not included in the copies.

For his less complicated compositions, such as the London *Adoration*, Pieter the Elder would not have needed a full-size cartoon but would have made sketches on a smaller scale. He would have worked up from a sketch the very free and creative underdrawing of the *Adoration*, which is much less precise than the underdrawing of the *Proverbs*. It seems plausible to suggest that, in cases where he had not made a full-size cartoon, he would have made a 'record copy' of the finished painting. Pieter the Younger's copy of the *Adoration* corresponds more closely with his father's finished picture than with its underdrawing; it must therefore have been taken from such a 'record copy'. It seems that Pieter the Elder anticipated the demand for versions or repetitions of his paintings and kept images of everything, or nearly everything, that he created.

Bruegel's technique may be admired here at its most characteristic and skilful. The paint is usually applied very thinly but it is sometimes impasted, for example in the black king's mantle, or stippled on with stiff brushes, for instance in the daub of the stable or the shadows in the foreground. Bruegel has employed *sgraffito* techniques in the patterns on the red tunic of the oldest king and elsewhere has used his brushes to remove as well as to lay in paint. Often he removes and lays in at one stroke, by turning his brush. He has also painted with his fingers, for he has left a fingerprint on the strut in the top right corner, and has blotted some of his glazes by removing excess paint with cloths – for example in the red drapery on the shoulder of the man behind the black king. Bruegel liked painting wet-in-wet. Working boldly and at great speed, he could do strange things. Here he lettered his signature so rapidly that he misspelt his name. At first he wrote BVEGEL, corrected by adding another B and converting the second B into an R. He was also capable of passages of immense delicacy, for instance the black king's eyes and finger-nails. His feeling for pattern never deserted him and informed even his most random-seeming brushstrokes. Few artists have rivalled Bruegel in his mastery of oil paint; none has surpassed him.

LC

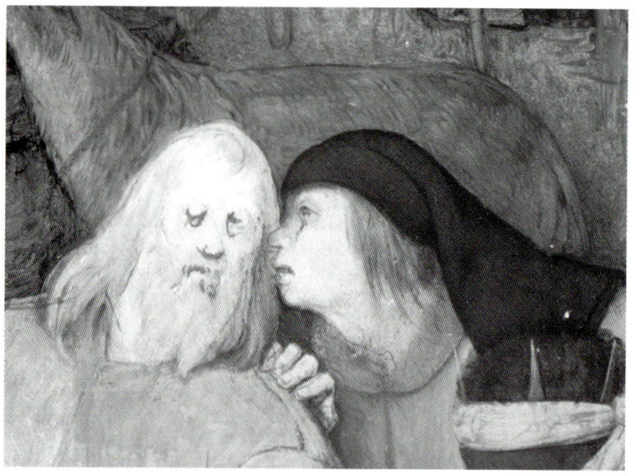

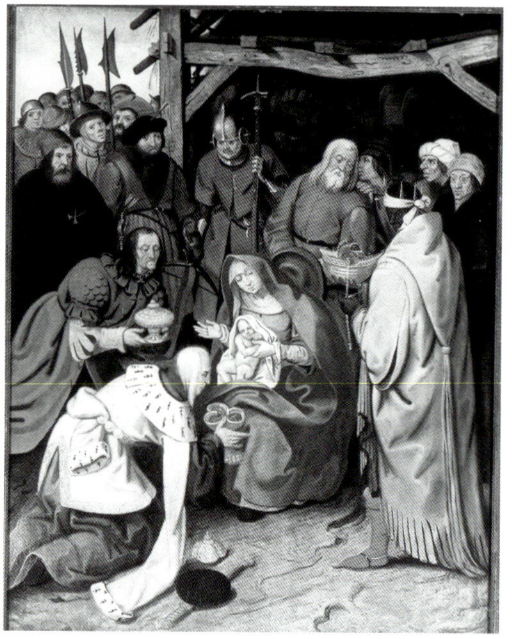

Fig. 303 (top)
Infrared photograph, detail of Fig. 297

Fig. 304
PIETER BRUEGHEL THE YOUNGER, Copy of the *Adoration of the Kings* by Bruegel the Elder, between 1616 and 1635?
Oil on panel, 108 × 86.5 cm
Sold London, Sotheby's, 19 April 1989, lot 24

Fig. 305
JAN BRUEGHEL, *Adoration of the Kings* [NG 3547], 1598
Bodycolour on vellum, 32.9 × 48 cm

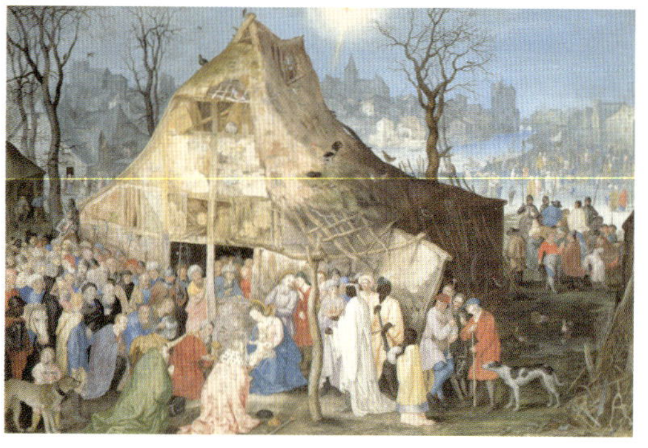

Technical Appendix

Infrared reflectography

Infrared reflectography involves the use of a television-type tube camera with a special coating sensitive in the infrared region of the electromagnetic spectrum. Most systems today use vidicon tubes produced by Hamamatsu which use a lead oxide–lead sulphide (PbO-PbS) composite target. According to the literature supplied by Hamamatsu these 'super infrared vidicons' (the N2606 series) are sensitive between 500 and 1900 nm (2200 nm in the case of the N2606-06). Different pigments are penetrated by different wavelengths of infrared and it has been found that for many paintings, especially those from the fifteenth and sixteenth centuries, the optimum range for obtaining good images of the underdrawing is a broad band stretching from 900 to 2000 nm. The PbO-PbS vidicon would therefore appear to be an ideal choice for such studies. However, as has been mentioned in the introduction, the vidicon suffers from a number of problems, inherent in the technology, which make the production of good clear images of underdrawings difficult, principally low resolution, geometric distortions and variations and fluctuations in sensitivity. Using computers for the assembly of infrared reflectogram mosaics has made it possible to reduce the effects of many of these problems.

The infrared reflectography described in this catalogue has all been carried out using a Hamamatsu C2400 system with an N2606 series infrared vidicon tube (mostly the 2606-06 tube). The camera is equipped with a 36 mm lens which allows paintings to be examined from close up. A Kodak 87A Wratten filter is fitted to the lens. This filter excludes visible light but allows all wavelengths above 900 nm to pass. As the vidicon tube is most sensitive in the 400–800 nm region, it is vital that visible light is not allowed to enter or the results would be dominated by the reflected visible light.

For examination in the studio at the National Gallery, paintings are placed on an electrically operated easel and can be moved horizontally and vertically in relation to the camera and lights. Lighting is provided by two Philips IRK 13/13X L8 infrared lamps in custom-made housings run from a purpose-built rheostat.

Perfectly good results can be obtained using other sources of light, for example tungsten halogen photographic lamps. The advantages of special infrared lights like those used at the National Gallery are that they give off less visible light to compete with the infrared, are more controllable and less hot.

Solid-state infrared imaging

Relatively recent advances in solid-state technology have seen the development of a number of thermal imaging devices. These were initially developed for use by the military but are being used increasingly in the public domain, for example as security cameras, and for a variety of industrial uses. Several of these cameras have been adapted for use in studying art works. Early trials carried out at the National Gallery of Art in Washington DC using a camera containing a platinum silicide (PtSi) detector showed that excellent results could be obtained. The penetration of some pigments was improved and the problems of geometric distortion and signal instability inherent in the vidicon system were eliminated.

PtSi detectors are sensitive between 1200 and 5000 nm, peaking between 2000 and 3000 nm. Research carried out in Washington has shown that for the detection of underdrawings there is no advantage in using wavelengths beyond 2500 nm, although the longer wavelengths can give other information about the painting, and this is an area of ongoing research. PtSi cameras configured to work in the 1200–2500 nm range are now being used in a number of museums in the US and Europe. Other solid-state arrays are also being developed for use in imaging art works, including indium gallium arsenide (InGaAs), which is sensitive between 900 and 1700 nm. This gives no great improvement in penetration of difficult pigments over the vidicon but does have the advantage of not suffering from geometric distortions or fluctuating sensitivity.

Computer assembly of infrared reflectogram mosaics

Whatever the means of recording the individual reflectograms, the mosaics are now very much clearer and easier to read thanks to the use of computers to join them together. The inherent problems of geometric distortion, overall lighting imbalance and fluctuations in sensitivities in reflectograms from vidicon systems can all be addressed to some extent by processing of the raw data images once they have been digitised. The result is an infrared reflectogram mosaic which is much more even and easy to read than the traditional hand-built mosaics.

Any image-processing software could be used to join the reflectograms together but probably the most popular commercially available program for this is Adobe Photoshop. There are also a number of other purpose-built pieces of software available (see bibliography for selected references). The infrared reflectogram mosaics in this catalogue have been assembled using VIPs-ip, a piece of software purpose-built at the National Gallery for joining and processing digital images. The program was originally written to be run on a Sun computer which uses the Solaris operating system. More recent versions can be run on a PC using Linux. The software is available free by downloading it from the Internet.

For further information and to download the software see the VIPs website www.vips.ecs.soton.ac.uk

RB

Notes

The Materials of Underdrawing

1 The studio of the woman painter Martia at the court of King Honour is described by Jean Lemaire de Belges, a writer serving at the court of Margaret of Austria, in the poem 'La Couronne Margaritique', composed between September 1504 and March 1505: *Oeuvres de Jean Lemaire de Belges*, ed. J. Stecher, 4 vols, Louvain 1882–91; Vol. IV, 1891, p. 158:

Leur ouvroir est tout fin plein de tableaux
Peints, et à peindre, et de maint noble oustil.
Là sont charbons, crayons, plumes, pinceaux,
Brousses à tas, coquilles par monceaux,
Pinceaux d'argent, qui font maint trait subtil . . .

At this date the word *pinceau* usually implies a pointed brush, made from hair from the tail of an animal such as sable; the connotation of 'pointed' explains the use of the word for a silver stylus. *Brousse* ['brosse'] would be a coarser, bristle brush for preparatory or larger-scale work. See also E. Duverger and D. Duverger-Van de Velde, 'Jean Lemaire de Belges en de Schilderkunst. Een Bijdrage', *Jaarboek van het Koninklijk Museum voor Schone Kunsten Antwerpen*, 1967, pp. 37–78, esp. p. 53.

2 One recent example where non-destructive analysis has been carried out is on a group of Florentine metal-point drawings: see B. Brejon de Lavergnée, O. Liesse, A. Duval and H. Guicharnaud, 'Dessins florentins du XVe siècle à la pointe métallique du musée des Beaux-Arts de Lille', *Techné*, 13–14, 2001, pp. 78–83; A. Duval, 'PIXE analyses of metal point drawings' *Proceedings of the 6th International Conference on Non-Destructive Testing and Microanalysis for the Diagnostics and Conservation of the Cultural Heritage, Rome, May 17th–20th 1999*, Rome 1999, pp. 1009–22.

3 'Methods and Materials of Northern European Painting in the National Gallery, 1400–1550', in L. Campbell, S. Foister and A. Roy (eds), *Early Northern Painting, National Gallery Technical Bulletin*, 18, 1997, pp. 6–55, esp. pp. 20–5; J. Dunkerton and M. Spring, 'The development of painting on coloured surfaces in sixteenth-century Italy', *Painting Techniques: History, Materials and Studio Practice; Contributions to the Dublin IIC Congress 7–11 September 1998*, ed. A. Roy and P. Smith, London 1998, pp. 120–30.

4 D. Bomford, A. Roy and A. Smith, 'The Techniques of Dieric Bouts: Two Paintings Contrasted', *National Gallery Technical Bulletin*, 10, 1986, pp. 39–57; A. Roy, 'The Technique of a "Tüchlein" by Quinten Massys', *National Gallery Technical Bulletin*, 12, 1988, pp. 36–43.

5 'Gossaert's *Adoration of the Kings*', in Campbell, Foister and Roy 1997 (cited in note 3), pp. 89–92.

6 'Methods and materials of Northern European painting in the National Gallery, 1400–1550', in Campbell, Foister and Roy 1997 (cited in note 3), pp. 28–9. The cutting of quills to make pens is discussed in Cennino d'Andrea Cennini, *Il libro dell'arte di Cennino Cennini*, commentato e annotato da F. Brunello, 2nd edn, Vicenza 1982, p. 15; *The Craftsman's Handbook: the Italian 'Il libro dell'arte'*, tr. D.V. Thompson, New Haven 1933 (Dover reprint, London and New York 1960), p 8. See also the manual on calligraphy by the sixteenth-century Bolognese cleric Fra Cherubino Ghirardacci (*c.*1543): *Modo di perfettamente scrivere del R.P. Maestro Fra Cherubino Ghirardacci Bolognese Eremitano* (Siena, Biblioteca Comunale degli Intronati, MS H.VII.39), in A.P. Torresi, *Tecnica artistica a Siena: Alcuni trattati e ricettari del Rinascimento nella Biblioteca degli Intronati*, Ferrara 1993, pp. 90–1, 100–1.

7 Cennini 1982 (cited in note 6), pp. 37–8, pp. 22–3 in 1933 English edn; M.P. Merrifield, *Original Treatises dating from the XIIth to XVIIIth Centuries on the Arts of Painting*, 2 vols, London 1849 (Dover reprint, New York and London 1967), Vol. I: Manuscripts of Jehan le Begue (Paris, Bibliothèque Nationale, MS 6741), Petrus de S. Audemar, 'De coloribus faciendis' (fourteenth century), no. 172, pp. 138–9; H.J. Leloux, 'Noordoostmiddel-nederlands in Keulen: een Keuls manuskript met laatmiddeleeuwse recepten voor verf en inkt voor het schrijven en verluchten van boeken', *Driemaandelijkse Bladen*, 29, 1977, pp. 11–31, see no. 14, p. 26; *Liber illuministarum pro fundamentis auri et coloribus ac consimilibus collectus ex diversis* [Munich, Bayerische Staatsbibliothek Cgm. 821; part I mid-fifteenth century; part II first decade sixteenth century], ff. 28–29r. This ink is described as a black that will flow 'out of the pen so one can draw what one wants'. See also R. Borghini, *Il riposo*, Florence 1584, p. 207 (reprinted by the Società Tipografica, Milan 1807: see Vol. 1, p. 242.).

8 Cennini 1982 (cited in note 6), p. 38, p. 22 in 1933 English edn; Borghini 1584 (cited in note 7), p. 207 (Vol. 1, p. 242 in 1807 edn); K. van Mander, *Het Schilder-Boeck*, Haarlem 1604, Chapter 12, no. 17, f. 47 v.; see also K. van Mander, *Den grondt der edel vry schilderconst*, ed. H. Miedema, 2 vols, Utrecht 1973, pp. 257, 597–8.

9 Borghini 1584 (cited in note 7), p. 207 (Vol. 1, p. 242 in 1807 edn).

10 Cennini 1982 (cited in note 6), pp. 126–7, p. 75 in 1933 English edn.

11 M. Zerdoun Bat-Yehouda, *Les encres noires au Moyen Age*, Paris 1983, pp. 91–6.

12 D. Cardon and G. du Chatenet, *Guide des teintures naturelles: plantes, lichens, champignons, mollusques et insectes*, Paris 1990, pp. 261–4, 291–2; H. Schweppe, *Handbuch der Naturfarbstoffe: Vorkommen; Verwendung; Nachweis*, Landsberg/Lech 1993, pp. 469–74. Many other plants producing hydrolysable tannins similar to those obtained from oak galls are also discussed. See also J.S. Mills and R. White, *The Organic Chemistry of Museum Objects*, 2nd edn, London 1994, pp. 150–2. For the chemistry of iron-gall inks see C. Krekel, 'The chemistry of historical iron gall inks; understanding the chemistry of writing inks used to prepare historical documents', *International Journal of Forensic Document Examiners*, 5, 1999, pp. 54–8.

13 Merrifield 1849 (cited in note 7) Vol. I, Manuscripts of Jehan le Begue, Petrus de S. Audemar, no. 200, pp. 158–9; in this recipe for ink it is stated that the presence of gum prevents the ink from running.

14 Merrifield 1849 (cited in note 7), Vol. I, Manuscripts of Jehan le Begue, no. 31, pp. 60–1, no. 47, pp. 68–9, no. 89, pp. 150–3, nos 199, 200, pp. 158–9, nos 303, 303a, pp. 288–93; *Artliche künst mancherley weyse Dinten un[d] allerhand Farben zubereyten*, in *Drey schöner künstreicher büchlein*, Leipzig 1532, 3rd treatise, ff. B viii v.–C iii v. (there are many different editions published in different towns, the tracts may be assembled in a different order). An example of a scribe's compilation is that of Ambr[u]ogio di Ser Pietro da Siena, *Ricepte daffare più colori*, 1462 (Siena, Biblioteca Comunale degli Intronati, MS I.II.19), ff. 99r.–106r., recipe no. XIX, ff. 104r.–v., in Torresi 1993 (cited in note 6), no. XIX, pp. 80–1; D.V. Thompson, 'The "Ricepte daffare più colori of Ambrogio di Ser Pietro da Siena"', *Archeion*, XV, 1933, pp. 339–47; A. Wallert, *Kookboeken en koorboeken*, PhD thesis, Rijksuniversiteit Groningen, Groningen 1991a, no. XVIII, pp. 30–3. Another example is that made by the Carthusian monk Bartolomeo da Siena (Siena, Biblioteca Comunale degli Intronati, MS L.XI.41), ff. 34v.–39r., in Torresi 1993 (cited in note 6), pp. 39–40; Wallert 1991a, pp. 34–9. See also Fra Cherubino Ghirardacci's manual on calligraphy in Torresi 1993, pp. 89–90. For other examples of recipes for inks from fifteenth- and sixteenth-century sources see Zerdoun Bat-Yehouda 1983 (cited in note 11), pp. 91–6; 186–211; *Liber illuministarum* (cited in note 7), ff. 93r.–97v., 115r.–118v., 29 r.; E. Berger, *Quellen und Technik der Fresko-, Oel und Tempera-Malerei des Mittelalters*, Munich 1897, pp. 143–76 (The Strassburg Manuscript): see no. 34, p. 163, and also *The Strasburg Manuscript: a Medieval Painter's Handbook*, trs. V. and R. Borradaile, London 1966, pp. 40–1; V. Boltz, *Illuminirbuch: wie man allerlei Farben bereiten, mischen und auftragen soll* (Basel 1549), ed. C.J. Benziger, Munich 1913 (rep. Schaan 1982), pp. 114–15; Leloux 1977 (cited in note 7), nos 7–9, p. 24, and A. Wallert, 'Instructions for Manuscript Illumination in a 15th Century Netherlandish Technical Treatise', *ACTA of the Congress on Medieval Manuscript Illumination in the Northern Netherlands, University of Utrecht, 10–13 December 1989*, Utrecht 1991b, pp. 447–56, esp. p. 449 (both these papers discuss Cologne, Historisches Archiv MS W 8° 293); E.E. Ploss, 'Ein Malerbüchlein aus dem Bamberger Karmelitenkloster', *Bericht des historischen Vereins für die Pflege der Geschichte des ehemaligen Fürstbistums Bamberg*, 100, 1964, pp. 331–46, esp. pp. 343–4; A.P. Torresi, *Il taccuino Antonelli. Un ricettario ferrarese del Quattrocento di tecnica artistica e fitoterapia*, Ferrara 1993 (Ferrara, Biblioteca Comunale Ariostea, Antonelli 861), pp. 47–53, 79–80.

15 Leloux 1977 (cited in note 7), nos 10–12, pp. 24–6; Wallert 1991b, p. 449, Berger 1897, p. 163, and Borradaile 1966, p. 40 (here apparently translated as gall apples) (all cited in note 14); *Middelnederlandse verfrecepten voor miniaturen en 'alderhande substancien'*, ed. W.L. Braekman, Brussels 1986 (Scripta 'Mediaeval and Renaissance Texts and Studies' 18): London, Wellcome Historical Medical Library, MS 517 (fifteenth century), no. 52, pp. 50–1.

16 R. White, J. Pilc and J. Kirby, 'Analyses of Paint Media', *National Gallery Technical Bulletin*, 19, 1998, pp. 74–95, esp. pp. 75–6, 87.

17 V. Biringuccio, [*De la pirotechnia*] *The Pirotechnia of Vannoccio Biringuccio*, trs. C.S. Smith and M.T. Gnudi, Cambridge, Mass., 1942 (1966 reprint; originally published Venice 1540), pp. 173–9, 413–14.

18 Cennini 1982 (cited in note 6), pp. 32–4, pp. 19–20 in 1933 English edn; Biringuccio 1942 (cited in note 17), p. 414.

19 Borghini 1584 (cited in note 7), p. 143 (Vol. 1, pp. 164–5 in 1807 edn). Two other methods described are almost identical to Cennini's.

20 Cennini 1982 (cited in note 6), pp. 126–7, p. 75 in 1933 English edn. Borghini comments on the fact that charcoal is a material that is easy to remove: Borghini 1584 (cited in note 7), pp. 175–6 (Vol. 1, p. 203 in 1807 edn).

21 Merrifield 1849 (cited in note 7), Vol. II: *Segreti per colori* (the Bolognese Manuscript), no. 386, pp. 594–5.

22 N. Penny and M. Spring, 'Veronese's Paintings in the National Gallery: Technique and Materials: Part I', *National Gallery Technical Bulletin*, 16, 1995, pp. 4–29, esp. pp. 17–18.

23 G. Vasari, *Le vite de' più eccellenti pittori, scultori e architettori, nella redazione del 1550 e 1568*, ed. R. Bettarini, annotated by P. Barocchi, Florence 1966–87, 'Introduzzione alle tre arti del Disegno, cioè architettura, pittura e scultura', Vol. 1, 1966, p. 134. See also *Vasari on Technique, being the Introduction to the three Arts of Design, Architecture, Sculpture and Painting, prefixed to the Lives of the most excellent Painters, Sculptors and Architects*, trs. L.S. Maclehose, ed. G. Baldwin Brown, New York 1960 (first published London 1907), p. 231.

24 Cennini 1982 (cited in note 6), p. 34, p. 20 in 1933 English edn.

25 Vasari 1966 (cited in note 23), Vol. 1, p. 118; p. 213 in English edn. See also Merrifield 1849 (cited in note 7), Vol. I, pp. ccxxv–vi; Borghini 1584 (cited in note 7), pp. 139, 206 (Vol. 1, p. 241 in 1807 edn).

26 F. Baldinucci, *Vocabolario toscana dell'arte del disegno* (Florence 1681), rep. Milan 1809, pp. 316–17, refers to *matita nera*, a sort of black stone, dug in France, but the best came from Spain. Giovanni Paolo Lomazzo refers to *pietra todescha*, German stone, but without description so the type of stone meant is unclear; he may even be referring to graphite: G.P. Lomazzo, *Trattato dell'arte de la pittura*, Milan 1584, Book 3, p. 192.

27 During the preparation of the experimental panels mentioned on p. 27, it was found that the mark produced by a stick of nineteenth-century red conté (consisting essentially of red iron-oxide pigment, probably synthetic) was easily visible as a dark line by infrared reflectography. Examination of the line under a microscope suggested that the conté has a high haematite content. It is conceivable that a drawing done using a natural red earth that happened to have a markedly high haematite content might also be visible in infrared reflectography.

28 Borghini 1584 (cited in note 7), p. 139 (Vol. 1, p. 160 in 1807 edn).

29 G. B. Armenini, *De' veri precetti della pittura* [Ravenna 1586, rep. 1587], ed. M. Gorreri, Turin 1988, pp. 71–2 (p. 56 in 1587 edn). English translation *Giovanni Battista Armenini on the True Precepts of the Art of Painting*, ed. and tr. E.J. Olszewski, [New York, Burt Franklin] 1977, p. 126.

30 P. Scarzella and P. Natale, *Terre coloranti naturali e tinte murali a base di terre; monografie e catalogo delle collezioni di terre coloranti e di campioni di coloriture a base di terre allestite al Politecnico di Torino*, Turin 1989; part 1, section 3, on the geology of earth pigments, and part 2, showing examples of the range of colours obtainable from earths of different regions, principally of Italy; M.P.

Merrifield, *The Art of Fresco Painting*, London 1846, pp. xiii–xxxiv.

31 Vasari 1966 (cited in note 23), Vol. 1, p. 118; pp. 212–13 in English edn; Baldinucci 1681/1809 (cited in note 26), p. 316.

32 Lomazzo 1584 (cited in note 26), Book 3, p. 192.

33 I. Sandner, 'Die Analyse von Unterzeichnungen auf Gemälden mit Hilfe der Infrarotreflektografie am Beispiel von Werken Lucas Cranachs d.Ä', *Deutsche Gesellschaft für Zerstörungsfreie Prüfung e.V.*, Berichtsband 45, Teil 1, Berlin 1994, pp. 193–202; G. Heydenreich, 'Artistic exchange and experimental variation: studies in the workshop practice of Lucas Cranach the Elder', *Painting Techniques: History, Materials and Studio Practice; Contributions to the Dublin IIC Congress 7–11 September 1998*, ed. A. Roy and P. Smith, London 1998, pp. 106–11, esp. p. 108.

34 See, for example, Merrifield 1846 (cited in note 30), pp. xxix–xxxiv; Cennini 1982 (cited in note 6), pp. 39, 73–80, esp. p. 76, pp. 23, 42–7, esp. p. 44, in 1933 English edn.

35 Vasari 1966 (cited in note 23), Vol. 1, p. 134, p. 231 in English edn; Borghini 1584 (cited in note 7), p.175 (Vol. 1, p. 203 in 1807 edn).

36 S. Andriessen, *Een schoon Tractaet van sommighe werckigende Alchemistische dinghen om Gout, silver te maken*, Amsterdam 1581, pp. xiiij vso–xv vso; *Middelnederlandse verfrecepten* 1986 (cited in note 15), MS 517, no. 46, p. 47. The latter text refers to the use of the chalk instead of, or with, pumice, which was also used for correcting drawings on paper: see Armenini 1988 (cited in note 29), p. 71 (p. 56 in 1587 edn), p. 126 in English edn.

37 Lomazzo 1584 (cited in note 26), Book 3, pp. 192–3.

38 B. Cellini, *Due trattati di Benvenuto Cellini, scultore fiorentino, uno dell'oreficeria, l'altro della scultura* (Florence 1568), Società Tipografica de' Classici Italiani, Milan 1811, (2nd treatise), p. 210; Armenini 1988 (cited in note 29), pp. 64, 123, 133 (pp. 49, 103, 114–15 in 1587 edn), pp. 120, 174, 183 in English edn. Lead white tempered with aqueous gum and applied with a brush was widely used for highlighting drawings: see Cennini 1982 (cited in note 6), p. 31, p. 18 in 1933 English edn; Borghini 1584 (cited in note 7), p. 140 (Vol. 1, p. 161 in 1807 edn).

39 Leonardo da Vinci, *The Literary Works of Leonardo da Vinci*, ed. J.P. Richter, 2 vols, London 1883, Vol. I, no. 612, p. 315. (From MS Forster II, here coded SKMII[1], 'Forster Library, South Kensington Museum', dated 1495: O': note written inside front cover.) Similar ingredients could be used to make a modelling material and conceivably there is some connection between the two: compare Armenini 1988 (cited in note 29), p. 117 (p. 96 in 1587 edn) pp. 167–8 in English edn.

40 The metals used are listed in *Liber illuministarum* (cited in note 7), f. 33 r: lead, tin, copper, silver. See also L. Rockinger, 'Zum baierischen Schriftwesen im Mittelalter', *Abhandlungen der königlich bayerischen Akademie der Wissenschaften, historischen Classe*, XII, Munich 1872/3, part 1, pp. 1–72, esp. p. 18. A translation by D.V. Thompson Jr is given in Cennini 1933 (cited in note 6), pp. 4–5. Cennini also mentions the use of silver, brass and a mixture of two parts lead, one part tin, beaten together with a hammer, pp. 5, 7–8 in this edn and Cennini 1982 (cited in note 6), pp. 9–10, 13–14; silver and the same lead-tin composition are mentioned by Borghini 1584 (cited in note 7), p. 139 (Vol. 1, p. 159 in 1807 edn). See also Merrifield 1849 (cited in note 7), Vol. I, Manuscripts of Jehan le Begue, Johannes Alcherius, 'De coloribus diversis' (1398, corrected 1411), no. 296, pp. 274–9, esp. pp. 276–7: brass (copper/zinc), bronze (copper/tin), copper, silver.

41 Small panels covered with parchment and prepared with gesso and lead white ground in linseed oil were used by tradesmen, writing with a stylus and erasing the letters with saliva (in the case of lead-point a piece of bread could be used). They were re-whitened when necessary. Parchment, like paper, could also be prepared with ground bone. See the references cited in note 40 above.

42 Cennini 1982 (cited in note 6), pp. 9–10, p. 5 in 1933 English edn.

43 Lead-tin alloy metal-point is thought to have been used for some of Botticelli's drawings for Dante's *Divine Comedy*; these were drawn on fine parchment and some have been painted, entirely or in part. See D. Oltrogge, R. Fuchs and O. Hahn, '*Finito* and *Non finito:* Drawing and Painting Techniques in Botticelli's *Divine Comedy*', *Sandro Botticelli. The Drawings for Dante's Divine Comedy*, Royal Academy of Arts, London 2000, pp. 334–41.

44 A. Dürer, *Dürer schriftlicher Nachlass*, ed. H. Rupprich, 3 vols, Berlin 1956–69; Vol. I, p. 157, lines 79–81. *Kohln* can apparently also be translated as coal, or a mineral black.

45 Dürer/Rupprich 1956 (cited in note 44), Vol. 1, p. 174, lines 21–2; for drawings made with black chalk see, for example, lines 31–3 and 53–5 on the same page.

46 Dürer/Rupprich 1956 (cited in note 44), Vol. 1, p. 157, line 39. The materials cost 4 *stübers*.

47 Dürer/Rupprich 1956 (cited in note 44), Vol. 1, p. 167, lines 292–4.

48 B. Heimberg, 'Zur Maltechnik Albrecht Dürers', in G. Goldberg, B. Heimberg and M. Shawe, *Albrecht Dürer: die Gemälde der Alten Pinakothek*, Munich 1998, pp. 32–53, esp. pp. 36–42; see also individual catalogue entries.

The Artists of 'the North'

1 J.R.J. van Asperen de Boer, J. Dijkstra and R. Van Schoute, *Underdrawing in the Paintings of the Rogier van der Weyden and Master of Flémalle Groups (Nederlands Kunsthistorisch Jaarboek*, vol.XLI, 1990), Zwolle 1992; A.P. Abrantes, I.Vandevivere et al., *Nuno Gonçalves, novos doumentos, Estudo da pintura portuguesa do Sec. XV*, Lisbon 1994; M.W. Ainsworth, *Gerard David, Purity of Vision in an Age of Transition*, New York 1998; exh. cat. *Van Eyck to Bruegel 1400 to 1550: Dutch & Flemish Paintings in the collection of the Museum Boymans-van Beuningen*, Rotterdam 1994.

2 'Le Livre du très chevalereux comte d'Artois et de la femme, fille du comte de Boulogne', Bibliothèque Nationale de France, Paris, MS fr. 11610: see François Avril and Nicole Reynaud, *Les Manuscrits à peintures en France 1440–1520* (exh. cat., Bibliothèque Nationale), Paris 1993, pp. 99–100.

3 See the letters to Pirckheimer written from Venice on 7 February and 8 September 1506 and reproduced in *Dürer, Schriftlicher Nachlass*, ed. Hans Rupprich, 3 vols, Berlin 1956–69, vol. I, pp. 44, 55.

4 C. White, *Dürer, The Artist and his Drawings*, Oxford 1971, pp. 52–3; Fedja Anzelewsky, *Dürer, His Art and Life*, Fribourg 1980, p. 42.

5 White, pp. 106–7; Anzelewsky, pp. 106, 118–19, both cited above.

6 Parallels may also be made with methods used in print design. Designers of woodcuts drew on the blocks; they were then passed to professional cutters, who carved away the wood around the drawn lines. Bruegel's *Wedding of Mopsus and Nisa* (New York) is a pen drawing on an applewood block with a white preparation: though it has been partially cut, most of the drawing is preserved: see Nadine M. Orenstein, ed., *Pieter Bruegel the Elder, Drawings and Prints* (exh. cat.), New York 2001, pp. 246–8 (No. 111). Latterly, engravings too were made by specialist engravers after highly finished drawings by specialist draughtsmen. Bruegel's wonderfully detailed and delicate pen-drawing of *Spring* (Vienna, Albertina; Fig. 58), dated 1565, was engraved five years later by Pieter van der Heyden: ibid., pp. 236–8 (Nos 105–6).

7 For example, the coloured drawings on parchment of *Alexander the Great in the Orient*, divided between the Historisches Museum at Bern and the British Museum; or the coloured drawings on paper of the *Trojan War* in the Louvre and the Bibliothèque Nationale de France: see A. Rapp Buri and M. Stucky-Schürer, *Burgundische Tapisserien*, Munich 2001, pp. 158–70, 313–19, 453–6.

8 For example, Vermeyen's cartoons on paper, now in the Kunsthistorisches Museum, Vienna, for the *Conquest of Tunis* tapestries: see H.J. Horn, *Jan Cornelisz. Vermeyen, Painter to Charles V and his Conquest of Tunis, Paintings, Etchings, Drawings, Cartoons & Tapestries*, 2 vols (Aetas Aurea, Monographs on Dutch and Flemish Painting, VIII), Doornspijk 1989, vol. II, pp. 344–5; W. Seipel, ed., *Der Kriegszug Kaiser Karls V. gegen Tunis, Kartons und Tapisserien*, Milan and Vienna 2000.

9 Campbell 1998 catalogue, pp. 174–211; the underdrawing and the changes are most accurately and fully described by Rachel Billinge, 'Examining Jan van Eyck's Underdrawings' in *Investigating Jan van Eyck*, ed. S. Foister, S. Jones and D. Cool, Turnhout 2000, pp. 83–96. On the interpretation of the changes made to the heads and figures, see L. Campbell, 'The Making of Early Netherlandish Painted Portraits' in *The Image of the Individual*, ed. N. Mann and L. Syson, London 1998, pp.105–12

10 L. Campbell, 'The Early Netherlandish Painters and their Workshops' in *Le Dessin sous-jacent dans la peinture, Colloque III, 6–7–8 septembre 1979, Le problème Maître de Flémalle–Van der Weyden*, ed. D. Hollanders-Favart and R. Van Schoute (Université Catholique de Louvain, Institut supérieur d'archéologie et d'histoire de l'art, Document de travail N° 11), Louvain-la-Neuve, 1981, pp. 43–61, pp. 46–50.

11 L. Campbell, 'The Art Market in the Southern Netherlands in the Fifteenth Century', *Burlington Magazine*, CXVIII, 1976, pp. 188–98, p. 191 and references. Such a shop window is visible in the background of the painting by Konrad Witz of *Saint Catherine and the Magdalen* in the Musée de l'Oeuvre Notre-Dame in Strasbourg: reproduction in P. Lorentz, *Jost Haller le peintre des chevaliers et l'art en Alsace au XV e siècle*, exh. cat., Musée d'Unterlinden, Colmar 2001, p. 49. H. Huth, *Künstler und Werkstatt der Spätgotik*, 2nd edn, Darmstadt 1967, p. 33.

12 F.G. Zehnder, 'Gotische Malerei' in *Köln. Altkölner Bilder von 1300-1550*, Cologne 1989, p. 22; for restrictions regarding a maximum of two in Ulm, Augsburg and Munich, see M. Baxandall, *The Limewood Sculptors of Southern Germany*, New Haven 1980, pp. 102–26 p. 108, note 43, p. 114.

13 See Baxandall, cited above, and *Gothic and Renaissance Art in Nuremberg, 1300-1500*, exh. cat., New York 1986 p. 60.

14 Lucas Cranach den Aelten Schuchardt I p. 88, Campbell, *Renaissance Portraits*, New Haven and London 1990, p. 184.

15 L. Grote, 'Dürer-Werkstatt und Dürer-Schule', *Meister um Albrecht Dürer Germanisches Nationalmuseum*, Nuremberg, 1961, pp. 11–16.

16 K. van Mander, *Het Schilder-Boeck*, Haarlem 1604, fol. 242v.

17 Campbell 1976, pp. 194–7; D. Ewing, 'Marketing Art in Antwerp, 1460–1560: Our Lady's *Pand*', *Art Bulletin*, vol. LXXII, 1990, pp. 558–84.

18 L. Campbell and J. Dunkerton, 'A famous Gossaert rediscovered', *Burlington Magazine*, CXXXVIII, 1996, pp. 164–73.

19 Infrared reflectograms, kindly sent by Peter Eikemeier, are reproduced by Campbell and Dunkerton, cited above, p. 171.

20 Richard Charlton-Jones kindly arranged for this picture to be examined at the National Gallery on 31 March and 1 April 1999, when a reflectogram was made.

21 See Campbell 1998 catalogue, pp. 25–8, on fifteenth-century Netherlandish 'pattern' drawings.

22 Van Mander 1604, cited in note 16, fol. 242v; K. van Mander, *Den grondt der edel vry schilderconst*, ed. H. Miedema, 2 vols, Utrecht 1973 vol. I, p. 229.

23 Campbell 1990, cited in note 14, pp. 2–3.

24 Giulia Bartrum of the British Museum Department of Prints and Drawings kindly enabled a comparison to be made between the drawing and an overlay taken from the painting by Rachel Billinge

25 F. Koreny, 'A coloured flower study by Martin Schongauer and the development of the depiction of nature from Van der Weyden to Dürer', *Burlington Magazine*, CXXXIII, 1991, pp. 588–95.

26 U. Nürnberger, *The Late Medieval Workshop of the Master of the St Bartholomew Altar: An Investigation of Underdrawings and Paintings*, PhD thesis, Indiana University 1997.

27 R. Budde and R. Krischel (eds), *Genie ohne Namen: Der Meister des Bartholomäus-Altars*, exh. cat., Wallraf-Richartz Museum, Cologne 2001, p. 548.

28 U. Nürnberger, *Zeitenwende. Zwei Kölner Maler um 1500. Jüngerer Meister der Heiligen Sippe. Meister des Aachener Altars*, exh. cat., Berlin 2000.

29 J. Chipps-Smith, 'Dürer as Teacher', *Nuremberg Renaissance City 1500–1618*, University of Texas at Austin, 1983, pp. 45–52.

30 G. Goldberg, B. Heimberg and M. Schawe, *Albrecht Dürer: die Gemälde der Alten Pinakothek*, Munich 1998.

31 K. C Luber, 'Albrecht Dürer's Maximilian Portraits: An Investigation of Versions', *Master Drawings*, 29, 1991, pp. 30–47.

32 C. Grimm, J. Erichsen, E. Brockhoff (eds), *Lucas Cranach: ein Maler-Unternehmer aus Franken*, exh. cat., Festung Rosenberg, Kronach, 1994, pp. 345–7.

33 Jochen Sander of the Städelsches Kunstinstitut Frankfurt kindly confirmed that a reduced overlay of the head of the Elector in the National Gallery portrait corresponded to the head in the altarpiece of the Holy Kindred in Frankfurt.

34 L. Campbell, S. Foister and A. Roy (eds), *Early Northern Painting, National Gallery Technical Bulletin*, 18, 1997, p. 108.

35 Van Even, 'Monographie de l'ancienne école de peinture de Louvain', Messager des sciences historiques, 1866, pp 241–338, esp. pp. 287–8. The dealer Ghysbrecht die Ketelbuetere had supplied *prynten ende beelderien* costing 3 Rhenish florins and 16 stuivers.

36 Noted by M. Levey, *National Gallery Catalogues: The German School*, London 1959, p. 67.

37 R. Budde and R. Krischel (eds), cited in note 27, p. 522.

38 J. Berg Sobré, *Behind the Altar Table. The Development of the Painted Retable in Spain, 1350–1500*, Columbia (Missouri) 1989, pp. 297–304.

39 See Huth, cited in note 11, pp. 132–3.

40 D. Tamis, 'The genesis of Albert Cornelis's "Coronation of the Virgin" in Bruges', *Burlington Magazine*, CXLII, 2000, pp. 672–80.

41 Though Vermeyen was to paint the cartoons 'de sa propre main', he was to employ 'scavans et souffisans compaingnons painctres des pays de pardeca, quoy qu'ilz luy coustent, affin que iceulx patrons soient faicts le mieulx que possible sera': see Horn, 1989, cited in note 8, vol. II, pp. 344–5; and Seipel, 2000, cited in note 8. One of the painters who assisted him was Pieter Coecke : see Iain Buchanan, 'Designers, weavers and entrepreneurs: sixteenth-century Flemish tapestries in the Patrimonio Nacional', *Burlington Magazine*, CXXXIV, 1992, pp. 380–4.

42 A very interesting *vidimus* survived into the nineteenth century of the *Baptism of Christ*, dated 1548 and attributed to Michel Coxcie. It was for a window in the church of St Rombout in Mechlin; on the reverse was a contract by which the glass-painter Melchior van Viaenen agreed to execute and install the window 'following this *vidimus*': see Y. Vanden Bemden, 'Michel Coxcie, créateur de vitraux', *Handelingen van de Koninklijke Kring voor Oudheidkunde, Letteren en Kunst van Mechelen*, vol. XCVI, 2, 1992, pp. 141–59, p. 150.

43 Berg Sobré, cited in note 38, pp. 288–97.

44 In 1490 the Brussels shoemakers, commissioning from Aert van den Bossche a painting of St Crispin, paid a large sum for a design ('bewoerp') and then a small sum 'te coste vander copien te makenen van sinte Crispijn tafele'. The painter received his final payment for the picture in 1494. See A.-M. Bonenfant-Feytmans, 'Aert van den Bossche peintre du polyptyque des saints Crépin et Crépinien', *Université Libre de Bruxelles, Annales d'histoire de l'art et d'archéologie*, vol. XIII, 1991, pp. 43–58, p. 55.

45 G.-M. Leproux, *La peinture à Paris sous le règne de François Ier* (Corpus Vitrearum, France, Etudes IV), Paris 2001, p. 191.

46 Leproux, cited above, p. 192.

47 P. Huvenne in the exhibition catalogue *Bruges et la Renaissance, De Memling à Pourbus, Notices*, Memlingmuseum, Bruges 1998, pp. 128–31 (with infrared reflectograms of the triptych and comments on further changes).

48 C. Muller, *Katalog der Zeichnungen des 15. und 16. Jahrhunderts. Teil 2A. Die Zeichnungen von Hans Holbein dem Jüngerem und Ambrosius Holbein*, Öffentliche Kunstsammlungen Basel Kupferstichkabinett. 1996, No. 157, pp. 106–8.

49 Berg Sobré 1989, cited in note 38, p. 48.

50 van Asperen de Boer, Dijkstra and Van Schoute, 1992, cited in note 1, pp. 137–43, 202–21.

51 *Earth* and the other paintings in the series are discussed in L. Campbell, 'Beuckelaer's *The Four Elements*, Four masterpieces by a neglected genius', *Apollo*, February 2002, pp. 40–6; the reflectograms are published here for the first time.

52 J. Dunkerton, A. Burnstock and A. Smith, 'Two Wings of an Altarpiece by Martin van Heemskerck', *National Gallery Technical Bulletin*, vol. 12, 1988, pp. 16–35.

53 J.M.C. Boreel and F.W.H. van Zon-Christoffels, 'Enkele aspecten van de schilderspraktijk in her atelier van Pieter Aertsen natuurwetenschappelijk nader bekeken', *Nederlands Kunsthistorisch Jaarboek*, vol. 40, 1989, pp. 167–96; Martin Bijl, Marija Zeldenrust and Wouter Kloek, 'Pieter Aertsen in het restauratie-atelier van het Rijksmuseum', *ibid.*, pp. 197–233.

54 M. Schawe, 'Albrecht Altdorfer's "Susanna im Bade" von 1526. Überlegungen zum Werkprozess', *Niederdeutsche Beiträge zur Kunstgeschichte*, 38, 1999, pp. 93–103.

55 Van Mander 1604, cited in note 16, fol. 244; van Mander-Miedema, vol. I, p. 234, cited in note 22.

56 J. Rowlands, *The Complete Paintings of Hans Holbein the Younger*, Oxford 1985, No L14, pp. 224–6

57 Campbell 1998 catalogue, p. 27.

58 S. Foister, *Drawings by Holbein from the Royal Library, Windsor Castle*; London and New York 1983; M. Ainsworth, '"Paternes for Phiosioneamyes", Holbein's Portraiture Reconsidered', *Burlington Magazine*, CXXXII, 1990, pp. 173–86.

59 L. Campbell, S. Foister and A. Roy (eds), cited in note 34, p. 27.

60 R. Duckwitz, 'The Devil is in the Detail. Pieter Bruegel the Elder's *Netherlandish Proverbs* and copies after it from the workshop of Pieter Brueghel the Younger' in *Brueghel Enterprises*, ed. Peter van den Brink (exh. cat., Bonnefantenmuseum, Maastricht and Musées Royaux des Beaux-Arts de Belgique, Brussels), Ghent and Amsterdam 2001, pp. 58–79.

61 H. Mielke, *Pieter Bruegel, Die Zeichnungen*, Turnhout 1996, p. 63 No. 57; for the paintings by Pieter the Younger, see K. Ertz, *Pieter Brueghel der Jüngere (1564–16378), Die Gemälde mit Kritischen Oeuvrekatalog*, 2 vols, Lingen 2000, pp. 205–6.

62 See the exhibition catalogue cited in note 60, p. 49 No. A.

63 J. Folie, 'Les oeuvres authentifiées des Primitifs flamands', *Bulletin de l'Institut royal du patrimoine artistique*, vol. VI, 1963, pp. 183–251, p. 235; P. Vandenbroeck, 'The Spanish *inventarios reales* and Hieronymus Bosch' and M. Renson, 'Genealogical Information concerning the Bronchorst-Bosschuysen Triptych' in *Hieronymus Bosch. New Insights into his Life and Work*, ed. J. Koldeweij, B. Vermet and B. van Kooij, Rotterdam 2001, pp. 48–63 and 92–5.

64 C. Grimm, 'A Rediscovered Work by Hugo van der Goes', *Journal of the Walters Art Gallery*, vol. XLVI, 1988, pp. 77–91.

65 Kupferstichkabinett, Dresden: A.E. Popham, *Drawings of the Early Flemish School*, London 1926, p. 28, plate 33 (as 'Dutch School about 1490'). A related painting of the *Crucifixion with Saints and Donors* exists in a private collection in Madrid (Elisa Bermejo Martinez, *La Pintura de los Primitivos flamencos en España* , vol. II, Madrid 1982, pp. 65–6, plates 65–9). Unfortunately, since no infrared photographs or reflectograms are available, nothing is known about the underdrawing.

66 A.L. Dierick, 'Jan van Eyck's Handwriting' in Foister, Jones and Cool, cited in note 9, pp. 79–82; S. Buck, 'An Approach to Looking at Eyckian Drawings', *ibid.*, pp. 183–95. For the differences between the drawing and the painting, see Campbell 1990, cited in note 14, pp. 170–1.

67 R. Billinge, H. Verougstraete and R. Van Schoute, 'The *Saint Barbara*' in Foister, Jones and Cool, cited in note 9, pp. 41–8.

68 Foister 1983, cited in note 58; S. Foister, M. Wyld and A. Roy, 'Hans Holbein's *A Lady with a Squirrel and a Starling*', *National Gallery Technical Bulletin*, 15, 1994, pp. 6–19, esp. pp. 10–11, 13, 16–17.

69 L. Campbell, 'Bosch, Christ Mocked (The Crowning with Thorns) NG 4744' in *Le Dessin sous-jacent et la technologie dans la peinture, Colloque XII, 11–13 septembre 1997: La peinture dans les Pays-Bas au 16e siècle, Pratiques d'atelier, infrarouges et autres méthodes d'investigation*, ed. H. Verougstraete, R. Van Schoute and A. Dubois, Louvain, 1999, pp. 29–35.

70 S. Buck, *Die niederländischen Zeichnungen des 15. Jahrhunderts im Berliner Kupferstichkabinett, Kritischer Katalog*, Turnhout 2001, pp. 55, 197–206, 388–9.

71 'Miserrimi quippe est ingenii semper uti inventis et numquam inveniendis.' This is taken from *De disciplina scholarium* by Pseudo-Boethius: see P. Vandenbroeck, 'Over Jheronimus Bosch. Met een toelichting bij de tekst op de tekening KdZ 549 in het Berlijnse Kupferstichkabinett' in *Bijdragen tot de geschiedenis van de Kunst der Nederlanden Opgedragen aan Prof. Em. Dr. J.K. Steppe*, ed. M. Smeyers, Louvain 1981, pp. 151–88.

72 'Dann er muss gar ein spröder vestand sein/der jme nit trawet auch etwas weyters zu erfinden/sonder ligt allwegen auff der alten pan/volgt allein anderen nach/vnd vndersteet sich nichten weitter nachzudencken.' Albrecht Dürer, *Vier Bücher von menschlicher Proportion*, Nuremberg 1528, fol. A ij. The dedication is reprinted, with modernised spelling, in H. Faensen, ed., *Albrecht Dürer, Schriftlicher Nachlass, Eine Auswahl*, Berlin 1962, pp. 173–6; this sentence is on page 174.

73 See also Campbell 1998 catalogue, pp. 31–2, on imitation and invention in Early Netherlandish painting.

Drawing in Italy

1 See definitions for '*Disegnamento*' and '*Disegno*', in *Vocabolario degli Accademici della Crusca*, reprint of 1612 edition (Gio. Alberti, Venice), Florence 1987, p. 281.

2 For Vasari's definition of *disegno*, see Giorgio Vasari, *Le Vite de' più eccellenti pittori scultori e architettori nelle redazioni del 1550 e 1568*, ed. R. Bettarini and annotated P. Barocchi, Florence 1966–87, 7 vols, I, pp. 111–13. For a translation, see *Vasari on Technique* [Florence, 1568], tr. L.S. Maclehose, New York 1960, pp. 205–6. For a summary of the conceptual history of *disegno*, see D. Summers, *Michelangelo and the Language of Art*, Princeton 1981, especially ch. XVII; also C.C. Bambach, *Drawing and Painting in the Italian Renaissance Workshop. Theory and Practice, 1300–1600*, Cambridge 1999, p. 16, and p. 377, n. 62.

3 *Di Cennino Cennini trattato della pittura, messo in luce la prima volta con annotazioni dal Cavaliere Tambroni*, Rome 1821. The standard editions used henceforth are: C. Cennini, *Il Libro dell'Arte*, with commentary and annotations by F. Brunello, Vicenza 1982; Cennino d'Andrea Cennini, *The Craftsman's Handbook, the Italian 'Il Libro dell' Arte'*, tr. D.V. Thompson, Jr, Dover edition, New York 1960. For literature on the dating of Cennino's treatise (recent scholarship favours a date in the late 1390s; Cennino's original manuscript is lost but three manuscript copies have survived), see Bambach, cited in note 2, p. 373, n. 7.

4 For Vasari's account of painting, 'Della Pittura', see Vasari (ed. Bettarini), I, pp. 111–72; Vasari (tr. Maclehose), cited in note 2, pp. 205–84.

5 G.B. Armenini, *De' veri precetti della pittura* [Ravenna 1586], ed. M. Gorreri, Turin 1988. An English translation is *Giovanni Battista Armenini on the True Precepts of the Art of Painting*, ed. and tr. E. J. Olszewski, New York [Burt Franklin] 1977.

6 Cennini (ed. Brunello), pp. 5–6; Cennini (tr. Thompson), pp. 2–3, both cited in note 3.

7 *Idem.*

8 Cennini (ed. Brunello), p. 8; Cennini (tr. Thompson), p. 4.

9 Cennini (ed. Brunello), pp. 109–10; Cennini (tr. Thompson), pp. 64–5.

10 Cennini (ed. Brunello), pp. 10, 110; Cennini (tr. Thompson), pp. 5, 65.

11 Cennini (ed. Brunello), p. 15; Cennini (tr. Thompson), p. 8.

12 Cennini (ed. Brunello), p. 8; Cennini (tr. Thompson), pp. 4–5.

13 Cennini (ed. Brunello), pp. 9–10; Cennini (tr. Thompson), pp. 5–8.

14 Cennini (ed. Brunello), pp. 10–13; Cennini (tr. Thompson), pp. 9–12.

15 Paper was made from pulping linen (for the highest quality of paper), cotton or rags, and its manufacture was dependent on the textile industry (itself undergoing a rapid expansion) for the supply of raw materials. See D. Hunter, *Papermaking: The History and Technique of an Ancient Craft*, Dover edition, New York 1978. See also, F. Ames-Lewis, *Drawing in Early Renaissance Italy*, New Haven and London 1981, p. 21 and p. 182, n. 2.

16 Ames-Lewis, cited above, pp. 38 and 128; plate 21.

17 For literature on the history of papermaking at Fabriano, see G. Finaldi, E. Harding and J. Wallis, *The Conservation of the Carracci Cartoons in the National Gallery*, London 1995, p. 20, n. 25.

18 Alberti's *De Pictura* was translated from the original Latin into Italian in 1436; the Latin version was first published in 1540, and the Italian translation in 1547. L.B. Alberti, *Della Pittura: Edizione critica*, ed. L. Malle, Florence, 1950. *On painting and On sculpture: The Latin texts of De Pictura and De Statua*, ed. and tr. C. Grayson, London 1972. *On Painting* (Italian text), tr. and commentary by John R. Spencer, New Haven and London 1966 (1st edn, 1956).

19 Alberti (ed. Malle), pp. 108–9; Alberti (ed. Grayson), p. 100, para. 57; Alberti (tr. Spencer), p. 94, cited above.

20 According to Ames-Lewis, cited in note 15, pp.22–3, and confirmed by archival documentation from elsewhere in Europe. Sources in both Northern Europe and Italy suggest that in the years around 1500 paper was approximately five times cheaper than parchment. We would like to thank Dominique Vanwijnsberghe of the Institut Royal du Patrimoine Artistique, Brussels, and Rupert Shepherd of Sussex University (Material Renaissance project) for help in establishing this statistic.

21 For a discussion of early Italian model-books and sketch-books, see Ames-Lewis, cited in note 15, pp.63–9. Also, J. Elen, *Italian Late-Medieval and Renaissance Drawing Books from Giovannino de' Grassi to Palma Giovane. A Codicological approach*, Leiden 1995.

22 On Pisanello, see L. Syson and D. Gordon, with S. Avery Quash, *Pisanello: Painter to the Renaissance Court*, exh. cat., National Gallery, London 2001.

23 Ibid., chapter v, especially pp.192–202; and pp.26–8.

24 See for example ibid., pp.167–71, and fig. 4.59.

25 C. Gould, *National Gallery Catalogues. The Sixteenth-Century Italian Schools*, London 1975 (rep. 1987), pp.109–10.

26 Cennini (ed. Brunello), pp.27–8; Cennini (tr. Thompson), pp.14–15, cited in note 3.

27 M. Hirst, *Michelangelo and his Drawings*, New Haven and London 1988, pp.4–6, 46 and 59; M. Hirst and J. Dunkerton, *Making and Meaning: The Young Michelangelo*, exh. cat., National Gallery, London 1994, p. 14, and plates 4–6.

28 Although Cennino recommended copying from nature 'above all other models', few drawings made from life (or indeed from the imagination) survive before the early fifteenth century. Cennini (ed. Brunello), p. 28; Cennini (tr. Thompson), p. 15, cited in note 3.

29 Alberti (ed. Malle), p. 109; Alberti (ed. Grayson), p. 100, para. 58; Alberti (tr. Spencer), pp.94–5, cited in note 18.

30 Vasari (ed. Bettarini), I, pp.114–15; Vasari (tr. Maclehose), p. 210, cited in note 2.

31 Vasari (ed. Bettarini), I, p.112; Vasari (tr. Maclehose), pp.207–8.

32 See *Léonard de Vinci, les études de draperie*, exh. cat., ed. F. Viatte with C. Monbeig Goguel and M. Pinault, Musée du Louvre, Paris 1989.

33 On prints and printmaking, see D. Landau and P. Parshall, *The Renaissance Print, 1470–1550*, New Haven and London 1994; for the later period, see M. Bury, *The Print in Italy, 1550–1620*, exh. cat., British Museum, London 2001.

34 P.L. Rubin and A. Wright, *Renaissance Florence. The Art of the 1470s*, exh. cat., National Gallery, London 1999, cat. no. 53.

35 J. Martineau (ed.), *Andrea Mantegna*, exh. cat., Royal Academy, London, Metropolitan Museum of Art, New York, 1992, cat. no. 79 and p. 54.

36 On prints of Raphael's designs made by Marcantonio Raimondi, Agostino Veneziano and Marco Dente da Ravenna, see Landau and Parshall, cited in note 33, pp. 120–46.

37 D. Ekserdjian, 'A print source for Botticelli. A devil by the Master E.S.', *Apollo*, CXLVIII, no. 441, November 1998, pp.15–16. For Pontormo's use of Northern art, see F. M. Clapp, *Jacopo Pontormo: His Life and Work*, New Haven 1916, pp. 37–46; J. Cox-Rearick, *The Drawings of Pontormo*, 2 vols, Cambridge, MA, 1964, rev. edn, New York 1981, pp.213–30.

38 Alberti (ed. Malle), p. 112; Alberti (ed. Grayson), pp.102–4; Alberti (tr. Spencer), p. 96.

39 Ames-Lewis, cited in note 15, p. 85.

40 J.P. Richter, *The Literary Works of Leonardo da Vinci*, London 1883, vol. 1, p. 287, para 571. See further ibid., p. 246, para 490 and p. 288, para 572.

41 *Idem*: 'for the forms and positions of objects are so infinite that the memory is incapable of retaining them, wherefore keep these as your guides and masters.'

42 Vasari (ed. Bettarini), I, pp.112–13; Vasari (tr. Maclehose), p. 208, cited in note 2.

43 Alberti (ed. Malle), p. 108; Alberti (ed. Grayson), pp.98–100, para. 56; Alberti (tr.Spencer), pp.93–4, cited in note 18.

44 Maso Finiguerra, for example, left 14 books of drawings at his death in 1464, stipulating that they should pass to any member of the family who continued in the trade (in the event they went to his brother, also a goldsmith): see D. Carl, 'Documenti inediti su Maso Finiguerra a la sua familia', *Annali della Scuola Normale Superiore di Pisa*, 3rd ser. 13, no. 2 (1983), pp. 507–54, noted in M. Haines, 'Artisan Family Strategies' in *Art, Memory and Family in Renaissance Florence*, eds. G. Ciappelli and P. Rubin, Cambridge 2000, p. 168. For Filippino Lippi's legacy, among which were 'zacchiere e disegni e quadernucci e scritture e schartabelli e lavori e libri de chomte sua e lettere', distributed between his three sons, one of whom was a goldsmith, see *idem*, 'Das Inventar der Werkstatt von Filippino Lippi', *Mitteilungen des Kunsthistorischen Institutes in Florenz*, XXXI, 1987, p. 389 [item 244].

45 Ames-Lewis, cited in note 15, pp. 11–12.

46 Ibid, pp.4–5; Gabinetto Disegni e Stampe, Uffizi, Florence, inv. no. 404E (from Vasari's *Libro de' Disgni*).

47 Ames-Lewis, cited in note 15, p. 12. On the provenance of the London sketchbook, see A.E. Popham and P. Pouncey, *Italian Drawings in the Department of Prints and Drawings in the British Museum. The Fourteenth and Fifteenth Centuries*, London 1950, I, p. 14, cat. 21. For other drawings in the Vendramin Collection, see the inventory published by A. Ravà, 'Il "Camerino delle Anticaglie" di Gabriele Vendramin', *Nuovo Archivio Veneto*, XXXIX (1920), pp.155–81.

48 Hirst 1988, cited in note 27, p. 106.

49 V. Birke and J. Kertész, *Die Italienischen Zeichnungen der Albertina*, 4 vols, Vienna, Cologne and Weimar 1992–7, IV, pp.2158–9. Inscribed in Dürer's hand (here translated): '1515, Raphael of Urbino, who is so much admired by the Pope, made this nude study and sent it to Albrecht Dürer to illustrate his hand to him.'

50 Hirst 1988, cited in note 27, ch. 10.

51 M. Hirst, *Sebastiano del Piombo*, Oxford 1981, ch.5.

52 P. Costamagna, *Pontormo*, Milan 1994, cat. nos 69 and 70; M. Hirst and G. Mayr, 'Michelangelo, Pontormo und das Noli Me Tangere', in *Vittoria Colonna: Dichterin und Muse Michelangelos*, exh. cat., ed. S. Ferino-Pagden, Kunsthistorisches Museum, Vienna 1997, pp.335–44. For a discussion of Michelangelo's sketches for *The Purification in the Temple* in the National Gallery, attributed to Venusti, see Gould, cited in note 25, p. 154.

53 L. Ragghianti Collobi, *Il Libro de' Disegni del Vasari*, 2 vols, Florence 1974. For subsequent bibliography, see Bambach, cited in note 2, p. 403, note 16.

54 For Titian's drawings see H. E. Wethey, *Titian and his Drawings*, Princeton 1987.

55 Vasari (ed. Bettarini), I, p. 117; Vasari (tr. Maclehose), p. 21, cited in note 2.

56 Hirst 1988, cited in note 27, p. 32; on Michelangelo's periodic destruction of his own drawings, see ibid., pp.14–19.

57 Vasari (ed. Bettarini), I, pp.117–18; Vasari (tr. Maclehose), p. 212, cited in note 2.

58 Vasari (ed. Bettarini), I, p. 118; Vasari (tr. Maclehose), p. 213.

59 Alberti (ed. Malle), p. 88; Alberti (ed. Grayson), p. 74, para 36; Alberti (tr. Spencer), p. 73, cited in note 18. Raphael, Del Sarto and Pontormo all adopted this practice.

60 *Francesco Salviati (1510–1563) ou la Bella Maniera*, exh. cat., ed. Catherine Monbeig Goguel, Rome and Paris 1998, pp.150–1, no. 37. Inscribed: 'di michelagnolo pitore fiorentino alias Salviati dic[h]iaro questo e[s]sere il disegno della tavola daltare che io [ho] promes[s]o fare a albizo delben[e] chome apare pe[r] uno chontrato rogato per M[esser] piero franc[es]co machalli notaio fiorentino ogi questo di di novembre'. The drawing, somewhat battered and folded, is squared for enlargement.

61 R.S. Miller, 'Documents for Francesco Salviati's "Incredulity of St Thomas"', *Dialoghi di Storia dell'Arte*, no. 6, June 1998, pp.122–5. The contract confirms that Albizzo was acting on behalf of the heirs of the deceased Tommaso Guadagni, another wealthy banker resident in Lyon, in whose possession it is recorded by Vasari.

62 Vasari (ed. Bettarini), I, p. 120; Vasari (tr. Maclehose), p. 214, cited in note 2.

63 On cartoons recorded in the collections of Vasari's contemporaries, see Bambach, cited in note 2, p. 276.

64 Vasari (ed. Bettarini), I, p.119; Vasari (tr. Maclehose), p. 213, cited in note 2.

65 Armenini (ed. Gorreri), p. 120; Armenini (tr. Olszewski), pp.170–1, cited in note 5: 'The sketches, the drawings, the models, the living models, in sum all the labours previously realized have as their only purpose that of being brought together on the spaces of the aforementioned cartoons.'

66 Armenini (ed. Gorreri), p.120; Armenini (tr. Olszewski), p.170.

67 Armenini (ed. Gorreri), p.120; Armenini (tr. Olszewski), p.171.

68 Hirst 1988, cited in note 27, p. 19.

69 Bambach, cited in note 2, pp.140–2.

70 Cennino (ed. Brunello), pp.143–4, and Cennino (tr. Thompson), pp.86–8, cited in note 3.

71 For a fuller account, and a reconstruction of the execution of this textile, see D. Bomford et al., *Art in the Making. Italian Painting before 1400*, London 1989, pp. 130–5.

72 Bambach, cited in note 2, pp.145–50; and E. S. Skaug, *Punch Marks from Giotto to Fra Angelico. Attribution, Chronology, and Workshop Relationships in Tuscan Panel Painting c.1330–1430*, Oslo 1994, vol. II, Appendix IV, pp.536–43.

73 Including some from the workshop of Andrea di Cione (Orcagna). See Bambach, cited in note 2, pp.158–64.

74 M. Castrichini, *Pisanello. Restauri e interpretazioni*, Todi 1996, p. 76 and p. 89, fig. 88; see also Bambach, p. 166.

75 R. Bellucci and C. Frosinini, 'Piero della Francesca's Process: Panel Painting Technique', *Painting Techniques, History, Materials and Studio Practice*, Contributions to the Dublin Congress of the International Institute for Conservation, 7–11 September 1998, A. Roy and P. Smith (eds), London 1998, pp. 89–93, esp. p. 89.

76 See, for example, Bellucci and Frosinini, cited above, p. 90, Fig 3.

77 For discussion of the use of pounced cartoons for the *Legend of the True Cross*, see Bambach, cited in note 2, pp. 22–30; and for the *Madonna del Parto* as well as the *Legend of the True Cross* see M. Matteini, A. Moles and M. Seracini, 'Indagini diagnostiche', pp. 232–58, esp. p. 281, S. Lazzeri, 'Ricognizione visiva', pp.259–66, esp. p. 263, and R. Franchi, M. Matteini, A. Moles and M. Seracini, 'Stato di conservazione e tecnica di esecuzione [del Madonna del Parto]', pp.367–79, esp. p. 367, all in Alinari (ed.), *Un progetto per Piero della Francesca*, Florence 1989.

78 For the use of *spolvero* by Domenico Veneziano, perhaps including the fragments of the Carnesecchi Tabernacle in the National Gallery, see Bambach, cited in note 2, pp.204–8.

79 J. Dunkerton and C. Plazzotta, 'Vincenzo Foppa's *Adoration of the Kings*' in *National Gallery Technical Bulletin*, 22, 2001, pp.18–28, esp. pp.21–2.

80 See L. Mattioli Rossi, ed., *Vincenzo Foppa. La Cappella Portinari*, Milan 1999, pp.264–71, for diagrams showing the presence of *spolvero*, especially for heads.

81 Bambach, cited in note 2, pp.235–6, suggests that the earliest full compositional cartoon to survive is that by Pesellino for a *Mystic Marriage of Saint Catherine* in the Gabinetto Disegni e Stampe degli Uffizi (inv. 1117 E). It is, however, very small, measuring 25.7 x 20.6 cm.

82 Bambach, cited in note 2, pp.219–20.

83 The documents concerning Tura's designs for tapestry are discussed more fully in J. Dunkerton, 'Cosmè Tura's Painting Technique' in S. J. Campbell, *Cosmè Tura. Painting and Design in Renaissance Ferrara*, exh. cat., Isabella Stewart Gardner Museum, Boston 2002, pp.107–51, especially pp.132–5.

84 For the construction of the cartoons, see S. Fermor and A Derbyshire, 'The Raphael tapestry cartoons re-examined', *The Burlington Magazine*, CXL, 1998, pp.236–50.

85 A. Nesselrath, *Raphael's School of Athens*, in the series *Recent Restorations of the Vatican Museums*, Vol. 1, Vatican City State, 1996, pp.15–18 and p. 100, fig. 100, and

Bambach, cited in note 2, pp. 39–40 and p. 287.

86 For detailed discussion of the 'substitute' cartoon, see Bambach, ch. 8.

87 See Nesselrath, cited in note 85.

88 See Bambach, cited in note 2, p. 97. The drawing has also recently been examined by the present authors with a stereo-binocular microscope at the British Museum.

89 Perugino's practice is discussed in detail, supported by many illustrations, including overlays of tracings made from paintings, in R. Hiller von Gaertringen, *Raffaels Lernerfahrung in der Werkstatt Peruginos*, Munich and Berlin 1999, esp. pp. 131–222. See also R. Hiller von Gaertringen, 'On Perugino's Re-uses of Cartoons', *Le Dessin Sous-Jacent et la Technologie dans la Peinture, Colloque XI*, 1995, R. Van Schoute and H. Verougstraete (eds), Louvain-la-Neuve 1997, pp. 223–30.

90 Curiously, only one fragment of such a cartoon has survived (for the head of Saint Joseph of Arimathaea in the *Lamentation* painted for Santa Chiara, Florence in 1495), and as yet only a few paintings have undergone infrared examination for the detection of *spolvero* dots.

91 Hiller von Gaertringen 1999, cited in note 89, especially Plate 19.

92 Hiller von Gaertringen 1999, Plates 26–7.

93 P. Scarpellini, *Perugino*, Milan 1984, p. 101, cat. no. 106; Hiller von Gaertringen 1999, pp. 154–6.

94 See D. Bomford and N. Turner, 'Perugino's Underdrawing in the *Virgin and Child adored by an Angel* from the Certosa di Pavia Altarpiece' in *Perugino, Lippi e la bottega di San Marco alla Certosa di Pavia, 1495–1511*, exh. cat., Pinacoteca di Brera, Milan, published Florence 1986, pp. 49–54.

95 See J.K. Cadogan, *Domenico Ghirlandaio. Artist and Artisan*, New Haven and London 2000, p. 249. Similarly all the surviving versions of a very popular circular composition of the Virgin and Child, accompanied by the Infant Baptist and angels in various permutations, appear to be by various, and often distinctly different, members of the workshop. The original design, however, may well have been Domenico's.

96 For a fuller discussion of Bellini's underdrawing practice see J. Dunkerton, 'Bellini's Technique' in *Cambridge Companion to Giovanni Bellini*, ed. P. Humfrey, Cambridge (forthcoming). For illustrations of Bellini underdrawings see A. Dorigato (ed.), *Carpaccio, Bellini, Tura, Antonello e altri restauri quattrocenteschi della Pinacoteca del Museo Correr*, Milan 1993, and R. Goffen and G. Nepi Scirè, *Il Colore Ritrovato. Bellini a Venezia*, exh. cat., Galleria dell'Accademia, Venice 2000.

97 For examples of the transmission of Bellini designs see A. Tempestini, in *Cambridge Companion to Giovanni Bellini*, ed. P. Humfrey, Cambridge (forthcoming).

98 L. Keith, 'Andrea del Sarto's *The Virgin and Child with Saint Elizabeth and Saint John the Baptist*: Technique and Critical Reputation', *National Gallery Technical Bulletin*, 22, 2001, pp. 42–53, esp. pp. 44–8.

99 Vasari (ed. Bettarini), I, p. 134; Vasari (tr. Maclehose), p. 231, cited in note 2.

100 M. Kemp (ed.), *Leonardo da Vinci and the Mystery of the 'Madonna of the Yarnwinder'*, exh. cat. National Gallery of Scotland, Edinburgh 1992, esp. pp. 16–20.

101 Giampietrino managed to utilise a drawing which seems originally to have derived from the figure of Leda in a lost composition by Leonardo for half-length paintings of both the naked Cleopatra, in a painting in the Louvre, Paris, and the richly dressed *Salome* in the National Gallery. Since the figures are on the same scale, the same cartoon was almost certainly adapted for both. This may have been transferred by pouncing – pounced dots have been observed on other paintings by Giampietrino – although no evidence could be found on the *Salome*. See L. Keith, 'Giampietrino, Boltraffio, and the Influence of Leonardo', *National Gallery Technical Bulletin*, 17, 1996, pp. 4–19, esp. pp. 6–10.

102 See J. Dunkerton, N. Penny and A. Roy, 'Two Paintings by Lorenzo Lotto in the National Gallery', *National Gallery Technical Bulletin*, 19, 1998, pp. 52–63, esp. pp. 53–5.

103 N. Penny, 'Two paintings by Titian in the National Gallery, London. Notes on technique, condition and provenance' in *Tiziano. Técnicas y restauraciones*, Actas del Simposium Internacional celebrado en el Museo Nacional del Prado los días 3, 4 y 5 junio de 1999, Madrid 1999, pp. 109–16, esp. pp. 109–11.

104 Several of Titian's drawings on paper included squaring grids, and this technique of enlargement may have been commonly practised in the workshop.

105 See L. Campbell, *Renaissance Portraits. European Portrait-Painting in the 14th, 15th and 16th Centuries*, New Haven and London 1990, p. 184.

106 According to Vasari, Bonsignori's heirs had a collection of such drawings. See Campbell 1990, p. 185. This drawing has also been attributed to Mantegna; see catalogue entry in J. Martineau (ed.), *Andrea Mantegna*, exh. cat., cited in note 35, 1992, pp. 339–41. The underdrawing on the painting is schematic and linear.

107 See D. Bull, '"Ginevra de' Benci" and the "Lady with an Ermine"', *Artibus et Historiae*, XIII, 1992, pp. 67–83, esp. pp. 80–1.

108 However, Bambach, cited in note 2, pp. 111–2, argues on the basis of a careful examination of the drawing that Leonardo's cartoon for a *Portrait of Isabella d'Este* (Département des Arts Graphiques du Musée du Louvre) was pricked for transfer by a later copyist.

109 Vasari (ed. Bettarini), p. 118; Vasari (tr. Maclehose), p. 212, cited in note 2.

110 For Cennino's instructions for underdrawing for fresco and panel painting see Cennini (ed. Brunello), pp. 75 and 126–7; and Cennini (tr. Thompson), pp. 43–4 and p. 75, cited in note 3.

111 A striking example of an early underdrawing shaded with broad washes is Giotto's *Virgin and Child Enthroned* from S. Giorgio alla Costa, Florence. See M. Ciatti and C. Frosinini (eds), *La Madonna di San Giorgio alla Costa di Giotto. Studi e restauri*, Florence 1995, esp. pp. 69–70 and 93–4.

112 For similar underdrawing by Giovanni di Paolo see J.J.A. Panders, *The Underdrawing of Giovanni di Paolo: Characteristics and Development*, doctoral thesis, University of Groningen, 1997.

113 For Duccio's underdrawing see Bomford et al., cited in note 71, pp. 80–1, 86, 89, 93–7.

114 Dunkerton and Plazzotta, cited in note 79, pp. 21–2.

115 For infrared reflectograms revealing the underdrawn features of the angels on the left (completely obscured by the green earth) see M. Hirst and J. Dunkerton, cited in note 27, p. 92.

116 Similarly the careful incision of all the armour in *Portrait of a Man in Armour* (NG 895), attributed to Granacci, may have been carried out so as not to lose the detail once the first underpainting had been laid in.

117 Charcoal underdrawing was observed for the figures, and black particles appear in some cross-sections; see N. Penny and M. Spring, 'Veronese's Paintings in the National Gallery. Technique and Materials: Part I', *National Gallery Technical Bulletin*, 16, 1995, pp. 4–29, especially p. 17. For very similar underdrawing of the architecture in Veronese's *Feast in the House of Levi* see P. Spezzani, *Riflettoscopia e indagini non distruttive*, Milan 1992, pp. 114, also *Paolo Veronese restauri*, exh. cat., Gallerie dell'Accademia, Venice 1988 (Quaderni della Soprintendenza ai Beni Artistici e Storici di Venezia, 15), pp. 86–96.

118 See J. Dunkerton, 'The Technique and Restoration of Bramantino's "Adoration of the Kings"', *National Gallery Technical Bulletin*, 14, 1993, pp. 42–61.

119 For the division of this picture between Filippino and Botticelli, see Rubin and Wright, cited in note 34, p. 290.

120 Michael Pacher may have visited Padua, probably in the 1460s. His paintings appear to show a knowledge of Mantegna's Eremitani frescoes and also, rather intriguingly, of some of the drawings in Jacopo Bellini's Drawing Books (see A. Rosenauer, 'Zur Frage der europäischen Bedeutung Michael Pachers'/ 'Il ruolo di Michael Pacher nell'arte Europea', in *Michael Pacher und sein Kreis. Ein Tiroler Kunstler der europäischen Spatgotik/ Michael Pacher e la sua Cerchia. Un artista tirolese nell'Europa del Quattrocento*, exh. cat., Neustift/Novacella, Bolzano 1998, pp. 37–47, esp. pp. 39–44). Connections between Pacher and Italy are always discussed in terms of the influence of Italian art on Pacher's compositions, but it is worth pointing out that his underdrawings were often as detailed and carefully shaded as those of Giovanni Bellini.

121 Bellini's *Lamentation over the Dead Christ* (Florence, Uffizi) is often taken to be an underdrawing that was never painted, but it was more probably intended as a form of grisaille, and it may even be identifiable with such a painting described by Ridolfi; see J. Dunkerton in *Cambridge Companion to Giovanni Bellini*, ed. P Humfrey (forthcoming), cited in note 96.

122 'a niuno lasciava mai vedere le sue opere se non finito del tutto': Vasari (ed. Bettarini), IV, p. 231; For a translation, see Vasari, *Lives of the Painters, Sculptors and Architects*, tr. G. de Vere, intro. and notes by D. Ekserdjian, London 1966, 2 vols, II, p. 868. This echoes Vasari's accounts of Michelangelo's self-protectiveness during the painting of the Sistine Chapel, and Franciabigio's destruction of his own work in the atrium of SS. Annunziata after the friars viewed his fresco before he deemed it finished.

123 C. Plazzotta and L. Keith, 'Bronzino's "Allegory": new evidence of the artist's revisions', *The Burlington Magazine*, CXLI, February 1999, pp. 89–99.

124 G. Gaye, *Carteggio inedito d'artisti dei secoli XIV, XV, XVI* (1839–40), II, pp. 330–1. Letter from Bronzino to Cosimo's maggiordomo Pierfrancesco Riccio dated 22 August 1545, republished in J. Cox-Rearick, *Bronzino's Eleonora Chapel in the Palazzo Vecchio*, Berkeley, Los Angeles and Oxford, 1993, p. 337, doc.13. Bronzino reports the Duke as saying: ' "Io la vogl[I]o in quell modo proprio come sta quella, et non la vogl[I]o più bella" quasi dicesse: "Non m'entrare in latra inventione, perchè quella mi piace."'

125 See J. Dunkerton and M. Spring, 'The Development of Painting on Coloured Surfaces in Sixteenth-century Italy', *Painting Techniques. History, Materials and Studio Practice*, Contributions to the Dublin Congress of the International Institute for Conservation, 7–11 September 1998, eds A. Roy and P. Smith, pp. 120–30.

126 For examples of X-radiographs of paintings by Dosso with white underdrawings see A. Rothe and D. Carr, 'Poetry with Paint', and A. Coliva, 'Dosso's works in the Galleria Borghese: New Documentary, Iconographical, and Technical Information', in P. Humfrey and M. Lucco, *Dosso Dossi. Court Painter in Renaissance Ferrara*, ed. A. Bayer, exh. cat., New York 1998, pp. 58 and 75; and for Tintoretto see J. Plesters, 'Tintoretto's Paintings in the National Gallery', *National Gallery Technical Bulletin*, 4, 1980, pp. 32–47, esp. pp. 40–1.

127 Vasari mentions white 'tailors' chalk; see Vasari (ed. Bettarini), p. 134, and Vasari (tr. Maclehose), p. 231, cited in note 2.

128 Almost 1,000 drawings by Parmigianino have now been identified; see C.C. Bambach, H. Chapman, M. Clayton and G.R. Goldner, *Correggio & Parmigianino. Master Draughtsmen of the Renaissance*, exh. cat., British Museum, London, and Metropolitan Museum of Art, New York 2000–1, p. 18.

129 Richter, cited in note 40, p. 306, selection no. 492.

130 For the *giornate* of the Sistine ceiling see G. Colalucci, 'The Technique of the Sistine Ceiling Frescoes', and F. Mancinelli, 'The Problem of Michelangelo's Assistants', in P. De Vecchi et al., *The Sistine Chapel. A Glorious Restoration*, New York 1994, pp. 26–35 and 46–57; for the lunettes see F. Mancinelli, 'Michelangelo at Work. The Painting of the Lunettes' in A. Chastel et al., *The Sistine Chapel. Michelangelo Rediscovered*, London 1986, pp. 218–59.

131 For some of the drawings for the lunettes see M. Hirst, '"Il modo delle attitudini". Michelangelo's Oxford Sketchbook for the Ceiling', in Chastel et al., cited above, pp. 208–17.

Bibliography

Within each section, general works are cited before the more specific, where this is appropriate; otherwise, or within this structure, arrangement is alphabetical by the surname of the (first) author or editor and then by date. A more comprehensive bibliography can be found in the series of colloquia with the general title *Le dessin sous-jacent dans la peinture* (see note, page 191).

General and introductory texts

M.W. AINSWORTH and M. FARIES, *Northern Renaissance Paintings: The Discovery of Invention, The Saint Louis Art Museum Bulletin*, N.S., XVIII, 1, 1986, esp. pp. 4–7.

J.R.J. VAN ASPEREN DE BOER, 'An introduction to the scientific examination of paintings', in J.R.J van Asperen de Boer and J.P Filedt Kok (eds), *Scientific Examination of Early Netherlandish Painting: Applications in Art History, Nederlands Kunsthistorisch Jaarboek*, 26, 1975, pp. 1–40, esp. pp. 8–12.

M. FARIES, 'Underdrawings in the workshop production of Jan van Scorel – A study with infrared reflectography', in J.R.J. van Asperen de Boer and J.P. Filedt Kok (eds), *Scientific Examination of Early Netherlandish Painting: Applications in Art History, Nederlands Kunsthistorisch Jaarboek*, 26, 1975, pp. 89–228, esp. pp. 92–7; these pages give a very clear introduction to the technique.

M. FARIES, 'Reshaping the Field: The Contribution of Technical Studies', in M.W. Ainsworth (ed), *Early Netherlandish Painting at the Crossroads: A Critical Look at Current Methodologies*, The Metropolitan Museum of Art, New York, and Yale University Press, New Haven and London 2001, pp. 70–105 (The Metropolitan Museum of Art Symposia series).

M. FARIES, *Discovering Underdrawings: A Guide to Method and Interpretation*, Turnhout, Brepols, in press.

W.A. REAL, 'Exploring New Applications for Infrared Reflectography', *Bulletin of the Cleveland Museum of Art*, 72, 8, December 1985, pp. 390–412.

The techniques of infrared photography and reflectography

A very basic introduction to the physics of light and other forms of radiation will be found in D. BURNIE, *Light*, published by Dorling Kindersley in association with the Science Museum, London 1992 (rep. 1999; Eyewitness Guide no. 75), esp. pp. 40–1.

W.S. TAFT and J.W. MAYER, *The Science of Paintings*, New York 2000, pp. 50–79, 125–7. A more advanced explanation of the physics of light and infrared radiation.

Infrared photography

From the National Gallery Laboratory, preface by Sir William Bragg, introduction and notes by I. Rawlins, London 1940; of historical interest for early published infrared photographs of two National Gallery paintings, Plates 42–7.

H.L. GIBSON, *Photography by Infrared: its Principles and Applications*, New York 1978 (3rd edn of *Photography by Infrared* by W. Clark, first published 1939).

R.A. LYON, 'Infra-Red Radiations Aid Examination of Paintings', *Technical Studies in the Field of the Fine Arts*, II, 4, 1934, pp. 203–12.

Infrared reflectography (IRR)

The following sub-sections include literature used for the Technical Appendix, p. **181**.

J.R.J. VAN ASPEREN DE BOER, 'Reflectography of paintings using an infra-red vidicon television system', *Studies in Conservation*, 14, 1969, pp. 96–118.

J.R.J. VAN ASPEREN DE BOER, *Infra-red Reflectography. A Contribution to the Examination of earlier European Paintings*, doctoral thesis, University of Amsterdam 1970.

J.R.J. VAN ASPEREN DE BOER, 'Examination by Infrared Radiation', in R. Van Schoute and H. Verougstraete-Marcq (eds), *Art History and Laboratory: Scientific Examination of Easel Paintings*, published on the occasion of the Xth Anniversary Meeting of the Pact Group at Louvain-la-Neuve, 1986, *PACT* (Journal of the European Study Group on Physical, Chemical and Mathematical Techniques Applied to Archaeology), 13, 1986, pp. 109–30.

M. FARIES and J.P. FILEDT KOK, 'Infrared Reflectography (IRR) and Art History: The Pioneering Years (1970–75)' in P. van den Brink and L. M. Helmus (eds), *Album Discipulorum J.R.J. van Asperen de Boer*, Zwolle 1997, pp. 9–18.

Digital infrared systems

D. BERTANI, M. CETICA, P. POGGI, G. PUCCIONI, E. BUZZEGOLI, D. KUNZELMAN and S. CECCHI, 'A scanning device for infrared reflectography', *Studies in Conservation*, 35, 1990, pp. 113–16.

C. METZGER, J. DELANEY, C. FLETCHER and E. WALMSLEY, 'A Platinum Silicide Camera applied in the Study of Underdrawings', *Le dessin sous-jacent dans la peinture, Colloque X: Le dessin sous-jacent dans le processus de création*, ed. H. Verougstraete and R. Van Schoute, Louvain-la-Neuve 1995, pp. 195–200.

J. VAN DER WEERD, R.M.A. HEEREN and J.R.J VAN ASPEREN DE BOER, 'A European 640 x 486 PtSi Camera for Infrared Reflectography', *Le dessin sous-jacent et la technologie dans la peinture, Colloque XIII: La peinture et le laboratoire: Procédés; Méthodologie; Applications*, ed. R. Van Schoute and H. Verougstraete, Louvain 2001, pp. 231–43.

Computer assembly of mosaics

R. BILLINGE, J. CUPITT, N. DESSIPRIS and D. SAUNDERS, 'A note on an improved procedure for the rapid assembly of infra-red reflectogram mosaics', *Studies in Conservation*, 38, 1993, pp. 92–8.

R. BILLINGE, 'Further Advances in the Computer Assisted Assembly of Infrared Reflectogram Mosaics', *Le dessin sous-jacent dans la peinture, Colloque X: Le dessin sous-jacent dans le processus de création*, ed. H. Verougstraete and R. Van Schoute, Louvain-la-Neuve 1995, pp. 77–80.

F. MAIRINGER, 'Die Infrarotreflektographische Untersuchung von Gemälden und die Erstellung von Bildmosaiken mittels des Programmpakets IREIKON', in I. Sandner (ed.), *Unsichtbare Meisterzeichnungen auf dem Malgrund. Cranach und seine Zeitgenossen*, exh. cat., Wartburg-Stiftung, Eisenach, Regensburg 1998, pp. 28–41.

P. PEYREDIEU DU CHARLAT, 'Assemblage de mosaïques infrarouges en restauration de peintures. Application utilisant les logiciels IPLab Spectrum et Hypercard', *Le dessin sous-jacent et la technologie dans la peinture, Colloque XI: Perspectives*, ed. R. Van Schoute and H. Verougstraete, with A. Dubois, Louvain-la-Neuve 1997, pp. 231–7.

T.M. RUSSO, 'Infrared Reflectography and Computer Image Processing: New Alternatives', *Le dessin sous-jacent dans la peinture, Colloque IX: Dessin sous-jacent et pratiques d'atelier*, ed. R. Van Schoute and H. Verougstraete-Marcq, Louvain-la-Neuve 1993, pp. 267–73.

The role of drawings, the transfer of the design and underdrawings in workshop practice

Some general accounts of workshop practice in Northern Europe and Italy, including the use of drawings and the preparation of the underdrawing on the surface to be painted, are listed below. With the exception of the study by Bambach (see below), the role of drawing in Italian workshop practice remains relatively little studied.

J. DUNKERTON, S. FOISTER, D. GORDON and N. PENNY, *Giotto to Dürer: Early Renaissance Painting in the National Gallery*, New Haven and London 1991, pp. 164–74.

J. DUNKERTON, S. FOISTER and N. PENNY, *Dürer to Veronese: Sixteenth-Century Painting in The National Gallery*, New Haven and London 1999, esp. pp. 222–35.

C.C. BAMBACH, *Drawing and Painting in the Italian Renaissance Workshop: Theory and Practice, 1300–1600*, Cambridge 1999; this book is of fundamental importance for an understanding of drawings and their role in workshop practice in Italy.

'Methods and Materials of Northern European painting in the National Gallery, 1400–1550', in L. CAMPBELL, S. FOISTER AND A. ROY (eds), *Early Northern Painting, National Gallery Technical Bulletin*, 18, 1997, pp. 6–55, esp. pp. 25–9, for workshop practice in Northern Europe.

J.R.J. VAN ASPEREN DE BOER, M. FARIES AND J.P. FILEDT KOK, 'Painting technique and workshop practice in Northern Netherlandish art of the sixteenth century', in J.P. Filedt Kok, W. Halsema-Kubes and W.Th. Kloek (eds), *Kunst voor de beeldenstorm: Noordnederlandse kunst 1525–1580*, exh. cat., Amsterdam 1986, pp. 106–16 (Dutch text, with illustrations, pp. 85–105); for sixteenth-century Early Netherlandish painting practice.

S. BUCK, 'Comparing Drawings and Underdrawings: The Possibilities and Limitations of a Method', *Le dessin sous-jacent et la technologie dans la peinture, Colloque XIII: La peinture et le laboratoire: Procédés; Méthodologie; Applications*, ed. R. Van Schoute and H. Verougstraete, Louvain 2001, pp. 201–12.

L. CAMPBELL, 'The early Netherlandish painters and their workshops', *Le dessin sous-jacent dans la peinture, Colloque III: Le problème Maître de Flémalle-van der Weyden*, ed. D. Hollanders-Favart and R. Van Schoute, Louvain-la-Neuve 1981, pp. 43–61.

L. CAMPBELL, 'Rogier van der Weyden and his Workshop' *Proceedings of the British Academy*, 84, *1993 Lectures and Memoirs*, 1994, pp. 1–24.

L. CAMPBELL, 'Introduction: Netherlandish painting in the Fifteenth Century', *National Gallery Catalogues: The Fifteenth Century Netherlandish Schools*, London 1998, pp. 18–35, esp. pp. 25–8 for pattern drawings and their use.

J. DIJKSTRA, 'On the Role of Underdrawings and Modeldrawings in the Workshop Production of The Master of Flémalle and Rogier van der Weyden', *Le dessin sous-jacent dans la peinture: Colloque VII: Géographie et chronologie du dessin sous-jacent*, ed. R. Van Schoute and H. Verougstraete-Marcq, Louvain-la-Neuve 1989, pp. 37–53.

J. DIJKSTRA, 'Methods for the Copying of Paintings in the Southern Netherlands in the 15th and Early 16th Centuries', *Le dessin sous-jacent dans la peinture: Colloque VIII: Dessin sous-jacent et copies*, ed. H. Verougstraete-Marcq and R. Van Schoute, Louvain-la-Neuve 1991, pp. 67–76.

S. JONES, 'The Use of Workshop Drawings by Jan van Eyck and his Followers', in S. Foister, S. Jones and D. Cool (eds), *Investigating Jan van Eyck*, Turnhout 2000, pp. 197–207.

Drawing in the Workshop

F. AMES-LEWIS, *Drawing in Early Renaissance Italy*, New Haven and London 1981.

F. AMES-LEWIS and J. WRIGHT, *Drawing in the Italian Renaissance Workshop*, exh. cat., University Art Gallery, Nottingham, and Victoria and Albert Museum, London 1983.

S. BUCK, *Die niederländischen Zeichnungen des 15. Jahrhunderts im Berliner Kupferstichkabinett: Kritischer Katalog*, Berlin 2001.

S. BUCK, 'An Approach to Looking at Eyckian Drawings', in S. Foister, S. Jones and D. Cool (eds), *Investigating Jan van Eyck*, Turnhout 2000, pp. 183–95.

F. KORENY, E. POKORNY AND G. ZEMAN, *Early Netherlandish Drawings from Jan van Eyck to Hieronymus Bosch*, exh. cat., Rubenshuis, Antwerp 2002.

J. MEDER, *The Mastery of Drawing*, tr. and rev. W. AMES, 2 vols (Vol. 1, text; Vol. 2, plates), New York 1978. Translation of *Die Handzeichnungen: Ihre Technik und Entwicklung*, Vienna 1919.

A. NOVA, 'Salviati, Vasari and the Reuse of Drawings in their Workshop Practice', *Master Drawings*, 30, 1992, pp. 83–108.

N.M. ORENSTEIN (ed.), *Peter Bruegel the Elder: Drawings and Prints*, exh. cat., Museum Boijmans Van Beuningen, Rotterdam/The Metropolitan Museum of Art, New York, New Haven and London 2001.

J. ROWLANDS and G. BARTRUM, *The Age of Dürer and Holbein: German Drawings 1400–1550*, exh. cat., British Museum, London 1988.

General accounts of underdrawings in paintings; collections of published infrared images

P. VAN DEN BRINK and L. M. HELMUS (eds), *Album Discipulorum J.R.J. van Asperen de Boer*, Zwolle 1997. A collection of essays, in Dutch and English, by former students of Professor van Asperen de Boer, compiled to mark his retirement.

General accounts discussing a range of artists or periods

H.W. VAN OS, J.R.J. VAN ASPEREN DE BOER, C.E. DE JONG-JANSEN and C. WIETHOFF (eds), *The Early Venetian paintings in Holland*, Maarsen 1978.

R. BILLINGE, 'The National Gallery-Leverhulme Infrared Reflectography Project: an Overview', *Le dessin sous-jacent et la technologie dans la peinture, Colloque XI: Perspectives*, ed. R. Van Schoute and H. Verougstraete, with A. Dubois, Louvain-la-Neuve 1997, pp. 109–15.

M.C. GALASSI, *Il disegno svelato: Progetto e immagine nella pittura italiana del primo Rinascimento*, Nuoro 1998.

M.P.J. MARTENS (ed.), *Bruges et la Renaissance: De Memling à Pourbus; Notices*, Vol. 2 of exh. cat., Memlingmuseum, Oud-Sint-Janshospital, Bruges 1998. (Vol. 1 of the catalogue contains introductory essays and colour illustrations of the exhibits, with brief catalogue entries; Vol. 2 contains more detailed catalogue entries, including infrared reflectograms for works by several painters. Only Vol. 1 is available in English under the title *Bruges and the Renaissance: Memling to Pourbus*.)

I. SANDNER (ed.), *Unsichtbare Meisterzeichnungen auf dem Malgrund. Cranach und seine Zeitgenossen*, exh. cat., Wartburg-Stiftung, Eisenach, Regensburg 1998.

M. SONKES, 'Le dessin sous-jacent chez les Primitifs flamands', *Bulletin de l'Institut Royal du Patrimoine Artistique*, XII, 1970, pp. 195–225 (see also entries under Comblen-Sonkes below).

P. SPEZZANI, *Riflettoscopia e indagini non distruttive: pittura e grafica*, Milan 1992.

R. SPRONK, 'More than meets the Eye. An Introduction to Technical Examination of Early Netherlandish Paintings at the Fogg Art Museum', *Harvard University Art Museums Bulletin*, V, 1 (Fall), 1996.

Museum catalogues and other large groups of images

L. CAMPBELL, *National Gallery Catalogues: The Fifteenth-Century Netherlandish Schools*, London 1998.

M. COMBLEN-SONKES and P. LORENTZ, *Corpus de la peinture des anciens Pay-Bas méridionaux et de la principauté de Liège au quinzième siècle, 17: Musée du Louvre, Paris, II*, Brussels 1995, and *19, Musée du Louvre, Paris, III*, Brussels 2001.

M. COMBLEN-SONKES, *Corpus of Fifteenth-Century Painting in the Southern Netherlands and the Principality of Liège, 18: The Collegiate Church of Saint Peter, Louvain*, Brussels 1996.

J.O. HAND and M. WOLFF, *The Collections of the National Gallery of Art Systematic Catalogue: Early Netherlandish Painting*, National Gallery of Art, Washington, and Cambridge University Press 1986.

J.O. HAND and S.E. MANSFIELD, *The Collections of the National Gallery of Art Systematic Catalogue: German Paintings of the Fifteenth through Seventeenth Centuries*, National Gallery of Art, Washington, and Cambridge University Press 1993.

J. SANDER, with S. KNOBLOCH, *Niederländische Gemälde in Städel 1400–1550* (Frankfurt-am-Main Städelsches Kunstinstitut), Mainz-am-Rhein 1993.

M. SCHAWE, *Rom in Augsburg. Die Basilikabilder aus dem Katherinenkloster*, Bayerische Staatsgemälde-sammlungen, Munich (n.d.).

M. SCHAWE, *Staatsgalerie Augsburg. Altdeutsche Malerei in der Katherinenkirche*, Bayerische Staatsgemäldesammlungen, Munich (n.d.).

C. STERLING et al. *The Robert Lehman Collection II: Fifteenth- to Eighteenth-Century European Paintings*, The Metropolitan Museum of Art, New York/ Princeton, Princeton University Press 1998.

C. STROO and P. SYFER-D'OLNE, *Catalogue of Early Netherlandish Painting in the Royal Museum of Fine Arts of Belgium. The Flemish Primitives*, Vol. I, *The Master of Flémalle and Rogier van der Weyden Group*, Brussels 1996; Vol. II (with A. Dubois and R. Slachmuylders), *The Dirk Bouts, Petrus Christus, Hans Memling and Hugo van der Goes Groups*, Brussels 1999.

Van Eyck to Bruegel 1400 to 1550: Dutch and Flemish Painting in the collection of the Museum Boymans-van Beuningen, Rotterdam 1994.

Individual artists

This section includes publications on underdrawings in the work of fifteenth- and sixteenth-century artists from Italy and Northern Europe, apart from those whose works are represented in the catalogue. For these painters see the bibliographies for the catalogue entries, pp. 189–91.

GERMAN

Albrecht Dürer

P. ACKROYD, S. FOISTER, M. SPRING, R. WHITE and R. BILLINGE, 'A Virgin and Child from the Workshop of Albrecht Dürer?', *National Gallery Technical Bulletin*, 21, 2000, pp. 28–42, esp. pp. 33–5.

G. GOLDBERG, B. HEIMBERG and M. SHAWE, *Albrecht Dürer: die Gemälde der Alten Pinakothek*, Munich 1998.

O. KOTKOVÁ, '"The Feast of the Rose Garlands": what remains of Dürer?', *The Burlington Magazine*, CXLIV, 2002, pp. 4–13, esp. pp. 4–5, 7.

K.C. LUBER, 'Albrecht Dürer's Maximilian Portraits: An Investigation of Versions', *Master Drawings*, 29, 1991, pp. 30–47.

Hans Holbein the Younger

M.W. AINSWORTH, '"Paternes for Phisioneamyes", Holbein's Portraiture Reconsidered', *The Burlington Magazine*, CXXXII, 1990, pp. 173–86.

M.W. AINSWORTH, 'Methods of Copying in the Portraiture of Hans Holbein the Younger', *Le dessin sous-jacent dans la peinture, Colloque VIII: Dessin sous-jacent et copies*, ed. H. Verougstraete-Marcq and R. Van Schoute, Louvain-la-Neuve 1991, pp. 11–13.

S. FOISTER, 'Workshop or Followers? Underdrawing in some Portraits associated with Hans Holbein the Younger', *Le dessin sous-jacent dans la peinture, Colloque IX: Dessin sous-jacent et pratiques d'atelier*, ed. R. Van Schoute and H. Verougstraete-Marcq, Louvain-la-Neuve 1993, pp. 113–24.

S. FOISTER, M. WYLD and A. ROY, 'Hans Holbein's *A Lady with a Squirrel and a Starling*', *National Gallery Technical Bulletin*, 15, 1994, pp. 6–19, esp. pp. 10–11, 13, 16–17.

The Housebook Master

J.P. FILEDT KOK (ed.), *Livelier than Life: The Master of the Amsterdam Cabinet, or the Housebook Master, ca. 1470–1500*, exh. cat., Rijksmuseum, Amsterdam 1985.

Wolf Huber

'Wolf Huber's *Christ taking Leave of his Mother*', in L. CAMPBELL, S. FOISTER and A. ROY (eds), *Early Northern Painting, National Gallery Technical Bulletin*, 18, 1997, pp. 99–112, esp. pp. 106–8.

Master of the Karlsruhe Passion

Die Karlsruher Passion: ein Hauptwerk Strassburger Malerei der Spätgotik, exh. cat., Staatliche Kunsthalle, Karlsruhe 1996.

ITALIAN

Antonello da Messina

J. DUNKERTON, 'North and South: Painting Techniques in Renaissance Venice' in B. Aikema and B.L. Brown (eds), *Renaissance Venice and the North. Cross currents in the Time of Bellini, Dürer and Titian*, exh. cat. Palazzo Grassi, Venice, Milan 1999, pp. 92–103 (also Cima da Conigliano).

Fra Bartolommeo

S. PADOVANI (ed.), *L'età di Savonarola. Fra' Bartolommeo e la scuola di San Marco*, Venice 1996, esp. pp. 300–5.

Giovanni Bellini

A. DORIGATO (ed.), *Carpaccio, Bellini, Tura, Antonello e altri restauri quattrocenteschi della Pinacoteca del Museo Correr*, Milan 1993.

R. GOFFEN and G. NEPI SCIRÉ (eds), *Il colore ritrovato. Bellini a Venezia*, Venice 2000.

M.R. VALAZZI (ed.), *La Pala Ricostituita. L'Incoronazione della vergine e la cimasa vaticana di Giovanni Bellini. Indagini e restauri*, Venice 1988.

Botticelli

M. CIATTI (ed.), *L'Incoronazione della Vergine del Botticelli: restauro e ricerche*, Florence 1990, esp. pp. 72–3, 87–100.

Vittore Carpaccio

P. LE CHANU, 'Les noms de couleur dans La Prédication de Saint Etienne de Vittore Carpaccio', *Techne*, 4, 1996, pp. 90–8. For an English version of this article see 'The Names of the Colors in the *Preaching of St. Stephen* by Vittorio Carpaccio', *Kermes* XI, 32, May–August 1998, pp. 46–52.

Y. SZAFRAN and A. WALLERT, 'The Technical Examination of the *Ordination of St. Stephen* by Vittore Carpaccio: Colours and Colour Notations', *Le dessin sous-jacent et la technologie dans la peinture: Colloque XI: Perspectives*, ed. R. Van Schoute and H. Verougstraete, with A. Dubois, Louvain-la-Neuve 1997, pp. 161–7.

Cima da Conegliano

J. DUNKERTON and A. ROY, 'The Technique and Restoration of Cima's "The Incredulity of S. Thomas"', *National Gallery Technical Bulletin*, 10, 1986, pp. 4–27, esp. pp. 5–8.

Vincenzo Foppa

J. DUNKERTON and C. PLAZZOTTA, 'Vincenzo Foppa's *Adoration of the Kings*', *National Gallery Technical Bulletin*, 22, 2001, pp. 18–28, esp. pp. 20–2.

M.C. GALASSI, 'Sul percorso di Vincenzo Foppa: un avvio all'analisi del disegno sottostante', *Commentari d'arte*, anno II, n. 5, 1996, published 1998, pp. 27–42.

M. C. GALASSI, 'Disegno sottostante e stesura pittorica di Vincenzo Foppa e Ludovico Brea nel *Polittico della Rovere*: due culture operative a confronto', in M. Capella, I. Gianfranceschi and E. Lucchesi Ragni (eds), *Vincenzo Foppa. Techniche d'esecuzione, indagini e restauri*, Atti del Seminario Internazionale di Studi, Milan 2002, pp. 183–96.

Garofalo (Benvenuto Tisi)

J. DUNKERTON, N. PENNY and M. SPRING, 'The Technique of Garofalo's Paintings at the National Gallery', *National Gallery Technical Bulletin*, 23, 2002, pp. 20–41, esp. pp. 27–30.

Ghirlandaio family and associates

M.C. GALASSI, 'The Re-Use of Design-Models by *carta lucida* in the 16th Century Italian Workshops: Written Sources and an Example from Michele di Ridolfo del Ghirlandaio', *Le dessin sous-jacent et la technologie dans la peinture, Colloque XII: La peinture dans les Pays-Bas au 16e siècle: Pratiques d'atelier; infrarouges et autres méthodes d'investigation*, ed. H. Verougstraete and R. Van Schoute, with A. Dubois, Louvain 1999, pp. 205–13.

Giovanni di Paolo

E. KLEIN, E. GORDON and K. FRENCH, 'Stylistic, technical and material developments in the paintings of Giovanni di Paolo', in A. Roy and P. Smith (eds), *Painting Techniques: History, Materials and Studio Practice; Contributions to the Dublin IIC Congress 7–11 September 1998*, London 1998, pp. 82–8, esp. p. 84.

J.J.A. PANDERS, *The Underdrawing of Giovanni di Paolo: Characteristics and Development*, doctoral thesis, University of Groningen 1997.

Filippino Lippi

M.C. GALASSI, 'Filippino Lippi's Underdrawing: The Contribution of Infrared Reflectography', *Le dessin sous-jacent et la technologie dans la peinture, Colloque XI: Perspectives*, ed. R. Van Schoute and H. Verougstraete, with A. Dubois, Louvain-la-Neuve 1997, pp. 153–9.

Lorenzo Lotto

J. DUNKERTON, N. PENNY and A. ROY, 'Two Paintings by Lorenzo Lotto in the National Gallery', *National Gallery Technical Bulletin*, 19, 1998, pp. 52–63, esp. pp. 53–5.

Lorenzo Monaco

M. CIATTI and C. FROSININI (eds) *Lorenzo Monaco. Tecnica e Restauro*. Florence 1998, esp. pp. 91–2.

Mantegna

K. CHRISTIANSEN, 'Some Observations on Mantegna's Painting Technique', in J. Martineau (ed), *Andrea Mantegna*, exh. cat., Royal Academy of Arts, London, and Metropolitan Museum of Art, New York 1992, pp. 68–78.

Masolino and Masaccio

K. STREHLKE and C. FROSININI (eds), *The Panel Painting of Masolino and Masaccio. The Role of Technique*, Milan 2002.

Michelangelo

J. DUNKERTON, 'Michelangelo as a Painter on Panel', in M. Hirst and J. Dunkerton, *Making and Meaning: The Young Michelangelo*, exh. cat., National Gallery, London 1994, pp. 83–133, esp. pp. 90–4, 109–11.

Pietro Perugino

R. HILLER VON GAERTRINGEN, 'On Perugino's Re-uses of Cartoons', *Le dessin sous-jacent et la technologie dans la peinture, Colloque XI: Perspectives*, ed. R. Van Schoute and H. Verougstraete, with A. Dubois, Louvain-la-Neuve 1997, pp. 223–30.

R. HILLER VON GAERTRINGEN, 'A *Madonna and Child with the Infant St. John* in the Städel. Between Perugino's Formulas and Raphael's Interest in Narrative', *Le dessin sous-jacent et la technologie dans la peinture, Colloque XII: La peinture dans les Pays-Bas au 16e siècle: Pratiques d'atelier; infrarouges et autres méthodes d'investigation*, ed. H. Verougstraete and R. Van Schoute, with A. Dubois, Louvain 1999, pp. 189–203.

R. HILLER VON GAERTRINGEN, *Raffaels Lernerfahrungen in der Werkstatt Peruginos: Kartonverwendung und Motivübernahme im Wandel*, Munich 1999.

Andrea del Sarto

D. BERTANI et al., 'Andrea del Sarto in riflettografia', in A. Cecchi and A. Natali (eds), *Andrea del Sarto*

1486–1530; Dipinti e disegni a Firenze, exh. cat., Palazzo Pitti, Florence, 1986–7, pp. 341–58.

L. KEITH, 'Andrea del Sarto's *The Virgin and Child with Saint Elizabeth and Saint John the Baptist*: Technique and Critical Reputation', *National Gallery Technical Bulletin*, 22, 2001, pp. 42–53.

Sebastiano del Piombo

K. LAING and M. HIRST, 'The Kingston Lacey "Judgment of Solomon"', *The Burlington Magazine*, CXXVIII, 1986, pp. 273–82.

Signorelli

T. HENRY, *Signorelli in British Collections*, exh. cat., National Gallery, London 1988.

R. OLSON, 'Signorelli's Berlin tondo: new Information (technical, stylistic, and iconographic)', *Arte Cristiana*, 779, 1997, pp. 99–108.

M. SEIDEL, 'Signorelli um 1490', *Jahrbuch der Berliner Museen*, XXVI, 1984, pp. 181–256.

Titian

C. HOPE and J.R.J. VAN ASPEREN DE BOER, 'Underdrawings by Giorgione and his Circle', *Le dessin sous-jacent dans la peinture, Colloque VIII: Dessin sous-jacent et copies, 8–10 septembre 1989*, ed. H. Verougstraete-Marcq and R. Van Schoute, Louvain-la-Neuve 1991, pp. 127–40.

B.W. MEIJER, 'Titian Sketches on Canvas and Panel', *Master Drawings*, 19, 1981, pp. 276–89.

M.C. GARRIDO and R. DÁVILA, 'La Virgen y el Nino con San Jorge y Santa Cataloina de Tiziano: estudio técnico y restauración', *Boletin del Museo del Prado*, VI, 1985, pp. 138–52.

M. JAFFÉ and KARIN GROEN, 'Titian's "Tarquin and Lucretia" in the Fitzwilliam', *The Burlington Magazine*, CXXIX, 1987, pp. 162–72, esp. p. 167.

H. LANK, 'Titian's "Perseus and Andromeda": restoration and technique', *The Burlington Magazine*, CXXIV, 1982, pp. 400–6.

G. NEPI SCIRÈ, 'Recenti restauri di opere di Tiziano a Venezia', *Tiziano*, exh. cat., Palazzo Ducale, Venice 1990, pp. 109–31.

Paolo Uccello

J. DUNKERTON and A. ROY, 'Uccello's *Saint George and the Dragon*: Technical Evidence Re-evaluated', *National Gallery Technical Bulletin*, 19, 1998, pp. 26–30.

Paolo Veronese

Paolo Veronese restauri, exh. cat., Gallerie dell'Accademia, Venice 1988 (Quaderni della Soprintendenza ai Beni Artistici e Storici di Venezia, 15).

NETHERLANDISH

M. FARIES, 'The First Examples of Titles in Underdrawing', *Le dessin sous-jacent dans la peinture: Colloque VII: Géographie et chronologie du dessin sous-jacent*, ed. R. Van Schoute and H. Verougstraete-Marcq, Louvain-la-Neuve 1989, pp. 45–6.

Pieter Aertsen and family

J.M.C. BOREEL and F.W.H. VAN ZON-CHRISTOFFELS, 'Enkele aspecten van de schilderspraktijk in het atelier van Pieter Aertsen natuurwetenschappelijk nader bekeken', *Nederlands Kunsthistorisch Jaarboek*, 40, 1989, pp. 167–96 (colour notations).

P. VAN DEN BRINK, 'Het Petrus en Paulus altaarstuk van Pieter Pietersz in Gouda. Verslag van een natuurwetenschappelijk onderzoek', *Nederlands Kunsthistorisch Jaarboek*, 40, 1989, pp. 235–62.

Joachim Beuckelaer and family

J. DIK, A. WALLERT, Y. SZAFRAN, H.M.J. MEIJERS, K.A.N. ABELSKAMP, R. LEENHEER AND H. KARS, 'The Technical Examination of Joachim Beuckelaer's "The Miraculous Draught of Fishes"', in J. Bridgland (ed.), *ICOM Committee for Conservation, 11th Triennial Meeting, Edinburgh, Scotland, 1–6 September 1996; Preprints*, London 1996, pp. 348–54, esp. p. 350 (colour notations).

M. WOLTERS, 'De Monogrammist HB geïdentificeerd: Huybrecht Beuckeleer', in P. van den Brink and L. M. Helmus (eds), *Album Discipulorum J.R.J. van Asperen de Boer*, Zwolle 1997, pp. 231–7.

Hieronymus Bosch

L. CAMPBELL, 'Bosch, *Christ Mocked (The Crowning with Thorns)*, NG 4744', *Le dessin sous-jacent et la technologie dans la peinture, Colloque XII: La peinture dans les Pays-Bas au 16e siècle: Pratiques d'atelier; infrarouges et autres méthodes d'investigation*, ed. H. Verougstraete and R. Van Schoute, with A. Dubois, Louvain 1999, pp. 29–35.

M. FARIES and J.R.J. VAN ASPEREN DE BOER, 'Covering-over or Covering-up: Some Instances of Re-use of Panels in Paintings after Hieronymus Bosch', *Le dessin sous-jacent et la technologie dans la peinture, Colloque XI: Perspectives*, ed. R. Van Schoute and H. Verougstraete, with A. Dubois, Louvain-la-Neuve 1997, pp. 7–17.

C. GARRIDO and R. VAN SCHOUTE, *Bosch at the Museo del Prado*, tr. J.F. Dodman, Madrid 2001 (Spanish title *Bosco en el Museo del Prado: El Estudio Técnico*).

Dieric Bouts

M.W. AINSWORTH, *Facsimile in Early Netherlandish Painting: Dieric Bouts's 'Virgin and Child'*, exhibition leaflet, The Metropolitan Museum of Art, New York 1993.

D. BOMFORD, A. ROY and A. SMITH, 'The Techniques of Dieric Bouts: Two Paintings Contrasted', *National Gallery Technical Bulletin*, 10, 1986, pp. 39–57, esp. pp. 46, 51–2.

L. DEPUYDT-ELBAUM, 'La restauration du Triptyque du Saint Sacrement de Dirk Bouts. La restauration, un moment privilégié', in B. Cardon, M. Smeyers, R. Van Schoute, H. Verougstraete and K. Smeyers (eds), *Bouts Studies: Proceedings of the International Colloquium (Leuven, 26–28 November 1998)*, Louvain, Paris and Sterling, Va, 2001, pp. 371–83.

N. GOETGHEBEUR, 'Le Triptyque de Saint Hippolyte de l'église Saint-Sauveur de Bruges', in Cardon et al. 2001, cited above, pp. 393–401.

P. SILVA MAROTO, 'Le dessin sous-jacent du Triptyque de la Vie de la Vierge de Thierry Bouts au Musée du Prado', in Cardon et al. 2001, cited above, pp. 357–69.

R. SPRONK, 'Three Boutsian Paintings in the Fogg Art Museum: Technical Examination and Art Historical Implications', in Cardon et al. 2001, cited above, pp. 423–49.

Robert Campin and associated works

L. CAMPBELL, D. BOMFORD, A. ROY and R. WHITE, '*The Virgin and Child before a Firescreen*: History, Examination and Treatment', *National Gallery Technical Bulletin*, 15, 1994, pp. 20–35, esp. pp. 27–9.

M. FARIES, 'Robert Campin and Stefan Lochner: Any Connection?', in S. Foister and S. Nash (eds), *Robert Campin: New Directions in Scholarship*, Turnhout 1996, pp. 137–47.

C. GARRIDO, 'The Campin Group Paintings in the Prado', in Foister and Nash 1996, cited above, pp. 55–70.

Antoon Claeissens

M.P.J. MARTENS (ed.), *Bruges et la Renaissance: De Memling à Pourbus; Notices*, Vol. 2 of exh. cat., Memlingmuseum, Oud-Sint-Janshospital, Bruges 1998, pp. 154–5.

Albert Cornelis

D. TAMIS, 'The genesis of Albert Cornelis's "Coronation of the Virgin" in Bruges', *The Burlington Magazine*, CXLII, 2000, pp. 672–80.

Colyn de Coter

C. PÉRIER-D'IETEREN, *Colyn de Coter et la technique picturale des peintres flamands du XVe siècle*, Brussels 1985.

Gerard David

M.W. AINSWORTH, 'Old Assumptions Reconsidered through Revised Methodologies', *Le dessin sous-jacent et la technologie dans la peinture: Colloque XI: Perspectives*, ed. R. Van Schoute and H. Verougstraete, with A. Dubois, Louvain-la-Neuve 1997, pp. 103–8.

M.W. AINSWORTH, *Gerard David: Purity and Vision in an Age of Transition*, New York 1998.

Cornelis Engebrechtsz.

J.P. FILEDT KOK, 'The Workshop Practice of Cornelis Engebrechtsz.: Some Preliminary Remarks', *Le dessin sous-jacent et la technologie dans la peinture, Colloque XII: La peinture dans les Pays-Bas au 16e siècle: Pratiques d'atelier; infrarouges et autres méthodes d'investigation*, ed. H. Verougstraete and R. Van Schoute, with A. Dubois, Louvain 1999, pp. 19–28.

Jan van Eyck

J.R.J. VAN ASPEREN DE BOER, 'A Scientific Re-examination of the Ghent Altarpiece', *Oud Holland*, 93, 1979, pp. 141–214.

J.R.J. VAN ASPEREN DE BOER, 'Some Technical Observations on the Turin and Philadelphia Versions of "Saint Francis Receiving the Stigmata"', in *Jan van Eyck: Two Panels of 'Saint Francis Receiving the Stigmata'*, Philadelphia Museum of Art, Philadelphia 1997, pp. 51–63.

R. BILLINGE and L. CAMPBELL, 'The Infra-red Reflectograms of Jan van Eyck's Portrait of Giovanni (?) Arnolfini and his Wife Giovanna Cenami (?)', *National Gallery Technical Bulletin*, 16, 1995, pp. 47–60.

R. BILLINGE, 'Examining Jan van Eyck's Underdrawings', in S. Foister, S. Jones and D. Cool (eds), *Investigating Jan van Eyck*, Turnhout 2000, pp. 83–96.

R. BILLINGE, H. VEROUGSTRAETE and R. VAN SCHOUTE, 'The *Saint Barbara*', in Foister et al. 2000, cited above, pp. 41–8.

P. COREMANS et al, *Les primitifs flamands. III. Contributions à l'étude des primitifs flamands. 2. L'Agneau Mystique au laboratoire: Examen et traitement*, Antwerp 1953. This classic study includes some infrared photographs of details of the painting, more recently examined using infrared reflectography by J.R.J. van Asperen de Boer 1979, cited above.

A.L. DIERICK, 'Jan van Eyck's Handwriting', in Foister et al. 2000, cited above, pp. 79–82.

M. FARIES, 'The Underdrawing in Jan van Eyck's Dresden Triptych', *Le dessin sous-jacent et la technologie dans la peinture, Colloque XII: La peinture dans les Pays-Bas au 16e siècle: Pratiques d'atelier; infrarouges et autres méthodes d'investigation*, ed. H. Verougstraete and R. Van Schoute, with A. Dubois, Louvain 1999, pp. 221–9.

Geertgen tot Sint Jans

T. VAN BUEREN and M. FARIES, 'The "Portraits" in Geertgen tot Sint Jans' Vienna panels', *Le dessin sous-jacent dans la peinture, Colloque VIII: Dessin sous-jacent et copies*, ed. H. Verougstraete-Marcq and R. Van Schoute, Louvain-la-Neuve 1991, pp. 141–150.

Jan Gossaert

'Gossaert's *Adoration of the Kings*', in L. CAMPBELL, S. FOISTER and A. ROY (eds), *Early Northern Painting, National Gallery Technical Bulletin*, 18, 1997, pp. 87–97, esp. pp. 89–91.

Martin van Heemskerck

J. DUNKERTON, A. BURNSTOCK and A. SMITH, 'Two Wings of an Altarpiece by Martin van Heemskerck', *National Gallery Technical Bulletin*, 12, 1988, pp. 16–35, esp. pp. 25–8.

M. FARIES, 'Attributing the Layers of Heemskerck's Cologne *Lamentation of Christ*', *Le dessin sous-jacent dans la peinture, Colloque X: Le dessin sous-jacent dans le processus de création*, ed. H. Verougstraete and R. Van Schoute, Louvain-la-Neuve 1995, pp. 133–41.

Juan de Flandes

C. GARRIDO, 'Le processus créatif chez Juan de Flandes', *Le dessin sous-jacent dans la peinture, Colloque X: Le dessin sous-jacent dans le processus de création*, ed. H. Verougstraete and R. Van Schoute, Louvain-la-Neuve 1995, pp. 21–9.

Lucas van Leyden

J.P. FILEDT KOK, 'Underdrawing and other Technical Aspects in the Paintings of Lucas van Leyden', *Nederlands Kunsthistorisch Jaarboek*, 29, 1978, pp. 1–184.

Quinten Massys

A. ROY, 'The Technique of a "Tüchlein" by Quinten Massys', *National Gallery Technical Bulletin*, 12, 1988, pp. 36–43, esp. pp. 38–9.

Jan Provoost

R. SPRONK, 'An Early Sixteenth Century *Last Judgement* by Jan Provoost', *Le dessin sous-jacent et la technologie dans la peinture: Colloque XI: Perspectives*, ed. R. Van Schoute and H. Verougstraete with A. Dubois, Louvain 1997, pp. 43–51.

Jan van Scorel

M. FARIES, 'Underdrawings in the workshop production of Jan van Scorel – A study with infrared reflectography', in J.R.J. van Asperen de Boer and J.P. Filedt Kok (eds), *Scientific Examination of Early Netherlandish Painting: Applications in Art History, Nederlands Kunsthistorisch Jaarboek*, 26, 1975, pp. 89–228.

M. FARIES and L.M. HELMUS, *The Madonna of Jan van Scorel 1495–1562: Serial Production of a Cherished Motif*, Utrecht 2000.

Rogier van der Weyden

'The materials and technique of five paintings by Rogier van der Weyden and his Workshop', in L. CAMPBELL, S. FOISTER and A. ROY (eds), *Early Northern Painting, National Gallery Technical Bulletin*, 18, 1997, pp. 68–86, esp. pp. 71–3.

J.R.J. VAN ASPEREN DE BOER, J. DIJKSTRA and R. VAN SCHOUTE, *Underdrawing in Paintings of the Rogier van der Weyden and Master of Flémalle Groups* (Nederlands Kunsthistorisch Jaarboek 41), Zwolle 1992.

D. DE VOS, *Rogier van der Weyden: The Complete Works*, Antwerp 1999.

The catalogue

Short bibliographies for the catalogue entries and references for specific points are given below.

1 **Stephan Lochner**

Saints Matthew, Catherine of Alexandria and John the Evangelist

B. BRINKMANN, 'Stefan Lochner's "Apostelmartyrien": Erste Ergebnisse der Gemäldetechnologischen Untersuchung', *Wallraf-Richartz Jahrbuch*, LVIII, 1997, pp. 159–72.

M. FARIES, 'Stefan Lochner's Darmstadt "Presentation in the Temple" and the Paris "Copy"', *Le dessin sous-jacent dans la peinture, Colloque VIII: Dessin sous-jacent et copies*, ed. H. Verougstraete-Marcq and R. Van Schoute, Louvain-la-Neuve 1991, pp. 15–24.

M. FARIES, 'Robert Campin and Stefan Lochner: Any Connection?', in S. Foister and S. Nash (eds), *Robert Campin: New Directions in Scholarship*, Turnhout 1996, pp. 137–47.

'A double-sided panel by Stephan Lochner', in L. CAMPBELL, S. FOISTER and A. ROY (eds), *Early Northern Painting*, *National Gallery Technical Bulletin*, 18, 1997, pp. 56–67, esp. pp. 58–9.

See also:

J. CHAPUIS, 'The Cologne *Last Judgement* and the Originality of Stefan Lochner's Graphic Style', *Le dessin sous-jacent et la technologie dans la peinture: Colloque XI: Perspectives*, ed. R. Van Schoute and H. Verougstraete, with A. Dubois, Louvain-la-Neuve 1997, pp. 53–60.

J. CHAPUIS, 'Thoughts on the Genesis of Stefan Lochner's *Last Judgement*', in P. van den Brink and L. M. Helmus (eds), *Album Discipulorum J.R.J. van Asperen de Boer*, Zwolle 1997, pp. 45–52.

M. FARIES, 'Stefan Lochners Unterzeichnungen: Erste Einsichten', in F.G. Zehnder, *Stefan Lochner Meister zu Köln*, Wallraf-Richartz-Museum, Cologne 1993, pp. 169–80.

W. HANSMANN, 'Beobachtungen zum frühen Arbeits-stadium am Altar der Stadtpatrone von Stefan Lochner im Kölner Dom', *Zeitschrift für Kunsttechnologie und Konservierung*, 2, 1, 1988, pp. 96–106.

2 Cosimo Tura
Saint Jerome

J. BENTINI (ed.), *San Giorgio e la Principessa di Cosmè Tura: Dipinti restaurati per l'officina ferrarese*, Bologna 1985, p. 19.

A. DORIGATO (ed.), *Carpaccio, Bellini, Tura, Antonello e altri restauri quattrocenteschi della Pinacoteca del Museo Correr*, Milan 1993.

J. DUNKERTON, 'Cosimo Tura as Painter and Draughtsman: The Cleaning and Examination of his *Saint Jerome*', *National Gallery Technical Bulletin*, 15, 1994, pp. 42–53.

J. DUNKERTON, 'Cosmè Tura's painting Technique' in S.J. Campbell, *Cosmè Tura: Painting and Design in Renaissance Ferrara*, ed. A. Chong, exh. cat., Isabella Stewart Gardner Museum, Boston 2002, pp. 106–51.

J. DUNKERTON, A. ROY and A. SMITH, 'The Unmasking of Tura's "Allegorical Figure": A Painting and its Concealed Image', *National Gallery Technical Bulletin*, 11, 1987, pp. 5–35.

M.C. GALASSI, *Il disegno svelato. Progetto e immagine nella pittura italiana del primo Rinascimento*, Nuoro 1998, pp. 130–1.

D. SCRASE, 'Cosimo Tura "The Crucifixion with the Virgin and St John"', *The Bulletin of the Hamilton Kerr Institute*, I, 1988, pp. 69–71.

M. TOFFANELLO, 'I pannelli di polittico di Cosmè Tura: Alcune osservazioni sull'ultima attività dell' artista', *Arte Documento*, 6, 1992, pp. 97–102.

M. TOFFANELLO, 'I pannelli di polittico e le ultime opere di Cosmè Tura: Altre osservazioni', *Arte Documento*, 8, 1994, pp. 41–50.

M. TOFFANELLO, 'I primi vent'anni di attività di Cosmè Tura alla luce dell'analisi tecnica', *Dialoghi di Storia dell'Arte*, 4–5, 1997, pp. 10–23.

M. TOFFANELLO, 'Cosmè Tura: Drawing and its Pictorial Complements' in S.J. Campbell, *Cosmè Tura*, Boston 2002, cited above, pp. 152–72.

3 Carlo Crivelli
The Dead Christ supported by Two Angels

M. DAVIES, *National Gallery Catalogues. The Earlier Italian Schools*, London 1961, pp. 153–6.

P. ZAMPETTI, *Carlo Crivelli*, Florence 1986.

For the early varnish covering the signature see J. DUNKERTON and R. WHITE, 'The Discovery and Identification of an Original Varnish on a Panel by Carlo Crivelli', *National Gallery Technical Bulletin*, 21, 2000, pp. 70–6.

For discussion of drawing practice in Paduan circles which are likely to have influenced Crivelli in the earlier part of his career, see H. CHAPMAN, *Padua in 1450s. Marco Zoppo and his Contemporaries*, London 1998.

For the drawing of *Saint Peter* attributed to Crivelli see A. MONGAN and P.J. SACHS, *Drawings in the Fogg Museum of Art*, Cambridge, Mass, 1940, Vol. I, pp. 9–10 (they also conclude that 'the drawing is an early copy from the painting').

4 Hans Memling
A Young Man at Prayer

For a full discussion of the painting see L. CAMPBELL, *National Gallery Catalogues: The Fifteenth Century Netherlandish Schools*, London 1998, pp. 370–3.

See also:

M.W. AINSWORTH, 'Hans Memling as a draughtsman', in D. de Vos (ed.), *Hans Memling: Essays*, Ghent 1994, pp. 78–87.

L. CAMPBELL, 'Memling's Creative Processes as seen in his Paintings in the National Gallery, London', *Le dessin sous-jacent dans la peinture, Colloque X: Le dessin sous-jacent dans le processus de création*, ed. H. Verougstraete and R. Van Schoute, Louvain-la-Neuve 1995, pp. 149–52.

M. FARIES, 'The Underdrawing of Memling's *Last Judgement Altarpiece* in Gdansk', in H. Verougstraete, R. Van Schoute, M. Smeyers and A. Dubois (eds), *Memling Studies: Proceedings of the International Colloquium, Bruges, 10–12 November 1994*, Louvain 1997, pp. 243–59.

M.P.J. MARTENS (ed.), *Bruges et la Renaissance: De Memling à Pourbus; Notices*, Vol. 2 of exh. cat., Memlingmuseum, Oud-Sint-Janshospital, Bruges 1998, pp. 20–2.

C. PÉRIER-D'IETEREN, 'La technique de Memling et sa place dans l'évolution de la peinture flamande du XVe siècle', in D. de Vos (ed.), *Hans Memling: Essays*, Ghent 1994, pp. 67–77.

C. PÉRIER-D'IETEREN and A. GODFRIND-BORN, 'Les trois versions de *La Vierge montant l'Homme de Douleurs* de Grenade, Melbourne et Bilbao', in H. Verougstraete, R. Van Schoute, M. Smeyers and A. Dubois (eds), *Memling Studies: Proceedings of the International Colloquium, Bruges, 10–12 November 1994*, Louvain 1997, pp. 323–37.

5 Master of the View of St Gudula
Portrait of a Young Man

For a full discussion of the painting see L. CAMPBELL, *National Gallery Catalogues: The Fifteenth Century Netherlandish Schools*, London 1998, pp. 346–53.

6 Workshop of the Master of the Life of the Virgin
The Conversion of Saint Hubert

H.M. SCHMIDT, *Der Meister des Marienlebens und sein Kreis: Studien zur spätgotischen Malerei in Köln*, Düsseldorf 1978 (Beiträge zu den Bau-und Kunstdenkmälern im Rheinland, Vol. 22).

A. SCHERER, 'Neues zum Meister des Marienlebens', in F.M. Kammel and C.B. Gries (eds), *Begegnungen mit Alten Meistern: Altdeutsche Tafelmalerei auf dem Prüfstand*, Nuremberg 2000, pp. 123–37.

7 Workshop of the Master of the Saint Bartholomew Altarpiece
The Virgin and Child with Musical Angels

U. NÜRNBERGER, *The Late Medieval Workshop of the Master of the Saint Bartholomew Altar: An Investigation of Underdrawings and Paintings*, PhD thesis, Indiana University 1997.

See also:

R. BUDDE and R. KRISCHEL (eds), *Genie ohne Namen: Der Meister des Bartholomäus-Altars*, exh. cat., Wallraf-Richartz-Museum, Cologne 2001.

U. NÜRNBERGER, 'Some Observations regarding the Chronology of the Oeuvre of the Master of the Saint Bartholomew Altar', *Le dessin sous-jacent dans la peinture, Colloque X: Le dessin sous-jacent dans le processus de création*, ed. H. Verougstraete and R. Van Schoute, Louvain-la-Neuve 1995, pp. 67–76.

U. NÜRNBERGER, 'A Newly Discovered Work by the Master of the Saint Bartholomew Altar', in P. van den Brink and L. M. Helmus (eds), *Album Discipulorum J.R.J. van Asperen de Boer*, Zwolle 1997, pp. 155–62.

8 Raphael
The Procession to Calvary

C. GOULD, *National Gallery Catalogues: The Sixteenth-Century Italian Schools*, London 1975 (1987 reprint), pp. 220–2. (This volume combines the 1959 edn of *The Sixteenth-Century Venetian School* and the 1962 edn of *The Sixteenth-Century Italian Schools excluding the Venetian.*)

J. MEYER ZUR CAPELLEN, *Raphael: A Critical Catalogue of his Paintings; Volume 1, The Beginnings in Umbria and Florence ca. 1500–1508*, tr. and ed. S.B. Polter, Landshut 2001, cat. no. 17D, pp. 178–82 (although we disagree with the conclusion that the cartoon transfer was undertaken by an associate).

For the San Antonio Altarpiece in general see K. OBERHUBER, 'The Colonna Altarpiece in the Metropolitan Museum, and Problems of the Early Style of Raphael', *Metropolitan Museum Journal*, 12, 1977, pp. 55–91; and J. MEYER ZUR CAPELLEN, *Raphael*, Landshut 2001, cited above, cat. no. 17, pp. 172–85.

9 Raphael
The Madonna and Child with the Infant Baptist (The Garvagh Madonna)

C. GOULD, *National Gallery Catalogues: The Sixteenth-Century Italian Schools*, London 1975 (1987 reprint), pp. 215–16.

J. DUNKERTON and N. PENNY, 'The Infra-red Examination of Raphael's "*Garvagh Madonna*"', *National Gallery Technical Bulletin*, 14, 1993, pp. 6–21.

For Raphael's Roman Madonnas see J.A. CROWE and G.B. CAVALCASELLE, *Raphael*, 2 vols, London 1882–5, Vol. 2, pp. 123–35; R. JONES AND N. PENNY, *Raphael*, London and New Haven 1983, p. 88.

See also:

R. HILLER VON GAERTRINGEN, *Raffaels Lernerfahrungen in der Werkstatt Peruginos: Kartonverwendung und Motivübernahme im Wandel*, Munich 1999.

C. MONBEIG GOGULE, 'Stylet et tracé sous-jacent dans les dessins de Raphaël', *Le dessin sous-jacent dans la peinture, Colloque VI: Infrarouge et autres techniques d'examen*, ed. H. Verougstraete-Marcq and R. Van Schoute, Louvain-la-Neuve 1987, pp. 99–101.

N. PENNY, 'Raphael's "Madonna dei garofani" rediscovered', *The Burlington Magazine*, CXXXIV, 1992, pp. 67–81, esp. pp. 72–6.

Raphael before Rome: Studies in the History of Art, National Gallery of Art, Washington, 17, 1986.

J. SHEARMAN and M.B. HALL (eds), *The Princeton Raphael Symposium: Science in the Service of Art History*, Princeton 1990 (papers from a conference held in Princeton in 1983).

10 Giorgione
The Adoration of the Kings

J. ANDERSON, *Giorgione: The Painter of 'Poetic Brevity'*, Paris 1997, esp. chapter III.

J. DUNKERTON, 'Developments in colour and texture in Venetian painting of the early 16th century' in F. Ames-Lewis (ed.), *New Interpretations of Venetian Renaissance Painting*, London 1994, pp. 63–76.

J. DUNKERTON, 'Bellini's Technique' in P. Humfrey (ed.), *Giovanni Bellini*, Cambridge University Press (forthcoming).

J. DUNKERTON, S. FOISTER and N. PENNY, *Dürer to Veronese: Sixteenth-Century Painting in The National Gallery*, New Haven and London 1999, esp. pp. 232–5.

C. HOPE and J.R.J. VAN ASPEREN DE BOER, 'Underdrawings by Giorgione and his Circle', *Le dessin sous-jacent dans la peinture, Colloque VIII: Dessin sous-jacent et copies, 8–10 septembre 1989*, ed. H. Verougstraete-Marcq and R. Van Schoute, Louvain-la-Neuve 1991, pp. 127–40.

P. JOANNIDES, *Titian to 1518*, New Haven and London 2001, esp. chapter 2.

For further discussion of the attribution of the *Holy Family* in the National Gallery of Art, Washington, see S.J. FREEDBERG, 'The Benson *Holy Family*: A Reconsideration', in P Rosenberg, C. Scallierez and D. Thiébaut (eds), *Hommage à Michel Laclotte*, Milan 1994, pp. 324–40.

11 Lucas Cranach the Elder
Saints Christina and Ottilia

Lucas Cranach der Ältere: Der linke Flügel (Innenseite) des Katherinenaltars von 1506, exh. cat., Gemäldegalerie Alte Meister, Dresden, Berlin 1996.

C. GRIMM, J. ERICHSEN and E. BROCKHOFF (eds), *Lucas Cranach: ein Maler-Unternehmer aus Franken*, exh. cat., Festung Rosenberg, Kronach, and Museum der bildenden Künste, Leipzig, Regensburg 1994.

See also:

G. HEYDENREICH, 'Artistic exchange and experimental variation: studies in the workshop practice of Lucas

Cranach the Elder', in A. Roy and P. Smith (eds), *Painting Techniques: History, Materials and Studio Practice; Contributions to the Dublin IIC Congress 7–11 September 1998*, London 1998, pp.106–11.

I. SANDNER, 'Die Analyse von Unterzeichnungen auf Gemälden mit Hilfe der Infrarotreflektografie um Beispiel von Werken Lucas Cranachs d. Ä', *Deutsche Gesellschaft für Zerstörungsfreie Prüfung e.V.* (Berlin), Berichtsband 45, Teil 1, 1994, pp. 193–202.

I. SANDNER (ed.), *Unsichtbare Meisterzeichnungen auf dem Malgrund. Cranach und seine Zeitgenossen*, exh. cat., Wartburg-Stiftung, Eisenach, Regensburg 1998.

12 Pontormo
Joseph with Jacob in Egypt

G. VASARI, 'Life of Pontormo', *Le vite de' più eccellenti pittori, scultori e architettori, nella redazione del 1550 e 1568*, ed. R. Bettarini, annotated by P. Barocchi, Vol. 5, Florence 1984, pp.316–17.

P. COSTAMAGNA, *Pontormo*, Milan 1994, cat. nos 19 (NG 6453), 20 (NG 6451), 21 (NG 6452), 22 (NG 1131), pp.28–9, 38, 125–30.

J. COX-REARICK, *The Drawings of Pontormo: A Catalogue Raisonné with Notes on the Paintings*, rev. edn, 2 vols, New York 1981: NG 6453, Vol. 1, pp. 117–18, cat. nos 19–21, Vol. 2, figs 24–7 and Addendum 19a, pp. 364–5, Plate 3a; NG 6451, Vol. 1, pp. 118–20, cat. nos 22–4, Vol. 2, figs 28–31 and Addendum 24a, pp. 365–6, Plate 3b; NG 6452, Vol. 1, pp. 120–2, cat. nos 25–8, Vol. 2, figs 32–5 and Addendum 26a, p. 366, Plate 4a; NG 1131, Vol. 1, pp.154–6, cat. nos 90–2, Vol. 2, figs 89–91 and Addendum 91a, pp.367–8, Plate 5.

J. DUNKERTON, S. FOISTER and N. PENNY, *Dürer to Veronese: Sixteenth-Century Painting in The National Gallery*, New Haven and London 1999, pp. 130–4, figs 153–4.

C. PLAZZOTTA and R. BILLINGE, 'The Underdrawing of Pontormo's *Joseph in Egypt*', *The Burlington Magazine*, in press (November 2002).

See also:

A. NATALI (ed.), *Rosso e Pontormo: Fierezza e Solitudine. Esercizi di lettura e rediconti di restauro per tre dipinti degli Uffizi*, Florence 1995.

13 Albrecht Altdorfer
Christ taking Leave of his Mother

M. SCHAWE, 'Albrecht Altdorfers "Susanna im Bade" von 1526. Überlegungen zum Werkprozess', *Niederdeutsche Beiträge zur Kunstgeschichte*, 38, 1999, pp.93–103.

See also R. BILLINGE and S. FOISTER, 'The Underdrawing of Altdorfer's "Christ taking Leave of his Mother"', *The Burlington Magazine*, CXXXV, October 1993, pp. 687–91.

14 Workshop of the Master of 1518
The Flight into Egypt

The Marienkirche 1518 Altarpiece and comparative works by other painters mentioned in the text are discussed in M.J. FRIEDLÄNDER, *Early Netherlandish Painting*, 14 vols, Leiden and Brussels 1967–76, Vol. XI, No. 70 (1518 altarpiece); Vol. XI, No. 72 (Dielegem triptych); Vol. XI, No. 71 (panels from the same series as *The Flight into Egypt*); Vol. VII, Nos 12, 13, 39 (paintings by Quinten Massys and followers); Vol. XII, No. 10 (workshop of the Master of the Magdalen Legend); Vol. XII, No. 9 (Ashwellthorpe Triptych).

On the Marienkirche 1518 Altarpiece see also F. HIRSCH, G. BAUMANN and F. BRUNS, *Die Bau- und Kunstdenkmäler der Freien und Hansestadt Lübeck*, Vol. II, *Petrikirche, Marienkirche, Heil.-Geist-Hospital*, Lübeck 1906, pp.225–8; J. WITTSTOCK, *Kirchliche Kunst des Mittelalters und der Reformationszeit* (Museum für Kunst und Kulturgeschichte der Hansestadt Lübeck, Die Sammlungen in St.-Annen-Museum), Lübeck 1981, p.180; M. HASSE, *Die Marienkirche zu Lübeck*, Munich and Berlin 1983, pp.70–2, 146–8.

For the Dielegem triptych see also M. KOYEN, 'Abbaye de Dielegem, à Jette-Saint-Pierre' in *Monasticon Belge*, IV, *Province de Brabant*, Vol. III, Liège 1969, pp.687–720.

For the iconography see M. MEISS and E.H. BEATSON, *La Vie de Nostre Benoit Sauveur Ihesuscrist & La Saincte Vie de Nostre Dame*, New York 1977, pp.26, 29.

For the reflectogram of the *Christ and the Doctors* underdrawing see A. GODFRIND-BORN, 'Le style et le rôle du dessin sous-jacent dans la genèse du *Triptyque de Marie-Madeleine* attribué au Maître de 1518', *Le dessin sous-jacent dans la peinture, Colloque X: Le dessin sous-jacent dans le processus de création*, ed. H. Verougstraete and R. Van Schoute, Louvain-la-Neuve 1995, pp.121–31, Plate 65.

Details of the underdrawing of parts of the 1518 altarpiece are illustrated in M.W. AINSWORTH and M. FARIES, *Northern Renaissance Paintings: The Discovery of Invention, The Saint Louis Art Museum Bulletin*, N.S., XVIII, 1, 1986, p. 34, Fig. 58 (reflectogram of a detail from the panel of the *Circumcision*), and C. PÉRIER-D IETEREN, 'Un dessin inédit du Maître de 1518 et les volets peints du retable I de Västerås', *Konsthistorisk Tidskrift*, LIII, 2, 1984, pp.47–52, esp. p. 51, Fig. 5 (infrared photograph, an incorrectly captioned detail from the Stuttgart predella panel of *The Angel appearing to Joseph*).

For the reflectogram of the Dielegem triptych underdrawing see A. BORN, 'Apport à l'étude du dessin sous-jacent et pratiques d'atelier du Maître de 1518' in *Le dessin sous-jacent dans la peinture, Colloque IX: Dessin sous-jacent et pratiques d'atelier*, ed. R. Van Schoute and H. Verougstraete-Marcq, Louvain-la-Neuve 1993, plate 75b; GODFRIND-BORN, 'Le style et le rôle du dessin sous-jacent dans la genèse du *Triptyque de Marie-Madeleine* attribué au Maître de 1518' 1995, cited above, plates 61–5.

15 Marinus van Reymerswale
Two Tax Gatherers

M.J. FRIEDLÄNDER, *Early Netherlandish Painting*, 14 vols, Leiden and Brussels 1967–76, esp. Vol. XII, No. 170, for the dates of the signed versions of *The Banker and his Wife* and Vol. VII, No. 53, for *The Banker and his Wife* by Quinten Massys.

A. MACKOR, 'Are Marinus' Tax Collectors collecting taxes?', *Bulletin du Musée National de Varsovie*, XXXVI, Nos 3–4, 1995, pp.3–13.

A. MACKOR, 'De schilder Marinus belicht stadgenoot Cornelis van der Mare: Reymerswale, Zuid-Beveland en de vloed van 1530', *Historisch Jaarboek van Zuid- en Noord-Beveland*, XXIV, 1998, pp. 77–93, esp. p. 84.

A. MONBALLIEU, 'The Lawyer's Office by Marinus van Reymerswael in the New Orleans Museum of Art', *Jaarboek van het Koninklijk Museum voor Schone Kunsten, Antwerpen*, 1972, pp. 101–41, esp. pp.104–6, 131–3 for the case of Cornelia Claes Dirixz. and the dispute over the pew.

M.P. NEUTEBOOM-DIELEMAN, *Reymerswale, Burgemeesters en Schepenen 1513–1631* (Nederlandse Genealogische Vereniging, Afd: Zeeland, Prae 1600 Club, Werkgroep voor de Studie van Middeleeuwse Genealogische en Historische Bronnen), Goirle 1989.

M.P. NEUTEBOOM-DIELEMAN, *Reymerswale, De stadsrekening van 1573* (Nederlandse Genealogische Vereniging, Afd: Zeeland, Prae 1600 Club, Werkgroep voor de Studie van Middeleeuwse Genealogische en Historische Bronnen), Goirle 1990.

M.P. NEUTEBOOM-DIELEMAN, *Reymerswale, Een Getuigenverklaring uit 1515* (Nederlandse Genealogische Vereniging, Afdeling Zeeland, Prae 1600 Club, Werkgroep voor de Studie van Middeleeuwse Genealogische en Historische Bronnen), Goirle 1991

The different versions of the *Two Tax Gatherers* are classified in L. CAMPBELL, *The Early Flemish Pictures in the Collection of Her Majesty The Queen*, Cambridge 1985, pp.115–17.

For the Dresden version of *The Banker and his Wife* see A. MAYER-MEINTSCHEL, *Gemäldegalerie Alte Meister, Katalog I, Niederländische Malerei, 15. und 16. Jahrhundert*, Dresden 1966, pp.49–51, plates 44–6.

For the underdrawing of the Paris version of the *Two Tax Gatherers* see R. BILLINGE, 'The National Gallery-Leverhulme Infrared Reflectography Project: an Overview', *Le dessin sous-jacent et la technologie dans la peinture: Colloque XI: Perspectives*, ed. R. Van Schoute and H. Verougstraete, with A. Dubois, Louvain-la-Neuve 1997, pp.109–15, esp. p.112.

16 Pieter Bruegel the Elder
The Adoration of the Kings

H. MARCQ-VEROUGSTRAETE and R. VAN SCHOUTE, 'Le dessin de peinture (dessin sous-jacent) chez Pierre Bruegel: L'Adoration des Mages de la National Gallery à Londres', in J.R.J van Asperen de Boer and J.P. Filedt Kok (eds), *Scientific Examination of Early Netherlandish Painting: Applications in Art History, Nederlands Kunsthistorisch Jaarboek*, 26, 1975, pp.250–67.

For Pieter Brueghel the Younger's copy of the *Adoration* see G. MARLIER, *Pierre Brueghel le jeune*, ed. Jacqueline Folie, Brussels 1969, pp.77–9; *Bruegel, Une dynastie de peintres*, exh. cat., Palais des Beaux-Arts, Brussels 1980, p. 145, No. 82; K. ERTZ, *Pieter Brueghel der Jüngere (1564–1637/38), Die Gemälde mit kritischem Oeuvrekatalog*, 2 vols, Lingen 2000, pp.306–7, 316–17.

For Jan Brueghel's copies of the painting see G. MARTIN, *National Gallery Catalogues, The Flemish School circa 1600–circa 1900*, London 1970, pp.13–15; K. ERTZ, *Jan Brueghel der Ältere (1568–1625), Die Gemälde mit kritischem Oeuvrekatalog*, Cologne 1979, pp.423–5, 565–6; the Brussels 1980 exhibition catalogue cited in the previous entry, p. 187, No. 120.

For the drawing known as *The Gooseherd* (reproduced on p. 38 above, Fig. 59) see H. MIELKE, *Pieter Bruegel, Die Zeichnungen*, Turnhout 1996, p. 63, No. 57; for the paintings by Pieter the Younger, see ERTZ, *Pieter Brueghel der Jüngere*, 2000, cited above, pp.205–6.

For the Brussels *Adoration* in water-colour see the Brussels 1980 exhibition catalogue cited above, p. 49, No. A.

Hieronymus Bosch's triptych of the *Adoration of the Kings* and what is known of its early history are discussed in J. FOLIE, 'Les oeuvres authentifiées des Primitifs flamands', *Bulletin de l'Institut Royal du Patrimoine Artistique*, VI, 1963, pp. 183–251, esp. p. 235; P. VANDENBROECK, 'The Spanish *inventarios reales* and Hieronymus Bosch', and M. RENSON, 'Genealogical Information concerning the Bronchorst-Bosschuysen Triptych' in J. Koldeweij, B. Vermet and B. van Kooij (eds), *Hieronymus Bosch. New Insights into his Life and Work*, Rotterdam 2001, pp. 48–63 and 92–5.

See also:

P. VAN DEN BRINK (ed.), *Brueghel Enterprises*, with contributions by D. Allart, P. van den Brink, C. Currie, R. Duckwitz, J. Folie, P. Fraiture and S. Harleman; exh. cat., Bonnefantenmuseum, Maastricht/Musées Royaux des Beaux-Arts de Belgique, Ghent-Amsterdam 2001.

R. VAN SCHOUTE and H. VEROUGSTRAETE, 'A painted wooden roundel by Pieter Bruegel the Elder', *The Burlington Magazine*, CXLII, 2000, pp.140–6, esp. pp.140–2.

NOTE (see p. 187)

This series of colloquia, organised under the auspices of the Laboratoire d'étude des oeuvres d'art par les méthodes scientifiques, Université Catholique de Louvain, has, since 1975, been held biennially in Louvain, Louvain-la-Neuve and, from 1997, Bruges. Each colloquium is dedicated to a specific topic; the ninth, held in 1991 and published in 1993, was on underdrawing and workshop practice. From *Colloque XI* (1995, published in 1997) onwards, the general title has been changed to *Dessin sous-jacent et technologie de la peinture*, reflecting a broadening of the subject field covered. *Colloques I–II* contains a detailed bibliography of published images or reflectograms of underdrawings and accounts of infrared examination up to 1978; this is continued (beginning with works published from 1979 onwards) from *Colloque VI* onwards and aims to provide a complete bibliography of the field as a whole.

Photo credits

All photographs © The National Gallery, London unless otherwise stated

ANTWERP
Museum Mayer van den Bergh
© A.C.L. Brussels
Fig. 279

BASEL
© Oeffentliche Kunstsammlung Basel
Fig. 80

BERGAMO
© Civica Biblioteca Angelo Mai, Bergamo
Photo: Studio Fotografico Dare
Fig. 94

BERLIN
Kupferstichkabinett
© Staatliche Museen zu Berlin. Bildarchiv Preussischer Kulturbesitz
Photo: Jörg P. Anders, Foto: 1992/108/407
Figs 45, 92

BREMEN
© Kunsthalle Bremen
Fig. 69

BRUGES
St. Jakobskerk
© Photo: Stedelijke Musea van Bruges
Fig. 79

BRUSSELS
© IRPA/KIK, Brussels
Figs 187, 188

CAMBRIDGE, MASS.
Courtesy of the Fogg Art Museum, Harvard University Art Museums
© President and Fellows of Harvard College, Harvard University
Photo: Allan Macintyre
Fig. 180

COLOGNE
Cologne Cathedral
© Rheinisches Bildarchiv, Cologne
Fig. 148
© Wallraf-Richartz-Museum, Cologne
Photo: Rheinisches Bildarchiv, Cologne
Figs 144, 147, 201, 209

DETROIT, Michigan
© The Detroit Institute of Arts, Detroit, Photograph 1994
Fig. 181

DRESDEN
Gemäldegalerie Alte Meister,
© Staatliche Kunstsammlungen Dresden
Fig. 243, 249
Photo: Klut, Fig. 292
Kupferstichkabinett
© Staatliche Kunstsammlungen Dresden
Photo: Pfauder
Figs 84, 248
Photo: Schurz
Figs 59, 86

ERLANGEN
© Graphische Sammlung der Universität Erlangen
Fig. 273

FLORENCE
Gabinetto dei Disegni e delle Stampe
© Photo: Archivi Alinari, Florence
Fig. 257
© Soprintendenza Speciale per il Polo Museale Fiorentino, Florence
Figs 93, 260, 261
Galleria Palatina, Palazzo Pitti
© Photo: SCALA, Florence
Fig. 119

FRANKFURT AM MAIN
© Städelsches Kunstinstitut, Frankfurt am Main
Photo: Ursula Edelmann
Fig. 149

HONOLULU, Hawaii
© Honolulu Academy of Arts Gallery
Fig. 277

LILLE
Musée des Beaux-Arts
© RMN, Paris
Photo: Quecq d'Henripret
Figs 57, 227, 228, 229, 230

LONDON
The British Museum
© Copyright The British Museum, London
Figs 61, 76, 99, 101, 103, 179, 218, 274

© Courtauld Institute Gallery, London
Fig. 142

© National Gallery, London
Courtesy of Sotheby's, London
Fig. 64

© Courtesy of Sotheby's, London
Photo: National Gallery Archives, Fig. 304

MANTUA
Palazzo Ducale,
© Photo: SCALA, Florence,
Fig. 162

MILAN
Pinacoteca di Brera
© Su concessione del Ministero per i Beni e le Attivitá Culturali, Milan
Fig. 158

MUNICH
Alte Pinakothek
© Bayerische Staatsgemäldesammlungen, Munich
Fig. 66

NEW YORK
© The Metropolitan Museum of Art, New York
Figs 5, 8, 185, 213, 214
© The Pierpont Morgan Library, New York
Fig. 215

NÜREMBERG
© Germanisches Nationalmuseum Nüremberg
Fig. 205, 208

OXFORD
© Copyright in these photographs reserved to the Ashmolean Museum, Oxford
Figs 121, 143

PARIS
© Bibliothèque Nationale de France, Paris
Figs 60, 189
© École Nationale Supérieure des Beaux-Arts, Paris
Figs 78, 263
Musée du Louvre
© RMN, Paris
Figs 267, 289
Photo: Michèle Bellot
Figs 32, 95, 105
Photo: J.G. Berizzi
Figs 97, 104

ROTTERDAM
© Museum Boijmans Van Beuningen, Rotterdam
Fig. 166

SIENA
Biblioteca Comunale degli Intronati
© Soprintendenza per il Patrimonio Storico Artistico e Demoetnoantropologico per le Province de Siena e Grosseto Siena
Figs 46, 47

ST PETERSBURG
© With permission from The State Hermitage Museum, St Petersburg
Figs 124, 126

THE HAGUE
Fig. 237
© Prof. Dr. J.R.J. van Asperen de Boer/Stichting RKD
The IRR research was done with a Grundig FA 70 television camera equipped with a Hamamatsu N 214 IR vidicon (1975); a Kodak wratten 87A filter cutting-on at 0.9 micron was placed between the vidicon target surface and the Zoomar 1:2 8/4 cm Macro Zoomatar lens. The television camera was mounted on a sturdy Linhof professional tripod with extension pieces, and a 90 cm sledge for moving the camera sideways. The monitor was a Grundig BG 12 with 875 television lines. Any documentation is done with a Nikon camera, a 50 mm macrolens, and Ilford film FP 4, ASA 125.
The IRR-assembly reproduced here was made with Adobe Photoshop 5.5 VIPs ip (at the National Gallery, London) and consists of images which were scanned on 1012 dpi with Polaroid SprintScan 35/Plus from photo negatives belonging to the archive of Prof. J.R.J. van Asperen de Boer at the RKD.

Fig. 208
© Prof. Dr. Molly Faries/Stichting RKD.
The IRR research was done with a Grundig 70 H television camera outfitted with a Hamamatsu N 214 IR vidicon (1981), a TV macromar 1:2.8/36mm lens, and Kodak wratten 87 A filter cutting on at 0.9 micron placed behind the lens, with a Grundig BG 12 monitor set at 875 lines. Any photographic documentation is done with a Canon A-1 35 mm camera, a 50 mm macrolens, and Kodak Plus X film and/or Ilford film, ASA 125. The IRR-assembly reproduced here was made with VIPs IP 9at the National Gallery, London) and consists of images which were scanned on 1012 dpi with Polaroid SprintScan 35/Plus from photo negatives belonging to the archive of Prof. Molly Faries at the RKD.

TRURO
© Royal Institute of Art, Truro
Fig. 75

UPTON, Warwickshire
Upton House, The National Trust
© Photo: The National Trust Picture Library, London
Figs 175, 176

VENICE
Galleria dell'Accademia di Belli Arti
© Soprintendenza per i beni artistici per Venezia e Laguna
Photo: Osvaldo Böhm
Fig. 102

VIENNA
© Albertina, Vienna
Figs 58, 67

WADDESDON, Buckinghamshire
© Waddesdon, The Rothschild Collection (The National Trust)
Photo: Mike Fear
Fig. 206

WASHINGTON, DC
© Conservation Department, National Gallery of Art, Washington, DC
Figs 235, 241. Infrared reflectogram (1.5-2.0 microns), computer assembly, captured with a Kodak PtSi infrared camera.
© National Gallery of Art, Washington. Board of Trustees, Photograph 2002
Figs 73, 232, 233
Photo: Dean Beasom
Fig. 100
Photo: Jose A. Naranjo
Fig. 221

WINDSOR
The Royal Collection
© 2002, Her Majesty Queen Elizabeth II
Fig. 120